VERY YOUNG CHILDREN WITH SPECIAL NEEDS

A Formative Approach for the Twenty-First Century

Vikki F. Howard
Gonzaga University

Betty Fry Williams
Gonzaga University

Patricia D. Port
Sacred Heart Medical Center

Cheryl Lepper
Gonzaga University
Illustrator

Merrill,
an imprint of Prentice Hall
Upper Saddle River, New Jersey   Columbus, Ohio

Library of Congress Cataloging-in-Publication Data

Very young children with special needs : a formative approach for the 21st century /
Vikki F. Howard . . . [et al.]; Cheryl Lepper, design and illustrations.
        p.   cm.
    Includes bibliographical references and index.
    ISBN 0-02-357211-6
        1. Handicapped children—Education (Early childhood)   2. Child development.
    3. Special education.   I. Howard, Vikki F.
    LC4019.3.V47   1997
    371.9' 0472—dc20   96-22334
                                                            CIP

Cover Photo: Randy Williams
Editor: Ann Castel Davis
Production Editor: Julie Anderson Peters
Production, Design, and Photo Coordination: Proof Positive/Farrowlyne Associates, Inc.
Cover Designer: Brian Deep
Production Manager: Pamela D. Bennett
Director of Marketing: Kevin Flanagan
Advertising/Marketing Coordinator: Julie Shough
Illustrations: Cheryl Lepper

This book was set in Optima by Proof Positive/Farrowlyne Associates, Inc. and was
printed and bound by R. R. Donnelley & Sons Company. The cover was printed by
Phoenix Color Corp.

 © 1997 by Prentice-Hall, Inc.
Simon & Schuster/A Viacom Company
Upper Saddle River, New Jersey 07458

Photo credits: Betsy Downey, Kathy Werfelmann, Randy Williams

Printed in the United States of America

10 9 8 7 6 5 4   3 2 1

ISBN: 0-02-357211-6

Prentice-Hall International (UK) Limited, *London*
Prentice-Hall of Australia Pty. Limited, *Sydney*
Prentice-Hall of Canada, Inc., *Toronto*
Prentice-Hall Hispanoamericana, S. A., *Mexico*
Prentice-Hall of India Private Limited, *New Delhi*
Prentice-Hall of Japan, Inc., *Tokyo*
Simon & Schuster Asia Ple. Ltd., *Singapore*
Editora Prentice-Hall do Basil, Ltda., *Rio de Janeiro*

This text is dedicated to the many children, students, colleagues, parents, and family members who have taught us well throughout our personal and professional lives. They set high standards for themselves and others, respected individual differences and needs, and committed themselves unselfishly to advocate for the care and education of children everywhere. It is their lessons we have tried to share in this text and from which we continue to learn.

Preface

This text is a collaborative effort, not only on the part of the authors, but also because of the contributions of the many parents, professionals, researchers, and students who have added to the growing body of knowledge about how to best serve very young children with disabilities and their families. It was our intention to synthesize perspectives and information from the fields of medicine, education, intervention, psychology, law, sociology, and family life for use by those who will work with infants, toddlers, and preschoolers with special needs. It was also our goal to challenge our readers to consider the future of early intervention and their role in shaping the field of early childhood special education as we move into the twenty-first century. The result is a text we hope will be a relevant and long-lasting resource.

The purpose of this text is to assist in the preparation of early childhood professionals who plan to engage in providing services and intervention to very young children with disabilities. Though early childhood special education teachers may make up the majority of readers who use this text, the term early childhood professional is used to address individuals in many disciplines, including health care, social work, physical and occupational therapy, child care, and those who are involved in interagency services to young children and their families.

The text opens with a Prologue in an effort to establish the current status of early childhood issues and to introduce how the text is organized. Chapter 1 provides an overview of the guiding philosophies of the text, which will be applied and reiterated throughout the two main parts of the book. Part One provides chapters that detail normal child development and the etiology of disabling conditions that affect the very young child with disabilities. Part Two addresses how intervention and support are provided to young children and how families might best be served. Throughout the book, families share their experiences and selected research is summarized in Case Studies and Close-Ups relevant to each chapter.

Very young children with special needs are the focus of this text, but to thoroughly understand and serve a child with disabilities, one must be knowledgeable of normal development, must understand how health and genetics affect potential, and must recognize the impact of the child's family and environment on realizing that potential. The text attempts to be interdisciplinary, inclusive, and family-focused.

ACKNOWLEDGMENTS

The authors wish to extend their deepest gratitude to the following people for their insight, inspiration, and encouragement. Though every person listed was extremely busy, they gave generously of their time and talents. There are no words adequate to express our thanks.

Editor: Ann Davis

Secretaries: Julia Bjordahl, Patty Crider, and Rosemary Hoskins

Contributing authors: Michelle Aurora, John Beck, Carl Bodenstein, Janet Katz, Jeannie Machado, Corrine McGuigan, T. F. McLaughlin, Joseph Terhaar, Joan VanBrocklin, and Edward Zigler

Editing: Julia Bjordahl, Mary Foutz, Gregg Godsey, and Stephanie Peck

The parents who shared their family histories and advice: David and Priscilla DeWolf, James and Judy Holden, Marsha and James Moore, Ann and Tom Simpson, and Tammy and Mitch Waritz

Student researchers in Early Childhood Special Education who provided us with the initial incentive, research, and ideas: Jean Agte, Susan Balenzano, Susan Banks, Becky Buehl, Michelle Daltoso, Pat Davis, Michele Dickerson, Colleen Fuchs, Maria Gianotti, Mary Jo Gilbert, Anita Glover, Carrie Guse, Lynn Harding, Nicole Huguenin, Mary Johnson, Megan Johnson, Tammy Keating, Jeannie Kennedy, Sylvia Kozyra, Amy Jo Kramp, Michelle Lallicker, Nancy Lennon, Marsha Moore, Michele Moskalonek, Katie Murphy, Michele Naccarato, Amy Nicholson, Jamie Parrish, Tricia Rossen, Kathy Rue, Elsa Stavney, Debra Tabacek, Marlene Visitacion, Teri Walker, Lisa Wardian, Dee Weeks-Nelson, and Cindy Yeager

Photographers: Betsy Downey, Kathy Werfelmann, and Randy Williams

Organizations that permitted our photographers to do their work: Gonzaga University's School of Education Preschool, Martin Luther King Center, Shriners Hospital, and Spokane Guilds' School

Reviewers who kindly read our manuscript and provided constructive comments:
David Anderson, Bethel College
Brent Askvig, Minot State University
Alice Donahue, Grand Rapids Community College
Barbara Lowenthal, Northeastern Illinois University
Maureen Norris, Bellarmine College

Contents

Chapter 3: Milestones of Development 75

Chapter 4: Development and Risking Conditions: Prenatal, Natal, and Postnatal 115

Chapter 6: Inborn Variations of Development   183

Chapter 7: Sensory Impairments and Infections   239

PART TWO   279

Chapter 8: Historical Interlude   281

Chapter 9: Families of Children with Disabilities   311

Chapter 10: Mandated Services for Young Children   343

Appendices

Glossary   473

Index   491

CASE STUDIES AND CLOSE-UPS

Early Childhood Services Today

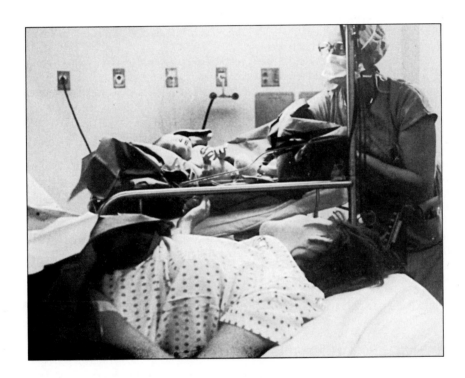

The potential possibilities of any child are the most intriguing and stimulating in all creation.—Ray L. Wilbur

The first cry in the delivery room, the sudden pause in what has been a growing frenzy of action and emotion, like a long exhalation of relief and joy; a baby is born. Parents beam, laugh, and cry; attendants share smiles and swing into action; and baby, bewildered and naked, draws in the first breath of life. Whatever this little one's life will be, it is begun; totally dependent on family, caregivers, educators, and the community. One new life, whose potential is determined not only by genetics, environment, and accidents of fate, but by the larger value and support society provides.

THE CHILD'S ECOLOGY

As members of the human community, we are each responsible for the other. Hence, with the birth of each baby, its development is entrusted to us—either in our direct and personal roles as professionals or in the communal connection we carry as members of the child's larger ecology. Each newborn offers both opportunities and responsibilities for the society it enters; each child is ultimately shaped by the complex relationships within its environment that support or diminish its development. Figure 1 illustrates these complexities.

A child's ecology may be seen as the systems or layers of the environment that affect its growth and development (Bronfenbrenner, 1976; 1977). A child's potential is not only affected by the close circle of its family and friends but also by the health of its neighborhood, by the services and resources available within its community, and by the customs of its culture. The first layer is also the most critical for the child—the immediate environment where children spend most of their time—in homes with friends, neighbors, or relatives, in family daycare settings, or in child-care centers.

At particular times in a child's life, relationships beyond this inner circle become important; these include interactions with parent or with teacher, therapist, physician, or other professionals. For example, a child may become seriously ill, and its recovery depends on the availability of a well-trained physician and a nearby hospital that is equipped and staffed to treat the child's ailment.

A third layer of society also impinges on or protects the young child; this layer might include local and state agencies, early intervention services, advocacy groups, neighborhood and community organizations, and churches. For example, a child may grow up in a city that provides and maintains community parks and playgrounds for children and offers summer activities that encourage safe and appropriate play close to the child's home. Finally, all children are affected by the distant but enveloping workings of our society—federal and state legislation, agency regulations, court rulings, societal attitudes, and the values and ethics of our culture. A good example of this final layer is our country's current concern for reducing child abuse and the resulting child protective services that are now available to all families.

A Child Interacts with and Influences Its System

A child is no passive cog within the wheels of these ecological systems. Just as the environment affects the child, the child interacts with and influences the system, in a transactional or bidirectional model (Sameroff & Chandler, 1975; Sameroff & Fiese, 1990). Suppose, for

Figure 1/ *The child's ecology may be seen as the layers that affect its growth and development.*

example, that a newborn enters our ecology with a low birth weight, chromosomal anomalies, and delayed development. These complications may disrupt the family structure, causing distress in the parents' marriage, reducing attention given to siblings, and causing rejection from relatives and neighbors. The child may require a longer hospital stay, specialized home nursing, and the services of multiple therapists. The parents may cope by developing collaborative programs with an early intervention team, becoming part of a community support group, and actively advocating for state services for children with special needs. Funds from state and federal sources may be obtained to provide specialized equipment, transportation, and education for the young child. Later, the child may be fully included in public education settings because federal and state mandates have guaranteed the child's equal opportunity for such services. Finally, adults with disabilities may require specialized housing, job adaptations, and community tolerance in social contexts—coming full circle to be active members of the community themselves.

We, as professionals, also actively contribute and interact within the child's ecology (Bailey & Wolery, 1992). It is the professional who responds to family concerns to formally diagnose a child's disabilities and to assist in determining eligibility for services available in the community. It is the professional who enters into a relationship with the child's family and caregivers and supports the family in the development of an educational service plan. It may be the professional who works with families to encourage local agencies to develop and deliver programs appropriate for this child and who is active in organizations that review and recommend legislative changes for the benefit of such children. It is the professional who is sensitive to family and child needs and who may be called to testify at court hearings or to review grant proposals and program amendments.

In order to be an effective professional, one must be a knowledgeable and active agent within a child's ecology. This implies understanding the influence of environment on behavior, being familiar with the array of typical environments, helping children adapt to environmental demands, and facilitating change within the environment itself (Bailey & Wolery, 1992). An effective professional recognizes the informal support systems available to families, works closely with the parents in decision making, establishes collaborative linkages within the community and with other agencies on the child's behalf, and knows the relevant laws and rationale that protect a child's rights and services. Finally, professionals serve as advocates for best practice and high quality services (Bailey & Wolery, 1992).

A typical preschool setting

As a culture, we have developed all the trappings to welcome and provide for babies, to ensure their safety, and to promote their growth. We have invented special foods and formula, designed special clothing and furniture, marketed countless toys and games, discovered vaccines to fight childhood diseases, and provided public education for all children. We fight in court for custody of our young ones, we fund public programs to give aid to dependent children and families, and we punish adults who mistreat or neglect children. Our media invest substantially in entertainment for children, professionals are certified and licensed to teach and care for children, and whole fields of psychology, medicine, and education deal only with issues of childhood.

1990s AND CHILD CARE

Child care has come of age in the 1990s in the United States. Legislative activity has escalated at both the federal and state levels, with expansion of Head Start, tax credits for families, and extension of Medicaid health insurance to all poor children. In 1991 alone, the federal government spent $8 billion on programs related to children's services (Hofferth & Phillips, 1991a). Since 1986, the Individuals with Disabilities Education Act (IDEA) has made it possible for all states to fulfill the mandate for preschoolers with disabilities ("DEC holds IDEA reauthorization hearing," January, 1994). It is clear we have come far from the days when children were frequently abandoned, sold into bondage, or abused (deMause, 1974).

On the other hand, as a society, we have also greatly failed our children. Though we think of ourselves as a nation that dearly loves and cares for its children, we lag behind almost all other industrialized nations in the world in terms of the quantity and the quality of child-care services we provide and the degree of financial support our government prioritizes for children. Hofferth and Phillips (1991b) quoted Marian Wright Edelman, head of the Children's Defense Fund, who warned,

> The inattention to children by our society poses a greater threat to our safety, harmony and productivity than any external enemy.

Demographic shifts occurring since 1970 have greatly increased the need for child care for normally developing children as well as for children with developmental disabilities (Landis, 1992). Increasing numbers of women in the labor force and the increasing numbers of single-parent families have contributed to a child-care crisis. By 1988, 56% of women in the United States with children under age six were employed (Sonenstein & Wolf, 1991). The rate is similar for women with children under age three (Landis, 1992).

Half of all children of working women, almost 9 million children, were cared for by a parent, relative, or in-home sitter; about 28% (5.3 million) were cared for in commercial day-care centers; and another 20% attended family daycare homes (Hofferth & Phillips, 1991a). The sheer number of children continues to increase because the number of women of child-bearing age is large. By 1995, 15 million preschoolers and 23.5 million school-aged children were expected to have working mothers (Hofferth & Phillips, 1991a). The National Center for Education Statistics (West, 1995) found that 31% of all children under age 6 were cared for in center-based programs and 18% were in home-based, nonrelative care.

The "Trilemma" of Child Care

A "trilemma" has been created by the large numbers of children for whom care is neither available, affordable, nor of sufficient quality (Culkin, Morris, & Helburn, 1991). Perhaps the most pressing of these problems is affordability (Culkin, et al., 1991). For example, the average family spends almost 11% on child care, the same proportion as they spend on food (Culkin, et al., 1991). Low-income families spend as much as 20% to 25% of their budget on child care (Hofferth & Phillips, 1991a). Further, affordability is directly related to quality of service because a primary means of reducing costs is to increase child-to-staff ratios and to offer low pay (Culkin, et al., 1991).

Abnormally low wages and benefits are given child-care staff, despite high levels of education and experience (Culkin, et al., 1991; Phillips, Howes, & Whitebook, 1991). In a survey by Phillips et al. (1991) almost 75% of teachers and 56% of assistant teachers at child-care centers reported having some college, and 65% had received specific early childhood course work; still, the average wage paid kept them at the poverty level. Consequently, it is not surprising that a recent sample of 1300 center-based child-care staff revealed a turnover rate of about 40% in child-care settings (Phillips, et al., 1991).

The issue of salaries for early child-care providers remains a critical one for the United States and, unfortunately, has no easy solution (Olmsted, 1992). Higher salaries might decrease the turnover rate, justify the higher education levels and preservice training, and allow states to increase staff educational requirements without causing staff shortages. Such requirements might attract qualified staff and increase the quality of services, but increased salaries would reduce affordability for families who are already strapped to support their current standard of living (Olmsted, 1992).

With labor representing the highest costs for care in centers, many facilities are able to exist only through dependence on subsidies provided by community or government sources. This dependency adds to the financial instability of the child-care delivery system (Phillips, et al., 1991). For example, since federal funding began to decline in 1981, both the quality and the number of children who could be served affordably also declined. By 1987, Head Start, the largest federally funded child-care program, was serving only 16% of the 2.5 million children eligible (Warger, 1988). Recognizing Head Start's inability to serve children adequately, Congress significantly increased its funding in 1990 (Bailey & Wolery, 1992),

Children with disabilities attending preschool

seeking to serve 40% of eligible children by 1991 and 100% by 1994 (Hofferth & Phillips, 1991b). However, by December of 1993, only 21% of eligible three-year-olds and 53% of eligible four-year-olds were being served ("Head Start quality, expansion guidelines released," February, 1994).

The quality of early childhood services is clearly related to funding issues but licensing standards also influence the quality of services. The current licensing systems used by states set minimum standards, but in many cases, these are lower than standards that research would suggest for positive child outcomes (Olmsted, 1992). All states have regulations for child-care centers, but regulations for family daycare homes vary widely. About half the states license home care, 8 states do not regulate homes or regulate them only for subsidized care, 3 have voluntary registration, and 13 states register but do not license homes (Olmsted, 1992). States also vary on which settings are exempt from regulations. For example, 12 states exempt all church-sponsored daycare centers, and 21 exempt all nursery schools and other part-day or full-day educational programs, other than those affiliated with public schools. Some states do not regulate programs run by private colleges and universities, programs run by the military, or programs that are parent cooperatives (Olmsted, 1992).

It is the paradox of childhood in our society today that we love our children greatly but fail to love them enough. It is the challenge of the early childhood professional to address the "trilemma" of availability, affordability, and quality of child care for all children. It is the further challenge of the early childhood educator to insist that our society also provide for the greater needs of families of children with disabilities.

1975 LANDMARK LEGISLATION

The Individuals with Disabilities Education Act (IDEA) was first passed under Public Law 94-142 in 1975 and has since evolved through several revisions. At the time, its passage provided landmark legislation that insured the free and appropriate education of all children with disabilities. Its impact was primarily on school-aged children. However, even in its first stages IDEA also recognized the importance of early intervention. IDEA was intended to apply to children ages 3 to 21, unless an individual state's law did not allow services to children at this young age. Financial incentives were built into IDEA to encourage the provision of services to preschoolers, and by 1985, 31 states had passed some form of preschool legislation (Bailey & Wolery, 1992).

In 1986, Congress amended IDEA, reauthorizing it under Public Law 99-457. The revised law extended all the act's rights and protections to preschoolers. When the newly revised IDEA was put in place in 1986, fewer than half the states had mandates for the education of preschoolers with disabilities; now all states have established such a mandate ("DEC holds IDEA reauthorization hearing," January, 1994). Since the passage of extended services through IDEA, more than 170,000 preschool children have been added to the daily rolls of those receiving special services. Almost 400,000 preschool children were served through IDEA programs and Chapter 1 funding in the 1990–1991 school year (Office of Special Education and Rehabilitative Services [OSERS], 1992).

In addition, Part H of the 1986 IDEA amendments established new incentives for services to children with disabilities who were less than three years old. By December of 1990, almost 200,000 infants and toddlers under age three were receiving early intervention through the assistance of federal funds (OSERS, 1992).

Provisions of IDEA do much to encourage the collaboration of parents and community agencies, including schools, in serving infants and toddlers with disabilities. The law makes clear that services are the responsibility of an interagency system and that resources should be shared ("DEC holds IDEA reauthorization hearing," 1994). Its emphasis is on delivery of services within the context of the family and in natural settings, which should encourage com-

A teacher working with children at preschool

munity-based, culturally sensitive, and family-driven services ("DEC holds IDEA reauthorization hearing," 1994). In addition, the new law allows states to address the early intervention needs of children who are born at-risk for developing later disabilities and delays.

Services Expand and Providers Are in Demand

The expansion of services to preschoolers, infants, and toddlers with disabilities has contributed to increasing difficulties in finding and retaining qualified personnel ("DEC holds IDEA reauthorization hearing," 1994). Shortages are a tremendous problem, particularly in rural areas. Of special importance is the preparation of early childhood providers who can work in inclusive, integrated settings, can use paraprofessionals well, and have skills in using collaborative and consultative models.

Personnel shortages are particularly acute for speech and language pathologists, physical therapists, occupational therapists, and special educators (OSERS, 1992). States reported that more than 14,000 special education teachers were employed in the 1990–1991 school year, just to work with three- to five-year-olds with disabilities, and that at least 2800 similar positions were unfilled. For every five special education preschool teachers employed, there was one job vacancy or a position filled by a less than fully qualified teacher (OSERS, 1992). The need for qualified personnel to serve very young children with disabilities increases every year as the number of children served increases.

The successful implementation of IDEA provisions for services to very young children depends greatly on the active involvement of qualified professionals. In identifying factors that have facilitated policy development for early intervention, several clearly rest on the advocacy and leadership of early childhood professionals. States most likely to be fully involved in serving young children with disabilities presented the following characteristics (among others):

1. A history of interest in and services to young children with disabilities and a history of legislative support for programs for young children

2. The presence of key people in different spheres of influence who had the power to bring about action

3. A vision of a service delivery system that had been clearly articulated and shared across four or five agencies, organizations, power sources, or constituencies

4. The existence or construction of mechanisms for planning and program coordination, such as interagency and intra-agency work groups

5. A climate of cooperation and trust among the various state agencies (OSERS, 1992, p. 61)

Such characteristics are present only when professionals have a basic understanding of the needs of children with disabilities and their families, are well-equipped with a solid knowledge-base in early childhood and special education, and are committed to a philosophy of inclusion and advocacy. This text attempts to prepare the reader to meet the challenges and opportunities presented in early childhood special education today. It attempts to provide both content and philosophy appropriate for professionals who will be working closely with families, collaborating within interagency systems, and providing services in natural settings designed for the integration of both typical children and children with disabilities. To do so, a text must not only convey substantial research and information but also communicate personal experiences and expectations.

INTRODUCING THE FAMILIES

It can be difficult to assimilate the kind of factual information provided in this text in a meaningful relationship to the individuals who are being directly served, young children with disabilities and their families. In order to assist in forming connections between theory and practice, several families agreed to share their stories within this text, and each chapter will feature vignettes of their experiences. Though a particular conversation may not fit perfectly into the context of every chapter, each brief interview serves as a reminder that the purpose of this text is grounded in a dedication to improve services to very young children and their families. A brief introduction to each family may help the reader establish a relationship.

Michael Moore is the youngest of six children, a handsome boy who failed to develop the cognitive, language, and motor skills of other children. He was diagnosed with infantile autism and has frequent severe seizures and significant developmental delays. Michael is currently integrated in a regular education public classroom in his neighborhood and rides the bus to school each day. Michael's father is an executive in mining, presently assigned to work in South America. Michael's mother is completing a master's degree in special education and will soon move Michael and his older sister to South America to be with their father.

Tommy Simpson was born with Down syndrome and currently attends a community-supported school for children under the age of three. Next year, he will make the transition to a public school preschool program. Mr. Tom, as his parents call him, lives with an older sister, his geologist father, Tom, Sr., and his mother, Ann, who works in public relations for a private university. Ann is also president of the parent's organization for Tommy's school and is active in the Down syndrome parent support group.

Jennifer Waritz is the second of three children. Jennifer has severe disabilities related to a newly identified syndrome: Kabuki syndrome. Jennifer uses a wheelchair and is dependent on others for all her daily needs. She is currently attending a public preschool program and is integrated in kindergarten on a part-time basis. Jennifer's mother and father describe themselves as a typical blue collar family. Mitch is a service manager for a scales manufacturer, and Tammy is a Parent Resource Coordinator for a parent advocacy agency.

Jennifer Waritz and her family

Robin DeWolf and her family

The Holden's youngest children: Courtney, April, and Reuben

Michael Moore plays the piano at home

Tommy Simpson and his family

Robin DeWolf is the third of four children and was born with Down syndrome. Her father is a law professor at a local university, and her mother has been able to be a full-time homemaker for her family. Robin's mother carried out infant stimulation and enrichment exercises with her at home, allowing Robin a traditional childhood in the care of her full-time mom. She now attends an integrated program in the public school.

The Holdens have raised seven children of their own and cared for almost 200 foster children over the years. James, a Choctaw Indian, and his wife, Judy, have served many young Native American children who have been exposed to drugs and alcohol during their mothers' pregnancies. They are in the process of adopting three of their youngest and most severely disabled charges. James' background as an early childhood special education teacher has helped considerably.

Throughout the text, these families will share their stories. Each brings a different perspective; all bring the wisdom of experience.

REFERENCES

Bailey, D. B., & Wolery, M. (1992). *Teaching infants and preschoolers with disabilities.* Upper Saddle River, NJ: Merrill/Prentice Hall.

Bronfenbrenner, U. (1976). The experimental ecology of education. *Educational Research, 5*(9), 5–15.

Bronfenbrenner, U. (1977). Toward an experimental ecology of human development. *American Psychologist, 32,* 513–531.

Culkin, M., Morris, J. R., & Helburn, S. W. (1991). Quality and the true cost of child-care. *Journal of Social Issues, 47*(2), 71–86.

deMause, L. (1974). The evolution of childhood. In L. deMause (Ed.), *The history of childhood.* New York: The Psychohistory Press.

DEC holds IDEA reauthorization hearing. (1994, January). *Early Childhood Report, 1*(1), 8–11.

Head Start quality, expansion guidelines released. (1994, February). *Early Childhood Report, 5*(2), 1–3.

Hofferth, S. L., & Phillips, D. A. (1991a). Child care policy research. *Journal of Social Issues, 47* (2), 1–13.

Hofferth, S. L., & Phillips, D. A. (1991b). The editor's page. *Journal of Social Issues, 47*(2).

Landis, L. J. (1992). Marital, employment, and child-care status of mothers with infants and toddlers with disabilities. *Topics in Early Childhood Special Education, 12,* 496–507.

Office of Special Education and Rehabilitative Services (ED). (1992). *Implementation of the Individuals with Disabilities Education Act. Fourteenth annual report to congress.* Washington, DC: Division of Innovation and Development.

Olmsted, P. P. (1992). Where did our diversity come from? *High/Scope ReSource, 11*(3), 4–9.

Phillips, D., Howes, C., & Whitebook, M. (1991). Child care as an adult work environment. *Journal of Social Issues, 47*(2) 49–70.

Sameroff, A. J., & Chandler, M. J. (1975). Reproductive risk and the continuum of caretaking casualty. In F. D. Horowitz, M. Hetherington, S. Scarr-Salapatek, & G. Siegel (Eds.), *Review of child development research* (Vol. 4, pp. 187–244). Chicago: University of Chicago Press.

Sameroff, A. J., & Fiese, B. (1990). Transactional regulations and early intervention. In S. J. Meisels & J. P. Shonkoff (Eds.), *Handbook of early childhood intervention* (pp. 119–149). Cambridge, England: Cambridge University Press.

Sonenstein, F. L., & Wolf, D. A. (1991). Satisfaction with child-care: Perspectives of welfare mothers. *Journal of Social Issues, 47*(2) 15–31.

Warger, C. (Ed.) (1988). *A Resource Guide to Public School Early Childhood Programs,* Alexandria, VA: Association for Supervision and Curriculum Development.

West, J. (1995). *Child care and early education program participation of infants, toddlers, and preschoolers. Statistics in brief,* Washington, DC: National Center for Education Statistics.

CHAPTER 1

Philosophy of Early Education

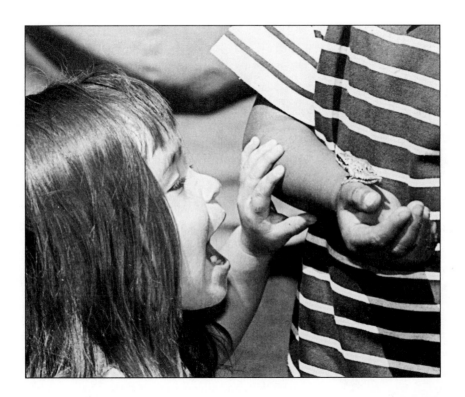

At the turn the century, early education for infants and children with special needs offers both promise and challenge. While the field is still young and discovering its knowledge-base, it is also established enough to be considered a necessary and important part of the educational system. Today, to a much greater degree than in the past, society acknowledges the need for early childhood services and values the quality of care and education provided for young children. Professional educators recognize the legitimacy and importance of study in the area of early development. Consequently, Congress has mandated the provision of services to preschool-aged children with disabilities and encouraged states to meet the needs of infants and toddlers with and at risk for developmental delays. Families can expect to become advocates for their children by providing continuous input into the manner of care received in child care, early intervention, and preschool services.

Exciting opportunities open in the field of early childhood special education bring serious responsibilities as well. Much is expected of early educators today. Professionals must be knowledgeable in issues important to families, must demonstrate skill in providing direct services to children, and can contribute to the growing body of knowledge about early development and care. The recent, impressive growth of early childhood special education is a legacy that all professionals can advance only by understanding the philosophy and knowledge-base of best practices. A **best practice** is a dynamic concept, changing in content as the technologies of service and education are extended through research and application. Early childhood educators should expect to be lifelong learners, keeping abreast of evolutionary changes and, at the same time, actively taking part in these changes. The current assumptions of best practice most important in the field of early childhood special education include the following:

1. A growing professional treats the field with an **attitude of science.** That is, individuals respect data-based information and evaluate the effects of new procedures, materials, or interventions by their impact on children and families being served.

2. An early childhood professional values the **inclusion** of children in natural settings where they engage in age-appropriate activities with peers of diverse backgrounds and abilities.

3. An effective professional is **culturally sensitive,** prepared to work with various populations and cultures in respectful and supportive ways.

4. A professional in early childhood education recognizes that very young children are a part of their larger family support systems and the environments that surround them. Such a professional may provide direct services to children, but only within the context of family needs and environmental demands, and in ways that will **empower the family.**

5. An early childhood professional works **collaboratively** with experts from other disciplines to develop and provide the comprehensive services very young children need.

6. Finally, early childhood special educators must practice their profession with the highest **ethical standards** for the children and families served. Professionals must serve as **advocates** for parents and children, politically and professionally, as well as through service to their communities.

Professionals now entering early childhood special education are in the enviable position of launching their careers with skills and attitudes others have taken years to identify and develop. This chapter will explore these key concepts in terms of their value to professionals. These concepts also will be woven throughout the content of the text.

THE IMPORTANCE OF AN ATTITUDE OF SCIENCE

Many professionals consider education to be an art; that is, a natural aptitude or ability granted a person at birth, which flowers with opportunity and experience. Some of this may be true; certainly most professionals in early childhood education were drawn into the field by the pleasure they found in working with young children and their families. Some gifted individuals possess talents that seem especially suited to working with infants, toddlers, and preschoolers. They display tolerance, playfulness, and a keen intuition for teaching. Others may be adept at com-

municating with children and parents, they may be more sensitive to others' needs, or they may be more skilled at working with diverse personalities and backgrounds. However, in all fields the factor separating hobby artists from professional artists is the quality of study and effort they put into developing their natural gifts, whether they be painting, dance, drama, or teaching. Inspiration comes not from spontaneity, but from a combination of knowledge, talent, and experience.

Professional artists enhance their talents by a reflective study of the work of other artists. They strive to identify principles that will improve their craft and advance the field for others. An artful teacher who relies on raw ability alone may take years to become skillful and helpful for a variety of students. Another artful teacher who reads the professional literature, experiments with and evaluates recommended materials and procedures, and holds an **attitude of science** builds on natural talent to efficiently become a versatile and effective teacher.

What Is an Attitude of Science?

An attitude of science deals with what is parsimonious and empirical. ~~Parsimony~~ is the adoption of the simplest assumption in the formulation of a theory or in the interpretation of data. That is, one would look for a simple explanation before investigating more complicated possibilities. For example, if a small infant wakes crying in the middle of the night, one would first see if the child was hungry or wet. One would not immediately jump to the conclusion that the child is suffering separation anxiety or is ill with an intestinal infection. "Parsimony does not guarantee correctness—because the simplest explanation may not always be the correct one—but it prevents our being so imaginative as to lose touch with the reality of observed data" (Alberto & Troutman, 1990, p. 4). Often, what is simplest is not the most interesting. For years, psychologists told mothers of children with autism that the latter were uncommunicative and developmentally delayed because the mother's relationship with her child during infancy had been cold and rejecting. This was an intriguing theory that grew from a complicated Freudian explanation based on psychotherapy with verbal adults, but it was not the most parsimonious. A great deal of mental suffering on the part of mothers, as well as misspent therapy, might have been saved if a parsimonious explanation had been investigated earlier. While there is still no explanation for the etiology of autism, parsimony might have led professionals to investigate biochemical or physical causes earlier if complex theories of attribution had not been so appealing to earlier psychologists.

In special education, many methods of intervention have evolved from complicated theories. Some theories, because they make assumptions about activities in the brain that can neither be seen nor measured easily, are untestable. One example of such a method is patterning or neural training. Thousands of parents were trained to use patterning techniques to "train the brains" of children whose disabilities ranged from mild to very severe. Experts claimed that if parents completed rigorous schedules (several hours per day) of precise movement exercises, their children's brains would begin to function normally. Later, this method was declared to be not only harmful in many cases, but a distraction from more practical and effective methods (Mercer, 1987). In fact, recent research suggests that much of early education, including physical movement exercises, should be conducted within the context of natural daily routines (Mallory & New, 1994). The latter offers a more parsimonious solution to families and children.

An attitude of science is also a "disposition to deal with the facts rather than with what someone has said about them. . . . Science is a willingness to accept facts even when they are opposed to wishes" (Skinner, 1953, p. 6). An attitude of science requires one to be **empirical** (that is, to rely on observation or experimentation) and to be guided by practical experience rather than theory alone. A teacher who is empirical tries out new materials and procedures with careful observation to determine their effect on children or families using them. Based on the outcomes of such experiments, teachers decide to continue or discontinue the use of individual procedures. For example, theory (or trend) may indicate that pastel colors have a warm and calming effect on infants, encouraging their attention. To evaluate this recommendation, an empirical teacher might place an infant in a plain crib with a pastel yellow, pink, and blue mobile and observe carefully to see how much the infant vocalizes, kicks, looks at the mobile, and so on. This teacher would then compare the same infant's behavior when the baby is placed in the same crib and room with a mobile of contrasting white and black. Scientific teachers experiment to find out if a theory really applies in a particular situation, rather than accepting a theory without a verifiable demonstration.

Of course, a teacher cannot function efficiently if every piece of advice must be directly tested or experienced before it is adopted. Fortunately, "science is more than the mere description of events as they occur. Rather, empiricism is an attempt to discover order, to show that certain events stand in lawful relations to other events" (Skinner, 1953, p. 6). Other teachers and researchers work to **replicate** results, that is, to demonstrate the same results with other children and in other settings. A scientific teacher can then review research to identify data-based procedures that have been verified repeatedly through experimentation and that should work in the teacher's own situation.

When the same results can be replicated reliably, and when there is a well-documented literature-base, the theory or principle has **predictive utility.** Such a theory provides accurate forecasts regarding how a child might respond in certain circumstances, thereby giving teachers a useful tool for supporting or modifying a child's behavior. This is not to say the data-based method selected will work with all children. However, the likelihood is increased that this method will work more often or effectively than an untested or unverified method. For example, the principle of **reinforcement** states that if a stimulus is a reinforcer, the behavior it follows is likely to increase in frequency. A teacher might find that giving requested items (a music box, for example) to Amy when she says "please" increases the rate of Amy's saying "please." The teacher might then use those items as consequences for Amy when she takes a step independently, predicting with some confidence that the music box (for example) will act as a reinforcer to increase Amy's independent walking.

"As the principle is tried over and over again and continues to produce the same results, we gain faith in it and the probability that it is indeed true for all behavior" (Whaley & Malott, 1971, p. 444). When a body of knowledge is advanced enough to provide a set of principles based on extensive research and experimentation, it becomes a **conceptual system.** A conceptual system shows researchers and teachers how similar procedures may be derived from basic principles. "This can have the effect of making a body of technology into a discipline rather than a collection of tricks. Collections of tricks historically have been difficult to expand systematically, and when they were extensive, difficult to learn and teach" (Baer, Wolf, & Risley, 1968, p. 97).

Look again at the example of Amy's saying "please." Using the music box as a consequence seems like a pretty good trick to Ms. Johnson, who is visiting that day. When she returns to her classroom, she tries the music box as a consequence for Joey to see if it will increase his babbling. Nothing happens. Ms. Johnson would have been more successful if she understood the principle behind the use of the music box. If she had the **concept** of reinforcement in her repertoire, she would have looked for some consequence that was already effective in increasing the rate of Joey's behavior. A brief observation might show that Joey reaches for a toy more frequently when the toy is squeezed to make a noise each time Joey reaches for it. Squeezing the toy as a consequence to increase Joey's babbling has a higher probability of success than playing the music box. Or, if Ms. Johnson recognized the concept that a child's frequently chosen activities or materials often act as reinforcers, she might have found that marshmallows, bouncing, or clapping would also be predictable reinforcers. Ms. Johnson's skills would have been much improved if she had a data-based conceptual system from which to work, and not just a "trick." Applied behavior analysis offers one data-based conceptual system that is of great value to educators. Behavioral approaches are parsimonious in that they deal with observable relationships between environmental stimuli, behavioral responses, and contingent consequences.

Table 1.1/ *Basic Principles of Applied Behavior Analysis*

Basic Principle	Contingent Consequence	Effect on Future Rate of Behavior	Example
Reinforcement	When a stimulus is presented (positive) or removed (negative) contingent upon a response,	the future probability of that response *increases.*	A child who chews his carrot carefully before swallowing is given ice cream immediately after and in the future he chews carefully more often. (positive reinforcement)
Punishment	When a stimulus is presented or removed contingent upon a response,	the future probability of that response *decreases.*	A child who hits his play partner is removed from the play activity and told to watch for five minutes before he is returned to the play activity, and in the future he hits less often.
Extinction	When the contingent stimulus for a previously reinforced response is no longer presented,	the future probability of the behavior *decreases.*	A child who takes toys away from others has in the past been allowed to keep playing with the stolen toys and her rate of stealing toys increased. Now the teacher makes sure she must return any toy taken from another child and her rate of stealing decreases.

"For a behaviorist, all learning principles are defined on the basis of what actually happens, not what we think is happening" (Alberto & Troutman, 1990, p. 23). The basic principles of behavior analysis were developed through extensive empirical testing and were replicated in thousands of classroom, clinic, and home applications. Therefore, the principles and procedures have a high degree of predictive utility and many successful interventions have been developed based on this conceptual system. Though it is not within the scope of this text to teach the principles of behavior analysis, a few examples drawn from this discipline will help to illustrate elements of a conceptual system. The basic principles of behavior analysis include reinforcement, punishment, and extinction, though these simple principles have been extended to dozens of procedures that help children learn (see Table 1.1). Yet this conceptual system, like all others, must be challenged by scientific educators to build on and improve their ability to match intervention to the needs of children and families served. The scientific teacher builds on natural talent for working with children, families, and professionals by drawing from a knowledge-base of concepts that work because they are parsimonious, empirically derived, and replicable.

THE IMPORTANCE OF FULL INCLUSION

While full inclusion may be, as some regard it, a passing fancy of modern time (Fuchs & Fuchs, 1994; Hilton & Smith, 1994), it is possible that at some point its challenge to this

Full Inclusion

generation of educators may also be viewed as a measure of their resolve to build a world that is more dignified, more just, more ethical, and more practical. Since schools and classrooms are microcosms of the society, the extent to which children are isolated from each other in schools reflects society's willingness and intent to isolate this same group of individuals outside the walls of the school (Gerrard, 1994).The justification for full inclusion is relatively simple compared to the task of putting this philosophy into practice. The following argument provided by Skrtic (1991) explains, in part, why implementation of inclusive practices is so controversial.

> When industrialization and compulsory school attendance converged to produce large numbers of students who are difficult to teach in traditional classrooms, the problem of school failure was reframed as two interrelated problems—inefficient organization and defective students . . . the field of special education . . . emerged as a means to remove and contain the most recalcitrant students in the interest of maintaining order in the rationalized school plant. (p. 152)

In fact, educators are so divided on this issue they cannot even agree on a label, let alone a definition, for this practice. The following is an attempt to define *full inclusion* for early intervention as it will be discussed throughout the remainder of the text.

What Is Full Inclusion?

Before the term *full inclusion* evolved, others were used in special education to refer to the placement of children with disabilities in the same physical setting as children without disabilities. These terms include *mainstreaming, least restrictive environment,* and *integration.* Because these terms do not always mean the same thing to different people, there is confusion among professionals and parents. The following is an attempt to define these terms as discrete practices, but in no way should this suggest that these definitions are widely accepted. **Mainstreaming** is when children who have a disability participate in programs designed for typical children in areas where their disability does not affect their performance as compared to the majority of their peers. In other words, whenever an adaptation to a program must take place in order for a child to be successful (e.g., different response requirement, more instruction, more resources), it is unlikely the child with disabilities will be included. Such segregation results in a reduction in the expectations of both the regular classroom teacher and the special education personnel. The result is sometimes a permanent sentence to the special education domain; a loss of the separated child's sense of self-worth associated with the label, the treatment, and the separation itself; and an easy target for deprecation by peers and adults (Wolfensberger, 1983).

Least Restrictive Environment (LRE) is the legal term used to define the rights of children with disabilities to be educated in settings where they are not segregated from children without disabilities. The law states:

> . . . to the maximum extent appropriate, handicapped children, including children in public or private institutions or other care facilities, are educated with children who are not handicapped, and that special classes, separate schooling, or other removal of handicapped children from the regular educational environment occurs only when the nature or severity of the handicap is such that education in regular classes with the use of supplementary aids and services cannot be achieved satisfactorily. (Section 612(5)B of P. L. 94-142)

The Individuals with Disabilities Act (IDEA) reaffirmed the right of preschoolers as well as infants and toddlers to an education in the least restrictive environment. However, the definition is vague enough that considerable discretion is given to decision makers. Consequently, phrases such as "to the greatest extent *possible*" and "*separation should occur* only when" are clauses through which some educators have found justification for placing children in more, rather than less, restrictive settings. In fact, it has recently been discovered that since the original passage of IDEA in 1975, a substantially larger percentage of children eligible for special education are served in *more,* rather than *less,* restrictive settings (Gerrard, 1994). For example, students with special needs who were served full time in the regular classroom (with modifications) decreased by 71% in the past 20 years. The legal mandate for Local Education Agencies (LEA) to provide a full continuum of services, which range from full-time placement in typical settings to institutionalization, guarantees that schools will maintain a parallel system of segregation.

Integration occurs when children with special needs are placed in specialized separate classrooms within a public school. Many preschool programs for children served through special education are located on the grounds or in the buildings of public elementary schools. Even though such children may have the opportunity to see, and even interact with, other children without disabilities, they are still viewed as exceedingly different because they have their own classrooms, their own buses, and their own recesses. This is especially true of preschool-aged children with disabilities, who seldom have peers of the same age who are educated within public schools. Instead, most preschool-age peers are either at home or in private preschool or daycare programs.

Additionally, children with disabilities are often excluded from school functions because they might be disruptive or because these activities are not deemed age-appropriate. The very fact that children with disabilities are grouped together highlights their differences and distances them from others. Furthermore, the fact that social interactions take place only when nondisabled peers are asked to be helpers or trained to be their "buddies" decreases the likelihood that natural reciprocal interaction will develop.

Integration is usually accompanied by the presence of students with disabilities in regular classroom environments for nonacademic activities. This recent practice increased the likelihood that peers might influence each other's social skill development through episodic positive interactions. Arranging for a preschool child with a disability to spend part of the day in a regular kindergarten class is an example of this type of integration. However, whenever a child is removed from the classroom, even for part of the day, the child is less likely to be viewed by peers as a true member of the class; rather, the child is viewed as a visitor, not belonging to the normal constituency of the group.

As with other developments in the evolution of Least Restrictive Environment, **full inclusion** is not simply a child's placement, but has to do with the integrity of the placement. When a child with a disability is placed in a regular setting without the delivery of the specialized services that define special education, everyone in the system loses—the teacher, the other students, the parents, and the children with disabilities themselves.

Full inclusion occurs when a student with a disability becomes a full-time member of a program the child might attend if he or she did not have a disability, and the child is not removed for the delivery of educational, social, or related services. Full inclusion means that every student, not just students with significant disabilities, or students with mild disabilities, or students with perceptual disabilities, has an opportunity to become a contributing member of a heterogeneous group of children. Students participate in all the regular daily routines of the classroom. These routines are modified through specialized instructional or curricular strategies to meet each child's individually determined functional, social, or educational objectives. Each student has multiple opportunities during the day for naturally occurring positive interactions with students without disabilities. The classroom teacher is the primary interventionist, and has frequent and regular consultation from educational specialists, from administrators, and from the children's parents—all of whom comprise a decision-making team supporting the classroom teacher. A child is fully included when there is access to routine curricular and extracurricular activities and the child is a part of not just the classroom, but the school and the community. In sum, full inclusion is supported education—support for the classroom teacher and support for the student.

Justification for Full Inclusion

The practice of full inclusion has been variously justified by identifying social, philosophical, ethical, legal, and empirical arguments. First, if children with and without disabilities are educated together, they learn important lifelong lessons and skills necessary for sustained positive relationships with each other. That is, if individuals are expected to get along in integrated environments as adults, then they must have opportunities to learn to get along as children (Salisbury, Palombaro, & Long, 1993). In fact, studies support the notion that facilitated inclusion models lead to a higher frequency of interactions and enhance the development of social and adaptive skills of children with disabilities (Coles & Meyer, 1991; Fox & Hanline, 1993; Hanline, 1993). For example, McGee, Paradis, and Feldman (1993) found that when children with autism were surrounded by children without disabilities, they displayed autistic behavior at a lower rate than when they were either with other children with autism or alone. When preschool children with disabilities attend inclusive programs, their peers are more accepting of them than of those in self-contained programs (Esposito & Koorland, 1989; Guralnick & Groom, 1988). An interview of children who were in an integrated classroom with a child with severe disabilities gave evidence of the importance of such relationships:

What is friendship?

Hong: "A friendship is the best thing out of all others that you could ever achieve in your whole entire lifetime."

Mario: ". . . in this world most people all need at least one friend to survive."

What have you learned from Jaime?

José: "He makes me feel good when I am sad, and when I get mad, he slows me down."

Zach: "I learned that he could fit in with everyone in the school and he wanted to be friends and he is my friend. Being friends with Jaime has its advantages. He is very nice, considerate, kind, polite, and my favorite, a cool kid." (Jubala & Bishop, 1994, pp. 38–39)

Second, since the late 1960s, the field of special education has promoted a philosophy of normalization, which is based on the practice of treating persons with disabilities as valuable members of society (Wolfensberger, 1972). When persons are segregated, labeled, or treated in any way that sets them further apart for their differences, then their worth is devalued (Lipsky & Gartner, 1989; Wolfensberger, 1983). When such a practice is commonplace, as it now is, individuals with differences begin to see themselves as less valuable and to behave in ways that match their devalued status. In this scenario, young children with disabilities can achieve their highest potential only when they are provided with normal opportunities. This rationale may be the most vulnerable, and the one that leaves inclusion open to criticism as a passing trend or frivolous sentimentality. Yet, Rainforth (1994) contended that, "philosophy is a powerful influence, perhaps *the* influence, on how individual needs of children can be met most appropriately" (p. 252).

Third, the United States legal system protects the equitable treatment of all citizens. The Equal Protection Clause of the Fourteenth Amendment to the Constitution provided the legal basis for the Civil Rights Act of 1965, which in turn set the stage to argue for equal treatment of persons with disabilities. In 1973, Congress wrote Section 504 of the Vocational Rehabilitation Act, indicating that no person can be discriminated against solely on the basis of the presence of a disability. The Least Restrictive Environment mandate of IDEA further added to the legal foundation for full inclusion. This collective legislation, however, has led to thousands of hearings in which parents and school districts have disagreed about the proper interpretation for specific children.

While it is important to justify full inclusion with an empirical basis, it is perhaps more important to identify strategies for improving the success of students within natural settings (Gerrard, 1994). As one father questioned, "Why must children 'prove' they are ready to be in regular classrooms? We do not ask that of any other members of our society" (J. Terhaar, personal communication, January 16, 1995). Though research on this topic is complex, preliminary findings indicate that children with and without disabilities perform at least as well in integrated settings as children who are separated based on the presence of a disability (Fox & Hanline, 1993; Hanline, 1993). Furthermore, a promising knowledge-base is evolving that provides a means of bringing services to children, rather than bringing children to services (Kamps, Leonard, Vernon, Dugan, & Delquádri, 1992). Not all research is supportive, however. For example, Cole, Dale, Jenkins, and Mills (1991) found that of 124 children with disabilities who were placed in inclusive settings, higher performing students performed better, while lower performing students tended to perform better in more segregated settings.

While these rationales seem to provide a sufficient basis for advocacy of full inclusion for all children with disabilities, there is a final and perhaps more compelling reason to eliminate the dual educational system that arbitrarily separates regular from special education. Full inclusion may be the only *practical* choice for children. Social policies in this country have led to poverty for more adults and children and have a direct impact on early childhood education. Poverty and its social consequences put children at risk.

There is no evidence that the number of young children in society who have special needs and are at risk of failure will decrease in the future. For example, primary teachers indicate a growing concern that fewer and fewer children enter their classrooms with the expected levels of skill and social competencies (Healy, 1990). It is impractical to think that all needy children could be served in segregated programs. Furthermore, it does not make sense to separate a smaller percentage of children who happen to actually be identified.

The final rationale for advocating inclusive preschool programs is related to personnel issues. Arguably, segregated early childhood special education programs pose the greatest challenge for teachers. Teachers must plan for and execute educational programs that provide individual instruction for students with a wide range of ages and disabilities. The growing number of children identified with significant behavioral problems increases the chaos in a classroom where children have limited language skills and only modest development of rule-governed behavior. The impossibility of managing such a classroom is likely to lead to teacher resignations, or perhaps more damaging, teacher burnout. By contrast, inclusive classrooms can absorb children with disabilities while those typical students who follow rules, play independently, and stay on task for reasonable lengths of time help adults by providing modeling and by requiring less management.

Opposition to Inclusion

Ample justification for full inclusion has not been matched with concomitant implementation. Reasons for this delay include practical as well as sociological barriers. Gerrard (1994) summarized six major objections to inclusion:

> ***Lack of input by regular educators:*** *Since inclusive efforts began in earnest in the late 1980s, there has been very little input or initiative from regular educators themselves. Yet, it is the expectation of parents of children with disabilities and special educators, the forces behind the movement, that changes take place in the regular education domain. Many regular educators resent the fact that major changes must take place in their classrooms when the practice of inclusion is really based on someone else's ideology.*

Lack of empirical evidence: Some view the inclusive movement as no more than a political policy. These educators argue that school decisions should not be regulated by politics, but by sound educational practices. It is predicted that the political nature of inclusive efforts destines the movement to failure.

Practitioner resistance: Opposition to inclusion by regular and special education teachers, who tend to prefer the pull-out model, is fierce. This resistance is likely due to educators being comfortable with what they know—and what teachers know—as separate schooling.

Educational reform: Teachers are pulled by seemingly opposing forces. While educational reform efforts are pressing teachers to improve educational achievement, there is also a demand on schools to be leaders in promoting equity.

Protection: Many educators and parents feel that separate schooling is necessary to protect children with disabilities from rejection by their nonhandicapped peers.

Impractical: Historically, children were removed from the regular classroom because it was believed that specialized education could not be conducted effectively in a general education setting. This argument is still compelling, as regular classrooms are seen as nonadaptable for inclusion. Hence, the needs of students with disabilities cannot be fully met there.

Perhaps, because these arguments have not been sufficiently addressed by proponents of full inclusion, the debate over full inclusion as a philosophy and a policy continues (Rainforth, 1994). While some schools have seized the opportunity to explore new delivery systems that permit inclusive education, a majority of educational programs either maintain or purposively reestablish more traditional segregated models. Programs that have been successful are those where individual communities have adapted methods and models of inclusion to fit their own educational structure. Hence, Thousand and Villa (1991) advocated that schools moving toward inclusion should allow "professional educators and community members . . . the flexibility and discretion to invent unique approaches and solutions to achieving . . . quality heterogeneous schooling" (p. 559). Forest (1988) further observed that schools committed to inclusion were characterized as "incredibly child centered systems with leadership which believes in team building, cooperation, collaboration, and learning. They are also systems that dare to talk about love and social justice" (p. 2).

There are many who claim schools can either have inclusion or appropriate individualized educational programming—but not both (Fuchs & Fuchs, 1994). That is, some feel that one must forfeit educational programming for social integration. In fact, there is the risk this will happen if inclusion is not properly planned and implemented, with children, as feared, "dumped" into regular classrooms (File & Kontos, 1993).

Sometimes things work out (Salisbury, et al., 1993), but too often administrators and practitioners rush to implement inclusive programs with limited understanding of and commitment to the philosophy, and they exercise too little patience and integrity in the process. Consequently, many children who are said to be "included" are placed in a typical setting where they are not wanted and where educators do not have the skills or support to provide an individualized education (Pudlas, 1993). Later, these same children, who, like their parents, have been humiliated, are sent back to special education programs. Educators say, "you see, inclusion doesn't work," when full inclusion, as defined here, was never attempted.

Representing a far different point of view are those who believe that persons should not only be recognized by their labels and segregated accordingly, but that they should develop cultures identified exclusively by a disability (Hallahan & Kauffman, 1994). For example a large percentage of deaf persons belong to the "deaf culture," a community in the broad sense that is socially, economically, and politically entwined (Singleton, 1992). Advocates of cultures of disability cite internal pride in their "differentness" and reject the intrusive imperi-

Michael Moore, Full Inclusion for the First Time

Interview with Marsha Moore

The thing that I remember most about Mike's first days of being fully included in a regular classroom was the day before school started. This sounds so silly, but it brings tears to my eyes. It was routine for the teachers to post the names of the children who were in their classes to the outside of their classroom doors several days before school started, so that the students would be able to anticipate their new teachers and see which friends would be in their classes for the upcoming school year. We had driven to school so our daughter, who was in fifth grade, could get the scoop on her teacher and classmates. Mike had already been assigned to a specific first-grade classroom, and we had been given the opportunity to meet with his teacher and visit his empty class-room several days before.

As we made our way around the school, we came to Michael's classroom. There on the door was posted the classroom list, and there in the list of alphabetical names in the boys' column was Michael's name! It sounds like such a simple thing, but he was finally a part of a "real" classroom. His sisters were thrilled and brought him close in hopes that he might recognize his name. They read him the names of the other children in the class. "Mike, look, this is *your* class!" they told him proudly. This symbol, just a simple class list, communicated to us that Michael finally belonged and was not just on the periphery of life. For some reason, that little list of names signified to us the beginning of commu-nity. Michael's name was neither at the top nor the bottom, but right where it should have been.

Anyway, we started school. I thought to myself, "This poor teacher, she really doesn't know what she's in for." But to my surprise, those little first graders just took Mike into their hearts and included him in all they did. They cared for him and would help him. Instead of an aide being at his side to keep him from self-stimming on his shoelaces and throwing his glasses to the ground,

the kids surrounded him and helped him to learn how the real world behaves.

Michael's gains have always been painfully slow for us, but he has made gains. He makes eye contact more consistently, initiates interaction with others, and attends to books. We can take him to church and even to full-length movies. He loves to eat out, and although he's not Mr. Manners, he no longer yells, or flaps his hands or bangs his head on the back of the chair. People are not offended by him. His behavior has changed.

Some people in the school district have told me this behavior change is probably just the result of maturation. They are not certain that full inclu-sion for Michael in the regular classroom has really made the difference in his behavior and think he would have probably changed as much if he had spent the last several years in a self-contained classroom. Well, I can guarantee he wouldn't be the same little boy without his friends by his side to model for him and remind him when he's out of line. He had been in a self-contained special edu-cation classroom from the time he was three until he was almost seven. His behavior had escalated from baby cries and back arching, when he started preschool, to hand flapping, face smacking, and loud inappropriate vocalizations as he progressed through the system. The older he got, the harder it became for us because he was bigger and stronger and much more noticeable! It was in the regular classroom that he came to know, through the assistance of his classmates, that these behaviors weren't acceptable. That's not to say that every-thing is perfect and we never regress a little, but things are much better.

I can't really know what inclusion has meant to Mike. He can't tell us. I only know what it has meant to us. It's great to belong to the neighborhood school and attend PTA and bake sales with the neighbors next door and down the street. It makes us happy to know that Mike has

(continued)

friends, not just assigned helpers.
This summer three of his classmates
came to visit, unannounced. They
had to come on their bikes because
it was quite a way, but they knew
where Michael lived and wanted
to come and see how he was doing.
In the morning when he walks down
the driveway to catch the bus, several
of his buddies leave the bus line and
run up the driveway to greet him. It takes a while
for Mike to get to the end of the driveway, but
he grins and prances when he sees them. He is
excited to get on the bus in the morning and

pushes himself to get up the bus stairs, just
because school is something he truly looks forward to. It's just important. It means a lot to us
and a lot to Mike.

alism of full inclusionist proponents who would dissemble this form of segregation. Likewise,
Hallahan and Kauffman argued that other disability groups (e.g., learning disabilities, behavior
disorders, etc.) would be better served through creation of subcultures based on the presence
of a disability.

University training programs themselves promote segregation. Rather than providing a
model of collaboration, personnel preparation is typically a parallel training system for regular
and special preschool educators (Gable, McLaughlin, Sindelar, & Kilgore, 1993). To be prepared, even attitudinally, for inclusion, general educators need more than the one or two
courses they typically take in special education (Wolery, et al., 1993). Furthermore, school
systems must make available the necessary resources for inclusion if they expect teachers to
adopt a positive attitude or to become effective educators of students with diverse needs
(Gemmell-Crosby & Hanzlik, 1994; Wolery, et al., 1993).

Research shows that both regular and special education preschool teachers who have
been provided sufficient preservice training for inclusion felt more confident about their abilities and had a more positive attitude toward teaching children with special needs (Gemmell-
Crosby & Hanzlik, 1994). Some of the more effective strategies that have been used and
should be taught in preservice or inservice training include team teaching (e.g., with regular
and special educators), direct service by special personnel within the regular classroom, cooperative learning, peer tutoring or confederacy training, use of parallel curricula, use of technology, and accompaniment by paraprofessionals (Gerrard, 1994).

Summary on Inclusion

Preschool programs, due to their ecology, may provide an ideal context for inclusion.
According to Mallory and New (1994), preschool classrooms are predicated on social activity.
Most early childhood programs are language and social skills based and have multiple daily
activities in which children are encouraged to learn from contextually relevant and problem-

based curricula. The use of principles of developmentally appropriate curriculum and authentic evaluation may be well suited for children with diverse needs.

Developmentally appropriate practice (DAP) emphasizes active exploration and interaction with learning activities and materials that are concrete, real, and relevant to young children (Bredekamp, 1987). Children's interests guide activities, and caregivers support success in completing tasks, reducing stress, and promoting self-esteem and self-control. The DAP approach may serve as a good context in which intervention for children with disabilities can be conducted, though one must also identify the needs of children with disabilities and continue to individualize for those children to be sure these needs are met (Bailey & Wolery, 1992).

Authentic assessment encourages gathering information about a child's skills and abilities from a variety of classroom and family sources. Teachers and parents may observe children with structured or informal instruments and checklists, keep anecdotal records, interview children, and examine child work samples across time in order to build a complete portfolio for the child and to identify strengths and areas that need support (Pike & Salend, 1995). These student-centered data add to the information collected through norm referenced testing and may give more realistic or complete bases for intervention.

Because of the compatibility of inclusive philosophy and socially mediated pedagogy in early childhood special education, opposition to inclusion should be less intense. Perhaps early childhood education can provide a model of inclusiveness for programs serving school-aged students.

THE IMPORTANCE OF BEING CULTURALLY SENSITIVE

The United States has long enjoyed a heritage enriched by diverse cultures, languages, and religions. For the most part, however, early settlers from European homelands dominated its cities, businesses, newspapers, churches, and so on to create a fairly standard image of a white, Christian, nuclear family in the United States. In recent years, however, trends in birthrates, immigration, family structures, and economics have greatly altered national **demographics** and will continue to do so in the future. Because families are the center of planning and provision of services to very young children, it is important that early childhood professionals acknowledge a broad, inclusive definition of family. Early childhood professionals must be prepared for the consequences of changes in society that contribute to increasing diversity among families served. It is unlikely these trends will reverse, yielding profound changes in the culture and the profession. While there is sometimes a temptation to dwell on the comfort of status quo, early educators are challenged to embrace the inevitable changes with both a determination to adapt and an appreciation for the gifts of diversity. An analysis of current and future population changes may lend greater appreciation to the need for a pluralistic perspective.

Population Trends

The 1990 census showed increasing ethnic and racial diversity in this country. Hispanic citizens number 21 million, a 44% increase since 1980. People of "other" races (mostly Asian) grew the fastest during the 1980s, up by 65%. African-Americans continue to make up about 12% of the total population of this country though Caucasians have fallen from an 86% to an 84% share of the total.

By the year 2000, one-fourth to one-third of the United States population will be African-American, Hispanic, or Asian (Allen & Turner, 1990; Feistritzer, 1987; Wehrly, 1988). By the year 2050, Caucasians will comprise barely 50% of the total United States population

(Martin & Midgley, 1994). In many of the largest urban counties and some nonmetropolitan counties, the shift has already occurred, with no single ethnic or racial group maintaining a majority (Allen & Turner, 1990). Thirty-three states already have K–12 minority enrollments of 20% or more, and minority enrollment has increased in 44 states in the last five years. All 25 of the nation's largest city school systems have "majority minorities" (Wehrly, 1988).

Today's immigrants, unlike those from previous periods in United States history, are most likely to come from Latin American and Asian countries, birth homes to 85% of all immigrants in the 1980s (Martin & Midgley, 1994). Today's immigrants are less well educated, poorer, and more likely to be unemployed than past immigrants. In fact, every year nearly two-thirds of legal immigrants live and work in the United States illegally before being granted legal status. Hispanics are by far the fastest growing minority group, largely due to current immigration rates (Martin & Midgley, 1994). Other factors contributing to demographic shifts are the birthrate, which is slightly higher in foreign-born families than for native-born citizens, and the fact that immigrant females tend to be younger than average native-born women. Hence, foreign-born women accounted for 15% of births nationwide in 1990, though they comprised just 8% of the total population. In California, the changes are greatest; in 1991, for example, 42% of all births were produced by foreign-born women (Martin & Midgley, 1994).

By the year 2000, there will be twice as many Hispanics in this country as there were in 1990, and by 2030, the increase will be fourfold (Exter, 1987). Hispanics, like most recent immigrant groups throughout history, suffer from the highest rates of poverty, have the highest school dropout rates, and are educated in the most highly segregated settings (Orum, 1986). Out of every 100 Hispanic children, 39 live in poverty. About 37% of Hispanics will not finish high school, and even in the primary grades, 28% will be enrolled below grade level for their age. Since Hispanic subgroups tend to concentrate in particular metropolitan areas, some children attend schools with 90% minority enrollment (Orum, 1986).

African-American enrollment in public schools increased 3% between 1972 and 1992, while Caucasian enrollment dropped 14% (Orfield, Schley, Glass, & Reardon, 1994). The latter does not represent an increased enrollment in private schools by Caucasian students as some believe, but an overall drop in the number of school-age Caucasian children in the United States.

Unfortunately, special education services are not proportionately representative of minority populations (Rounds, Weil, & Bishop, 1994). Hispanics, African-Americans, and American Indians tend to be overrepresented in special education (Williams, 1992). This is due to many confounding factors that tend to correlate with minority status, including limited parental education, language differences, and lack of resources, all of which may contribute to an endless cycle of educational disadvantage. Though difficult to estimate precisely, the disastrous impact of institutional biases in testing, curriculum, social expectations, and teaching strategies on the appropriate education of minority children is apparent.

Jonathan Kozol (1992), after visiting inner city schools across the country, charged that, "The dual society, at least in public education, seems in general to be unquestioned. . . . In public schooling, social policy has been turned back almost one hundred years" (p. 4). After two decades of improvement in the desegregation of schools during the 1960s and 1970s, a reversal in this trend is occurring. The changes, while not obvious until the late 1980s, were attributed to Justice Department efforts during the early 1980s to abolish enforcement of desegregation policies (Orfield, et al., 1994). Thus, demographic shifts (see Figure 1.1) in the schools may be part of a deliberate effort to reverse patterns of social integration established since 1965.

Early educators must be sensitive to cultural differences that may be of concern to specific culturally diverse groups (Heward, 1996). For example, Caucasian teachers generally place a high value on eye contact when talking with a student, but many African-Americans engage in conversation without making eye contact at all times; they may even participate in unrelated activities while still paying attention to a conversation. Hispanic children may be reluctant to ask for help because they are accustomed to their families responding to nonverbal cues when help is needed. Hispanic children may work well in group projects but may not be motivated to strive

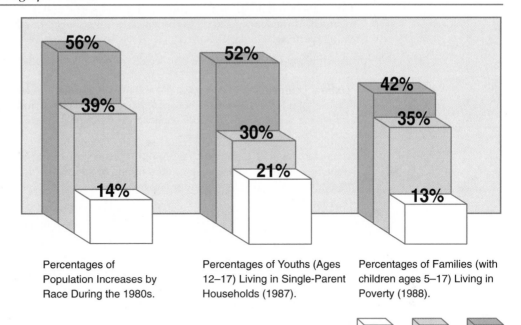

Percentages of Population Increases by Race During the 1980s.

Percentages of Youths (Ages 12–17) Living in Single-Parent Households (1987).

Percentages of Families (with children ages 5–17) Living in Poverty (1988).

Key: White Hispanic Black

Source: Data compiled from the U.S. Census Bureau 1987 "Marital Status and Living Arrangements" report, and the 1988 "Money, Income, and Poverty in the United States" report.

for individual gain. Asian-American parents may be reluctant to seek help for a child with disabilities, preferring instead to handle a child's abnormal behaviors within the family. American Indian children with disabilities may be so absorbed within the family and community that it is difficult to identify and provide services to these children. These and many other differences may interfere with a teacher's understanding of the family and communication between school and home unless early educators work hard to learn about a child's culture and customs.

The National Association for the Education of Young Children makes clear that meeting the challenge of diversity is an essential component of quality early childhood education programs (Jones & Derman-Sparks, 1992). Their criteria state that staff must treat children of all races, religions, and cultures with respect and consideration. To do this successfully, teachers need to recognize attitudes and approaches that interfere with meeting these criteria (Jones & Derman-Sparks, 1992):

1. Teachers believe they are not prejudiced, but in fact everyone learns prejudices through practices and stereotypes that are all around and must notice them and act to correct them. For example, inappropriate images of American Indians abound in alphabet books, cartoons, and Westerns.

2. Teachers are proud of being colorblind, when in fact they are merely fitting all children into a Euro-American mold that does not encourage children to value their own origins.

3. Teachers believe that Caucasian children are unaffected by diversity issues, when in fact even in classes where all the children are Caucasian, these children need to learn to live in a society that is ever-increasing in its diversity.

4. Teachers assume that the minority children they teach are "culturally deprived," have inadequate or inferior parenting, use incorrect language, and don't know how to be American. These teachers need to recognize the importance of other cultures' child-rearing practices.

Early childhood professionals are also legally responsible for delivering services to families in a culturally competent manner (IDEA Amendments of 1991, sec 678b[7]). Roberts (1990) defined **cultural competence** as "a program's ability to honor and respect those beliefs, interpersonal styles, attitudes and behaviors both of families who are clients and the multicultural staff who are providing services" (p. 4). More explicitly, five essential criteria contribute to cultural competence (Cross, Bazron, Dennis, & Issacs, 1989):

1. *Acknowledging and valuing differences.* This value stresses respect for individual uniqueness, while developing an understanding of the manner in which race, culture, and ethnicity influence families and children.

2. *Conducting a cultural self-assessment.* Practitioners must be aware of their own culture and the manner in which such beliefs shape their personal and professional behavior.

3. *Recognizing and understanding the dynamics of difference.* Practitioners need to recognize that factors such as racism, social status, and the long history of race relations in this country influence the substance and quality of interactions between individuals of different cultures. For example, a Caucasian teacher might expect that African-American parents would be somewhat distrustful, and it may take a long time before rapport is established (Rounds, et al., 1994).

4. *Acquiring cultural knowledge.* Teachers who work with families of children with disabilities need to have a good understanding of these families' cultural backgrounds. At the same time, this understanding must be tempered with the ability to view families individually, because of variations within groups.

5. *Adapting to diversity.* Early childhood educators must adapt to the needs and styles of family cultures. These adaptations include using culturally unbiased assessment practices, recognizing the importance and role of service providers within a culture, and understanding the "ethnic realities" of disability.

Economics

One-fourth of children in this country are born into poverty, compared to only one in eight adults (Feistritzer, 1987). The consequences of childhood poverty are multiple. Poor children are more likely to have a low birth weight, more likely to die in the first year, more likely to suffer hunger or abuse, and less likely to have adequate medical care. The rates at which children are judged by teachers to need remedial or special education are much higher for children in poverty than for children from families with greater economic resources (Hodgkinson, 1985).

The likelihood that a child will live in poverty tends to parallel the data on children from minority families; one in three African-Americans, compared to one in ten Caucasians, lives below the poverty line ("Black and White in America," 1988). At present, 90% of the increase in children born into poverty is attributed to households headed by an African-American or Hispanic woman (Hodgkinson, 1985). African-American children are more than twice as likely to die in infancy as Caucasians and nine times as likely to be neurologically impaired (Congress of the United States, 1987). It is no wonder that African-American children are three times as likely as Caucasians to be identified as mentally retarded by the public schools (Kozol, 1990).

Children from impoverished families are more likely to be abused and neglected (Wolock & Horowitz, 1984). There has been a 333% increase in the reporting of child abuse in the United States since 1980 (Hegar & Scannapieco, 1995), a statistic paralleled by rising rates of poverty. Not only is child abuse related to poverty, but abuse increases with the amount of poverty (Pelton, 1978). Child neglect is even more closely linked to poverty than child abuse, with neglect occurring between two and ten times as often. Neglect is also more likely to cause death than child abuse (Wolock & Horowitz, 1984).

Homeless families make up a new subgroup living in poverty. Estimates of the number of homeless range from 600,000 to 3 million ("Saving the Children," 1988; Anderson & Koblinsky, 1995). Homeless families are rapidly crowding single homeless people out of shelters, with families accounting for 28% to 43% of the urban homeless ("Saving the Children," 1988), even though most major cities turn away approximately 30% of families who apply for shelter because they have insufficient facilities (Anderson & Koblinsky, 1995). These temporary shelters are characterized as overcrowded with little privacy, high noise level, and limited stays (Anderson & Koblinsky, 1995).

A 1989 estimate put the number of homeless children at 500,000 (Kozol, 1990). A five-fold increase in homeless children was seen in Washington, D.C., in 1986 alone. Nearly half the occupants of homeless shelters in New York City in 1987 were children, whose average age was only six years (Kozol, 1990). The make-up of homeless families could almost be predicted, since a large majority of families are homeless for economic reasons (Anderson & Koblinsky, 1995). Female-headed families constitute 90% of homeless families, and three-quarters of the families are from minority racial or ethnic groups.

A study of homeless children found that 18% of homeless children under age five exhibited impaired gross motor coordination and 15% demonstrated impaired fine motor function (Bassuk & Rubin, 1986). The study also found that at five years of age homeless children exhibited sleep problems, shyness, withdrawal, and aggression similar in level to children diagnosed as emotionally disturbed. More than half of homeless children displayed behavior disturbances and a third showed levels of depression indicating a need for further psychiatric evaluation (Bassuk & Rubin, 1986).

Though most of these children are not literally starving, they do present a steady stream of physical ailments aggravated by neglect, such as ear infection, asthma, and anemia. Since these children are housed in temporary shelters and move frequently, they usually have no established residence and often do not attend school. Shocking numbers of homeless children do not receive their inoculations and for that reason alone are not admitted to school. Those who do attend school are likely to be two years below grade level (Kozol, 1990). Like ethnicity statistics, the impact of homelessness on child development is entwined with other ecological variables (e.g., economics, family configuration, violence in community, etc.). Still, the characteristics of children in homeless situations indicate that many will require the services of early childhood special education.

In working with homeless families, Anderson and Koblinsky (1995) proposed the following practices:

1. Incorporate the principles of family centeredness and interdependence in service delivery;

2. Recognize diversity among families rather than treating them as a homogenous group;

3. Foster family stability, making sure families maintain current support systems, and help to establish new support networks;

4. Empower families to become self-sufficient, respecting individual dignity and including them in the development and implementation of service plans; and

5. Strengthen neighborhoods and communities through actively helping families to maintain ties with their old neighbors or relatives.

Early educators must be especially sensitive to the needs of poor and homeless children when designing programs (McCormick & Holden, 1992). That is, programs for young homeless children must be maximally flexible about scheduling, opening at earlier times and closing later, and providing respite care for parents. Programs should provide transportation or funds to cover transportation expenses. They should provide social and case-management services and emphasize special attention for specific developmental delays and emotional problems that poor and homeless children may exhibit. Staff of such programs must be sensitive to the support and encouragement needed by parents.

Family Composition

Most people recognize that the traditional nuclear family is not predominate today, but perhaps many do not fully comprehend how much diversity exists. In the 1960s, 60% of American families could be described as traditional, with two parents, one at home, and two or three children. Now only about 7% can be considered traditional (Carlile, 1991). By the year 2000, it is expected that 60% of all children in the United States will spend some part of their lives in single-parent homes (Carlile, 1991). These statistics are significant since research indicates that children in families headed by both parents, biological or adoptive, tend to do better in terms of social adjustment and academic performance than children in either **blended families** or those headed by a single parent (Thomson, Hanson, & McLanahan, 1994). Most of the differences in children's outcomes are, however, explained by economic disadvantage. In other words, adoptive families and those headed by two biological parents tend to be more economically stable; and it is the resources, not the family configuration, that place children at social and academic risk. Interestingly, Thomson et al. (1994) found that in most cases parental childrearing behaviors have much less to do with children's outcomes than family income and parents' educational levels.

Poverty is particularly prevalent among families headed by single mothers. By 1986, the number of female-headed families reached more than 6 million, with one out of four children under age 18 living in a single-parent household (Congress of the United States, 1987). Of all female-headed families, 34% are poor, with this group constituting the fastest growing segment of poverty's subgroups. Unfortunately, this incidence correlates with minority status; about 55% of all African-American children and about 33% of Hispanic youth live with a single parent (Duany & Pittman, 1990).

Many single mothers became pregnant while still teenagers and never married. In 1984, 56% of teen births were out of wedlock, compared with only 15% in 1960. Each year more than 550,000 teenagers have children. In addition to environmental risk, babies of teenagers are more likely to be of low birth weight and to suffer birth defects (Spencer, 1985). Teenage mothers are also more likely to deliver premature babies. The high incidence of teenage pregnancy is one contribution to America's infant-mortality ranking, the highest among the 20 industrialized countries of the world (Spencer, 1985). Teenage mothers tend to come from low-income households and chances are that their mothers or sisters were teenage mothers.

Whether Caucasian, African-American, or Hispanic, teens whose families live in poverty and who have poor basic skills are at great risk of early childbearing; about 20% become parents before age 19 (Duany & Pittman, 1990). Yet, birth rates for unmarried minority women ages 15 to 24 years remain much higher than those for Caucasian women (Dorfman, 1988). For example, almost half of births to Hispanic teens are to women 17 or younger (Duany & Pittman, 1990). Once pregnant, teenage mothers tend to drop out of school to have their babies. Most never finish their education and many come to depend on public assistance to survive. Even normal infants of teenage parents may be delayed by the time they begin school due to a mother's lack of parenting skills, lack of education and job skills, and consequent poverty and isolation (Spencer, 1985).

As the number of single-parent and working poor families increases, more and more mothers of young children are compelled to enter the labor force (Olmsted, 1992). Consequently, even if the number of three- to six-year-old children in the United States does not increase, the number of children who need child care will continue to increase. The proportion of children under age six with mothers who work is estimated at 66% (Hofferth &

Jennifer Waritz, Family Hardship

Interview with Tammy Waritz

In my job as a parent advocate, I see families with many difficulties to overcome. One of the biggest problems for families of children with disabilities is finding financial resources. There are a lot of families who don't have insurance and their incomes are not low enough to meet the federal guidelines to get medical assistance, so they're really struggling to figure out how they're going to pay for the services their children need.

For a number of years, our family has made sacrifices that no family should ever have to make. Some of the things that Jennifer requires are common needs for a child with disabilities and we had to be flexible enough to ensure she received what she needed. The cost of her equipment is incredible. For example, the braces that she has on her feet have to be replaced at least once a year, sometimes twice a year, and it costs seven hundred dollars each time. We just got a brand new seat and back for her wheelchair, and it was a thousand dollars. Jennifer's chair alone cost $3500.

Our family got to a point of desperation, and my husband and I separated so that our income could be low enough to receive state funding for Jennifer's needs. At the time Jennifer had been denied state funding, we were only $147 over the monthly eligibility limit on our income. We were stuck; we were struggling just to make enough money for food, shelter, and clothing; even with two blue-collar people working. It wasn't like we had a lot of money and we were trying to cheat the system out of something. We felt like we were being punished because we had this child with special needs and we didn't have jobs that paid twenty dollars an hour.

Finally, our situation reached a point where I had to break down publicly. I knew there were income waiver programs available and that Jennifer met the federal criteria for such a waiver, but the state agency would not approve one. I was crying

uncontrollably one day, and I told them on the phone, "My family cannot continue to live like this. We can't afford to have a single-parent household. Furthermore, it's not right that I have to continue turning down raises at work to keep the financial assistance we have. If my family cannot access a waiver, you're going to have to place Jennifer because we cannot continue to live the way that we're living."

The need for medical funding literally put us in the position to choose between Jennifer and our family, though she is part of our family. I begged, "Please don't make us make that choice." I don't know how many lawyers we saw, on a consultation kind of basis, and they never charged us anything, but they all said, "There's nothing your family can do, you just don't have an option."

Finally, the state granted an exception to policy to give us a waiver for Jennifer. She is now deemed as an individual household of one, so that our income no longer counts against her eligibility for Social Security Supplementary Income (SSI) and

(continued)

*JENNIFER IN
HER WHEELCHAIR*

Medicaid. For us, the SSI, which is the check that she gets, wasn't important. It didn't matter to us whether she got one penny of financial assistance as long as she got the medical help she needed.

I think that it was fortunate I was well informed, assertive, and articulate, and I also think that's why I do the work that I do. Outside my job as a parent advocate, I'm very active legislatively, and I'm thankful that I've had a supportive husband who recognized that's a need I have. We are better off because I've learned to be politically active. It's my crusade. I don't want other families to have to experience what we've gone through. I can help to lessen that hardship because I've impacted the system in changes that go beyond Jennifer to reach other families in need.

This year my husband and I filed for divorce. The stress on the family for the last nine years has taken its toll. Certainly not all of our marital difficulties were caused by challenges in state agencies, but a family can only endure so much hardship before its foundation is eroded. I believe my family has now paid the ultimate sacrifice to a system that was set up to help and support but fell short in doing so.

Phillips, 1987). The number of children who spend a significant amount of each day in professional care places greater responsibility on early educators to provide appropriate experiences for these children and their families.

As many as 30% of children from divorced families live in stepfamilies, the other 70% live with their mothers or fathers alone (Clarke-Stewart, 1989). Divorce, however, does not account for all family diversity. Children may be living with grandparents, in foster care, or in residential facilities. The foster care systems in the United States are overwhelmed by the numbers of children who need assistance (Hegar & Scannapieco, 1995). This is partly because the total number of foster families dropped from 147,000 to 100,000 between 1984 and 1990 (National Commission on Foster Family Care, 1991). Many infants and young children spend the early part of their lives in "boarder" nurseries, temporary shelters where shift changes and high ratios of children to caretakers decrease the possibility of healthy attachments (Griffith, 1992). Children lucky enough to be placed in foster care may find untrained foster parents overwhelmed by the demands of caring for children with special needs and may consequently be returned to institutional placement (Griffith, 1992).

An emerging family option, developed out of necessity, is **kinship care** (Hegar & Scannapieco, 1995). Defined broadly, **kin** may include extended family, such as grandmothers and aunts, as well as other members of a community who are close to a family. Primary reasons for kinship care are parental drug abuse and neglect. Yet, full-time living arrangements with kin tend to have significant advantages over traditional foster care options. Children who stay with kin tend to be more stable and are associated with fewer behavioral problems than those in foster-care, even though most kinship caregivers live in poverty themselves (Iglehart, 1994).

What can professionals do to assist children whose lives are complicated by divorce or separation, who are surviving with a single parent, or whose lives in some other way no longer fit the "traditional" image? Several actions may be appropriate (Carlile, 1991), though empirical research is meager. Teachers should use instructional activities that teach children about the many different types of family structures in today's society. Numerous books deal with divorce, single parenting, grandmothers as guardians, and so on, and can be used to show different kinds of families. Teachers should modify their language and actions to match existing family patterns—inviting a grandparent to Open House, making a Mother's Day card for an aunt, speaking with foster parents at child conferences. Professionals need to make special efforts to keep communication open with both parents or other appropriate guardians. This may mean adjusting conference times, making evening telephone calls when working parents are home, or sending out multiple copies of announcements. Finally, professionals need to recognize they can provide a kind of safety net of consistency and support as children go through transitions in family situations. Yet, none of these expectations are as simple as they might appear. In order to be comfortable in this role, professionals must be secure in their own lives and careers.

Summary on Diversity

This nation is rapidly becoming a people of color, with significant growth in minority populations in virtually every region of the country. Though the United States has moved forward in defining equity, justice, and multiculturalism, the country has done a poor job in translating these attitudes into improved educational achievement (Wells, 1988). In fact, due to significant political shifting during the 1980s, culturally diverse families have drifted further behind the mainstream economically, educationally, and perhaps most importantly, in terms of hope for improvement. Historical mistreatment of minority populations has contributed to the growth of a high risk group who tend to have a considerable disadvantage in the education system (Bempechat & Ginsburg, 1989).

To conclude that educational underachievement and other social problems are caused by racial characteristics would be inaccurate and inappropriate. The correlation between race and educational disadvantage is far more complicated, as multiple factors influence members of racial minorities in this country (Williams, 1992). Educators need greater preparation in working with families who are at risk. Family service planning and case management must become a natural part of all educational planning. Early childhood professionals need to be familiar with local resources and be able to empower families to identify and access community services. Special service delivery must reach beyond the traditional services of the school building to locations on the streets, in shelters, and within community centers. Traditionally delivered services are unlikely to reach those in greatest need if they are offered only within the agency setting. Likewise, such services will provide only part of what is needed unless they are given in conjunction with social services support. Team management and social support should include family counseling, financial assistance, job training, family planning, and housing.

As educators address the needs of the increasing numbers of children who are at risk, more comparisons will be made between minority children and children of the dominant culture. Because race is certain to be emphasized, these comparisons may unfairly foster a view that minority students are inferior and incompetent, particularly when cultural differences are viewed as deficits (McLoyd, 1990). Yet, minority status is confounded by socioeconomic class, and poverty alone is a critical factor limiting educational attainment (Sewell & Hauser, 1976). Early childhood professionals must be careful to document the ways in which minority children achieve educationally and find methods to promote the ecological, situational, and cultural factors that encourage success. Professionals must also collaborate with other service providers to work constantly for the elimination of bigotry and discrimination, which may limit opportunities available to all children and families within this diverse population.

THE IMPORTANCE OF SERVING CHILDREN IN THE CONTEXT OF A FAMILY

Empowerment is a term widely used in social science fields. According to Koren, DeChillo, and Friesen (1992), various definitions have been offered for **empowerment** over the past 15 years: "the reduction of powerlessness . . . gaining, developing, seizing, enabling or giving power . . . the ability to influence people, organizations, and the environment affecting one's life . . . attaining control over one's life and democratic participation in the life of one's community" (p. 306). Within organizations, such as early childhood programs, one should attempt to provide families with three levels of empowerment:

1. the *personal* level, where individuals feel a sense of self-efficacy;

2. the *interpersonal* level, which is the ability to influence others; and

3. *political* empowerment, the ability to effect social change and engage in social action (Gutierrez & Ortega, 1991).

Like *full inclusion,* the term *empowerment* has become a cliché, empty and scorned by those who are wary of passing fads and those who might agree with the definition, but have observed empty promise (Brinker, 1992). Early childhood professionals are challenged by law to be more inclusive of families in intervention for young children with disabilities (Sass-Lehrer & Bodner-Johnson, 1989). Bailey, Huntington, Simmeonson, and Yoder (1992) found, however, that professionals across disciplines are ill prepared for this responsibility. Moreover, Brinker (1992) claimed the field's current knowledge-base regarding family dynamics is so weak that early childhood professionals are likely to fail in most situations when exploratory empowerment practices are attempted. In fact, Brinker (1992) was so cynical that, like opponents of full inclusion, he believed family empowerment philosophy to be motivated more by "political correctness" than by sound pedagogical practice. Even parents sometimes have rejected the term *empowerment,* which to them infers that professionals are condescendingly "granting" them power that belonged to them in the first place (Healy, Keesee, & Smith, 1989).

The fact that federal law requires families in early intervention to be assessed for the purpose of establishing goals for intervention implies an intent to "fix" families so they can become capable, care-giving units. While recent literature cautions against such clinical intrusiveness in families, current practices for older school-age children might be used to predict the challenge (Bailey, 1989). Twenty years after IDEA first mandated schools to include parents as equal partners in the educational process, parents largely remain either passive or adversarial in planning their children's education (Benson & Turnbull, 1986; Goodman & Bond, 1993; Turnbull & Turnbull, 1990). In fact, a recent study by Yanok and Derubertis (1989) found little difference between the level of participation by parents of children in regular and special education.

These findings indicate those parents who are involved in special education would be so with or without the law. A similar pattern has already been acknowledged in early intervention programs. For example, Minke and Scott (1993) found that parents rarely suggested goals in Individualized Family Service Plan (IFSP) meetings, and when they did, those goals sometimes did not appear in the final document. Even when intensive efforts were made to involve parents, there tended to be a disturbing lack of participation (Fallon & Harris, 1992).

Harry (1992) concluded that the very fact that professional behavior is prescribed by legal mandate precludes spontaneous, honest, and effective interactions. Ironically, early childhood special education law may achieve the opposite effect intended by Congress. The precise structure of special education, including clinical eligibility, written documentation of standardized tests and instructional plans with their related jargon, and "written notification" to parents, places educators and parents in two different worlds: an objective-clinical one for educators and a personal-subjective one for parents. Early interventionists are at great risk of concentrating on the "letter of the law" rather than on the "spirit of the law."

What Is a Family?

Best practice for working with families who have children with disabilities is based on the **family systems model** (McDonnell & Hardman, 1988). This model defines the consumer of services as the family unit rather than simply a child with a disability. Each family member is affected by other family members and events that might influence those persons. For example, if a child with a disability requires extraordinary medical attention, other siblings may be affected by loss of parental attention, perhaps by loss of financial support once available for activities or things, and by more responsibilities around the home. Similarly, the amount of involvement in programs associated with a child with a disability will be affected when caregivers are required to work extra hours to make rent payments, when they lose a job because

Figure 1.2/ *Ecological Mapping of the Child and Family*

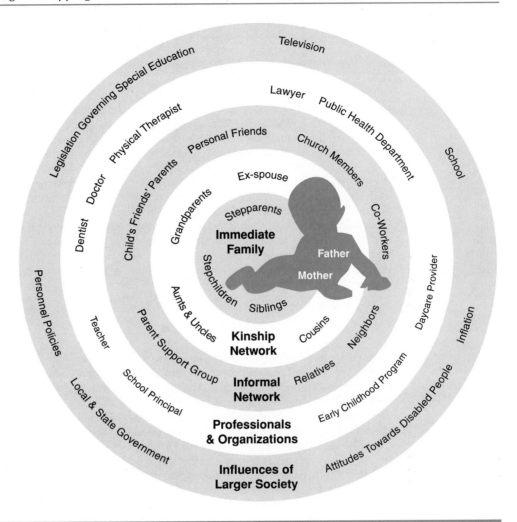

Source: Adapted from Dunst, C., Trivette, C., & Deal, A. (1988). *Enabling and empowering families: Principles and guidelines for practice*, p. 78. Cambridge, MA: Brookline.

of the need to take time off, or if they experience marital conflict. Professionals, ignorant or neglectful of the family system, will likely become frustrated when concentrating solely on the needs of a child who has been identified for services. This child-centered model (see Figure 1.2), while convenient and compatible with most professionals' training, has not been terribly effective for families who do not already possess considerable self-efficacy.

Definitions of *family* are influenced by culture, politics, economics, and religion. Consequently, in early childhood professions there is no consensus on criteria for membership in families (Brinker, 1992). Yet, the issue is not moot, since the scope of early childhood work relies on such a definition. For example, a broad definition of family (e.g., parents, siblings, grandparents, child-care providers, involved relatives and close friends of the family, all of whom influence the development of the child in question) would require that all these persons be considered in the development of a family service plan. A more narrow definition (e.g., blood relatives who live in the child's dwelling) reduces the scope of intervention required but may also limit possible benefits for children with special needs.

Clearly, a traditional definition of family as a nuclear construct will not suffice. According to Healy, Keesee, and Smith (1989), a family is comprised of parents and any family or nonfamily members who have an important care-giving responsibility. This simply stated definition is consistent with the family systems model, which acknowledges all important influences on individuals within families. Still, society is struggling with "moral" issues related to the "goodness" or "rightness" of diverse family structures (Ingrassia & Rossi, 1994). However, early childhood educators can little afford to be exclusive or negative when defining families. Family configurations include foster families, adoptive families, nuclear biological families, single parent families, extended families, and same gender parents families.

While it is difficult to define families, the next step—involvement of all family members—is even more difficult. For example, *the* parent in parent-professional interactions has almost exclusively referred to mothers (Davis & May, 1991). In recent history, society has engaged in practices that denigrate fathers, focusing on paternal attributes incompatible with the best child-rearing practices (Lillie, 1993). Morgan (1993) claimed that mothers are, in part, responsible for exclusion of fathers, as women attempt to protect this one domain over which they tend to possess more power than men. Again, early educators can be most effective when they move beyond popular opinion in interactions with families. A true "family-centered" approach to early childhood compels professionals to find ways to permit fathers to be involved in decision making and child care (Davis & May, 1991; Lillie, 1993; McBride, B. A. & McBride, R. J., 1993).

Empowerment

Families are empowered when their needs are met and most of the credit goes to the families themselves. When a professional can boast, "Look, they don't need me to make decisions for them, locate information, or access services," then a family is empowered. Fostering empowerment will require that educators practice in a way that they never have before. As Buysse and Wesley (1993) acknowledged, these changes cause substantial disequilibrium for early childhood educators whose roles are being reformed. Social service professionals, in particular, feel useful, wanted, even *necessary* when they can do things "for" families. It is not unusual for professionals to "need to feel needed." Yet, this very practice of apparent benevolence builds in paternalism and dependency (Dunst, Trivette, & Deal, 1988).

The desire to feel needed eventually leads to behavior that supports service providers, and agencies begin to feel that it is families' responsibility to serve them. Agencies can become didactic and judgmental, labeling families as "good" or "dysfunctional" based on the agencies' definitions of what is best for children with disabilities and their families. It is not uncommon for educators and even other parents to prescribe how each family should feel, how long they should "grieve," what steps they should take to become "involved," and how they should serve professionals' needs (McGill-Smith, 1992).

Changes in the verbal behavior of service providers should reflect a new philosophy based on the preservation of families' dignity. For example, one might do away with the psychology of "death" as it relates to families with members with disabilities (Bragg, Brown, & Berninger, 1992). Professionals often label a parent who refuses to accept the opinions of professionals as "in denial," or families who seek another opinion as "bargainers," and perhaps most often to label parents who express their rights as "angry." Learning the "stages of grief" and thinking that all family behavior can fit into this model of inferred maladjustment brings one no closer to understanding family members. In fact, Hodapp and Zigler (1993) found that families of children with severe disabilities face problems that are "the same, only more so" than other families.

Furthermore, there is increasing evidence that families with children with disabilities exude considerable resilience, and that family resources quickly "kick in" to compensate for their new stress (Krausse, 1991). Treating families as if they are disabled because their child is disabled "undermines the intent and the effect" of family centered services (Bailey, 1989; Bromwich, 1981). Krausse (1991) proposed an alternative view of families, which he refers to as the "family adaptation hypothesis." This hypothesis rejects the concept of pathological maladaptation associated with the presence of a child with a disability (grief model) and acknowledges the hardiness of families to cope both initially and over time. The fundamental assumption of empowerment is that *families are the center.* All decisions move from the center outward; all action by the periphery is to serve the center (see Figure 1.2).

The goal of empowerment is to enable families to make decisions and take action serving their self-selected needs. According to Dunst et al. (1988):

> To the extent that professionals do not recognize and explicitly consider empowerment of families as the goal of intervention, they are more likely to fool themselves into believing they have done a good job when in fact they have lost an opportunity to enable and empower the family and perhaps even created dependencies by engaging in noncontingent helping. (p. 7)

Noncontingent helping is defined as providing services or support for families while expecting no proactive behavior on the part of families. While seemingly "helping" families, professionals actually usurp opportunities for empowerment when family members are given no responsibility. Dunst et al. (1988) further contended that empowerment requires the fulfillment of three criteria:

1. Taking a **proactive stance;** enabling experiences and attribution of change to help the seeker. A proactive stance is one in which professionals assume that families are either competent *or* capable of becoming competent. Assuming that some families are incompetent and unable to change renders a professional useless for those children and their families.

2. *Creating opportunities* for families to display their strengths in order to gain new competencies is the responsibility of helping systems. "A failure to display competencies is not due to deficits within the person but rather failure of the social system to create opportunities" (Dunst, et al., 1988, p. 4).

3. The third empowerment criterion is met when professionals *enable families to acquire a sense of personal control* over family affairs. "It is not simply a matter of whether or not family needs are met, but rather the manner in which needs are met that is likely to be both enabling and empowering" (Dunst, et al., 1988, p. 4).

Bromwich (1981) identified the following guidelines for building trust and offering support to families in ways that will lead toward empowerment:

1. *Enabling parents to remain in control:* Practitioners should remain conscious of their role as "guest" in families' lives. Parents who feel they are in control will be more likely to take active responsibility and gain confidence and competence.

2. *Avoid the "authority-layman" gap:* Rapport can be best established when there is reciprocity in interactions, which is fostered by *active listening* on the part of practitioners. Listening to parents illustrates that value is placed on their contributions and leads to greater confidence. When practitioners assume the role of authority, parents may become dependent or view intervention as intrusive.

3. *Identify and respond to parents' priorities and goals:* Families whose own priorities are respected and supported are more likely to invest in related responsibilities than those who simply acquiesce to the priorities of professionals. Moreover, self-selection of goals, supported by practitioners, will empower parents to become lifelong advocates for their own families.

4. *Building on parents' strengths:* Practitioners should observe and identify strengths of families. Reinforcement of these strengths should further enable families.

Building a climate for parent-professional partnerships is perhaps the field's greatest challenge. There is still much unknown. To say that the understanding of this relationship is in its infancy would be too generous (Brinker, 1992). Most discouraging is the fact that those families who may benefit the most from family empowerment (i.e., minorities and low income families) are the least likely to receive empowering services (Rueda & Martinez, 1992). Research efforts leading into the twenty-first century should be devoted to identifying methods of supporting the philosophy of empowerment and the spirit of IDEA (Nelson, Howard, & McLaughlin, 1993).

THE IMPORTANCE OF WORKING COLLABORATIVELY

An infant or toddler whose medical condition, developmental delay, or physical disability is so severe that it comes to the attention of caregivers and service providers at an early age is likely to present more complex needs than a child who does not demonstrate a disability until he or she is of school age. Very young children with medical, cognitive, or physical complications are typically at risk for developing disabilities in related developmental areas. For example, a child with abnormal muscle tone may have trouble learning to walk, may have motor problems related to eating difficulties, may not develop necessary motor movements to produce intelligible speech, and, with poor tools for communication, may be unable to demonstrate her cognitive abilities. This child has one primary disabling condition, poor muscle tone, yet the intervention services of a physical therapist, occupational therapist, speech therapist, special educator, and parent are all necessary. While it was common practice in the past, it is unlikely that any one professional could serve this child well (Haring & McCormick, 1990). Consequently, very young children with special needs are likely to have a team of specialists attending to different aspects of their care and development. An **interdisciplinary approach** combines expertise from many disciplines to scrutinize a child's various aspects of development, combining interpretation, synthesis, planning, and practices to design a plan that will promote a child's overall development (Healy, et al., 1989).

When a number of professionals collaborate with a family, careful teamwork becomes absolutely necessary. Without careful coordination, there might be unnecessary duplication of services and paperwork, lack of communication with important parties, an increase in confusion and contradiction, and resultant poorer services to children and their families. A successful team approach must be organized to produce timely and accurate assessment, comprehensive and effective intervention, clear and inclusive communication, and regular evaluation and review. An effective team approach is reached only through mutual trust and respect, practice, and hard work.

Several approaches to teaming have worked well, as long as fundamental guidelines are respected. First, **consensus building** is more effective than an authoritative structure. When various professionals gather with parents, each comes with differing levels of professional status and biases. It is hard to set priorities unless each participant is willing to listen carefully to all parties and to "give and take" in regard to their particular areas of expertise. In situations with a breakdown of give and take, team coordination is at an impasse. One father described his experience as a member of his son's individualized education planning (IEP) team (McCauley, personal communication, January 25, 1994). He requested that the team include toilet training on Sean's IEP, even though the teacher reported that his son had not had any "accidents" at school. Mr. McCauley acknowledged this observation but contended that Sean continued to have difficulty at home, and wanted to have his toileting routine continued at school. The educators refused to listen to Mr. McCauley's priorities (including the toileting training) and the IEP process eventually

Time as a Resource and Constraint for Parents of Young Children with Disabilities: Implications for Early Intervention Services

Society has high expectations for families who are supposed to provide shelter, food, clothing, safety, and education for their members. Time is an important element in allowing a family to fulfill all its responsibilities, and for families of young children with disabilities, time can become a precious commodity. As early childhood intervention increasingly involves the family in the planning and provision of services to young children, it is critical that professionals look closely at how families view the time required for intervention and the constraints they face.

Families of 21 children of varying disabilities and severity and 19 professionals representing different disciplines participated in focus groups to discuss questions regarding family-centered intervention. A moderator in each group asked a variety of questions:

1. What defines successful partnerships and program implementation in early intervention?
2. What contributes to or impedes developing successful partnerships and program implementation?
3. How, if at all, has the early intervention program supported your child and family?
4. Think of a professional who has worked well with you and your family. What made that relationship successful?
5. Think of a professional who has not worked well with you and your family. How would you describe that relationship?
6. What would you like professionals to know about building successful partnerships with families?

Though no direct questions were asked about time, this factor was identified as critical by both parents and professionals and was discussed in several dimensions.

Parents identified four issues that support their efficient and effective use of time:

1. To parents, it was important that therapy and education activities fit into a family's routine and environment.
2. Parents believed that they knew their children best and that professionals should listen to parents and use their information as data for intervention decisions.
3. Several parents discussed how communication devices for their children (e.g., tape recorder, computer, or other technology for therapy and education activities, etc.) aided the effective use of parents' time.
4. Finally, parents asked that professionals provide sufficient time for the long process of developing and maintaining a relationship with a professional.

Parents also identified four issues that placed constraints on their time and effectiveness:

1. They cited the lack of coordination among professionals as a time waster, and recommended that parents be used more as efficient conduits of information across professionals.
2. Parents also felt overwhelmed with what they were being asked to do in their busy lives in terms of therapeutic and educational activities that left them with little time for their other children.
3. A third concern was the lack of services in local communities that caused parents to drive long distances and spend several hours a day to obtain services in different locations.
4. Finally, parents found problems related to a lack of flexible and family-centered scheduling. In scheduling appointments or services, professionals acted as if families had enough income for one parent to

(continued)

be a full-time caregiver to be available during the day, when often both parents worked daytime jobs and lost wages to keep appointments.

The implications of this study are several. Families want to be respected as competent, contributing members of the team with knowledge to share. Professionals need to be realistic in terms of the time and energy families can expend in providing intervention. Services need to be accessible in home communities with flexible scheduling to accommodate families' responsibilities. Certainly time and consistency are required for developing productive long-term relationships between parents and professionals.

Source: M.J. Brotherson & B.L. Goldstein (1992). *Topics in Early Childhood Special Education, 12,* 508–527.

reached an impasse. This conflict might have been avoided had members of the team valued the input of all members and tried to accommodate as many priorities as possible from each member.

Each professional must be flexible and willing to share roles as well as information. Consider a child who presents a language delay; the teacher, the physical therapist, and the parents must all work to develop the child's language whether that is within that person's area of expertise or not. This team approach requires that each member has some working understanding of other disciplines or at least a willingness to implement suggestions made by other professionals. For example, both the speech therapist and the teacher should learn how to position a motor-involved child in the most appropriate way during all aspects of the child's home or school day. This will require some instruction and modeling by the physical therapist.

Finally, effective group process is essential for insuring a positive team experience. **Group process** includes making all participants comfortable in sharing their concerns and desires, listening carefully to all members of the team, valuing the input of all members of the team, and making decisions based on consensus. For example, parents are often intimidated when meeting with a large group of professionals and may hesitate to speak honestly and clearly regarding their priorities. If coerced into silence by intimidation or lack of opportunity, parents may leave a meeting unhappy with the planning and uncommitted to the work a plan involves. To decrease anxiety, parents should be greeted when they arrive, perhaps offered refreshments and comfortable seating, and introduced to all members of the team. These practices may seem overly zealous to some. As one educator put it, "This is not a social gathering! Do you get refreshments when you go to a law office or a dental office?" While this objection is reasonable, the goals of early childhood special education may be incompatible with the client-expert practices of many other professions. Certainly one would want to avoid the intimidation and sterility of legal and dental visits.

Professionals should refrain from using technical jargon or should take care to explain terminology carefully to other members of the team. Written plans should never be formally completed ahead of time, nor should parents be expected to sign-off at the time of the meeting. Soliciting parent suggestions and input before decisions are made is a necessary (and legally required) component of the group process. One person should act as a facilitator to make sure a meeting begins promptly, to keep the discussion on task, to see that all members have a chance to give input or to object when appropriate, and to restate or summarize when agreement has been reached. Before a meeting ends, everyone present should know what will happen next, who is responsible for each part of a plan, and when the team will meet again to review progress.

Teaming Models

There are three basic team models or arrangements, and they vary in the degree to which team members are able to work together. **Multidisciplinary teams** are made up of members who work independently in providing assessment and direct services to a child and meet to share their goals and progress reports, though there is little direct coordination of efforts. For example, the psychologist may meet with a child to test intelligence and achievement levels, then meet with the team to report his results and recommendations for treatment. Members in an **interdisciplinary model** may conduct their assessments and plan goals together, but continue to provide direct services on an independent basis. For example, the speech therapist may observe while the psychologist is testing a child and check-off speech sounds, or phonemes, that the child can say, rather than duplicating the testing in a separate speech session. In a **transdisciplinary model,** professionals share roles and may combine their assessment and treatment tasks so that any one individual may be carrying out the responsibilities of a different professional. For example, the classroom teacher may be using a phoneme check-off instrument to obtain information for the speech therapist or may carry out a language program the speech therapist has recommended.

Of particular benefit to a child served by a team approach is that each team member sees the child's problem from his or her own perspective. "Early childhood education has always been an interdisciplinary field with a commitment to the education of the whole child; an understanding of the child as a complete human being is basic to the development of a program concerned with each area of development and learning" (Spodek, Saracho, & Lee, 1986). Sometimes a teacher may be intimidated by the knowledge of other specialized team members; however, the generalist perspective that a teacher brings is a necessary part of team dynamics. Specialists have in-depth knowledge of their discipline, but teachers are better able to see the whole child as he or she functions in a variety of settings, both socially and physically.

The team configuration used in a particular situation will depend on the administrative policy of the school and service agencies involved and on the comfort and cohesiveness of the professionals serving a particular child. There is no question, however, that teaming across disciplines is a necessary part of services to young children. The greater the ability of the team

Table 1.2/ *Team Models*

Team Model	Strengths	Weaknesses
Multidisciplinary Team	• Involves more than one discipline in planning and services • Pools expertise for group decision-making • Reduces mistakes and biases	• May not promote a unified approach to intervention • May lack team cohesion and commitment
Interdisciplinary Team	• Activities and goals complement and support other disciplines • Allows commitment to unified service plan • Information flow is coordinated through a case manager • Encourages interaction within many disciplines	• Professional "turf" may be threatened • Inflexibility by professionals may reduce efficiency • Role of case manager may be ambiguous, case manager may become autocratic
Transdisciplinary Team	• Encourages role sharing • Provides a unified, holistic plan for intervention • Allows a more complete understanding of the child • Leads to professional enhancement and increased knowledge and skill	• Requires participation by many experts • Places largest responsibility on the teacher as case manager • Requires a high degree of coordination and interaction • Requires more time for communication and planning

to interact, to share roles, and to inform each other across disciplines, the more unified and complete a child's services are likely to be. Table 1.2 summarizes the strengths and weaknesses of each of these models.

Collaboration in Early Intervention

Collaboration with other professionals is apparently not as easy as it seems. In fact, many teachers report that their jobs are made most difficult by lack of cooperation among their peers and themselves. A study of teachers' and prospective teachers' preferences for collaboration may aid understanding of issues involved in planning (Morrison, Walker, Wakefield, & Solberg, 1994). Teachers with the highest level of self-efficacy were the most amenable to collaborative problem solving. Ironically, those teachers who most believed they were capable of teaching a broad range of skills in the classroom were the most willing to work collaboratively. For example, the student teachers in this study were less willing than the practicing teachers to work with and gain assistance by other professionals. One might conclude from this study that an important barrier to collaboration is a sense of intimidation by other professionals. Yet, collaboration by all professionals, with other professionals as well as with parents, is a necessary prerequisite to an effective program.

In early intervention, the challenge of integrating services for families demands the most of collaborative efforts. As family needs increase, the need for increased services increases—as does the need for greater coordination of disciplines (see Figure 1.2). For example, families with multiple needs cannot be well served by autonomous narrowly defined programs. Take the following example:

> Paulette is a young 28-year-old mother and about-to-be grandmother living on Aid to Families with Dependent Children (AFDC), with four children by three fathers, none of whom is part of the household physically or financially. Paulette never finished high school. Her son, Mark, 14 years old, was a chronic truant in school, and in and out of trouble in the neighborhood, which finally earned him a sentence to the Maryland Training School for Boys. Since his release, his case worker has been trying to place him in a suitable school but without success. Her oldest daughter, Tessie, is pregnant at age 13, repeating her maternal family pattern. She wants to drop out of school, but a neighbor told her about a special school for pregnant girls and Paulette is trying to get admission. The eight-year-old daughter, Marie, is doing satisfactory school work, but Paulette has noticed her late returns from school with unexplained spending money. There is a real concern that Marie is earning her money as a "spotter" for neighborhood drug dealers. The two-year-old baby of the family has started exhibiting symptoms of lead paint poisoning, caused by nibbling on flaking paint chips in their apartment. Unchecked and untreated, this could result in permanent brain damage. This is a family beset with behavioral, health, educational, housing, and financial problems. At least five different public agencies in five separate locations have some knowledge of and contact with this family. Fourteen different workers in those agencies have attempted to offer assistance during the past two years, each concerned with the specialized service agency but with little or no knowledge of efforts by the other professionals (Levitan, Mangum, & Pines, 1989, p. 21).

This family's needs can be viewed from an ecological systems model described by Bronfenbrenner (1986). The most immediate needs, schooling for Tessie and Mark, supervision for Marie, and prevention of paint eating for the baby, are at the **microsystem** level. At the **mesosystem** level, there is a linkage between microsystems, such as a linkage between Paulette and the schools, or between the schools and the juvenile justice system. The **exosystems** are those affecting families, but with no direct relationship with agencies, such as church and neighbors. Finally, families are influenced by **macrosystems,** broad social values and belief systems of cultures and subcultures. Interdependency of agencies serving families from these multiple perspectives is a crucial philosophy. A formal link between professionals/agencies and early childhood programs serving Paulette and her family should be the service coordinator. This person is responsible for assessment of family and child needs, coordination of planning for intervention and delivery of services, as well as monitoring of services delivered.

Programs that are successful at integrating these services are correlated with such broad based family needs as decreased birthrates in adolescents, lower incidences of low birth weight babies, increased school participation by parents, decreased drug abuse and behavior problems, increased financial self-sufficiency, and higher IQ and test scores (Voydanoff, 1994). Clearly, one professional or agency cannot possibly address all these areas. In a metaanalysis, Schorr and Both (1991) concluded that successfully integrated systems had the following attributes:

1. Comprehensive, flexible, and responsive

2. Child is part of family and family is part of community

3. Well trained staff, who are accepting enough to build trusting relationships

4. Persistent and responsive to the needs of those families at greatest risk

5. Well-managed, with energetic and committed professionals whose attitudes and skills are well-defined. Professionals are willing to take risks, tolerate ambiguity, work with diverse populations, and operate with a collaborative management style

6. Client centered

In summary, collaboration as a philosophy is possible only when professionals are able to separate their own needs from those of clients, and are nonjudgmental, open-minded, and committed to providing families with the very best services possible.

THE IMPORTANCE OF ETHICAL CONDUCT AND ADVOCACY

What does ethical conduct and advocacy have to do with philosophy? Many decisions educators make, including their daily activities in a classroom, are based on a set of personal ethics or personal philosophy. Professionals, charged with working with families of very young children with disabilities, should be held to the highest ethical standards. When this is the case, conclusions can be drawn: (1) educators should know and follow the **ethical standards** of their profession; and (2) educators should actively **advocate** for issues that will encourage society to respond to the needs of families and children with disabilities in an ethical fashion.

Ethical professional behavior means that one will be the best early childhood professional that one can be and will support others in providing quality services with the highest ethical standards. Professional organizations serving children have already articulated high ethical and accreditation standards for those who provide services to young children. A prime example is the Code of Ethical Conduct developed by the National Association for the Education of Young Children (1989). These standards for ethical behavior in early childhood education describe professional responsibilities in regard to children, families, colleagues, the community, and society. The first principle presented in the Code expresses its ideals well: "Above all, we shall not harm children. We shall not participate in practices that are disrespectful, degrading, dangerous, exploitative, intimidating, psychologically damaging, or physically harmful to children. This principle has precedence over all others in this Code" (National Association for the Education of Young Children, 1989).

Advocacy Issues

For what should one advocate? The president of the Association of Child Advocates, Eve Brooks, suggests getting involved with what is closest to one's heart (Himelfarb, 1992). That may mean working and playing with one's own children or helping others in need. It may mean voting regularly and intelligently, writing one's congressman, or participating on state councils or research projects. *Putting People First* (Clinton & Gore, 1992) identified national priorities for children that few could argue against. These goals included the following:

1. Guarantee affordable quality health care through maternal and child networks and programs.

2. Revolutionize lifetime learning by fully funding Head Start, improving the K–12 education systems, and providing opportunities for college and vocational experience.

3. Make homes, schools, and streets safer for children by reducing violence and providing drug education.

4. Support pro-family and pro-children policies through tax credits for families, family and medical leaves, child-care network, and tough child-support legislation.

Obtaining good child care is a nationwide problem due to short supply, lack of affordability, poor regulation, frequent staff turnover, and little staff training (Ryan, 1992). An estimated 23 million children in the United States require child care. Of this number, only 8.3 million attend licensed daycare settings required to meet minimum standards for health, safety, and curriculum; the remaining 14.7 million are placed in unlicensed settings that may or may not provide adequate care. Many other children are left with friends and relatives, or even left unsupervised (Ryan, 1992). The consequences of poor child care are often troubling, leaving very young children at risk for molestation, physical injury, and even death (Hoyt & Schoonmaker, 1991). Since an enormous population of children require child care while their parents work, society must take responsibility for insuring the well-being of children in child care (Hoyt & Schoonmaker, 1991).

Although the federal government sets standards for many aspects of daily life, the regulation of child care is left to state governments. Consequently there is a tremendous variety among state laws and enforcement levels (Hoyt & Schoonmaker, 1991). In fact, the Children's Defense Fund (1993, December) reported that nearly half the children in child care outside their own home are not protected by any state regulations at all. Even when states have regulations on the books, many are not able to properly inspect centers and enforce these regulations (Hoyt & Schoonmaker, 1991). In any case, as many as 80% to 90% of daycare settings are unlicensed. Yet, even a license on the wall does not guarantee appropriate care is being provided, and eight states reported that they could not even respond to all the parent complaints they received.

Who should monitor the quality of child care provided? Who should insist on high standards for programs for young children and who should police the enforcement of these standards? Parents are often ill-equipped to do so because they are victims of a provider's market; the short supply of openings available and the high cost of quality day care tend to make parents settle for affordability (Hoyt & Schoonmaker, 1991). It is absolutely essential that early childhood professionals advocate for appropriate, high quality services to very young children. Professionals have the education, the commitment, and the positions to insist that standards for child care be adequate and that society contribute to the health, safety, and education of all children regardless of race, handicapping condition, or economic status.

Another issue that will have an impact on early childhood special education is the reform of public assistance policies at state and federal levels that require single mothers (and families) on public assistance to work and limit the length of time for which families are eligible. Such policies will most assuredly increase the need for low-cost child care. To date, policy makers have not addressed this need. Therefore, it is possible that the lack of child care will result in higher rates of child neglect, homelessness, and need of special services. A professional should be an informed citizen and participate in advocacy for families through voting, writing or using electronic mail to contact congressional representatives, sending letters to the editor of the local newspaper, and using other effective ways to inform the public of issues important to families of young children with disabilities.

How to Get Involved in Advocacy

There are numerous ways one can become involved in child advocacy (Himelfarb, 1992). Many community organizations have an interest in child issues—from Parent Teacher Associations to Kiwanis Clubs, Junior Leagues, and religious charities. Every state now has at least one organization devoted to child advocacy as well. These organizations may track state legislation, monitor voting records of elected officials, lobby for child issues, and fund research and education aimed at improving children's circumstances. A phone call or letter will put one in contact with a number of national organizations working on behalf of children. Among these are the following:

Association of Child Advocates, 716-924-0300

Children's Defense Fund, 1-800-CDF-1200

Parent Action, 410-PARENTS

Child Welfare League of America, 1-800-8KIDS80

Child Care Action Campaign, 212-239-0138

A profession is more than a job. It is a long-term commitment to a field. In early childhood education, that commitment is to the well-being of children, and that well-being cannot be insured if efforts are confined to one's classroom, playground, or home. The health, safety, and education of children are dependent on society and its efforts to protect children from discrimination, poverty, disease, abuse, violence, and ignorance. Marian Wright Edelman, President of the Children's Defense Fund, gave this advice on life: "Hang in with your advocacy for children and the poor. The tide is going to turn. . . . Don't think you have to be a big dog to make a difference. You just need to be a persistent flea. . . . Enough committed fleas biting strategically can make even the biggest dog uncomfortable and transform even the biggest nation, as we will transform America in the 1990s" (Edelman, 1991).

IMPLICATIONS FOR THE TWENTY-FIRST CENTURY

This chapter has summarized six of the major assumptions of early childhood special education. Over the past three decades, since early childhood education seriously began its business of serving children with special needs and their families, an increasingly liberal philosophy has evolved, in sharp contrast with the social changes in an increasingly conservative society. Already, this clash in direction has meant the closure of many early intervention programs and the reduction of funds for preschool special education programs. An assumption not discussed in this chapter is that of efficacy. There is little doubt as to the efficacy of early childhood services for very young children with special needs (Baer, 1987). Years of research have demonstrated that money and time spent in the first year of life save money and reduce the effects of developmental delays later in life (White & Casto, 1985). This is especially true of children with mild delays or those who are at risk for delays. An analogy to automobile maintenance can be made. If a problem is detected early and repaired quickly, the cost and effort are small. However, if the problem is allowed to persist, the automobile will suffer extensive damage that will be more costly and difficult to repair.

When funding for special education was generous, as in the 1970s and 1980s, schools could afford the "wait and treat later" approach because funding was available for remedial and special education. In the 1990s, money for special education has shrunk, and it will continue to diminish in the twenty-first century. Therefore, more than ever, professionals must remind budget makers that their dollars are best spent on early childhood education.

STUDY GUIDE QUESTIONS

1. What are the two important elements of an attitude of science?

2. What is the value of a conceptual system?

3. How does applied behavior analysis meet the criteria for a good conceptual system?

4. Identify three characteristics of full inclusion that differentiate it from mainstreaming, LRE, or integration.

5. What are the benefits of full inclusion?

6. What barriers impede the movement toward full inclusion?

7. How has the population of the United States changed in regard to racial distribution?

8. What impact do changing demographics have on education?

9. State two reasons sensitivity to cultural differences is important in early childhood education.

10. What are the detrimental effects of childhood poverty?

11. How have families changed in recent years?

12. What can teachers do to support children from nontraditional families?

13. Why is it inappropriate to conclude that minority children are abnormal or incompetent?

14. What problems accompany a philosophy of empowerment?

15. How is family defined within a family systems model?

16. Why is noncontingent helping not helpful?

17. Describe how a professional effectively relates to empower a family.

18. What can professionals do to ensure that a team works well together?

19. Describe the differences among the three primary team models.

20. Give examples of how you could relate to a single mother of a child with Down syndrome that would contribute to a successful collaborative team.

REFERENCES

Alberto, P. A., & Troutman, A. C. (1990). *Applied behavior analysis for teachers,* (3rd ed.). Upper Saddle River, NJ: Merrill/Prentice Hall.

Allen, J. P., & Turner, E. (1990). Where diversity is. *American Demographics, 12*(8), 34–38.

Anderson, E. A., & Koblinsky, S. A. (1995). Homeless policy: The need to speak to families. *Family Relations, 44,* 13–18.

Baer, D. M. (1987, March). A behavior-analytic query into early intervention. Paper presented at the 19th Banff International Conference on Behavioral Science: Early Intervention in the Coming Decade. Banff, Alberta.

Baer, D. M., Wolf, M. M., & Risley, T. R. (1968). Some current dimensions of applied behavior analysis. *Journal of Applied Behavior Analysis, 1,* 91–97.

Bailey, D. B. (1989). Case management in early intervention. *Journal of Early Intervention, 13,* 120–134.

Bailey, D., Huntington, G., Simmeonson, R., & Yoder, D. (1992). Preparing professionals to serve infants and toddlers with handicaps and their families: An integrative analysis across eight disciplines. *Exceptional Children, 10,* 26–34.

Bailey, D. B., & Wolery, M. (1992). *Teaching Infants and Preschoolers with Disabilities.* Upper Saddle River, NJ: Merrill/Prentice Hall.

Bassuk, E., & Rubin, L. (1986). Homeless children: A neglected population. *American Journal of Orthopsychiatry, 57,* 279–286.

Bempechat, J., & Ginsburg, H. P. (1989). Underachievement and educational disadvantage: The home and school experience of at-risk youth. *Urban Diversity Series No. 99.* Washington, DC: Office of Educational Research and Improvement.

Benson, H. A., & Turnbull, A. P. (1986). Approaching families from an individualized perspective. In R. H. Horner, L. H. Meyers & H. D. Fredericks (Eds.), *Educating learners with severe handicaps: Exemplary service strategies* (pp. 127–157). Baltimore: Paul H. Brookes.

Black and white in America. (1988, March 7). *Newsweek.* pp. 18–23.

Bragg, R. M., Brown, R. L., & Berninger, V. W. (1992). The impact of congenital and acquired disabilities on the family system: Implications for school counseling. *The School Counselor, 39,* 292–299.

Bredekamp, S. (Ed.) (1987). *Developmentally appropriate practice in early childhood programs serving children from birth through age 8.* Washington, DC: National Association for the Education of Young Children.

Brinker, R. P. (1992). Family involvement in early intervention: Accepting the unchangeable, changing the changeable, and knowing the difference. *Topics in Early Childhood Special Education, 12*(3), 307–332.

Bromwich, R. (1981). *Working with parents and infants: An interactional approach.* Austin, TX: PRO-ED.

Bronfenbrenner, U. (1986). Ecology of the family as a context for human development. *Developmental Psychology, 22,* 732–752.

Brotherson, M. J., & Goldstein, B. L. (1992). Time as a resource and constraint for parents of young children with disabilities. *Topics in Early Childhood Special Education, 12,* 508–527.

Buysse, B., & Wesley, P. W. (1993). The identity crisis in early childhood education: A call for professional role clarification. *Topics in Early Childhood Special Education, 13,* 418–429.

Carlile, C. (1991, Summer). Children of divorce: How teachers can ease the pain. *Childhood Education,* 232–234.

Children's Defense Fund. (1993, December). Family Support. *CDF Reports,* pp. 5–9.

Clarke-Stewart, K. A. (1989, January). Single-parent families: How bad for the children? *NEA Today,* 60–64.

Clinton, B., & Gore, A. (1992). *Putting People First.* New York: Times Books. 47–51.

Cole, K. N., Dale, P. S., Jenkins, J. R., & Mills, P. E. (1991). Effects of preschool integration for children with disabilities. *Exceptional Children, 58,* 36–45.

Coles, D. A., & Meyer, L. H. (1991). Social integration and severe disabilities: A longitudinal analysis of child outcomes. *The Journal of Special Education, 25,* 340–351.

Congress of the United States. (1987). United States children and their families: Current conditions and recent trends, 1987. House Select Committee on Children, Youth, and Families (Stock No. 052-070-06299-1). Washington, DC: United States Government Printing Office.

Cross, K. L., Bazron, B. J., Dennis, K. W., & Issacs, M. R. (1989). *Towards a culturally competent system of care: A monograph on effective services for minority children who are severely emotionally disturbed.* Washington, DC: Child and Adolescent Service System Program (CASSP) Technical Assistance Center, Georgetown University Child Development Center.

Davis, P. B., & May, J. E. (1991, Spring). Involving fathers in early intervention and family support programs: Issues and strategies. *CHC,* 87–91.

Dodd, P., & Gutierrez, L. (1990). Preparing students for the future: A power perspective on community practice. *Administration in Social Work, 14*(2), 63–78.

Dorfman, C. (1988). Youth indicators 1988: Trends in the well-being of American youth. National Center for Education Statistics, (Eds.), Washington, DC: Superintendent of Documents, U. S. Government Printing Office.

Duany, L., & Pittman, K. (1990). Latino youths at a crossroads. *Adolescent Pregnancy Prevention Clearinghouse Report* (ISSN: 0899-5591). Washington, DC: Children's Defense Fund.

Dunst, C., Trivette, C., & Deal, A. (1988). *Enabling and empowering families: Principles and guidelines for practice.* Cambridge, MA: Brookline.

Edelman, M. W. (1991). Ten lessons to help us through the 1990s: The state of America's children. *The Measure of Our Success.* Beacon Press, 13–15, 19, 20.

Esposito, B. G., & Koorland, M. A. (1989). Play behavior of hearing impaired children: Integrated and segregated settings. *Exceptional Children, 55,* 412–419.

Exter, T. (1987). How many Hispanics? *American Demographics, 9*(5), 36–39, 67.

Fallon, M. A., & Harris, M. B. (1992). Encouraging parent participation in intervention programs. *The Transdisciplinary Journal, 2*(2), 141–146.

Feistritzer, C. E. (1987). Schools learn a lesson. *American Demographics, 9*(11), 42–43.

File, N., & Kontos, S. (1993). The relationship of program quality to children's play in integrated early intervention settings. *Topics in Early Childhood Special Education, 13,* 1–16.

Forest, M. (1988, Winter). Full inclusion is possible. *Minnesota UAP Impact, Minnesota Affiliated Program on Developmental Disabilities, 1.*

Fox, L., & Hanline, M. F. (1993). Learning within the context of play: Providing typical early childhood experiences for children with severe disabilities. *Journal of the Association for the Severely Handicapped, 18,* 121–129.

Fuchs, D., & Fuchs, L. S. (1994). Inclusive schools movement and the radicalization of special education. *Exceptional Children, 60,* 294–309.

Gable, R. A., McLaughlin, V. L., Sindelar, P., & Kilgore, K. (1993). Unifying general and special education teacher preparation. *Preventing School Failure, 37,* 5–10.

Gemmell-Crosby, S., & Hanzlik, J. R. (1994). Preschool teachers' perceptions of including children with disabilities. *Education and Training in Mental Retardation and Developmental Disabilities, 29*(4), 279–290.

Gerrard, L. C. (1994). Inclusive education: An issue of social justice. *Equity and Excellence in Education, 27*(1), 58–67.

Goodman, J. F., & Bond, L. (1993). The Individualized Education Program: A retrospective critique. *The Journal of Special Education, 26,* 408–422.

Griffith, D. R. (1992, September). Prenatal exposure to cocaine and other drugs: Developmental and educational prognosis. *Phi Delta Kappan,* 30–34.

Guralnick, M. J., & Groom, J. M. (1988). Peer interactions in mainstreamed and specialized classrooms: A comparative analysis. *Exceptional Children, 54,* 415–425.

Gutierrez, L., & Ortega, R. (1991). Developing methods to empower Latinos: The importance of groups. *Social Work with Groups, 14*(2), 23–43.

Hallahan, D. P., & Kauffman, J. M. (1994). Toward a culture of disability in the aftermath of Deno and Dunn. *The Journal of Special Education, 27*(4), 496–508.

Hanline, M. F. (1993). Inclusion of preschoolers with profound disabilities: An analysis of children's interactions. *Journal of the Association for the Severely Handicapped, 18,* 28–34.

Haring, N. G., & McCormick, L. (1990). *Exceptional children and youth.* Upper Saddle, NJ: Merrill/Prentice Hall.

Harry, B. (1992). *Cultural diversity, families, and the special educational system: Communication and empowerment.* New York: Teachers College Press.

Healy, J. M. (1990). *Endangered minds: Why children don't think and what we can do about it.* New York: Touchstone.

Healy, A., Keesee, P. D., & Smith, B. S. (1989). *Early services for children with special needs: Transactions for family support.* Baltimore: Paul H. Brooks Publishing.

Hegar, R., & Scannapieco, M. (1995). From family duty to family policy: The evolution of kinship care. *Child Welfare, 75*(1), 200–217.

Heward, W. L. (1996). *Exceptional children.* (5th ed.). Upper Saddle River, NJ: Merrill/Prentice Hall.

Hilton, A., & Smith, T. E. C. (1994). Inclusion as a philosophy which leads to loss of vision: A response to Rainforth's philosophy versus student need? *Education and Training in Mental Retardation and Developmental Disabilities, 29,* 253–255.

Himelfarb, S. (1992, November). You can make a difference for America's children. *Parents,* pp. 221–224.

Hodapp, R. M., & Zigler, E. (1993). Comparison of families of children with mental retardation and families of children without mental retardation. *Mental Retardation, 31*(2), 75–87.

Hodgkinson, H. L. (1985). *All One System: Demographics of Education—Kindergarten Through Graduate School.* Washington, DC: Institute for Educational Leadership, Inc.

Hofferth, S. L., & Phillips, D. A. (1987). Child care in the United States, 1970 to 1995. *Journal of Marriage and the Family, 49,* 559–571.

Hoyt, M. & Schoonmaker, M. E. (1991, October, 15). The day care delusion: When parents accept the unacceptable. *Family Circle,* pp. 81–87.

Iglehart, A. P. (1994). Kinship foster care: Placement, service, and outcome issues. *Children and Youth Services Review, 16*(1–2), 107–121.

Ingrassia, M., & Rossi, M. (1994, February). The limits of tolerance? *Newsweek,* p. 47.

Jones, E., & Derman-Sparks, L. (1992). Meeting the challenge of diversity. *Young Children, 47*(2), 12–18.

Jubala, K., & Bishop, K. (1994). By June, given shared experiences, integrated classes, and equal opportunities, Jaime will have a friend. *Teaching Exceptional Children, 27*(1), 36–39.

Kamps, D. M., Leonard, B. R., Vernon, S., Dugan, E. P., & Delquadri, J. C. (1992). Teaching social skills to students with autism to increase peer interactions in an integrated first-grade classroom. *Journal of Applied Behavior Analysis, 25,* 281–288.

Koren, P. E., DeChillo, N., & Friesen, B. J. (1992). Measuring empowerment in families whose children have emotional disabilities: A brief questionnaire. *Rehabilitation Psychology, 37*(4), 304–321.

Kozol, J. (1990; Winter, Spring). The new untouchables. *Newsweek,* pp. 48–53.

Kozol, J. (1992). S*avage inequalities: Children in America's schools.* New York: Harper Perennial.

Krausse, M. W. (1991). Theoretical issues in family research. Paper presented at the Annual meeting of the American Association on Mental Retardation, Washington, D. C. (ERIC Document Reproduction Service No. ED 337 923).

Levitan, S. A., Mangum, G. L., & Pines, M. W. (1989). *A proper inheritance: Investing in the self-sufficiency of poor families.* Washington, DC: The George Washington University.

Lillie, T. (1993). A harder thing than triumph: Roles of fathers of children with disabilities. *Mental Retardation, 31,* 438–442.

Lipsky, D., & Gartner, A. (1989). *Beyond separate education: Quality education for all.* Baltimore: Paul H. Brookes.

Mallory, B. L., & New, R. S. (1994). Social constructivist theory and principles of inclusion: Challenges for early childhood special education. *Journal of Special Education, 28*(3), 322–337.

Martin, P., & Midgley, E. (1994). Immigration to the United States: Journey to an uncertain destination. *Population Bulletin, 49*(2), 2–47.

McBride, B. A., & McBride, R. J. (1993). Parent education and support programs for fathers. *Childhood Education, 70,* 4–8.

McCormick, L., & Holden, R. (1992). Homeless children: A special challenge. *Young Children, 47* (6), 61–67.

McDonnell, A., & Hardman, M. (1988). A synthesis of "best practice" guidelines for early childhood services. *Journal of the Division for Early Childhood, 12,* 328–341.

McGee, G., Paradis, T., & Feldman, R. S. (1993). Free effects of integration on levels of autistic behavior. *Topics in Early Childhood Special Education, 13*(1), 57–65.

McGill-Smith, P. (1992). Can't get on the train without a ticket. *Teaching Exceptional Children, 25,* 49.

McLoyd, V. C. (1990). Minority children: Introduction to the special issue. *Child Development, 61,* 263–266.

Mercer, C. D. (1987). *Students with learning disabilities.* (3rd ed.). Upper Saddle River, NJ: Merrill/Prentice Hall.

Minke, K. M., & Scott, M. M. (1993). The development of Individualized Family Service Plans: Roles for parents and staff. *The Journal of Special Education, 27,* 82–106.

Morgan, R. (1993). *The word of a woman.* New York: W. W. Norton.

Morrison, G. M., Walker, D., Wakefield, P., & Solberg, S. (1994). Teacher preferences for collaborative relationships: Relationship to efficacy for teaching in prevention-related domains. *Psychology in the Schools, 31,* 221–231.

National Association for the Education of Young Children. (1989). Code of Ethics. Author.

National Commission on Family Foster Care. (1991). *The significance of kinship care: Blueprint for fostering infants, children, and youths in the 1990s.* Washington, DC: Child Welfare League of America.

Nelson, D., Howard, V. F., & McLaughlin, T. F. (1993). Empowering parents to become advocates for their own children with disabilities. *B. C. Journal of Special Education, 17*(1), 62–72.

Olmsted, P. P. (1992). Where did our diversity come from? *High/Scope ReSource, 11* (3), 4–9.

Orfield, G., Schley, S., Glass, D., & Reardon, S. (1994). The growth of segregation in American schools: Changing patterns of separation and poverty since 1968. *Equity and Excellence, 27*(1), 5–8.

Orum, L. S. (1986). *The education of Hispanics: Status and implications.* Washington, DC: National Council of La Raza. (ERIC Document Reproduction Service No. ED 274 753).

Pelton, L. (1978). Child abuse and neglect: The myth of classlessness. *American Journal of Orthopsychiatry, 42,* 608–617.

Pike, K., & Salend, S. J. (1995). Authenic assessment strategies: Alternatives to norm-referenced testing. *Teaching Exceptional Children, 28*(1), 15–20.

Pudlas, K. A. (1993). Integration: Students and teachers at risk? *B. C. Journal of Special Education, 17,* 54–60.

Rainforth, B. (1994). Philosophy versus student need? A reply to Smith and Hilton. *Education and Training in Mental Retardation and Developmental Disabilities, 29,* 251–252.

Roberts, R. (1990). *Developing culturally competent programs for families of children with special needs* (2nd ed.). Washington, DC: Georgetown University Child Development Center.

Rounds, K. A., Weil, M., & Bishop, K. K. (1994). Practice with culturally diverse families of young children with disabilities. *Families in Society, 75,* 3–15.

Rueda, R., & Martinez, I. (1992). Fiesta Educativa: One community's approach to parent training in developmental disabilities for Latino families. *Journal of the Association for the Severely Handicapped, 17*(2), 95–103.

Ryan, M. (August 30, 1992). Who's Taking Care of the Children?" *Parade Magazine,* pp. 3–5.

Salisbury, C. L., Palombaro, M. M., & Long, C. A. (1993). On the nature and change of an inclusive elementary school. *Journal of the Association for the Severely Handicapped, 18,* 75–84.

Sass-Lehrer, M., & Bodner-Johnson, B. (1989). P. L. 99–457: A new challenge to early intervention. *American Annals of the Deaf, 134*(2), 71–77.

Saving the children (1988, January 25). *Newsweek.* pp. 58–59.

Schorr, L. B., & Both, D. (1991). Attributes of effective services for young children: A brief survey of current knowledge and its implications for program and policy development. In L. B. Schorr, D. Both, & C. Copple (Eds.), *Effective services for young children: Report of a workshop* (pp. 23–47), Washington, DC: National Academy Press.

Sewell, W. H., & Hauser, R. M. (Eds.). (1976). *Schooling and achievement in American society.* New York: Academic Press.

Singleton, P. (1992). We Can! Empowerment of people who are deaf. *OSERS News in Print, 5*(2), 12–15.

Skinner, B. F. (1953). *Science and human behavior.* New York: Macmillan Publishing.

Skrtic, T. M. (1991). The special education paradox: Equity as the way of excellence. *Harvard Educational Review, 61*(2), 148–205.

Spencer, C. M. (1985). Children of teenage parents: A review of the literature. Springfield, Illinois: Illinois State Board of Education. (ERIC Document Reproduction Service No. ED 260 830).

Spodek, B., Saracho, O. N., & Lee, R. C. (1986). *Mainstreaming young children.* Newton, MA: Allyn and Bacon.

Thomson, E., Hanson, T. L., & McLanahan, S. S. (1994). Family structure and child well-being: Economic resources vs. parental behaviors. *Social Forces, 73*(1), 221–242.

Thousand, J. S., & Villa, R. A. (1991). A Futuristic view of the REI: A response to Jenkins, Tious, and Jewel. *Exceptional Children, 57*(6), 559.

Turnbull, A., & Turnbull, R. (1990). *Parents, professionals, and exceptionality.* Upper Saddle River, NJ: Merrill/Prentice Hall.

Wehrly, B. (1988). Toward a multicultural partnership in higher education. Macomb, IL: Western Illinois University, (ERIC Document Reproduction Service No. ED 308 731).

Wells, A. S. (1988). *Urban teacher recruitment programs.* New York, NY: Columbia University, Institute for Urban and Minority Education, (ERIC Document Reproduction Service No. ED 312 318).

Whaley, D. L., & Malott, M. E. (1971). *Elementary princip es of behavior* (2nd ed.). Englewood Cliffs, NJ: Prentice-Hall.

White, K., & Castro, G. (1985). An integrative review of early intervention efficacy studies with at-risk children: Implications for the handicapped. *Analysis and Intervention in Developmental Disabilities, 5,* 7–31.

Williams, B. F. (1992). Changing demographics; Challenges for educators. *Intervention in Schools and Community, 27* (3), 157–163.

Wolery, M., Holcombe, A., Venn, M., Brookfield, J., Huffman, K., Schroeder, C., Martin, C., & Fleming, L. (1993). Mainstreaming in early childhood programs: Current status and relevant issues. *Young Children, 78*–83.

Wolfensberger, W. (1972). The principle of normalization in human services. Paper presented at the National Institute on Mental Retardation, Toronto.

Wolfensberger, W. (1983). Social role valorization: A proposed new term for the principle of Normalization. *Mental Retardation, 21*(6), 234–239.

Wolock, I., & Horowitz, B. (1984). Child maltreatment as a social problem: The neglect of neglect. *American Journal of Orthopsychiatry, 54,* 530–543.

United States Conference of Mayors. (1993). *A status report on hunger and homelessness in America's cities: A 26-city survey.* Washington, DC: Author.

Voydanoff, P. (1994). A family perspective on services integration. *Family Relations, 44,* 63–68.

Yanok, J., & Derubertis, D. (1989). Comparative study of parental participation in regular and special education programs. *Exceptional Children, 56,* 195–199.

In order to effectively serve young children, one must understand normal development and recognize the delays and deviations from a typical path that might require treatment or intervention. Many factors can have an impact on development—some of them environmental, some genetic. Illness, injury, or a lack of resources can all contribute to developmental delay or risk of delay. A well-prepared early childhood professional understands these elements, knows how to learn more about them, and can effectively share this information with families who are influenced by them. This part of the text focuses on normal development and the social, genetic, and medical complications that may affect it.

Principles of Human Development

2

The wonder of nature, responsible for the changes that take place between human conception and the first years of school, largely awaits scientific explanation. Our understanding of human development is predominantly confined to describing the surprisingly predictable processes and stages through which the human species matures. Psychologists, linguists, biologists, geneticists, sociologists, educators, and other researchers continue to look for explanations of this fascinating phenomenon. Even without those answers, however, our present knowledge of human growth is vital to fields serving families with very young children.

IMPORTANCE AND USE OF KNOWLEDGE OF HUMAN DEVELOPMENT

Importance to Families

The greater the degree to which families develop an understanding of their children, the greater will be their level of competency in caring for and making decisions regarding their children. One important goal of early childhood professionals must be to convert state-of-the-science knowledge of human development to understandable and practical information that can be used by families. Yet, families of infants and preschoolers vary considerably in their curiosity and understanding of human development. While some families study their children's growth by consulting developmental resources (e.g., books, videos, pamphlets, health professionals, etc.), others develop a keen understanding from simple informal observation of children over time. Both processes result in knowledge critical to decision making related to:

1. the need for professional involvement when the rate and/or pattern of development seems atypical;

2. tolerance and management of children who progress through stages or transitions differently from expectations;

3. selection of activities and toys that are appropriate for the developmental level of children and will foster maturation to the next levels; and

4. avoidance of unhealthy advice that may be contrary to our present understanding of child development.

While child rearing is far from an exact science, it is clear that the better prepared parents are for changes through which their children are likely to proceed, the more likely they are to make sound decisions and take positive action.

Importance of Knowledge to Professionals

A thorough understanding of human development is fundamental to the competency of early childhood professionals. Without basic knowledge of the principles and stages through which infants and preschoolers pass, educators would be unable to communicate with parents, assess children, design instruction, set expectations, select intervention strategies, or evaluate child and program progress. Parents turn to early childhood professionals for information and assistance, thus expecting them to be experts in normal development. To satisfy this need, educators must have at least a knowledge of developmental patterns for physical growth, as well as of cognitive, language, and social/emotional growth.

Using Knowledge to Answer Questions   Professionals are sometimes expected to be able to resolve controversial issues related to development: Should children be given a pacifier? How long should breast feeding continue? Should one continue toilet training for a child who is physically mature but resistant to training? In order to answer such questions, early childhood professionals must have a thorough knowledge of the popular as well as the professional literature related to child development.

Using Knowledge in Parent Training   In addition to an educator's acquisition of knowledge of human development, there is an emerging expectation that professionals be willing and able to give that knowledge to parents. Furthermore, professionals will be most successful in partnerships with parents if they are sensitive to the degree to which families are eager and able to acquire such an understanding. Professionals will be most efficient when able to impart knowledge in a manner that is practical to families (e.g., informal brochures, resource guides, videotapes).

Using Knowledge in Assessment   In early childhood, eligibility for special services is traditionally determined by the degree to which a child's rate or pattern of development varies from the norm. Thus, children's behaviors are compared to the behaviors that would be expected of a same-age peer, based on the present level of knowledge of normal human development. Professionals should be able to detect those children who are at risk for delays or those who actually have delays in development. Many children who might otherwise benefit from early intervention services could be overlooked by unprepared professionals.

Using Knowledge for Intervention   Perhaps the greatest use of our knowledge of human development is in the identification of appropriate intervention objectives and the subsequent selection of intervention strategies. Because human development is largely predictable, it is possible to take a child's present behavior and select the probable emerging behavior based upon knowledge of a child's current performance. Selecting a target behavior that is too simple or too difficult for a child would bias that child's success and, subsequently, lessen the professional's effectiveness.

Intervention strategies must also be appropriate for a child's developmental level. Professionals should be capable of matching materials to children's cognitive levels, giving instructions to match a child's linguistic understanding, determining how long a child can be expected to attend, and knowing the degree of social interaction that can be expected.

Effective educators collect continuous data to inform themselves of individual child success as well as overall program progress. To determine if a teaching procedure is working well, one must be able to differentiate progress due to growth and development from that which has been enhanced by parental or teacher intervention. This understanding enables educators to select appropriate measures of progress. Resulting information helps professionals make decisions regarding the effectiveness of treatment as it relates to the developmental progress of children.

Knowledge of normal human development, paired with a knowledge of conditions that may lead to developmental disabilities, enables professionals to estimate the potential effects of a particular disability on a child. For example, an educator might anticipate that a child with a moderate degree of athetoid cerebral palsy will experience delays in expressive language and motor development. The probability of such problems should prompt this child's team to focus on intensive communication intervention and physical and occupational therapy, as well as to project the potential need for assistive devices as the child matures.

The need to cultivate a thorough understanding of how humans develop is underscored by the difficulty of such an undertaking. It often takes professionals many years to master this knowledge. Fortunately, many resources regarding development are available to assist in making day-to-day and long-term decisions. While these resources are no substitute for mastery, they provide a useful supplement to a soundly established basic understanding of human development. Some basic principles of development are well established in the literature, and knowledge of these guidelines assists professionals in making daily decisions.

PRENATAL GROWTH AND DEVELOPMENT

By the time children are born, they have already undergone an average of 38 weeks of development. This period is divided into three stages: ovum, embryo, and fetus. For two weeks following the time of conception, the **ovum,** or fertilized egg, travels down one of the fallopian tubes and eventually attaches to the wall of the uterus, where it remains throughout the prenatal period.

The **embryonic stage** begins in the third week, when cell differentiation permits the emergence of a central nervous system and a circulatory system, and is completed by the end of the eighth week, when ossification of the bones begins. During the embryonic phase, the heart, lungs, digestive system, and brain develop from unspecified cells to well-defined structures. Muscular and nervous system development accompanies these structural changes. Additionally, hands, feet, fingers, and toes are formed, as well as facial features such as eyelids and ears.

The embryonic period is the most vulnerable stage of pregnancy. For one thing, many women are unaware of their pregnancies at this point, and may inadvertently cause harm to the fragile embryo. Many embryos spontaneously abort when they detach from the uterine wall and are expelled. During this early period, harmful substances (e.g., cigarette smoke, radiation) or trauma can also disrupt the structural development taking place in an embryo. Hence, embryonic damage may result in spontaneous abortion, miscarriage, or development of a birth defect.

Supporting the developing embryo, and later the fetus, are the **placenta,** umbilical cord, and amniotic sac (see Figure 2.1). The placenta is a fleshy mass made up of villi or projectiles that insert themselves into the lining of the uterus. The largest and most important of these is the **umbilical cord,** which joins the bloodstream of the embryo at the site of the child's abdomen to the bloodstream of the mother via the uterine lining. This connection permits the exchange of critical substances between the maternal bloodstream and the fetus. Though the fetal and maternal blood do not mix, it is the passage of nutrients, oxygen, and other gases through the umbilical cord to the fetus that allows the unborn baby to survive. At the same time, fetal waste products such as carbon dioxide and other metabolites pass back through the umbilical cord to be excreted by the mother. Though the placenta also serves as a barrier to large molecules and potentially harmful substances, it is not infallible. The placenta, unable to differentiate healthy from damaging chemicals, permits some dangerous drugs (including alcohol), hormones, and bacterial and viral organisms to cross into the bloodstream of the developing human.

Another important structure is the **amniotic sac,** which contains liquid amniotic fluid and surrounds the embryo. This sac, made pliable by the encapsulated fluid, protects the vulnerable embryo from physical shocks a mother might experience and maintains a constant temperature for the fetus.

Figure 2.1/ *Developing Fetus in Prenatal Environment*

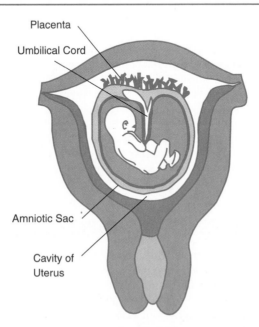

Placenta

Umbilical Cord

Amniotic Sac

Cavity of Uterus

The final and longest stage of development is the **fetal stage,** which begins in the ninth week and lasts through the ninth month. While each system was primitively developed during the embryonic stage, these systems undergo rapid growth and increase in complexity through differentiation during the final period (see Figure 2.2). At 12 weeks, a fetus resembles a human figure, and spontaneous movement of the limbs may be observed. By 16 weeks a mother can usually feel movement in the infant referred to as "the quickening." At 16 weeks, a fetus can also open and close its mouth and eyes, and grows fingernails and hair.

The age at which a fetus is considered viable, or would have the potential to live outside the womb, is about 26 to 28 weeks (24 weeks is considered the cutoff for viability). To permit independent survival, a fetus must have developed reflexes such as sucking and swallowing, and the lungs must be sufficiently developed to produce surfactant, which allows breathing without collapse of the lungs. During the final two months of pregnancy, the central nervous system, including the brain, continues to develop greater differentiation, and the fetus grows rapidly in height and weight.

Figure 2.2/ Phases of Fetal Development

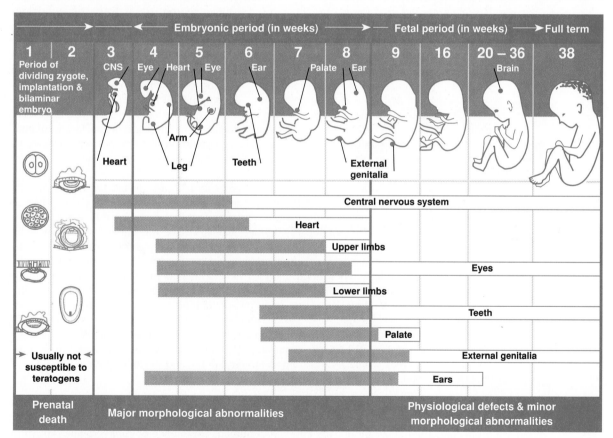

- **Indicates common site of action of teratogen.**
Dark band indicates periods of high sensitivity;
light band indicates stages that are less sensitive to teratogens.

Source: Adapted from Moore, K. L. (1983). *Before we are born: Basic embryology and birth defects, 2nd ed.* W. B. Saunders. Reprinted with permission.

CHILD GROWTH AND DEVELOPMENT

Child **development** occurs when the complexity of a child's behavior increases (Allen & Marotz, 1989). Others may observe signs of a child's genetic inheritance through changes in physical and behavioral characteristics. Though some of these characteristics are solely determined by genetic code (e.g., eye color), others are influenced to some, as yet unknown, degree by other factors. Characteristics that are determined by both genetic and environmental factors tend to progress, though variant in rate, in a continuous and predictable pattern.

Maturation is the universally observed sequence of biological changes that take place as one ages. Maturation permits the development of psychological functions. For example as the brain develops in the early months of life and becomes capable of understanding and producing language, infants who are exposed to language gradually develop this ability. If either language stimulation or neurological growth is missing, language would not develop.

Normal development refers to a sequence of physical and psychological changes that are very similar for all children. Within individual children, the extent to which environment is likely to influence this sequence, or the extent to which children will realize their potential, has been referred to as **range of reaction** (Zigler & Stephensen, 1993). Favorable conditions enable children to reach the high end of their potential, while unfavorable conditions can depress development toward the lower end of the range of a child's potential.

Major indexes of developmental accomplishments, such as "Casey just took his first step yesterday" or "Adam just learned to say 'mama'!", are used to measure developmental progress. These indexes, which are identified across developmental areas (e.g., language or social skills) and across years, are referred to as **developmental milestones.** Established milestones are based on the average age at which children acquire skills or pass through stages. For example, an average child begins to take the first step at 12 months, and begins to say "mama" at 9 months. The milestones at which children are expected to achieve skills are determined by taking a representative sample of children and determining the average age that they acquire those skills.

Norms are statistically determined standard (normal) age levels for developmental milestones. For example, the norm for independent sitting is six months. Some children sit earlier, and others take longer than six months to acquire this skill, but on the average, infants learn to sit by themselves about midway through their first year. It is important to stress, however, that norms are simply averages, around which there is a **range of normalcy.** Typically developing children who acquire developmental skills earlier or later than the norm will still be considered normal. It is when acquisition of developmental milestones occurs sometime beyond the range of normalcy that parents and educators should be concerned about a child's progress. For example, if a child is not sitting independently (norm is 6 months; range is 4–8 months) by 10 months of age, parents should seek professional advice. Children who exceed the norms in several areas or the expected ranges in a few areas may be **at risk** for developmental delays. Significant delays in acquisition of developmental milestones in one or more developmental areas would indicate **developmental delay** and eligibility for early childhood special education.

Patterns of Growth

From conception throughout early adulthood, humans experience physical growth. The most obvious index of growth is in size, as measured by changes in height and weight. Height and weight measures increase rapidly during fetal development and early childhood. An increase in birth weight of 300% is expected by the time a child is 12 months of age, while height is expected to increase 200% by 24 months of age. This rate of growth slows after the first year to an almost linear rate until adolescence. While some children grow in spurts, others appear to grow steadily throughout childhood. In addition to individual genetic differences in rate and pattern of development, factors such as nutrition and health influence growth outcomes. Children from economically advantaged families tend to grow faster than children from poorer families who tend to have poor nutrition and more frequent illnesses.

Size

Body proportion also changes as a child ages. At birth, a child's head accounts for approximately one fourth of the total body height and weight. Gradually, the proportion of the head to the body decreases, while the proportion of the legs gradually increases (see Figure 2.3). Ossification or hardening of the bones is another function of growth, beginning during the prenatal period. This skeletal development is necessary for posture and strength. During early infancy, the bones of the legs and arms are fragile, and unable to support an infant's weight. As hardening of the bones takes place, the extremities straighten and one-year-olds are able to bear weight in standing and walking.

Developmental Patterns

Three universal patterns of physical growth govern motor development. **Cephalo-caudal** is the sequence in which growth and development of motor skills occurs progressively downward from head and neck, to the trunk, hips, and legs, and finally to the feet and toes. Children first gain head and neck control, which enables them to hold their heads steady and look around; then they gain trunk control, which allows infants to turn from back to tummy, to sit,

Figure 2.3/ *Changes in Body Proportions*

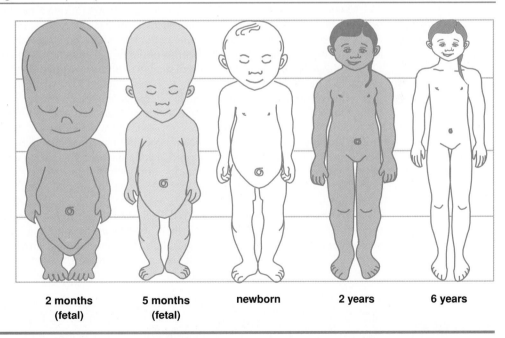

| 2 months (fetal) | 5 months (fetal) | newborn | 2 years | 6 years |

Source: Adapted from Zigler, E. F., & Stevenson, M. F. (1993). *Children in a changing world: Developmental and social issues, Second Edition.* Pacific Grove, CA: Brookes/Cole.

and so on. A second principle, ~~proximo-distal~~ sequencing, refers to development that prgresses from the center of the body, outward toward the extremities. Legs and arms, being closer to the midline of the body, can be controlled earlier than toes and fingers, as seen by gross movements of extremities in the play of young infants. A child will reach (arm movement) before grasping because the hands are farther from the center of the body, and finger control comes later.

Refinement is a third principle that is also referred to as simple-to-complex or gross-to-fine development. A child's motor development is initially concentrated on large muscle groups for sitting and walking, and then on small muscle group control for such things as scribbling and writing with a crayon. Understanding these three principles helps adults predict a child's development so that intervention is appropriately concentrated on present and emerging stages of development.

Physical Growth

At birth, an infant should be capable of independent functioning that is separate from its mother. Even though organ systems are not all fully developed, they should function well enough to permit growth and development. Deviations from the normal progression of growth may indicate a health problem, but more often are normal deviations that relate to genetic predisposition. Again, though the normal *sequence* of growth and development is known, the individual timing of certain milestones is not always predictable.

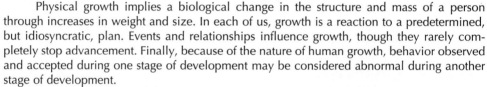

Physical growth implies a biological change in the structure and mass of a person through increases in weight and size. In each of us, growth is a reaction to a predetermined, but idiosyncratic, plan. Events and relationships influence growth, though they rarely completely stop advancement. Finally, because of the nature of human growth, behavior observed and accepted during one stage of development may be considered abnormal during another stage of development.

Major organ systems develop at different rates and at different times. All of the major systems are established during fetal life and, by birth, have developed to the point where adaptation of the systems to extrauterine life can occur. Major organ systems include the respiratory, cardiovascular, gastrointestinal, renal, neurological, skeletal, and integumentary systems. Each of these systems controls different activities of normal physiological functions that are critical to a normal life.

The **respiratory system** is made of many complex structures that enable human beings to both take in oxygen, essential for cellular life, and give off carbon dioxide (a by-product of cellular function). The lungs are the main organs of the respiratory system, though healthy cardiovascular functioning is critical to normal functioning of the lungs. Adequate nutrition is necessary for normal lung growth. This factor can be very important when dealing with certain infants and children, such as those with cerebral palsy, who suffer from diseases that affect either the lungs themselves or a child's ability to sustain adequate caloric intake.

The **cardiovascular system** is comprised of the heart and the blood vessels that extend throughout the body connecting all cells to their source of nutrition. A fetal heart begins to beat at approximately four weeks of gestation. This development provides the link necessary for the placenta to adequately provide oxygen and nutrition to a fetus. These nutritional elements (oxygen, glucose, etc.) are then carried to the fetus and circulated throughout the body by the fetal circulatory system.

After birth, the act of independent respiration changes the normal blood flow. This transition occurs when the lungs expand, changing the pathway of blood to the lungs for oxygenation. Newborns consequently become self-reliant in the physiology of oxygen and carbon dioxide exchange. Deviations in development of heart structure or of the pathways for blood flow can have very significant effects on the growth of a child.

The **renal system** consists of the kidneys and bladder, as well as the tubes that connect these organs. The cardiovascular system directs blood flow through the renal organs, where the products of cell reproduction and death are absorbed from the bloodstream and excreted from the body through urine. Adequate kidney function is essential for survival, for without these organs waste cannot be eliminated. As a consequence, other vital organs would be destroyed by the toxic build-up of waste products. Kidneys, generally not completely developed by birth, mature throughout the first year of life.

The **gastrointestinal system** (GI system) both processes and absorbs nutrients taken in with food to maintain metabolism and to support growth. The system includes the mouth, esophagus, stomach, and small and large intestines. The GI system also is involved with excretion of both digestive residue and waste products absorbed from the blood as it passes through the intestinal tract. A functioning gastrointestinal system is essential for life. Failure to develop, or malformations of this system, can produce significant problems related to malnutrition and failure to thrive.

Prior to birth, the **neurological system** is the fastest growing system. Rapid brain growth occurs between 18 and 20 weeks of gestation and again at about 30 weeks through the first 12 months of postnatal life. In fact, it is estimated that the brain achieves at least two-thirds of its adult size by the time an infant has reached one year of age (Beck, Moffatt, & Lloyd, 1973; Langman, 1975). Head circumference is an index of brain growth. Typically, measurements of the head change rapidly during the first year of life then slow down during subsequent years.

During the first six months of life, the brain cortex increases in size and function, as **neurons** (cells responsible for receiving and sending messages) of the brain increase in number and connectedness to other neurons. Immediately after birth, the brain's cortex has little control over neonates' activities. Primitive reflexes, controlled by peripheral nerves and the brain stem, generally guide the activity of very young infants (see Figure 2.4). As growth and development occur, the brain, through its developing pathways, exerts increasing control over the reflex activity of infants, facilitating the acquisition of more complex abilities. Cortical control requires the development of a **myelin** sheath on the nerves. This sheath permits electrical impulses to move quickly along the nerve fiber or axon (see Figure 2.5). That is, the more myelinization there is, the more efficient or rapid the nervous system becomes at sending/receiving messages. Hence, myelinization of the nervous system is required before complex motor skills can be developed. Lack of

Figure 2.4/ *Location of Voluntary and Reflexive Motor Control in the Brain*

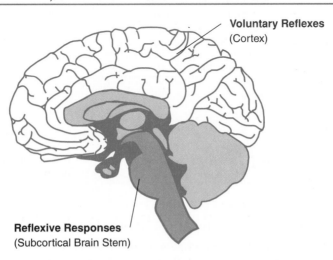

Voluntary Reflexes
(Cortex)

Reflexive Responses
(Subcortical Brain Stem)

myelinization or damage to the myelin sheath leads to motor disorders such as cerebral palsy. Myelinization is also required before visual discrimination can be accomplished.

Increases in body size require both new *bone growth* and the maturation of existing bone structures. The development of new skeletal cells and connective tissue leads to this linear growth. Through maturation, tissues consolidate into a permanent shape that provides structure for the body. Bone growth follows a genetic plan that continues for up to 20 years after birth (Beck, et al., 1973). Many diseases that affect children may affect bone growth. For example, chronic lung disease in premature infants increases the possibility for decreased food intake leading to poor nutrition that can adversely affect bone growth.

Muscle growth also has a role in childhood development. Muscle fibers, which have been laid down in fetal life, remain constant in number throughout the lifespan, but increase in size at varying times. Growth periods are probably most apparent during adolescence, when hormonal changes in puberty stimulate the muscle fibers to increase in size. By contrast, muscles that are unused in childhood will shrink in size, ultimately leading to **atrophy** with eventual loss of muscle function.

The **integumentary system** has many component structures. These include nails, hair, sebaceous glands, sweat glands, ligaments, tendons, and fat tissue. The skin is the largest organ in the body. It provides protection and structure to an individual, prevents the loss of body contents, and impedes the entrance of hazardous agents. The skin also conserves heat when the external temperature is low and allows for heat loss when the external temperature is high. In addition, the skin's ability to prevent water loss is essential for maintaining the body's steady state. This efficiency in protecting and preventing heat loss is underdeveloped in very young or immature infants. Maturity improves the ability of this system to control or prevent heat loss and maintain a normal fluid balance.

Dentition (tooth formation) is another process of growth. Primary and secondary tooth formation can be categorized into stages that consist of growth, calcification, eruption, and tooth loss. Ages at which teeth erupt are inconsistent among children, but the order in which they erupt is fairly constant (see Figure 2.6). With the exception of the first molar the teeth erupt from the incisors, or front teeth, backward in order to the molars. Still significant delays in eruption may be indicative of nutritional factors or other health problems.

Weight is a growth variable that is influenced by many factors. Heredity, gestational age, maternal conditions, and environmental influences all affect weight. Weight and height, in combination, make it possible to determine normal ranges of growth for different populations. Periodic measurements of weight and height are monitored using standard charts to determine an individual child's rate of growth according to the norm (see Figure 2.7). This information is useful in determining where a particular child stands in relation to other chil-

Figure 2.5/ *Neural Transmission of Myelinated Axon*

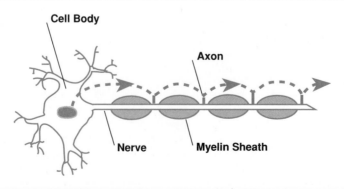

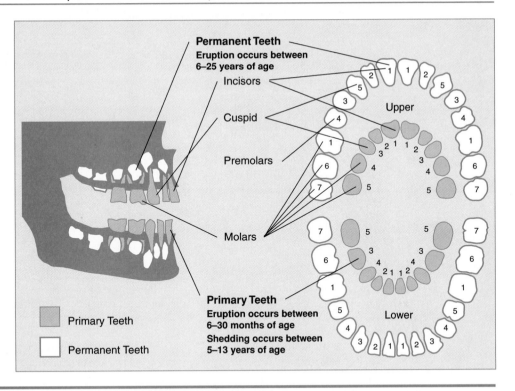

dren of the same age. Children who deviate from the norm are categorized as "large for age" or "small for age." These deviations give information related to the overall health of a particular child and indicate potential or real problems.

Growth parameters follow age-related guidelines. However, age stages are arbitrarily determined and do not generally take into account individual differences. Therefore, it is more important to follow the weight gain in a particular child than to make assumptions about health based solely on where a child lies on the standard growth curve.

Typical stages of growth include the **prenatal period** (from conception to birth), the **neonatal period** (from birth to 30 days of age), the **infancy period** (from 30 days to 12 months), the **toddler** stage (from 1 year to 3 years), the **early childhood** stage (from 3 years to 6 years), the **middle childhood** stage (from 6 years to 12 years), and the **adolescent** stage (from 13 years to 18 years). As mentioned, the prenatal growth period consists of the embryonic and the fetal stage of development. During prenatal care, obstetricians can determine if growth complications that may lead to problems during the neonatal period are present. During the neonatal period, babies attain stability from intrauterine to extrauterine life. Infants must transition completely from fetal circulation patterns, during which they relied on their mothers for all their metabolic needs, to assuming much of the responsibility for meeting their own needs. An average newborn weighs between 7 and 7 1/2 pounds (3175 to 3400 grams), is usually 18–21 inches long, and has a head circumference of 12–15 inches (Allen & Marotz, 1989). These newborns generally lose about 7% to 10% of their body weight during the first two to three days of life, but gradually regain that weight and stabilize their ongoing weight gain to approximately an ounce per day. **Neonates** have poor temperature control, requiring external heat management, such as extra blankets, to maintain a normal temperature of 98.6°F (37°C). Poor

Figure 2.7 / *Sample Growth Charts Showing Normals for Infant Weight/Height*

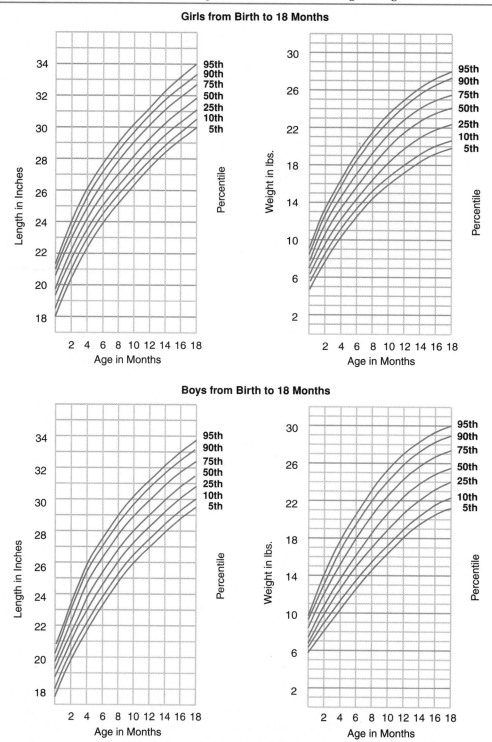

heat control is related to the insufficient fat stores under the skin, which produce fuel for maintaining body temperature (Dahn & James, 1972). Neonates also have a rapid heart rate and a fast but somewhat inconsistent breathing pattern. Because of their small stomach size, neonates eat small amounts frequently. Breast-fed infants may eat as often as every hour.

The infancy period (from 30 days to 12 months) is also a time of very rapid physical growth. By one year, normally progressing infants have tripled their birth weights and are approximately one-and-a-half times their birth heights. The head and chest circumferences have equalized. Heart rates continue to be elevated but are less rapid, and the respiratory pattern is well established. By this time (two to three months), infants can maintain temperature stability and fat stores are sufficient to preserve heat. Skeletal and muscle growth has also occurred, enabling infants to progress through the developmental tasks that are appropriate for this age, especially those related to gross motor skills. Primary tooth eruption usually occurs, and by 12 months infants have an established pattern of three meals daily with an additional feeding before going to bed for the night. Most infants sleep approximately 12 hours each day.

Toddlers (from 12 to 36 months) generally weigh four times their birth weight (26–32 pounds) and are about 32 to 33 inches tall at the end of this stage. Head circumference is increasing, though more slowly now, and primary dentition is usually complete (Allen & Marotz, 1989). Toddlers have food preferences and may not exhibit much of an appetite. In spite of this, many toddlers' abdomens protrude and their extremities appear to have an excess of fat. Toddlers' heart rates may continue to be slightly elevated, though heart rate is decreasing to an average of about 100 beats per minute. The respiratory rate continues at about 25 breaths per minute with use of the abdominal muscles. Many toddlers have inconsistent sleep patterns and are reluctant to go to bed.

Early childhood is the period between three and six years of age. It is during this time that children begin a steady linear growth rate that will continue until adolescence. Three-year-olds will have attained about 50% of their adult height. Weight gain also continues on a steady curve, though growth may be slowed due to an enormous amount of physical activity. This increased physical activity and the increase in linear growth both require calories that are diverted away from weight gain. Brain growth has achieved approximately 90% of its total, with the head circumference reaching approximately 90% of the adult size. Organ growth continues along the same steady curve as external physical growth. The average heart rate continues at about 100 beats per minute, with the average respiratory rate between 21 and 23 breaths per minute. Young children may begin to lose their primary teeth in early childhood.

PRINCIPLES AND PATTERNS OF DEVELOPMENT

The following section provides a brief summary of several principles of normal development that have been derived from decades of observation of infants and young children. These principles represent our current knowledge and beliefs about human patterns of physical and behavioral development. These principles probably will be revised or replaced in the future as our understanding of very young children grows. Still, what we now know allows early childhood professionals to plan intervention and to advise parents. Assessment tools, instructional strategies, and curricular materials are based on the principles of development that follow.

An Infant Is a Highly Competent Organism

As research emerges on child development, it becomes increasingly clear that even newborns possess complex skills. Young infants are capable of learning new behaviors, solving problems, and adapting to changes in their environment. Abilities that enable neonates to use perceptual and cognitive abilities to acquire vast knowledge were unrecognized by early researchers. These competencies are observed across developmental domains, including

Children Exposed to Cocaine: Characteristics and Implications for Research

The 1990 president's National Drug Control Strategy report estimated that 100,000 babies who have been prenatally exposed to cocaine are born each year. Williams and Howard (1993) summarized the damage such exposure presents for today's young children. Medical research has established risks for both cocaine-using pregnant women and their unborn children. Infants prenatally exposed to cocaine may experience a marked failure to adapt to their physical and social environment; a lack of appropriate interaction with caregivers; and language, cognitive, and motor abnormalities that clearly place them at risk. Such infants are highly irritable, difficult to comfort, and hypersensitive to stimuli. Initial results of follow-up on these infants have suggested that some will suffer long-term educational and behavioral disabilities.

Little, however, has been documented concerning the characteristics of children 18 months and older who were exposed to cocaine prenatally. Furthermore, well-controlled research on the long-term effects of cocaine exposure may be very difficult. The risk taken in assigning blame to cocaine alone is that our society might continue to ignore issues of a more social and/or contributing nature. The long-term effects may be due to complications of the cocaine user's lifestyle as well. Such confusing variables include:

1. *A lack of prenatal care:* It has been found that women using drugs were more likely to have lower than average weight to height ratios, to have evidenced sexually transmitted disease, and to have poorer prenatal histories.
2. *Premature birth:* Cocaine causes vasoconstriction of the uterus and has been linked to a higher incidence of premature births.
3. *Prenatal polydrug use:* Alcohol, marijuana, barbiturates, heroin, and methamphetamine are also frequently used in combination with cocaine. Each of these drugs alone is a known or suspected toxin that may cause prenatal injury.
4. *The natural home environment:* Because of the lack of treatment options for women who are addicted to drugs, a very large percentage of mothers remain addicted or return to drug use following treatment. The potential for and actual incidences of child abuse are high in families in which drugs continue to be used.
5. *Poverty:* Without question, the issue of poverty can be the most significant contributing factor in postnatal potential. Outcomes for children associated with poverty alone include malnourishment, attention deficit disorder, significant developmental lags, increased crime and violent behavior, and a constellation of other preventable behaviors.
6. *Racial inequities:* Even though drug use pervades all segments of society, persons from low income and minority groups are overrepresented. Minority students largely comprise a high-risk group at a considerable disadvantage in the education system. This is unfortunate since minority status is confounded by socioeconomic class, and poverty alone may be the critical factor limiting educational attainment.
7. *Social welfare:* Finally, and perhaps most significantly, the child welfare system has become responsible for placing and monitoring 30% to 50% of all infants who were prenatally exposed to cocaine. A result of the overwhelmed welfare system is that children often are shifted from foster home to foster home after brief

(continued)

stays with a single family. Failure of children to bond or show affection is a reasonable if not probable outcome. Children who have been described as "cocaine babies" may be more accurately described as suffering from "vulnerable child syndrome." Despite all the foregoing, it must be mentioned that some researchers feel a majority of children who have been prenatally exposed to cocaine will not have long-term developmental problems. There is much to be said about the apparent resiliency of high-risk infants, but research alone can answer the question of potential for children exposed to cocaine.

Source: Betty Fry Williams and Vikki Howard. (1993). *Journal of Early Intervention, 17,* 61–72.

social, perceptual, motor, and cognitive domains. With increased understanding of infants, changes in educational policy and practices reflect a recognition of the need to match a child's ability with appropriate levels of stimulation. For example, a wind-up mobile was once thought to be appropriate stimulation for a "passive" infant. Now mobiles that jingle or turn only when the infant touches the mobile are considered more appropriate since they help infants establish cause-and-effect and encourage them to take control of their environments.

Infants Are Socially Interactive

In the past, research and intervention policies focused primarily on the intellectual development of young children. More recently, educators have recognized that not only is social interaction a critical area of development but it also influences development in intellectual growth. In fact, it is possible that social competencies may be a more accurate predictor of later abilities than cognitive abilities. Evidence suggests that the need for social attachment is a biological drive. Animal and human research provide examples of failures to establish social relationships in early life that result in significantly abnormal behavior.

MacDonald (1992) theorized that warmth and human affection is emerging as a distinct developmental and biological construct that merits further research. According to MacDonald, human affection provides motivation for children to be compliant and accepting and correspondingly encourages adults to invest in their children. For example, in the past, parents were sometimes advised to feed a child on a fixed schedule at three-hour intervals. Considering the interactive nature of development, parents are now trained to respond to a child's cues to feed or stop feeding based on the child's facial expressions, vocalizations, or activity levels. Parents try to read a child's intent and respect the child's social communication. A child who has not experienced such interactions on a regular basis may learn to be a passive participant.

Infants Are Active Learners

Historically, infant development was thought to be externally governed by the interaction of biological inheritance and environmental influences. Today, developmentalists believe infants are not merely passively modified but play an active, if not always intentional, role in their own development. Early give-and-take interactions between infants and caregivers provide the context for a child to learn control over the environment.

For example, observers have referred to the turn-taking activity that often takes place between mother and infant during breast feeding as the burst-pause sequence. It is thought that an infant instinctively initiates this interaction by pausing briefly during feeding. The mother in turn jiggles the child gently. When the child resumes suckling, seemingly contingently, the mother's behavior is reinforced, and early conversation-like interactions are established. Thus, much of what a child learns is dependent on the child's initiation of interactions with the environment. Hence, a child's play and exploration is essential for development. Along with the emerging research demonstrating the active nature of young children, early educators have altered intervention strategies to build in more child-initiated activities and fewer highly structured teacher-directed activities.

Infant Development Is Multidimensional

The process by which infants' skills become more complex and integrated is a nonarbitrary sequence. Rather, this highly organized process unfolds predictably as children simultaneously grow physically and develop cognitively and socially. Traditionally, child development has described six major areas of functioning: cognition, language, motor skills, perceptual abilities, social skills, and personal/self-help skills. Other functions of interest include self-regulation and temperamental styles. While no area of functioning operates or develops in isolation, it is clear that categorical sequences of subskills define the building blocks on which the acquisition of more specialized abilities can be predicted.

Each developmental domain has been described by listing sequential milestones children progress through in early childhood. It is critical, however, to recognize that behaviors in each area have an impact on behaviors in other domains, as skills develop across domains at the same time. For example, children with Down syndrome often have cognitive delays. Their ability to problem-solve is complicated by poor language development, which is also typically delayed. Articulation difficulties further compound the linguistic problems. A child with Down syndrome who needs help may not be able to request it in an understandable way. As a consequence, social interactions are affected. Three domains are therefore delayed.

Developmental Sequencing Is Universal

Developmental milestones describe a universal sequence of steps through which children progress (see Figure 2.8). Though not all children progress through the steps at precisely the same age, the pattern of development is very reliable. When there are significant deviations in this pattern of development, a child may be at-risk of developmental disability.

Skills Become More Specialized

As children develop, they are able to integrate more refined skills in one area with newly acquired skills in another to perform coordinated behaviors. For example, infants learn to recognize an adult's voice as their auditory discrimination improves. At the same time, facial muscle control increases to the point where a child can smile voluntarily. The result is a specialized ability to smile at "mom" when she is speaking. This acts as a way to enhance social relationships. In early childhood, children scribble nondiscriminately. Gradually, they refine this skill so that they can copy lines and circles. As children near school age, they integrate their emerging cognitive knowledge of alphabet letters with their newly refined fine motor skills. Thus, the specialization of these two domains results in handwriting.

Plasticity

One of the remarkable aspects of development is the **plasticity** of the human brain, by which alternate neural pathways can be formed to compensate for deficits in other portions of the brain. Damage to a specific area of the brain (e.g., language) often results in another portion of the brain developing the function of the damaged section. Another example of this flexibility is seen in infants who are blind or deaf but acquire necessary developmental skills by focusing on alternate channels of understanding. Some researchers theorize that plasticity is possible only before the brain has completed myelinization.

While acknowledging the principle of brain plasticity, Healy (1990) described a process through which human brains become "hardwired." Based on neural research with lab animals, it is clear that permanent neural pathways are established through early (as well as later)

Figure 2.8/ *Typical Motor Development Sequence*

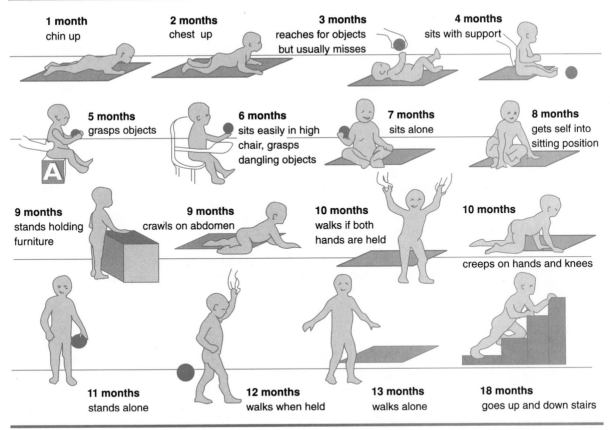

1 month
chin up

2 months
chest up

3 months
reaches for objects
but usually misses

4 months
sits with support

5 months
grasps objects

6 months
sits easily in high
chair, grasps
dangling objects

7 months
sits alone

8 months
gets self into
sitting position

9 months
stands holding
furniture

9 months
crawls on abdomen

10 months
walks if both
hands are held

10 months

creeps on hands and knees

11 months
stands alone

12 months
walks when held

13 months
walks alone

18 months
goes up and down stairs

Source: Adapted from Mussen, P. H., Conger, J. J., Kagen, J., & Huston, A. C. (1990). *Child development and personality (7th ed.).* New York: Harper & Row.

learning experiences. Experiences affect both the function and the structure of brains. Once neural pathways are formed, it is increasingly difficult to reorganize them. Therefore, it is only uncommitted brain tissue that can be molded to adapt to environmental demands. According to Healy (1990) and other researchers, youth in our society are increasingly being exposed to experiences in learning that vary from those experienced by children in the past. Hence, neural pathways or hardwiring are thought to be so different that these youth may be unable to learn and think in the same manner as previous generations. For example, Healy contended that reading, literacy, and language skills are noticeably deficient in today's youth—a direct consequence, she claimed, of early experiences that developed incompatible pathways or failed to develop necessary neural pathways of the brain.

Critical Learning Periods

Interactional and developmental theorists contend that critical sensitive periods during which a child is biologically *most* ready to learn certain new behaviors occur throughout human development. When environmental events provide the right conditions for a particularly sensitive period, developmental progress can be maximized. However, when experiences fail to match a child's predisposition for learning, the window of opportunity is missed. Though a child will not necessarily fail to acquire the new skills, learning will take much longer than otherwise possible.

Paired with the theory of "peak" periods of learning is the need to provide diverse learning experiences involving all sensory systems. Many factors can upset the formula of optimal development. For example, infants are able to make diverse vocal sounds (phonemes), some of which will not be used later as children develop native language specific sound production repertoires. Young children learn to discriminate the sounds used by others in conversation from those sounds never used. If, however, a very young child develops chronic ear infections during a critical period, the child may have difficulty acquiring the sounds necessary for speech.

Children Undergo Several Transitions

It is typical for children to undergo stages of **transition** when there are spurts of growth and development that may be followed by unpredictable behavior or regression. For example, changes in a daily pattern, such as beginning at a new daycare center, may result in behavior problems that are generally short lived. As children cognitively become more inquisitive, more mobile, and more verbal in the latter half of their second year, their behavior also becomes more unpredictable. Until toddlers come under the control of certain rules of conduct that are difficult to teach two-year-olds, they are in transition. This transition is affectionately referred to as the "terrible twos." The resolution of these problems, referred to as **consolidation,** occurs when the disorganized behavior is replaced by more advanced developmental skills. For example, a child may become better behaved when babbling is replaced by the more sophisticated means of communication, conventional words.

Individual Differences Among Children

Children differ in such characteristics as temperament and gender, making each child unique. **Temperament,** or one's adaptation to everyday events, is partially innate and partially learned. Thomas and Chess (1981) concluded that temperament is a relatively constant trait throughout life and identified nine categories of temperament: activity level, persistence, sensitivity to environmental stimuli, mood, approach to or withdrawal from new situations, adaptability to change, intensity of response to stimuli, regularity of routines, and distractibility. Differences in temperament affect the manner in which adults interact with infants and children and often result in such labels as "difficult" or "easy" baby. These responses, in turn, influence the development of a child's temperament. For example, if a cuddly, active, and smiling infant is reinforced by similar adult behaviors, the child is likely to continue being a socially rewarding companion.

Expectations of infants according to gender are obvious, even in newborns, as adults handle and talk to infants differently based on a child's sex (Rheingold & Cook, 1975). This social training appears to be so powerful that children learn to label their own and other's gender before they are able to label objects or tasks that are nongender related (Bussey & Bandura, 1992). Girls and boys develop behaviors and attitudes compatible with subtle as well as explicit expectations of their respective sex roles. Bussey and Bandura found that early gender-regulated behavior was related to the anticipated social sanctions of others (approval or disapproval), and as children grow older, they develop personal standards to which they apply their own self-imposed sanctions. Influences such as toy selection, play activities, playmates, adult modeled behavior, and exposure to television all affect the degree of children's compliance to sex-role expectations.

DEVELOPMENTAL DOMAINS

As mentioned earlier, six primary domains are considered discreet components of child development. While various sources label the domains differently, all refer to the same basic

The Process of Acceptance

Interview with David DeWolf

I have heard some parents express great resentment when someone says to them, "Oh, you must be such special parents because God gave you this little bundle." The parents' attitude is, "Who are they to say that?" Those parents think, "This is a lot of work, and don't give me your piety. God doesn't do this to people." But, actually this came closer to my own feelings than a sense that this was a tragic accident or something for which I wanted people to feel sorry for me.

One of the things that just weighed on my own mind at first was the fear that Robin's disability would be destructive to my parenting or that it would be a wall between us; that Robin's disability would be something that would be a bad thing from a parenting perspective. My fear was that I wouldn't be able to love her—I wouldn't be able to love her completely. I was afraid she would be different from my other children in that respect and that I would be saddled with this cross to bear. The worst fear was that I would be expected to treat her like my own child, but I wouldn't feel that way and I'd be trapped as though in a bad marriage. I was afraid I'd be trapped in a bad parenting relationship.

If you've never had a child with a disability, you don't know. You don't know, any more than you try to imagine in your mind, what would happen if your spouse got hit by a truck and lay dead or in a coma. Would I continue to love him or her, or would I want out? As long as your spouse was an attractive, wonderful person, you'd like to think, I married for better, for worse, in sickness and in health. But I've never been tested in that way, and so I don't know.

So early in the first couple of days, the thing that I think was the scariest thought was not that I'd go broke, or not that I'd be up nights. There was no other burden that I found so scary. The scariest thing was that I'd be a parent of somebody that I really didn't want.

We got a call a couple days after Robin's birth from another parent of a child with Down

syndrome who provided me with an entrée back into the normal world. I think that the difficult thing for the parent of a child with a disability is to feel cut off from the sense of being like everybody else, and suddenly facing all the uncertainty and anxiety that having a child born with a disability produces. The man who called me had a twenty-two-year-old son with Down syndrome. He took me to lunch and showed me pictures and told me about how much fun he had and that he was just a normal kind of father. He happened to be a headmaster of a private school, and had an educational background that I could identify with. I could see myself in his shoes.

The basic message was, "Hey, this works. It's okay, you'll just take it in stride." I found that to be a kind of thing I could hold onto. Even with all of the other doubts put into my mind, here at least there was an example that there was no reason to think that my relationship with Robin would be that much different from my other children. And within a matter of days just the physical, biological, chemical reaction between a parent and a child was all there. Early on, I was able to say, this one's going to be okay, this will be fine.

My wife's family were more understanding than my own. Her grandmother was still alive when Robin was born. My wife's grandmother had a son with Down syndrome, so they had a special kind of understanding about that. I think her response was positive in the special way only a parent who also has a child with the same disability can affirm. I think Priscilla has also been closer to contemporaries in the same situation. We had friends from when we were living in Oklahoma who were extremely supportive. Priscilla's personal experience was greater and made Down syndrome less an issue for her. Priscilla needed to know what to do to help Robin, but there was never a worry about whether she would fit in our family.

Acceptance is a lifelong process of coming to terms with loss. It's like any other thing; your

(continued)

hair turns gray, or it falls out as you age; you lose things and people that you care about; but you adjust. I think the adjustment comes for us when we reach milestones in Robin's life that are different because she has Down syndrome. For example, we had one experience with very dear friends of ours, neighbors, who have a daughter who was instrumental in Robin's development of her speech and many other qualities. At one point, they pulled back from the relationship because their daughter had spent so much time with Robin that they were concerned that their daughter was becoming more like Robin rather than the other way around. That was very painful for us, both because I think there was some stereotyping of Robin, but there was also some overprotective denial on our part.

Right now, Robin is just on a slower clock. There has been no point at which we said, "Gee, she's lost out on this because she has Down syndrome." I think as she gets older and there will be things that are not available to her—that she'd like to get a driver's license or she'd like to get married or whatever it is that she would like to do that can't happen in the time frame that she would like, or may not be appropriate for her. Those will be times that will be tough to deal with.

It's hard to imagine Robin as an adult. I guess what I'd have to hope for her would be a supportive environment. I think she has everything she needs to be happy and fulfilled, when she's in a context of people who care about her and provide her with a family atmosphere. The greatest fear I would have is that she'd be deprived of that because of our becoming unavailable or too old or too sick or whatever, that we couldn't provide that for her. And/or that she wouldn't develop the skills and connections so that she could make that world for herself. I don't see Robin, because of her nature, as ever being independent—in the sense that I'm not very good at being independent; I've

done poorly left by myself. I need other people to keep me going, cheer me up, keep me company, and give me a good kick in the rear end when I need it. Robin is also like that, only more so. For Robin to be by herself would be a shameful waste of an incredible personality. She's a people person.

Of course, that's not something that you can control over her lifetime. What the world will look like in 40 years—who knows? What kind of world will she inherit at that point? We've talked before in terms of how much independence you prepare your children for. On the one hand it would be possible to get her ready to be independent, and yet, to me, that would involve a premature closure of the very sort of open characteristics of her personality that I think are who she is, and who she is at her most fulfilled. For that matter, most of the rest of us are most fulfilled when we live in a family. So, I guess I want to preserve that as long as I can and hope and have some faith that in the end, when we're no longer able to fulfill that role, that something or somebody or somehow else, she will have some successor to us.

sequences identified as cognition, social skills, language skills, motor skills, perceptual abilities, and self-help skills. Though described separately here, there is a direct functional relationship between changes in one area and development in the other domains.

Cognition

A child's evolving intellectual abilities include increasingly complex problem solving behaviors. A neonate's cognitive behavior is primarily reflexive, though infants learn very quickly to make sense of the relatedness of events and their own behavior, enabling them to exert voluntary control over personal behavior. The cognitive processes involved include memory, discovery, interpretation, sorting and classification of information, making comparisons, inductive and deductive reasoning, understanding language, and predicting the consequences of current events. Critical to cognition is the ability to take previously learned knowledge and use it to solve novel problems. It is with a mixture of delight and anxiety that parents discover that the latch to a child-protection gate has been opened by a young child who has not yet learned to avoid the dangers beyond the gate.

The most widely referenced theoretical analysis of cognitive development is that of Jean Piaget. After intense observation of his own children, Piaget made remarkably accurate observations of stages through which children progress from birth through early childhood. The **sensorimotor stage** stretches from birth to age two and represents children's primitive exploration of their environment, wherein children attempt to integrate sensory information with their own movement. This stage is followed by the **preoperational stage,** during which children reason through the use of linguistic input and personal knowledge. From age two to six, conceptual knowledge rapidly expands as children begin to engage in imitation, fantasy play, and self-regulation.

Social Skills

From the first hours of infancy, a child establishes the building blocks for sustained social relationships with others. Social skills involve a range of behaviors that define how children feel about themselves and their relationship with others. As mentioned earlier, increasing knowledge of infant attachment suggests that early social competency is critical to later cognitive, linguistic, and social development. The extent to which adults foster bonding affects infants' sense of security in their relationships with others. Individual characteristics of infants (e.g., temperament, health) also influence the course of social interactions. However, a metanalysis of attachment research that investigated the influence of maternal problems (e.g., maltreatment or mental illness) and child problems (e.g., resistance to approach by caregiver or physical disability) concluded that maternal behaviors toward children play a much more important role in attachment of secure relations than those of children (van IJzendoorn, Goldberg, Kroonenberg, & Frenkel, 1992). Included within this domain are self-esteem, play behavior, sex roles, independence, moral development, rule-governed behavior, and cultural values. As children age, their personalities are defined by the social behaviors shaped in early childhood.

Language Skills

Communication between an infant and others begins at birth when neonates send messages that are interpreted. Though initially those messages are unintentional, children typically acquire all the major components of a complex symbol system of communication by the age of three. Symbols include spoken words, sign language, written words, and other forms of translating ideas into a commonly understood communication system. This symbolic system, which is comprised of a set of rules for structure and content, is referred to as **language.** Two subcategories of language are expressive (the production of messages) and receptive (understanding communication) language. Most children learn to use oral-motor functions to produce **speech,** though not all communication or language is produced through spoken words. Humans also communicate with gestures, facial expressions, and body language.

Language will not develop in the absence of social contexts, and it is a direct reflection of the sophistication of cognitive development. As children's knowledge of objects, events, and relationships in their environment expands, they acquire words to express this knowledge. Moreover, social relationships provide the motivation for individuals to use language and learn new forms of communication. These observations reflect the strong interdependence of developmental domains.

Motor Skills

Physical development involves the increased control, coordination, strengthening, and complexity of **neuromuscular** functioning. As the brain matures, muscles strengthen, bones harden, and infants' ability to move about their environment improves. Like communication, motor movement is solely reflexive at birth. The presence of primitive reflexes at birth is a sign that neonates are neurologically intact. As infants mature, these reflexes are replaced with more adaptive postural reflexes and voluntary control over movement. Failure to integrate primitive reflexes will inhibit normal and adaptive movement and is a clear sign of neurological damage.

Typically, motor development is separated into gross and fine motor abilities. Gross motor skills involve the movement and control of large muscle groups for sitting, crawling, and walking. By contrast, fine motor control refers to the refined movement of small muscle groups, such as those in the hands, face, and toes. During the first year of life, children learn to master the control of large muscle groups. Children later learn to walk faster and run, to throw a ball with more precision, and to balance, even while walking on a sidewalk curb.

The refinement of fine motor skills is dependent on several factors, including the maturation of gross motor abilities. The movement of small muscle groups to perform such actions as grasping and manipulation of objects with the hands also requires the integration of perceptual abilities. To enable children to build block towers and tie their shoes, the coordination of muscle movement and perceptual abilities becomes more critical. For example, a child will use sight to identify the color, shape, size, and position of the blocks, and for best balance, touch to adjust a block placed on the tower.

Perceptual Skills

The parallel nature of perceptual development and development in other domains may already be obvious. Even so, this area of inquiry has yielded the most remarkable discoveries regarding the once grossly underestimated competencies of very young infants. **Perceptual abilities** involve a child's ability to make use of information received through the six senses or modalities: auditory, visual, kinesthetic, gustatory, olfactory, and tactile (see Table 2.1). While these abilities can be defined discretely, humans rarely use one sense in isolation. Rather, multiple modalities are finely coordinated to permit movement, to understand communication, and to eat.

Normally developing infants quickly learn to **habituate,** which allows them to use environmental information in an efficient manner. This ability permits humans to identify and attend to critical sensory stimuli, such as a favorite toy or person, while selectively ignoring irrelevant stimuli, such as the sounds from a radio, texture of clothes touching one's body, and smell of Dad's cologne. The capacity to screen interfering stimuli is an essential element of normal development. In fact, recent studies appear to indicate that habituation in infants is one of the most reliable early predictors of later intelligence scores (McCall & Carriger, 1993).

Self-Help Skills

As children mature motorically, linguistically, cognitively, and perceptually, they begin to integrate these skills to perform daily maintenance routines referred to as self-help skills, or adaptive

Table 2.1/ *Patterns of Perceptual Development*

Sense	Ability at Birth	Patterns of Development
Visual	Research indicates range from 20/800 to 20/150; discriminates colors; shows preference for patterns and three-dimensional images	20/100 at 1 year; 20/60 at 2 years; 20/20 at 5 years; 180 visual arc at 3 months; adult-like focus at 4 months; discriminates age and gender at 5 1/2 months; recognizes face from different angles at 7 months
Auditory	40 dB threshold; startle response; habituation to sound; soothed by rhythmic music	Discriminates speech sounds (ba/pa) at 4–14 weeks; 20 db threshold at 3–8 months; localizes to sound and shows preference for female voices at 4–6 months
Gustatory	Little research; prefers sugar solution to water	
Olfactory	Little research; appears to respond differentially to odors	
Tactile	Reflexive responses to touch; differential sensitivity by body parts; discriminates warm and cold	Decreased response threshold across first 5 days; by 3 days learns to habituate and is conditioned to tactile stimulation; thermal regulation at 1 1/2 weeks; discriminates objects tactually by 10–12 months

Source: Adapted from Hanson, M. J., & Hanline, M. F. (1984). Behavioral competencies and outcomes: The effects of disorders. In M. J. Hanson (Ed.), *Atypical infant development* (pp. 109–142). Austin, TX: PRO-ED.

behaviors. Eating, dressing, toileting, and grooming are self-help skills that are the functions that emerge from competencies in the other developmental domains. For example, children will not learn to eat finger food until they are able to grasp an object and bring it to their mouth, can discriminate food from nonfood, and have well-developed swallow reflexes. Sleep patterns and eating patterns both influence and are influenced by individual and environmental factors. Normally, in early infancy, sleeping and eating predominate. A gradual reduction in the dominance of these basic human functions permits children to spend proportionately greater time interacting with their environment, which in turn frees energy for the acquisition of new abilities.

FACTORS INFLUENCING DEVELOPMENT

The heredity versus environment debate, regarding the relative influence of a child's genetic potential for growth and development compared with the impact of environmental factors, continues. While few would argue that one or the other is unimportant, agreement as to the absolute proportion of influence of each to developmental progress is not imminent. Toward that end, many twin and adoption studies have been conducted to measure the influence of genes and environment (see Figure 2.9). The most revealing studies have been those conducted with identical twins who were raised in different environments and then assessed at a later time. For example, in one study of separated fraternal and identical twins, Bouchard, Lykken, McGue, Segal, and Tellegen (1990) estimated that heredity was 70% responsible for intelligence, while Vandenburg (1962) found a hereditary contribution of only 16%. Though high variability exists in the degree to which heredity is believed to influence such measures as intelligence and personality, it is clear that genetics plays no small part in determining such behaviors (Vandenburg, 1971).

On the other hand, adoptive studies have revealed that environment also plays a substantial role in influencing behavior. For example, Honzik (1957) found an average 20-point IQ improvement in adopted children as compared to those who were raised by their less affluent biological mothers. Similarly, Schiff, Duyme, Dumaret, and Tomkiewicz (1982) discovered an average 14-point IQ improvement in children adopted into upper-income professional families as compared to their parents who were unskilled workers. Though the search for the definitive resolution of heredity versus environment will continue for many decades, it can be assumed that to a large extent children's development across domains can be altered by the manipulation (intentional or not) of environmental factors.

Economics

Demographics and economics of families will influence such factors as nutrition, nurturing and education, and health care. A decline in the average family income leading to poverty is related to increases in mental health disorders, child abuse, lack of prenatal care, malnutrition, poor educational outlook, and exposure to environmental hazards, such as lead poisoning. As can be seen in Figure 2.10, poverty leads predictably to conditions that affect child development. In the United States one in four children live in poverty, with the trend toward poverty increasing in the last two decades.

Figure 2.9/ *Comparative Studies of Performance of Gestational and Fraternal Twins*

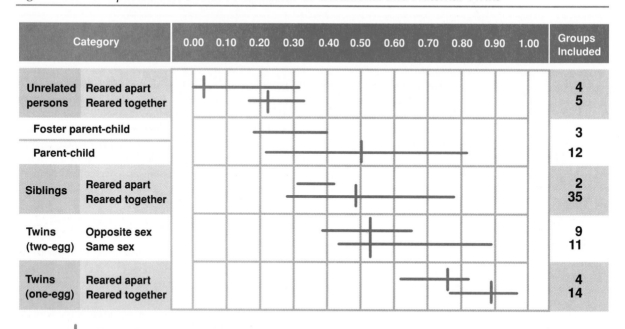

Source: Adapted from Zigler, E. F., & Stevenson, M. F. (1993). *Children in a changing world: Developmental and social issues, Second Edition*, p.106. Pacific Grove, CA: Brookes/Cole.

Pathways of Poverty

Lack of Food

undernutrition during pregnancy

low birth weight, spina bifida, anencephaly, and related birth defects

poor nutritional status (indicated by stunted growth)

lower academic test scores

iron deficiency

anemia and problems with problem-solving, motor coordination, attention, concentration, and long-term IQ scores

Family Stress

perceived financial hardship

parent stress and depression

family conflict, less effective parenting behavior, marital strain and breakup

child behavior problems, aggressiveness, delinquency, learning problems

Neighborhood Problems

exposure to crime

post-traumatic stress symptoms, limited opportunities to go outside

inferior schools, fewer job opportunities

lower achievement, lack of hope, dropping out, not attending college, joblessness, lack of job benefits, low wages

exposure to toxic chemicals and pollution

cancer, lung damage, brain damage, school failure, behavior problems, damaged immune systems, and disease

Fewer Resources for Learning

inferior child care

stress (measured by stress hormone levels), and aggressive behavior, less active or friendly

unaffordable text books and school fees

dropped out, withheld diplomas, less participation in school activities

fewer stimulating family trips, hobbies, camps, or extracurricular activities

lower school achievement

home and work responsibilities

"more mind wandering and less exerting effort in school," lower school enrollment and attainment

financial barriers to college

lower school attainment

Housing Problems

homelessness

infant mortality, chronic diarrhea, asthma, delayed immunizations, family separation, missed school

frequent moving

not completing high school

utility shut-offs

home fire deaths

water leakage

mold, cockroaches

asthma

peeling paint, falling plaster, fewer opportunities to clean and repaint

lead poisoning low birth weight, hearing loss, brain and kidney damage, reading disability, lower IQ scores, dropping out of school, attention deficit and hyperactivity disorders

crowded housing

stress, less opportunity for rest, infections

illness

crowded housing (combined with lack of neighborhood parks and facilities)

few places to play, children playing in street

injuries

Source: Adapted from Sherman, A. (1994). *Wasting America's future: The Children's Defense Fund report on the costs of child poverty* (p.12). Boston: Beacon Press.

Family Configuration and Lifestyle

To suggest that changes in American society threaten the survival of the "traditional family" is to perpetuate the myth that such an institution ever existed. Still, youth in America are increasingly growing up in families whose lifestyles have altered patterns of social nurturance (see Figure 2.11). In part because of changes in the lifestyle of families, childrearing has become progressively more difficult in American society. In support of this conclusion are data from The Fordham Institute for Innovation in Social Policy, which found that the social health of children (i.e., the extent of child abuse, poverty, teen suicide, etc.) has become progressively poorer almost every year since data were first gathered in 1970 (Miringhoff, 1989).

The instability of today's American families is evident in demographic data. Divorce affects approximately half of all American children (Glick & Lin, 1986). Single-parent families, usually headed by the mother, increased from 22% in 1974 to 34% in 1987 (Children's Defense Fund, 1988). These families are disproportionately impoverished, isolated from families and friends, and include small children. While poverty and isolation are the most salient concerns for such families, the absence of either a dominant female or male adult figure in a child's life influences patterns of development, particularly in social and personal areas. The reconstitution of divorced families in blended or extended families results in socialization patterns that may affect children's loyalty to others, values, adaptability, and self-esteem. Research indicates that divorce has a variable influence on children, depending on such factors as age and gender of children, the presence of siblings, the psychological status of custodial parents, the intensity and outcome of custody battles, and the reconstitution of families in subsequent marriages (Monahan, Buchanan, Maccoby, & Dornbusch, 1993).

Research on the developmental effects of adopted children indicates that several factors, such as family structure, the adoptive family's adjustment to infertility problems, age of the adopted child, and support of extended family members, interrelate to influence a child's development (Berry, 1992). Simon and Alstein (1987) found that adopted children tended to receive poorer grades than children born into the family, while Bohman and Sigvardsson (1985) found significantly higher rates of maladjustment in adopted children—particularly males—as compared to children raised by their biological parents.

Child Care

Since World War II, the percentage of women, especially those with children, who work outside the home has gradually increased. While overall 70% of all women with children work outside the home, the percentage of women with children under six who work outside the home has increased from 11.9% in 1950 to 56.8% in 1987 (Hoffman, 1989). Raising children while working full time places stress on both parents, especially when the working mothers are expected to fulfill all the traditional responsibilities (Hoffman, 1989). Yet, the fact that mothers work outside the home in greater proportion does not automatically mean that children are less well nurtured. Vandell and Ramanan (1992) made a longitudinal analysis of work patterns of low-income women and related factors. These authors found that the earlier women went to work after childbirth and the more recently (relative to the time of the study) they worked, the better off the family was. These women were more educated and more intelligent, the family was less likely to exist in poverty, and the quality of home life was higher; finally, their children were more likely to do well in school academics.

Psychological Factors

The maintenance of a nurturing environment is as important to child development as health care and nutrition. From the first days of life, adults begin to nurture children through breast feeding, eye contact, smiling, kissing, and vocalizations, which in turn establish an attachment

Figure 2.11/ *The Effects of Childhood Poverty on High School Completion Percentages (Longitudinal study of income dynamics based on 1,705 children ages 0–6 originally tested in 1968; outcomes measured at ages 21–27.)*

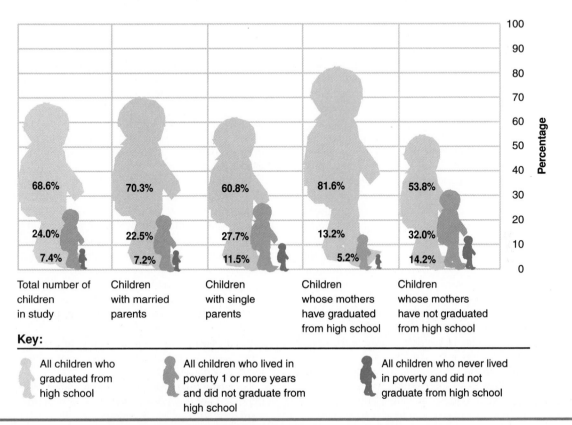

	Total number of children in study	Children with married parents	Children with single parents	Children whose mothers have graduated from high school	Children whose mothers have not graduated from high school
	68.6%	70.3%	60.8%	81.6%	53.8%
	24.0%	22.5%	27.7%	13.2%	32.0%
	7.4%	7.2%	11.5%	5.2%	14.2%

Key:

All children who graduated from high school

All children who lived in poverty 1 or more years and did not graduate from high school

All children who never lived in poverty and did not graduate from high school

Source: Adapted from Sherman, A. (1994). *Wasting America's future: The Children's Defense Fund report on the costs of child poverty* (p. xxiii). Boston: Beacon Press.

between infant and caregiver referred to as **bonding** (Siegel, 1982). Unlike other species, however, human babies resiliently retain the capability of bonding, even if parents miss opportunities in the first days and weeks of life. As infants grow, other psychological factors begin to influence development. Erikson (1963) wrote that one of the primary tasks of infants in their first year of life was to develop a sense of trust, which comes out of predictable and positive responses of caregivers and siblings.

When adult behavior is either unpredictable or predominantly aversive in nature, young infants learn mistrust in relationships with others. The extent to which adults engage in frequent and sustained reciprocal play, and where adults "enter the child's world," are said to be crucial to the development of social communication/language (McDonald, 1989). Hence, parental style is important to nurturance of children. Adults who use warm and gentle tones to give directions and provide frequent positive feedback supporting appropriate behaviors develop the strongest levels of attachment. Kennedy (1992) analyzed the childrearing strategies of parents whose children were rejected by their peers and found that mothers had spent

Working with the Foster Care System

Interview with James Holden

I have been an early childhood special education teacher, and now I teach a regular sixth grade, but my wife and I started taking foster children before I was ever trained in education. We've probably had a couple hundred foster children over the course of our marriage. We did foster care for years, when our family was smaller, but as our own family increased to seven children, we retired from foster care for a while. At the time, we didn't feel we had a voice in what was happening to the foster children. When foster children were placed, the decisions on what was going to happen with them were pretty much controlled and dictated by the state.

For example, when we first started, in the mid 1960s, there was not a lot of emphasis on disabilities. All the children were just foster children and there wasn't really a thought given to the special needs a lot of those children had. The only special service I can remember being considered was the notion that counseling would fix whatever was wrong with foster children. Many of the children we dealt with, even then, were of mixed ethnic backgrounds, or coming out of divorce situations, so there were some emotional needs that got in the way of education. When you would have children like that, you'd have a hard time.

We had not had foster children for some time when I went back to school and became a certified special education teacher. I took a teaching position on an Indian reservation and that was when we got back into the foster system. These children would show up at our house anyway. Sometimes parents would get to the point where they didn't feel like they could take care of their children, so they would bring them to our house, and we'd watch over them for a few days. Usually this was in a crisis situation. The school district superintendent's wife worked for the Department of Social and Health Services on the reservation, so in an emergency situation she would always place a few children with us. Finally, someone at the tribe said, "Well you're doing it anyway, you might as well get a license"; so that's what we did.

All the foster children from the reservation were high needs children. Many had parents who had used drugs or alcohol during pregnancy; the children were chemical effect, fetal alcohol syndrome, or alcohol impacted children. All kinds of differing abilities go with these problems. We no longer live on the reservation and now the children we receive tend to have health impairment or emotional problems.

Medical care is paid for through the foster care system, which is a big bonus. The difficulty is making sure you get children with special needs to the right people. The treatment can be more traumatic than just leaving them alone. For example, taking Rueben and April to an office for physical therapy is more traumatic than trying to do it yourself at home because you're taking them off of their schedules and they're being exposed to a lot of people. You also expose them to more illness and they're already medically fragile, so they can become undone by this. Doing something in an unfamiliar setting can be very stressful for these children.

Many times you get children with problems that have not been diagnosed, so you're starting from ground zero. Each child is so individual, the evaluation process can be overpowering. I know a lot of foster parents just say, "Hey, it's not worth the effort," or "I just don't have the time to do it." As the children get older you're often looking at some kind of counseling or therapy as well. Getting services is very time intensive and distracting from a normal life, whatever that is.

We often have had five foster children at one time. With the kinds of high needs children we have, that's about all a family can handle. Right now we have two children who have cystic fibrosis and fetal alcohol effect, and the other three who we're adopting who are all chemically impacted from crack cocaine. My wife and I are a team. I try to deal with the bureaucracy, arrange the medical treatment, and the diagnostic testing, but she does the every day nitty-gritty care of the children.

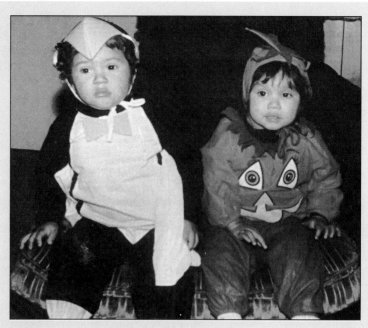

Right now, the foster care system is overloaded with these kinds of children, and many of them are not in appropriate homes. Many of the foster parents are simply not trained adequately to deal with high needs children. When they hit school, many foster parents are going to feel, "Hey, we've done our job, now do yours." If the evaluation process doesn't start until then, the child has already lost three years before we do anything with them.

Foster parents in this area have organized to try to make changes in the system. They would like to see ongoing training about ways to identify suspected abuse or neglect, and continuing training with substance abuse impacted children. AIDS is another huge part of what we're going through right now. The system will put a child with AIDS or suspected AIDS in your home and will not give you that information. I've also had a couple of children who had hepatitis and they did not tell us. Those can be scary things because you're really in jeopardy. Family contact is very intimate at that level, there's no way to avoid it—so something needs to be done. Again we're balancing confidentiality rights with the rights of the caregiver, and we as a society haven't come to grips with that.

All in all, I feel the foster parent association and the state foster care workers work very well together to try and provide for the best care available. But this will be an ongoing and important battle to win for the children. If we don't fight for these children, who will?

less time teaching social skills to their children and were more likely to use punishment and used less reasoning to explain discipline. At the same time, the fathers and mothers of these children did not value or spend time in child-centered activities.

Infants and young children must also be given the freedom to explore their environments and to experiment and play with appropriate toys or materials (Allen & Marotz, 1989). For decades it has been recognized that the absence of stimulation or deprivation of experiences negatively affects development (Skeels, 1942; 1966). In Skeels's original research, 25 infants were selected from an overcrowded orphanage; 13 of them were sent to an institution to be cared for by adult women with mental retardation who provided the children with a stimulating and responsive environment. Though initially testing an average of 22 IQ points lower than the 12 infants remaining in the orphanage, a year and a half after placement in the institution, the children raised by women with mental retardation gained an average of 28 IQ points. Meanwhile, the children who remained in the overcrowded orphanage lost an average of 26 IQ points in the same interval of time.

Education

Perhaps no discipline that influences child development is further from achieving professional consensus than education. It is undisputed that American schools fail to meet the expectations of the public. The following list represents some tenuous educationally related factors that have been found to differentially influence a child's development (McLaughlin & Vacha, 1992):

1. the opportunity for preschool educational services, especially for children who are raised in poverty

2. educational level of parents

3. structure and curriculum focus of educational program

4. safety of child in school

5. opportunity for success and positive experiences in school

6. consistency of school attendance and mobility

7. value of a child's education to parents

8. a parent's knowledge of the educational system

Ethnicity

Although cross-cultural research is in its infancy, it has revealed that universality exists in many aspects of development, just as differences have been observed in the rates of that development. For example, infants within the same culture seem to behave similarly, while behaving as a group differently than children from other cultures (Lester & Brazelton, 1982). In the past, educators tended to evaluate the development of all children according to the norms established with white, middle-income children. Similarly, educational priorities favor the values of the dominant culture. For example, cooperative group behavior is highly valued in most minority groups, while Caucasians tend to value independence and competition. More recently, it has been realized that this practice gives undue priority to a single culture, while simultaneously and arbitrarily devaluing the practices of other cultures that may differentially affect child development.

Technology

Two major influences of the technological expansion in the last half of the twentieth century are television and the computer. While computers are quickly becoming household tools for both adults and children, the long-term influence of this technology on child development is yet undetermined. Television, on the other hand, has been the center of controversy for decades. The potential influence of television cannot be underestimated, as it has been found that no other activity consumes as much time for American children as watching television (Nielson, 1988).

Of particular concern to parents and child advocates have been the correlational findings linking programming and commercials on television to aggression in children (Pearl, Bouthilet, & Lazar, 1982), unhealthy eating habits (Finn, 1977), and unwise buying tendencies (Baecher, 1983). A reduction in children's academic capacity when greater than three hours per day were spent watching television was identified by Beentjes and VanderVoort (1988). However, Henggeler, Cohen, Edwards, Summerville, and Ray (1991) concluded that family contexts (maternal life events stress and paternal marital satisfaction), when correlated with television viewing time, might be interrelated with academic performance of children (support for and active participation in studying). Though computers and television are sources of concern when overused to entertain, as in computer and video games and in many television forums, both also have the potential to be valuable learning tools.

HUMAN DEVELOPMENT IN THE TWENTY-FIRST CENTURY

Knowledge and practice in the twenty-first century will be dramatically influenced by changes in technology in ways that we cannot begin to predict. Theories of human development will change more rapidly as technology enables researchers to investigate and solve riddles previously inaccessible to observation. In the past, cognitive, linguistic, and social behaviors have been largely explained by guesses about what goes on underneath one's skin, rather than by knowledge of actual neurological or endrocrinological processes. Technology will enable researchers to observe more closely, measure more accurately, and replicate more reliably, the molecular-level changes that are likely to hold answers to human development.

Based on this new knowledge, early childhood educators can help families to select and design programs that more reliably influence children's acquisition of desirable behaviors. Concomitantly, professionals will need to learn more about family systems, so that we are able to respond sensitively and effectively to diverse characteristics. This issue is infinitely more complex and intractable than the mind-boggling changes in technology that we are likely to encounter in the coming decades. If our past is an accurate indicator, then progress in working effectively with families so that they can be empowered to facilitate their children's development is likely to proceed slowly.

Technology is also likely to influence children's development in a more direct way. Increasingly, human activities are interwoven with computers. Computers have and will continue to take over traditional routines of daily life. It is possible that such basic activities as reading, teaching, and shopping will be replaced by computers. These changes will not only

Children's early learning experiences influence the development of their neural pathways

influence what children need to learn, but can also influence *if* and *how* they will learn. That is, if children's early learning experiences vary significantly because of interactions with technology, their neural pathways will become hardwired differently than today's youth, who have had different kinds of experiences.

All of these changes will take place without our having gained an understanding of the importance of early experiences. For example, is it necessary for children to learn to read? Even if technology replaces this skill, which is considered necessary for survival in the twentieth century, will the loss of literacy affect future generations' chances of survival? Will the neural pathways used to read be formed in other ways, or will these pathways be replaced by other hardwiring more adaptive to the demands of the twenty-first century? The risk we have taken, without the consent of children, is that some types of early learning experiences will be critical for survival—but not sustained because of our fascination with technology.

STUDY GUIDE QUESTIONS

1. Name ways in which parents' decisions will require knowledge of human development.

2. In what areas of development must educators have knowledge?

3. How does an educator use knowledge of development to carry out identification of objectives and intervention strategies?

4. Briefly explain development during the embryonic stage.

5. Describe development of the fetus throughout the fetal stage.

6. What are the developmental requirements for a viable fetus?

7. Would you expect the same rate of growth across all children?

8. Would you expect the same pattern of growth across all children?

9. List and explain the three universal patterns of growth governing motor development.

10. Why is continual monitoring of physical growth important in the early years of life?

11. What is the function of the cardiovascular system and its relationship to the respiratory system?

12. Explain the function of the renal system.

13. Why is the gastrointestinal system important to physical growth?

14. Describe the relationship between myelinization and neurological development.

15. How is bone maturation related to growth?

16. Why is the integumentary system important—especially in early childhood?

17. How is physical growth measured?

18. Identify the seven stages of growth.

19. Describe a "normal" newborn in the first days of life.

20. What would be a "normal" infancy growth pattern?

21. What is meant by "competent organism"?

22. According to MacDonald (1992), what does emotional warmth or affection provide for humans? What may result if a child does not experience such affection?

23. In what way is child development sequential and universal?

24. Explain the remarkable plasticity of the human brain.

25. What is the theory of peak periods of learning?

26. What is the relationship between transition and consolidation? Define each in your explanation.

27. Define *temperament*. List the nine categories of temperament.

28. What are the six developmental domains? Provide a brief analysis of each.

29. Define *language* and the two subcategories of language. What is the main diffference between language and speech?

30. Discriminate between fine and gross motor control.

31. Why is the ability to habituate essential to normal development?

32. Give a unique example of a self-help skill that is reliant upon competencies in other domains.

33. Briefly summarize the heredity/environment debate. What are some reasonable conclusions regarding the influence of environment?

34. Briefly explain how the following influence a child's development: economics, family configuration and lifestyle, and child care.

35. Several factors influence bonding. Name three of these.

36. There are several educational factors believed to influence a child's growth. List five of these factors.

37. Why is it important to evaluate a child's development according to relevant culture, rather than according to dominant culture?

38. What are the correlational findings between television exposure and children's behavior?

REFERENCES

Allen, E. A., & Marotz, L. (1989). *Developmental profiles: Birth to six.* Albany: Delmar.

Baecher, C. M. (1983). *Children's consumerism: Implications for education.* Paper presented at the Bush Center in Child Development and Social Policy, Yale University, New Haven, CT.

Beck, F., Moffatt, D., & Lloyd, J. (1973). *Human embryology and genetics.* Oxford: Blackwell Scientific Publications.

Beentjes, J. W., & VanderVoort, T. H. (1988). Television's impact on children's reading skills. *Reading Research Quarterly, 23,* 389–413.

Berry, M. (1992). Contributors to adjustment problems of adoptees: A review of the longitudinal research. *Child and Adolescent Social Work Journal, 9,* 525–540.

Bohman, M., & Sigvardsson, S. (1985). A prospective longitudinal study of adoption. In A. R. Nicol (Ed.), *Longitudinal studies in child psychology and psychiatry.* New York: Wiley.

Bouchard, T. J., Lykken, D. T., McGue, M., Segal, N. L., & Tellegen, A. (1990). Sources of human psychological differences: The Minnesota study of twins reared apart. *Science, 250,* 223–228.

Bussey, K., & Bandura, A. (1992). Self-regulatory mechanisms governing gender development. *Child Development, 63,* 1236–1250.

Children's Defense Fund. (1988). *A children's defense budget: An analysis of the president's FY 1986 budget and children.* Washington, DC: Author.

Children's Defense Fund. (1994). *Wasting America's future: The Children's Defense Fund report on the costs of child poverty.* Washington, DC: Author.

Dahn, L., & James, L. (1972). Newborn temperature and calculated heat loss in the delivery room. *Pediatrics, 49,* 504–506.

Erikson, E. H. (1963). *Childhood and society* (2nd ed.). New York: W. W. Norton.

Finn, M. (1977). *The politics of nutrition education.* Unpublished dissertation, Ohio State University, Columbus.

Glick, P. C., & Lin, S. (1986). Recent changes in divorce and remarriage. *Journal of Marriage and the Family, 48,* 737.

Hanson, M. J., & Hanline, M. F. (1984). Behavioral competencies and outcomes: The effects of disorders. In M. J. Hanson (Ed.), *Atypical infant development* (109–142). Austin, TX: PRO-ED.

Healy, J. M. (1990). *The endangered mind: Why children can't think and what we can do about it.* New York: Touchstone.

Henggeler, S. W., Cohen, R., Edwards, J. J., Summerville, M. B., & Ray, G. E. (1991). Family stress as a link in the association between television viewing and achievement. *Child Study Journal, 21,* 1–10.

Hoffman, L. W. (1989). Effects of maternal employment in the two-parent family. *American Psychologist, 44,* 283–292.

Honzik, M. P. (1957). Intellectual resemblance of adopted children to true and adopted parents and of children to their own parents. *Child Development, 28,* 25–228.

Kennedy, J. H. (1992). Relationship of maternal beliefs and childrearing strategies to social competence in preschool children. *Child Study Journal, 22,* 39–60.

Langman, J. (1975). *Medical embryology. Human development—normal and abnormal (3rd ed.).* Baltimore: The Williams & Wilkins Co.

Lester, B. M., & Brazelton, T. B. (1982). Cross-cultural assessment of neonatal behavior. In D. A. Wagner & H. W. Stevenson (Eds.), *Cultural perspectives on child development.* San Francisco: Freeman.

MacDonald, K. (1992). Warmth as a developmental construct: An evolutionary analysis. *Child Development, 63,* 753–773.

McCall, R. B., & Carriger, M. S. (1993). A meta-analysis of infant habituation and recognition memory performance as predictors of later IQ. *Child Development, 64,* 57–79.

McDonald, J. D. (1989). *Becoming partners with children: From play to conversation.* San Antonio, TX: Special Press.

McLaughlin, T. F., & Vacha, E. F. (1992). The social, structural, family, school, and personal characteristics of at-risk students: Policy recommendations for school personnel. *The Journal of Education, 174(3),* 9–25.

Miringoff, M. L. (1989). *The index of social health 1989: Measuring the social well-being of the nation.* Tarrytown, NY: Fordman Institute for Innovation in Social Policy.

Monahan, S. C., Buchanan, C. M., Maccoby, E. E., & Dornbusch, S. M. (1993). Sibling differences in divorced families. *Child Development, 64,* 152–168.

Moore, K. L. (1983). Before we are born: Basic embryology and birth defects (2nd ed.). Philadelphia: W. B. Saunders.

Mussen, P. H., Conger, J. J., Kagen, J., & Huston, A. C. (1990). *Child development and personality.* New York: Harper & Row.

Nielson, A. C. (1988). *Nielson report on television.* Northbrook, IL: Author.

Pearl, D., Bouthilet, L., & Lazar, S. J. (Eds.). (1982). Report by the Surgeon General on Television Violence. *Television and behavior: Ten years of scientific progress and implications for the eighties.* Washington, DC: Government Printing Office.

Rheingold, H. L., & Cook, K. V. (1975). The content of boys' and girls' rooms as an index of parents' behavior. *Child Development, 46,* 459–463.

Schiff, M., Duyme, M., Dumaret, A., & Tomkiewicz, S. (1982). How much could we boost scholastic achievement and IQ scores: A direct answer from a French adoption study. *Cognition, 12,* 165–196.

Sherman, A. (1994). *Wasting America's future: The Children's Defense Fund report on the costs of child poverty.* Boston: Beacon Press.

Siegel, E. (1982). A critical examination of studies of parent-infant bonding. In M. H. Klaus & M. O. Robertson (Eds.), *Birth, interaction, and attachment: A round table.* Skillman, NJ: Johnson & Johnson.

Simon, R. J., & Alstein, H. (1987). *Transracial adoptees and their families: A study of identity and commitment.* New York: Praeger.

Skeels, H. M. (1942). A study of the differential stimulation on mentally retarded children: A follow-up report. *American Journal of Mental Deficiency, 46,* 340–350.

Skeels, H. M. (1966). Adult status of children with contrasting life experience: A follow-up study. *Monographs of the Society for Research in Child Development, 31* (3).

Thomas, A., & Chess, S. (1981). The role of temperament in the contributions of individuals to their own development. In R. M. Lerner & N. A. Busch-Rossnagel (Eds.), *Individuals as producers of their development: A life-span perspective.* New York: Academic Press.

Vandell, D. L., & Ramanan, J. (1992). Effects of early and recent maternal employment on children from low income families. *Child Development, 63,* 938–949.

Vandenburg, S. G. (1962) — See Encyclopedia of Education (1970). Deighton (Ed) p. 125.

Vandenburg, S. G. (1971). What do we know today about the inheritance of intelligence and how do we know it? In R. Canero (Ed.), *Intelligence: Genetic and environmental influences.* New York: Grune & Stratton.

van IJzendoorn, M. H., Goldberg, S., Kroonenberg, P. M., & Frenkel, O. J. (1992). The relative effects of maternal and child problems on the quality of attachment: A meta-analysis of attachment in clinical samples. *Child Development, 63,* 840–858.

Williams, B. F., & Howard, V. F. (1993). Children exposed to cocaine: Characteristics and implications for research. *Journal of Early Intervention, 17,* 61–72.

Zigler, E. F., & Stevenson, M. F. (1993). *Children in a changing world: Developmental and social issues, Second Edition.* Pacific Grove, CA: Brookes/Cole.

Milestones
of Development

Understanding the principles of human development is prerequisite to interpreting the milestones that mark the developmental progression of infants and young children, including those with and at risk for developmental disabilities. Maturation across developmental domains is characterized by behavioral markers or key **milestones.** For practitioners working with young children with disabilities, this knowledge should be constantly at the ready—available for ongoing assessments of the headway children are making. In the absence of this knowledge, an educator's barometer of normalcy tends to drift. For example, early childhood special educators often admit that when they have an opportunity to observe typically developing children, they are reminded of the severity of their own students' delays. While the point is not to highlight individual differences, misinterpretation of development can lead to lowered expectations, oversight of potential problems, inaccuracy in educational programming, and miscommunication with families and other professionals. Since drift is possible, even for well-trained professionals, early childhood professionals should continuously recalibrate by revisiting developmental milestones.

In this chapter, our descriptions in each of five areas of development—motor, cognitive, language, social, and self-help—are accompanied by little theory. The absence of theory is intentional but is not meant to diminish its importance to the field of early childhood special education. Entire courses, indeed entire disciplines, have been devoted to these theories. This text's purpose, however, is to provide the elementary basis for making judgments about a child's performance in relation to typical developmental patterns and rates.

MOTOR DEVELOPMENT

Motor development provides the physical basis for movement, posture, and balance, which are critical prerequisites for acquiring concrete knowledge, producing speech, exploring the environment, carrying out daily self-help activities, and socializing with others. Normal development allows children to accomplish organized, purposeful, and efficient movement. This movement is dependent on the integration of the central nervous system and the muscular system acting together on skeletal structures (Bigge, 1991). Delayed or dysfunctional motor development can greatly influence when and how well children reach expected milestones. Consequently, it is important that early childhood professionals understand motor development, recognize deviations from norms, and know appropriate intervention services that may support a child's individual motor needs.

Reflexes

Primitive reflexes are developed in utero and are present in the early months of life. They are responsible for involuntary motor responses to specific stimuli. For infants with intact neurological systems, the presentation of a given stimulus, such as a touch to the cheek, is predictably followed by a motor response; in this case, the head turns toward the touch and is known as the rooting reflex. Primitive reflexes may be a kind of natural "hardwiring" that equips the child with basic motor patterns and established neurological pathways. While thought to be useful prenatally (Fetters, 1984), primitive reflexes have limited utility to infants after birth. As infants mature, most primitive reflexes are neurologically **integrated,** giving the child control over them. Primitive reflexes gradually disappear and are replaced by **postural,** or adaptive, reflexes. When this does not happen, persistent primitive reflexes can interfere with a child's development of voluntary movement.

It is generally agreed that reflexes are key to normal motor development. According to Nelson (1969), "The most important and constant evidence of neurological abnormality in an infant is the absence of reflex patterns appropriate to age, or the persistence, reappearance or exaggeration of patterns either less mature or otherwise inappropriate to his age" (p. 1267). In fact, the presence of primitive and adaptive reflexes provides a prediction of developmental potential. Therefore, early childhood educators should be aware of reflex patterns so that noticeable deviations in development can be spotted. Since the objective of subsequent neuromotor intervention is to limit the influence of atypical reflexive development, early identification provides the greatest promise of mediating motor problems.

Primitive Reflexes   The **moro reflex** is the most commonly used index of reflexive maturity and is present at birth (see Figure 3.1). When a child's head is suddenly dropped backwards, the child's arms fly back and out in a symmetrical **abduction** (away from body) and **extension** (straightening of the joints); then the child's arms flex and return to the body in **adduction** (toward body), as if to embrace someone. Abnormal neurological maturation is indicated when the moro response:

a. is absent in the neonatal period

b. is asymmetrical

c. persists beyond three to four months of age

The **asymmetrical tonic neck reflex (ATNR),** also commonly assessed, is sometimes referred to as the "fencer's reflex." When a child's head is turned to one side, the extremities of the same side are extended, while the extremities on the opposite side of the body are **flexed** (bent at the joints) (see Figure 3.2). In normally developing infants, the response is usually partial or incomplete. On the other hand, when the response is well-defined and easily provoked, this is usually a sign of some negative neurological involvement. The ATNR reflex begins to disappear in the first few months.

Other primitive reflexes seen at birth include the rooting, grasp, startle, and stepping reflexes. The **rooting reflex** occurs when an infant's cheek is lightly stroked. In response, a child will turn its head toward the touch. Stimulating the palm of an infant's hand will elicit the **grasp reflex,** or flexion of the hand. A **startle reflex** occurs when a sudden noise or movement causes children to thrust their arms outward and then pull them back. It is apparent that if these involuntary responses were to persist, they would interfere with normal motor routines. For example, if the grasp reflex persisted, individuals would never be able to voluntarily release objects once placed in the hand's palm. The disappearance of these reflexes, mostly within the first four to six months of life, is a necessary transition referred to as **reflex integration.**

Several reflexes could interfere with walking and are typically integrated within the first six months. By holding a child in a vertical position so that the feet touch the surface, one can elicit the **stepping reflex** (see Figure 3.3). This step-like response encourages many parents to inaccurately conclude that their children are precociously ready to begin walking. The **Babinski reflex** is stimulated by stroking the sole of an infant's foot. If the Babinski reflex is present, infants will respond by spreading their toes. A third commonly assessed reflex of the lower extremities is the **plantar reflex.** The latter is observed when pressure applied to the ball of an infant's foot is followed by flexion of the toes around the stimulus, as if to grasp the object.

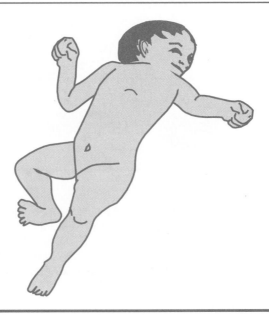

The **sucking** and **swallowing reflexes** are adaptive reflexes that are present at birth, though still immature. These reflexes work in harmony when mature and are usually well-developed by six months of age. When they are fully developed, a child has good tongue control and lip closure when sucking. These reflexes are paired with the ability to move food from the front to the back of the mouth, and to control the path of food to the esophagus (rather than trachea), and to move food down the esophagus to the stomach.

Figure 3.3/ *The Stepping Reflex*

Postural Reflexes   While much of human movement is voluntary, a significant part of balance is reflexive. Unlike primitive reflexes, which interfere with movement if persistent, **postural reflexes** actually supplement movement and help to prevent injury. A **parachute reflex** (see Figure 3.4) results when an infant is held horizontal and prone, and then lowered toward the floor. As if to break the fall, infants will extend their arms and legs toward the surface. Several reflexes evolve that permit children to maintain an upright position, as infants learn to sit and stand. An **equilibrium reflex** is stimulated whenever a child moves or is pushed out of a midline (vertical) position. Resisting gravity, the equilibrium reflex involuntarily causes the body to realign its trunk vertically. Similarly, when an infant's trunk is pushed out of an upright position either to the side, front, or back, the **head righting reflex** will attempt to hold the head in an upright position. A final and complementary reflex is referred to as **protective extension.** In this case, an infant, pushed out of midline from either a sitting or standing position, will reach out (extension) and attempt to protect itself from falling. Children will first learn to protect themselves from falls to the front, then from falls to the sides, and finally from falls to the rear.

Muscle Tone   Posture, consistency of muscles, and joint range of motion are all affected by dimensions of muscle tone. Three categories are generally used to define a child's muscle tone: normal, hypertonic, and hypotonic. Infants with abnormally high or tight muscle tone **(hypertonia)** show restricted ranges of motion. By contrast, **hypotonia,** or very loose tone, is seen in children who show little strength to resist gravity or joint movement. While the former have very tense muscle consistency, the latter tend to have flaccid muscle tone. Both hypertonicity and hypotonicity are indexes of neurological insult and are also likely to result in delayed if not abnormal motor development.

Assessment of muscle tone can be accomplished by comparative analysis of range of motion. One test of muscle tone is head rotation, in which the head is passively turned when **flexed** and when **extended.** The Scarf sign is a second test of muscle tone. In this test a child's arm is extended across the chest toward the opposite shoulder. In both cases, the degree to which movement is permitted or prohibited gives an index of the neurological maturity: in normally developing children, the range of motion must be neither too loose nor too tight for the chronological age of a child.

Gross Motor Development

A review of the principles of physical development will provide a means for understanding the progress of gross motor development. In Chapter 2, it was noted that children's muscle control progresses from head to toe (cephalo-caudal), from gross to fine, and from the center of the body

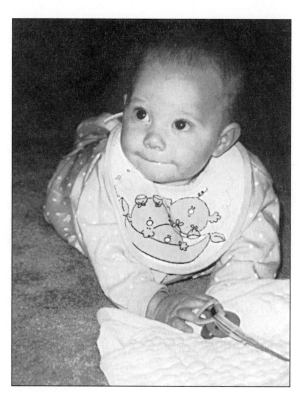

Typical prone propping position

toward the extremities (proximo-distal). The first of these, head to toe, is most useful in determining which skills one would expect to emerge next, based upon the present level of maturity.

Head Control   A newborn has very little intentional body control, yet does move its arms, legs, head, fingers, and toes reflexively. Because newborns are unable to independently support the weight of their heads, caregivers provide these babies with substantial head support. Soon, neck muscles develop sufficient strength and tone for turning the head from side to side in a **supine** (lying on the back) position and for greater ability to hold the head up in an upright or horizontal position. This head control becomes stronger until, eventually, infants raise their heads off a surface from a supine position and turn their heads from side to side in a **prone** (on the tummy) position. An infant is said to have gained good head control when, as the infant is tilted side to side and front to back, there is no head lag and the posture of the head remains upright. A test for head control is the facilitated sit-up. A caregiver places a child supine and, taking the arms, pulls the child to a sitting position. If an infant is able to raise its head independently so the head stays parallel to the trunk, there is no head lag.

Shoulder Control   Though overlap exists in the development of neck and shoulder control, the latter cannot fully develop without an infant first achieving complete head control. At approximately two to three months of age, infants begin to assist themselves in turning their heads from side to side by propping their chests on their forearms. As muscle control is gained, infants are able to prop themselves higher and for a longer time, eventually pushing up on fully extended arms and hands (proximo-distal principle in effect). Prone propping is paralleled by supine use of the arms, in which children begin to reach, first a few inches and then with fully extended arms, for exciting objects. At this age, infants will begin to play with mobiles hung over their beds and to reach for near objects while lying on their tummies. When infants have well-developed shoulder control, they are able to turn themselves from prone to supine and back the other way. Usually, it is the front to back roll that emerges first since infants get an assist from the their extended arms. However, by the fourth or fifth month, most infants are able to do both well since trunk control is also emerging.

Trunk Control In observing infants across the first six months of their lives, it is clear that the development of sitting posture closely accompanies the stages of body control described above. An infant placed in a sitting position will droop from the waist to the head, exhibiting little resistance to gravity. At two months, an infant can hold its head upright in a sitting position and, at four months, can hold its upper body upright, but will fall over when a caregiver releases support on the waist. By six months, most infants will be able sit independently, though they may not be able to catch themselves in a fall because protective extension reflexes are still immature. A strong sitter, at eight months, will independently be able to get in and out of a sitting position, will be able to reach for objects on the floor without falling over, and can stay upright when pushed gently in all directions. The last protective reaction to develop is extension to the rear, and even at eight months, an infant is vulnerable to head injuries from falls backward.

Hip Control When an infant is independently able to get in and out of a sitting position, it is because some hip control has developed. At this time, an infant in a prone position will begin to **crawl** by coordinating its arms and legs to move across the floor or other surface. While hip control may have developed sufficiently to permit coordinated leg movement, weight bearing by the hips has yet to mature. When weight bearing is possible, infants then resist gravity by raising their heads and lifting their trunks off the floor on their hands and knees (some infants go straight to hands and feet in a "bear crawl"). By coordinating movement of the extremities, infants of nine to ten months creep from this elevated position.

Refinement of gross motor skills includes development of recreation skills

Lower Body Control   The final major gross motor development is upright mobility. Once hip control is fully developed, infants are capable of balance and stability on extended legs. Initially, standing may be possible only when knee joints are hyperextended. By 10 to 12 months though, most children can stand upright while holding on to a support. This evolves into **cruising,** or stepping sideways while holding on to furniture or some structure for support. Before long, a competent cruiser can be expected to **transfer** short distances between furniture by taking short steps without holding on. Finally, a child begins to take, first a few, and then several, independent steps.

Refinement   Once a child has learned to walk independently, the remainder of gross motor movement can be considered a refinement of the most critical skills of this domain. In fact, early childhood professionals tend to place relatively less emphasis on this domain (see Table 3.1) and more on cognitive and language skills after a child has begun to walk well. Refinement includes walking up and down stairs, running, standing on one leg, skipping, jumping, and development of recreation skills. While a child could be quite functional in life without most of these skills, a delay in development of gross motor coordination could be an early signal of generalized developmental problems later in life.

Fine Motor Skills

Like gross motor skills, fine motor development follows a predictable pattern. The most relevant principle is gross-to-fine motor skill maturation. For example, you would not expect a child to be capable of grasping objects intentionally until the child had gained shoulder control and was reaching with some accuracy. It can also be predicted that control of grasping progresses from the palm of the hand to the finger tips (proximo-distal).

Table 3.1/   *Refinement of Gross Motor Development*

12–18 months	Creeps up and down stairs. Runs. Throws a ball overhand. Pulls a toy behind when walking. Walks backwards.
18–24 months	Kicks a ball. Squats. Bends at the waist to pick something up without falling. Walks up stairs alone, placing both feet on each step.
3 years	Rides a tricycle by pedaling with alternating feet. Catches a large bounced ball. Long jumps on two feet. Runs smoothly with changes in speed.
4 years	Catches a thrown playground ball against the body with arms. Walks up and down stairs alternating feet and holding rail. Jumps over a string held slightly off the floor. Walks to the rhythm of music.
5 years	Catches a bounced ball. Skips by alternating feet. Jumps rope two or three consecutive times. Rides a bike with training wheels. Skates forward a few feet. Hits a ball with a bat or stick.

Eye Contact and Facial Expression   In conformity with head-to-toe development, fine muscle control of the eyes is one of the first observable fine motor skills to begin developing. Within the first few days of life, neonates may be observed matching maternal eye movement. Infants will also scan visual stimuli and are known to attend first to the edges of an object and patterned stimuli. Yet, neonates have difficulty **tracking,** following moving objects with their eyes, and they lose contact once an object has been moved away from their midline. In just a few weeks, however, infants begin to track objects that are moved gradually from side to side and, eventually, will track 180 degrees by moving their heads to prevent loss of eye contact. Tracking also develops in a vertical direction, and infants maintain eye contact for increasingly sustained periods of time. Both range and duration of eye contact are important to mobility, fine motor coordination, and language development.

Reaching   At birth, an infant's reach and grasp are entirely reflexive. Intentional reaching from a supine position begins at about two months, after an infant has gained some control at the shoulders. Infants will initially reach toward objects with minimal coordination and may bat or swing at an object but do not grasp it. Instead, a predominant flexor pattern holds the hands in a fisted position. By four months, an infant's reach has become more coordinated, and the infant will unhesitatingly move its arm and hand in the direction of a desired object.

Grasping   At the point where reaching has become a refined movement, grasping becomes intentional, now permitting infants to acquire and hold objects. Still, the unintegrated grasp reflex does not permit infants to intentionally release objects. The most primitive grasp is referred to as the **palmar grasp** (see Figure 3.5), in which a child acquires an object by scooping it into the palm with all fingers extended. Obviously, this grasp prevents an infant from manipulating an object in any precise fashion and play with the object is unsophisticated. Later, infants will

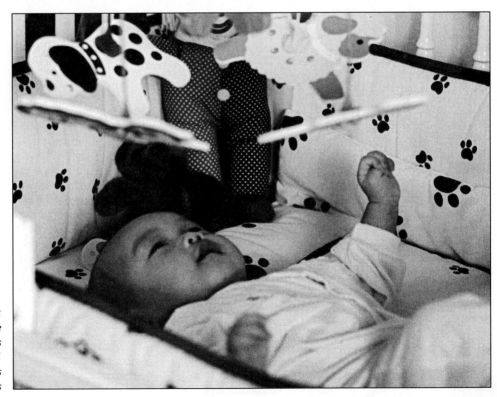

A predominant flexor pattern: the infant holds its hands in a fisted position and swipes at objects

Figure 3.5/ *The Palmar Grasp (A) and the Pincer Grasp (B)*

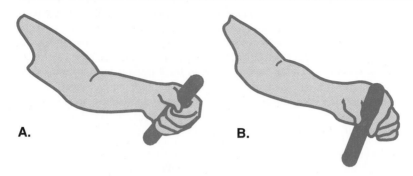

A.   B.

be able to pick up and hold an object by opposing the palm with the tips of all fingers. Still there is no differentiation of finger use. A major milestone is reached when infants are able to grasp by opposing their thumbs with other fingers. This development, the **prehensile grasp,** is a feature unique to humans and other primates. First, the thumb opposes all the fingers, then the second and third fingers, and finally a **fine pincer grasp** (see Figure 3.5) is achieved.

Refinement of fine motor abilities is observed throughout the preschool years (see Table 3.2). The gradual refinement is facilitated by increased speed, strength, and coordination of small muscle groups. This ability is closely integrated with cognitive and perceptual development. Infants learn to pick up small objects and use their index finger to point to and probe objects. Toddlers begin to put simple puzzles together and to scribble with a crayon. Later on preschoolers learn to draw, to cut with scissors, and to form objects with clay.

LANGUAGE DEVELOPMENT

One of the most amazing phenomena of human life is the development of language. In just three-years time, infants progress from almost total reflexive responding to the development of adult-like speech. Yet, even in the first few days, infants **communicate;** they send messages that are understood by caregivers. For most children, this communication will later conform to a set of rules that guide how ideas are formed into words and put together in sentences. These symbolic systems, known as **languages,** differ across cultures. Furthermore, language can be communicated in writing, orally through **speech,** and manually (e.g., American Sign Language). All these systems have something in common. Individuals who share the language conform to the standard rules, enabling them to communicate very efficiently. However, humans do not send and receive messages through language alone. Unconventional language—body language, facial expressions, grunts, laughter, wincing, and so on—all communicate powerful messages that are "read" by the listener.

Just as musculo-skeletal movement is reflexive at birth, so is the majority of neonatal communication. A newborn communicates basically in two ways—crying and not crying. Within two years, however, this child will have developed all the basic constructs of human adult language. Several theories attempt to explain the nature of linguistic development. The various theories can be viewed as complementary, contradictory, or supplemental. In fact, our current understanding of language seems to borrow from each of the most prominent theories (McCormick & Schiefelbusch, 1990). The following principles of language development are generally agreed upon by linguists.

Table 3.2/ *Refinement of Fine Motor Development*

12–18 months	Holds crayon from radial side of hand. Turns pages of a cardboard book. Places a peg in a pegboard. Builds a tower with two blocks. Places a round form in a formboard.
18–24 months	Imitates a crayon stroke. Imitates vertical and circular strokes. Completes puzzle with circle, square, and triangle.
2 years	Builds tower with four to six blocks. Turns door knobs or TV handles by twisting wrist. Unscrews nesting toys. Turns pages one at a time. Holds a crayon with thumb and forefinger.
3 years	Cuts with scissors on a line. Holds pencil with adult-like tripod grasp (resting on third finger). Folds paper. Winds up toys.
4 years	Completes puzzle of three to five pieces. Moves paper and cuts out simple shapes (e.g., triangle). Draws a person with two body parts. Makes crude clay objects having two or three parts. Screws together threaded objects.
5 years	Prints first name. Completes puzzle of 11 to 15 pieces. Copies small case letters. Colors within lines. Opens lock with a key. Hits a nail with hammer.

- Humans are born with a certain capacity to acquire language. The nature of this function is still not agreed on. Chomsky, as well as later psycholinguists, believed that humans are prewired for language structure, while pragmatic theorists believe that infants are intrinsically motivated to engage in social exchanges (McCormick & Schiefelbusch, 1990).

- Children acquire language according to a universal pattern, which is observed across children of different languages, cultures, families, and disabilities (Chaudhary & Suparna, 1991).

- Children generally develop an understanding of the meaning of concepts before they learn to use the corresponding words. Moreover, a child's **receptive language** (words they understand) is almost always more highly developed than a child's **expressive language** (words they use).

- Social exchanges are a necessary context for language development. The nature of these exchanges is also important; among other things, caregivers should be sensitive to communicative attempts, should engage in balanced turn-taking, and should match their communication to the child's linguistic ability.

- Children's language development is facilitated through modeling by adults, repeated practice of sounds and words, and differential reinforcement (i.e., attending to understandable language and not attending to indecipherable language).

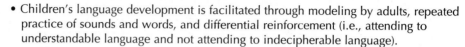

The remainder of this section will be a description, rather than an explanation, of language development in children from birth to six years of age. Interactional theorists describe language as three interrelated components: form, content, and use. The **form** of language refers to its structure: phonology, syntax, and morphemes. Language **content** refers to a child's knowledge of the words and the interrelationship between words. Both receptive and expressive language are considered in language content. Finally, language **use,** or pragmatics, is the way in which children communicate in social contexts.

A second way of viewing language is according to its sophistication. Pragmatic theorists identify three stages of linguistic development: perlocutionary, illocutionary, and locutionary. In the **perlocutionary** stage (birth to 6–8 months), infants' language is unintentional and unconventional (e.g., crying, grunting, cooing, etc.). In the **illocutionary** stage (8 to 15 months), infants communicate intentionally but are still using mostly unconventional means (e.g., pointing, facial expressions, etc.). The **locutionary** stage identifies infants who communicate both conventionally and intentionally (i.e., words, phrases, etc.). While these categories provide useful descriptors, they are not discrete. That is, while children are making the transition from one stage to the next, there is considerable overlap in communication abilities.

Language Form

Three aspects of language are generally considered when discussing language form. **Phonology** is the study of speech sounds. When considering the linguistic development of infants, the evolution of **phonemes** (speech sounds) follows a predictable pattern. The rules that govern structural patterns of language utterances and sentence grammar are referred to as **syntax.** Finally, **morphological** development refers to the evolution of word structure and word parts such as prefixes and suffixes.

Phonological Development The sounds made by neonates are nonspecific crying, grunting, and gurgling. Without training or direction, caregivers are typically able to differentiate types of crying sounds to determine if an infant is wet, tired, hungry, or otherwise uncomfortable. While in the perlocutionary stage, infants begin to make vowel sounds within the first few months. Vowel sound production is referred to as **cooing.** Vowels are physically the easiest sounds to make since they require little motor control or use of the articulators (tongue, lips, palate, and teeth).

Infants begin to **babble** by about four months of age as they gain greater oral motor control. Babbling is a combination of consonant and vowel sounds (C-V and V-C) and progresses from simple to complex sound production. In the early babbling stages, infants produce a variety of sounds, some of which are not a part of their native language. Later, sounds not used in children's native language(s) drop from their repertoire and may be very difficult to acquire at an older age. By the end of the first year, infants' first words begin to appear; many of these are monosyllabic C-V or V-C combinations, for example "up" or "ma-ma." Sounds that are heard during babbling are not necessarily carried over to the locutionary stage. Thereafter, consonant sound production progresses along a continuum of easy to hard, relative to oral-motor complexity (see Table 3.3). Nasal sounds ("n") and stop sounds ("g," "d") are generally used in early word production. Glide sounds ("w") appear later but are generally acquired by three to four years of age. Sounds like "s," "v," and "z" are the most difficult, and sometimes do not appear before seven or eight years of age.

Phonetic sounds made in isolation are of less interest to adults than the combination of sounds in words. Children produce words that increase in understandability as initial sounds, ending sounds, and middle sounds of words are put together with precision. The transition to real words is remarkably fleet. At 18 months, infants' speech is only about 25% intelligible, but it should be approximately 65% intelligible by two years of age, when toddlers begin to

Table 3.3/ *Sequence of Phonological Acquisition* *

Age	Sounds Produced
By age 3	p, m, h, n, w
By age 4	b, k, g, d, f, y
By age 6	t, ng, r, l, s
By age 7	ch, sh, j, th (unvoiced) as in *thick*
By age 8	s, z, v, th (voiced) as in *this*
Later	zh

* The age of acquisition may vary by as much as 3 years.

Source: Adapted from McCormick, L., & Schiefelbusch, R. L. (1984). *Early language intervention.* Upper Saddle River, NJ: Merrill/Prentice Hall.

produce two-word utterances. At four years of age, children have acquired most phonetic sounds and are producing almost totally intelligible sentences.

Syntax   Without direct instruction, children acquire the rules of spoken syntax with surprising accuracy. It is not until after children already speak with correct syntax that the rules of grammar are specifically taught. In the initial months of the locutionary stage, infants rely primarily on one-word utterances, and toward the end of their second year, they rely on successive single-word utterances. Infants do not begin to put words together in presentences until late in their second year. However, this linguistic development represents a major accomplishment in a child's communicative power. The significance of two-word utterances is that these telegraphic phrases possess more meaning than either word uttered in isolation. That is, two-word phrases convey the meanings of word A and word B, plus the meaning of each words' relationship to the other. This phenomenon is referred to as a **semantic relationship.** Examples of simple two-word phrases used include noun-verb: "baby eat"; verb-noun: "give ball"; noun-noun: "Daddy ball").

Sentence structure becomes complex in several ways in children's third year. At about 27 months, children begin to ask questions, though initially only by intonation. Children may ask some "wh-questions" at this time, but initially not with the verb transposed (e.g., "Where car is going?"). Wh-questions emerge in correspondence with conceptual knowledge and receptive understanding of the same types of questions. "Who," "what," and "where," which have more concrete referents, precede "when," "how," and "why." Queries that require transposition of verbs occur when children have begun to use auxiliary verbs and copulas or linking words (e.g., "*Is* the bike outside?"). Tag questions are also complex interrogative forms added on after other question forms have appeared (e.g., "We are having ice cream, aren't we?").

Negative sentences also follow a pattern of increasing complexity as they gradually approximate accurate syntactic rules. To the frustration of adults, negative statements are among the highest frequency utterances made by toddlers. Children first make negative comments by placing a negative marker at the beginning of a sentence. This is followed by placing the negative marker inside the sentence next to the relevant verb, but without the use of copulas and auxiliary verbs. Finally, though not until about age four, children begin to accurately use inflections and negative markers together.

Stage I.   *No* want milk.

Stage II. Kitty *no* eat candy.

Stage III. I *can't* fix the bike.

Complex sentences contain at least one independent clause and at least one subordinate or dependent clause. Sentences with more than one independent clause are referred to as **compound sentences.** Both advanced types of sentences combine two or more ideas in a single sentence through the use of conjunctions, relative pronouns, or other linguistic linkages. "And" is the first conjunction to appear and is observed in children as young as 25 months of age, though initially the "and" joins nouns (e.g., "me and Mommy") rather than clauses. **Relative clauses** that modify subjects (e.g., "I like the doll *that has the green hair*") appear later. By three or four, many children are using compound and complex sentences by adding elements to the beginning or end of kernel sentences. Still later (4 to 13 years of age), children add clauses internally to sentences in a process referred to as **embedding** (e.g., "I saw the girl *who is in my class* at the park").

Morphological Development

A **morpheme** is defined as the smallest part of a word that possesses meaning. Morphemes that can stand alone with meaning are referred to as **free morphemes,** while those that cannot stand alone are referred to as **bound morphemes.** Of the two, free morphemes appear first in infants' language as their first words (e.g., bottle, Mommy, ball, cup, etc.). Not until much later (beginning at about 24 months) do bound morphemes (inflections) begin to appear (e.g., -ed, -ing, pre-, etc.). The latter, along with auxiliary verbs, are referred to as **morphological inflections** and emerge along a predictable pattern (see Table 3.4).

An index of the sophistication of a children's language is based upon the frequency of morphemes in their utterances. **Mean Length Utterance (MLU)** is calculated by dividing the number of morphemes in an utterance by the number of utterances (at least 50). An MLU of 1.0 is observed when infants are at the one-word-phrase stage. By the time children have MLUs of 3.0 or higher, they are usually incorporating at least some morphological inflections into their phrases. When a child's MLU is greater than 4.0, the score is no longer a valid index of language development.

Table 3.4/   *Sequence of Acquisition of Morphological Inflections*

1. Present progressive (eat*ing*)
2/3. Prepositions (in, on)
4. Plural (boot*s*, shoe*s*)
5. Irregular past tense (came, went)
6. Possessive (Daddy's chair)
7. Copula, uncontractible of "to be" ("there *you are*")
8. Articles (a, the)
9. Regular past tense (jump*ed*)
10. Third person singular, present tense, regular (jump*s*)
11. Third person singular, present tense, irregular (does, has)
12. Auxiliary, uncontractible (can, will)
13. Copula, contractible ("It's mine.")
14. Auxiliary, contractible ("I'll take it.")

Source: Adapted from Wiig, E. H., & Semel, E. M. (1980). *Language assessment and intervention for the learning disabled.* Upper Saddle River, NJ: Merrill/Prentice Hall. p. 28.

Language Content

As mentioned earlier, content develops along two parameters: receptive and expressive language. The former typically progresses at a more rapid rate but is not necessarily a prerequisite for expressive development. In other words, children sometimes use words in their speech before they understand their meaning.

Receptive Language   The first sign that children are capable of learning speech has been documented in infants' first days of life. Bertoncini, Bijelac-Babic, Jusczyk, Kennedy, and Mahler (1988) discovered that infants would alter their pattern of sucking when a tape emitting phonetic sounds ("ba") suddenly changed to a new sound ("da"). This ability to discriminate sounds is a necessary prerequisite to speech production. Within the first few months, a mother might notice that her child will become quiet or pause at the sound of mom's voice but not at that of a stranger's voice. Later, when infants develop some head control, they will turn their heads toward sounds by **sound localization.** As skillful and perceptually sophisticated as these babies appear, it is not until the end of children's first year that they begin to acknowledge specific words. This is evident when children respond differentially to their names. Not surprisingly, one of the first words recognized by infants is the word "no." By the end of their first year, infants recognize a few high-frequency words and can demonstrate this skill by looking directly at the named objects. One-year-olds are also learning to follow simple commands like "wave bye-bye," or "give me a kiss." However, these commands are often accompanied by gestures or signals.

The next six months are a turning point in children's receptive language, as infants learn to follow simple novel commands that do not have gestures, such as "put the toy on the table" or "give mommy a drink." Likewise, at 16 months, infants point to body parts upon request. It is at this stage that parents learn the advantage of knowing how to spell words out to each other.

Until their second year, infants' word understanding is referent specific. During their second year, these same infants begin to categorize concepts by making gradually more sophisticated generalizations (Oviatt, 1982). For example, they learn that cats and dogs belong to a category of animals. Later, they learn that even though horses have some of the same characteristics as dogs, they do not belong to the same class. Still, two-year-olds are bound by literal interpretation of adult language and are unable to solve the figurative meaning behind clichés, metaphors, or analogies. By three, young children can both interpret and use figurative speech. A child might be overheard saying, "Rover is a *pig*." Anaphoric terms, such as "this," "that," "it," and "there," are difficult terms to master, though three-year-olds are typically able to solve such directions as "put the spoon *there*." Four-year-olds can understand passive sentences (e.g., "I had wanted to take you to the park") but use them infrequently in conversation. A six-year-old is quite good at solving subtle messages in language, such as sarcasm and humor that rely on irony (Winner, 1988). Since children's language is still literal, transparent metaphors, such as "hold your tongue," might be understood by these youth, though it is not until much later that children are able to decode opaque metaphors, such as "smell the roses" (MacArthur, 1990).

Expressive Language   Documenting the development of expressive language is easier since one does not have to make inferences about the invisible cognitive processes that underlie this form of communication. Though children represent meanings much earlier, the first real words do not generally appear much before a child's first birthday. Interestingly, studies involving children who are deaf reveal that the first words are signed well before the first birthday and, on the average, before the first spoken words would be expected. It is supposed that the physiological demands of signing are easier than those of speech, suggesting that children are cognitively capable of speech earlier than they are physically capable. Universally, the first words that infants use represent salient features of children's immediate environments. Actions and objects dominate early words, though nouns appear to be more easily learned and more frequently used than verbs. This makes sense, since objects have a concrete referent, while actions are not permanent and their dimensions change with each event. For example, "jumping" can

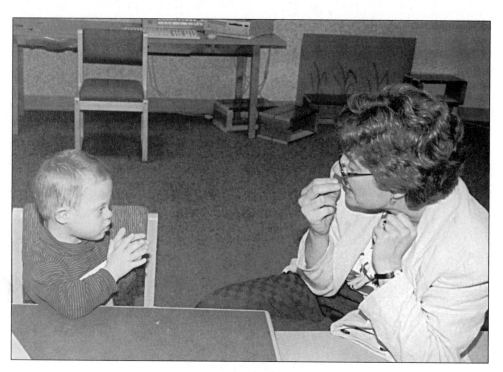

Tommy and his mother signing to each other

only be labeled when someone jumps, and then the action is gone. Additionally, jumping can be on one foot or two feet, executed by mom or dad, a few inches or over a high jump, and so on. Words that represent objects that move or are acted upon in a variety of different ways (e.g., baby doll) are more frequently used than objects that do not move (e.g., wall).

At 18 months, when infants typically possess a 50-word vocabulary of mostly nominals, their language content begins to change significantly. It is at this juncture in development that children begin naming many different objects that are less salient and less important. Some have referred to this transition as a "naming spurt," and it corresponds with a sudden sharp increase in children labeling everything they see (Gopnik & Meltzoff, 1992). This milestone also seems to be the threshold for combining words into successive single-word utterances and semantic relations. Finally, at about this stage, a sharp rise in the use of both verbs and adjectives has been observed (Klink & Klink, 1990).

At two years, toddlers have acquired a vocabulary of about 300 words. With words paired together in telegraph-like sentences, children use only key words (e.g., "baby up" stands in for "the baby is standing up"). A rapid growth in novel semantic relations takes place in children's second year. For example, Braine (1963) documented novel use of two-word utterances of a toddler. In successive months the child used 24, 54, 89, 250, 1400, and 2500 new phrases.

Perhaps because of their limited repertoire of words, toddlers commonly **overextend** the use of words. For example, these children might mistakenly refer to all men as "Daddy" since men have physical characteristics similar to their fathers. At the same time, these toddlers might alternately look at Dad and his friend Bob when they hear their names, reflecting a lag in production as compared to cognitive understanding. **Underextensions** occur when categories are defined too narrowly. For example, very young children might use the word "chair" to refer to their highchairs and the dining room chairs but do not include the rocking chair or kitchen stool in this category. It is also common for children to use known words idiosyncratically to fill in for concepts for which they have no words.

Preschool programs commonly spend much time teaching young children color terms, a behavior that maintains very little functional value when compared to the many other conceptual categories available. Little ones can typically supply a color of an object to the request "What color is this?" by age two, though not necessarily accurately. Colors closest to primary (e.g., red-reds) are learned most easily (Andrick & Tager-Flusberg, 1986). More complex content reflecting concepts that are not concrete typically do not appear much before a child's third birthday. For example, time and space are relative terms, and words used to reflect these concepts begin to appear at about age four when concepts such as "before," "after," "next to," "in front of," "first," and "last" are observed.

Though a child's vocabulary development is influenced, to some unknown but significant degree, by experiences, the normal rate of word acquisition has been described (Reed, 1994). By two years a child typically uses 300 words, 1000 by three years, 1500 by four years, over 2000 by five years, and nearly 3000 words by age six. By contrast, a child's receptive vocabulary is approximately 20,000 to 24,000 words by age six.

Language Use

The final category of language function, language use, is more difficult to define, assess, and plan for instruction. This aspect of language refers to the effectiveness of the speaker in establishing and maintaining mutually rewarding interactions with others. Some children have very well-developed language form and content but are simply unable to engage others in conversations. Even as adults there are people who, for example, can talk and talk but are not desirable conversation partners because they are insensitive to the subtle rules of communication that make interactions mutually rewarding.

Three types of behavior comprise language use. **Speech acts** are the speakers' intentions or purposes for communicating. People communicate to give information, ask questions, make requests, tell a story or entertain, make protests, and show surprise, among other things. When communicating with others, people also make judgments about the listener that allow modifications to the content and style of the communication. These **presuppositions** include, but are not limited to, assessments of social status, educational or developmental level, and the intimacy of relationships. For example, one estimates the level of interest that the listener might have in a particular topic as well as the degree of background knowledge that the listener holds. If these judgments are inaccurate, one could talk over someone's head or, conversely, offend someone by appearing condescending. Finally, conversations have subtle rules, that may vary from culture to culture, that allow humans to converse in a reciprocal manner. **Conversational postulates**, as these rules are called, include skills in initiating conversations, balanced turn-taking, questioning, repairing a breakdown in conversations, maintaining interactions, and closing a conversation.

The earliest appearance of language use is in the form of conversational postulates. For example, neonates have been observed engaging in reciprocal turn-taking with caregivers in the first days of life. Eye blinking and mouth and tongue movements can become routinized back-and-forth actions between a child and caregiver. However, it will be several more years before these skills become refined. A child of nine months will play many reciprocal games, demonstrating conversation-like turn-taking (e.g., peek-a-boo). This turn-taking skill is used primitively in dialogues when a child is 18 to 24 months of age.

During the period when children first begin to use intentional communication (illocutionary and locutionary) many of their language intentions are nonverbal. For example, a child may point to a favorite doll. Yet, the purposes of this intent could be several. The child might be making a request to acquire the toy, telling mom that the doll is nice, protesting the removal of the doll, or asking if the doll is hungry. In context, a parent can interpret these limited regulatory requests. Even at this age, these same one-year-old speakers have been observed altering their communication for their listeners.

*Four-year-olds
exhibit a variety of
conversation skills*

By the latter half of the second year, children begin to use language for a variety of new functions that integrate regulatory purposes with interactional skills. At two years of age, children have learned that a single utterance can serve more than one function. Because conversation has now taken on a social purpose, toddlers need to maintain conversational topics. However, many conversations break down as children appear to flit in and out of a conversation more often than they stay on topic. Limited skills, such as repeating or imitating words or parts of words used in the previous sentence, are used to maintain conversations. These children might fix a topic breakdown by attempting to articulate with greater clarity. By contrast, four-year-olds are capable of carrying on a conversation for several minutes, discussing the same or related topics. Skills used to fix topic breakdowns include rephrasing sentences, shortening utterances, and expanding their sentences.

Three- and four-year-old children will adapt their communication based on their perceived assessment of the listener's prior knowledge. They may give more or less information based on the extent of previous experiences their listeners are judged to possess. Furthermore, these preschoolers can be observed altering the length of sentences, affect (e.g., facial expression, voice intonation, body language), and language content when interacting with younger children or infants (Shatz & Gelman, 1973).

Factors Affecting Language Development

Multiple factors can affect the rate and pathology of linguistic acquisition. For example, many developmental disabilities can directly affect language form. Clefts of the lip and/or palate and oral-structural anomalies associated with Down syndrome influence phonological production. Cerebral palsy may result in reduced respiratory capacity that hampers speech production as well. Other developmental disabilities affect children's rate of learning and slow the acquisition of content and use. Autism, for example, is linked with aberrations in all areas of language development.

Though patterns of language development are universal (see Table 3.5), there are some cultural and sociocultural factors that influence the rate of acquisition of language (Wood, 1992). For example, Chaudhary and Suparna (1991) found that children differed across nuclear and extended families, with children from single units having more rapid language development. Idiosyncrasies in parenting also influence language development. Schacter and Straye (1982) described a specialized manner of interaction between mothers and infants

Table 3.5/ *Milestones of Language Development*

Birth	Responds to noises (activity stops). Cries frequently. Makes vowel-like sounds "e" and "a."
1 month	Vocalizes. Responds to voices. Uses special cry for hunger. Vocalizes pleasure.
4 months	Imitates simple gestures. Repeats syllables (da-da-da). Localizes sounds. Uses vowel sounds "o" and "u." Expresses displeasure without crying.
8–11 months	Produces consonant sounds in babbling. Stops activity momentarily when told "no." Combines two syllables in vocal babbling "ba-da." Babbles using adult-like intonation. Shows understanding of some words. Waves "bye-bye." Plays "peek-a-boo" and "pat-a-cake."
12 months	Says 5–10 words. Points to familiar objects when named. Expresses wants. Says "no" with authority.
18 months	Points to 2 or 3 pictures named. Names familiar objects upon request. Uses intelligible speech 25% of time. Imitates last word spoken. Uses own name in conversation.
24 months	"Sings" along with music. Uses plurals. Uses two-word phrases. Responds to choices. Utterances have communicative intent. Uses intelligible speech 65% of time. Overextensions ("goed," "feets").
3 years	Knows a few songs and approximates correct pitch. Can carry on a conversation. Uses four-word sentences. Uses past tense (-ed) and present tense (-ing). Asks wh-questions. Uses pronouns I, her/him, hers/his, she/he. Uses intelligible speech 80% of time.
4 years	Says "excuse me" to interrupt conversation. Retells story read by someone else. Carries out instructions containing prepositions. Participates in group songs. Defines words. Tells what simple things are made of.

Table 3.5/ *Milestones of Language Development (cont.)*

5 years	Knows birthday, phone number and parents' names.
	Uses five-word sentences.
	Describes events in past/future with logical sequence.
	Answers questions related to a spoken content or story.
	Begins to understand abstract concepts.
	Uses compound sentences with two main clauses.

called "motherese." Tactics of motherese were found to be correlated with the rate of language development and include use of extensions, shortened sentence length and simplified vocabulary, repetitions or rewording, and talking about events within a child's world. Though gender differences do exist in communication with infants, Klink and Klink (1990) concluded that fathers also engage in "motherese."

COGNITION

The process by which human beings learn has been under inquiry and discovery for hundreds of years. The acquisition of knowledge, also known as **cognition,** is a complex phenomenon in which infants, children, and adults are constantly learning about their world. This development allows human beings to learn to reason (both concretely and abstractly), to think logically, and to organize information about their environment in a way that will bring order to their world. Cognitive development is closely tied to the other developmental domains. Failure to follow the normal developmental pathway can result in difficulties in social and emotional development and produce blocks to the development of communication skills.

Bringing understanding to cognitive development has resulted in the evolution of many theories about learning and the conceptual frameworks that correlate with those theories. Ensuing controversy over incompatible theories, as well as questions left unanswered, both frustrate and fascinate students. Most theories are based on observations of behaviors that can be related to age, maturity, and environment. Explanations typically hypothesize a link between observed behaviors and unobservable processes. For example, if an infant loses interest in a toy that has dropped off the highchair (the observed behavior—looks away or plays with something new), one can hypothesize that the child has not yet learned that objects still exist when out of sight of the observer (the process—object permanence). All models of cognitive development deal with how humans gather information, process it in both short-term and long-term memory, and relate it back in a relevant fashion to be used in determining and executing action.

Children appear to be born with the innate ability for learning, but this potential is developed only through interaction with the environment. Using their senses to gather and process information leads to the ability to understand relationships between themselves, objective reality, and the world at large. Furthermore, development of the intellect occurs jointly with physical growth, development of motor skills, language development, and learning social skills. Children progress serially through stages of cognitive development—learning skills and having insights in which ideas fit into their pictures of the world.

The **habituation paradigm** is a method that has been developed to measure memory in infants by utilizing a more scientific approach than that of casual observation (Fagan, 1973; Fantz, 1964; Friedman & Carpenter, 1971). Habituation is a response measure in which a repeated stimulus initially elicits a response, but after becoming accustomed, humans will

Acceptance

Interview with Marsha Moore

When we were finally given a diagnosis for Michael, it was not good. The prognosis we were given was infantile autism with moderate to severe mental retardation. We were told that because we had a large family and much responsibility to our other children, we should consider applying for institutional placement for Michael in the state institution for the mentally handicapped. It would be several years before space would come available. Four or five years was a long time and by then we may be ready.

You know, to be honest, it was almost a relief to hear someone say that there was a place where "trained personnel" could take care of your child on an ongoing daily basis. After all, it was obvious that, after a year of sleepless nights and frazzled emotions, we were not prepared to care for him! We thought about this possibility for less than a half hour. This was truly not an option for us. We never did put our name on the waiting list. I can't help sometimes wondering what our lives would be like if we had.

The time that we received Michael's diagnosis was the saddest time in our lives. Somehow, it seemed almost too painful to feel such deep sorrow for very long. It didn't hurt as much to be angry. Part of our anger focused on the medical establishment. What stupid, uncaring human beings they were! How could anyone even suggest institutionalizing this beautiful little boy of ours? How can they predict Michael's future? We'll show them. We will prove them wrong!

I also felt resentment and anger towards others who seemed to be enjoying their lives in ways that I thought would never again be possible. Did they know how precious their "perfect" children were?

I put on a happy face for everyone outside the home, but often even a casual remark would hurt me deeply. Friends, who were trying to be upbeat, would tell me how lucky I was to "at least" have five "other" beautiful, healthy children, as if Michael was a puppy and the deformed runt of the litter or something, as if that should make me happy. To me, there was no consolation.

We worried about how our extended family would react, but they were all very supportive. I think my mom and dad knew how devastated we were, but I don't think my brother and sisters had a clue as to what our family was going through. We tried to keep a stiff upper lip when they'd call. We'd talk about other things and not really cry or complain or go into detail over the phone. I think everything was very gradual for them, seeing Michael over a period of time and realizing he wasn't changing.

After the diagnosis, I remember working for hours out in the yard and just crying and crying and crying. I felt sorry for myself, I felt sorry for Jim, I felt sorry that the kids would always have a retarded brother. I couldn't imagine how Mike would be when he was 10, just like I really can't imagine what he'll be like when he's 20. When you have a typical child, you imagine an adult and you assume he's going to be bright and handsome and charming. But with Michael, I was so fearful. What would he be like when he was five years old or ten years old? The thought of having to bathe a ten-year-old child, having to change his diaper, and wipe his runny nose was almost scary. I thought, "I don't want this. This wasn't included in my grand scheme of life."

Michael is 10 now and I'm not horrified by his needs and he's not repulsive to me. Its just part of my routine in life. It doesn't mean that I don't ever feel discouraged and that I don't ever feel sad when I look at him and compare him to other little boys his age, but the sadness isn't as intense now as it was in the beginning. I find so much more pleasure in just Mike and how he is right now. I just enjoy him for the dumb little things he does; like the smile that he gives me out of the corner of his eyes sometimes.

(continued)

MICHAEL MOORE
AND HIS DAD

There is still the burden of taking care of a child with severe disabilities. Michael was up this morning at 4:30 A.M., and would not go back to sleep, so Jim brought him into bed with us. I can't sleep when the both of them are in bed with me. So I got up and I went to the grocery store this morning at 5:00 A.M. It's not what a typical family would be experiencing at this time in their life, but it's our life, and I think you learn to just grow to enjoy and appreciate even the little things he does. I really can't imagine Mike any other way.

ignore the stimulus. For example, playing children may stop playing when the vacuum cleaner is first turned on, but after a short time, they will ignore the sound and begin once again to attend to more salient stimuli. Changing the stimulus will again elicit a response. An infant's decreased response to the initial stimulus is not fatigue or an inability to attend consistently but is related to memory (Franz, 1964). Studies done by Friedman and Carpenter (1971) reliably demonstrated memory responses in infants under three days of age, determining that short-term memory is probable in very young infants. That is, infants possess both short- and long-term memory long before they can verbally express or demonstrate such ability.

Theories of Cognition

Jean Piaget is the most well-known theorist associated with the **cognitive-developmental** approach. Piaget was originally trained as a biologist and applied many biological principles and methods to the study of human development. Many of the terms he introduced to psychology were drawn directly from biology (Slavin, 1994). He based his earliest theories on careful observation of his own three children. His theory is appreciated because of the ease in adapting constructs of the model to the descriptive observations of infants and their learning processes.

Piaget's model identified four distinct stages of cognitive development he referred to as sensorimotor, preoperational, concrete operational, and formal operational (see Table 3.6). Each stage is characterized by the emergence of new abilities and the reorganization of a child's thinking about the world. Piaget held that development precedes learning and that the developmental sequence for cognitive skills is largely fixed (Slavin, 1994).

The **sensorimotor** stage of development integrates gross and fine motor development with the senses of sight and hearing. This stage (birth to age two) consists of simple learning governed by sensations. Primitive reflex activity progresses to repetitive activity and, later, to imitation. In the reflexive stage, repetitive action of the reflexes allows infants to eventually draw associations between their activity and a response. As an example, sucking (initially

Table 3.6/ *Piaget's Stages of Cognitive Development*

Stage	Approximate Ages	Characteristics
Sensorimotor	Birth to 2 years	*Reflex activity* (0–1 mo.): Reflexive movement in sucking/swallowing, etc. *Primary circular reactions* (1–4 mo.): Repetition of movements becomes more coordinated toward end of period. *Secondary circular reactions* (4–8 mo.): Can focus on outside world; repetition of movements that produced interesting stimulation. *Coordination of secondary schemes* (8–12 mo.): Can generalize use of acquired actions to solve new problems. *Tertiary circular reactions* (12–18 mo.): Exploration of and experimentation with environment through previously learned schemes. *Invention of new means through mental combinations* (18–24 mo.): Ability to comprehend that one thing can represent another thing.
Preoperational	18–24 months to 7 years	Stored imagery or representational thought characterized by deferred imitation. Symbolic ability characterized by pretend play and language development. Egocentrism—unable to view the world from another's perspective.
Concrete Operations	6–8 years to 12 years	*Decentration:* Focus on several attributes of object simultaneously. *Reversability* of mental operations. Use of *logic* to solve problems. *Conservation:* Amount does not change with change in shape. *Relational thinking:* e.g., larger, shorter, etc. Understands *hierarchical relationships* and that objects can belong to more than one class.
Formal Operations	12 years and up	Versatile flexible thinking process. Reasoning about hypothetical problems. Systematic searching for solutions to problems. Abstract thinking.

Source: Adapted from Hanson, M. J. (1984). *Atypical infant development.* Austin, TX: PRO-ED; Mussen, D. H., Conger, J. J., Kagan, J., & Huston, A. C. (1990). *Child development and personality.* New York: Harper Row.

reflexive) on a nipple produces a milk flow and consequently leads to a feeling of fullness. Later, infants understand (have gained knowledge about) the relationship between the act of sucking and the outcome. Such experiences are used by the developing intellect as a foundation for advancing along a progressive course to the next stage.

Primary circular reactions are sequential progressions, evolving out of early sensorimotor experiences. This is the beginning of voluntary behavior. Deliberate activity begins when infants learn that certain behaviors can elicit specific responses. **Accommodation** begins with an infant incorporating and adapting actions with the recognition that certain activities produce a specific response. An infant may begin to cry upon hearing the voice of its mother, having learned from previous experience that the general response to crying is mother picking up and cuddling the infant. This is the beginning of the recognition of sequence and is an early experience with cause and effect.

Secondary circular reactions are a continuation and reinforcement of the primary circular reactions. It is during this period that both the quality and quantity of activity can be identified. Activities such as grasping progress to shaking (as with a rattle) that produces both movement and noise. An infant learns during this progression that degrees of shaking produce different qualities of sound. It is also during this time period that infants learn separateness from other objects in their environment and realize that their environment can be controlled by their own behavior. During this stage infants can demonstrate imitation, object permanence, and attachment, which are memory-related behaviors (Cohen & Gelber, 1975).

Imitation, the repetition of a sound or activity or both actions and sounds of another individual, implies there has been storage of information within an infant's brain. In fact, studies by Butterworth and Hopkins (1988) determined that infants probably have the capacity at birth for imitation; observations of even very young infants showed they can imitate the facial expressions of caregivers. This initially may be a reflexive activity but through the progression of learning is broadened and becomes more sustained to include not only expressions but verbalization and motor activity.

Object permanence can be described as the demonstration of knowledge that an object exists even though it can no longer be seen. Infants between four months and eight months will search for an object if it is at least partially exposed. Infants between eight months and one year of age will seek out an object even if it cannot be visualized at all (Ault, 1977). For example, when a rattle is placed under a blanket, an eight- to twelve-month-old infant recognizes that the rattle still exists and will actively attempt to remove the blanket and expose it. This implies that short-term memory functions and is being demonstrated on the basis that knowledge exists even without the reality of observation.

Attachment is also a strong indicator of memory in infants. Fear of strangers appears to develop between six and eight months of age and involves recognition memory. This implies that infants draw from an experience-base that recognizes the comfort in familiarity and a lack of trust in the unfamiliar. Whether this is based on sight, smell, or sound remains unclear, though it is obvious that long-term memory is being demonstrated (Seamon, 1980).

Coordination of secondary schemata and its application to new situations is the last stage of Piaget's sensorimotor development and precedes transition to the next level of learning. This stage occurs between 18 months and two years of age. Increased gross motor skills and past experience with achievements in behaviors increase an infant's ability to interact with the environment. An increased understanding of object permanence accompanies the initiation of intellectual reasoning. Infants can recognize that an object has singular properties that are separate from the individual possessing the object. An example of this ability is the recognition that a ball will roll even if not necessarily pushed by a person having possession of the ball. Infants at this stage begin to actively engage in manipulating their environment by attempting to remove barriers that detain them from reaching a desired goal. Toward the end of this period expressive language skills are emerging that increase the ability of young children to successfully interact with their environment.

The **preoperational stage** in cognitive development (2–7 years) is characterized by rapid intellectual development. During this period of development children view the world only in direct relationship to themselves. They seem to be unable to view a situation from a perspective other than their own, and their thinking processes are generally concrete. They are increasingly able to use language to express ideas and use toys symbolically to replace objects in play (e.g., using a broom as a "horse"). Finally, children in the preoperational stage begin to understand the relationships between size, time, and weight, and their thought processes are intuitive, based on just knowing without reasoning.

Though the final stages of Piaget's theory extend beyond early childhood, they are introduced here to show the longitudinal nature of his observations. **Concrete operations** (7–11 years) is the stage of logic. It is during this period that children can classify, sort, and organize facts about their world to use in problem solving. They continue to solve problems concretely based on perception since most have not yet developed abstract thinking. In looking at the development of memory in children at this stage, the processes of selective attention, strategies used for retention, and the duration of memory must be explored. There is no doubt that age makes a difference in the abilities of children to both attend to learning and remember what has been learned before. During this process, children also develop the ability to build on past memories and use their current environment for new learning.

Formal operations (11 years to adulthood) is the stage of adaptability, flexibility, and abstraction. During this stage, adolescents can make hypotheses and use them to think in theoretical and philosophical terms. These individuals are aware of the contradictions in life, can analyze them practically, and can act upon the conclusions.

Long-term memory ability in children is variable. Use of selective attention processes and strategies improves with age. There is no comparison between the ability of children and adults to process information and recall the same information over time. Flavell (1971) and Flavell, Friedrichs, and Hoyt (1970) determined that maturation is necessary for the development of individual awareness about memory and the relationship of meaning to performance. However, Flavell et al. (1970) also determined that young children recognize their limitations. Through this determination children learn how to use available resources to succeed in the learning process, which in turn allows them to become more adaptive to their environment (see Table 3.7).

SOCIAL DEVELOPMENT

Social development is part of the developmental progression that governs the emergence of individual emotions and personality. Human beings are constantly involved in a dynamic relationship with other human beings and their environment. This involvement is essential for survival. People need social relationships in order to learn the rules for adapting to community norms that govern living within a society. Rules, however, are not always constant. Part of the developmental progression is learning how to seek the information necessary to learn current rules and to recognize the steps that may be necessary when old rules change and new rules are adopted.

Such rules are learned through interactions with adults and other children. Among other factors, heredity, culture, economics, and the community differentially influence social development. Developmental delays can occur when infants and young children are seriously deprived of early social nurturance by caregivers. Through nurturance, caregivers provide reliable stimulation to the senses, establishing a mechanism for the development of a trust relationship. This reciprocal confidence in primary caregivers is the first step toward being able to expand and develop other attachment relationships. In more dramatic cases, infants who do not experience "mothering" with some sort of consistency fail to gain weight regardless of appropriate caloric intake, are lethargic, and do not show a normal developmental progression. Some of these infants may even die if the emotional isolation occurs over a long enough period of time.

Infants initially require an individual caregiver to provide a relationship in which learning the social rules occurs. Providing the cues for what will be the personality development of an infant, this nurturing person (or persons) represents a major influence in early infancy. This influence frequently remains as one of the most significant relationships throughout the life span of a person.

Table 3.7/ *Milestones of Cognitive Development*

Age	Behavior
1 month	Responds to voices. Inspects surroundings.
4 months	Shows anticipatory excitement. Plays with rattle. Repeats new behaviors. Plays with hands and feet.
4–8 months	Finds partially hidden object. Indicates continuation of play by repeating movement. Touches adult to restart activity. Reaches for second object. Anticipates trajectory of object. Imitates familiar action. Finds hidden object. Plays 2–3 minutes with single object. Recognizes names of family members.
8–12 months	Imitates new action. Responds to simple request with gestures (e.g., "point to ____") Uses "tool" to retrieve object. Knows "no." Responds to simple verbal request.
12–18 months	Enjoys looking at a book. Shows understanding of category. Places round, and later square, piece in a puzzle. Stacks toys. Imitates "invisible" gesture. Matches objects. Points to named objects. Brings objects from another room on request. Identifies at least one body part.
18–24 months	Points to pictures named. Activates mechanical toys. Plays with modeling clay and paints. Matches object to pictures. Sorts objects. Understands personal pronouns and adjectives. Matches sounds to photo of animals.
24–36 months	Understands the concept of one. Identifies clothing items for different occasions. Engages in simple make-believe play. Matches shapes and colors. Knows gender. Identifies body parts with function. Sorts shapes. Completes puzzle of three or four pieces. Begins to understand long and short.

Age	Behavior
3 years	Completes 10% of a task with little supervision. Counts to three orally. Draws a circle in imitation. Knows most prepositions. Locates big and little. Sorts by size.
4 years	Remains on task for 10 minutes with distractions present. Knows more and less, many and few. Matches coins. Draws a line between two parallel lines. Places three simple pictures in a sequence. Identifies objects that do not belong. Determines three ways that objects are similar or different.
5 years	Completes 50% to 75% of task independently. Determines when a task is complete. Names letters and alphabet sounds. Counts orally to 10. Names penny, nickel, and dime. Reads and writes numerals to 3. Relates today, tomorrow, and yesterday to days of the week. Copies letters and numbers. Prints own name. Colors within lines. Makes judgments in time and speed. Draws a picture to illustrate three pieces of information. Reads simple three-letter words paired with pictures. Reads numerals on a clock face. Names days of the week. Counts orally to 100. Draws a person with three to six body parts.

Social skills appear at an early age with the ability of an infant to recognize family members. These skills continue to mature throughout one's life span as different social skills are necessary at different ages. For example, it is acceptable for toddlers to hug family members and acquaintances lavishly, but in adolescence, such displays of affection are usually viewed as immature. Normal social development is achieved when an individual exercises the rules of social conduct acceptable for a given age, gender, economic status, and culture.

Human beings are accustomed to receiving "rewards" for appropriate social behaviors. This is a learned response from early infancy when interactions between infants and significant caregivers include feedback of a physical nature that becomes associated with an activity generally perceived as pleasurable. As an example, an infant initially responds physically by body movement and then with vocalization upon hearing the caregiver approach, and this activity results in the infant being picked up and cuddled. Infants soon learn which of their behaviors initiate desired responses in caregivers and incorporate these activities into their interactions with other human beings.

Engineering the Fetal Brain

Some parents are willing to take great measures to ensure that their children will be intellectually advanced and culturally and physically gifted. To shape their children, such parents enroll their progeny at very early ages in a variety of preschool activities, including infant swimming instruction, preschool music lessons, and formal academic instruction in mathematics, foreign languages, and reading. While the developmental appropriateness and pedagogical wisdom of preschool "superkid" programs may be debated, there is evidence that such programs do provide many children with an educational head start. Now, enthusiastic parents are being encouraged to begin their children's education even earlier—in the womb. This very early intervention approach is a direct attempt to influence cognitive development in the womb.

Under normal conditions, a fetus's brain is constantly stimulated. In addition to the sound of mother's heartbeat and the sensation of maternal and fetal movement, the amniotic fluid provides variations in odors and tastes. In fact, there is some evidence that nonhuman species can acquire taste and smell preferences in utero.

Source: Healy, J. M. (1990). *The endangered mind: Why children can't think and what we can do about it.* New York: Touchstone.

Human fetuses may also learn to discriminate some familiar voices, as demonstrated after birth. These findings, though limited, have spawned a rash of programs, including one called "Prenatal University," marketed for expectant families.

Methods of teaching prenatally include such unusual tactics as holding an alphabet flash card to the mother's abdomen and shining a light through the card while verbally pronouncing the alphabet letter name. Other methods are less dramatic: pregnant women wear stereo headsets and play auditory programs intended to stimulate fetuses' brains; other prospective mothers read and reread stories aloud.

Early childhood education as described above is a considerable leap of faith, given the modest results of just a few research studies. Most researchers believe that our understanding of fetal brain development is so limited that we are better off to leave the process to nature. It is possible that misguided attempts to engineer brain development prenatally could actually cause harm by distorting natural mental growth. According to one expert, "For heavens sake, nature has created the perfect environment; why should we mess around with it?"

Young children with disabilities are at risk for the development of distorted social skills. Because all developmental areas are interlinked, an impairment in one area can significantly alter the ability of an infant or child to initiate or respond to interactions in ways that build or maintain social relationships. Physical impairments, such as cerebral palsy, may prohibit postures or gestures that progress to social interactions. Caregivers need to learn to read the signals of infants or children with disabilities and use these signals in their interactions with the child. Teaching families relevant mechanisms to establish relationships with their disabled children is one of the initial responsibilities of an early childhood educator.

As in other areas of human development, research and understanding of social development are influenced by theory. For example, Erik Erikson (1968, 1980), a psychoanalytic theorist, posited that humans progress through eight discrete stages of psychosocial development (see Table 3.8). Each stage represents contrasting constructs that form a continuum. That is, at the beginning of each stage, a person's psychosocial behavior is negative or immature; by the end of each stage, desirable resolution has occurred. At each stage, individuals can be characterized as "working to resolve" the contrasting elements. For example, infants are working to resolve mistrust into trust of other humans.

Table 3.8/ *Erikson's Stages of Psychosocial Development*

Ages	Psychosocial Crises	Significant Relationships	Psychosocial Emphasis
Birth to 18 months	Mistrust vs. Trust	Mother	To get To give in return
18 months–3 years	Shame vs. Autonomy	Father To let go	To hold on
3–6 years	Guilt vs. Initiative	Basic Family	To make (= going after) To "make like" (= playing)
6–12 years	Inferiority vs. Industry	Neighborhood and school	To make things To make things together
Adolescence	Role Confusion vs. Identity	Peer groups and models of leadership To share being oneself	To be oneself (or not to be)
Young adulthood	Isolation vs. Intimacy	Partners in friendship, sex, cooperation	To lose and find oneself in another
Middle age	Stagnation vs. Generativity	Divided labor and shared household	To take care of
Old age	Despair vs. Integrity	Mankind or my kind	To be, through having been To face not being

Source: Adapted from Slavin, R. E. (1994). *Educational psychology theory and practice*, p. 54. (4th ed.). Boston: Allyn & Bacon.

Social Play

Play is the medium through which infants and toddlers acquire and execute social relationships. It is within play activities that people behave just to enjoy or amuse themselves. Yet play is a significant precursor for both physical and mental growth and for the acquisition of normal social maturation. Playing is a form of self-expression and is required in the normal dynamic of growth as a significant part of social development (see Table 3.9).

Play is universal and crosses all the physical and social boundaries of the world (Piers, 1972). Activities that are both fantasy and real constitute play. Play can be individual or collective, can involve a small or large group, and can occur anywhere and at any time. Play activities can be divided into three general groups: motor (physical exercise, action toys, etc.), intellectual (mental activities such as card and board games), and sensory (spectator activities, such as track meets, ball games, etc.). Very young children, between two and four years, generally prefer to engage in motor play activities.

Though some claim that neonates have little personality, observations of newborns reveal that they begin to engage in simple play within hours of birth. As mentioned earlier, reciprocal interactions involving facial expressions, eye movements, and sounds begin very early and serve as reinforcers to caregivers, who are drawn to this "playful" little being. Infant interactions with their environment generally remain within the context of relationships with their primary caregivers. **Social-affective play** may involve stretching or turning an infant's arms or legs, patting or stroking, and presenting bright objects or introducing sounds to elicit responses, such as cooing (Hughes, 1975; Johnson & Medinnus, 1974; Neisworth & Bagnato, 1987). An infant's typical response to social play is pleasure that is derived from nurturing relationships with familiar people. Thus, play provides a context for learning that emotional responses from caregivers can be provoked by smiling, cooing, and other such behaviors. In fact, some refer to play as "the work" of young children (MacDonald, 1989).

Table 3.9/ *Milestones of Social-Play Development*

Age	Behavior
1–6 months	Smiles. Regards face. Establishes eye contact. Laughs. Discriminates strangers.
6–12 months	Enjoys frolic play. Lifts arms to mother. Shows separation anxiety. Cooperates in social games. Tests parental reactions during bedtime. Likes to be in constant sight and hearing of an adult.
12–18 months	Is difficult to discipline independent behavior. Displays frequent tantrums. Needs and expects routines. Shows a sense of humor. Tends to be messy. Enjoys being the center of attention. Hugs and kisses parents.
18–24 months	Shows jealousy at attention to others. Desires control of others. Enjoys solitary play. Attempts to comfort others in distress.
2 years	Distinguishes self as separate person. Strongly possessive; dependent; clings and whines. Frustration tantrums peak. Enjoys parallel play. Values own property, and uses the word mine. Begins to obey and respect simple rules. Takes pride in own achievements and resists help.
3 years	Plays games with another person. Takes turns in games 25% to 50% of the time. Responds to and makes verbal greetings. Plays with one or two others. Cooperates with others in group activities.
4 years	Behaves according to the desires of others. Volunteers. Conforms to group decisions. Takes turns in games 75% of the time. Verbalizes feelings before physical aggression.
5 years	Tries again after change or disappointment. Leaves provoking situations. Sacrifices immediate reward for delayed reward. Accepts friendly teasing; comforts a playmate in distress. Cooperates in group games with loose rules. Protects other children and animals. Offers help to others voluntarily.

Jennifer Waritz, Acceptance

Interview with Tammy Waritz

I hate the word *retarded*. I just hate that word, and kids use it so cruelly. My children know I really dislike that word, but some of their friends use it. Just the other day, one my daughter's friends said "retarded," and Cathy just looked at her, very calmly, and said, very nicely, "We don't use that word in our home." Then she explained to her friend that Jennifer is very special to us and that it's important for us to respect her. I think Cathy's friend will remember that and may think twice next time.

When Cathy was in kindergarten and first grade, she would ask me if she could take Jennifer for show-and-tell. That was really hard for me at first because it was like we were going to put Jennifer on display, but I recognized that Cathy had a need for her friends to know about her sister and for them to feel comfortable with her sister. I think, too, that she was very proud of her sister. Whenever we visited one of Cathy's classes, I always found a book that was written for her age group, and I would share the book, and we would talk about Jennifer. The students would ask questions like, "Is she ever going to walk? Will she ever talk? Can I catch what she has? Is it OK to touch her?" Just questions that kids need to ask and need to have answered.

After that, when Cathy's friends started coming over, they would say, "Can we take Jennifer for a walk?" Jennifer was always out and about with the neighborhood kids. It was a nice experience and those kids' lives will forever be changed because of that experience.

We used to expect Jennifer to live with us the rest of her life, and thought we could take care of her

until we died. As she's gotten older, and we have gotten older, we've come to know that's not realistic. Your kids grow up, some go off to college, some get jobs; eventually many get married and they have children of their own. Jennifer is different from our other children because she will require 24-hour adult care for the rest of her life. I don't think that she will ever be independent enough to prepare her own food or bathe herself. She'll always need to have someone there to help her, but this should not keep her from experiencing life on her own.

This is reality; we struggle with so many demands. We work full-time, and there's still the house to be cleaned, the laundry, and cooking dinner every night. For a long time, we just wanted to take one day at a time, and we still do, but we're beginning to look further ahead. We don't even know what Jennifer's life expectancy is. We think that she's developing seizures again, so

(continued)

*JENNIFER WARITZ
AND HER GRANDMOTHER*

that'll certainly have an impact on her health. She does have atrophy in her brain, and no one seems to know what that could mean for her. Her future remains questionable; however, we still need to continue planning and moving forward.

Though we do just take one day at a time, we've started the separation process with Jennifer, as hard as it has been for us to do this. Even though she is so young, it got to the point, because of her physical involvement, that we were really limited where we could go and what we could do. We recognized that we were taking normal and healthy family activities away from our other children. Now Jennifer leaves our home one weekend a month and goes to a respite provider so that we can provide more attention and time to our other children. For two weeks during the summer, she's gone as well, and we go camping or do things our other children like to do but that are not necessarily accessible when we have Jennifer. It is hard to think that you have to exclude one of your family members in order to do that, but when you care for a child with disabilities, you're constantly adjusting and readjusting your lifestyle.

Once infants have begun to develop voluntary motor skills, play progresses to acquiring new skills. Manipulating objects repetitively elicits repeated pleasure that commonly accompanies success. On the other hand, play can produce frustration when attempts to learn new skills are not immediately successful (Brooks-Gunn & Lewis, 1982). By the time infants reach one year of age, they are able to participate in imitative games. These may include repetitive games, such as pat-a-cake, itsy-bitsy spider, and peek-a-boo. Such games generally involve an infant and an adult, but they are setting the stage for the later initiation of play with other children. Though

Mother and infant engaged in social-affective play

these initial social relationships are necessary to the development of social skills, children generally learn many of the rules of social conduct from other children. Peers are less tolerant of deviations from an established standard than are adults who can reason beyond what is obvious. Social play in the preschool years can be categorized into five sequential stages: solitary play, spectator play, parallel play, associative play, and cooperative play (Cass, 1971). The rate of progress at which an individual child transcends these stages is dependent upon both the opportunities a child has for interactions and the integrity of the social contacts that are available.

In some cases, children with greater economic stability may have the advantage because more social contacts are arranged to provide the opportunities for engaging play experiences and may allow for a more rapid progression. For example, in established supervised play groups, parents have the means to take the initiative in providing toys and games that promote peer interactions.

Solitary play involves both isolation and independence. This play experience can involve an individual child within the same physical area as a group of children. Children involved in solitary play are involved with their own activities and their own group of toys. They enjoy the physical presence of other children but do not speak to other children, nor do they attempt to decrease the physical distance between play areas. They also show no interest in the activities of other children that differ from their own activities. Young children will also engage in solitary play in their own homes while with a caregiver. Though engaging in independent play, a child may frequently move the activity to the vicinity of the caregiver.

Spectator play is also frequently referred to as onlooker play. This occurs when a young child observes the play activities of other children but makes no attempt to enter in the activity. This play may involve conversation about the nature of the activity between the observer and child involved.

Parallel play also involves independent play between children in a group. Children play with toys that are like those of the children around them but of their own choosing and in their own fashion. This play involves children playing beside each other but not with each other. Toddlers frequently engage in parallel play, which is consistent with their world view that objects have properties independent of involvement. Additionally, toddlers' language development is just beginning to allow for verbal expression in social context.

Associative play occurs between the ages of 3 to 4 years. Individual children will play with other children, engaging in similar or even identical activities. Without adult facilitation, associative play generally lacks organization. Though toys may be shared, each member acts without regard for the group wishes since no group goal has been established. When an individual child initiates an activity, the entire group will typically follow this lead. During this stage, there may be occasional attempts by individual children to control both group behavior and group membership. Four-year-olds begin to establish strong preferences for associates and may begin to have a "best friend." This "friend" may change frequently during the course of a play experience, depending upon the direction of the play. Hence, children have learned initial strategies to gain power over other children; yet these young children are incapable of wielding power wisely. For example, it is typical of children of this age to be bossy and selfish, to begin to taunt and name-call, and to boast and bend the truth a little.

Cooperative play occurs when activities are organized. Children involved in cooperative play are engaged in a goal-directed activity that has been planned by the group to accomplish some defined end. Formal games become important during this stage, and the end goal frequently involves some competition. Group members have designated roles that are generally both assigned and directed by one or two accepted "leaders" of the group. Even at this age, children develop a great sense of either belonging or not belonging to cooperative play groups. During this final stage of play development, there may be gender splits with children seeking membership in same-sex groups.

Play enhances skill development in both motor activities and emotional development. Active play develops muscle control, cognitive development, and socialization. Through play,

Toddlers frequently engage in parallel play

children learn about their physical world and its relationship to themselves. Intellectual stimulation is provided through manipulation of shapes and work with texture, color, and size. Children can experiment with abstract thought through fantasy and fabrication within the acceptable context of creativity without being diverted by conformity to a norm of the society. Play becomes less spontaneous and more structured with age. Because children are not as tolerant of violations of codes within their own play group, externally initiated codes of behavior for the group facilitate learning of acceptable social behaviors. Truth, honesty, fair play, self-control, and leadership skills are learned within the group and provide an important mechanism for teaching the standards of the society and personal accountability for individual actions.

SELF-HELP SKILLS

Traditional skills falling into the domain of **self-help** include independent feeding, dressing, toileting, and personal responsibility (see Table 3.10). In the 1991 Amendments to the Individuals with Disabilities Education Act (P.L. 101-119), the term *self-help* was changed to **adaptive** skills. Both terms refer to the same set of skills and either may be used by various assessment tools and curriculum packages. The acquisition of skills that enable children to interact independently with their environment is linked closely to both motor development and cognitive skill development. For example, children will not independently use the toilet until they:

1. have gained sufficient muscle control to stay dry for an hour or two at a time

2. can move themselves to the toilet

Table 3.10/ *Milestones of Self-Help*

1–4 months	Coordinates sucking, swallowing, and breathing. Recognizes bottle.
4–8 months	Swallows strained or pureed foods. Feeds self a cracker. Holds own bottle.
8–12 months	Drinks from held cup. Finger feeds. Sleeps 10–12 hours. Cooperates in dressing.
12–18 months	Cooperates in washing and drying. Undoes bows and snaps. Has regular bowel movements. Indicates when wet or soiled. Cooperates in dressing.
18–24 months	Sits on "potty-chair." Unzips, zips, removes unlaced shoes. Washes and dries hands partially. Helps with simple household tasks. Prefers certain foods.
24–36 months	Delays sleeping by demanding things. Understands and stays away from common dangers. Undresses with assistance. Washes hands and brushes teeth. Uses toilet with assistance, daytime control.
4 years old	Takes responsibility for toileting. Serves self and helps set table. Dresses with supervision. Uses spoon and fork well. Uses toilet regularly without asking. Puts comb and brush in hair. Puts shoes on correct feet. Knows front from back.
5 years old	Drinks from water fountain; serves self and carries tray. Carries liquid in open container without spilling. Wipes self after toileting. Uses comb/brush; washes face and ears in bath and dries with towel. Zips up front opening of clothing. Dresses and undresses functionally without being told.
6 years old	Cuts and spreads with knife; cuts with knife and fork. Independently washes and dries hands after toileting. Bathes, showers, and "cleans up" independently. Washes own hair. Selects and uses clean and protective clothing. Ties shoes. Turns clothing right side out. Uses proper tooth brushing strokes.

3. are cognitively aware of the "signs" of urgency to void

4. know what action to take to avoid an "accident"

Historically, planning for instruction of self-help skills has followed a strict developmental model, but more recent research illustrates that skills once thought to be prerequisites could be skipped for children with significant developmental disabilities. While recognizing this, the following description of self-help skills is based upon knowledge of typical developmental patterns.

Independent Eating and Drinking Skills

As in all other areas of development, a neonate eats and drinks reflexively only, though parents might swear there is some intent involved when a hungry infant wakes parents throughout the night and keeps them further vigilant during the day with demands to be fed. It is this aspect of child care that is most exhausting for parents, as infants demand food five to eight times a day, requiring approximately 30 minutes time for each feeding.

Though the sucking reflex is present at birth, it is not until infants are four months old that they suck voluntarily with enthusiasm and vigor. Young infants consume exclusively liquid diets of either breast milk or formula for the first four to six months. At about this time, infants begin to take some responsibility for eating by holding their bottle. Simultaneously, solid pureed foods will be tolerated, though infants may remain very passive, not offering to close their lips around the spoon or to push food from the front of the tongue toward the back of their mouths.

A dramatic transition of independence takes place at about eight months of age. Infants, who now have well-developed fine motor skills, will drink from cups with help, will feed themselves finger foods (crackers, etc.), and may refuse to drink from their bottles. Very grown

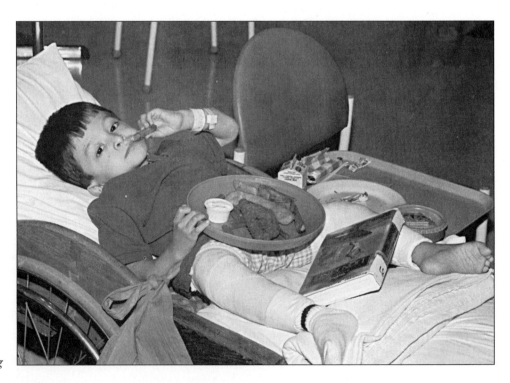

Child self-feeding

up now, these infants should be on the same eating schedule as adults though, like adults, enjoying between meal snacks.

By age two, toddlers are often independent eaters and drinkers. This does not mean that they can do so with grace. Using a spoon, toddlers can feed themselves. However, this level of independence is often paired with independent decision making. It is not uncommon for toddlers to maintain a narrow range of food preferences or to go through stages where they eat very little.

Three-year-olds eat well with a spoon and may be able to use a fork to stab foods. These youngsters now display some very sophisticated skills at the table, serving themselves drinks or portions of food. Additionally, vegetables become a food to avoid. Independence in the use of utensils is achieved by four years of age. Four-year-olds also enjoy helping prepare meals and are able to make simple meals, such as cereal and toast, independently by age five.

Dressing Skills

The first indication that infants are thinking about dressing skills is when they begin to tug at their feet and incidentally pull off socks or shoes. At about the same time, approximately nine months, significant progress in dressing is made when infants assist with dressing by lifting their arms to remove or put on a shirt, stepping into a pair of suspended pants or shoes, and holding still during diapering. Since undressing is easier, toddlers take off jackets, shoes, socks, and unbuttoned pants at about 18 months. Though they will try earlier, children have little success in dressing even in articles of clothing that are easy to put on (pants, loose shoes) until they are about two years of age. A two-year-old may learn to fasten large buttons and small front buttons by three years of age. Zippers and buckles are more difficult fine motor tasks that may be mastered at age four or five. Usually by the time children are four, they will be able to dress by themselves, though it is not until age five that most dressing errors (putting clothes on backwards or inside out) are recognized and self-corrected. Complex dressing tasks such as tying shoes and fixing stuck zippers emerge at five years of age but may not be mastered until age six or seven.

Toileting Skills

Toilet training begins at birth, as muscle control is gradually gained. A very young infant is seldom dry, dribbling small quantities of urine almost constantly. Gradually, muscle control permits infants to sustain first brief, and then longer, periods of dryness. By eight months, infants begin to stay dry for reasonable lengths of time and may communicate their recognition of "wetness" by pulling at their diapers. Parents should not, however, consider toilet training until at least 18 months or later if a child does not stay dry for an hour or more.

One index of sufficient bladder control is whether toddlers remain dry during their naps. Bowel control is more easily achieved than bladder control, as infants begin to have routine bowel movements one or two times a day by eight months of age. Training for bowel control can begin at 12 months and may be accomplished as early as 18 months. This process is often not completed until age three, though it is typically more easily accomplished by girls than boys. By five years of age, children can be expected to independently care for all toileting needs, including wiping and washing hands afterwards.

Personal Responsibility

Children can be expected from an early age to begin to take on responsibility for themselves. Toddlers, for example, can follow directions to pick up their toys, though this behavior might not become habitual until some years later. Two-year-olds will put their coats away regularly when the routine is expected. By three years of age, children can take on a variety of responsibilities, such as wiping up spills, helping to clear the table, and placing dirty clothes in a hamper.

Parents should begin brushing an infant's teeth as soon as the primary teeth begin erupting. As infants gain sufficient fine motor control, parents can ask infants to attempt to imitate tooth brushing. Though cleanliness is not the goal, as caregivers follow after children and brush with precision, children learn valuable patterns of routine daily care. Bathing and washing are similar responsibilities that can be transferred to young children. By age four, children should be able to bathe themselves and brush their teeth with acceptable proficiency. While four-year-olds are unpredictable, five-year-olds are generally happy to assist in the completion of jobs around the home. Given chores, children tend to be cooperative and reliable.

FORMATIVE ANALYSIS FOR THE TWENTY–FIRST CENTURY

There is little question that the twenty-first century will bring changes in our culture, both friendly and unfriendly, that will influence the capacity of children to progress from one milestone to the next. In fact, changes may be so great that the dimensions of behavior that are now considered indexes of healthy growth will be obsolete. New expectations could evolve from changes in technology and medicine or from environmental catastrophe.

Perhaps more will be expected, perhaps less, but surely different priorities will be selected for adaptation and survival in a world that is changing too fast to describe. Will some parents continue along the current trend of expecting infants to accomplish more and more at earlier ages? Will they want children to walk at 6 months or to play the violin at 11 months? Or, will more and more parents adopt the current philosophy of "developmental appropriateness" and expect less and less of children—favoring an emphasis on "natural" evolution of learning? Perhaps the coming generation of children will struggle so hard to adapt to or survive increases in poverty, threats to safety, and diminished educational resources that such questions will seem esoteric.

STUDY GUIDE QUESTIONS

1. Describe the relationship between primitive reflexes and normal motor development.

2. What is the most commonly used index of reflexive maturity? Explain this reflex.

3. Name and describe the primitive reflexes seen at birth.

4. What is the main difference between primitive reflexes and postural reflexes? Name and describe postural reflexes.

5. Name and describe the three categories generally used to define muscle tone.

6. Explain the development and evaluation of head control.

7. Describe the development of trunk control at two, four, six, and eight months.

8. Describe the sequence and age milestones of hip control.

9. Explain the progression of development from reflex to reaching to grasping.

10. Describe the sequence of refinement skills of the fine motor domain.

11. What are the five principles of language development?

12. How is the composition of language described by interactional theorists?

13. How is the composition of language described by pragmatic theorists? Describe the three stages.

14. Explain the three aspects of language considered when discussing form.

15. Explain the phenomenon of semantic relationship.

16. Briefly outline the general development of sentence structure.

17. What is a morpheme? How do we measure the sophistication of language?

18. Describe the receptive language abilities of a child around the following ages: 1 year, 18 months, 2 years, 3 years, 6 years.

19. As children begin to develop expressive language, actions and objects dominate their vocabulary. Explain why this may be so.

20. Describe the "normal" rate of vocabulary acquisition from three to six years of age.

21. To what does "language use" refer?

22. Describe a child's language use at the following ages: neonate, 9 months, 1 year, 18 months to 2 years.

23. Define cognition.

24. Identify a common link between theories of cognitive development.

25. Explain the habituation paradigm and discuss its importance in cognition theory.

26. Describe the four phases of Piaget's model of cognitive development.

27. Define accommodation.

28. What is the importance of imitation in cognitive development?

29. Define attachment.

30. Name three factors that may influence social development.

31. Define play.

32. Discuss the three groups of play activities.

33. Identify and discuss the five stages of play.

34. How do children learn social behavior through play?

35. List the traditional skills that fall into the domain of self-help.

36. Describe a child's eating and drinking repertoire at the following ages: 4–6 months, 8 months, 2 years, 3 years, 4 years, 5 years.

37. Describe a child's dressing skills at the following ages: 9 months, 18 months, 2 years, 4 years, 5+ years.

38. When should training of bowel and bladder begin? Complete?

39. At what age should tooth brushing begin?

REFERENCES

Andrick, G. R., & Tager-Flusberg, H. (1986). The acquisition of colour terms. *Journal of Child Language, 13,* 119–134.

Ault, R. (1977). *Children's cognitive development.* New York: Oxford University Press.

Bertoncini, J., Bijelac-Babic, B., Jusczyk, P. W., Kennedy, L. J., & Mahler, J. (1988). An investigation of young infants' perceptual representations of speech sounds. *Journal of Experimental Psychology, 117,* 21–33.

Bigge, J. (1991). *Teaching individuals with physical and multiple disabilities* (3rd ed.) Upper Saddle River, NJ: Merrill/Prentice Hall.

Braine, M. D. (1963). The ontogeny of English phrase structures: The first phrase. *Language, 39,* 1–13.

Brooks-Gunn, J., & Lewis, M. (1982). Affective exchanges between normal and handicapped infants and their mothers. In T. M. Field & A. Fogel (Eds.), *Emotion and early interaction,* (pp. 161–188). Hillsdale, NJ: Earlbaum.

Butterworth, G., & Hopkins, B. (1988). Hand-mouth coordination in the newborn baby. *British Journal of Developmental Psychology, 6,* 303–314.

Cass, J. (1971). *Helping children grow through play.* New York: Schocken Books.

Chaudhary, N., & Suparna, N. (1991). Early language learning in a multilingual environment. *Early Child Development and Care, 76,* 135–143.

Cohen, L., & Gelber, R. (1975). Infant visual memory. In L. Cohen & P. Salapatek (Eds.), *Infant perception: From sensation to cognition, Vol I.* New York: Academic Press.

Erikson, E. H. (1968). *Identity, youth and crisis.* New York: Norton.

Erikson, E. H. (1980). *Identity and the life cycle* (2nd ed.). New York: Norton.

Fagan, J. (1973). Infant's delayed recognition memory and forgetting. *Journal of Experimental Child Psychology, 16,* 424–450.

Fantz, R. (1964). Visual experience in infants: Decreased attention to familiar patterns relative to novel ones. *Science, 146,* 668–670.

Fetters, L. (1984). Motor development. In M. J. Hanson (Ed.), *Atypical infant development* (pp. 313–358). Austin, TX: PRO-ED.

Flavell, J. (1971). First discussant's comments: What is memory development the development of? *Human Development, 14,* 272–278.

Flavell, J., Friedricks, A., & Hoyt, J. (1970). Developmental changes in memorization processes. *Cognitive Psychology, 1,* 324–340.

Friedman, S., & Carpenter, G. (1971). Visual response decrement as a function of age in human newborn. *Child Development, 42,* 1967–1973.

Gopnik, A., & Meltzoff, A. N. (1992). Categorization and naming: Basic-level sorting in eighteen-month-olds and its relation to language. *Child Development, 63,* 1091–1103.

Hanson, M. J. (1984). *Atypical infant development.* Austin, TX: PRO-ED.

Healy, J. H. (1990). *The endangered mind: Why children can't think and what we can do about it.* New York: Touchstone.

Hetherington, E. M., & Parke, R. D. (1979). *Child psychology: A contemporary viewpoint* (2nd ed.). New York: McGraw-Hill.

Hughes, J. (1975). *Synopsis of pediatrics* (4th ed.). St. Louis: C.V. Mosby Co.

Johnson, R., & Medinnus, G. (1974). *Child psychology: Behavior and development* (3rd ed.). New York: Wiley & Sons, Inc.

Klink, M., & Klink, W. (1990). The influence of father caretaker speech on early language development: A case study. *Early Child Development and Care, 62,* 7–22.

MacArthur, F. (1990). Miscommunication, language development and enculturation in L. P. Hartley's "The Go Between." *Style, 24* (1), 103–112.

MacDonald, J. (1989). *Becoming language partners with children.* San Antonio: Special Press.

McCormick, S., & Schiefelbusch, R. L. (1990). *Early language development.* Upper Saddle River, NJ: Merrill/Prentice Hall.

Mussen, D. H., Conger, J. J., Kagan, J., & Huston, A. C. (1990). *Child development and personality.* New York: Harper Row.

Neisworth, T., & Bagnato, S. (1987). *The young exceptional child: Early development and education.* New York: Macmillan Publishing Co.

Nelson, W. E. (1969). *Textbook of Pediatrics* (9th ed.). Philadelphia: W. B. Sanders Co.

Oviatt, S. L. (1982). Inferring what words mean: Early development in infant's comprehension of common object names. *Child Development, 53,* 274–277.

Piers, M. W. (Ed.) (1972). Play and development: A symposium. New York: W.W. Norton.

Reed, V. A. (1994). *An introduction to children with language disorders.* New York: Macmillan.

Schacter, F., & Straye, A. (1982). Adults talk and children's language development. In S. Moore & C. Cooper (Eds.), *The young child: Reviews of research.* Washington, DC: National Association for Young Children.

Seamon, J. G. (1980). *Memory and cognition: An introduction.* New York: Oxford University Press.

Shatz, M., & Gelman, R. (1973). The development of communication skills: Modifications in the speech of young children as a function of the listener. *Monographs of the Society for Research in Child Development, 38* (Serial No. 152).

Slavin, R. E. (1994). *Educational psychology theory and practice.* (4th ed.). Boston: Allyn & Bacon.

Wiig, E. H., & Semel, E. M. (1980). *Language assessment and intervention for the learning disabled.* Upper Saddle River, NJ: Merrill/Prentice Hall.

Winner, E. (1988). *The point of words.* Cambridge, MA: Harvard University Press.

Wood, D. (1992). Culture, language, and child development. *Language and Education, 6*(2), 123–140.

Development and Risking Conditions:
Prenatal, Natal, and Postnatal

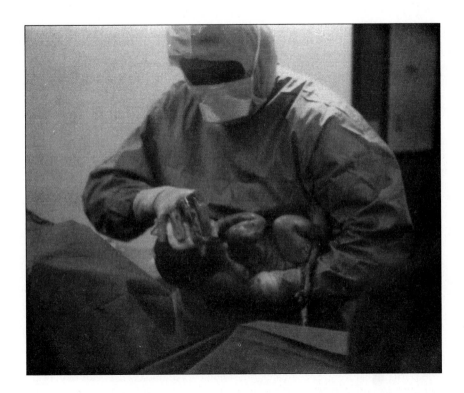

This chapter is a discussion of many maternal and infant conditions that may result in disabilities for the infant. Included is information about fetal development that provides a basis for understanding how interruptions in the process could result in physical or psychological deviations from the norm. Educators should possess a knowledge base about these conditions to better serve the families with whom they interact.

The physical connections between mothers and their infants that exist before pregnancy, during pregnancy, during the labor and delivery process, and during the immediate period after birth can affect the later physical and developmental health of children. **Prenatal** refers to the period before conception through **gestation. Natal** conditions affect the mother or the infant during the labor and delivery process, and **postnatal** conditions affect the mother or the infant after delivery and during the first 30 days of extrauterine life. A fourth term, **perinatal,** is commonly used to designate a period that actually overlaps all of the preceding periods. Technically, the perinatal period begins at the 29th week of gestation and ends between the first and fourth weeks after birth. At any time during any of these periods, problems may arise that can compromise the physical or cognitive growth of the infant. While knowing the cause or timing of injury seldom guides early childhood professionals as they design intervention plans, this knowledge can be useful to families in understanding their children.

PRENATAL GROWTH AND DEVELOPMENT

Prematurity is when a developing fetus is born prior to the 37th week of gestation. It is important to distinguish between premature infants and those who are of low birth weight, small for gestational age, or have intrauterine growth retardation. Though babies from all these categories are at-risk due to their size and other factors, premature infants have a unique set of risk factors associated with immature physical development corresponding to the gestational age of the baby.

Viability is the gestational age when a fetus can survive outside of the womb with or without medical or technological intervention. With current medical practice, a fetus is considered viable at a gestational age greater than 23 weeks beyond conception. In fact, the survival of premature infants is directly related to advances in neonatal medical technology. With the improved survival rates of premature infants, it has become possible to identify a normal progression of preterm growth and development. Consequently, researchers have also investigated interventions aimed at improving the quality of survival and assisting families to meet the needs of their medically fragile infants.

While infants born between the 33rd and 36th week of gestation have increased risk compared to full-term infants, those born at less than 32 weeks are at extreme risk for significant developmental delays. The corresponding fragility of underdeveloped organ systems, particularly the brain, affects both physical growth and neurological development. Indexes used to project fetal physical growth are gestational age, birth weight, and medical conditions. Maternal and fetal conditions (e.g., maternal hypertension or fetal anomalies such as a heart defect) can either independently or collectively influence fetal growth. In spite of preexisting conditions, appropriate interventions can alleviate or control high-risk medical conditions, while permitting infants to progress along a corrected growth curve established specifically for infants born prematurely. Specifically, physiological parameters for heart rate, respiratory rate, blood pressure, urine production/excretion, fluid needs, and caloric needs for growth have standard indexes for preterm infants. These parameters are specific to gestational age, though progress can be further influenced by the medical conditions with which individual infants are faced.

EFFECTS OF PREMATURITY ON BODY SYSTEMS

Fetuses who will eventually be born prematurely proceed along the same predetermined pattern as that of term fetuses until birth itself interrupts this normal course of development. Though this interruption does not change the normal developmental sequence, it does have an impact on the *schedule* over which development occurs. That is, premature infants are born with underdeveloped organs, which are not sufficiently capable of meeting the demands of independent life without the support of the mother's womb. The following is an analysis of the particular organ systems that are compromised when infants are born prematurely. Note that all systems, while described in a discrete manner, are essentially linked, with insult to one or more systems affecting the development of other systems.

Respiratory System

Surfactant is a chemical agent needed for independent breathing that is not produced in sufficient quantity until the last four to five weeks of pregnancy. This chemical prevents the lungs from sticking together during expiration. Without surfactant the lung surfaces stick together, causing the small airsacs to collapse. The tiny airsacs, called alveoli, permit normal exchange of oxygen and carbon dioxide. Collapsed alveoli cause oxygen deficiency, leading to lung disease and, if serious enough, death. Respiratory function can be further compromised by an immature nervous system. Since respiratory function is governed by nerve impulses, weak or absent stimulation (as is the case in prematurity) results in very inconsistent patterns of breathing. Consequently, it is common for preterm infants to experience **apnea,** in which an infant stops breathing for periods of seconds or minutes.

Cardiovascular System

Blood vessels in premature infants are unusually fragile and break easily. This fragility increases the risk of bleeding into the brain (intracranial bleeding or stroke) or other vital organs. A second condition associated with an immature cardiovascular system is **anemia,** since underdeveloped bone marrow is unprepared for the body's demand to produce red blood cells. These conditions place additional stress on the young heart, which is poorly equipped to meet the body's demands for oxygen and nutrients.

Neurological System

The younger the fetus, the greater the probable impact on a developing neurological system. In particular, the relationship between cardiovascular proficiency and neurological functioning is critical. The more premature the infant, the more likely it is that the blood/oxygen supply to the brain will be compromised. Hence, the brain, which itself is immature and consequently vulnerable to any interruption in the vital oxygen and nutrient supply, can incur permanent damage to its cells. Furthermore, as mentioned, the immature neurological system is incapable of sending or receiving messages efficiently. Thus, other systems in the body, all of which are dependent upon the nerve network for adequate functioning, have decreased ability to respond to the body's demands.

Renal and Gastrointestinal Systems

In addition to being affected by their own immaturity, the kidneys and gastrointestinal systems are seriously affected by compromised cardiovascular and neurological systems. The kidneys are unable to maintain normal sodium and calcium levels or to sufficiently filter waste. The gastrointestinal tract is capable of absorbing nutrients, but the large bowel is too short, so the passage of food is too rapid to permit sufficient absorption. Furthermore, this system is fragile, and injury occurs frequently. Interestingly, when the cardiovascular system is weakened (as in prematurity) infants' bodies make unilateral decisions regarding an organ's importance to survival. Accordingly, the gastrointestinal system is not considered critical to an infant's preservation, so blood flow is detoured away from the intestine to provide increased blood to the brain, heart, and kidneys. Fortunately, milk-feeding places demands on the bowels to break milk down for its nutrients and, consequently, promotes maturation and thickening of the bowel walls.

Muscular System

Studies have documented the developmental evolution of tone, deep tendon reflexes, pathologic reflexes, and primitive reflexes for infants born between 24- and 32-weeks gestation. These data are used to guide evaluation of the developmental progression of preterm infants and to assist with prediction of follow-up needs. The somewhat standard sequence also helps nursery staff design interventions for limiting harmful influences, such as noise and light. Ironically, while motor development in full-term infants follows a pattern of upper extremities to lower extremities (cephalo caudal) and from the center of the body to the extremities (proximal to distal), the preterm developmental progression of tone and reflexes emerges in the opposite directions (Allen & Capute, 1990).

Micropremature infants (24–26 weeks of gestation) show generalized flexion of the lower extremities at birth. Though tone has not emerged, these infants are consistent in reflex patterns. Emergence of lower extremity tone, deep tendon reflexes, primitive and pathologic reflexes is seen at approximately 31-weeks gestation. Upper extremity tone and reflexes emerge at approximately 34 weeks (Allen & Capute, 1990). These parameters give providers the opportunity to determine whether these infants are following a progressive course typical of gestational age or whether they are experiencing delays.

Skeletal System

Linear growth is one of the most critical measures in determining the progression of a normal growth curve in premature infants. In spite of adequate weight gain, infants who exhibit decreased linear growth (should expect 0.5 cm to 1 cm of linear growth per week) deviate from the normal expectation. Poor nutrition contributes to bone growth deficiency, which is necessary for linear growth. Most importantly, calcium loss in the newly forming bone structures (rickets) will delay both growth and maturation. A premature infant's inability to adequately coordinate sucking and swallowing is one cause of nutrient deficiency, though medical conditions can further exacerbate the problem.

Integumentary System

The skin in premature infants is extremely fragile. For a very premature infant, the skin surface provides no protection from heat or water loss and no barrier against infection. These infants are also at-risk for the development of yeast infections on the skin surface. The infection can then progress into the blood stream through breaks in the fragile surface. External heat sources (i.e., **isolettes**), filtered air, and good hygiene practices are necessary to provide both warmth and protection for these infants.

INDEXES OF GROWTH IN PREMATURE INFANTS

As with term infants, weight is an unpredictable measure of both gestational age and maturity. Premature infants who have been under physiological stress during pregnancy will exhibit signs of lower birth weight, along with less-advanced organ function. Head circumference, as a measure of brain growth, is used to make growth predictions. **Corrected gestational age** (gestational age versus chronological age) is used to determine if appropriate growth and development is occurring. This is determined to be accurate at least through the first year of life. Prematurity affects growth and development, sometimes only during early life, and sometimes produces effects that will alter the course of an individual's entire life. Recognition of the normal progression provides the opportunity for planning interventions and aligning resources that will promote development to the maximum potential of the affected infant.

Neurobehavioral Assessment of High-Risk Infants in the Neonatal Intensive Care Unit

High-risk infants have a lower threshold for sensory input than other infants and show difficulty tolerating handling and interaction. These infants have poor neurobehavioral organization and thus have problems coping with environmental stimulation. For example, the high-risk infant may not move smoothly from deep sleep to quiet alertness. This infant may not respond in healthy ways to normal physiological functions. When parents seek to interact with such infants, it is stressful for both, and the parents may feel rejected by their infants and powerless in the overwhelming environment of the neonatal intensive care unit.

Fortunately, caregivers can modify how they approach high-risk infants to improve their levels of neurobehavioral organization. Studies have found that when parents and other caregivers are sensitized to what stresses the child and modify their interactional styles according to infant cues, the results are shorter hospitalization, decreased severity of medical problems, and improved parent-infant interaction. In addition, infants' developmental status at discharge and follow-up is markedly improved.

In order to determine stressors in the high-risk infant's environment, a thorough assessment should be undertaken. During assessment, a therapist presents graded intensities of sensory input and levels of handling and interaction and notes how the infant responds. The therapist looks for signs of instability in the infant. These might include the following stress signals:

- Autonomic: alterations in breathing, color changes, gastrointestinal upsets, tremors/ startles, coughing, sneezing, yawning, seizures
- Motoric: low tone, high tone, hyperflexion, frantic/diffuse activity
- State-Related: whimpering, grimacing, irregular breathing, twitching, glassy eyes, hyperalertness, irritability, worried alertness, fussing
- Interaction: gaze aversion, tuning out, staring

Different evaluation instruments are appropriate for this assessment, based on the child's gestational age. The Neonatal Behavioral Assessment Scale (NBAS) was designed for full-term healthy infants from 36- to 44-weeks gestation. The Assessment of Preterm Infant Behavior (APIB) scale is an extension and refinement of the NBAS and is appropriate for preterm infants. The Naturalistic Observations of Newborn Behavior system was developed after APIB but is based on the same concepts. It is appropriate for infants who cannot tolerate the greater handling and manipulation required by the APIB. Finally, the Infant Behavioral Assessment was developed to assess infants from birth to six months of age for the specific purpose of prescribing interaction styles to match infant behaviors.

Source: Margaret Q. Miller and Mary Quinn-Hurst. *The American Journal of Occupational Therapy*, June 1994, *48*, pp. 506–513.

MATERNAL CONDITIONS AFFECTING PREGNANCY OUTCOMES

Preconceptual Maternal Conditions

Conditions exist in some women that will affect their own health as well as the development and overall health of a fetus if pregnancy occurs. Actively educating women to these conditions and encouraging them to seek health care and counseling before becoming pregnant is a practice that early educators can adopt. Some of these conditions are diabetes, hypertension, heart disease, drug and alcohol addiction, obesity, age, and some genetic conditions (e.g., cystic fibrosis, PKU, etc.). Attention to risk factors and providing available interventions significantly reduce the risks to both the mother and infant.

Socioeconomic factors play an important role in the prevention of prenatal and natal complications. Poverty influences both living conditions and physical conditions that increase the incidence of prematurity. Limited economic opportunities frequently lead to poor prenatal care, poor diet, and increased complications of pregnancy (e.g., pregnancy-induced hypertension), all of which may lead to premature delivery. Consideration of socioeconomic issues prior to becoming pregnant, with an exploration of available resources, decreases the incidence of complications of pregnancy. Table 4.1 summarizes these conditions.

Prenatal Maternal Conditions

Pregnancy is the condition of the maternal uterus carrying a fetus. A **term** pregnancy averages approximately 280 days (10 lunar months or 40 weeks) and terminates in the delivery of a **viable** fetus that is capable of independent life. Delivery prior to the 37th week of pregnancy is considered to be **premature.** Viability within the context of current technology exists at about 23-weeks gestation.

The number of times a woman has been pregnant (**gravida**) and the number of live infants that she has delivered at greater than 20-weeks gestation (**parity**) is important information in giving prenatal care. That is, the more times a woman has been pregnant, the greater risk for problems associated with the pregnancy than for those who have been pregnant fewer times. These problems may include faster labors with quick and uncontrolled deliveries, failure of muscle contraction of the uterus with significant bleeding, and malpositioned placentas. Previous premature delivery also increases the probability of a subsequent pregnancy ending in premature delivery and earlier in the gestation than the previous delivery.

Table 4.1/ *Preconceptual Maternal Conditions Affecting Neonatal Outcomes*

Condition	Outcome
Chronic disease	Variable effect on the fetus; determination of the condition prior to a pregnant state will decrease the potential effect on the infant
Poverty	Influences both living conditions and physical conditions that increase the incidence of prematurity
Age	Mothers younger than 20 and older than 40 years have an increased risk of spontaneous abortion, toxemia of pregnancy, prematurity, and congenital abnormalities in a fetus
Drug and alcohol use during pregnancy	Produces infants who have lower birth weight, potential addiction, feeding problems, and the possibility of developmental delays and disabilities
Smoking cigarettes	Decreased birth weight and problems associated with decreased blood flow to the placenta
Nutrition	Malnutrition results in decreased available stores of nutrients to the developing fetus; overweight mothers have a higher incidence of gestational diabetes and hypertension
Bacterial and viral infections	Can lead to a multitude of disabilities for the fetus and neonate

Age is an important factor that can be related to the increased incidence of both premature delivery and appearance of physical and genetic abnormalities in the infant. Young women less than 20 and women over 40 have an increased risk of spontaneous abortion, toxemia of pregnancy, premature delivery, and congenital abnormalities in the fetus. These mothers frequently have other risk factors present that increase the possibility of pregnancy complications, for example, socioeconomic factors in young women and health problems (preexisting hypertension, diabetes) in older women.

Socioeconomic standing is an important factor in the incidence of premature delivery. This includes race, culture, shelter, food, money, and social support structures. Studies show that young, single mothers with few support networks have both an increased incidence of unplanned pregnancy and a higher incidence of premature delivery and low birth weight infants (Report of Consensus Conferences, 1987).

Nutrition is one of the most significant factors associated with maternal/infant well-being. Poor nutritional habits along with variations in such preexisting conditions as obesity or malnutrition will severely affect a fetus both during gestation and following birth. Maternal behaviors that promote malnutrition (e.g., anorexia) result in decreased stores of nutrients for the developing fetus. These infants may be born with growth retardation (greater than two standard deviations below the norm on the growth chart) and may have brain injury due to diminished oxygen and nutrition supply caused by a poorly functioning placenta (Villar, do Onis, & Kestler, 1990).

Maternal obesity (20% over the standard weight) can also produce both maternal and fetal problems. Overweight mothers have a higher incidence of developing gestational diabetes (increased blood sugar during pregnancy), which can produce vascular and kidney changes that increase the risk for development of other chronic diseases following the pregnancy. These women are also at higher risk for hypertension during the pregnancy, which increases the possibility of growth retardation in the fetus. Infants born to obese mothers may be large, thereby increasing problems with delivery. Maternal obesity may also produce hypoglycemia (low blood sugar) in the infants, leading to serious neonatal problems.

Maternal **infections** can play a significant role in fetal outcomes. Both bacterial and viral infections can cause a multitude of disabilities for the fetus and neonate. Meningitis, cytomegalovirus, rubella, toxoplasmosis, and many other maternal infections as well as their impact on newborns are discussed elsewhere in this text. Many of these can be avoided by prenatal education and attention to behaviors that place a mother at risk for contacting an infection.

Chronic diseases in mothers may have an effect on a fetus. These conditions include kidney disease, cancer, thyroid disease, Rh sensitization, hypertension, cardiovascular disease, diabetes, genetic disorders (e. g., PKU), respiratory disease (e.g., cystic fibrosis), neurologic disorders (e.g., multiple sclerosis), infectious disease (e.g., hepatitis), psychiatric disorders, and mental retardation. Some of these conditions have a known effect on developing fetuses, and through appropriate prevention measures, risk to the fetus can be decreased.

Utilization of **prenatal care** in which a woman's pregnancy is monitored by a health care professional is statistically the most important factor in decreasing problems associated with any of the maternal conditions. For example, early and consistent care decreases the incidence of prematurity associated with risk factors (Committee to Study Outreach for Prenatal Care, 1988). At the same time, lack of prenatal care is one of the most reliable predictions that problems will occur. Many of the conditions discussed on the following pages could be identified through good prenatal care, thereby reducing risks to mother and infant.

SUBSTANCE ABUSE AND PREGNANCY OUTCOMES

Since **substance abuse** during pregnancy is associated with many disabling newborn conditions and is entirely preventable, more detailed discussion is focused in this area. Alcohol, drugs, and cigarettes are all considered **teratogens.** A teratogen is an agent introduced into the mother's womb that causes either physical or neurological harm to an embryo or fetus. While a range of environmental substances are dangerous, the most common will be discussed here.

Fetal Alcohol Syndrome

Though the in utero effects of alcohol have been acknowledged for centuries (Weiner & Morse, 1988), it was not until the 1970s that the term **Fetal Alcohol Syndrome (FAS)** was officially attached to the constellation of characteristics now considered criteria for this syndrome (Jones, Smith, Ulleland, & Streissguth, 1973; Jones & Smith, 1973). It is estimated that 350,000 infants are born annually in the United States with a lifelong disability caused by prenatal exposure to alcohol (Stevens & Price, 1992). These statistics make FAS the leading known cause of mental retardation.

Children born with FAS may not be identified at birth, and if suspected at some later point, must be medically diagnosed with the syndrome. The three primary characteristics of FAS are:

1. growth deficiency

2. abnormal facial features

3. central nervous system dysfunction
   (Burgess & Streissguth, 1992)

Additionally, the physician must find strong evidence of maternal alcohol consumption during pregnancy (Burgess & Streissguth, 1992). If some, but not all, of the characteristics mentioned are present at birth, and if the mother is known to have been a heavy drinker during pregnancy, these infants will be labeled **Fetal Alcohol Effects** (FAE). Though the latter is not a medical diagnosis, both the cause and the effects may be as serious as in FAS. Fetal Alcohol Effect may also be referred to as Alcohol Related Neurodevelopmental Disorder (ARND).

Infants with FAS are short for their chronological age and tend to weigh less than average. As these children age, they do not tend to catch up to their peers, but they are more likely to be closer to expected weight than height (Streissguth, LaDue, & Randels, 1988). Facial characteristics commonly attributed to FAS include a short, upturned nose, thin lips, wide set eyes, flat midface, epicanthic folds, and ear anomalies (Streissguth, et al., 1988).

The average IQ of individuals with FAS was found to be around 68 (borderline mental retardation), with a range of 20 to 105 (Streissguth, et al., 1988). When academic content is concrete (in early elementary), children with FAS or FAE may do quite well. However, abstract content causes such children to experience increasing difficulties (Burgess & Streissguth, 1992). It is because of the transition in intermediate school years to more abstract content that children with FAS or FAE tend to plateau in terms of academic achievement (Streissguth, et al., 1988).

It is the behavioral characteristics of FAS that are the most distressing for caregivers. Typical behavior patterns may or may not be associated with neurological damage sustained by vulnerable fetuses. That is, for a majority of infants and preschoolers with FAS or FAE, postnatal environments are chaotic and sometimes transient. These conditions alone could cause the kinds of abnormal developmental behaviors seen in children with FAS or FAE. Behaviors seen within this population (not necessarily in all children with FAS or FAE) include hyperactivity and impulsivity, language and communication difficulties (especially in pragmatics), noncompliance, immaturity, and difficulty in self-regulation, judgment, and decision making (Burgess & Streissguth, 1992). Children with FAS or FAE appear to be immune to subtle kinds of consequences (e.g., praise, reprimands) that help others regulate their behavior. Furthermore, this combination of behaviors makes children particularly challenging to parents and educators. For example, children who are hyperactive tend to get into situations in which they are frustrated and become aggressive. Yet, it is difficult to isolate consequences that are effective in changing this impulsive behavior. As these children reach adolescence, their behavior may become more serious, as lack of judgment leads them to steal and lie (Burgess & Streissguth, 1992). These behaviors cause significant concern in terms of adaptation to vocational and community settings.

Etiology   The cause of FAS and FAE is always alcohol consumption during pregnancy. Alcohol crosses the placenta and enters the fetal blood stream. A fetus's immature liver and neurological systems are less capable of metabolizing the alcohol than a mother's systems. Consequently, the alcohol becomes toxic. There is no known safe level of alcohol intake below which point it can be said that a developing fetus would be safe. However, it is probable that such factors as the timing, duration, and overall health of a mother (e.g., age, nutrition, genetics, etc.) interact with the amount of alcohol consumed to influence fetal development (Stevens & Price, 1992). Though the incidence of FAS and FAE is relatively high in some ethnic groups (i.e., American Indians and Native Alaskans), the toxic risk of alcohol to a fetus appears to be the same for all women (Burgess & Streissguth, 1992).

Treatment   FAS and FAE are disabilities that require the mobilization of multiple agency resources. For example, families may require drug rehabilitation before they can be expected to nurture a child with so many needs. An early interventionist may be asked to mediate services by foster care, child protection, mental health, drug rehabilitation, public schools, public assistance, corrections, and public health. None of these agencies working in isolation is likely to be effective in meeting the plethora of needs of families who have children with FAS. Early intervention for children should center around social language, learning weak-rule governed behavior, and sustained attention (Howard, Williams, & McLaughlin, 1994).

Prenatal Exposure to Drugs

Some have suggested that the single most challenging educational problem of the twenty-first century will be the aftereffects of maternal use of recreational drugs during pregnancy. Already, estimates indicate that between 11% and 25% of all newborns in the United States have been exposed to cocaine or other drugs (Chasnoff, 1989). One drug—alcohol—has already been discussed. The other major drugs of choice (as of this writing) are cocaine/crack, methamphetamine, marijuana, and tobacco.

Cocaine/Crack and Methamphetamine   The physiology of these drugs on adults and fetuses is similar, though the drugs themselves vary considerably in price, availability, and addictiveness. Crack is the least expensive and is a crystallized form of cocaine (the powder form). Furthermore, crack provides a more powerful, though shorter lived, high, and is significantly more addictive than either cocaine or methamphetamine. These drugs release neurotransmitters in the synaptic clefts (short gaps) of neurons (Williams & Howard, 1993). The excess chemicals are then picked up by a user's blood stream, where these chemicals (dopamine and norepinephrine) cause the vessels to constrict, resulting in hypertension. In a pregnant woman, the placenta itself constricts, reducing oxygen flow to the fetus.

An intraventricular hemorrhage is bleeding in the brain.

Likewise, fetuses directly exposed to cocaine that crossed the placenta experience similar "highs" along with associated side effects. Since the fetus is unable to metabolize or break down the drug as easily as mom has done, cocaine can stay in a fetal system for up to four times as long as in an adult's system. Primary risks to a fetus include premature birth, placenta previa (Handler, Mason, Rosenberg, & Davis, 1994), abruptio placenta, spontaneous abortion, and neurological damage (Chasnoff, 1987). Intrauterine growth retardation, significantly lower birth weights, shorter gestational periods, and smaller head circumferences have also been associated with the maternal use of cocaine during pregnancy (Chasnoff, Burns, Burns, & Schnoll, 1986). Echograms of the brains of infants who had been exposed to cocaine show residual lesions caused by intraventricular hemorrhaging or stroke (Chasnoff, et al., 1986). However, for most infants, the long-lasting consequences of drug use during pregnancy are generally obscure to neurological diagnosis.

A neonate born to a drug-using mother will not always show signs of prenatal exposure, just as some infants born to alcohol abusers do not. However, those that do have a recognizable constellation of behavioral characteristics. No abnormal attributes in appearance are associated with prenatal cocaine or methamphetamine effects. Neonates who are obviously affected appear to be going through withdrawal: they have an irritating high-pitched cry, clonic tremors, hyperextension, and hypersensitivity to environmental stimuli; are difficult to calm or may sleep extensively (18–24 hours); exhibit excessive movement (resulting in abrasions on their hands and knees), apnea, and gaze aversion (Williams & Howard, 1993). These withdrawal features may persist for a few days, weeks, or months. Perhaps the most enduring and disturbing behavior is hypersensitivity to stimuli, which in some children will remain a serious problem for years.

In infancy and early childhood, though research is still scarce, long-term effects continue to be behavioral. Dixon and Bejar (1989) speculated that the type, location, and distribution of neurological lesions might cause disabilities that could not be clinically identified during infancy or early childhood but would appear later as more complex visual-motor and social-cognition skills are required. The most prominent and widely discussed feature of babies who are drug-affected is their inability to predict or attend to normally effective consequences. Consequences that either punish or reinforce others (e.g., praise or reprimands), do not seem powerful enough to influence the behavior of some of these children. Perhaps as a result, parents report that some children become destructive, aggressive, oppositional, and mean-spirited.

Other associated problems include hyperactivity, attentional deficits, social skills problems, language deficits (especially in language interaction skills), some perceptual difficulties or learning disabilities, and gross motor immaturity. It has also been mentioned by many caregivers that children with long-term effects will experience "behavioral crisis." At the point when environmental demands become too overwhelming to cope with, these children will "lose it" and engage in intensive acting out. One grandmother reported that (unrestrained) her child would run back and forth across a room running into the wall, turning around and running into the opposite wall until she was literally exhausted. Children who are prenatally exposed to cocaine and methamphetamine are not more likely than the general population to have intellectual deficits, but school problems often result from the traits listed above.

Care for children with the symptoms just mentioned needs to be intensive. Yet, parents of these children are often in crisis themselves and unable to cope. Like many children with FAS or FAE, a large percentage of children with prenatal drug exposure are cared for by extended family or foster care families. Even here, families often report that the children are exceedingly challenging and strategies that were used to raise other children have little effect on drug-affected children. To date, the most consistently recommended measures are behavioral self-control training, minimizing environmental stimuli while gradually increasing ability to habituate, use of consistent routine, and language training in natural settings.

Cigarette Smoking Cigarette smoking in North America decreased significantly from the 1970s to the 1980s, with men representing the largest group of quitters or abstainers (Fried, 1993). In fact, during the same period of time, there was a slight, but not appreciable, decrease in the incidence of smoking by women in their childbearing years (Fried, 1993). Furthermore, Fried noted that an increase in the relative proportion of heavy smokers favored women (57% to 31% for men). Almost a third of women over 20 smoke, and approximately 25% of women continue to smoke during their pregnancy (Floyd, Zahniser, Gunter, & Kendrick, 1991). Though cigarettes contain over 2000 active ingredients, nicotine is considered the most deleterious (Zuckerman, 1991).

For unborn children, exposure to tobacco that crosses the placenta causes vasoconstriction of the blood vessels and subsequent hypoxia or reduction of oxygen-carrying capacity of the hemoglobin, due to an increase of carbon monoxide, which binds with the hemoglobin

(Floyd, et al., 1991; Zuckerman, 1991). Beginning very early in pregnancy, this process can have a degenerative effect (i.e., necrosis and reduced thickness) on the integrity of the placenta (Jauniaux & Burton, 1992). Several outcomes that increase infant morbidity and mortality have been associated with maternal smoking before or after birth; these include placenta previa (Handler, et al., 1994), stillbirth, premature abruption, and Sudden Infant Death Syndrome (Fried, 1993). The immediate risks of smoking on newborns include preterm delivery, intrauterine growth retardation, and low birth weight (an average of 200 grams less than infants not exposed to tobacco) (Hakim & Tielsch, 1992; Floyd, et al., 1991; Hanrahan, et al., 1992; Zuckerman, 1991).

Strabismus is a visual condition in which the eyes do not focus together.

There also appears to be a direct dose response relationship between the amount of smoking and the reduction of birth weight (Floyd, et al., 1991; Zuckerman, 1991). It has been estimated that for every additional five cigarettes smoked per day, the newborn's birth weight is lowered by 26% (Kleinman & Madans, 1985). However, when mothers stop smoking either before or during pregnancy, the risk of problems goes down (Floyd, et al., 1991). Apparently, the third trimester of pregnancy is the period most vulnerable to the harmful effects of nicotine (Fried, 1993). For example, Hakim and Tielsch (1992) found that the incidence of strabismus was higher in infants of women who smoked, but only if these women smoked throughout pregnancy.

Prenatal exposure to tobacco is also correlated with a high incidence of lung disease (i.e., bronchitis, pneumonia, tracheitis, and laryngitis), respiratory illnesses, and middle-ear disease (Floyd, et al., 1991; Hanrahan, et al., 1992). Moreover, smoking causes a reduction in breast milk volume and is perhaps the reason why heavy smokers are less likely to breast feed and tend to wean their children sooner (Fried, 1993). As with Down syndrome, the risk of smoke related problems for neonates seems to increase as the age of mothers increases (Wen, Goldenberg, & Cutter, 1990).

Though the findings are somewhat controversial, Lazzaroni et al. (1990) found a 16 g reduction in birthweight and 0.05 cm reduction in birth length for every hour that a non-smoking mother was exposed to second-hand smoke during pregnancy. Also challenged was the finding that the risk of childhood cancer increased substantially for children of women who smoked during pregnancy, even though they were exposed to several known carcinogens (Stjernfeldt, Lindsten, Berglund, & Ludvigsson, 1986).

In analysis of infant development, there is again a relationship between the amount of smoking done by mothers and the degree of developmental delay. In general, children born to heavy smokers tend to do worse on standardized tests of development than infants born to light smokers or nonsmokers (Fried, 1993). Long-term effects of smoking (again dose dependent) indicate that when exposed, children do less well in cognitive and language domains (Zuckerman, 1991). Others have documented an increased incidence of hyperactivity, attention deficit disorders, and learning disabilities (Floyd, et al., 1991; Fried, 1993).

For cigarette smoking, as with other drugs, we should caution that neurologically vulnerable infants may do just as well as uncompromised infants when exposed to responsive caretaking; "...responsive caretaking appeared to be a protective factor for those preterm children with biologic vulnerability" (Zuckerman, 1991, p. 34). In fact, numerous intervening variables interact with prenatal smoking. For example, J. L. Jacobson, S. W. Jacobson, and Sokol (1994) argued that when controlled for drinking alcohol, childhood stature was not affected by smoking at all. Nevertheless, it is impossible to separate the isolated and conglomerate effects of teratogens. In the meantime, it is most reasonable to assume the worst and attempt to eliminate the potential harmful effects of nicotine during and after pregnancy.

Marijuana Use of marijuana during pregnancy is substantially lower than cigarette smoking. Fried (1993) reported that use to be between 1% for heavy users and 6% for infrequent users. When marijuana is smoked, more than half of the psychoactive ingredients are absorbed in the blood and tend then to accumulate in the fatty tissues of the body (Zuckerman & Bresnahan, 1991). Like cigarettes, marijuana increases the maternal carbon monoxide levels

A Parent's Perspective on Fetal Alcohol Syndrome

Interview with James Holden

Part of the difficulty with the diagnosis of fetal alcohol syndrome is there are so many variables we don't know. We don't know how much the parents were drinking, and we know these children often had absolutely no prenatal care. April's mother just showed up at the hospital, had the baby, checked herself out and left.

April was 2–3 months old when we got her. She was in a good home, but a court order had deemed the home was not a culturally appropriate home. They wanted her in a Native American home. But, here again, I think part of the trouble of the system is that, although they offer a wide variety of training for foster parents, those folks really didn't know what to look for. They really didn't know what the danger signs would be. We got this child, and we knew instantly this was not the child we had been led to believe we would be receiving.

She slept all the time and wouldn't take any nourishment. Her little arms and legs were scrawny, and she couldn't do anything that was developmentally appropriate for her age. At three months, you would expect to see her head moving, and she should be responding to light or sound, but she was lethargic; she'd just lie there and not do anything.

Within three or four weeks she started waking up, and we knew immediately it was going to be a battle. She was so flighty even then. As soon as she started waking up, she would start quivering even when we were holding her. She didn't like to be held, to be walked, to be rocked, to be touched, or to be cuddled. We couldn't do anything to comfort her, so she did a lot of screaming.

In addition to April, we also adopted April's cousin, Rueben, and her half-sister, Courtney. As we get closer to an educational experience for these children, we considered Head Start and ECAP, which are great programs, but they're already so heavily weighted with children of color

and children of poverty that we fear our Indian children won't have appropriate models. When we get children in kindergarten who have no social skills, who can't work with large groups or small groups, who are hyperactive, and a lot are on medications, our teachers are just totally overwhelmed.

Our children receive occupational and physical therapy and speech therapy at home. So with three of them, we have our own little group, but there's not much interaction with other children their age. And that really concerns us, because I know there's a lot of children like that out there.

As soon as the children turn three, the therapists may want us to take them in to their offices. You can't blame them; they're getting overloaded too; there are so many of these children. So we have to find treatment for them somewhere, and we would prefer that they be in smaller sessions but with some other children on a consistent basis. I don't see anything like that. Most of the therapists

HOLDEN CHILDREN AT THE OCEAN

want one-on-one. So, as far as working in small groups, these children aren't doing that yet.

These children won't get into the early childhood program in the schools until they're four, unless they're identified as developmentally impaired. Our district has a propensity to identify only those children who have neurological or physical handicaps as eligible for preschool services.

Every time I go to a foster care meeting, or see other foster care folks, we're all saying the same thing. We're talking about terribly, chemically impacted children. These are children who desperately need some kind of intervention for social and behavioral issues, but until they're four, we often can't get services unless they also have a pronounced physical disability.

in the blood, while directly reducing the amount of oxygen passing to the bloodstream. Both these physiological events decrease fetal oxygenation.

Though a few studies have been conducted, there is no consistent finding that maternal use of marijuana would compromise a fetus's or newborn's neurological system (Fried, 1993). Weak evidence indicates that birth weight is negatively influenced by prenatal marijuana smoking (Fried, 1993). Furthermore, Fried (1993) reported that neonates displayed behavior consistent with neurological insult: tremors, heightened reflex response, high-pitched crying, and delayed visual habituation. These observations were consistent with, though much less dramatic, than observations of children prenatally exposed to cocaine and alcohol. Long-term developmental growth seems to be unaffected until later childhood (age 4 to 5), when some evidence suggests deficits in memory and verbal ability (Fried & Watkinson, 1990). These findings have not been consistently replicated and may reflect differences in factors other than marijuana smoking.

COMMON CONDITIONS OF GESTATION

The following conditions are frequently seen during gestation. They lead both to the need for advanced intervention for the pregnant woman and also account for the greatest majority of premature deliveries. Education of the pregnant woman, through prenatal care, to look for signs of complications can decrease the incidence of problems to the fetus. Table 4.2 summarizes these conditions.

Placenta Previa

Placenta previa is a condition in which the placenta implants in the bottom segment of the uterus instead of the top segment. A normal site of implantation of a fertilized egg is in the upper half of the uterus. When a previa occurs, the placenta implants over the opening of the cervix. Many factors may initiate the onset of sudden and excessive maternal bleeding. These may include contractions of the uterus, intercourse, and excessive fetal activity. This bleeding is generally not painful but can result in a large blood loss over a very short period of time and places the unborn infant at high risk for in utero death from loss of placental function.

Many pregnant women who have a placenta previa will have multiple episodes of bleeding through the second and third trimesters of the pregnancy. Ultrasound is often conducted after the woman has had an episode of bleeding and then seeks care to determine the cause. This will diagnose the condition. Women with known previa are placed in the hospital and on bed rest until the gestation is sufficient for the fetus to be capable of independent breathing after birth. This is to assure that immediate care is available for both the woman and the unborn infant should sudden, excessive bleeding occur from the placenta. The babies are then delivered by cesarean section, and those women who have received consistent care generally are able to carry their infants close to term before delivery is necessary.

Table 4.2/ *Conditions of Gestation*

Condition	Characteristics
Placenta previa	The placenta implants in the bottom segment of the uterus instead of the top segment. Requires bed rest until the fetal gestation is sufficient for independent breathing after birth.
Abruptio placenta	The placenta separates from the wall of the uterus prematurely. Causes decreased availability of oxygen and nutrition, decreased blood flow to the fetal brain with decreased tissue perfusion, and even fetal death.
Toxemia of pregnancy	Causes an elevation in maternal blood pressure, decrease in urine output, and decreased ability of the kidneys to conserve protein and salts, which contributes to swelling of the extremities that may advance to the liver and brain. Reduces blood flow to the uterus, and the placenta then begins to shrink in size causing fetal growth retardation.
Gestational diabetes	Increased blood sugar that is initiated by the pregnancy. Infants may have complex heart defects, be very large size for age, require increased gestation for lung maturation to occur, and experience an increased rate of respiratory distress syndrome.
Rh sensitization	Occurs when a pregnant female who has a negative blood Rh-is exposed to positive blood Rh from her fetus. Thereafter, the mother carries an activated antibody against Rh-positive, which will attack any fetus with positive blood Rh. The result of fetal exposure to the maternal antibody is profound fetal anemia requiring blood transfusions.
Premature rupture of the membranes	The water sack that surrounds the fetus breaks prior to the 37th week of pregnancy, often initiating premature delivery. Risk of infection is high.
Premature labor	Onset of regular uterine contractions that produce cervical dilatation prior to the 37th week of gestation. Attempts are made to control the progression of labor until transfer can be made to a facility with a critical care nursery.

Abruptio Placenta

Abruptio placenta is a condition in which the placenta separates from the wall of the uterus prematurely, which is before delivery of the fetus. This can occur at anytime during the gestation and to varying degrees of separation. The impact on both the mother and the fetus can be significant. Partial separation of the placenta will result in vaginal bleeding, which may be small or large, and is generally associated with abdominal pain in the mother. The fetus may be affected by a decreased placental blood flow and may respond by either a drop or an increase of the fetal heart rate. This change in blood flow may have a significant impact on the long-term outcome for the infant. Effects may include decreased availability of oxygen and nutrition, decreased blood flow to the fetal brain, and even fetal death. Chronic abruptions will result in growth retardation along with any of the fetal factors of an acute abruption.

Acute and total abruptio placenta will result in fetal death. When the placenta fully separates from the uterine wall, the fetus loses the supply of oxygen and nutrients that are essential to sustain life. This condition also has significant maternal effects. Many women who have a total abruption lose the ability to maintain their own cardiovascular integrity. Blood clotting is affected, increasing the risk of bleeding from many systems, and may even result in the death of the mother.

Toxemia of Pregnancy (Pregnancy-Induced Hypertension)

A major problem associated with premature delivery is referred to as **toxemia of pregnancy.** This condition presents a variety of symptoms that produce variable effects in individual pregnancies. The exact cause of the cluster of symptoms and why they occur during pregnancy remains unknown, though factors that increase an individual's vulnerability to toxemia have been identified.

As many as 10% of all pregnancies have some evidence of toxemia of pregnancy. This ratio may increase to as high as 25% in mothers who are diabetic. Maternal mortality rates from this condition may be as high as 2%, with fetal mortality rates being approximately 20% (Besinger, Repke, & Ferguson, 1989). Toxemia of pregnancy is present more frequently in very young, pregnant women and during a woman's first pregnancy. Most of the fetal effects are a result of significant prematurity that stems from the urgency to deliver the baby to prevent maternal death and to save the infant.

Symptoms of toxemia generally include an elevation in maternal blood pressure, a decrease in urine output, and a decreased ability of the kidneys to conserve protein and salts. The kidney disorder contributes to swelling in the extremities that may advance to the liver and brain. Blood vessels constrict causing increased blood pressure and constriction of the blood vessels that provide blood flow to the uterus. The placenta then begins to shrink in size causing fetal growth retardation. This process does not happen quickly; rather, it occurs over an extended period of time.

The effects of toxemia of pregnancy on the long-term health of the mother are variable. Chronic conditions may result from the acute illness. These may include permanent kidney and liver damage and, in extreme cases, may leave neurological damage, including stroke or seizures. The fetus will be affected with the multitude of problems that may affect a premature infant.

Maternal Diabetes

Diabetes in a pregnant woman can be present prior to the pregnancy or come about during gestation. Infants of diabetic mothers, regardless of the onset, are at significantly higher risk for natal and postnatal complications.

Gestational diabetes is a condition of increased blood sugar that is initiated by the pregnancy. It is usually diagnosed during the second trimester of the pregnancy through laboratory analysis and is generally controlled through diet but, occasionally, may require the use of supplemental insulin. The condition disappears after delivery occurs and does appear to be a predictive factor for the development of age-onset diabetes later in the mother's life. Mothers who experience gestational diabetes during one pregnancy are also at an increased risk of developing the condition during subsequent pregnancies.

Preexisting diabetes in a woman, who then becomes pregnant, raises many issues for maternal care during gestation. The physiological changes that occur in the human body during gestation have a significant effect on the ability of a woman to maintain normal control of her diabetic condition. Nutritional factors and supplemental insulin needs are inconsistent during the course of the gestation and will, in turn, affect fetal well-being. Precise control of diabetes decreases the risk to a fetus, but this requires a multidisciplinary approach to the pregnancy and a mother who is committed to providing every opportunity to her fetus for normal growth and development.

Infants of diabetic mothers have an increased risk for congenital abnormalities. The most frequently occurring anomalies are complex heart defects. Babies may also be born very large for the gestational age, which increases the possibility for birth trauma. Many of these infants also require a longer gestation for lung maturation to occur and, without this advantage, have an increased rate of respiratory distress syndrome. These infants will also have significant problems with blood sugar control and tend to have difficulty in initiation of normal feedings after birth. That is, they tend to have a decreased ability in the first few days of life to coordinate their sucking, breathing, and swallowing mechanisms which make feeding consistent.

Rh Sensitization

Understanding of the pathophysiology of blood groupings and antibody/antigen responses requires study that is not part of the purpose of this textbook. It is enough to have familiarity with the notion that each human being has a blood grouping that has been inherited from her or his parents. They, in turn, pass the genetic framework to their children. There are situations that arise in which the antigen of the mother and that of the unborn fetus are not compatible. When this occurs, the mother produces antibodies against the fetal blood.

Rh sensitization occurs when a female who has a negative blood Rh is exposed to positive blood Rh. This may occur during a blood transfusion or as a result of a pregnancy when the partner has a positive Rh blood type. Sensitization may occur with any pregnancy, even those that end in miscarriage at a very early gestation. The positive Rh antigen crosses the placenta, and the maternal response to this foreign protein is to produce antibodies against the perceived invasion. This is a normal response of a healthy immune system.

The initial pregnancy in which Rh-positive and Rh-negative blood are involved is not affected, but subsequent pregnancies, in which the mother now has an activated antibody against Rh-positive, will be affected if the fetus has a positive blood Rh. The result of fetal exposure to the maternal antibody is profound fetal anemia. If not diagnosed and treated in utero, the fetus may die or have multiple systems affected by the anemia.

Progress in medical technology and public awareness has significantly decreased both the occurrence of Rh sensitization and the effects of the process on the development of an affected infant. Health care providers have become more aware of all the mechanisms by which mothers may become Rh sensitized and make every effort to treat girls and women of childbearing age in ways that avoid sensitization.

Treatment consists of giving blood transfusions in utero or exchanging the fetal blood to prevent the breakdown of the normal blood cells. Either of these interventions support the affected fetus until the gestation has progressed to viability or the ability of the fetus to breathe outside the uterus has been determined. Severely affected infants may also require exchange transfusions because of the high levels of bilirubin that build up in the bloodstream as a result of the breaking apart of the affected red blood cells. Transfusion is done to prevent the effects of high bilirubin concentrations on normal brain development. Severe mental retardation may occur with very high levels of bilirubin. Prevention of sensitization is now possible with RhoGAM. This destroys any positive cells that enter the maternal circulation, preventing the mother from producing antibodies that will eventually destroy the blood cells of the unborn fetus.

> An antibody is a protein serving the body's immune system. Each type of antibody defends against a specific invader or antigen. Antigens include foreign proteins, bacteria, cancerous cells, and other types of potentially harmful substances. The antibodies produced to fight an antigen adhere to and interact with only the antigen that caused their production.

Premature Rupture of the Membranes

Premature rupture of the membranes is a common initiating factor in premature delivery. The water sack that surrounds the fetus breaks prior to the 37th week of pregnancy. This may either initiate the onset of uterine contractions and subsequent delivery or place the woman and fetus at risk for infection with the loss of the protective barrier around the infant.

The reasons for premature rupture may vary. Though most instances are not explained, an infant who has acquired an infection is thought to initiate the process in many cases. Even with a ruptured sack, the placenta and infant continue to produce fluid, and the woman continues to leak fluid throughout gestation, until delivery occurs. Any bacteria (or virus) that may be present in the vaginal tract of the mother can find their way into the uterus and come into contact with the fetus. Careful observation of the mother and infant for signs of distress or infection can delay a potential delivery. Infants who experience a decreased fluid volume through premature loss of the sack, or because of decreased fluid production, are at risk of interruption of normal physical growth related to the alterations in the environment. However, rupture of the membranes tends to speed up the process of maturation of the lungs in a fetus. An infant's self-protective mechanisms sense impending delivery and actually accelerate the maturation process.

Premature Labor

Regular uterine contractions that produce dilatation of the cervix signal the onset of labor. When contractions and dilatation occur prior to the 37th week of gestation, it is defined as **premature labor.** It is estimated that as many as 10% of all gestations may have episodes of premature labor (Seel, 1986). This rate increases when women are at risk due to aforementioned socioeconomic factors and inadequate prenatal care. Women receiving care tend to be educated regarding warning symptoms of labor and are more likely to seek help before labor has progressed to the point of making premature delivery unavoidable. Many women will have regular uterine contractions prior to delivery. This may result from uterine weight, fetal movement, stress, diet, exercise, and many other factors. However, unless there is cervical change and movement of the cervix from a posterior to an anterior position, premature labor may not be occurring.

Premature labor can be controlled with medication and bed rest. Careful monitoring of maternal conditions and the status of the fetus are critical in any situation in which an attempt is being made to stop labor. If the labor is progressing and delivery is unavoidable, current technology allows for acceleration of fetal lung maturity with medication (within 36–48 hours), which allows a woman undergoing premature labor to deliver her infant with decreased risk. Still, attempts are made to control the progression of labor until the mother can be transferred to a tertiary care center, where the fetus can be delivered directly into a critical care nursery equipped to handle very small infants. These efforts have decreased the impact of premature delivery on the newborn.

> A tertiary care center is a large medical facility that offers comprehensive health care services.

MATERNAL/INFANT NATAL COMPLICATIONS

Labor is precarious for an infant, who is expected to pass from the dependent world of dark, warm liquid to a world that is bright, cold, and dry and requires an independent ability to both breathe and excrete waste products. The physiological adaptations are easier when the labor and delivery process does not place additional stress upon the infant.

Labor is the process in which the mother and fetus work together toward the goal of delivery of the infant. The uterus provides the contractions that produce pressure on the emerging part of the fetus to dilate the cervix. Dilatation is necessary to provide a passage for the infant from the protective environment of the uterus into the world. Labor requires that both the mother and infant participate to successfully complete the process.

Factors may occur that influence the ability of either the mother or the fetus to be effective during the labor and delivery process (see Table 4.3). Maternal factors may include an ineffective labor pattern that:

1. does not produce the uterine pressure necessary for dilatation to occur

2. has too few uterine contractions

3. is accompanied by high-risk maternal conditions, such as toxemia of pregnancy

All place the mother at risk during the labor process. Fetal conditions may also influence the course of the labor and delivery. The normal position for delivery is head down. It is

Table 4.3/ *Maternal/Infant Natal Conditions*

Condition	Characteristics
Dysfunction of labor and/or delivery	Ineffective labor pattern, too few uterine contractions, or maternal conditions that place the mother at-risk for a normal labor process. These may be malposition of the fetus, large size for gestation, and congenital defects that prevent proper positioning.
Prolapsed or entangled cord	The length of time the flow is obstructed can be a critical factor in determining whether the fetus will asphyxiate in utero and die or whether blood flow will be resumed at a point when neurological damage may occur, but the fetus will survive the insult.
Hypoxic-ischemic brain injury	Hypoxia, decreased oxygen levels, and ischemia, death of the cells and tissue due to decreased blood flow, can occur together or separately. Such neurological damage generally includes severe mental retardation, intractable seizures, and spasticity.
Meconium aspiration syndrome	The fetus either gasps before delivery (usually from asphyxia), or meconium is aspirated into the trachea and airways with the first breath of the infant whose mouth and nose have not been cleared of the amniotic fluid that contains meconium particles. This initiates a state of pneumonia.

possible for a fetus to present in an abnormal position. The fetus may be breech (bottom first), transverse (sideways), large for gestation, or have congenital defects that prevent proper positioning to occur. The health status of the fetus also influences its ability withstand labor.

Dysfunctional labor may be improved with the use of medication to increase both the number and strength of uterine contractions. However, if medication is not effective, then delivery by cesarean section may be necessary. Medication must be closely monitored to make sure that the fetus can withstand the increased uterine pressure. In large-for-age infants, their shoulders may fail to pass below the mother's pubic bone, which can cause cord compression that, in turn, may lead to asphyxia. Assessment of the maternal pelvis (by examination) and the estimated fetal size (by ultrasound), prior to the onset of labor, may prevent shoulder dystocia. Anticipation of this occurrence may lead health care providers to surgically deliver the infant.

Prolapsed Cord/Entangled Cord

The **umbilical cord** is the lifeline by which a fetus is connected to the placenta, which is connected to the mother. This structure contains one large blood vessel and two smaller vessels that carry oxygenated blood and nutrients from the fetal side of the placenta to the fetus. The two small vessels return blood with fetal waste products to the fetal side of the placenta, where an exchange takes place across a membrane to the maternal side of the placenta. The cord vessels are protected by a thick membranous cover and a thick jelly-like substance on the inside.

The length of any umbilical cord varies. Length of the cord may be a factor in the likelihood of becoming entangled. In many normal vaginal deliveries the umbilical cord is wrapped around the neck of an infant or, occasionally, around other areas of the body, such as the chest or abdomen. Monitoring equipment used during labor can give care providers information that an umbilical cord may be entangled with an infant's body parts.

If an infant is wrapped up in its own cord, there may be slight and transient decreases in the fetal heart rate during a contraction. Occasionally a fetus may become entangled in the cord during the gestation, decreasing blood flow through the cord. The length of time the flow is obstructed can be a critical factor in determining whether the fetus will asphyxiate in utero and die or whether blood flow will be resumed to permit the fetus to survive the insult. Even though neurologic damage is likely, infants are born without any indications of an in utero insult but display obvious and profound symptoms of neurological deficits after delivery. Symptoms of damage may include seizures, abnormalities in muscle tone, and the absence of primitive reflexes.

Abnormal positioning of a fetus may cause the umbilical cord to fall from the uterine cavity (prolapsed cord) after the mother's water has broken. The normal position of a fetus for a vaginal delivery should be head down. When the fetus is breech (bottom first) or transverse (lying on the side), space is available for a cord prolapse.

Prolapse of the umbilical cord places a fetus at risk for loss of blood flow due to cord obstruction. The presenting part of the fetus can come to rest on the cord and blood flow either significantly decreases or may stop completely. The fetus then experiences asphyxia, and death occurs rapidly. If prolapse occurs, the emerging part of the fetus must be manually held off the cord, allowing for blood flow, and delivery by cesarean section is done immediately. Infants who are delivered rapidly can expect normal recovery, but if a prolapsed cord occurs outside of the health care setting, even if the infant survives, significant neurological damage is likely.

NEONATAL CONDITIONS

Hypoxic–Ischemic Perinatal Brain Injury

Hypoxia (decreased oxygen levels) and **ischemia** (death of the cells and tissue due to decreased blood flow) can occur together or separately. This condition accounts for the largest group of infants with severe nonprogressive neurological deficits that happen prior to and during delivery. Permanent changes in the neurological structure of the brain matter follow such injuries. Such neurological damage generally includes severe mental retardation, intractable seizures, and spasticity.

Hypoxic-ischemic brain injury can occur during gestation or during the labor and delivery process. Any situation that causes a decrease in blood flow or oxygen supply or an increased level of carbon dioxide can result in the condition. The cycle is repetitive, unless intervention (change of position or supplemental oxygen) increases the blood flow again. Infants do not have the reserves of larger children and adults, and smaller decreases in central blood pressure may severely impact blood flow to the brain.

Infants who have experienced either prenatal or natal asphyxia syndrome may have problems with independent respiration and hyperactive responses to the environment. Seizures are often observed between 12 and 72 hours after birth. The earlier the onset of the seizures, the greater the insult on the neurological status of the infant. As many as 80% of these infants experience severe mental retardation, and 50% exhibit spastic quadriplegia (McCormick, 1989).

Brain damage from asphyxia can be determined by diagnostic imaging methods. Death of the brain neurons results in the transformation of brain matter into fibrous tissue. This injured brain matter is ultimately replaced in many areas by cysts and these can be located by scanning methods. Other affected areas of the brain can be identified through the seizure patterns that emerge. Certain seizure patterns are known to evolve from specific brain areas.

Meconium Aspiration Syndrome

Meconium is the accumulation of fetal waste products that collect in the bowel during gestation. The rectum should not relax until after the infant is delivered, but when a fetus experiences asphyxia or when an infant is overdue, the muscles of the rectum relax and meconium is passed by the infant into the amniotic fluid. This results in a green staining of the fluid, which is generally obvious with rupture of the bag of waters. Even mild asphyxia can initiate the passage of meconium and set the infant up for possible aspiration syndrome. This material contains fetal waste products as well as fetal sludge (skin, hair, cells, etc.), which can be swallowed or absorbed through the intestinal wall.

Meconium aspiration syndrome occurs when a fetus either gasps before delivery (usually from **asphyxia**) or when meconium is aspirated into the trachea and airways with the first breath of the infant whose mouth and nose have not been cleared of the amniotic fluid that contains meconium particles. This aspiration can lead to pneumonia, which may be mild to severe. Multiple physical problems can result from aspiration syndrome, affecting the respiratory system, the cardiovascular system, and the neurological system. Permanent neurological dysfunction is common. Chronic lung disease will also place infants at risk for a multitude of neonatal problems.

POSTNATAL CONDITIONS

Many of the postnatal complications that infants encounter are a result of prematurity. In addition, infants affected with congenital abnormalities, congenital infections, acute infections, birth trauma, and many other factors will be found within the neonatal intensive care units in this country. The following discussion addresses only a select few of the conditions that affect these infants. Those discussed frequently result in outcomes that place these infants and young children in early intervention programs. Table 4.4 summarizes these postnatal complications.

Prematurity

Prematurity is one of the biggest issues affecting pregnancy outcomes in our society. Infants delivered before the 37th week of gestation account for a major portion of the health care dollars being spent within the United States (Seel, 1986). Maternal factors that affect gestation have been discussed earlier in this chapter. Interventions to deal with these risk factors will decrease the incidence of premature delivery.

Gestational age is a critical factor in determining what problems a particular premature infant may encounter. Pregnancy dating is not a perfect science and lacks the ability to determine precisely in which week of gestation a particular infant may be (Kline, Stein, & Susser, 1989). Technology currently makes it possible for survival of infants as young as 23-weeks gestation, but these infants have the potential of a multitude of problems that affect them at birth and within the first weeks of life and may follow them into their future. Progression along the continuum of gestation decreases the incidence of the effects of prematurity.

Birth weight, along with gestation, is a more useful indicator of outcome than gesttional age alone. Infants who are both premature and growth retarded (or small for gestational age) have two factors that threaten their prognoses. Infants born at less than 2800 g (6 lb 3 oz) at 38-weeks gestation are considered **low birth weight.** These infants may experience many of the problems commonly associated with premature infants, to varying degrees. These problems may include respiratory distress, apnea (breathing pauses), poor temperature control, and problems with nutrition. Though survival rates for this group are as high as 95%, developmental delays are a concern (Paz, et al., 1995). Such delays may result in lower cognitive ability and poorer school achievement.

Table 4.4/ *Postnatal Conditions*

Condition	Characteristics
Prematurity	Infants delivered before the 37th week of gestation. Consequently, those infants who are both premature and growth retarded (or small of gestational age) have two factors that influence their prognoses.
Intraventricular hemorrhages	Bleeding that may cause brain damage.
Apnea of prematurity	Pauses in breathing due to position or to neurological lapses.
Respiratory distress syndrome	Difficulty breathing caused by the absence of, or a deficiency in the amount of, surfactant present in the lungs of the infant.
Bronchopulmonary dysplasia	Chronic lung disease of infancy.
Patent ductus arteriosus	A cardiac defect that frequently occurs in the very low birth weight and extremely low birth weight infant. This condition can result in increased respiratory distress.
Hypothermia	Low body core temperature, which places the infant at risk for other physical problems, such as increased respiratory distress, low blood sugar, and possibly, intraventricular hemorrhage.
Retinopathy of prematurity	Retinas of premature infants subjected to excess oxygen show an overgrowth of connective tissue surrounding blood vessels. This overgrowth ultimately damages vision.
Anemia	There is a deficiency in the number of red blood cells available to the infant.
Poor nutrition	Difficulty with sucking, swallowing, and breathing coordination and feeding apnea requires either continuous tube feeding or intermittent tube feedings.
Periventricular leukomalacia	A condition of brain development and function that is related to cerebral blood flow both prior to delivery and during the neonatal period; most frequently seen in premature infants; most common and most profound symptom is spastic diplegia.
Failure to thrive	Inability of the infant to maintain or gain weight sufficient for healthy growth and development.

Infants delivered at less than 1500 g (3 lb 5 oz) are considered **very low birth weight.** Such infants may be both premature and/or growth retarded. These infants are at-risk for respiratory distress, bleeding within the brain and surrounding structures, infections, apnea, nutritional problems, and potential visual defects. Infants who are considered growth retarded, within this context, may be at-risk for developmental delays due to a history of extended insufficiency of the placenta to supply adequate nutrition to the fetus during the pregnancy (Low, et al., 1981).

Infants delivered at less than 750 g (1 lb 10 oz) are considered **extremely low birth weight.** Survival rates for these very fragile infants have steadily increased over the last 10 years, and now, the expectation for survival is around 70%. Of these survivors, greater than 45% require some special services that includes special education (Hack, et al., 1994). These infants have the highest risk factors for poor or delayed outcomes. All of these infants will have

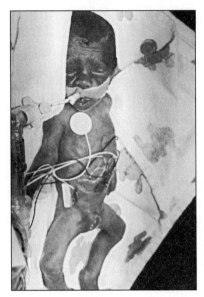
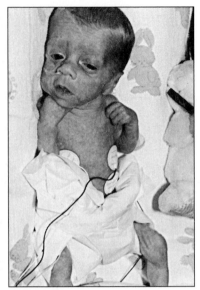
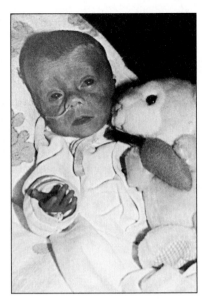

A. 25-week preterm infant on day two of life weighing 800 g (1 lb 12 oz).

B. Same infant at 4 weeks weighing 1200 g (2 lb 10 oz).

C. Infant at 8 weeks weighing 1900 g (4 lb 3 oz) and ready to go home.

Surfactant is a substance secreted by the lungs which permits them to expand.

respiratory distress syndrome (immature lung disease). Even with the advent of artificial surfactant, chronic lung disease and long-term oxygen dependency are the standard.

Extremely low birth weight infants frequently have some degree of intraventricular bleeding, which may cause brain damage. The effects of the bleeding are variable with deficits including a wide range of developmental delays. Visual and hearing deficits are common with these very immature infants. Retinopathy of prematurity (ROP) is a common occurrence caused by the need for long-term oxygen therapy (for apnea of prematurity) and capillary fragility, which may lead to bleeding in the capillaries that supply the retina of the eye. Hearing loss is common and is related to drug therapy necessary for survival and the neurological impact from bleeding or decreased oxygen.

Infection is a frequent complication for the extremely low birth weight infant. The immune system does not become functional for several months after birth, leaving the infant at significant risk for any environmental or human bacteria or virus. Many of the common care needs of the infant, such as intravenous feedings and airway support, place the infant at-risk for the development of an infection.

Nutrition is a major complicating factor with extremely low birth weight infants. The gastrointestinal tract requires the initiation of oral feedings before maturation can occur. The ability of these infants to tolerate oral feedings is extremely variable. Lung disease places the intestine at risk for perforation because of chronic decreased blood flow and lower oxygen levels supplying the system. Lung growth is necessary for healing and this will be compromised in the presence of inadequate nutrition. The interventions to provide sufficient calories for growth impact other organs, such as the liver or kidneys. Long-term, intravenous therapy leads to poor liver function. Failure of the infant to be able to feed increases the potential for total system failure that can ultimately lead to death.

Respiratory Distress Syndrome (RDS)

Respiratory distress syndrome is a common condition found in the premature infant. It is caused by the absence of, or a deficiency in, the amount of surfactant (naturally occurring chemical, lung soap) present in the lungs of the infant. Surfactant increases the surface tension of the lung, allowing the small airways (alveoli) to open and stay open with the respiratory

The Ethics Of Microprematurity

Not a day goes by when current technology does not provide the mechanisms for successful delivery room resuscitation of a fetus that weighs less than 600 g (1 lb 5 oz). The sequence of events that lead to the need to deliver at such a small size and at such a young gestation (usually less than 25 weeks) have changed only slightly over the last 50 years, but the ability of health care providers to respond to the unique physical and psychological needs of these tiny, fragile infants has expanded the horizons of humanity. We now have the capability to provide interventions during the early, critical weeks of life that *may* allow these infants to grow and develop into productive members of our society. In spite of advances, of the approximately 80% who survive, about 20% will have significant neurological deficits, and about 60% will have learning disabilities that require some special education services. Only about 20% of the total population of micropremature infants will emerge from the experience without apparent affects.

How did this happen? The commitment of the United States of America to place a man on the moon opened the doors for a technological explosion that has impacted more than the aviation and electronics world. The need to provide a safe environment for the people involved in the space program led to the development of monitoring systems that overflowed the intended parameters of use into health care. These systems allowed health care providers to expand the knowledge-base about human physiology, and nowhere was this expansion more evident than in the arena of premature and sick newborn care. The ever-increasing base of information being learned from each success provides the groundwork not only for successes in the future but also for the continuation of our ability to preserve life in spite of overwhelming odds.

Fifteen years ago an infant delivered at 1000 g (2 lb 3 oz) stood a 50% chance of dying within the first week of life. This may have been from either immature lungs or bleeding into the brain. Many of the survivors had visual disturbances and evidence of cerebral palsy. The development of artificial surfactants, along with the increased knowledge about premature physiology has moved back the horizon to an unbelievable point. The cost of reaching this point has been enormous. Expenditures of both resources and health care dollars on a small group of individuals is straining the resources available to provide service to the populace at large. Are there answers to the current dilemma? Just how far is society willing to go? Does this discussion only include the tiny premature infant, or does it go beyond that to include the aging population and the belief that immortality is achievable?

The first step toward affecting the problem is a change in the mindset of our society. The belief that prenatal care alone influences pregnancy outcomes must supersede the belief that pregnancy is an absolutely normal human experience that does not require interventions from the scientific community. Though critics of current obstetric practices in this country criticize health care methods, they fail to acknowledge the magnitude of maternal and infant death rates prior to the establishment of a standard of maternity care in this country. Unless we would care to regress to a period where infant mortality rates are substantially higher than they are today, early prenatal care that is continuous and inclusive of newborn care and parenting skills must be available at all levels. This is the first line of defense toward decreasing the number of micropremature deliveries and the long-term costs in both money and resources that are necessary to provide care to these individuals. Current research shows that consistent prenatal care does not necessarily decrease the number of premature deliveries, but it does increase the gestation age at which

(continued)

these infants are delivered and the long-term effects of the premature condition. Larger infants with fewer problems both decrease the cost and improve the long-term quality of life for the involved family.

The major problem that needs to be addressed is what priorities does this society want to establish for its future? Many resources are not replaceable. The expanding horizon is placing an increasing burden on society to support increasing numbers of infants that are salvaged but not saved by the current technology. It is not fair to ask families to bear the burden of providing continuous care to these infants and children without significant support in both time and resources from society. At what point does society support the decision to provide comfort measures and compassion in those cases where advanced interventions appear futile or produce more discomfort than help, with the ultimate end as futile as the beginning? Health care providers, educators, theologians, politicians, and families must come together and initiate discussion about a course for the future.

An essay by P. Port MSN, ARNP/NNP

Dignity, compassion, and caring must be at the core of discussions about our future. It is not reasonable that individuals with high economic security have a larger say in the plan for the future than individuals who are faced with the daily struggle for economic survival. Premature delivery of extremely low birth weight infants can be found in any segment of society, and any discussion of policy must include all segments of our culture.

Reduction in the incidence of micropremature deliveries should be the goal of any plan for the future. Provisions for education and availability of services for those most affected (i.e., young, single, poor, and less educated) are crucial to any discussion having a vision for the future. Questions about age, gestation, weight, and condition also must be addressed. Society must come to terms with our reality in the future. We must be willing to discuss mortality and morality within the context of dignity and compassion and arrive at some general consideration for the course of the future. Regardless of the decisions that evolve in a plan for the future, all positions should have an equal voice in making the hard decisions.

effort of the infant. Decreased amounts, or the absence, of this chemical allow the airways to collapse upon themselves with expiration, and the infant is not able to generate enough pressure to reopen the collapsed segments of the lung. This creates the condition in which there is decreased lung tissue available for the work of providing oxygen to cells and releasing carbon dioxide into the environment. This low oxygen state can ultimately result in neurological damage along with the advent of stiff lungs that require very high pressures to reexpand the collapsed segments.

Infants suffering from respiratory distress syndrome present symptoms of respiratory failure. These include an increased respiratory rate, retraction of the space between the ribs, audible grunting noise when breathing, and a blue-tinged or pale color to the skin, in spite of supplemental oxygen. If the symptoms persist without appropriate intervention, the infant will eventually tire of the effort and quit breathing. Mechanical ventilation is used to treat this disease, as are artificial surfactants, which are given directly into the lungs through a tube placed in the trachea.

Mechanical ventilation has certain risks that are inherent in its use. These include lung damage from increased artificial pressure, tearing of small airways resulting in air leaks between the external lung surface and the rib cage (pneumothorax), bleeding into the lungs from increased pressure, damage to the small capillaries that are part of the circulation pathway (pulmonary hemorrhage), and cystic changes that occur in the airways from pressure (pulmonary interstitial emphysema), all of which can ultimately lead to chronic lung disease of infancy (bronchopulmonary dysplasia). The oxygenation needs of the infant with extreme prematurity frequently lead to chronic lung disease. Cautious use of the ventilator and artificial surfactants decreases the risk factors of respiratory distress syndrome, but many premature infants continue to die or have chronic lung changes from this disease.

Bronchopulmonary Dysplasia (BPD)

Chronic lung disease of infancy is called **bronchopulmonary dysplasia (BPD).** This is the condition in which lung injury has occurred during the treatment of premature lung disease. This can be from the effects of positive pressure from extensive oxygen use. Occasionally a term infant who has had meconium aspiration or acute pneumonia from infection may contract BPD. Health care providers who treat these infants are very aware of the potential implication of the treatments but are committed to provide the necessary intervention for acute respiratory failure and then deal with the effects over the course of the first two to three years of life.

Most extremely low birth weight infants will develop BPD. Estimates place this figure at as high as 80%, with most requiring home oxygen therapy through the first year of life. Aggressive treatment of the accompanying health care problems allows for the possibility of recovery, and many infants show normal lung function over the course of early childhood.

> Symptoms of cardiac failure include weakness, fatigue, swelling, exercise intolerance, and shortness of breath.

Infants with BPD show symptoms of respiratory distress. These include an increased respiratory rate, increased effort for breathing that may be displayed by retraction of the space between the ribs, the use of abdominal and neck muscles to breathe, the need for supplemental oxygen, and pale or dusky skin color. Additional symptoms may be poor tolerance for activities of daily living and symptoms of cardiac failure, which result from the strain placed on the heart and liver by chronic low oxygen levels and the need to maintain circulation through the injured lungs.

Bronchopulmonary dysplasia can also show up as a cluster of health problems for affected infants. These include, but are not limited to, problems with both acute and chronic infections, cardiovascular problems (including high blood pressure), kidney stones, vitamin and mineral deficiencies (which may result in bone fragility), feeding problems, and poor growth. This combination of factors then places these infants at significant risk for developmental delays and often for problems with bonding. The emotional problems are most likely related to repeated and prolonged hospitalizations and irritability that is frequently seen in infants with chronic air hunger from lung disease.

Infants experiencing the effects of BPD can recover. Aggressive attention to the nutritional needs (allows for new lung growth) and the respiratory needs (prevents further deterioration), as well as medication to control cardiovascular effects, provide the time for healing to occur. When incorporated into the efforts of professionals, there is the need for early intervention to allow the child to develop normally within the constraints of his or her physical limitations.

Another significant problem associated with this disease is the dramatic impact on family structure. Many of the care needs of the infant may require skilled nursing. This may mean the addition of strangers to the inner family. Family systems that are already stressed may not survive the additional burdens this chronic disease places on individuals.

Patent Ductus Arteriosus (PDA)

Patent ductus arteriosus (PDA) is a cardiac defect that frequently occurs in the very low birth weight and extremely low birth weight infant (see Appendix A). This condition can result in increased respiratory distress for these infants and may have to be treated with medication or, in some cases, surgically closed at one of the most vulnerable periods, within the first week or two of life.

Neutral Thermoregulation

Low birth weight infants do not have the physical or physiological mechanisms to maintain body temperature. Heat loss occurs rapidly in these infants through convection (heat loss with the delivery of unwarmed gases such as oxygen), conduction (heat loss to unwarmed surfaces such as a mattress), evaporation (heat loss through fluid loss through the skin), and radiation (heat loss through dissipation from the body into the air). **Hypothermia** (low body core temperature) then places the infant at-risk for other physical problems, such as increased respiratory distress, low blood sugar, and possibly, intraventricular hemorrhage. Efforts are taken to preserve body temperature during any interaction with the very immature infant.

Temperature regulation may continue to be a problem for infants with chronic diseases. Poor regulatory mechanisms in infants with neurological deficiencies places them at risk for cold stress in what may appear to be a normal environment. Other conditions that may produce temperature instability are any conditions in which there is decreased blood flow to the skin. This may occur in children who have congenital heart defects or acute and chronic infections or in infants who have problems with lung disease.

Intraventricular Hemmorhage (IVH)

The neurological system is one of the most vulnerable in any infant. This is particularly true for the premature infant. Many factors that affect the blood flow to the brain and surrounding structures may ultimately result in breaking vessels in the capillary bed or leaking of the cell membrane, allowing bleeding to occur. The area of bleeding, the amount of affected area, the age and weight of the infant, and many other physical factors determine the amount of potential damage to function that may occur.

Intraventricular hemorrhage (IVH) may occur rapidly or the bleeding may be slow. Bleeding that is acute and rapid tends to have greater impact on the overall stability of the infant in the acute phase. The bleeding may be so severe as to require blood transfusion to replace blood loss, or it may even result in such rapid deterioration of the overall status of the infant that death may occur.

A ventricular peritoneal shunt is a tube that runs from the fluid-filled cavities of the brain (ventricles) to a cavity in the abdomen, where the extra fluid can drain and thereby reduce pressure on the brain.

Intraventricular hemorrhages are categorized into four grades. The grade of the hemorrhage can be predictive for the long-term outcome of the child, though this is not always accurate. For example, a grade four IVH frequently results in hydrocephalus, or swelling of the fluid-filled cavities in the brain, and the subsequent need for placement of a ventricular peritoneal shunt. These infants require ongoing developmental follow-up after discharge from the hospital and are at significant risk for serious developmental delays.

Many factors that can influence low birth weight infants may result in intraventricular bleeding. Extremes of temperature with rapid fluctuation causes dilatation and constriction of blood vessels, which may cause leakage or rupture of the vessels. Changes in blood pressure affect blood flow in the fragile vessels, also resulting in breakage or leaking. One of the most critical factors is the acid balance of the blood. Infants who are acidotic (high levels of blood acid) are predisposed to fragility of the vessels, which increases the risk of bleeding (Dijxhoorn, Visser, Touwen, & Huisjes, 1987). Acid buildup can occur with lung disease (high carbon dioxide levels and decreased oxygen), low blood sugar, infections, and temperature instability, among other factors. Careful planning of care and attention to handling of infants who are at-risk is critical to decreasing the incidence of serious hemorrhage in the extremely low birth weight infant.

Apnea of Prematurity

Premature infants have a very high incidence of irregular breathing patterns. Pauses in breathing are called **episodes of apnea.** These may be apparent at birth for those infants that do not require ventilation or may develop over the first few days of life. This apnea results from central nervous system immaturity or may be a result of posture in the small infant. Many cases may actually be attributed to a combination of both factors. When pauses occur, the infant's response is generally a decrease in the baseline heart rate. This may be a small decrease or it may be substantial. Many infants will require stimulation by caregivers or, if the apnea is particularly severe, may require mechanical ventilation.

Initial apnea in the infant may not be severe. It is the case in which the infant does not self-stimulate (autoregulatory effect from the nervous system) and proceeds to more profound states of apnea that creates conditions requiring intervention to prevent decreased oxygen to the brain, heart, and kidneys. Failure to appropriately intervene can lead to secondary apnea (respiratory failure/arrest), which is more difficult to reverse. Apnea can lead to the build-up of acid in the blood, placing affected infants at-risk for bleeding into the brain.

Several interventions are possible to decrease the incidence of apnea. These may include continuous external stimulation, such as an oscillating mattress and medications that stimulate the central nervous system to regulate respiration. These methods may be necessary for the first few months of life, until the nervous system has matured sufficiently to have acquired more consistent regulatory control. Many premature infants may be discharged from the hospital with continuous cardiac/respiratory monitoring and medication, provided their caregivers have been educated to appropriately respond to apnea events.

Retinopathy of Prematurity (ROP)

Low birth weight infants face the possibility of damage to their vision because of their size and gestational age. This factor is variable, depending on the ventilation needs of the infant and the necessity for the use of supplemental oxygen during visual maturation.

Retinopathy of prematurity (ROP) was identified as a condition of prematurity in 1951. Retinas of premature infants that were subjected to excess oxygen showed an overgrowth of connective tissue surrounding blood vessels. This overgrowth ultimately obstructed the lens and destroyed the integrity of the normal vascularization process. This condition was initially controlled with the use of less oxygen, but decreased oxygen increased infant mortality rates and created a significantly higher incidence of cerebral palsy. Today, oxygen is administered liberally in an effort to save increasingly smaller premature infants. The mature retina is not affected by increased oxygen use. This is why few term infants have ROP. When given supplemental oxygen, premature infants must be closely monitored in order to keep arterial blood oxygen levels within a range to prevent hypoxia, while minimizing risk of eye damage from the oxygen.

Retinopathy of prematurity is currently categorized into four stages. This parameter of measurement allows the practitioner the knowledge to intervene, when appropriate, and also to counsel families about the implications for future vision and visual needs of the child during the first few years of life. Stage One and Stage Two damage generally resolves completely without treatment. Stage Three damage may require laser treatment, while Stage Four damage will require surgery to attempt to reattach the retina. Most infants who proceed to Stage Four will have significant visual defects from this disease in spite of the surgical intervention.

Anemia

Anemia is the condition in which there is a deficiency in the number of red blood cells available to the infant. This can result either because of a failure in the production of cells or because cells are being used or destroyed faster than they can be replaced. Prematurity results in infants who are affected with anemia for both of these reasons.

Since premature infants have immature bone marrow, production of red blood cells, which takes place in the marrow, is inhibited until the marrow has matured. In addition to the inability to produce new cells, premature infants are nutritionally deficient, especially in iron, which also leads to decreased blood cell production. Even with supplemental iron in the diet, premature infants often are unable to take in sufficient amounts of oral feedings to meet requirements. Infants may become symptomatic with anemia as demonstrated through decreased activity, poor feeding, increased apnea, and slowed weight gain. Premature infants require multiple blood transfusions during their initial weeks of life. Parents now have the option of requesting a Directed Donor in many hospitals. This program allows parents and close family members to donate blood to be used by the individual infant, thus decreasing parent anxiety over multiple blood transfusions.

Nutrition

The ability to eat and then utilize food sources is critical to life. Alterations in either physical or physiological processes that affect eating or digestion place a child at-risk for the development of delays or for an increase in the impact of an existing disability on the course of the child's life. Adequate fluids, sufficient caloric intake of essential proteins, fats, and carbohydrates, as well as vitamins and minerals are essential for growth and development.

Term infants are born with primitive reflexes that allow them to initiate a suck and to coordinate breathing and swallowing. These reflexes disappear as maturation occurs, and the act of eating becomes voluntary. Premature infants, dependent upon gestation, may not have matured to the point of a primitive reflex state. Oral feeding for these infants is not possible. As maturity occurs, these reflexes emerge and learning to eat becomes possible.

Chronic disease in premature infants impacts both the ability to learn to eat orally and the utilization of food sources for growth. Disease requires an increase in caloric intake for maintenance of a minimal state of health and for growth to occur. The combination of events increases the risks that the infant will fail to grow.

Premature infants require a minimum of 120 Cal/kg of body weight each day for growth to occur. Chronic disease will require up to 150 Cal/kg of body weight for the same growth pattern to occur. The expectation is that the infant will gain approximately 15 g (1/2 oz) to 30 g (1 oz) of weight every day. This allows for the linear growth and brain growth that is critical to a normal developmental progression.

Difficulty with sucking, swallowing, and breathing coordination requires tube feedings. Nonnutritive sucking (pacifier) initiates a learning drive in which nutritive sucking becomes possible as a learned behavior. Factors such as fatigue, illness, and congenital defects affect the rate and success of learning.

Occupational therapy may be necessary within the neonatal period to assist in planning care for the premature or sick infant who is feeding poorly and not gaining weight. Many interventions may be tried to provide opportunities for the child to successfully feed. Infants who cannot take a minimal requirement of fluids and/or calories for normal growth may require further interventions to assist in the feeding process. This may involve the placement of a gastrostomy tube or a gastric button through which feedings can be given directly into the stomach, bypassing the esophagus. Even infants who are receiving primary nutrition through a feeding tube are continually orally stimulated to teach them oral feeding.

Failure to Thrive

Failure to thrive can be described as the condition of growth failure in infancy and early childhood. Parameters for determining adequate growth are dependent upon placement in standard growth charts that are guidelines for a normal growth curve. Infants and young children who fall at least two standard deviations below the norm over a designated time period (generally two months) are suggestive of growth failure. This condition may be the result of a multitude of problems that affect the infant. These include, but are not limited to, inadequate economic means for adequate food, chronic disease (congenital heart defects, BPD, etc.), genetic disorders, emotional distress, and abuse. The signs of failure to thrive include decreased weight, decreased height, small head size, and any combination of these. Prolonged failure will ultimately affect brain growth, leading to more complex problems.

CASE STUDY

Adopting High Needs Children

Interview with James Holden

Rueben is one of the foster children we've recently adopted. We brought him home from the hospital, and he is now three years old. Rueben is of mixed ethnic background with an Hispanic father and a Native American mother. He was born full-term, but his mother was using drugs during her pregnancy, though we have never been told what chemical was involved. Rueben developed a seizure disorder early on and also has had a variety of respiratory problems, including asthma and reflux.

When we'd had Rueben for about four weeks, he was released to his grandparents' custody. When he was moved, he went into an emotional withdrawal. He basically gave up and wouldn't eat anything, so he was returned to us in a couple of days. When we got him back, he was in a full fetal position, and it took us about three or four weeks to get him calmed down again. He is still easily alarmed, he doesn't want to be separated from what he knows, doesn't want to be left with anyone else, and he doesn't like strangers or crowds. As we look down the road, we see educational issues looming large in this child's life.

We also adopted two more of our foster children, both relatives of Rueben's. April is also three years old, and she is Rueben's first cousin. She appears to have fetal alcohol syndrome and may be chemically impacted as well. Even at three years of age, she still has pretty marked tremors, a lot of upper torso rigidity, and very low muscle tone development. She is very hyperactive, and has a short attention span. April still has the high-pitched screaming that seems to go with children who are chemically impacted. She doesn't like strangers or crowds, and she sometimes engages in self-stimming activities. She'll take a wet cloth and scrub the same thing for a long period of time.

April is getting a little better, but she's difficult. At this point, she appears to have some pretty good processing skills, and we don't see the traits of mental retardation that usually go with fetal alcohol syndrome, though she does have the physical indicators in her eyes and face. As with Rueben, she's on medication, which is administered through a patch, to calm her down. Without the medication, April was all over the place and was a danger to herself. She wore a helmet when she was younger because she was constantly crashing.

Our third adoptee is Courtney who is the half sister of Rueben. We were called and told, "We have Rueben's half sister in the hospital; would you like her, with a view to adopting her?" Her mother had shown up at the hospital, had the child, and left. We were told she was a normal child. As we were dressing her to take her home, we noticed she had a huge bandage, and she was all wrapped around the middle. Naturally, it made us somewhat curious, so we asked and the nurse said, "Oh, she had an ovarian cyst at birth that they had to remove." When we got her home, she was just a doll, just so cute, but within a short period of time, we began to see problems. She doesn't respond to light or to sound. When she is disturbed, she's like the other two; there's no self-calming mechanism.

Within six months, we had her in the hospital for a test to determine if she could perceive sound waves. The professional and medical folks put the diagnosis in neutral terms; she appears to have some midbrain dysfunction. We don't really know what that is, but if we look it up, it's probably going to scare us. Now that she's two years old, it's fairly obvious to most folks that she is partially blind and partially deaf. She will hold her arms up for anyone to hold her, and it's not until she's in your arms that she is close enough to realize you are not who she thought you were.

Courtney's a very small child with a quick smile, and one of the problems we've had in the school system with these children is that once they are dressed nicely and clean and well-kept, they just float through the system. The kind of comments you get are, "We're having behavioral problems, we're having this, we're having that, but they're such cute little Indian children that..." You just cringe, because

(continued)

*HOLDEN CHILDREN
AT THE OCEAN*

it's probably not in the best interests of the child to allow them to go through life viewed that way.

Courtney still has tremors and muscle tone difficulties, which would indicate there are neurological problems we're dealing with. But after a while you wonder, how many doctors can you have them to, and have them evaluated before you just say, "We're going to have to wait; time will tell."

We have seen some remarkable things with Rueben and April over time. I think the important thing is that we don't look at the history and give up. I am a firm believer that the environment is going to make all of the difference in the world. Sometimes we look at children, even the normal children in my classroom, and we're so overwhelmed by their environment that we forget we're supposed to be in the treatment business. If you can get these children into the right kinds of programs, you can achieve a great deal.

We've taken a lot of children home from the hospital. We were a receiver home for three or four years, where we just had nothing but infants for 8 to 10 days, and then they'd find a home for them. That was kind of fun, because you didn't form any attachments, but when you end up with babies for ten months instead of ten days, it's hard not to form attachments for them.

I'm not sure why we sought adoption. I guess we formed such an attachment for these children, we found ourselves fighting for them. We said, "Hey, this is not right, there's only one hope this child has for a normal existence, and that is if we take on the battle. On the reservation, you see so many high needs children, and you get tired of, "Well, we want them in a culturally appropriate home." That's fine, but make sure that home is also appropriately safe emotionally, physically, and every other way.

Failure to thrive may be termed as either organic (specific physical causation) or as nonorganic (without specific physical cause). Many physical conditions that result in poor growth can be treated with a resultant improvement in growth rates. These interventions may include increasing caloric intake through dietary changes, medications, and the treatment of other physical factors that may impact growth, such as chronic ear infections.

Nonorganic failure to thrive is the more commonly occurring condition. Nonorganic factors that influence the ability of an infant to grow normally include economics, ignorance, poor parenting skills, and ongoing family stresses. Feeding problems arise in these situations, resulting in prolonged malnutrition and, if not corrected, may lead to delayed mental development and, in the most severe cases, may even lead to death of the infant. Many of these infants appear to lose the will to live during periods of profound depression. This can be positively affected most significantly by a nurturing attitude in a consistent caregiver.

The ability to impact failure to thrive in infancy is dependent upon the age at onset, the cause, and the requirements for treatment. The earlier the infant is affected, the poorer the long-term outcome. The initiation of adequate nutrition improves overall growth, but determination of the developmental impact may take a prolonged period. Comprehensive interdisciplinary planning is necessary in severe cases of failure to thrive. Specialized dietary preparations and specialized feeding techniques may be necessary to counteract the behaviors of the infant and its aversion toward feeding. Prolonged nutritional deficits will place the child at-risk for learning problems that may affect gross motor skills, expressive language, and social skills.

POSSIBILITIES FOR THE TWENTY-FIRST CENTURY

One of the greatest challenges for society over the next decade will be to identify and plan interventions for decreasing the impact of prematurity on infants, and their families, and to influence life choices that affect the health of future children. This plan should include education toward prevention, resources toward providing assistance to families involved with children with special needs, and discussion among disciplines regarding approaches that promote optimal functioning among affected children.

STUDY GUIDE QUESTIONS

1. Discriminate between the terms prenatal, natal, perinatal, and postnatal.

2. Explain how prematurity influences the vulnerability of different body systems.

3. Describe the impact of maternal conditions (e.g., age, weight, socioeconomic status, etc.) on fetal growth.

4. What are the defining characteristics of FAS?

5. Why are children with FAS such an enigma to families and professionals?

6. Explain the way in which cocaine and methamphetamine influence a mother and fetus physiologically.

7. What are the "withdrawal" symptoms of neonates affected by cocaine/methamphetamine?

8. Explain the relationship between possible long-term behaviors associated with cocaine/methamphetamine and their treatment.

9. Summarize the influence of tobacco on unborn infants.

10. Is marijuana smoking harmful to a fetus?

11. Describe the following conditions of pregnancy in terms of mechanism and risk to fetuses: placenta previa, abruptio placenta, toxemia

of pregnancy, maternal diabetes, premature rupture of membranes, and Rh sensitization.

12. During labor itself, there are several conditions that place neonates at risk. Identify and describe these.

13. Explain how hypoxia-ischemia places a newborn at risk for developmental delays.

14. What is meconium, and when does it pose a threat to infants?

15. Discriminate between low, very low, and extremely low birth weight.

16. What is the relationship between RDS and BPD?

17. Explain the heat regulation concerns of premature infants.

18. A major concern to early childhood professionals of premature infants is IVH. Explain.

19. Define apnea and describe its relationship to prematurity.

20. ROP is a common outcome of the treatment of prematurity. Explain.

21. What is the relationship between nutritional needs of premature infants and anemia.

22. Define "failure to thrive" and explain the difference between organic and nonorganic failure to thrive.

REFERENCES

Allen, M., & Capute, A. (1990, Supplement). Tone and reflex development before term. *Pediatrics, 393–399.*

Besinger, R.E., Repke, J.T., & Ferguson, J.E. (1989). Preterm labor and intrauterine growth retardation: Complex obstetrical problems with low birth weight infants. In Stevenson, D.K., & Sunshine, P. (Eds.), *Fetal and neonatal brain injury. Mechanisms, management & risks of practice* (pp. 11–33) Toronto: BC Decker Inc.

Burgess, D. M., & Streissguth, A. P. (1992). Fetal Alcohol Syndrome and Fetal Alcohol Effects: Principles for educators. *Phi Delta Kappan, 1,* 24–30.

Chasnoff, I. J. (1987, May). Perinatal effects of cocaine. *Contemporary OB/GYN,* pp. 163–179.

Chasnoff, I. J. (1989, July). *National epidemiology of perinatal drug use.* Paper presented at the conference on Drugs, Alcohol, Pregnancy and Parenting, Spokane, WA.

Chasnoff, I. J., Burns, K. A., Burns, W. J., & Schnoll, S. H. (1986). Prenatal drug exposure: Effects on neonatal and infant growth and development. *Neurobehavioral Toxicology and Teratology, 8,* 357–362.

Committee to Study Outreach for Prenatal Care. (1988). *Prenatal Care: Reaching Mothers, Reaching Infants,* Institute of Medicine, Washington, DC: National Academy Press, 2–7.

Dijxhoorn, M.J., Visser, G.H.A., Rouwen, B.C.L., & Huisjes, H.J. (1987). Apgar score, meconium and acidemia at birth in small for gestational age infants born at term, and their relation to neonatal neurological morbidity. *British Journal of Obstetrics and Gynaecology, 94,* 873–879.

Dixon, S. D., & Bejar, R. (1989). Echoencephalographic findings in neonates associated with maternal cocaine and methanphetamine use: Incidence and clinical correlates. *The Journal of Pediatrics, 115,* 770–778.

Floyd, R. L., Zhniser, M. P. H., Gunter, E. P., & Kendrick, J. S. (1991). Smoking during pregnancy: Prevalence, effects, and intervention strategies. *Birth, 18*(1), 48–53.

Fried, P. A. (1993). Prenatal exposure to tobacco and marijuana: Effects during pregnancy, infancy and early childhood. *Clinical Obstetrics and Gynecology, 36* (2), 319–337.

Fried, P. A., & Watkinson, B. (1990). 36- and 48-month neurobehavioral follow-up of children prenatally exposed to marijuana, cigarettes, and alcohol. *Journal of Behavioral and Developmental Pediatrics, 11,* 49.

Hack, M. Taylor, G., Klein, N., Eiben, R., Schatschneider, C., & Mercuri-Minich, N. (1994). School-age outcomes in children with birth weights under 750 grams. *The New England Journal of Medicine, 331*(3), 753–759.

Hakim, R. B., & Tielsch, J. M. (1992). Maternal cigarette smoking during pregnancy: A risk factor for childhood strabismus. *Archives of Ophthamology, 110,* 1459–1462.

Handler, A. S., Mason, E. D., Rosenberg, D. L., & Davis, F. G. (1994). The relationship between exposure during pregnancy to cigarette smoking and cocaine use and placenta previa. *American Journal of Obstetrics and Gynecology, 170*(3), 884–889.

Hanrahan, J. P., Tager, I. B., Segal, M. R., Tosteson, T. D., Castile, R. G., Vunakis, H. V., Weiss, S. T., & Speizer, F. E. (1992). The effect of maternal smoking during pregnancy on early infant lung function. *American Review of Respiratory Disease, 145*(5), 1129–1135.

Howard, V. F., Williams, B. F., & McLaughlin, T. F. (1994). Children prenatally exposed to alcohol and cocaine: Behavioral solutions. In R. Gardner, D. M. Sainato, J. O. Cooper, T. E. Heron, W. L. Heward, J Eshleman, & T. A. Grossi (Eds.), *Behavior analysis in education: Focus on measurably superior instruction* (pp. 131–146). Belmont, CA: Brooks/Cole.

Jacobson, J. L., Jacobson, S. W., & Sokol, R. J. (1994). Effects of prenatal exposure to alcohol, smoking, and illicit drugs on postpartum somatic growth. *Alcoholism: Clinical and Experimental Research, 18*(2), 317–323.

Jauniaux, E., & Burton, G. J. (1992). The effect of smoking in pregnancy on early placental morphology. *Obstetrics & Gynecology, 79*(5), 645-648.

Jones, K. L., & Smith, D. W. (1973). Recognition of the Fetal Alcohol Syndrome in early infancy. *The Lancet, 2,* 999–1001.

Jones, K. L., Smith, D. W., Ulleland, C. N., & Streissguth, A. P. (1973). Pattern of malformation in offspring of chronic alcoholic mothers. *The Lancet, 2,* 1267–1271.

Kleinman, J. C., & Madans, J. H. (1985). The effects of maternal smoking, physical stature, and educational attainment on the incidence of low birthweight. *American Journal of Epidemiology, 121,* 843–855.

Kline, J., Stein, Z., & Susser, M. (1989). *Conception to birth: Epidemiology of prenatal development. Monographs in epidemiology and biostatistics, Vol.14.* New York: Oxford University Press.

Lazzaroni, F., Bonassi, S., Manniello, E., Morcaldi, L., Repetto, E., Ruocco, A., Calvi, A., & Cotellessa, G. (1990). Effect of passive smoking during pregnancy on selected perinatal parameters. *International Journal of Epidemiology, 19*(4), 960–966.

Low, J., Galbraith, R., Muir, D., Killen, H., Pater, B., & Karchmar, J. (1982). Intrauterine growth retardation: A study of long-term morbidity. *American Journal of Obstetrics and Gynecology, 142,* 670–677.

McCormick, M.C. (1989). Long-term follow-up of infants discharged from neonatal intensive care units. *Journal of the American Medical Association, 261,* 24–31.

Miller, M.Q., & Quinn-Hurst, M. (1994). Neurobehavioral assessment of high-risk infants in the neonatal intensive care unit. *American Journal of Occupational Therapy, 48,* 506–51.

Paz, I., Gale, R., Laor, A., Danon, Y.L., Stevenson, D.K., & Seidman, D.S. (1995). The cognitive outcome of full-term small for gestational age infants at late adolescence. *Obstetrics & Gynecology, 85(3),* 452–456.

Report of Consensus Conferences. (1987). *American Nurses' Association: Access to Prenatal Care: Key to Preventing Low Birthweight,* Kansas City, MO: American Nurses' Association, 24–32.

Seel, E.G. (1986). Outcome of very very low birth weight infants. *Clinics of Perinatology, 13,* 451–459.

Stevens, L. J., & Price, M. (1992). Meeting the challenge of educating children at-risk. *Phi Delta Kappan, 1,* 18–23.

Stjernfeldt, M., Lindsten, J., Berglund, K., & Ludvigsson, J. (1986). Maternal smoking during pregnancy and risk of childhood cancer. *The Lancet, 2,* 519–520.

Streissguth, A. P., LaDue, R. A., & Randels, S. P. (1988). *A manual on adolescents and adults with Fetal Alcohol Syndrome with special reference to American Indians* (2nd ed.). Seattle, WA: University of Washington Press.

Villar, J., do Onis, M., & Kestler, E. (1990). The differential neonatal morbidity of the interauterine growth retardation syndrome. *American Journal of Obstetrics and Gynecology, 163,* 151–158.

Weiner, L., & Morse, B. A. (1988). FAS: Clinical perspectives and prevention. In I. J. Chasnoff (Ed.), *Drugs, alcohol, pregnancy and parenting* (pp.127–148). Lancaster, UK: Kluwer Academic Publishers.

Wen, S. W., Goldenberg, R. L., & Cutter, G. R. et al. (1990). Smoking, maternal age, fetal growth, and gestational age at delivery. *American Journal of Obstetric Gynecology, 162,* 53–58.

Williams, B. F., & Howard, V. F. (1993). Children exposed to cocaine: Characteristics and implications for research and intervention. *Journal of Early Intervention, 17(1),* 61–72.

Zuckerman, B. (1991). Drug exposed infants: Understanding the medical risk. *The Future of Children, 1(1),* 26–35.

Zuckerman, B., & Bresnahan, K. (1991). Developmental and behavioral consequences of prenatal drug and alcohol exposure. *The Pediatric Clinics of North America, 38(6),* 1387–1406.

Conditions Affecting the
Neurological Function

CHAPTER
5

arly childhood special educators are often a family's first link to intervention services and, consequently, also a first bridge between medical treatment and other professional therapies. It is critical, therefore, to have both substantive knowledge and reference information regarding the most common conditions that are associated with neurological damage. Though educators cannot be as intensely trained as medical personnel, a basic understanding of medical procedures and conditions is necessary in order to be conversant with other professionals and with parents.

Early childhood special educators may also find themselves in the role of interpreter for parents and for others who need to understand the medical nature of a child's neurological condition in order to plan effective intervention. Educators can refer to this text to refresh their own understanding of a condition, as well as to help parents interpret information given by health professionals. Though health professionals are often very direct and thorough, a parent's own ability to "hear" such information can be limited by the normal, initial emotional responses to a child's trauma or poor prognosis. Later on, early childhood special educators may be called upon to fill in missing information when parents are better able to "hear" and to understand.

This chapter is devoted to understanding conditions that may affect a child's neurological functioning. This understanding includes knowledge of diagnostic testing, etiological factors resulting in damage to the nervous system, and characteristics of specific medical conditions common to early childhood special education. The neurological system is comprised of the central nervous system (brain and spinal cord) and the peripheral nervous system (12 cranial nerves and motor/sensory nerves in the extremities). Neurological impairments can be so subtle that they can be detected by neither medical nor educational diagnostic techniques. On the other hand, significant damage to the nervous system can affect functions in all developmental domains, including movement, communication, social interactions, and cognitive functioning. Specific permutations of brain damage can also vary. Children with similar etiologies may have seizures, cerebral palsy, mental retardation, or attentional deficits. Some forms of damage to the neurological system occur very early in fetal development; other children may be affected long after birth. Causes of neurological damage include prenatal exposure to toxins, birth trauma and infections, as well as other factors.

DIAGNOSTIC TOOLS

The first step in identifying various medical or disabling conditions is often medical testing. These tests can be expensive, time-consuming, and frightening for families engaged in the process. A simple understanding of the diagnostic tools involved can help alleviate a parent's concern or lack of understanding. Diagnostic tools involve both **invasive** procedures, in which a body system must be penetrated, and **noninvasive** methods, in which the body is not penetrated.

X rays   One of the oldest noninvasive tools used to evaluate an individual's condition is the X ray. X rays are a form of invisible electromagnetic energy that have a short wavelength and are produced by passing a current of high voltage through a Coolidge tube to bombard a target. Because of their very short wave length, X rays are able to penetrate most substances, some substances more easily than others. The density of the tissue and the voltage power used affect the degree to which certain tissue is penetrated by the X rays. These rays make certain substances fluoresce so that the size, shape, and movement of organs can be observed. The X rays themselves are invisible to the human eye but can be captured as an image on a specially coated film by using an instrument called a fluoroscope.

X rays are useful in detecting foreign bodies and fractures or for illuminating radioactive substances that have been introduced to the body. For example, radioactive dye may be injected into a vessel, and X rays can trace the resultant pathway.

Excessive exposure to X rays, especially over a short period of time, can pose a serious health hazard. X rays have the potential to damage living cells, especially those that are dividing rapidly. The risks include damage to bone marrow and other blood-forming organs, damage to genes resulting in genetic/chromosomal mutations (which can be passed to future generations), onset of fetal death or malformation, and the development of cataracts. Such damage is avoided by using the lowest possible radiation doses, by using a lead shield to protect tissue that is not of concern, and by avoiding X rays when there is any possibility of pregnancy. X-ray technicians wear a film badge to monitor their total exposure to radiation. Ironically, while exposure to X rays over a long period of time can be carcinogenic, a primary treatment of cancer is radiation therapy, which is used to destroy cancerous cells.

Computerized Axial Tomography   The Computerized Axial Tomography (CAT scan, also commonly known as CT) was developed in 1972 and was proclaimed the most important diagnostic device to be invented since X rays were first introduced. While operating on similar physical principals as an X ray (radiology), a CAT scan is 100 times more powerful than its predecessor. To conduct this exam, individuals are placed in a circular chamber and are bombarded with focused X rays coming from several planes (e.g., cross-sectional, horizontal). A detector, positioned opposite the X-ray source (scanner), picks up the X rays, which have been absorbed at different rates, depending on the density of the tissue through which they have passed. These measurements are reconstructed using a computer to produce clear, three-dimensional images of body tissue and structure on an oscillating screen. Computerized Axial Tomography scans are used to distinguish interior body structures, lesions, bleeding in the brain, hydrocephalus, and tumors. An advantage of CAT scans over X rays is their ability to detect structures not visible on conventional tests and their ability to evaluate the targeted body part from many different angles simultaneously. Though more expensive and more risky (due to radiation exposure) than ultrasonography, CAT scans are considerably more accurate in detecting such problems as tumors or abscesses (see Figure 5.1).

Magnetic Resonance Imaging   Magnetic resonance imaging (MRI) is a relatively new technology that is now used widely in the diagnosis of abnormalities in cardiovascular, orthopedic, and neurological systems. Unlike CAT scans and X rays, magnetic resonance imaging does not rely on radiation, thereby reducing the risks of radiation exposure. Instead, a powerful magnetic force is used to attract ions within cells toward the edges of an organ. An image of those ions lined up on the edges of an organ reveals whether an anomaly has occurred, for example, the growth of a tumor, torn cartilage, or a fracture (see Figure 5.2).

During imaging, a patient lies very still inside a massive, hollow, cylindrical magnet. Children may be given a powerful sedative or even general anesthetic for the average half-hour examination. Short bursts of magnetic power are emitted. These cause the hydrogen atoms in the patient's tissues to line up parallel to each other like little magnets. The machine detects this alignment as an image and a computer processes the information in much the same way as a CAT scan but shows normal and abnormal tissues with greater contrast. The test is particularly valuable for studying the brain and spinal cord, identifying tumors, and examining the heart and major blood vessels.

Figure 5.1/ *CAT scans produce several views or slices of observed body part, as in this illustration of the brain.*

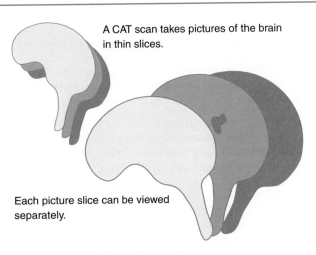

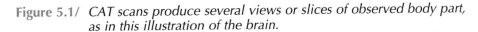

A CAT scan takes pictures of the brain in thin slices.

Each picture slice can be viewed separately.

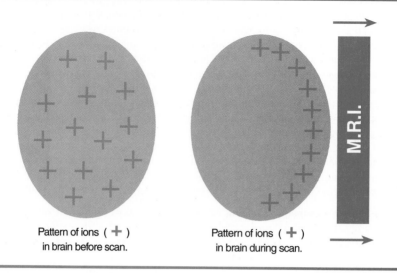

Pattern of ions (+)
in brain before scan.

Pattern of ions (+)
in brain during scan.

Functional Imaging While X rays, CAT scans, and MRIs are useful in analyzing gross anatomical abnormalities, they are not useful in monitoring actual chemical activity. Two relatively new techniques, which have been used largely for research purposes until recently, are capable of measuring this function. Positron emission tomography (PET) and single photon emission computer tomography (SPECT) are noninvasive techniques that are particularly valuable for evaluating neurological disorders.

PET scanning detects positively charged particles that have been labeled with radioisotopes and injected into the blood. Because of their instability, these substances are taken up in greater concentration by areas of tissue that are more metabolically active, such as tumors. Detectors linked to a computer make a picture of how the radioisotopes are distributed within the body. PET scans can detect brain tumors, locate the origin of epileptic seizures, and examine brain function. Similar to the CAT scan, in producing images of the brain in several planes, the PET scan makes a biochemical analysis of metabolism rather than anatomy. PET scanning equipment is expensive to buy and operate, so it is currently available in only a few urban centers, but its contributions are so valuable that it is likely to become more widespread in the future.

PET and SPECT are safe procedures. They require only minute doses of radiation and carry virtually no risk of toxicity or allergy. Advances in radioisotopic scanning depend on the continuing development of radioactive particles specific to certain tissues.

Ultrasonography In this noninvasive procedure, high-frequency sound waves (inaudible to the human ear) are passed through a patient's skin and focused onto the organ of interest. The sound waves travel at variable speeds depending on the density of the tissue through which they are passing. For example, the waves travel through bone much faster than they travel through muscle. The sound waves bounce back to the transducer as an echo and these sounds are then amplified. A computer processes these echoes into electrical energy and displays them on a screen for interpretation. The images are displayed in real time, producing motion on a television screen. The images can then be translated into photographs for permanent examination. A distinct advantage of ultrasound over other techniques is the absence of risk incurred by exposure to radiation as in some other diagnostic techniques (see Table 5.1).

> A radioisotope is an unstable atom that releases a stream of subatomic particles.

Ultrasonography is frequently used during pregnancy to view the uterus and fetus. The technique helps in early pregnancy to establish fetal gestational age, determine if there is a multiple pregnancy, evaluate fetal viability, confirm fetal abnormalities, and guide amniocentesis. Later in pregnancy, an ultrasound may be carried out if the growth rate of the fetus seems slow, if fetal movements cease or are excessive, or if the mother experiences vaginal bleeding.

In the newborn child, ultrasound can be used to scan the brain to diagnose hydrocephalus, brain tumors, or brain hemorrhage and to determine if other organs, such as the kidneys, appear normal. A type of ultrasound is also used in echocardiography to investigate disorders of the heart valves. Doppler ultrasound is a modified version of ordinary ultrasound that can look at moving objects, such as blood flowing through blood vessels and the fetal heart beat in pregnancy.

Electroencephalography   Electroencephalography (EEG) is a conventional noninvasive procedure used to detect normal and abnormal electrical activity within the brain. EEGs detect, amplify, and measure electrical activity on the scalp produced by the brain's neurons. The analysis is typically conducted in a small room designed to eliminate electrical interference and distractions. Small electrodes are placed in a definitive pattern on the scalp but do not produce shock or otherwise aversive stimuli. While the results directly measure only surface activity, changes in electrical activity do effectively represent the activity of deeper structures. These impulses are recorded as brain waves on moving strips of paper.

This diagnostic technique is commonly used to detect the presence of abnormal brain activity that might be related to seizures. Different types of seizures emit differential brain waves. During testing, after an initial baseline is completed, various forms of stress, such as deep breathing or bright lights, may be introduced in order to elicit brain wave patterns typical of seizure disorders.

While EEGs are useful diagnostic tools, they are also more unreliable than many techniques and should be interpreted with caution. For example, approximately 20% of individuals who do not have brain damage will have abnormal readings on electroencephalography. On the other hand, a significant portion of individuals with seizures or other kinds of brain damage will have unaffected EEGs.

The EEG can also be used to evaluate hearing loss. Sounds are introduced through earphones, and the subsequently evoked electrical potentials are amplified via EEG and can then be separated from other electrical activity by computers. The resulting record reveals whether sound has been perceived by the brain.

Arteriogram   Arteriograms, also known as angiograms, are used to examine the blood flow through vessels and organs. Dye is injected into the blood stream while X rays are taken to document the route that the blood flows. Arteriograms are helpful in the diagnosis of con-

Table 5.1/   *Comparison of Diagnostic Tools*

Tool	Risk of Radiation	Powerful Tool	Multiple Analyses	Expense
X ray	X	limited	NA	low
CAT scan	X	X	X	high
Ultrasound	none	limited	X	low
MRI	none	X	X	high
PET/SPECT	low	X	X	high
EEG	none	X	X	high

genital heart defects, such as patent ductus arteriosus, a ventricular septal defect, or tetralogy of Fallot. Cerebral angiography is used to identify abnormalities in blood vessels supplying the brain or to help visualize a tumor prior to surgery.

Arteriograms are not without risk. The dye usually produces a sensation of warmth which may be felt to a greater (and unpleasant) degree in the part of the body where it has been injected. Also, severe allergic reactions to the dye have been common, though new agents are being introduced to reduce the risk of a severe reaction (Clayman, 1989).

Endoscopy   Examination of a body cavity is often done by means of an endoscope, a tube-like instrument with lenses and a light source attached. Modern electronics provides systems that permit physicians to film organ systems of the body. Minuscule cameras, guided by fiber optics, are threaded through channels in the body to identify damage, growths, or blockages. An arterioscope is used to take pictures of the heart. Colonoscopy is conducted when there is suspected damage to the large intestine.

Endoscopy is safe and can be repeated at frequent intervals. Often endoscopy replaces major surgery that would once have been done to view an organ or to take a biopsy sample. Endoscopy is valuable in treatment as well as diagnosis. It is sometimes used to remove polyps (small growths), to retrieve swallowed objects, to provide local application of drugs, and to assist in sterilization operations.

NEUROLOGICAL DISABILITIES

Cerebral Palsy

Cerebral palsy is one of the most common disabilities in our society. It encompasses a broad category of nonprogressive neuromuscular conditions affecting muscle tone, movement, reflexes, and posture. Cerebral palsy results from brain injury sustained during the early stages of development, and though the damage to the brain itself gets no worse during an individual's life, children may develop deformities across time. The original injury to the brain must occur before 16 years of age for the condition to be classified as cerebral palsy.

The incidence of cerebral palsy (approximately 1.5–2.7 per 1000 live births in developed countries and much higher in developing countries) has not changed significantly since the 1960s, even though modern medicine has improved the prognosis of premature infants below 2500 g (5-1/2 lbs) (Rosen & Dickinson, 1992). The rate continues to be high because of the concomitant success in decreasing the mortality of even smaller babies, who do not respond as well as more mature infants to intensive, life-saving medical treatment. For example, from the early 1970s to the mid 1980s, the survival rate of infants with birth weights below 1500 g (3 lbs 5 oz) improved in developed countries from 15%–40% to 75% (Rosen & Dickinson, 1992). In fact, since 1960, there has been a 20% increase in the incidence of cerebral palsy as a result of newborn intensive treatment of very low birth weight infants (Bhushan, Paneth, & Kiely, 1993). However, it is not just premature birth that causes cerebral palsy. Brain damage causing cerebral palsy may occur before, during, or after birth. The physical traits and etiological conditions of persons with cerebral palsy are diverse.

Cerebral palsy is categorized according to the site of cerebral damage, the extent of brain damage, and the parts of the body affected by that damage. Whatever the origin, cerebral palsy causes a functional miscommunication between a person's movement intentions and the subsequent motor responses of the limbs or trunk.

Affected Site   Cerebral palsy can be described by the extent of involvement (affected) if one imagines the body dissected vertically and horizontally (see Figure 5.3). **Hemiplegia** occurs when one side of the body is affected (double hemiplegia involves both sides, with one side

Jennifer Waritz, Searching for a Diagnosis

Interview with Tammy Waritz

Jennifer was born in Montana, in a small rural railroad town. I was very sick throughout my pregnancy, and I can remember saying, "It's just not right, something's wrong." We couldn't get a heartbeat until about six months into the pregnancy, although we had done an ultrasound, so we knew she was there. Everybody thought that she was going to be a big baby and that everything was going to be okay and that I was just being paranoid.

Jennifer's delivery was a repeat Cesarean section, but when she was born, she was blue and immediately began having seizures. Of course, being in a rural area, nobody really knew what was going on, and they just whisked her away before we had an opportunity to hold her. She was placed in the incubator with IVs everywhere and a heart monitor, because she frequently stopped breathing and had to be resuscitated. The doctor, a long-time family friend, was almost in tears when he said, "I don't know what's wrong with Jennifer, but I don't think she's going to make it through the night." I received this message alone in my hospital room.

Jennifer remained in the hospital for another two weeks. The hardest part was to leave her there and to go home without the baby that we had been anticipating for nine months. I returned to the hospital every day for feedings, but it just got to the point that we decided we needed to take her home, regardless.

Jennifer was so fragile; she only weighed 5 pounds 2 ounces and had absolutely no sucking reflex at all. She dropped almost one pound within the first 24 hours; she was so frail, had very low muscle tone (like a limp rag doll), and was almost lifeless. At one point, we were asked to use an alarm blanket that would go off if Jennifer quit breathing. It was really a hard decision to make, but we knew that we would lie awake every night waiting for that buzzer to go off. We felt that if it was her time to go, it was her time to go, so we declined to use the alarm.

We didn't know of anybody else who had a child with these concerns, so there was a period of time when we carried a lot of guilt. We used to think, "What did we do, what did we do? Why did this happen to us? Why is she like this? Why, why, why, why, why?" All these "why" questions, and there were no answers. Not once did we ever get a name and a number of another family who had already experienced all this grief. It would have been most beneficial for us to have been able to talk to someone who really could say, "I understand, and know what you're feeling and going through."

It took us a good three months just to settle in with Jennifer and to feel comfortable and accepting of her. Then, the search was on. We needed to know what Jennifer's condition was; what her diagnosis was. We got connected with a genetics specialist, who told us that Jennifer had a rare condition where the surface of the brain is smooth and she would probably die before the age of two. We were told that if she lived, she would be so severely involved that it would be an extreme burden on the family and that we should consider placing her in an institution. I cried all the way home that day. My husband had an even harder time, and he began to withdraw from Jennifer because he was afraid that he would get too attached and then lose her.

Several months later, I asked the specialist to retest. They found that she did have the ripples on the surface of the brain, but that she had microcephaly; her brain was smaller, but there was definitely a clear cranial pattern. I was told she would be severely disabled; Jennifer is moderately to severely involved, both mentally and physically.

Jennifer (now age 17) has very little speech; she can feed herself, but requires assistance in order to do that. She has to have total assistance to get dressed and bathed, and she's completely incontinent, so she requires diapering. She's mobile in her chair, and she can crawl around and pull herself up onto furniture. Her tests indicate functions somewhere between 12 and 18

(continued)

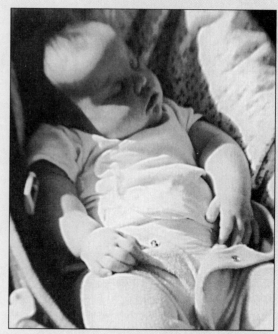

months of age. Socially, she is very much aware and very connected to her environment and probably at a 24-month or above level. That's been our saving grace; she has been such a pleasant child.

Jennifer's condition was just labeled as cerebral palsy, though we were told, "We really don't think that this is what it is, but this is the best term that we can use for her right now." We went through five years of thinking that she had cerebral palsy, but every doctor we saw said, "This is the funniest looking case of cerebral palsy that I have ever seen." Finally we were told that Jennifer's features looked very similar to children who have Kabuki makeup syndrome, so we went to another genetics specialist.

As soon as we walked into the room, the geneticist became very excited. I mean if this man could have done backflips, he probably would have. He was thrilled, "Oh my! Oh my! This is it! This is it!" He started shouting down the hall, "Bring me those papers my colleague in Germany sent me." The research was all on children with Kabuki makeup syndrome, and this colleague of his in Germany was following one of the first Caucasian children to be diagnosed with it and had just sent him this information.

The geneticist looked for all the distinguishing features of Kabuki makeup syndrome: the little lines and the loops in the fingers, the S-shaped eyebrows, the way the corners of her lips turn down, the way her eyes appear to be bigger than her eye sockets, and the retardation in her bone growth. Jennifer demonstrated the syndrome, and they consider her to be one of the most involved cases of the children they know. At the time of her diagnosis, there were only 69 other children who had actually been diagnosed, and most of those were in Japan.

We were pleased to have an answer, to have this diagnosis, but we didn't know anybody else with the same syndrome. There are a whole group of people who have cerebral palsy, and we had been really connected with them. We thought, "Oh, no, now what do we do?" But it was such a relief just to have someone say, we're

almost 100% sure that this is what she has, that these are the features that match this disorder, and we feel comfortable diagnosing her with this. In the meantime, the research is still continuing. The specialists think there is a large number of undiagnosed cases out there and that as the information gets out, Kabuki makeup syndrome will become a common diagnosis, like Down syndrome, and will also have an identified genetic link.

I have met only one other child with Kabuki makeup syndrome. It was such a relief to get that diagnosis and to have a clearer picture of what Jennifer's possible outcomes could be, instead of just guessing all of the time. It was probably even good that I had heard all the worst predictions possible, because I have accepted those things, and I know that's as bad as it could ever be for Jennifer. So every improvement that Jennifer makes, even the smallest improvement, is like a huge milestone for us because we're just one step beyond the possibility of her needing institutionalization; we've been successful at keeping her with us at home, just as we would either of our other children.

more severely impaired, and the arms more affected than the legs) and is caused by traumatic brain injury in the opposite side of the brain. In **paraplegia,** the lower extremities are affected, and in **quadriplegia** (or tetraplegia), all four extremities are involved. Similarly, all four extremities are affected in **diplegia,** with greater involvement of the legs than the trunk and arms. Finally, **monoplegia** and **triplegia** have involvement of one and three extremities, respectively.

Characteristics of Cerebral Palsy   Though definitions vary, the type of cerebral palsy can generally be classified according to the type of muscle movement or muscle tone abnormality manifested. The most common descriptions of the types of cerebral palsy indicate the state of muscle tone, the area of injury within the central nervous system, and the quality of muscle control.

High muscle tone, or **hypertonia,** occurs when the pyramidal tract (the motor cortex and spinal cord) is damaged. Hypertonia eventually limits joint movement because of shortened muscles and ligaments. If this muscle tightness is severe, it contributes to the development of deformities of the spine, joint dislocation, and contractures (Bigge, 1991).

Hypotonia refers to low muscle tone and weakness. Infants born with cerebral palsy are initially hypotonic, but if their floppiness persists through the first year without the development of other tone problems, generalized hypotonia is diagnosed. Hypotonia is often correlated with cognitive deficit. For example, children with Down syndrome are typically hypotonic. Hypotonic infants tend to rely on external support and are delayed in the development of motor skills. They also have poor posture and hypermobile joints.

The pyramidal nerve fibers originate in the brain and pass through the spinal cord to attach to motor cells in the body. When cerebral damage occurs outside the pyramidal nerve group, it is said to be **extrapyramidal,** and the resulting condition is called **athetosis,** or **dyskinesia.** Rather than being responsible for initiation of movement, extrapyramidal nerves are responsible for controlling and coordinating posture, tone, and locomotion. Dyskinesia affects approximately 20% of all children with cerebral palsy. Athetosis, or variable muscle tone, ranges from rigid to flaccid. Injury, often due to jaundice, is responsible for athetosis, which affects all four extremities. Slow worm-like or writhing movements, more pronounced in a child's head and hands, are accentuated when children attempt to move and when they become emotional. Children with athetosis may have difficulty sitting, walking, eating, and speaking. Typically, the excessive movement associated with athetosis is not observed until the second year of life, even though abnormalities in tone, reflexes, and posture can be diagnosed earlier.

With **ataxic** cerebral palsy, which is very rare, children have difficulty balancing well while walking. The cerebellum is the site of injury in this type of cerebral palsy (Bigge, 1991). **Ataxia** interferes with coordination in balancing and hand use. The individual bobbles while

> Jaundice is caused by a build-up of bilirubin (hyper-bilirubinemia) in the basal ganglia.

Figure 5.3/ *Categorization of Cerebral Palsy by Body Part(s)*

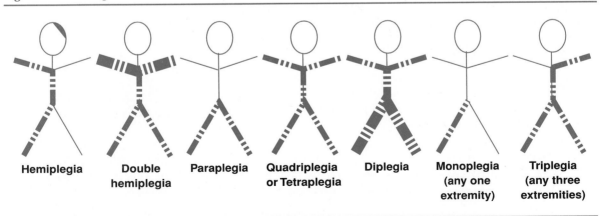

Hemiplegia — Double hemiplegia — Paraplegia — Quadriplegia or Tetraplegia — Diplegia — Monoplegia (any one extremity) — Triplegia (any three extremities)

standing and walking and tends to overshoot a target. Children with ataxia tend to exaggerate movement in an effort to balance, and the constant effort to stabilize can cause rigid movement.

Spastic cerebral palsy, in which the muscle tightens and resists efforts to move, is the most common type and results from injury to the pyramidal tract of the brain, usually due to hemorrhaging after premature birth or severe brain damage (perhaps caused by prolonged oxygen deprivation). Spastic movement has been characterized as a "jackknife" response, in which joints express hyperresistance to extension or flexion up to a certain threshold, and then resistance is suddenly released. The status of a child's tone may change over time; many children have hypotonia in infancy, and this progresses to spasticity.

Naturally, all movement, including that of both large and small muscle groups, can be affected by cerebral palsy. The diagnosis of just one type of cerebral palsy is rare (Bigge, 1991), and it is typical to encounter a diagnosis such as "mixed spastic/athetoid quadriplegia with underlying ataxia." Early in development, signs of neuromuscular damage include the absence of primitive reflexes or the later failure to integrate these reflexes. Hence, development of head control, crawling, sitting, and walking tends to be delayed.

Severity of Involvement A diagnosis of cerebral palsy is almost meaningless unless it is also paired with a description of the degree of **involvement** or the degree to which a child is affected motorically. Variations of motor involvement range from mild to severe, based on the degree to which a child's impairment interferes with independent motor and functional behaviors. Descriptions of the general characteristics of children with mild, moderate, and severe motor involvement are presented in Table 5.2.

Associated Characteristics of Children with Cerebral Palsy Because cerebral palsy results from damage to the central nervous system, interference with normal movement is almost always accompanied by collateral damage to other biological functions such as hearing and cognition. Furthermore, the motor involvement itself affects functioning in a number of skill areas. For example, self-help skills, such as feeding and dressing, are limited by the degree of motor dysfunction.

Table 5.2/ *Diagnostic Criteria for Severity of Cerebral Palsy*

Severe Handicap

1. Total dependence in meeting physical needs
2. Poor head control
3. Deformities, present or potential, that limit function or produce pain
4. Perceptual and/or sensory integrative deficits that prevent the achievement of academic and age-appropriate motor skills

Moderate Handicap

1. Some independence in meeting physical needs
2. Functional head control
3. Deformities, present or potential, that limit independent function or produce pain
4. Perceptual and/or sensory integrative deficits that interfere with achievement of academic and age-appropriate motor skills

Mild Handicap

1. Independence in meeting physical needs
2. Potential to improve quality of motor and/or perceptual skills with therapy intervention
3. Potential for regression in quality of motor and perceptual skills without intervention

Source: Adapted from Grove, N., Cusick, B., & Bigge, J. (1991). Conditions resulting in physical disabilities. In J. Bigge (Ed.) *Teaching individuals with physical and multiple disabilities* (pp. 1–15). Columbus, OH: Macmillan.

Difficulty in feeding children with cerebral palsy, especially those with dystonia, is common (Dahl & Gebre-Medhin, 1993). It has been found that approximately 50% of children with cerebral palsy experience feeding problems and 48% have growth retardation (Thommessen, Kase, Riis, & Heiberg, 1991). The most common feeding problems include poor self-feeding, poor swallowing and chewing from oral-motor dysfunction, and inordinately long feeding sessions. Frequent vomiting, dental problems that cause pain and infection, rumination, reflux, and poor appetite are also not uncommon (Dahl & Gebre-Medhin, 1993; Fee, Charney, & Robertson, 1988). Diets tend to be restricted in texture and taste, as many children are given pureed or powdered foods, which are easy to prepare and feed (Reilly & Skuse, 1992). Subsequently, children's energy intake and nutritional status are frequently compromised; two-thirds of the children studied by Dahl and Gebre-Medhin (1993) were below the 10th percentile for energy intake. To assist in monitoring a child's diet, Fee et al. (1988) identified several physical characteristics that can indicate to a caretaker a child might be malnourished (see Table 5.3). Feeding difficulties apparently begin at birth when a large percentage of infants have difficulty sucking during nursing (Reilly & Skuse, 1992). From direct observations of mealtime, Reilly and Skuse (1992) described typical mothers' behavior as mechanical and lacking in verbalization. They concluded that the stress associated with difficult feeding reduced mothers' typical nurturing. Although maternal behavior returned to normal levels as soon as mealtimes were completed, the loss of this valuable opportunity may be significant in terms of social and linguistic development.

Table 5.3/ *Signs of Malnutrition*

Body Part Affected	Observable Physical Symptoms of Malnutrition	Possible Nutritional Inadequacy
Overall body	Low body weight, short stature, edema (swelling)	Calories Protein
Hair	Looseness, sparseness, dullness	Protein
Skin	Xerosis (dryness), follicular keratosis (growth, e.g., wart, lesion), Solar dermatitis (inflammation) Petechiae, purpura (easy bruising and tiny red patches)	Vitamin A Niacin Ascorbic Acid
Subcutaneous tissue	Decreased subcutaneous tissue	Calories
Nails	Spoon shaped appearance	Iron
Eyes	Dry conjunctiva, keratomalacia (cell death of the cornea)	Vitamin A
Lips	Cheilosis (fissures and dry scaling of the lips)	Iron B-complex vitamins Riboflavin
Gums	Swelling, bleeding	Vitamin C
Tongue	Glossitis	Niacin, folate, riboflavin, vitamin B_{12}
Skeletal system	Bone tenderness	Vitamins C and D
Muscles	Decreased muscle mass	Protein, calories

Source: Adapted from Fee, M. A., Charney, E. B., & Robertson, W. W. (1988). Nutritional assessment of the young child with cerebral palsy. *Infants and Young Children, 1(1),* 33–40.

The overall growth patterns of children with cerebral palsy are substantially depressed when compared to standardized measurements. While measurements are within the normal range by 12 months of age (when corrected for gestational age), many infants have fallen well behind their nondisabled peers in both height and weight (Reilly & Skuse, 1992).

Seizure Disorders   Approximately one-third of children with cerebral palsy also have some form of epilepsy. Children with spasticity are most likely to experience seizures, while children with athetosis are least likely. The most common types of epilepsy observed are tonic-clonic and partial complex seizures.

Mental Retardation   The average incidence of severe mental retardation in accompaniment with cerebral palsy is 25%. By contrast, the majority of children with cerebral palsy have IQs above 50, in spite of the inherent bias built into intelligence tests when used for children with motor impairment. Taken as a group, however, children with cerebral palsy are more likely to have delayed development in sensorimotor behaviors (Cioni, Paolicelli, Sordi, & Vinter, 1993). This makes sense, since these infants and preschoolers are prevented from exploring and interacting with their environments to the same extent as children who have no motor involvement. Figure 5.4 illustrates the comparative results of children with cerebral palsy and nondisabled, same-age peers on measures of cognitive development.

Some types of cerebral palsy are more likely than others to be associated with intellectual deficits. For example, hemiplegia is rarely associated with cognitive deficits when it is not paired with seizures (Vargha-Khadem, Isaacs, Ver Der Werf, Robb, & Wilson, 1992).

Etiology of Cerebral Palsy   It has been held that premature birth and birth complications, such as asphyxia, constitute major causes of cerebral palsy. On the other hand, this assumption has been debated on the grounds that many children who experience birth-related problems do not show signs of motor involvement later in childhood (Grant, Joy, O'Brien, Hennessy, & McDonald, 1989). Further, it does not appear that cesarean delivery reduces the risk of cerebral palsy (Scheller & Nelson, 1994). Even Freud speculated that **Central Nervous System** (CNS) abnormalities preceded both birth complications and the asphyxia commonly associated with cerebral palsy. This stand was supported by a major study conducted by the National Collaborative Parental Project (Eicher & Batshaw, 1993), which revealed that fewer than 10% of all cases of cerebral palsy were the result of asphyxia alone.

Two opposing characteristics of the brain are associated with the long-term prognosis of children who have received neurological insult during the fetal or neonatal period. The developing brain is especially vulnerable to trauma or physiological disruptions. On the other hand, very young nervous systems are more plastic and may repair or compensate for damage at a rate and effectiveness that cannot be matched by older children and adults (Farmer, Harrison, Ingram, & Stephens, 1991). As a consequence, abnormal CAT scans at birth can appear normal 12 months later, with no apparent residual motor or cognitive damage (Eaton, Ahmed, & Dubowitz, 1991). Still, 36% of all cases of cerebral palsy are associated with a birth weight below 2500 g (5-1/2 lbs), and 30% of all cases were attributed to brain damage before or during birth (Rosen & Dickinson, 1992). To illustrate the diversity of circumstances associated with cerebral palsy, Veelken, Schopf, Dammann, and Schulte (1993) delineated the known and probable causes of 53 children with cerebral palsy who had very low birth weight. Table 5.4 provides a sample of these causes, which range from rupture of the umbilical cord to obstruction of the tracheal tube. The resultant motor impairments range from spastic hemiplegia to severe spastic triplegia.

In addition to birth related injury, congenital causes are cited as a second large category responsible for cerebral palsy, though causation in many cases is based on speculation. Naeye, Peters, Bartholomew, and Landis (1989) studied over 40,000 live births, of which 150 (0.37%) were diagnosed with cerebral palsy between birth and age seven. Of those with quadriplegia, 53% had a probable congenital cause, while 35% of the nonquadriplegic cases had a verifiable con-

Figure 5.4 A/ *Results Obtained by Infants with Cerebral Palsy on Tests of Object Permanence Compared with Mean Scores of Unaffected Subjects*

Figure 5.4 B/ *Results Obtained by Infants with Cerebral Palsy on Tests of Causality Compared with Mean Scores of Unaffected Subjects*

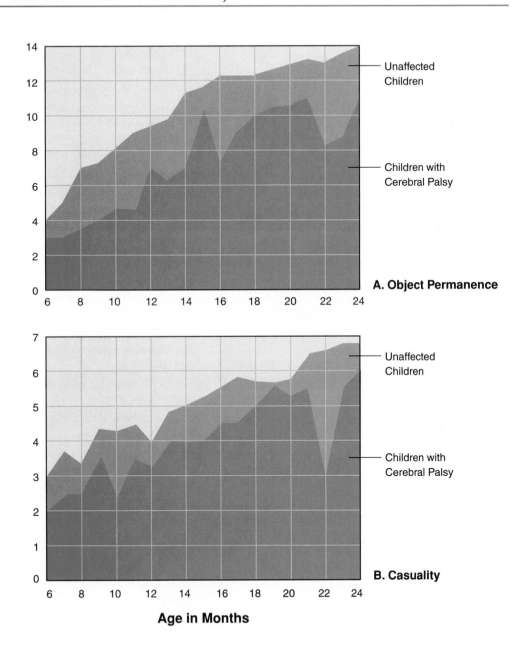

A. Object Permanence

Unaffected Children

Children with Cerebral Palsy

B. Casuality

Unaffected Children

Children with Cerebral Palsy

Age in Months

Source: Adapted from Cioni, G., Paolicelli, P. B., Sordi, C., & Vinter, A. (1993). Sensorimotor development in cerebral-palsied infants assessed with Uzgiris-Hunt Scales. *Developmental Medicine and Child Neurology, 35,* 1055–1066.

Table 5.4/ *Causes of Cerebral Palsy in Very Low Birth Weight Infants*

Type of CP	Timing of Brain Injury	Event Related to Injury
Spastic diplegia, moderate dystonia	Prenatal	Maternal epilepsy, placental bleeding
Dystonia	Prenatal/delivery	Gross cephalic deformity, lifeless at birth
Spastic diplegia, moderate	Delivery	Cord rupture during cesarean section, hypovolemic shock
Spastic diplegia, moderate	Delivery	Marginal placenta, hypovolemic shock
Spastic quadriplegia	Delivery	Cord prolapse, lifeless at birth
Spastic diplegia, severe	Delivery	Severe and prolonged bradycardia, refusal of cesarean section
Spastic hemiplegia	Delivery/ immediate postnatal	Stained amniotic fluid; no resuscitation efforts within 30 minutes after birth
Spastic diplegia, moderate	Neonatal	Intraventricular hemorrhaging; cerebral depression
Dystonia	Neonatal	Repeated resuscitations on day 6 following artificial airway obstruction
Spastic diplegia, moderate	Neonatal	Heart arrest on day 3, resuscitation
Spastic quadriplegia	Neonatal	Severe hypoxia; artificial airway tube obstruction on day 3
Spastic quadriplegia	Later	Encephalopathy of unknown origin in infancy, neurological deterioration
Spastic diplegia, mild	Later	Bacterial meningitis on day 42, neurological and sonographic deterioration
Spastic quadriplegia	Later	Skull fracture, subdural hematoma, neurological deterioration
Spastic diplegia, moderate	Prenatal	Severe placental bleeding, severe decelerations on cardiotocography
Spastic diplegia, moderate	Delivery/ neonatal	Vaginal delivery despite breech presentation, infection with strep B
Spastic diplegia, moderate	Immediate postnatal	Severe cardiac depression after birth
Spastic diplegia, moderate	Immediate postnatal	Cardiac depression after birth, delayed airway management despite severe signs of respiratory distress syndrome
Severe diplegia, moderate	Immediate postnatal	Defect of incubator heating and respirator during transportation resulting in hypothermia and ineffective ventilation
Spastic diplegia, moderate	Neonatal	Hyperkalemia on day 2, fall of hematocrit, intraventricular hemorrhage grade on ultrasound
Spastic diplegia, moderate	Neonatal	Severe apnea and bradycardia on day 2 after extubation
Spastic diplegia, moderate	Neonatal	Dramatic clinical deterioration with seizures day 8
Spastic diplegia, severe	Neonatal	Septicemia with thrombocytopenia on day 2; cardiac arrest, resuscitation on day 4

Source: Adapted from Veelken, N., Schopf, M., Dammann, O., & Schulte, F. J. (1993). Etiological classification of cerebral palsy in very low birthweight infants. *Neuropediatrics, 24,* 74–76.

genital origin. Hence, birth asphyxia accounted for just 14% of the cases of cerebral palsy in the quadriplegic group and a negligible percentage of cases (0.01%) in the nonquadriplegia group.

Cerebral palsy can result from neurological damage after birth as well. Infections such as bacterial meningitis and encephalitis can cause severe neurological damage. Anoxia caused by submersion syndrome (water accidents) or near-suffocation is another cause of cerebral palsy. Prenatal abnormalities such as a reduced blood supply to the placenta, cysts, and abnormal brain development are also associated with cerebral palsy. To a small degree, genetic and metabolic disorders contribute to the incidence of cerebral palsy. Finally, environmental toxins such as prenatal exposure to radiation, industrial waste, and alcohol exposure have been associated with cerebral palsy (Eicher & Batshaw, 1993).

However, it is still apparent that a large percentage of cases of cerebral palsy have no known etiology. It is these cases that sometimes result in unfortunate speculation and self-blaming by families. Professionals may inadvertently add to parent's guilt by asking probing questions about prenatal and perinatal history. In most cases, while such information might be interesting, it is of no functional use and may be better left unprobed.

Treatment of Cerebral Palsy Though many infants and preschoolers with cerebral palsy receive center-based treatment in the form of physical and occupational therapy or special education, these are also usually paired with expectations that parents complete home programs. Much research has been conducted on the efficacy of home programs; yet there continues to be a general lack of follow-through on the part of parents that is not reflective of parents' overall interest in their children's welfare (Hinjosa & Anderson, 1991). Instead, this lack of participation may be due to expectations set by therapists that were perceived by parents to be unrealistic. The following are excerpts from interviews of parents taken by Hinjosa and Anderson (1991):

> I would do it but then, as a mother, I would get frustrated...I was feeling like, "Wow, what is wrong with me?" It was like I was just tired, and it's like they said, "Don't try to take an hour and do it. Do it, like, when you are changing his Pampers, or when you are doing this." But, with me, when I finish his Pampers, I have to move on to something else. 'Cause I have the other child here, I can't, you know, do that. (Irene, p. 275).

> The other therapist told me, "Don't let her walk." I mean, that's like saying, "Don't let her eat." because I can't watch her all the time, and she wants to walk, you know. If it is going to make her become independent and this is what she wants to do, I'm going to let her do it! (Carol, p. 276).

In general, Hinjosa and Anderson (1991) made the following recommendations to therapists regarding expectations for family home intervention:

- Explore the needs of parents and assist them in developing their own interventions, which should foster their own creativity and reinforce their efficacy as the primary caregiver.

- Provide follow-up positive support and feedback related to family solutions and implementation of their own plans.

- Assist parents in developing activities that are consistent with the total family needs and that are realistic.

- Implement collaborative goal selection and treatment plans that are sensitive to a family's daily schedules, and recognize that parents may be unable to follow through as consistently as is recommended.

Research efforts conducted to determine the overall effectiveness of early intervention for infants and preschoolers with cerebral palsy yield mixed findings. Turnbull (1993) concluded that, while some children do no better than could be expected given natural maturation, overall those with and at-risk of cerebral palsy who receive physical therapy experience substantially greater motoric development than those without physical therapy. Other researchers found that young children who received physical therapy alone, progressed at least as well in all domains as those who received short-term infant stimulation and physical therapy (Palmer, et al., 1990).

For children with cerebral palsy, management of physical development is a primary focus in early intervention, as well as later education. Physical therapists may be the primary or only specialists working with families. Their role is to monitor physical development, detect changes in orthopedic status, and to plan and implement specific motor development strategies (Dormans, 1993). It may be necessary for children to wear day and/or night braces, to undergo corrective surgery, or to be fit for orthopedic equipment such as crutches, a walker, or a wheelchair. The goal of physical development however, is to facilitate the greatest amount of movement while concurrently working to diminish interfering abnormal movement or reflexes.

The primary focus of physical management is often positioning and handling. **Positioning** refers to the treatment of postural and reflex abnormalities by careful, symmetrical placement and support of the child's body. Efforts are made to adapt seating and standing equipment so that a child's skeleton can be aligned in a posture that is as normal as possible and to inhibit the effects of primitive reflexes. Parents and teachers can be trained in proper positioning techniques, but an occupational or physical therapist should be consulted for the specific needs of an individual child.

For example, a child with cerebral palsy who still has a dominant asymmetrical tonic neck reflex (ATNR) would extend the limbs on the side of the body toward which the head is turned and flex the limbs on the side of the body that is opposite. If the child is allowed to fall into this position much of the time, some muscles of the body would shorten and might cause contractures that would eventually deform the affected bones and joints. Furthermore, the child's face might be in an awkward position for speech, eating would be difficult, and the child would not be able to bring objects to the midline for functional use.

This child would best be seated in a device adapted to prevent looking to one side, thus inhibiting the ATNR. This might be done by placing blinders to the side of the child's head so that the child looks straight ahead. Any person feeding or talking with the child would approach from directly in front of the child. Now, the limbs could be used at midline in a symmetrical fashion.

A child with low muscle tone might be positioned in a standing device that provides a slight forward incline and straps to support the child's weak muscles and to encourage flexion of the head and arms. This postioning would allow stimulation of the child's weight bearing joints and limbs and keep the child upright to interact with other children and adults.

Handling involves preparation of a child for movement and positioning. A child who is hypertonic and very stiff may be difficult to dress, for example. If the parent or therapist provides gentle shaking or stroking of the child's arms before putting on a shirt, it will be much easier to bend the child's elbow and pull the shirt over as needed. Even soft lighting and music may relax the child's muscle tone in preparation for such an activity. Accurate assessment of an individual child's need for handling is best carried out by an occupational or physical therapist.

In addition to physical therapy, a nutritionist should be involved with families whose children have compromised nutritional intake. However, some general considerations for all children with oral-motor involvement were advised by Fee et al. (1988): frequent short feedings, development of a structured feeding program by a physical and occupational therapist, and increased caloric concentration of food, including nutritional formula supplements.

Seizures

As many as 1 in 10 persons has a seizure at least once in a lifetime. In childhood, approximately 1 in 100 chiidren experiences recurring seizures (Laybourn & Hill, 1994). Seizures are the result of abnormal electrical discharges in cerebral neurons. Different types of seizures result from cortical involvement of different regions of the brain. The physiology of seizures, irrespective of type, is an imbalance between the usual coordinated efforts of neurons that are

excited (activated to perform a function) and those that are **inhibited** (prevented from activating when not needed). When there is either excessive excitatory activity or depressed inhibitory activity (or a combination of both), a seizure may result.

While a person who has a seizure may have **epilepsy,** this is not necessarily the case. Epilepsy is a condition in which seizures are recurrent. Though epilepsy is not provoked by external sources (e.g., metabolic disturbances, exposure to poison, or severe insult to the central nervous system) seizures may be caused by such events. According to Brunquell (1994), all humans have a threshold for seizures, beyond which a clinical seizure will occur. Most person's thresholds are so high that normal life challenges will not push them past these limits. On the other hand, those with multiple daily seizures have very low thresholds as compared to persons who have less frequent seizures. Individual threshold levels are presumed to be both genetically determined and interactive with environmental events (Brunquell, 1994).

There are three categories of epileptic seizures recognized in the International Classification of Epileptic Seizures: **partial** (those that commence from a portion of one cerebral hemisphere), **generalized** (those that involve activation of both cerebral hemispheres), and **unclassified** seizures. In **simple partial seizures**, individuals may be conscious, while consciousness is impaired with **complex partial seizures.** Either of these two conditions may progress to a **partial seizure with secondary generalization,** in which an individual totally loses consciousness.

Of the seizures described above, generalized seizures are the most commonly discussed in educational literature, and these include the following: **absence** (petit mal), **tonic, clonic, tonic-clonic** (grand mal), **myoclonic,** and **atonic** seizures (see Table 5.5). In each of these seizures loss of consciousness is a classification criteria.

Several known causes of seizures have been identified. Most diagnoses are related to

Table 5.5/ *Types of Seizures*

Type of Seizures	Description
Absence	Sudden interruption of ongoing activity and the assumption of a blank stare for 1 to 15 seconds. Usually normal intelligence. Good response to therapy, though many have poor social adaptation and difficulty sustaining attention.
Tonic	Rigid muscular contraction, often fixing the limbs in some strained posture.
Clonic	Alternate contraction and relaxation of muscles, occurring in rapid succession.
Tonic-clonic	Rigid muscular contraction followed by the appearance of clonic activity.
Myoclonic	Sudden, brief, shock-like muscle contractions. Usually normal intelligence, but may experience delays in social development.
Temporal lobe (psychomotor)	Repetitive movements such as chewing, lip smacking, rocking. May have bizarre sensory/emotional changes.
Atonic	Sudden reduction in muscle tone. In more severe cases, persons may slump to the ground.
Infantile seizures	Long-term prognosis is very poor, mental and neurological damage affect over 80% of cases.
Febrile seizures	Tonic-clonic seizures result from high temperatures. Usually do not require medication and terminate when fevers are gone.

factors also associated with other forms of neurological damage. Factors associated with the risk of seizures include perinatal trauma, fetal distress, congenital and postnatal infections (e.g., cytomegalovirus, meningitis, and influenza), teratogens, malformations or tumors, head injuries, and chromosomal abnormalities (e.g., juvenile myoclonic epilepsy resulting from an anomaly of the short arm of chromosome 6).

The relationship between seizures and mental retardation seems to be related to the presence of associated neurological disabilities or severe cognitive delay (Goulden, Shinnar, Koller, Katz, & Richardson, 1991; Shepherd & Hosking, 1989). It seems that the risk of seizures in persons with mild mental retardation who do not have cerebral palsy or other types of disabilities is low (Goulden, et al., 1991). Laybourn and Hill (1994) referred to the relationship between seizures and other risk factors as "epilepsy-only" and "epilepsy-plus." Children in the latter group tend to have a poorer overall prognosis, including greater intellectual impairment, resistance to drug treatment of seizures, and other physical disabilities.

On the other hand, the effects of seizures themselves on cognitive functioning are associated with the type, age of onset, and frequency of seizures. Overall, children with seizures tend to have diminished concentration and mental processing (Dam, 1990). Generally speaking, the earlier the onset of seizures, the poorer the prognosis. Furthermore, each seizure has the potential for causing further brain injury due to a depletion of neurological metabolites. Children are most at-risk of further brain injury when seizures are prolonged for 15 minutes or more, in a condition referred to as **status epilepticus.**

There is some indication that children with seizures are more likely to have behavior problems than children without epilepsy. In general, Austin, Risinger, and Beckett (1992) found five factors which increased the likelihood of behavior problems:

1. female gender

2. families that had high levels of stress

3. families that perceived themselves as having low levels of mastery over family events or outcomes

4. families with little extended family support

5. high frequency of seizures

Approximately 4% of children experience **breath-holding spells** (Morelle, 1993). While these are not seizures, they are involuntary. Usually appearing before 18 months of age, breath-holding tends to disappear by age five. Typically, breath-holding proceeds from a stressful event (e.g., crying or anger) to a change in color, and then to a forceful inspiration. At other times, the breath-holding may be prolonged enough to lead to loss of consciousness, slow pulse, and incontinence. The cause of breath-holding episodes is unclear, though the incidence overlaps with some tonic-clonic seizures (Morelle, 1993), and Procopis (1992) reported a family history in about a third of cases. Medication, though sometimes prescribed, is generally neither necessary nor effective (Procopis, 1992). To assist parents, professionals should provide reassurance and information. For some children, whose temper tantrums precipitate episodes, behavioral intervention may be necessary, though the aim is to change the precipitating behavior and not the breath-holding which is involuntary.

Treatment   Medical treatment of epilepsy includes the use of several drugs (see Table 5.6). Drugs affect children differently than they do adults. For example, Phenobarbital may cause some children to become hyperactive, whereas this drug is generally a sedative in adults (Dichter, 1994). Because of this effect, and the tendency of Phenobarbital to adversely affect cognitive functioning and memory, its use is not recommended for younger children (Dichter, 1994). Sometimes with prescribed medication, a child's seizures will be resistant to a first attempt. Adding a second drug may be successful in eliminating or reducing seizures. However, in 30% of cases, seizures cannot

Table 5.6/ *Drugs Prescribed for the Treatment of Epilepsy*

Category A. Drugs prescribed to compensate for depressed inhibitory neuron functioning

Generic Drug Name	Common Product Name	Use
Barbiturates	Phenobarbital	Sedation; generalized seizures
Valproic Acid	Depakene	Multiple seizure types
Diazepam	Valium	Adjunct for generalized seizure control with other medications
Ethosuximide	Zarontin	Petit mal seizures
Vigabatrin	Sabril	Experimental drug, decreases by 50% seizures that are resistant to other therapy

Category B. Drugs used to counter hyperactive excitatory processes

Generic Drug Name	Common Product Name	Use
Carbamazepine	Tegratol	Partial and generalized tonic-clonic seizures
Phenytoin	Dilantin	Partial and generalized tonic-clonic seizures; experimental for individuals who are therapy resistant
Gabapentin	Neurontin	Individuals who are therapy resistant
Lamotrigine	Lamictal	Experimental for individuals who are therapy resistant
Paraldehyde	Paral/Paraldehyde	Used rectally to stop threatening prolonged seizures

be controlled through medication (Brunquell, 1994). Recent medical advances have made surgery a more viable option for persons with seizures that cannot be effectively controlled by medication (Fish, Smith, Quesney, Andermann, & Rasmussen, 1993). Procedures (i.e., video EEG, CAT scans, MRI, and PET) that have helped evaluate those who are and those who are not candidates for surgery, concomitant with improved surgical techniques, make the procedure safer than in the past. In general, surgery is more effective in improving one's quality of life if done in childhood than if delayed until adulthood (Brunquell, 1994).

Families of children with seizures can be assisted in several ways. As with other children with disabilities, there may be a tendency of parents to treat children with seizures differentially. For example, the potential hazard of having a seizure in traffic, near water, or in other dangerous situations may cause parents to become overcautious. Furthermore, when a seizure happens to occur concurrently with some action, such as enforcement of a family rule, parents may experience guilt and anxiety over future compliance requirements. The social and emotional effect of these family responses may affect sibling and peer relationships. Professionals can offer advice on the importance of consistency in child-rearing practices and normalcy of daily routines. Research indicates that children's overall developmental prognoses are best when they receive high-quality medical treatment and minimal use of drugs (Laybourn & Hill, 1994). Yet, professional educators themselves appear to lack sufficient information on seizures and often lack information regarding the needs of specific children with seizures (Laybourn & Hill, 1994). Since seizures are so common in the early childhood special education population, this knowledge deficit can prevent professionals from serving children and families well. Minimally, professionals should be well-versed on the protocol for treating children with generalized clonic-tonic seizures and aware of the symptoms of common types of seizures (see Table 5.7).

Multidisciplinary services indicated for children and families of children with seizures include medical, counseling, social skills programming, family support, education, and advocacy (Laybourn & Hill, 1994). According to Laybourn and Hill (1994), recent literature on family dynamics has paralleled early childhood philosophy. That is, historically, families were often viewed as needing the assistance of "experts" to help them overcome the emotional and psychological trauma and fear of public attitudes regarding their child's disability. Current efforts contrast this perspective, and focus on the positive aspect of services, which concentrate on the practical financial and medical needs of families. The latter perspective is based on actual data gathered from families who seemed to react sensibly to their children's disabilities and found friends, relatives, and professionals to be sympathetic and helpful.

In contrast, group programs designed to help parents cope with children with epilepsy are perhaps less successful. Hoare and Kerley (1992) established group counseling programs for a large number of parents whose children had recently received a diagnosis of epilepsy. Only 35% of parents expressed interest in the therapy, and only 12% actually attended, with a high rate of attrition in the latter group. A majority of the parents indicated they were not concerned with public attitudes but desired more information about epilepsy and its management. In summary, professionals may be overly concerned with parental coping and not sufficiently concerned with becoming an information resource for parents.

Attention Deficit Hyperactivity Disorder (ADHD)

The term *attention deficit* has been recognized for at least the last half century. In a 1902 address to the Royal College of Physicians, G. F. Still described 20 children in his clinical practice who were aggressive, defiant, and resistant to discipline; these children were excessively emotional or passionate and showed little self-control (Barkley, 1990). Furthermore, these children were described as impaired in attention and quite overactive. The primary symptoms of ADHD have changed very little since 1902, as was evident in the DSM-III-R Diagnostic Criteria for Attention Deficit Disorder, with and without hyperactivity, published by the American Psychiatric Association in 1987. However, in 1994, the terminology relating to ADHD changed with the APA's publication of the *Diagnostic and Statistical Manual of Mental Disorders* (1994). There is much controversy and disagreement among professionals as to the utility and meaning of this term (Bender & McLaughlin, 1995). In spite of this disagreement, descriptions of behaviors associated with the condition have remained remarkably consistent. The overall incidence of ADHD has increased markedly in the past few years. Furthermore, increasing numbers of very young children with ADHD are being identified. Many preschoolers are now medicated daily with drugs intended to reduce activity levels and improve concentration.

Characteristics Primary symptoms of ADHD include inattention, impulsivity, and hyperactivity. Recently Barkley (1993) postulated another primary symptom—poor delay of response. Inattention manifests itself when children fail to attend and concentrate on the task at hand. Preschool children often move from activity to activity, rapidly shifting their attention from one thing to another. If you ask them what they are supposed to be doing, many times they cannot tell you. These children also appear to be distracted by their own thoughts as well as the behaviors of other children and adults. What can be somewhat frustrating and promising is that these children will concentrate for longer periods of time in highly enjoyable activities such as going skiing for the first time.

Table 5.7/ *Treatment Protocol for Generalized Tonic-Clonic Seizures*

The typical seizure is not a medical emergency, but knowledgeable handling of the situation is important. When a child experiences a generalized tonic-clonic seizure, caregivers should follow these procedures.

- Remain calm. Take time to reassure others that the child will be fine in a few minutes; if appropriate remind other children of the correct conduct under these circumstances.
- Carefully lower the child to the floor and clear the area of anything that could hurt her or him.
- Put something flat and soft (like a folded blanket) under his or her head, so it will not bang on the floor as the body jerks.
- Since you cannot stop the seizure, let it run its course. Do not try to revive the child and do not interfere with the child's movements.
- Turn the child gently onto her or his side. This keeps the airway clear and allows saliva to drain away:
    Do not try to force the mouth open.
    Do not try to hold on to the tongue.
    Do not put anything in the mouth.
- When the jerking movements stop, let the child rest until he or she regains consciousness.
- Breathing may be shallow during the seizure, and may even stop briefly. In the unlikely event that breathing does not begin again, check the child's airway for an obstruction and give artificial respiration (remember—no objects in the child's mouth).
- Some children recover quickly after this type of seizure and others require more time. A short period of rest is usually advised. If seizures are routine, caregivers should encourage children and families to maintain daily activities with as little disruption as possible.

Source: Adapted from *Epilepsy School Alert*, Epilepsy Foundation of America, 1987, Washington, DC, Author.

Impulsivity has been viewed as another primary symptom. This can be seen when these children behave in ways that appear to others as though they do not understand the consequences of their actions. These children get into difficulty because they respond too soon and come to decisions too rapidly. They interrupt at meals, cannot take turns at preschool, and interrupt the play of others a great deal of the time.

The third primary symptom of ADHD is hyperactivity. This characteristic is the most widely known and easiest to recognize. Most parents and caregivers describe this characteristic as "always on the go," " in constant motion," "never sitting still," or "always fidgeting, talking, or making noise."

The newest characteristic suggested by Barkley (1993) replaces inattention with disinhibition or poor delay of response. Barkley feels that children with ADHD cannot delay their actions sufficiently and have little use for delay intervals between tasks. Barkley's contribution is based on the earlier work of Bronowski (1967, 1977), who postulated that as our language evolved, humans developed the skill to delay their response to a signal, message, or event. This ability is said to be part of the evolutionary changes of the frontal lobes. Frontal lobe differences can be seen in preschool children who cannot delay between tasks or activities or who respond too quickly to stimuli. There have been several secondary characteristics associated with ADHD, including poor school performance, learning disabilities, delays in speech and language development, poor problem solving abilities, and slightly more difficulties in sensory and motor skills.

Etiology   Since the first edition of Barkley (1981) as well as early classic texts in the field (e.g., Ross & Ross, 1976; Safer & Allen, 1976), considerable research as to the etiology of ADHD has been carried out. This research has been somewhat inconsistent and conflicting in outcomes. Most of the senior researchers in the field view the cause of ADHD as having multiple etiologies (Barkley, 1990; Lerner, Lowenthal, & Lerner, 1995). Various data-based correlates of ADHD have included exposure to toxins in the environment (Marlowe, 1986), gender favoring males (Barkley, 1990), differences in the brain's ability to use glucose fast enough to maintain normal thought (Zametkin, et al., 1991), and inheritability (Anastoploulos & Barkley, 1991). In addition, several theories that have no empirical support, ranging from diet (Conners, 1980) to sugar sensitivity (Milich, Wolraich, & Lindgren, 1986), have been with us for some time and continue to appear in the popular press at this writing. In summary, ADHD is probably a neurobiological disorder that has a strong hereditary and environmental basis. This disorder starts early in childhood and will follow the person for the rest of his or her life (Barkley, 1990; Lerner, et al., 1995).

Treatment   There is a wealth of data regarding the effective treatment of infants and children with ADHD. The information available today is clearly more empirically sound and is directed at both parents and professionals. The primary treatment of preference has been and continues to be stimulant medication therapy. Medication has been shown to be highly effective and of assistance to young children with ADHD (Barkley, 1990). The two most common medications employed have been Cylert (Pemoline) and Ritalin (Methylphenidate). Even with such positive outcomes, the use of medication therapy is not without side-effects that caregivers need to monitor (e.g., tics, weight loss, insomnia, stomachaches, headaches, dizziness, nail biting, reduced speech, irritability, nightmares, sadness, and staring). Recent research has indicated that over half of some children tested displayed the most common side-effects during medication therapy as well as with **placebo** conditions (Barkley, DuPaul, & McMurray, 1991). When two dosages of Ritalin were taken (3 mg/kg versus 5 mg/kg), the most common side-effects were decreased appetite, insomnia, anxiousness, irritability, and proneness to crying under either dosage level. However, many of these side-effects were also found during the placebo phase of the research.

Another common intervention with young children with ADHD has been to employ behavioral parent training in the home (Barkley, 1990). As students become older, behavioral interventions, such as token economies and behavioral contracting, and self-management procedures, alone or in combination with stimulant medication, have been effective at school (Abramowitz, Eckstrand, O'Leary, & Dulcan, 1992; O'Leary, Pelham, Rosenbaum, & Price, 1976; B.F. Williams, R. L. Williams, & McLaughlin, 1991).

Several excellent texts are available for parents who have children with ADHD. These texts are readable and provide parents and caregivers with data-based procedures to assist their children with ADHD. Some of the more notable texts include *Attention Deficit Hyperactivity Disorder* (Greenberg & Horn, 1991), *Dr. Larry Silver's Advice to Parents on Attention Deficit Hyperactivity Disorder* (Silver, 1993), and *Attention Deficit Disorder: ADHD and ADD Syndromes* (Jordan, 1992). In addition there is a wealth of information for teachers and other care providers to assist children with attention deficit hyperactivity disorder. Recent texts include *Attention Deficit Hyperactivity Disorder: A Handbook for Diagnosis and Treatment* by Barkley (1990), *Attention Deficit Disorders and Hyperactivity in Children* by Accardo, Blondis, and Whitman (1991), and Lerner's et al. (1995) text, *Attention Deficit Disorders: Assessment and Teaching.*

A placebo drug is an inactive substance given to persons without their knowledge of the false prescription. The placebo is given to determine if persons benefit because they think they are being aided by a drug, or if the drug itself makes a difference.

CONGENITAL PHYSICAL MALFORMATIONS

Neural Tube Defects

The most critical time for development of the nervous system is between the third and fifth week of gestation (Avey, 1965). It is during this time that the neural groove closes and forms the vertebral column, which houses the spinal cord and is joined to the other soft tissue structures surrounding the nerves. Any disturbance in the developmental sequence will result in incomplete closure. The resulting abnormality can be severe (anencephaly), moderately severe (myelomeningocele), or less severe (meningocele and spina bifida occulta).

Spina bifida is the term used to describe an incomplete spinal column and the relationship of the spinal cord and contents to the defect. The term is frequently used interchangeably with any of the neural tube defects. These include spina bifida occulta, meningocele, and myelomeningocele. Spina bifida affects about 1 out of every 1000 live births in the United States (Marlow & Redding, 1988). Treatment is dependent on the level along the spine at which the defect is located, as well as on the existence of other complications (e.g., hydrocephalus or urinary tract involvement).

Anencephaly   Anencephaly is a congenital malformation in which the brain does not develop and the skull, which would normally cover the brain, is absent. A membrane occasionally covers blood vessels that do develop within the cavity where the brain should be contained. This defect is one of the most commonly occurring neural tube defects and frequently occurs in conjunction with other midline defects of the spinal cord and the spine, which covers the cord.

Anencephalic infants will either be stillborn or die shortly after delivery. Prenatal diagnosis is possible by ultrasound and/or by a laboratory test for maternal or amniotic fluid alpha-fetoprotein (AFP). This protein increases in both the mother's blood stream and in the amniotic fluid when a neural tube defect is present. Genetic counseling is available for families who experience this condition and can be especially valuable when planning future pregnancies.

Development of anencephaly occurs between the 16th and 26th day after conception (Shapiro, 1990). No single factor seems to be responsible for the malformation, though genetic influence may be associated. There is a 5% recurrence rate within families (Shapiro, 1990). Environmental factors have also been linked correlationally to this malformation.

Current medical procedures related to anencephaly have raised some ethical dilemmas. Advances in medical technology have provided the means to defer death in these infants, and concurrently, the ability to successfully transplant organs to otherwise compromised newborn infants. These advances have created situations in which families of prenatally diagnosed anencephalic infants are being given the choice of initiating advanced life support with their doomed infants to provide the opportunity to use normal organs for transplant. Other issues currently under discussion are related to the fetal tissue from such infants being used to treat chronic and debilitating illness (e.g., Parkinson's disease). The implications of these situations continue to be debated within society.

Details about other neural tube defects that occur infrequently may be found in Appendix A. These include:
Arnold-Chiari malformation
holoprosencephaly
porencephaly
agenesis of the corpus callosum

Spina Bifida Occulta   The normal spinal cord is fully protected by bony structures called vertabrae (see Figure 5.5). Spina bifida occulta is an often unnoticed condition in which there is a defect in the vertebrae covering the spinal cord. There is neither exposure of the neural membranes nor evidence of nerve tissue in the defect (see Figure 5.6). Spina bifida occulta is a common occurrence. It is estimated that from 5% to 25% of the general population has some degree of the defect (Matson, 1969). Many cases of spina bifida occulta go undetected. Others are picked up by chance on an X ray that may be done for some other reason. Those that are discovered generally show a skin abnormality that brings attention to the defect. These skin anomalies may include abnormal hair tufts over the coccyx (tailbone) area, a dimple in this area, a "port wine" birth mark, or a cyst. Most individuals do not have any neurological symptoms that accompany the defect.

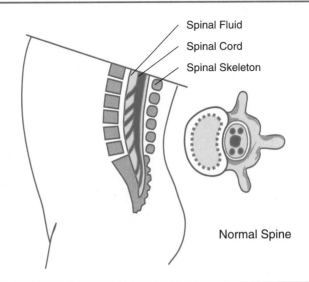

Spinal Fluid
Spinal Cord
Spinal Skeleton

Normal Spine

Some children with spina bifida occulta have symptoms of neurological deficits. These symptoms may include an abnormal gait, positional deformities of the feet, and problems with **incontinence** of urine or stool. Many times these do not become apparent until there is a period of rapid growth. The spinal cord involved in the defect is immobile and therefore does not elongate with the growth of the child. This places tension on the nerve, and symptoms then appear. Treatment is dependent on the noted symptoms and their severity.

Incontinence refers to loss of control when emptying the bowel or bladder.

Meningocele Meningocele is a neural tube defect that generally appears in the lumbar area (near the base of the spine). It is a soft tissue mass that is covered by skin and does not contain nerves or nerve roots. The cerebral spinal fluid (CSF) and meninges are affected in this defect (see Figure 5.7). Meningoceles are sometimes associated with genetic syndromes (Kousseff, 1984).

A meningocele is surgically repaired during the first few days of life. There is generally no paralysis or sensory loss and hydrocephalus rarely occurs. Occasionally there will be breakdown of the skin covering the defect, which increases the risk of infection of the spinal tract. There are sometimes nerve roots trapped within the sac, and this may cause weakness of the legs, but full recovery generally accompanies repair of the defect.

Myelomeningocele Of all the defects that occur under the heading of spina bifida, myelomeningocele occurs the most frequently and has the most significant of the long-term effects. In myelomeningocele, both the spinal cord and its covering, the meninges, push through the skeletal defect to the surface (see Figure 5.8). As with the other forms of spina bifida, this can occur at any level along the spine. The higher the defect occurs in relationship to the head, the more severe the complications for an infant.

There is no known cause for myelomeningocele. Researchers suspect that a combination of factors that include heredity, environment, and possibly vitamin deficiency may be responsible for the occurrence of neural tube defects (Mill, 1989; Mulinare, 1988). The intake of folic acid during pregnancy via prenatal vitamins is known to reduce the incidence of neural tube defects. Neural tube defects occur more frequently in Caucasians and appear to have an increased incidence in the southeastern United States (Alexander & Steg, 1989).

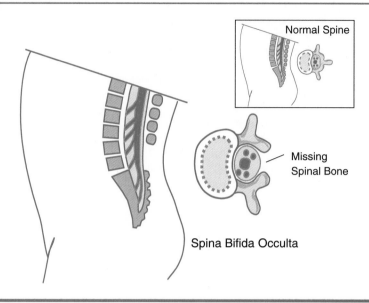

Spina Bifida Occulta

Myelomeningoceles differ in size as well as location. They may be as small as a dime or as large as an apple. The size of the defect is not always the key to the complications that may arise. Severe neurological involvement may accompany a small defect as well as one that is large.

At birth, the defect may be covered with a thin membrane. This is frequently broken during the birth process and cerebral spinal fluid leaks from the open area, placing the infant at significant risk for meningitis. A broken membrane also increases the need for surgery within the first few days of life.

Figure 5.7/ *Internal Schema of Meningocele*

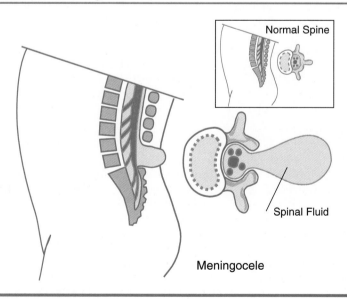

Meningocele

Surgical repair of a myelomeningocele replaces the contents of the exposed sac into the spinal column and closes the defect. Occasionally the defect may be so large that it requires a skin graft to cover the open area of the back. Within the next one- to two-week period, at least 90% of these infants will require a shunt in order to treat hydrocephalus which appears as part of the abnormality (National Institute of Neurological and Communicative Disorders and Stroke, 1986).

Prior to 1960, most infants affected with myelomeningocele were sent home and managed without the benefit of surgery. Fewer than 20% survived the first two years of life, with the majority dying within the first month (Laurence, 1964). In 1959, the University of Sheffield in Sheffield, England, developed a comprehensive plan for the treatment of affected infants. This plan included repairing the spinal defect within the first few days of life, placing a shunt for hydrocephalus, and establishing a home program, using the services of a team of surgeons, physicians, physical therapists, and social workers (Sharrard, Zachary, Lorber & Bruce, 1963). The two-year survival rate increased to over 70% but presented the community with a whole new set of problems. These included providing services for surviving children who had severe disabilities, degrees of bladder and bowel dysfunction, and lower extremity paralysis. These are the problems that continue to affect children with myelomeningocele.

Common problems experienced by infants and children with a repaired myelomeningocele include genitourinary and orthopedic abnormalities. These problems are anticipated within the neonatal period and realized during infancy and early childhood. Defects in the upper lumbar spine area will affect hip flexion and may confine the child to a wheelchair;

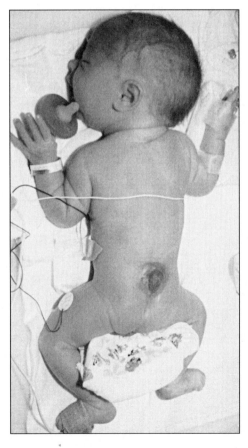

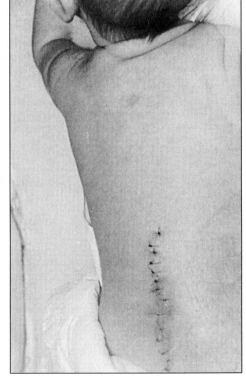

Myelomeningocele before surgery (left)

Myelomeningocele after surgery (right)

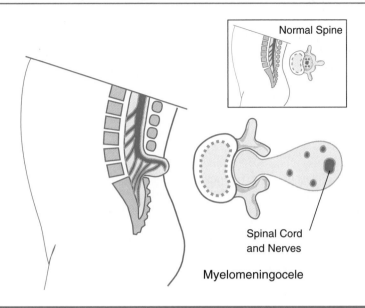

Normal Spine

Spinal Cord
and Nerves

Myelomeningocele

An ostomy is a surgically created opening through the abdomen. In the case of the bladder, the ostomy permits drainage of urine into a pouch which is placed over the opening.

Duodenal atresia is a birth defect where the small bowel is closed and therefore does not allow food to move from the stomach to the large intestine.

whereas, defects in the lower lumbar spine area may allow the child to walk with the aid of braces and crutches. Regardless of the level of the defect, many of these children also have club feet that often require casting.

Many affected children have significant problems with the genitourinary system. Because of the nerve involvement in the lumbar spine, the bladder frequently is atonic (without tone). The bladder becomes distended with urine and lacks the nerve impulses required to empty itself. This buildup of urine provides the perfect setting for bacteria to grow and chronic urinary tract infections place the child at risk for kidney disease. In addition, many of these children lack the nerve impulses for normal bowel control. Rectal muscles lack tone, allowing stool to leak, increasing the opportunity for contamination of the urinary tract with bacteria from feces. These children are also at-risk for problems with skin breakdown, both from decreased circulation and decreased sensation below the level of the defect. Consequently there is a higher rate of chronic infections. Caregivers must be educated regarding the best method of promoting adequate bladder and bowel function to decrease the risks of chronic problems. Methods of prevention may include insertion of a bladder catheter, learning to place downward pressure on the lower abdomen to empty the bladder, administration of antibiotics, or in severe situations, the creation of an **ostomy.**

Many children with myelomeningocele have average to above-average intelligence. This is dependent upon the presence of malformations within the brain that correlate with the defect (e.g., Arnold-Chiari malformations). Opportunities must be provided to allow for these children to reach their full potential in the presence of extensive physical disabilities.

Infants born with myelomeningocele, as with Down syndrome and **duodenal atresia,** are those who initiated what is known as the Baby Doe legislation. These laws were enacted by the Federal Government to protect the rights of infants with birth defects to receive definitive care for correctable defects and supportive care for problems related to defects that are not correctable but are compatible with life. Health care providers and educational systems are mandated by law to serve the needs of these children. In spite of the multiple problems experienced by infants and families affected with myelomeningocele, the expectation of parents for their children can generally be a happy and independent life.

Microcephaly

Microcephaly means very small head and brain. This condition can be either primary or secondary depending on the reasons for the limited brain growth. Primary microcephaly generally occurs during the first or second trimester of pregnancy and can result from genetic malformations, chromosomal abnormalities, or exposure to toxic agents: e. g., radiation, chemicals such as drugs or alcohol, and infections. Secondary microcephaly usually occurs during the last trimester of pregnancy, during the labor and delivery process, or during the period of early infancy. Some of the factors responsible for secondary microcephaly are infections, birth trauma, inborn errors of metabolism, and decreased oxygen supply related to many different causes. Either primary or secondary microcephaly may result in only minor developmental delays or may range to profound disabilities and mental retardation.

Small head size in infants is usually identified with a head circumference that falls at least two standard deviations below the mean on a standard growth chart for age. Microcephalic head size also tends to be disproportionate to both the weight and the linear growth of a child. In spite of the significant difference, many of the chromosomal abnormalities that cause small head size have varying degrees of disability. Still, many of these conditions are also associated with other physical and developmental disabilities, such as cataracts and skeletal abnormalities.

The most common development of microcephaly after the second trimester of pregnancy is related to hypoxic-ischemic cerebral injury. This generally occurs during the birth process or during the neonatal period and is caused by decreased blood flow to the brain, which in turn, decreases oxygen levels (hypoxia) and causes cellular death (ischemia) from lack of oxygen and glucose. Many affected infants are full term and initially have a head circumference that is within normal parameters for height and weight. Conditions that cause hypoxic-ischemic brain dysfunction may be trauma or infection. Development of microcephaly following such events has a major impact on the long-term neurological outcome of an infant. The neurological impairment that occurs generally includes cognitive impairment, cerebral palsy, seizures, and cerebral atrophy (Hill, 1991; Volpe, 1987).

There is no treatment for microcephalus. Many of the children with minor impairment show some degree of autism and many are hyperactive. Both conditions increase the need for carefully planned educational opportunities that address the individual needs of a child and also assist parents with the difficult job of raising a child with special needs.

Hydrocephalus

Hypdrocephalus is a condition where there is an excessive accumulation of cerebrospinal fluid in the **ventricles** of the brain. These four ventricles are fluid-filled sacs that occupy space within and around the brain mass. The cerebrospinal fluid bathes the brain and spinal cord, providing both protection and nutrition. Though capillary circulation throughout the brain is the main source of nutrition and the elimination of waste products, there is additional diffusion of nutrients from the cerebrospinal fluid to the brain tissue.

Hippocrates was one of the first physicians to describe hydrocephalus. He felt that chronic seizures caused the condition and that treatment should be laxatives, vegetable ingestion, and sneezing (Rocco, 1985). Failure of these treatments would then require surgical intervention that consisted of opening the skull extending to the brain material itself. Additional treatment involved the frequently used approach to any disease process—"bloodletting" (Rocco, 1985).

Untreated hydrocephalus causes the head to increase in size beyond two standard deviations above the mean on the standard growth chart. Swelling of the ventricles can be caused by an obstruction in the drainage system, an overproduction of spinal fluid, or a failure in reabsorption of cerebrospinal fluid into the general circulation. When the ventricles fill with excess fluid, they become massively dilated, placing pressure on the brain matter. If left unchecked, the brain structures may become permanently damaged, and mental retardation will occur.

Hydrocephalus may also be caused by the presence of a tumor or head trauma. Long-term outcomes for infants either born with hydrocephalus or who develop it after birth are dependent on the cause of the problem, presence of any other neurological problems, and the time frame from onset until a diagnosis is made and treatment is initiated (Jansen, 1988). Early diagnosis and treatment significantly improves the possibilities for normal development and the prevention of mental retardation. Head ultrasounds, computerized tomography, and magnetic resonance imaging are the methods used for definitive diagnosis. The medication Diamox can sometimes aid in controlling the condition without surgical intervention by pulling excess fluid into the circulatory system, where it can be excreted by the kidneys.

Failure to control hydrocephalus medically may ultimately result in the need for surgical intervention in which a temporary or permanent shunt is placed between the ventricles and the abdominal space. Shunting procedures require the surgical placement of a soft pliable plastic tube between the ventricle and either the heart or the peritoneum (a closed sac lining the abdomen). Generally, the peritoneal cavity is used in children because it provides the opportunity to loop extra catheter tubing into the abdominal space, allowing a child to grow without needing replacement of the system. Most shunts have a small bubble reservoir that is seeded under the skin, usually behind the ear. This reservoir contains a one-way valve that controls the amount of cerebrospinal fluid that can be drained from the ventricle at any one time depending on the pressure within the ventricle. This reservoir also provides a method of checking on the flow of the system; this is especially useful when a shunt failure is suspected. The ease with which the valve can be pumped (gently pushed) is an aid to evaluating the shunt for free flow of fluid. Symptoms of shunt failure are similar to those of increased pressure from obstruction. This tube must be watched carefully for blockage. Symptoms of tube obstruction may include a decreased level of consciousness, vomiting, temperature instability, seizures, and if the pressure gets high enough, loss of brain mass and even death.

Hydrocephalus may be evident on prenatal ultrasound, or it may be completely without evidence at birth. However, infants affected with significant blockage prior to birth, which has been identified by prenatal testing, may require delivery by cesarean section to attempt to preserve functional brain material and also decrease the risk of injury to a mother attempting to deliver an infant with a very large head by the vaginal route. Many cases of significant prenatal

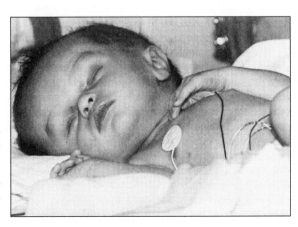

Hydrocephalus blockage before surgery (left)

Hydrocephalus shunt after surgery (right)

hydrocephalus will result in brain wasting from pressure during the developmental process. Surgical intervention in these cases is done not to protect the brain, but for comfort to an infant and to assist families in providing adequate physical and emotional care.

Hydrocephalus frequently occurs with other neural tube defects, such as myelomeningocele. In the latter, initial repair of the spinal defect is the first stage of surgical care, and placement of a ventricular/peritoneal shunt is the second stage. Closure of the primary defect (myelomeningocele) causes obstruction of cerebrospinal fluid that results in the need for a shunt.

Hydrocephalus is a life-long disorder. Management of the shunt, observations for function, and awareness of the symptoms of possible infections are requirements of not only the family and care providers but also of educators who may be working with these children. Awareness of symptoms that may be displayed by an individual child is part of the educational plan.

The cognitive and psychosocial development of children varies significantly, depending on the underlying cause of the hydrocephalus. Many children with hydrocephalus have normal intellectual development (Amacher & Wellington, 1984). Frequent shunt infections, plugged shunts, and other malfunctions may affect development of an otherwise normal brain. Early evaluation of possible developmental delays is necessary, and many of these children benefit from early childhood developmental stimulation programs. Shunt tubing is versatile and can withstand normal childhood activities. It is essential that children participate as fully as possible in age-appropriate activities so that the illness not be an unnecessary deterrent to full enjoyment of life.

APPROACH FOR THE TWENTY-FIRST CENTURY

Each child affected with a neurological disability, regardless of the cause, has an individual response to his or her condition. Continuing research into causes of neurological disabilities, both physical and functional will provide educators with the knowledge-base to devise new and innovative approaches to interactions with each child and family. Prevention is the goal, but providing optimal care to affected families is a more realistic short-term objective.

One area in which early childhood professionals must become more knowledgable is that of attentional deficits. With the present rise in incidence, which is recognized at an earlier and earlier age, children with very significant management needs cause havoc in preschool programs for children with special needs. In fact, this young population of children, who tend to be so disruptive, is more difficult to manage than older children because their language and cognitive skills are less well developed, and therefore, they are less able to understand rules and their consequences. On the other hand, because the time it takes to remediate behavioral problems is proportionate to the length of time that the behavior has been in a child's repertoire (a ratio of three months treatment for every one month that the behavior has occurred), very early treatment is crucial. One approach that holds much promise as a method of assessing and identifying effective strategies for preschool children is functional analysis (Peck, et al., in press). Using this method, the factors that motivate and sustain undesirable behavior are carefully observed and measured. When these factors are identified, systematic attempts are made to alter the conditions that maintain such behaviors. More research, however, is clearly needed. Therefore, future efforts in early childhood special education should be devoted to research in behavioral management of significant behavior problems, training of professionals to use such strategies, and, perhaps, widespread application in early childhood settings.

STUDY GUIDE QUESTIONS

1. Why should early childhood special educators know the etiologies and courses of disabling conditions?

2. Differentiate between invasive and noninvasive procedures. Give an example of each.

3. What are the medical uses of X rays? What precautions should be taken when X rays are used?

4. In what ways do CAT scans provide more information than X rays?

5. What are the advantages of the MRI over CAT scans and X rays?

6. Describe how PET scans are carried out. What special information do PET scans provide?

7. What are the primary medical uses of ultrasound?

8. What kind of information does an EEG provide?

9. What are arteriograms used for? What are the risks involved?

10. When might endoscopy be used?

11. What is cerebral palsy?

12. How has modern medicine maintained the incidence of cerebral palsy?

13. Differentiate each of the following: hemiplegia, paraplegia, quadriplegia, and diplegia.

14. Differentiate hypertonia and hypotonia.

15. Briefly describe the characteristics of athoetosis, ataxia, and spasticity.

16. Compare and describe cerebral palsy that is severe, moderate, or mild.

17. What nutritional and feeding problems often accompany cerebral palsy?

18. In addition to feeding problems, what other conditions are often presented with cerebral palsy?

19. How should therapists work with parents of children with cerebral palsy?

20. What is meant by positioning and handling?

21. How are seizures activated?

22. Define epilepsy.

23. Differentiate each of the following types of seizures: absence, tonic-clonic, and myoclonic.

24. How do seizures affect cognitive functioning?

25. Summarize the chapter's advice about assisting families of children with seizure disorders.

26. What should one do if a child experiences a tonic-clonic siezure?

27. What are the characteristics of ADHD?

28. What are the recommended treatments for ADHD?

29. What is anencephaly?

30. What are the effects of spina bifida occulta?

31. How is meningocele treated? What are the long-term effects?

32. What is myelomeningocele?

33. How is myelomeningocele treated?

34. What physical problems are common for children with repaired myelomeningocele?

35. What is the Baby Doe legislation?

36. What is microcephaly, and what causes it?

37. What is hydrocephalus?

38. How is hydrocephalus controlled?

REFERENCES

Abramowitz, A. J., Eckstrand, D., O'Leary, S. G., & Dulcan, M. K. (1992). ADHD children's responses to stimulant medication in two intensities of a behavioral intervention program. *Behavior Modification, 16,* 193–203.

Accardo, P. J., Blondis, T A., & Whitman, B. Y. (Eds.). (1991). *Attention deficit disorders and hyperactivity in children.* New York: Marcel Dekker, Inc.

Alexander, M., & Steg, N. (1989). Myelomeningocele: Comprehensive treatment. *Archives of Physical Medicine and Rehabilitation, 70*(8), 637–645.

Amacher, A., & Wellington, J. (1984). Infantile hydrocephalus: Long-term results of surgical therapy. *Child's Brain, 11,* 217–229

American Psychiatric Association. (1987). *Diagnostic and statistical manual of mental disorders* (3rd ed., revised). Washington, DC: Author.

American Psychiatric Association. (1994). *Diagnostic and statistical manual of mental disorders* (4th ed., revised). Washington, DC: Author.

Anastopoulos, A. D., & Barkley, R. A. (1991). Biological factors in attention deficit disorder. *CH. A. D. D. ER, 5,* 1.

Austin, J. K., Risinger, M. W., & Beckett, L. A. (1992). Correlates of behavior problems in children with epilepsy. *Epilepsia, 33*(6), 1115–1122.

Avey, L. (1965). *Developmental anatomy: A textbook and laboratory manual of embryology, (7th ed.).* Philadelphia: W.B. Saunders Co.

Barkley, R. A. (1981). *Hyperactive children: A handbook for diagnosis and treatment.* New York: Guilford.

Barkley, R. A. (1990). *Attention deficit hyperactivity disorder: A handbook for diagnosis and treatment.* New York: Guilford.

Barkley, R. A. (1993). A new theory of ADHD. *The ADHD Report, 1*(5), 1–4.

Barkley, R. A., DuPaul, G., & McMurray, M. (1991). Attention deficit disorder with and without hyperactivity: Clinical response to three dose levels of methylphenidate. *Pediatrics, 87,* 519–531.

Bender, W. N., & McLaughlin, P. J. (1995). The ADHD conundrum: Introduction to a special series on attention deficit/hyperactivity disorder. *Intervention in School and Clinic, 30,* 196–197.

Bhushan, V., Paneth, N., & Kiely, J. L. (1993). Impact of improved survival of very low birth weight infants on recent secular trends in the prevalence of cerebral palsy. *Pediatrics, 91*(6), 1094–1100.

Bigge, J. L. (1991). *Teaching individuals with physical and multiple disabilities* (3rd ed.). Columbus, OH: Macmillan.

Bronowski, J. (1967). *Human and animal languages. In honor of Roman Jakobson* (Vol. 1). The Hague, Netherlands, Mouton.

Bronowski, J. (1977). *Human and animal languages. A sense of the future* (pp. 103–131). Cambridge, MA: MIT Press.

Brunquell, P. J. (1994). Listening to epilepsy. *Infants and Young Children, 7*(1), 24–33.

Clayman, C. B. (1989). T*he American Medical Association Encyclopedia of Medicine.* New York: Random House.

Cioni, G., Paolicelli, P. B., Sordi, C., & Vinter, A. (1993). Sensorimotor development in cerebral palsied infants assessed with the Uzgiris-Hunt scales. *Developmental Medicine and Child Neurology, 35,* 1055–1066.

Conners, C. (1980). *Food additives and hyperactive children.* New York: Plenum.

Dahl, M., & Gebre-Medhin, M. (1993). Feeding and nutritional problems in children with cerebral palsy and myelomeningocoele. *Acta Pediatrica, 82,* 816–20.

Dam, M. (1990). Children with epilepsy: The effect of seizures, syndromes, and etiological factors on cognitive functioning. *Epilepsia, 31*(4), 26–29.

Dichter, M. (1994). The epilepsies and convulsive disorders. In K. J. Isselbacher, E. Braunwald, J. D. Wilson, J. B. Martin, A. S. Fauci, & D. L. Kasper (Eds.), *Harrison's principle of internal medicine* (13th ed.) (pp. 2223–2333). New York: McGraw-Hill.

Dormans, J. P. (1993). Orthopedic management of children with cerebral palsy. *Pediatric Clinics of North America, 40*(3), 645–657.

Eaton, D. G. M., Ahmed, Y., & Dubowitz, L. M. S. (1991). Maternal trauma and cerebral lesions in preterm infants. Case reports. *British Journal of Obstetrics and Gynecology, 98,* 1292–1294.

Eicher, P. S., & Batshaw, M. L. (1993). Cerebral palsy. *Pediatric Clinics of North America, 40*(3), 537–551.

Epilepsy school alert. (1987). Epilepsy Foundation of America. Washington, DC, Author.

Farmer, S. F., Harrison, L. M., Ingram, D. A., & Stephens, J. A. (1991). Plasticity of central motor pathways in children with hemiplegic cerebral palsy. *Neurology, 41,* 1505–1510.

Fee, M. A., Charney, E. B., & Robertson, W. W. (1988). Nutritional assessment of the young child with cerebral palsy. *Infants and Young Children, 1*(1), 33–40.

Fish, D. R., Smith, S. J., Quesney, L. F., Andermann, F., & Rasmussen, T. (1993). Surgical treatment of children with medically intractable frontal and temporal lobe epilepsy: Results and highlights of 40 years' experience. *Epilepsia, 34*(2), 244–247.

Goulden, K. J., Shinnar, S., Koller, H., Katz, M., & Richardson, S. A. (1991). Epilepsy in children with mental retardation: A cohort study. *Epilepsia, 32*(5), 690–697.

Grant, A., Joy, M. T., O'Brien, N. O., Hennessy, E., & MacDonald, D. (November, 1989). Cerebral palsy among children born during the Dublin randomized trial of intrapartum monitoring. *The Lancet,* 1233–1235.

Greenberg, G. S., & Horn, W.F. (1991). *Attention deficit hyperactive disorder: Questions and answers for parents.* Champaign, IL: Research Press, Inc.

Grove, N., Cusick, B., & Bigge, J. (1991). Conditions resulting in physical disabilities. In J. Bigge (Ed.), *Teaching individuals with physical and multiple disabilities* (pp. 1–15). Columbus, OH: Macmillan.

Hill, A. (1991). Current concepts of hypoxic-ischemic cerebral injury in the newborn. *Pediatric Neurology, 7,* 317–325.

Hinjosa, J., & Anderson, J. (1991). Mother's perceptions of home treatment programs for their preschool children with cerebral palsy. *The American Journal of Occupational Therapy, 45*(3), 273–279.

Hoare, P., & Kerley, S. (1992). Helping parents and children with epilepsy cope successfully: The outcome of a group programme for parents. *Journal of Psychosomatic Research, 36*(8), 759–767.

Jansen, J. (1988). Etiology and prognosis in hydrocephalus. *Child's Nervous System, 4,* 263–267.

Jordan, D. R. (1992). *Attention deficit disorder: ADHD and ADD syndromes, (2nd ed.).* Austin, TX: PRO-ED, Inc.

Kousseff, B. (1984). Sacral meningocele with conotruncal heart defects: A possible autosomal recessive trait. *Pediatrics, 74,* 395–398.

Laurence, K. (1964). The natural history of spina bifida cystica. *Archives of Diseases of Childhood, 39,* 41–50.

Laybourn, A., & Hill, M. (1994). Children with epilepsy and their families: Needs and services. *Child Care Health and Development, 20,* 1–14.

Lerner, J. W., Lowenthal, B., & Lerner, S. R. (1995). *Attention deficit disorders: Assessment and teaching.* Pacific Grove, CA: Brooks/Cole Publishing Co.

Marlowe, M. (1986). Metal pollutant exposure and behavior disorders: Implications for school practices. *Journal of Special Education, 2*(2), 251–262.

Marlow, D., & Redding, B. (1988). *Textbook of pediatric nursing 6th ed.* Philedelphia: W.B. Saunders Co.

Matson, D. (1969). *Neurosurgery of infancy and childhood.* Springfield, IL.: Charles G. Thomas Publ.

Milich, R., Wolraich, M., & Lindgren, S. (1986). Sugar and hyperactivity: A critical review of the findings. *Clinical Psychology Review, 6,* 493–513.

Mill, J. (1989). The absence of a relationship between the periconceptional use of vitamins and neural-tube defects. *New England Journal of Medicine, 321,* 430–435.

Morelle, M. J. (1993). Differential diagnosis of seizures. *Neurologic Clinics, 11*(4),737–754.

Mulinare, J. (1988). Periconceptional use of multivitamins and the occurrence of neural tube defects. *Journal of the American Medical Association, 260,* 3141–3145.

Naeye, R. L., Peters, E. C., Bartholomew, M., & Landis, J. R. (1989). Origins of cerebral palsy. *American Journal of Diseases of Children, 143,* 1154–1161.

National Institute of Neurological and Communicative Disorders and Stroke. (1986). *Spina bifida: Hope through research.* Bethesda, Md: National Institute of Health.

O'Leary, K. D., Pelham, W. E., Rosenbaum, A., & Price, G. H. (1976). Behavioral treatment of hyperkinetic children: An experimental evaluation of its usefulness. *Clinical Pediatrics, 15,* 510–515.

Palmer, F. B., Shapiro, B. K., Allen, M. C., Mosher, B. S., Bilker, S. A., Harryman, S. E., Meinert, C. L., & Capute, A. J. (1990). Infant stimulation curriculum for infants with cerebral palsy: Effects on infant temperament, parent-infant interaction, and home environment. *Pediatrics Supplement, 85*(3), 411–415.

Peck, S. M., Wacker, D. P., Berg, W. K., Cooper, L. J., Brown, K. A., Richman, D., McComas, J. J., Frischmeyer, P., Millard, T. (in press). Choice-making treatment of young children's severe behavior problems. *Journal of Applied Behavior Analysis.*

Procopis, P. G. (March, 1992). Breath-holding attacks in children. *Modern Medicine of Australia,* pp. 36–37.

Reilly, S., & Skuse, D. (1992). Characteristics and management of feeding problems of young children with cerebral palsy. *Developmental Medicine and Child Neurology, 34,* 379–388.

Rocco, C. (1985). *Historical background: The treatment of infantile hydrocephalus.* Boca Raton: CRC Press.

Rosen, M. G., & Dickinson, J. C. (1992). The incidence of cerebral palsy. *American Journal of Obstetrics and Gynecology, 167,* 417–423.

Ross, D. M., & Ross, S. A. (1976). *Hyperactivity: Research, theory and action.* New York: John Wiley & Sons.

Safer, D. J., & Allen, R. P. (1976). *Hyperactive children: Diagnosis and management.* Baltimore: University Park Press.

Scheller, J. M., & Nelson, K. B. (1994). Does cesarean delivery prevent cerebral palsy or other neurologic problems of childhood? *Obstetrics & Gynecology, 83*(4), 624–630.

Shapiro, K. (1990). Anencephaly. In Buyse, M. (Ed.). *Birth defects encyclopedia* (pp.139–140). Dover, MA.: Center For Birth Defects Information Services, Inc.

Sharrard, W., Zachary, R., Lorber, J., & Bruce, A. (1963). A controller trial of immediate and delayed closure of spina bifida cystica. *Archives of Diseases of Childhood, 38,* 18–25.

Shepherd, C., & Hosking, G. (1989). Epilepsy in school children with intellectual impairments in Sheffield: The size and nature of the problem and implications for service provision. *Journal of Mental Deficiency Research, 33,* 511–514.

Silver, L. B. (1993). *Dr. Larry Silver's advice to parents on attention-deficit hyperactivity disorder.* Washington, DC: American Psychiatric Press, Inc.

Thommessen, M., Kase, B. F., Riis, G., & Heiberg, A. (1991). The impact of feeding problems on growth and energy intake in children with cerebral palsy. *European Journal of Clinical Health, 45,* 479–487.

Turnbull, J. D. (1993). Early intervention for children with or at risk of cerebral palsy. *American Journal of Diseases of Children, 147*(1), 54–59.

Vargha-Khadem, F., Isaacs, E., Ver der Werf, S., Robb, S., & Wilson, J. (1992). Development of intelligence and memory in children with hemiplegic cerebral palsy. *Brain, 115,* 315–329.

Veelken, N., Schopf, M., Dammann, O., & Schulte, F. J. (1993). Etiological classification of cerebral palsy in very low birthweight infants. *Neuropediatrics, 24,* 74–76.

Volpe, J. (1987). *Neurology of the Newborn.* Philadelphia: W.B. Saunders.

Williams, B. F., Williams, R. L., & McLaughlin, T. F. (1991). Treatment of behavior disorders by parents and in the home. *Journal of Developmental and Physical Disabilities, 3,* 385–407.

Zametkin, A. J., Nordahl, T. E. Gross, M., King, A. C., Temple, W. E., Rumsey, J., Hamburger, S., & Cohen, R. M. (1990). Cerebral glucose metabolism in adults with hyperactivity of childhood onset. *New England Journal of Medicine, 323,* 1361–1367.

CHAPTER 6

Inborn Variations of Development

When one considers all the ways in which human development, from embryology to birth, might vary, the fact that so many children are born without apparent disabilities is miraculous. This chapter is devoted to the description of variations in development that originate before a child's birth. These variations do not insinuate devaluation, inferiority, or undesirability of persons born with differences. Rather, the variations in development result in patterns of physical and/or behavioral character that enable us to group children as distinctly different. Sometimes specific treatments are implicated when a child has membership in a certain group. For example, children with cystic fibrosis usually receive postural drainage treatments because respiratory congestion is always a symptom of the disease. Usually, however, membership in itself tells us very little about the specific treatments to be used for a child because individual differences are so great. Furthermore, most treatments are not universally effective for all children with the same characteristics. Anyone who has worked with children with autism can verify that determining what reinforcers, activities, and instructions work for one child will provide little guidance for another child who is given the same label. This chapter includes an introduction to basic genetics, which helps in understanding the etiologies of various genetic deviations of development. The third section of this chapter is devoted to common disabilities that have no known etiology. It is probable that most of these disorders will eventually be linked to genetics. Finally, metabolic and medical factors that affect very young children are described. This chapter intentionally includes more information than will seem necessary for a foundations text. This is intended as a reference for later use by early childhood professionals. It is clear from working with parents that the more they can learn about their child's disability, the more capable they feel. Thus, it is the responsibility of professionals to become as knowledgable as possible and to be able to help parents seek further information and resources.

Still, it should be noted that the following descriptions are generalizations based on current understanding of groups of children with categorical disabilities. It would be a mistake to assume that one could make any specific educational or programmatic recommendations for individual children based on the characteristics and types of treatments described in the following chapter. This general information provides a broad beginning point. Beyond that, families and early childhood professionals must define programs based on the unique characteristics of children and their families.

GENETICS

Genetics is the study of heredity and variations in the characteristics of organisms, both plant and animal. In humans, genetic research provides us with information about development and diseases. Understanding gene physiology and function in relation to human growth and development is necessary to understand how individual variability occurs. Treatment and sometimes prevention of unwanted variations (i.e., disabilities and diseases) are made possible by recognizing the role that both genes and the environment play in human development.

Chromosomes are the basic genetic units, which stay constant in number within a species and across generations. The first link between **genes** and chromosomes was made in 1911 by T. H. Morgan, using saliva from a fruit fly (Risley, 1986). Genes are regions of a chromosome made up of molecules that collectively define a particular trait. **Genetic mapping** is a process of connecting specific genes to individual chromosomes and chromosomal regions (Guyer & Collins, 1993). For example, the gene for muscular dystrophy is located on the "p21" region of the X chromosome. The gene is labeled Xp21. By contrast, Prader-Willi syndrome occurs when a region of the 15th chromosome is missing or deleted. The deleted region is called 15q11-13.

Recently, the study of genetics has been facilitated by new technologies. As a result, the genes responsible for many inherited traits such as Huntington's disease, fragile X syndrome, Duchenne muscular dystrophy, and cystic fibrosis have been isolated. Isolating and identifying genes, understanding their mutations, and learning about their protein products have increased knowledge about disabilities and diseases. This molecular approach is unlike past approaches to genetics, thus the term "new genetics" has been applied (Thompson, McInnes, & Willard, 1991).

The Human Genome Project is an example of new genetics. This is an international project whose goal it is to map and sequence the entire genetic code of human chromosomes by the year 2005. Mapping the human genome will lead to prediction, understanding, and, eventually, to the prevention or curing of many human disabilities and diseases (NIH, 1990). This knowledge brings with it numerous ethical questions about how such information should be used. Public dialogue, education, and policies are needed to address the social, legal, and ethical implications of the Human Genome Project. To date, however, participation by society at large in directing this project has been very limited.

Behavioral genetics represents another emerging area of genetics. This subdiscipline is so named because researchers seek the identification of genes associated with behaviors, such as violence, mental illness, and alcoholism. A majority of studies, however, refute the notion that genes, by themselves, cause behavior. Many geneticists warn that research in behavioral genetics should be reviewed critically. It is agreed that scientific and popular media should emphasize that rarely do genes alone determine behavior; rather, genes interact with the environment to cause variations in behavior. "Genes act in environments, and as a result, changing the environment can often change the effect of the gene" (Billings, Beckwith, & Alper, 1992, p. 236).

Cellular Activity of Genetics

The human body contains more than a billion miles of deoxyribonucleic acid (DNA), with an average cell possessing more than a meter of this substance. DNA is a nucleic acid compound that carries the chemical coding needed to transmit genetic information from generation to generation. A chromosome is a chain of DNA. Human cells possess a total of 46 chromosomes, or 23 pairs of chromosomes (see Figure 6.1). That is, each member of a chromosome pair has

Figure 6.1/ *Drawing of the Individual Chromosomes Arranged Sequentially in Pairs by Size, Shape, and Banding Pattern. Patterns 1–22 are autosomes (created by mitosis). Pattern 23 is one pair of sex chromosomes (created by meiosis).*

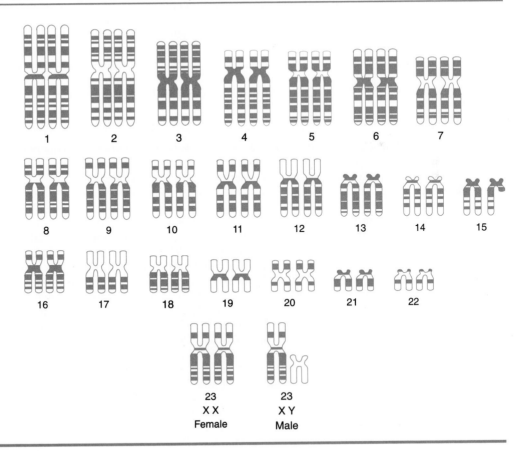

matching genes at the same location and in the same sequence. Of the 23 chromosomal pairs, 22 are called **autosomes.** The 23rd pair is comprised of two sex chromosomes: X and Y. The X and the Y chromosome combination determines the gender of an individual—XX in females and XY in males.

Alleles are one of two alternative versions of a gene, with complimentary alleles residing on each of the two chromosomes in a pair. A **homozygote** pair will inherit identical alleles for a certain trait, such as two genes for cystic fibrosis. A **heterozygote** has two different alleles for a particular trait, such as one normal gene and one gene for cystic fibrosis. **Genotype** refers to the combination of alleles inherited for a particular trait within an individual; **phenotype** refers to the observable expression, or appearance, of the genotype in an individual. When speaking of whole chromosomes, the term **karyotype** is used to describe the number and configuration of the chromosomes. Some genetic testing is done to examine the whole chromosome for variations that may indicate problems. For example, when a child is suspected of having Down syndrome, an analysis of the child's karyotype will be conducted to determine if there is an extra chromosome or extra chromosomal material causing this genetic difference.

The purpose of cell division is to ensure growth, development, and repair of an organism. The two types of cell division are mitosis and meiosis (see Figure 6.2). **Mitosis** produces two identical daughter cells each containing the full set of 46 chromosomes. This occurs in all body cell reproduction. Chromosomes replicate and the cell divides once to create two identical cells, as in the regeneration of skin cells. **Meiosis** produces sex cells, called germ cells, or **gametes,** each with only one half the full complement of chromosomes (one from each chromosome pair). These cells are involved in reproduction. A sperm is a male gamete, and an ovum is a female gamete. When these cells join during conception, the resultant cell(s) will have a full set of chromosomes—one of each chromosome pair from each parent. Abnormalities in chromosome number or structure can arise during either of these processes of cell division. An example is Down syndrome, in which the 21st chromosome, usually in maternal meiosis, does not divide, resulting in three 21st chromosomes, or trisomy 21.

Single Gene Disorders

Single gene inheritance is the type of inheritance described by Mendel's principles. Such variations are mutations of genes. This may involve one or both genes of a chromosome pair. Examples of single gene disorders are cystic fibrosis, hemophilia, and sickle cell anemia. The occurrence of abnormalities varies. For example, in hemophilia, the occurrence rate is 1 in 10,000 live births. By contrast, sickle cell disease occurs once in every 400 live births among African-Americans (Thompson, McInnes, & Willard, 1991).

There are about 4000 observable single gene characteristics, 3000 of which are considered genetic disorders. In several hundred of these diseases, the biochemical defect has been identified, and in many, as mentioned above, the responsible gene has been isolated (Thompson, et al., 1991). Single gene disorders are transmitted from one generation to another in three ways: recessive, dominant, and sex linked. A **recessive** gene is one whose genetic information is typically overruled by genetic information of a more **dominant** gene. Usually, it takes two recessive genes, one from each chromosome of a pair, in order for the trait to be expressed. On the other hand, only one dominant gene is typically needed for that gene's trait to be expressed. The terms *recessive* and *dominant* describe only the phenotypic expression, or observable trait; they do not describe what is happening at a molecular, or biochemical, level. For example, in the case of inheritance of a single recessive gene, the characteristic trait(s) of the disorder is usually not expressed. Nevertheless, at the biochemical level both the dominant and recessive genes are being expressed. The phenotype may also be a combination of recessive and dominant genes acting together (Thompson, et al., 1991). **Sex linked** disorders are transmitted on either the X or Y chromosomes. However, most sex linked disorders

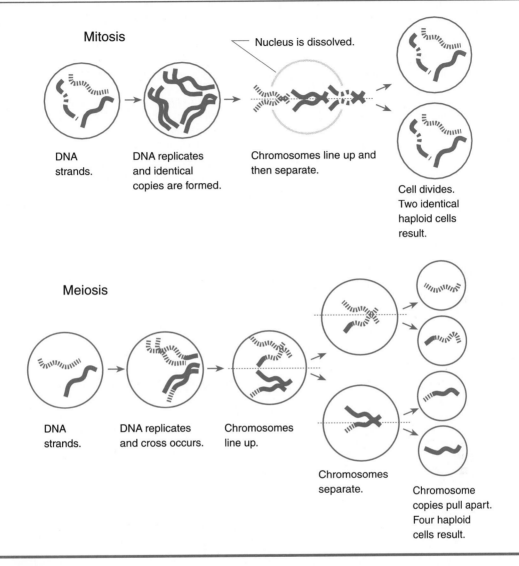

Mitosis

Nucleus is dissolved.

DNA strands.

DNA replicates and identical copies are formed.

Chromosomes line up and then separate.

Cell divides. Two identical haploid cells result.

Meiosis

DNA strands.

DNA replicates and cross occurs.

Chromosomes line up.

Chromosomes separate.

Chromosome copies pull apart. Four haploid cells result.

are inherited on the X chromosome. Hemophilia and color blindness are examples of sex linked genetic differences.

Recessive Gene Interitance Tay Sachs, phenylketonuria (PKU), cystic fibrosis, and sickle cell anemia are a few of the many recessive single gene disorders (see Figure 6.3). As mentioned, usually a recessive gene is expressed only if it is inherited from both parents. For example, if the recessive gene for sickle cell anemia is inherited from both parents, the person will show signs of the disease. In this case, the offspring have a 25% chance of receiving two recessive genes and, consequently, of having the disorder. If just one affected gene is inherited, the person will not show signs of the disease except at the biochemical level. This is because the gene is paired with a dominant gene, and the dominant gene is the one phenotypically expressed. This person is a **carrier,** and although carriers have no signs or symptoms of the disease, they may transmit the gene to their offspring. There is a 50% chance of inheriting one gene and becoming a carrier and a 25% chance of not inheriting the gene from either parent.

Dominant Gene Inheritance Huntington's disease, familial hypercholesteremia, and some forms of muscular dystrophy are examples of dominant single gene disorders (see Figure 6.4). Dominant genes are phenotypically expressed whenever they appear. Persons having just one of the genes will show signs of the disorder. Therefore, if one parent has the dominant gene and the other parent does not, the offspring have a 50% chance of receiving the dominant gene. Early identification of the possession of dominant gene disorders can help parents decide whether or not to prevent the inheritance. At this time, prevention of transmission can only occur when parents decide not to reproduce or, once conception has taken place, to abort a fetus with a genetic disease.

Recessive and dominant traits are not strictly determined by the presence or absence of a normal/abnormal gene. As with most things in nature, heredity is not so simple. If one normal and one mutant gene are present, then the result of their combined production of genetic material is what determines the dominant or recessive nature of the trait (Thompson, et al., 1991). For example, if there is enough gene product between the two genes to provide for normal functioning, then the mutant gene and its related disorder are overruled and therefore recessive. For the sake of illustration, let's say hypothetically that syndrome Q needs 56

Figure 6.3/ *Pattern of Inheritance of Autosomal Recessive Genes*

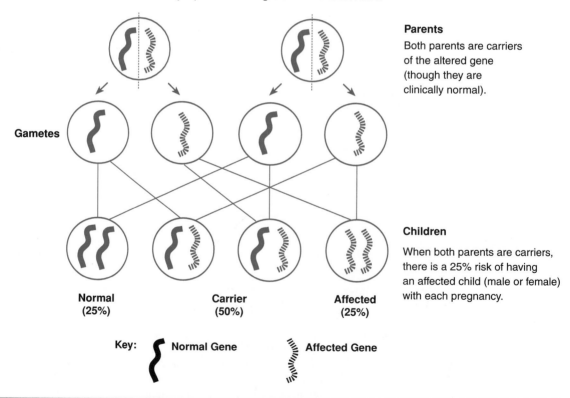

Autosomal Recessive Inheritance Pattern

Disorders are caused by a pair of altered genes on the autosomes.

Parents
Both parents are carriers of the altered gene (though they are clinically normal).

Gametes

Children
When both parents are carriers, there is a 25% risk of having an affected child (male or female) with each pregnancy.

Normal
(25%)

Carrier
(50%)

Affected
(25%)

Key: Normal Gene   Affected Gene

units of normal gene product in order for the syndrome to be expressed. From the mother, who is a carrier of the mutant gene, the fertilized cell receives 10 units of normal gene product and 40 units of mutant Q gene product. From the father, who is not a carrier, the fertilized cell receives 50 units of normal gene product. Since there are 60 units of normal gene product, the offspring of this union will yield sufficient gene product for the gene trait to function normally. In this child, the gene for syndrome Q is recessive.

If there is not enough genetic product between the two chromosomes to function normally, then the gene and the disorder are said to be dominant. For example, in sickle cell anemia, a recessive gene produces abnormal hemoglobin. If that gene is inherited from each parent, then the blood will make abnormal hemoglobin. In this case, the person has sickle cell anemia. On the other hand, if one abnormal gene and one normal gene are inherited, the blood will contain some normal and some abnormal hemoglobin. Although both genes are functioning, the person will show no symptoms of the disorder because there is enough normal hemoglobin produced to out-weigh the effects of the abnormal gene. These individuals do not have sickle cell anemia, but they are carriers of the recessive gene and can therefore transmit the gene to their children.

Sex Linked Inheritance   Sex linked disorders have the affected gene on either the X or Y chromosome. Most sex linked disorders are related to the X chromosome. Hemophilia and

---

Figure 6.4/ *Pattern of Inheritance for Autosomal Dominant Genes*

Autosomal Dominant Inheritance Pattern

Disorders are caused by a single altered gene on one of the autosomes.

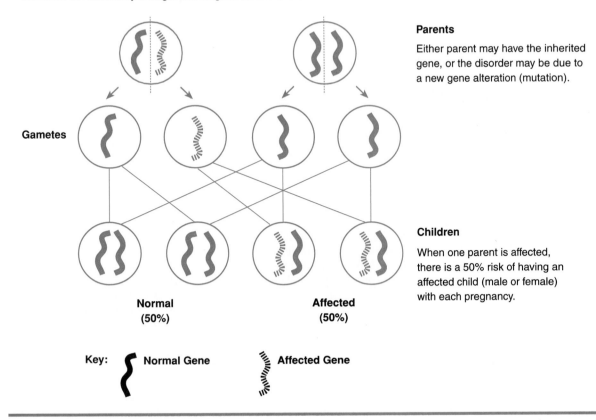

Gametes

Parents

Either parent may have the inherited gene, or the disorder may be due to a new gene alteration (mutation).

Children

When one parent is affected, there is a 50% risk of having an affected child (male or female) with each pregnancy.

Normal
(50%)

Affected
(50%)

Key: { **Normal Gene**   **Affected Gene**

X-linked Recessive

Either parent may have the gene present on the **X**-chromosome.

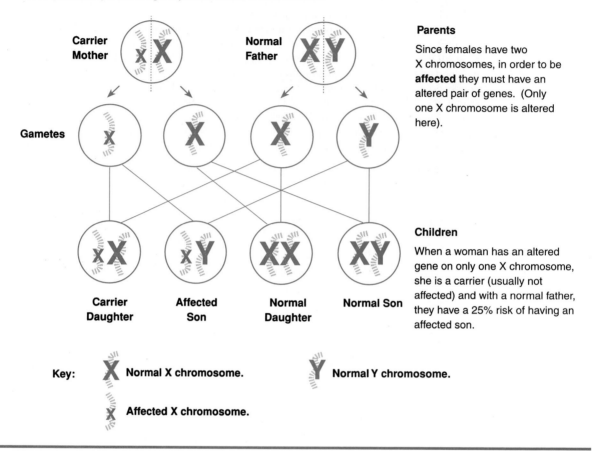

Parents

Since females have two X chromosomes, in order to be **affected** they must have an altered pair of genes. (Only one X chromosome is altered here).

Children

When a woman has an altered gene on only one X chromosome, she is a carrier (usually not affected) and with a normal father, they have a 25% risk of having an affected son.

Key:

X Normal X chromosome.   **Y** Normal Y chromosome.

x Affected X chromosome.

Duchenne muscular dystrophy are examples. The incidence of these types of disorders is highest in male offspring. Males inherit X linked diseases from their mothers, the source of their X chromosome. In males, such diseases are usually more significant since there is no complementary X chromosome. Females, with two X chromosomes, are usually not affected because the second X chromosome compensates for the recessive gene on the affected X chromosome. Only a few genetic disorders are X linked dominant. In this case, an affected male parent passes the disorder on to all daughters but none of the sons. This is because the son receives his X chromosome from the mother and the Y from the father. The daughter, on the other hand, receives one of her two X chromosomes from the father and, because it is dominant, will have the disorder. However, such diseases are usually of a less severe nature in females because they possess two X chromosomes. The normal X chromosome helps counteract the abnormal member of the pair (see Figure 6.5). Fragile X and Duchenne muscular dystrophy are similar in that females are usually carriers, but may show mild symptoms of the disorders. In these cases, the unaffected/normal X chromosome may not completely compensate for the affected X chromosome, and some form of the disorder is manifest.

Figure 6.6/ *Chromosome Disorders*

Some Chromosome Abnormalities

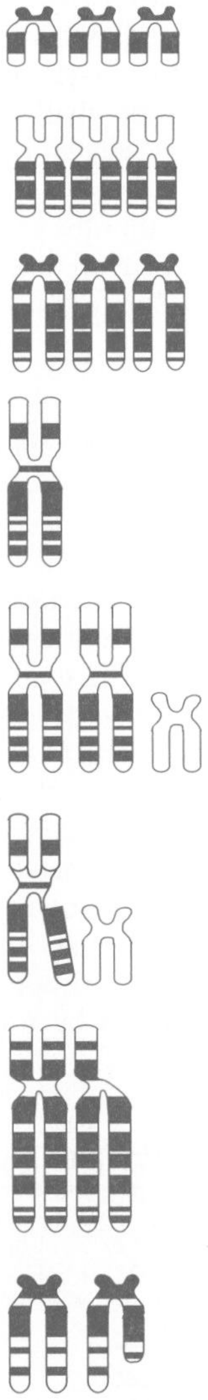

Abnormality	Karyotype	Disorder
Extra #21 chromosome		Down syndrome (Trisomy 21)
Extra #18 chromosome		Trisomy 18
Extra #13 chromosome		Trisomy 13
Girl with only one X chromosome		Turner syndrome (45, XO)
Boy with an extra X chromosome		Klinefelter syndrome (47, XXY)
Long arm of X chromosome is tenously attached		Fragile X syndrome
Deletion of the short arm of one #5 chromosome		Cri du chat syndrome
Deletion of part of the long arm of the #15 chromosome		Prader-Willi syndrome

Chromosome Disorders

In **chromosome disorders,** whole chromosomes or chromosome segments are responsible for a problem rather than a single gene or combination of genes (see Figure 6.6). These variations can include an extra chromosome, extra chromosome material, structural abnormality, or absence/deletion of a chromosome. Turner syndrome is an example in which there is a whole or partial absence of one of the two X chromosomes. Chromosome disorders of this nature are common, occurring in 7 out of every 1000 births. It is estimated that 50% of all spontaneous abortions in the first trimester are due to these chromosomal abnormalities.

Multifactorial Disorders

Multifactorial disorders account for two types of genetic problems: congenital disorders and the predisposition to a disease, usually with onset in adulthood. Congenital disorders account for malformations such as cleft palate, spina bifida, and various heart anomalies. Prenatal environmental factors may also be involved in these disorders. Many diseases do not appear until adulthood. These are exacerbated by a probable genetic predisposition to acquire the disease. A few examples that are currently believed to be affected by genetic predisposition include heart disease, obesity, arthritis, some forms of cancer, and metabolic problems, such as diabetes mellitus. It is also believed that lifestyle moderation, such as diet and exercise, can affect the course of some of these diseases.

Genetic Testing

One American in 100 is born with a serious genetic disorder, which may be chromosomal, sex-linked, or multifactorial (March of Dimes [MOD], 1992). Genetic testing and counseling are conducted for people who have questions and concerns about problems that may affect their offspring. There are several reasons to consider genetic testing: family history of genetic disorders, a child with a genetic disorder, two or more miscarriages or a baby that died in infancy, ethnic origin (e.g., sickle cell anemia is more prevalent among African-Americans), first cousins planning to have a child together, and pregnancy of a woman over age 35.

Analysis of blood samples can detect genetic disorders. Hemophilia, Tay Sachs disease, cystic fibrosis, sickle cell anemia, and Duchenne muscular dystrophy are detected in this way. Blood samples also show if a person is the carrier of a recessive gene that could be passed on to offspring. Amniocentesis, chorionic villus sampling, and, more recently, fetal blood sampling from the umbilical cord are prenatal tests that can be used for early detection of abnormalities (Sach & Korf, 1993). **Amniocentesis** is a painful and risky procedure that removes fluid from the sac surrounding the fetus. A long, thin needle is inserted through the abdomen to withdraw approximately four teaspoons of amniotic fluid (see Figure 6.7). Of every 400 amniocentesis tests performed by a qualified physician, one spontaneous abortion is

Figure 6.7/ *Drawing of Amniotic Fluid to Test Prenatally for Fetal Variations of Development*

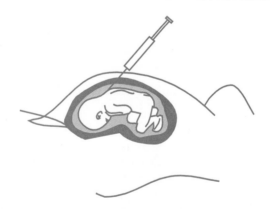

likely to occur. Amniocentesis can reveal chromosomal, metabolic, and biochemical disorders. For example, DNA tests can be conducted to detect such problems as cystic fibrosis or sickle cell anemia. Down syndrome is the most common chromosomal problem detected with this procedure. **Chorionic villus sampling** (CVS) is conducted vaginally or abdominally and requires a small tissue sample from the chorion or outer sac that surrounds the fetus. Chorionic villus sampling can be conducted earlier in fetal development than amniocentesis, but the risk to a fetus is higher. **Fetal blood sampling** (also called percutaneous umbilical blood sampling) can be conducted even earlier than CVS, and detects the same problems. A needle is guided into the abdomen, through the uterus to the umbilical cord, from which a blood sample is withdrawn.

Other prenatal tests include ultrasound and alpha-fetoprotein screening (AFP). Ultrasound is used to visualize the fetus and its developing organs. Congenital malformations, such as spina bifida, can be detected using this procedure. Alpha-fetoprotein screening is a blood test conducted to detect neural tube disorders, such as malformations of the spinal cord, the spinal column, and the brain. This test, however, produces many false positives since the level of AFP fluctuates during pregnancy. For this reason, AFP testing is usually used as a screening tool leading to further diagnostic tests, such as those mentioned above.

Gene Therapy

Though gene therapy is presently in its experimental stage, the next decade may provide treatment for various genetic disorders. One type of gene therapy introduces a normal gene into a cell nucleus to replace an abnormal gene. The cell can then function normally. For example, in diabetes mellitus, in which the body is unable to produce insulin, a gene that provides the genetic information needed to initiate insulin production could be introduced. However, the inserted genes are not passed on to the next generation because normal genetic material is not placed in the germ cells. For now, because such therapy is so exploratory, education and caution are necessary to facilitate judgment regarding the relative benefits and risks of therapy compared to the prognosis for the disease (Haan, 1990).

Germ line therapy introduces genes into the germ or sex cells, as well as into the somatic cells. The consequences of this therapy may be profound. Future generations would be influenced if such therapy is successful, and stability of the entire gene pool could be compromised by eliminating certain genes while potentially creating other new abnormalities. For this reason, and because it is believed that there is a risk of serious ethical abuse, most geneticists agree that this type of therapy should not be undertaken (Hann, 1990; Sach & Korf, 1993), even if it could be successful in reversing the effects of a serious genetic defect in some children.

GENETIC VARIATIONS IN DEVELOPMENT

Cystic Fibrosis

Cystic fibrosis is the most common fatal genetic disease in the United States. Approximately 1 in 1500–2000 white infants (Cystic Fibrosis Foundation [CFF], 1987a) and 1 per 17,000 African-American infants born in this country are afflicted with the disease. Cystic fibrosis affects the **exocrine glands,** which secrete body fluids, causing them to produce a thick, sticky mucus that eventually clogs the lungs and blocks functioning of the pancreas. Also affected are the sweat glands, which produce perspiration containing two to five times the normal amount of sodium (Anfenson, 1980; CFF 1987a).

Characteristics Individuals with cystic fibrosis produce an excessive amount of thick, sticky mucus (CFF, 1987a). In the lungs and respiratory tract, this mucus blocks airways and interferes with breathing, eventually resulting in respiratory failure. This mucus further inhibits the pancreas from releasing necessary digestive enzymes. Consequently, children with cystic fibrosis are unable to sufficiently metabolize fats and proteins. The sweat glands's tendency to excrete abnormally high amounts of sodium provides the basis for the "sweat test," the primary diagnostic measurement for cystic fibrosis. Because of an excessive release of salt, exposure to fevers and extreme heat are two conditions that can be especially harmful (CFF, 1987a). Heat can cause serious loss of sodium and may result in confusion, seizures, and other electrolyte imbalance problems.

As a consequence of these physiological disturbances, children with cystic fibrosis have chronic symptoms of persistent coughing, recurrent wheezing, repeated episodes of pneumonia, excessive appetite, poor weight gain or even weight loss, projectile vomiting, and a slightly protruding abdomen (CFF, 1987a). The progression of cystic fibrosis symptoms varies across individuals with the disease. Some children may be affected primarily in the respiratory system; in others the pancreas and digestive systems might be more significantly affected. No diagnostic tests have yet been devised to predict the course that will be taken in specific patients with cystic fibrosis (CFF, 1987a). In the past, it was very unusual for those affected by cystic fibrosis to live long enough to go to school; most died in infancy (Krener & Adelman, 1988). However, with recent treatment advances, there has been a substantial improvement in life expectancy. Current average life expectancies are approximately 23 years for women and 28 years for men (Dibble & Savedra, 1988).

Dibble and Savedra (1988) described numerous secondary physical complications that have emerged concomitant with improved survival of patients with cystic fibrosis. For example, there is an increased incidence of respiratory dysfunctions: lung infections, bloody mucus, and pneumothorax (rupture in the lung releasing air into the chest cavity). As the life expectancy of patients with cystic fibrosis increases, so does the probability of their developing diabetes; as many as 40% to 60% of persons with cystic fibrosis may acquire hyperglycemia.

Etiology   Cystic fibrosis is an **autosomal** recessive gene, transmitted genetically to offspring when both parents are carriers. In the United States, an estimated 12 million people, or 1 in 20, are carriers of the cystic fibrosis gene (CFF, 1987b). Carriers inherit a single cystic fibrosis gene located on one of the two number 7 chromosomes ("Gene that," 1989). For these individuals, the second chromosome 7 remains unaffected and blocks the expression of the harmful gene. A child afflicted with cystic fibrosis has two cystic fibrosis genes, one present on each chromosome 7 (CFF, 1987b).

Treatment   Diagnosis of cystic fibrosis is usually made by the second or third birthday, though for some children symptoms may go undiagnosed for months or years. Treatment of cystic fibrosis involves a multidisciplinary approach to address the numerous issues likely to arise for both child and family (Pediatric Pulmonary and Cystic Fibrosis Clinic [PPCFC], 1987). Professionals likely to be included on the team are a medical director, nurse, physical therapist, clinical pharmacist, respiratory therapist, nutritionist, social service worker, geneticist, and possibly others, all of whom will work together with a patient with cystic fibrosis on long and short term treatment goals (PPCFC, 1987). Anfenson (1980) identified typical family routines in daily treatment of children with cystic fibrosis:

1. adequate nutrition with a high carbohydrate and protein diet, adequate salt intake, pancreatic enzyme preparations, supplemental doses of fat soluble vitamins, and adequate fluid intake

2. prevention of infection through frequent bronchial drainage treatments, aerosol inhalation therapy, use of antibiotics, and a mist tent while sleeping or resting

3. promoting healthy development by encouraging normal social relationships, reinforcing self-image, continued contact with supporting agencies, continuous support

when children are hospitalized, and emphasis on a child's identity as a "typical child" whenever appropriate

Although treatment practices are limited and a cure still undiscovered, many advances have been made in the 1980s and 1990s. Since the 1989 identification of the abnormal protein causing cystic fibrosis, many new treatment methods have been researched. Such experimental methods as genetically bypassing the problems caused by the abnormal protein or therapeutically altering the defective protein in the bloodstream are being investigated ("Scientists Forecast," 1989). One other experimental approach is gene therapy, considered "the ultimate 'correction' strategy" ("New Treatments," 1989). Gene therapy entails replacing or correcting either the entire cystic fibrosis gene or the part of chromosome 7 that is defective ("New Treatments," 1989).

In the preschool years, children with cystic fibrosis may or may not display symptoms that affect their daily lives. Some children may have frequent and serious lung infections that could interfere with typical social and cognitive opportunities. Monitoring developmental progress and providing enriching educational programs should be a priority for educators of young children with cystic fibrosis. Other than constraints that might be placed on children by their medical condition, intervention should be developmentally and socially relevant.

Though cost varies from one family to another, depending on the severity and stage of the disease, family economics are almost always strained by this disease (Stullenbarger, Norris, Edgil, & Prosser, 1987). The cost of hospitalization is so high that families without medical insurance usually suffer financial crisis (CFF, 1987c). The social effects of cystic fibrosis on the entire family can also be difficult. Parents, siblings, and the children themselves are emotionally affected. Though families of children with disabilities are as resilient to life's challenges as other families, and though new technology offers unprecedented hope for a cure to cystic fibrosis, adjusting to the possible loss of a child or sibling with cystic fibrosis can begin as early as preschool. Finally, genetic counseling has also proven to be an effective means to alleviating fears and guilt in parents of children with cystic fibrosis (MOD, 1987).

Down Syndrome

Down
Syndrome

Down syndrome was one of the first causes of mental retardation to be categorized as a syndrome. Identified in 1866 by Langdon Down, the syndrome has variously been termed cretinism, unfinished or ill-finished child, and mongolism. Down referred to the syndrome as a retrogression to the Mongoloid race, since children and adults resembled persons of this ethnic group in several phenotypic ways. This name remained common in educational and medical communities until the 1960s, when it was replaced with the more dignified label Down syndrome. The prevalence of Down syndrome ranges from 1 in 600 to 1 in 1000 live births. This incidence makes Down syndrome the second largest genetic cause of mental retardation, after fragile X syndrome.

Characteristics Though more than 50 traits have been associated with Down syndrome, individuals with this disability may have a few or many of the known characteristics (Fishler & Koch, 1991). Mental retardation ranging from mild to severe is present in almost all individuals with Down syndrome. However, with changing educational practices over the last century, children's educational opportunities combined with innovative teaching methods have greatly improved the cognitive expectations and achievements of children with Down syndrome. Phenotypic characteristics include short stature and clubbed short fingers, epicanthal folds (skin at inner corner of eye forms a fold, making eye *appear* to be slanted), sloping forehead, flat **occipital** lobe, ruddy cheeks, speckled iris, malformed ears, flat nose bridge, upward tilt to nostrils, simian line in palm (a single deep wrinkle running across the width of the palm), third toe longer than second, gap between big toe and next one. A high palate and small oral cavity often lead to tongue protrusion.

Do We Value Diversity or Do We Value Normalcy:
Ethical Considerations for the Twenty-first Century

Down syndrome is the most visible and well known of inborn errors of development. Perhaps because of these features, children and adults with Down syndrome are often at the center of legal and ethical debates. Prenatal diagnosis, abortion, passive euthanasia, and cosmetic surgery are all battles fought by parents of children with Down syndrome.

Parents of children with Down syndrome often seek ways to reduce the stigma associated with this chromosomal anomaly. Cosmetic surgery for this group of individuals involves "tongue reduction...and is often accompanied by implants to the bridge of the nose, chin, cheeks, and jawbone, as well as Z-plasty on the eyelids to eliminate the characteristic epicanthal fold" (May & Turnbull, 1992, p. 29). The first known instance of plastic surgery to change the facial features of an individual with Down syndrome occurred in 1969 (Otermin-Aquirre, 1969).

May and Turnbull (1992) surveyed 100 plastic surgeons on their opinions regarding the use of cosmetic reconstruction of the facial features of individuals with Down syndrome. Of the 100 surgeons, 24 had performed the surgery themselves. Both experienced and inexperienced surgeons believed that the surgery should only be conducted in circumstances in which there is potential to improve eating, speech, breathing, and social acceptance.

Plastic surgery is neither risk free nor certain in its outcome. Little research has actually been conducted to determine whether there is improved social acceptance or physical ability. In fact, in one study in which parents perceptions of their children's physical, personal, and social functioning were measured, there was no difference between those parents of Down syndrome children who had the surgery and those parents of children who had not (Kravetz, Weller, Tennebaum, Tzuriel, & Mintzker, 1992). From this study conducted in Israel, where the surgery is not uncommon, it seems that the surgery did not have the desired impact. Moreover, there is still a need to examine whether it is appropriate to alter individuals' appearance to make them more acceptable, rather than to work toward altering a basic social flaw. May and Turnbull cautioned that professionals have a significant role in decision making, and their own biases influence the type of information given to parents.

Medical conditions also commonly accompany this disability. Neonates often have life threatening conditions, such as duodenal atresia (small bowel is partially or fully blocked) and patent ductus arteriosis, in which the duct connecting a fetus's blood system to the maternal blood supply does not close automatically after birth. Because of these and other medical conditions, the life expectancy of children with Down syndrome was only 9–12 years in the early part of this century. Chronic heart problems and depressed immune response resulting in frequent upper respiratory infections often led to premature death. In a more recent analysis, Eyman, Call, and White (1991) concluded that while medical problems do affect the overall life expectancy of persons with Down syndrome, restricted mobility and poor eating patterns of infants are more significant risk factors. Most individuals who do not have significant associated disabilities have an overall life expectancy of greater than 50 years.

One of the most dominant physiological characteristics is hypotonia, or low muscle tone. Consequently, infants with Down syndrome typically have delayed motor and speech development. Children also have a high incidence of hearing impairments with a tendency

A child with Down syndrome

toward high-frequency hearing losses (Marcell & Cohen, 1992). Because the hearing losses tend to be conductive, the susceptibility of these children to middle ear disease may be a related factor. Visual impairments are also more common in children with Down syndrome than in typically developing children.

As the life expectancy of individuals with Down syndrome improves, researchers have identified specific areas of premature aging. These differences range from the innocuous, such as accelerated aging and turnover of red blood cells (Wachtel & Pueschel, 1991), to the dangerous, as with premature deterioration of the thyroid function, leading to hypothyroidism in a large percentage of adults with Down syndrome (Pueschel, Jackson, Giesswein, Dean, & Pezzullo, 1991). Of greatest concern is the tendency toward premature dementia in middle age, leading to behavioral deterioration (Evenhuis, 1990).

Etiology   The discovery of chromosomes quickly led to the identification of genetic anomalies causing Down syndrome. Instead of the normal complement of 23 pairs of chromosomes in each cell (46 total), most individuals with Down syndrome have an extra 21st chromosome, and 47 total chromosomes. The three 21st chromosomes, referred to as **trisomy 21,** are always associated with at least a few of the physical or behavioral characteristics described earlier. In addition, two other chromosomal defects can cause Down syndrome:

1. A **translocation** trisomy is the existence of extra chromosomal material that has become attached to another chromosome. The size of the misguided genetic material may vary from a piece of one arm to an entire chromosome.

2. In **mosaicism,** a portion of cells have 46 chromosomes and another percentage (usually 10% to 12%) of the cells have the extra 21st chromosome (47).

The genetic history of each of these types of Down syndrome also varies. In typical trisomies, the extra 21st chromosome is associated with **nondisjunction** during meiosis (see Figure 6.8). In other words, when cell division takes place to create either an ovum or sperm, there is an incomplete detachment of the 21st pair, with one cell receiving 22 chromosomes and the other 24. In Down syndrome, the cell with 24 chromosomes (including the extra 21st) combines with a normal compliment of 23 chromosomes.

Translocation trisomies are typically genetically transmitted from a carrier parent to an affected child, and occur in approximately 5% to 10% of cases of Down syndrome. Research indicates that the different causes of Down syndrome described above are associated with differences in developmental and physical characteristics (Fishler & Koch, 1991; Johnson & Abelson, 1969). Specifically, Fishler and Koch (1991) observed that, on the average, children with mosaicism and translocations, had fewer physical traits associated with Down syndrome and greater intellectual potential (Fishler & Koch, 1991). This finding conflicts, however, with Johnson and Abelson (1969), who found that individuals with mosaicism had the lowest average intellectual functioning of the three types of Down syndrome.

Why some **gametes** have aberrant cell division, resulting in extra chromosomes, is still unknown. However, for some time, researchers recognized the contribution of maternal age to the incidence of Down syndrome. Generally speaking, as women grow older, the odds of conceiving a child with Down syndrome grow progressively more favorable. Women older than 35 years of age are considered high risk and may generally be advised to undergo prenatal testing such as amniocentesis when pregnant. A second factor associated with the incidence of Down syndrome is maternal exposure to low level radiation over a long period of time. Neither maternal age nor radiation exposure is an explanation for nondisjunction, but knowing their relationship to Down syndrome is useful in genetic counseling for women considering pregnancy.

Figure 6.8/ *Diagram of Cell Division Leading to Down Syndrome: Nondisfunction during meiosis results in disproportionate chromosome distribution. A normal cell (23 chromosomes) combines with an abnormal one (24 chromosomes) to produce trisomy 21.*

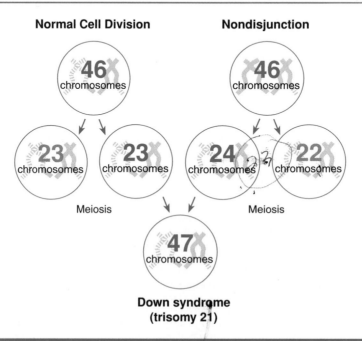

The Diagnosis

Interview with Tom and Ann Simpson

Tommy Simpson was born with Down syndrome. I was only thirty-four when he was born, and since we did not anticipate any problems, I hadn't had any extra tests or anything like that. When I was seven months pregnant, the doctor thought the baby might be breech so he suggested I have an ultrasound to determine his position. The medical technician took a long time doing the ultrasound; he checked and rechecked his figures two or three times, then told us the doctor would need to talk to us. Later, we were told the doctors suspected the baby was a dwarf.

By the time the baby was born, we knew there might be something wrong, but I had decided it really didn't matter. I was just worried about having the baby and making sure we loved him. The rest didn't seem to matter so much, and I remember my labor coach thought that I was wrong. She said, "If there are any problems, you should have the information, know about it. You should be investigating." I just felt that I wanted to wait until the baby was born and then deal with it.

No heart problems had been found, so we expected no problems with the birth itself. My mom came out a week and a half before the baby was born so she and I ran all over town and had a lot of fun. I taught class the evening he was born, came home, and by about eleven o'clock, I knew the baby was coming. We went to the hospital, and my labor was pretty easy. I don't think the nurses expected anything unusual; I don't think there was anything on my chart.

The birth came quickly. Smack! And not even the resident was there. I was just so happy, and the nurses were really proud they had delivered him. He had come easily, but he was very blue and almost inert. The nurses worked on him and even when he was picked up, he was still very inactive. I remember looking at him, his skin was ruddy and he didn't open his eyes. He was quiet, he didn't really cry, just complained a bit.

By the time the doctor and my labor coach rushed in, it was all over. The doctor looked at the baby, and checked me over, but he didn't say anything. Still, I think he suspected. He said he was going to call the genetics counseling expert.

The baby came, but he wouldn't nurse and he opened one eye just a little bit. The nurses had to put him under special lights because he had jaundice. The genetics counselor and his assistant wanted to talk to my husband and me together. Now, I knew there was something wrong. When I called Tom, he literally ran out of the house and left the door wide open, even in the cold. I held the baby and tried to get him to nurse, as they were talking to us. I was sharing the room with another woman, my labor coach was there, and the nurses were there. It was a difficult moment, and I didn't have any privacy.

The doctor said they thought the baby had Down syndrome, and we'd heard of it, but we really didn't know what it meant. I remember we all started bawling, even with my roommate on the other side of the room, and it seemed so weird. I would have done things differently, but at the time when it's happening to you, you just take what's coming no matter how uncomfortable it is.

After the nurses knew, they switched us to a private room, but I wished they'd put a no visitors order in. I still had too many visitors and calls. We'd all waited for this baby for a long time, and not that many people expected anything to be wrong, so people kept calling and coming. I didn't deal with that very well. We all cried; everybody was so sad. The worst thing was the baby wasn't doing very well.

His breathing was high and shallow and he never nursed. The nurses had to keep sticking him for blood samples, because his skin was so thick, and he had a heart murmur so they thought he might have a heart problem. He went into the intensive care unit that evening. I cried, and cried, and cried, and cried. It was ten o'clock at night, and I didn't want to call my husband and mother because I knew they were both tired. I

(continued)

TOMMY SIMPSON AND HIS DAD

went down to see Tommy in the nursery about two in the morning, but it was so hard having him taken away.

People would visit me, and I would try to be sociable, and that was difficult too. Most people were understanding when I told them the baby had Down syndrome, but I didn't really talk too much about it. You know it's funny, because now it's not upsetting to me, but those first few months I was terribly upset. I could cope, but I was really upset about it and had a hard time talking about it. Now it seems like he's a neat little kid, and we love him for just who he is, but it was so hard at first.

After Tommy was born with Down syndrome and we went home from the hospital, my mom acted as my gatekeeper. She was great. She hardly let anyone talk to me by phone, and I really appreciated that because I didn't feel like talking to too many people.

One of my sisters called and said, "Well it's not like it's a tragedy or anything."

But I thought, "Oh, honey, it is; this is."

She reminded me she'd volunteered for Special Olympics, and she had a friend with a child who had Down syndrome, and I said, "Did you know them when the baby was born?"

No, she'd met them when the child was five years old. I said, "Ask them what it was like when their child was born."

But my sister went on, "Oh, it's no big deal, it's not a tragedy, it's great."

I told her, "You need to understand that you've invalidated all of my feelings. Ask your friend."

Later she talked to her friend who confided that she had felt much of the same thing. I learned you do work through it, but you also have to recognize that sadness and disappointment are valid. It is a tragedy. Tommy is not going to go to college; he's not going to do a lot of things. He is a neat kid. But he's not going to do those things that you don't realize you expect for your child in your life.

Other Trisomy Disorders While Down syndrome is the most common live birth trisomy, other trisomy conceptions are common, and some occur even more frequently than trisomy 21. However, most of these chromosomal anomalies are spontaneously aborted because their characteristics are incompatible with life. Other fetuses may survive the pregnancy but may be stillborn or will likely die within a few days or weeks of birth. Trisomies 13, 16, and 18 are the most common of these chromosomal anomalies.

Treatment Early intervention for children and their families should focus on several dimensions. For parents, education regarding the etiology and long-term outcomes is needed. Parents may want to read literature or be put on mailing lists for magazines or newsletters, join support groups, or join the National Down Syndrome Society, a powerful advocacy group.

Intervention goals for children will likely be comprehensive, with early emphasis on motor and language development. Physical and occupational therapists and communication specialists should be involved. Speech development is often impeded by both cognitive delays and oral structural problems. However, Steffens, Oiler, Lynch, and Urbano (1992) found that the patterns of vocal development in children with Down syndrome paralleled those of normally developing children, even though the average rates of development in the former were slightly slower. Augmentative communication (sign language, communication boards, and other devices) can reduce frustration and enhance language development. Feeding may also be an issue, since children tend to be underweight in infancy. Later, as toddlers and preschoolers, hypotonicity and slow metabolic rates sometimes contribute to an excessive weight gain (Chad, Jobling, & Frail, 1990). According to Chad et al., regular exercise should be scheduled to both reduce body fat and correspondingly increase energy levels.

There is increasing evidence that, with certain instruction (i.e., early intervention, use of behavior analytic methods, and integration), many preschool and elementary students are able to stay at or above grade/age expectancies in some academic areas, notably in reading (Rynders & Horrobin, 1990). As children with Down syndrome grow older, their relative intellectual abilities diminish compared to the rate of progress made by typical children (Rynders & Horrobin, 1990). Even so, children with Down syndrome now being served in public schools are accomplishing feats once believed impossible. The potential of such children (indeed all children) is undoubtedly limited by our own boundaries in educational technology.

Fragile X Syndrome

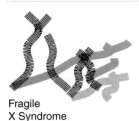

Fragile
X Syndrome

Until recently, the prevalence of mental retardation in males had been explained by social and behavioral gender differences (De La Cruz, 1985). The identification of fragile X syndrome challenged that assumption. This syndrome was first identified in 1969 when Lubs discovered the genetic abnormality in the X chromosomes of a mother and her son. Now, fragile X syndrome is considered the leading known cause of mental retardation (Dykens, Hodapp, Ort, & Leckman, 1993; Keenan, et al., 1992; Santos, 1992). Fragile X is believed to account for 40% of the X-related forms of mental retardation and 10% of all cases of mental retardation (Rogers & Simensen, 1987). Additionally, fragile X may be even more prevalent than these statistics indicate since many carriers who have the anomalous chromosome but do not have mental retardation go undiagnosed (Santos, 1992; Sudhalter, Cohen, Silverman, & Wolf-Schein, 1990). Yet, many early childhood professionals do not have a good understanding of this disability. Wilson and Mazzocco (1993) found that only 36% of professional educators responding to a survey had knowledge of fragile X, while 64% were knowledgable about Down syndrome, which appears to be less prevalent.

Characteristics Females who are affected by fragile X generally express either mild to moderate forms of mental retardation or, as carriers, may have some form of learning disability (De La Cruz, 1985; Sudhalter, et al., 1990; Wolff, Gardner, Paccia, & Lappen, 1989). Males, on the other hand, tend to range from borderline to profoundly mentally retarded (De La Cruz, 1985; Sudhalter, et al., 1990; Wolff, 1989). Of males with the fragile X chromosome, 80% express mental impairment, whereas only 30% of females with the fragile X chromosome are mentally retarded (Kennan, et al., 1992). Furthermore, longitudinal documentation indicates a steady deterioration in mental functioning as these children age (Keenan, et al., 1992; Santos, 1992; Simensen & Rogers, 1989). Unvalidated theories regarding this alleged decline include progressive neurological deterioration (Santos, 1992), increased emphasis on cognitive/reasoning skills as children age (Santos, 1992), and failure of the rate of intellectual growth to keep pace with expectations of standardized IQ tests (McClennen, 1992). Fragile X has a specific pattern of learning characteristics. Strengths include relatively strong language and visual skills, while weaknesses include difficulty with verbal organization (grammar) and math (De La Cruz, 1985; Keenan, et al., 1992). Males in particular have difficulty in processing novel sequential information, short-term memory, and problem solving that requires complex generalization (Reiss & Freund, 1990).

Most children with fragile X have a normal appearance at birth (Keenan, et al., 1992). Prominent physical features are most apparent in postpubertal males. Characteristic features in adults include a long face, large ears, prominent forehead, underdevelopment of the midface region, prominent jaw, and enlarged testicles (De La Cruz, 1985; Meryash, 1985; Santos, 1992; Simensen & Rogers, 1989). Meryash (1985) also noted that a majority of individuals with fragile X tend to be short in stature. The variability in facial features of females with fragile X makes it difficult to use physical features as an index in diagnosis (Rogers & Simensen, 1987).

As with intelligence, researchers have recorded a progressive degeneration of adaptive behavior in males with fragile X syndrome (Dykens, et al., 1993). After making steady gains in adaptive behavior until early adolescence, skills then begin to decline. Several behavioral phenomenon are associated with the syndrome, though considerable variability exists among individuals with fragile X. Many express distinctly autistic-like characteristics, such as unusual hand mannerisms (hand flapping and hand biting), stereotypic behaviors (rocking), and speech and language disorders (perseveration, echolalia, dysrhythmia, and inappropriate speech) (Keenan, et al., 1992; Meryash, 1985; Sudhalter, et al., 1990). Other traits include hyperactivity, attentional deficits, bizarre responses to their surrounding environments, hypersensitivity to environmental stimuli, emotional problems, motor delays, poor eye contact, and social avoidance (ARC Facts, 1988; Hagerman, 1992; Keenan, et al., 1992; Meryash, 1985; Santos, 1992; Simensen & Rogers, 1989; Wolff, et al., 1989). Wolff et al. (1989) described a unique form of greeting behavior in males with fragile X syndrome characterized by gaze avoidance and social distancing. Females may also have social difficulties, including problems with peer relationships, shyness, and a tendency to withdraw and act uncomfortable around others (McClennan, 1992). While social skills tend to be most affected by the fragile X chromosome, other adaptive behaviors appear to be especially well developed relative to mental impairment (Dykens, et al., 1993). Whether institutionalized or not, males have strong daily living skills in areas such as toileting, personal grooming, and domestic responsibilities.

Etiology   Fragile X syndrome derives its name from the form of its mutation on the X chromosome. The "fragile" site on the X chromosome is located on the long arm at the Xq27 gene (Keenan, et al., 1992; Meryash, 1985; Rogers & Simensen, 1987; Simensen & Rogers, 1989). This long arm may be separated or connected by only a thin strand (Meryash, 1985). Though most prevalent in males, fragile X, more so than any of the other X-related chromosomes, also affects females (Meryash, 1985; Simensen & Rogers, 1989). Sudhalter et al. (1990) noted that 1 in 1350 males and 1 in 2033 females have the hereditary abnormality. However, since females possess two X chromosomes, the one intact X chromosome tends to overrule the effects of the fragile X chromosome. Santos (1992) explained the incidence of fragile X characteristics in females as a selective inactivation of the normal X chromosome, which then allows expression by the other X chromosome at the fragile site. By contrast, males have only one X chromosome and are therefore always vulnerable to the defective genetic anomaly.

Fragile X is of a familial nature, transmitted from generation to generation in a unique fashion (Santos, 1992; Wolff, et al., 1989). The defective chromosome is most commonly transmitted by the mother who may be affected or unaffected; however, it has been noted that unaffected males may transmit the fragile X chromosome to their daughters (Santos, 1992). Furthermore, genetic studies of families with the fragile X chromosome revealed that as the affected chromosome is transmitted from generation to generation, the incidence of fragile X syndrome *increases in frequency and severity* (Black, 1992).

The fragile X chromosome travels through families in an unusual manner. A typical family pedigree is one in which all children of female carriers of the syndrome have a 50% chance of inheriting the gene from their mothers. Males who are carriers will pass the gene to their daughters, but obviously may not pass the gene to their sons. When a male carrier passes the abnormal gene to his daughter the likelihood of mental retardation is low. On the other hand, mental retardation is common (55%) in the daughters of females who inherited the abnormal fragile X gene from their carrier fathers (Meryash, 1985; Santos, 1992). Therefore, mental retardation is more likely to occur when the female transmits the mutated X chromosome.

Treatment   Fragile X syndrome is rarely detected at birth and may not be identified until school age in affected children with mild disabilities. Among the various professionals that should be involved in treatment are health professionals, child study teams, therapists, and educators (Keenan, et al., 1992). Medical treatment of the syndrome itself is limited, though stimulant medication, such as Ritalin, has been somewhat effective in controlling behaviors associated with hyperactivity and attentional deficits (Santos, 1992). The primary treatment for fragile X syndrome is educational, with early childhood special education providing the greatest promise for long-term adaptive and intellectual benefits. Because there is considerable variability within the population of individuals with fragile X syndrome, components of educational programs should be designed to fit children's behavioral needs and not the disability itself. It is likely that components would include functional skills training, physical therapy, and speech therapy (ARC Facts, 1988; McClennan, 1992; Meryash, 1985).

Muscular Dystrophy

Duchenne MD

Several hereditary muscle wasting diseases fall under the category of muscular dystrophy (see Table 6.1). The most common form of progressive muscular disease is Duchenne muscular dystrophy. Approximately 1 in every 3500 males is born with Duchenne muscular dystrophy (Shapiro & Specht, 1993). A milder but similar disorder, Becker muscular dystrophy, affects 1 in 30,000 male children. Though the severity of this disease is most prominent during the school age years, its onset is generally early childhood.

Characteristics   The course of Duchenne muscular dystrophy follows a fairly predictable pattern (Lynn, Woda, & Mendell, 1994; Shapiro & Specht, 1993). Usually in early childhood (ages three to six), children begin to have weakness in gross motor activities like running and jumping, and they fall often. The disability is positively identified when children rise from the floor using the Gower's maneuver or are unable to get up without using their arms for support. Children tend to waddle when walking and gradually develop **scoliosis** (spine curvature of the lower back). This misalignment of the body is a primary cause of respiratory disease, as the bellows of the lungs are compromised by the child's posture. As the muscles weaken, **contractures** form in the lower extremities. Between the ages of 8 and 12, children physically deteriorate rapidly and usually are unable to walk by the age of 12. Many children with Duchenne muscular dystrophy develop some degree of mental retardation, ranging from mild to moderate, due to the course of the disease. By middle to late adolescence, muscle tissue is almost completely replaced by fat or fibrous tissue. Children usually die before the age of 20, due to respiratory and heart failure. However, some individuals live into their 20s and are able to go to college or seek other occupations.

Those children with muscular dystrophy who are able to walk after the age of 15 are categorized with Becker muscular dystrophy (Lynn, et al., 1994). Such individuals tend to have a much slower disease progression and may live to be 40 or 50 years of age.

Etiology   Duchenne muscular dystrophy and Becker muscular dystrophy are both X-linked recessive inheritance patterns. Males who receive the affected genes (p21 region of X chromosome) are severely affected, while females who carry the gene are either normal or only mildly affected (Shapiro & Specht, 1993). Though females who carry the genetic mutation pass it on to 50% of their offspring, the gene responsible for Duchenne muscular dystrophy is randomly inactivated in half of the males who receive it. Approximately one-third of all cases of Duchenne muscular dystrophy are the result of a new mutation of the Xp21 gene and not the result of family history.

Presence of the disease is most often medically diagnosed by taking a blood sample and a muscle biopsy. The former test is conducted to determine if there is an elevated level of an enzyme (creatine phosphokinase) that is released when muscle cells deteriorate. However, this test is unreliable, making identification of carriers and prenatal screening difficult. New tests are being developed that may prove more accurate (Sancho, et al., 1993).

Table 6.1/ *Inherited Muscle Disorders*

Muscle Disorder	Age of Onset	Description
Muscular Dystrophy		
Duchenne muscular dystrophy	Early childhood	Progressive muscle wasting
Becker muscular dystrophy	Early childhood	Gradual muscle wasting
Emery-Dreifuss muscular dystrophy	First few years of life	Very slowly progressive muscle wasting
Myotonic dystrophy	Adult	
Infantile facioscapulohumeral	Infancy	Progressive wasting; initially muscular dystrophy of upper extremeties and facial musculature
Limb-girdle dystrophy	20 to 30 years of age	Weakness of shoulders and hips
Oculopharyngeal dystrophy	40 to 60 years of age	Dysfunction in swallowing
Congenital Myopathies		
Nemaline (rod) myopathy	Neonatal or adult	Mild to severe muscle weakness; sometimes fatal in infancy
Central core myopathy	Infancy	Hypotonia; delayed motor development
Centronuclear myopathy	Early childhood	Hypotonia; often fatal in infancy
Metabolic Myopathies		
Acid maltese deficiency	Infancy to 30/40	Mild to severe; excess build-up of glycogen in organs and muscles
Mitochondrial myopathies	Infant to adult	Hypotonia; generalized weakness
Periodic paralysis	Childhood to adolescence	Mild; recurrent attacks of muscle weakness

Source: Tabulated from Shapiro, F., & Specht, L. (1993). The diagnosis and orthopaedic treatment of inherited muscular diseases of childhood. *The Journal of Bone and Joint Surgery, 75*(3), 430–454.

Myotonic Diseases   Like muscular dystrophy, myotonic diseases affect muscle function. Though several disorders fall within the category, all forms of myotonic disease have a delayed relaxation of muscles after contraction, such as the inability to release a hand grip (Ptacek, Johnson, & Griggs, 1993). These muscle disorders also have a genetic etiology. Though most forms of myotonia are mild (e.g., myotonia congenita), a few rare types are very severe and associated with a high mortality (e.g., some forms of myotonic dystrophy). Generally, there are no deformities associated with this disease, and it is frequently not recognized until adulthood (Shapiro & Specht, 1993).

Treatment   There is presently no available treatment that will slow the progress of muscle wasting in children with Duchenne muscular dystrophy. However, treatments are available to assist families and children to cope with the disease. Sometimes, surgery for scoliosis is done to improve children's comfort and appearance, though this is not believed to return muscle strength nor prolong walking. Sometimes the aggressive use of tendon-transfer operations and bracing can prolong children's ability to walk for one to three years (Shapiro & Specht, 1993). While seemingly a modest goal, this accomplishment can be very meaningful to children and their families.

Several types of experimental research are investigating complex treatments for children with muscular dystrophy (Shapiro & Sprecht, 1993). Somatic cell therapy involves implanting normal muscle cells into the muscles of boys with Duchenne muscular dystrophy. So far, there is insufficient evidence to determine if such attempts will assist in the recovery of muscle function. Drug therapy, such as the use of Prednisone, is experimental in nature and often accompanied by undesirable side effects.

Severe symptoms of muscular dystrophy and related **myopathies** may begin in early childhood. For early educators, the goals of intervention are very different than for children with cognitive disabilities. Management of muscular function and alignment requires the ongoing participation of a physical therapist. Early interventionists should seek family input in determining educational priorities. Activities should be planned to maximize motor and cognitive functioning. Family support and interagency coordination will assist families to make short- and long-term decisions regarding the education and care of their child.

Prader-Willi Syndrome

Prader-Willi
syndrome

Prader-Willi syndrome was first labeled in 1956 (Prader, Labhart, & Willi, 1956), even though a review of case histories shows that the unusual characteristics of Prader-Willi syndrome were often noted incidentally by institutional staff and physicians prior to naming the disability (Goldman, 1988). Along with mental retardation, the most salient condition of this disability is an obsession with eating, leading to lifelong obesity, with or without dietary restrictions.

Characteristics   A three-stage developmental pattern is used to describe the characteristics of children with Prader-Willi syndrome: neonatal, childhood, and adolescent (Donaldson, et al., 1994). The neonatal stage is characterized by sticky saliva, hypotonia, small genitalia, an unusually weak or absent cry, abnormally large head circumference, feeding problems often necessitating a gastric tube, and failure to thrive (Aughton & Cassidy, 1990; Donaldson, et al., 1994). In addition, there are subtle facial features that can sometimes be used in diagnosis during infancy: a narrow face, "almond shaped" eyes, and a thin down-turned upper lip (Aughton & Cassidy, 1990).

In the childhood stage (after 1.5–2 years), overeating emerges as the dominant trait of children with Prader-Willi syndrome. Subsequent obesity tends to be characterized by excessive fatty tissue in the hips, breasts, thighs, and abdomen, resulting in a pear-like shape (Donaldson, et al., 1994). Physical characteristics associated with Prader-Willi syndrome include short stature, a slight slant to the eyes, and small hands and feet (Aughton & Cassidy, 1990). Children also have a tendency to bruise easily and develop cavities on their primary teeth (Donaldson, et al., 1994).

During adolescence, the third stage of development, significant behavior problems often arise: faked seizures, obsessiveness, lying and cheating, stubbornness, argumentativeness, distractibility, use of obscene language, noncompliance, and hot temperament (Dykens, Hodapp, Walsh, & Nash, 1992a). While the intellectual functioning of those with this disorder varies considerably (James & Brown, 1993), there is typically some degree of mental retardation, though predominantly borderline with a mean IQ of about 62 (Curfs, Wiegers, Sommers, Borghgraef, & Fryns, 1991). In an analysis of their adaptive behavior, individuals with this disorder tended to be relatively good at self-help skills and weak in social skills (Dykens, et al., 1992a). Specifically, youth tend to have relative success in reading and weakness in mathematics (Dykens, et al., 1992b). The extent of maladaptive behavior tends to be inversely related to intellectual functioning of persons with Prader-Willi syndrome (Dykens, et al., 1992a). In the past, many individuals with Prader-Willi syndrome were institutionalized (even those with IQs in the low normal range), possibly because of their intractable social behaviors.

Etiology   There is a genetic origin, which is both unique and complex, to most known cases of Prader-Willi syndrome. Approximately 50% to 60% of individuals with Prader-Willi syndrome are missing (deletion) a portion (15q11-13 region) of the long arm of the 15th chromosome. Deletions of 15q resulting in Prader-Willi syndrome are *paternal* in origin in most cases. Though fathers are thought to be carriers (Kennerknecht, 1992), they do not themselves have the syndrome as persons with Prader-Willi syndrome are infertile (Butler, 1990). Deletions of 15q11-13 do occur in offspring of female carriers, but interestingly, these children do not have Prader-Willi syndrome but another more rare anomaly called Angelman's syndrome. The latter, sometimes referred to as the "happy puppet" syndrome, is characterized by ataxia, seizures, severe mental retardation, absence of speech, frequent unprovoked laughter, and abnormal gross motor movement (Kennerknect, 1992; Reed & Leff, 1994).

Treatment   James and Brown (1993) cited findings of high stress in parents of children with Prader-Willi syndrome (nearly twice as high in fathers as compared to fathers of children with Down syndrome). They concluded that ongoing support might be needed to preserve the families of children with Prader-Willi (see Table 6.2 regarding interventions for children with Prader-Willi).

The tendency to overeat is sometimes indulged by parents who give in to resistant or oppositional behavior; the latter also being typical of these children. Not only does this management style compound the problem of obesity, but it teaches children that they can get food for their insatiable appetite by acting out. Additionally, children will engage in covert and ingenious methods of foraging for food—sometimes resorting to inedible alternatives—to subvert the inevitable dietary restrictions placed upon them. Yet, even with very low calorie diets (1000–1200 calories per day), persons with Prader-Willi will tend to gain weight.

Since obesity can begin to occur as early as six months of age, and usually by the toddler stage, early intervention can play a large role in helping parents to establish a lifelong vigilance over dietary habits of their children. Prevention is a key to avoidance of obesity since maintenance diets have a daily recommended intake that is 60% of the normal recommended caloric diet (Butler, 1990). Effective and recommended methods range from locking cupboards and refrigerators to increasing and maintaining high levels of physical activity in children who tend to have very low energy expenditure due to reduced activity (Donaldson, et al., 1994). Cooperation and consistency in management tactics between parents and other caregivers is crucial. In extreme cases, surgical management of obesity has been effective (Donaldson, et al., 1994).

Sickle Cell Disease

Sickle Cell

Sickle cell disease causes its victims to experience chronic and often painful episodes for which there is currently no cure and only limited treatment. Though sickle cell disease does affect individuals of other ethnicity to a much smaller degree, this genetic disorder affects 1 in every 400 African-American infants (Gil, Abrahms, Phillips, & Williams, 1992). Furthermore, because most of the largest cities in the United States have a high ratio of African-American residents, the incidence of sickle cell disease is likely to be higher in urban than in rural areas (Brown, Armstrong, & Eckman, 1993).

Characteristics   The name of the disorder is derived from its principal characteristic. Abnormal sickle shaped red blood cells proliferate and eventually clog the blood supply system (see Figure 6.9) causing unpredictable acute and chronic tissue death in all major organs of the body (necrosis) (Thompson, Gil, Abrahms, & Phillips, 1992). The most prominent feature of sickle cell disease is chronic pain. Approximately 20% of individuals with sickle cell disease have frequent and severe painful episodes referred to as **sickle cell crisis** (Shapiro, 1989). This pain is most likely to occur in one's abdomen, back, extremities, and

Table 6.2/ *Highly Effective Interventions for Children with Prader-Willi Syndrome*

Domain	High Frequency Interventions— Highly Effective	Low Frequency Interventions— Highly Effective
Medical	Monitoring by a specialist	Eye surgery
Dietary	Nutritionist/dietitian consultation	
Allied health	Ophthalmology	Chiropractic
Environmental	Remove food from availability	Locks on food cupboards Lock on kitchen door No food preparation responsibilities No food allowed outside dining area
Behavioral	Take away reinforcers Time out Praise	
Developmental	Swim programs Speech/language intervention Early childhood special education	Music therapy/training
Social	Integrated (regular) youth group participation	
Parental	Parent support group Family baby-sitting Private baby-sitting Respite care	Stress counseling

Source: Adapted from T. N. James and R. I. Brown. (1993). Prader-Willi syndrome: Quality of life issues in home, school and community. *Australia and New Zealand Journal of Developmental Disabilities, 18*(4), 253–260.

chest. Several other complications can accompany sickle cell disease: pneumococcal infections, meningitis, stroke, spleen dysfunction, enuresis, delayed physical growth, and bone inflammation and decay (Hurtig & Viera, 1986). Liu, Gzesh, and Ballas (1994) found a high incidence of clonic-tonic seizures and history of strokes in adults with sickle cell disease.

Because research is so limited, few conclusions are made regarding cognitive and behavioral associates of sickle cell disease (Brown, et al., 1993). Four physiological aspects of sickle cell disease have been documented, which Brown and colleagues believe can eventually compromise an individual's cognitive functioning:

1. numerous tiny strokes in the central nervous system, specifically the brain

2. anemia

3. malnutrition

4. a compromised blood supply to the brain

Figure 6.9/ *The Sickle Cell Process*

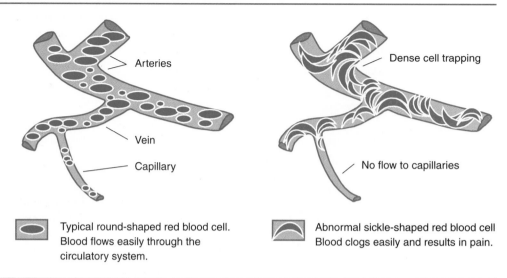

Arteries

Vein

Capillary

Dense cell trapping

No flow to capillaries

Typical round-shaped red blood cell. Blood flows easily through the circulatory system.

Abnormal sickle-shaped red blood cell Blood clogs easily and results in pain.

Source: Adapted from Nagel, R. L. (1993). Sickle cell anemia is a multigene disease: Sickle painful crises, a case in point. *American Journal of Hematology, 42,* 96–101.

In spite of these potentially harmful conditions, research to date indicates that children with sickle cell disease appear to suffer no loss of intelligence and no reliably measured deficit in academic performance as compared to peers without sickle cell disease (Brown, et al., 1993). Furthermore, it seems that, psychologically, children with sickle cell disease may be no more likely to experience coping problems than children who are healthy (Armstrong, Lemanek, Pegelow, Gonzalez, & Martinez, 1993). On the other hand, extensive testing of preschoolers with sickle cell disease revealed significant deficiencies in both motor and cognitive readiness skills on the *Pediatric Examination of Educational Readiness* (Chua-Lim, Moore, McCleary, Shah, & Mankad, 1993). In this same study, measurements using the *McCarthy Scales of Children's Abilities* confirmed that intellectual abilities were within normal range. Brown et al. (1993) noted that such research is complicated by variables that, in themselves, could account for academic and social problems, namely, poverty or social class, absenteeism caused by frequent hospitalizations, family structure, and absence of support networks. All these characteristics are associated with cognitive and social difficulties; they also happen to be disproportionately characteristic of minority populations.

Etiology   Sickle cell disease is genetically transferred to the child. The disease is caused by a mutation of genes on the 11th chromosome (Nagel, 1993). According to Pollack (1993), 8% of the African-American population carries the sickle cell gene. Three types of sickle cell disease exist (Brown, et al., 1993; Pollack, 1993). Sickle cell anemia, the most severe, is homozygous (both 11th chromosomes affected) and is caused by two abnormal genes on the 11th chromosome. Two other heterozygous (only one 11th chromosome contains sickle cell anomaly) genotypes (HbSC and HBS-thalassemia) also result in some form of sickle cell disease. Nagel (1993) explained that the latter result from a multigene interaction, with different gene combinations producing a gradient in severity of the disease across affected individuals. Therefore, the course of the disease is unpredictable, ranging from mild to severe symptoms (Chau-Lim, et al., 1993).

Treatment   The highest mortality rates from sickle cell disease are in the first five years of life because of suceptibility to infections, and again near adulthood because of multiple system

Table 6.3/ *Foods High in Iron for Children with Anemia with or without Sickle Cell Disease*

Raisins	Iron fortified and Vitamin B fortified cereals
Dried fruits	*Vitamin C rich foods
Pasta salad with beans	Dark leafy green vegetables
Chicken	Fish
Lean hamburger	Beans
Egg dishes	Peas/lentils

*Vitamin C is not itself rich in iron but encourages absorption of iron from other foods.

failure (Serjeant, 1985). Newborn screening and aggressive medical care have increased the life expectancy and quality of life of patients with sickle cell disease. However, very little is known about sickle cell disease, in spite of the fact that it is two times more prevalent than cystic fibrosis and nine times more common than phenylketonuria (PKU) (Brown, et al., 1990). Brown et al. noted that research on sickle cell disease lags far behind that of other congenital illnesses, implying that there is a link between the oversight of researchers and the ethnicity of its victims.

Diet may be a concern in children with sickle cell disease (see Table 6.3) who tend to expend energy more quickly and to possess less body fat than other children (Gray, et al., 1992). Furthermore, children may need to take vitamin supplements for zinc and Vitamin A (Gray, et al., 1992).

Pain coping methods, as with other types of chronic pain, often involve positive thinking/self-statements (Thompson, et al., 1992). However, for preschoolers, the degree to which such an intervention might work is limited by their cognitive development. Those who have knowledge of the course of their illness and some sense of control over treatment are more likely to fair better than those who are more fatalistic (Werthorn & McCabe, 1988). This is an example for which empowerment is both necessary and ethical.

Parents of children with sickle cell disease may cope with medical and disciplinary problems differently than parents of healthy children. Armstrong et al. (1993) found that in families in which there was significant lifestyle disruption, parents tended to cope by focusing on their child's medical rather than emotional needs. However, parents of children with sickle cell disease also tended to be more aware of effective and less punitive disciplinary practices than parents of healthy children. These parents endorse the use of praise and mild punishment, perhaps because of their reluctance to inflict any more pain than necessary on children who already suffer from random and unavoidable pain caused by the disease itself.

Tay-Sachs Disease

Tay-Sachs disease is an inherited autosomal recessive genetic disorder found predominantly in families with Jewish/Middle Eastern heritage. The mutation causes an enzymatic deficiency and subsequent excessive build-up of **lipids** in the central nervous system. The progressive neurologically degenerative disease leads to hypotonia, blindness, profound psychomotor mental retardation and dementia, seizures, and eventual death in infancy or early childhood (Kaback, et al., 1993; Schneiderman, Lowden, & Rae-Grant, 1978). According to Kaback et al. (1993), extensive screening and intensive genetic counseling have combined to significantly decrease the incidence of this syndrome in the past two decades. In fact, the combination of preventative efforts and abortion have almost completely eradicated Tay-Sachs from North America. Therefore, it is unlikely that early childhood professionals of the coming decades will work with families in which children have Tay-Sachs. It is also possible that the technology that has led to the near eradication of Tay-Sachs will reduce the incidence of other fatal or severely disabling diseases. For example, some forms of muscular dystrophy, cystic fibrosis, or sickle cell anemia could be selectively removed from the gene pool in the coming decades.

Thalassemia

Thalassemia occurs as a result of a genetic deficit that causes an insufficient amount of amino acid compounds to be produced. This lack of **polypeptides** results in a decreased production of **hemoglobin.** Consequently, the ingestion of iron, either through diet or with supplemental agents, can cause increased problems because this disease causes iron to accumulate within the body instead of being used in production of hemoglobin. More importantly, children affected with this disorder suffer from anemia that may range from mild to severe. Occasionally, thalassemia occurs in conjunction with sickle cell disease.

Characteristics   Children with thalassemia fail to thrive. They have a very pale appearance, poor appetites, and they frequently show signs of developmental delays, sometimes leading to mental retardation. Adults who have this disease have increased incidence of heart conditions because of the long-standing effects of iron accumulation within the body.

Treatment   Children affected with thalassemia require early evaluation and intervention for identified delays. Treatment of the disease itself is directed toward any symptoms that occur. There is no cure. Family education regarding diet control to reduce the amount of iron ingested, health maintenance, and educational needs should be initiated during early infancy and reinforced as children grow. The usual treatment for those children with severe anemia is routine blood transfusions. Occasionally the anemia may be so severe that removal of the spleen may be considered to decrease the rate of destruction of healthy blood cells.

Turner Syndrome

Turner Syndrome

Henry Turner first described Turner syndrome in 1938 (Williams, Richman, & Yarbrough, 1992). Found only in women, this disorder results when one of the two X chromosomes is absent (50%–55%), partially absent (12%–20%), mosaic where only a portion of the cells have a missing X chromosome (30%), or in rare instances, translocated. In most cases, there is a single X chromosome, and the characteristics of Turner syndrome are more severe than in partial or mosaic cases. The incidence of Turner syndrome is relatively rare, occurring in 1 to 4 cases per 10,000 live births (Hall & Gilchrist, 1990).

Characteristics   Girls and women with Turner syndrome are short in stature and fail to develop ovaries. One of the diagnostic characteristics of Turner syndrome is immature development of reproductive organs, with most women being infertile. Additionally, webbing of fingers, toes, and/or neck is not uncommon. Some individuals with Turner syndrome have kidney (Williams, et al., 1992) or heart abnormalities, such as coarctation of the aorta (see Appendix A) (Downey, et al., 1991).

The reported average IQ ranges from 90 to 95 (range 50–140), which is well within the normal intellectual range, though slightly lower than average (Rovet, 1990, 1993). Moreover, a distinctive pattern of cognitive functioning has been observed in girls with Turner syndrome (Downey, et al., 1991; Rovet, 1993; Williams, et al., 1992). Visual memory and visual-constructional reading and arithmetic abilities tend to be significantly lower than that of typical children. In school, children with Turner syndrome tend to have lower academic achievement than their peers (though not significantly lower than siblings), and as adults, they generally attain significantly lower occupational status.

Individuals with Turner syndrome tend to have delayed social maturity, possibly stemming from peer interactions that are disrupted by the odd appearance and unusually short stature of these girls. Furthermore, McCauley, Kay, Ito, and Treder (1987) found deficits in social awareness skills, such as being able to "read" facial affect. In spite of these findings, Rovet (1993) noted that adolescent girls with Turner syndrome tended to view themselves as intelligent, well behaved, and having normal appearance. Nevertheless, children with Turner syndrome do seem to have a higher incidence of significant behavior problems than their peers (McCauley, et al., 1987).

Etiology Turner syndrome is not considered to be familial. Therefore, after one child is born with Turner syndrome, subsequent pregnancies do not carry an increased risk of the disorder (Hall & Gilchrist, 1990). Unlike Down syndrome, absence of the X chromosome is not thought to be associated with maternal age. This may be because the absent X chromosome is paternally (father) initiated approximately two-thirds of the time (Mathur, et al., 1991) and has been associated with advanced paternal age (Hall & Gilchrist, 1990).

Interestingly, most fetuses (98% to 99%) with a missing sex chromosome spontaneously abort, as compared to a spontaneous abortion ratio of 15% of all conceptions (Hall & Gilcrhist, 1990). Hence, Turner syndrome has been estimated to represent as many as 1% of all conceptions. This disability can often be identified prenatally by ultrasound and confirmed through either amniocentesis or chorionic villus sampling.

Temple and Carney (1993) hypothesized that the absence or reduction of sex hormones, normally stimulated by both X chromosomes, adversely affects brain development during fetal growth. The impact of hormone deficiency is thought to be quite specific, resulting in the unique cognitive profile described above. That is, Turner syndrome is thought to be the result of absence of a "Turner" gene(s) rather than the absence of the X chromosome *per se* (Zinn, Page, & Fisher, 1993). In cases where two normally functioning chromosomes are present, these genes "turn on" growth production hormones necessary for healthy fetal development.

Treatment Early intervention and family support may contravene some of the expected social and cognitive problems associated with Turner syndrome. Preschool intervention might focus on readiness for mathematics and reading skills and opportunities to model and reinforce appropriate social skills. However, because of the type of intellectual deficits described above, it is very likely that cognitive problems will not surface until children begin academic tasks in school.

When girls with Turner syndrome reach puberty, hormonal replacement is usually recommended. The replacement therapy may continue into adulthood. In rare cases, spontaneous menstruation begins, and these girls are more likely to be fertile than others.

SYNDROMES WITH UNKNOWN CAUSES

Though the syndromes described above have a known etiology, there are a host of other disabling conditions whose origin continues to baffle researchers. In fact, a large majority of children have no known cause for their mental retardation. Environmental deprivations, such as nutrition, affection, and stimulation, may be the primary cause of most cases of mental retardation. On the other hand, it is likely that those syndromes that are distinctly articulated (e.g., autism) from others have some type of genetic or multifactorial origin.

Autism

Although autism is relatively rare (6–10 persons per 10,000), it is a highly visible disability. In fact, the characteristics of autism are neither discrete nor unchallenged. Some children who are identified with autism in infancy or early childhood are later identified with other disabilities. Other children who have not been labeled autistic possess behaviors termed "autistic-like." According to the American Psychiatric Association (1987), autism is classified as a pervasive developmental disorder (PDD). Historically, however, such terms as childhood schizophrenia, childhood psychosis, atypical personality disorder, and symbiotic psychosis were used to identify persons who are now labeled autistic.

Eaves and Hopper (1987–88) identified five broad categories that characterize children with autism: expressive affect, passive affect, anxiety/fear, cognition, and cognitive indifference. **Cognitive indifference,** thought to be the key diagnostic factor for autism, includes such behaviors as gaze avoidance, blank expression, lack of emotion, preference for solitude, avoidance of physical contact, hand and body movement (finger flicking, rocking, head banging, and staring at body parts), sensory stimulation by repetitive manipulation of objects, and bizarre compulsive behavior (e.g., excessive fascination with a texture or spatial arrangement).

Expressive affect includes those behaviors related to interactions or relative associations with others: distorted affect (e.g., laughs inappropriately, no pain response, smiles for no reason, hallucinations or superstitions, masturbation, and hypersenstitivity to smells. **Passive affect** is seen in behavior in which individuals are self-involved: hoarding objects, meticulousness, toe walking, and overreaction to environmental events. Relatively few persons with autism exhibit **extreme fear or anxiety,** but those who do may believe harmless objects to be dangerous or fear loud noises or crowds.

About two-thirds of children with autism are identified in infancy when caregivers note such behaviors as disinterest in toys, indifference to caregivers or physical contact, aberrant sleep patterns, excessive crying, irritability and stiffness, and an avoidance of eye contact (Mauk, 1993). Development may appear normal in the other third of children with autism until 12 to 18 months of age, at which point language and social skills may regress (Mauk, 1993).

Finally, most persons with autism have some degree of mental retardation. In fact, 40% of individuals with autism have IQs below 50. Though the range is very broad, the combination of mental retardation and other behavioral and language disabilities often results in profound developmental needs. According to Eaves (1992), autistic development is not consistent with developmental patterns in other forms of mental retardation, but can be "described as strange, distorted, even bizarre" (p. 70). **Savant** behavior, in which an individual shows extreme aptitude in one area (e.g., music or mathematics) along with autism, is very rare.

Etiology   There is no known cause of autism, though historically parents, mothers in particular, were blamed for their child's autistic behaviors. It was believed that women who failed to show love and nurturance psychologically impaired their child to such a degree as to cause autism. Thankfully, today, few women are accused of this misguided and harmful assumption. Yet, researchers are not much closer to identifying the cause of this mysterious disability. In fact, autism may not be a distinct disability in most cases; rather, it could be a set of characteristics that accompany other causes of mental retardation (Cantu, Stone, Wing, Langee, & Williams, 1990; Mauk, 1993). For example, autism is often associated with chromosomal anomalies, such as Cri du chat, fragile X syndrome, Williams syndrome, Down syndrome, XXY, congenital rubella, and PKU (Mauk, 1993). Nongenetic disorders also resemble autism; these include Rett syndrome, fetal alcohol syndrome, severe mental retardation, severe deafness and blindness, and deaf-blindness (Mauk, 1993).

Among the theories regarding the etiology of autism are metabolic disorder, birth trauma, infections of the central nervous system, and genetic anomaly. All these theories, however, have either been discredited (as in maternal neglect) or remain unvalidated. Mauk (1993) concluded that current evidence leads to a hypothesis that autism is the expression of multiple etiologies. In other words, there may be no such thing as "autism," but many different brain disorders may be expressed similarly enough to fall under the autism umbrella (see Table 6.4).

Treatment   One of the first steps to treatment is the exclusion of other potential causes of autistic behavior. For example, Eaves (1992) noted that the self-abuse in autism may mimic the tongue, finger, and lip biting of those with Lesch-Nyhan syndrome or otitis media, which commonly leads to head banging. Given present behavioral and medical technology, autism

Table 6.4/ *Frequency of Secondary Disabilities Associated with Autism*

Associated Characteristics of Persons with Autism	
Deafness	20%
IQ above 100	5%
IQ in 70–100 range	20%–30%
Severe Mental Retardation	30%–35%
Mild Mental Retardation	30%–35%
Seizure Disorder	25%
Affect Isolation	88%
Perceptual Inconsistencies (visual/hearing/touch)	80%
Stereotypy/Twiddling	82%
Self-Injury	65%
Nonverbal	50%
Echolalia	75%

is a lifelong condition, usually requiring very substantial resources. Treatment is likely to be complex, and no single intervention strategy will work with all children. In fact, even for a single child a strategy that seems to be effective at one point may lose its potency over time or overnight. Behavioral intervention, involving systematic training, has been most effective in teaching new sets of skills while reducing intrusive behavior. However, even those methods are rigorous, slow, and difficult to maintain over long periods. With the intense behavioral characteristics and limitations of technology, autism is one of the most demanding of developmental disabilities for families. The availability of multidisciplinary personnel, including a communications specialist, early childhood educator, social worker, counselor, respite care worker, and behavioral specialist, is desirable.

Cornelia de Lange Syndrome

Cornelia de Lange syndrome is a complex disorder also known as Brachmann de Lange syndrome. An immediately recognizable set of physical attributes provides the basis for diagnosis of Cornelia de Lange syndrome. These characteristics include **microcephaly,** low birth weight, long eyelashes, thin lips, small thin downturned nose, and small face, head, hands, and feet (Hawley, Jackson, & Kurnit, 1985). The absence or deformity of bones or limbs of the upper body is also common.

Mental retardation ranging from moderate to severe is almost always associated with Cornelia de Lange syndrome. Furthermore, one study found hearing losses in 100% of a sample of 45 individuals with Cornelia de Lange syndrome (Sataloff, Spiegel, Hawkshaw, Epstein, & Jackson, 1990). Delays in language development would be expected based on the two preceding characteristics. Yet, the type and severity of language delays are unpredictable. Many individuals have limited or no verbal communication skills. Others develop a repertoire of words that is superior to typical children's language skills (Goodban, 1993).

Stereotypic behavior is usually associated with Cornelia de Lange syndrome, sometimes evolving into self-mutilative behavior so severe that individuals are often institutionalized. Bryson, Sakati, Nyhan, and Fish (1971) reported IQ ranges between 12 and 30 for institution-

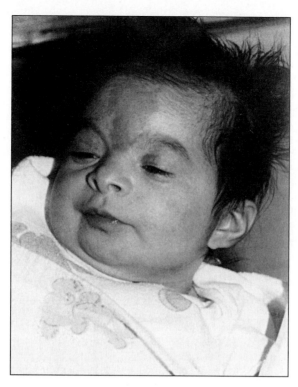

*Child with
Cornelia de Lange
syndrome*

alized adolescents with Cornelia de Lange syndrome. Though none of the individuals engaged in self-destructive behavior during their preschool years, all had caused severe life-threatening damage to themselves as a result of biting, scratching, head banging, and so on. Since none of the management or medical treatments was effective in diminishing the self-destructive behavior, it is believed that self-mutilation may be caused by some type of metabolic deficiency (Bryson, et al., 1971).

Though the specific etiology of Cornelia de Lange syndrome is unknown, there is believed to be a genetic cause. A large percentage of cases have abnormal chromosomal patterns, but to date no consistent genetic errors have been detected (Lakshaminarayana & Nallasivam, 1990). The latter hypothesize that Cornelia de Lange syndrome is not the result of a specific genetic mutation; rather, it may be the result of a predisposition for chromosomal change.

Rett Syndrome

Rett syndrome was first acknowledged as a separate class of characteristics in the 1960s, though the term itself was not coined until the 1980s (Perry, 1991). Since initial descriptions were professionally introduced, the number of individuals with this syndrome has grown to over 2000. Originally thought to be female gender specific, Rett syndrome was later found in males, and no known sex-related differences have been observed (Burd, Randall, Martsolf, & Kerbeshian, 1991). A 41-member international panel (Rett Syndrome Diagnostic Criteria Work Group) listed nine criteria that must all be present for a child to be identified with this disorder (Perry, 1991). The following diagnostic characteristics are obligatory for inclusion in the syndrome at this writing:

1. Apparently normal prenatal and perinatal period

2. Apparently normal psychomotor development for at least the first 6 months

3. Normal head circumference at birth

4. Deceleration of head growth between 5 months and 4 years

5. Loss of acquired purposeful hand skills between 6 and 30 months

6. Development of severely impaired expressive and receptive language, and severe psychomotor retardation

7. Stereotypic hand movements such as hand wringing/squeezing, clapping/tapping, mouthing, and "washing"/rubbing automatisms. These hand movements are so constant that they disrupt almost all functional activity—manipulating toys, eating, and so on.

8. A disturbance in children's ability to coordinate movement according to intention

9. Tentative diagnosis until 2 to 5 years of age

While these characteristics are present in all children identified with Rett syndrome, several other characteristics are common. These supporting characteristics include seizures, breathing dysfunctions (i.e., apnea, hyperventilation), abnormal brain activity measured on EEGs, hypertonicity, teeth grinding, scoliosis, small feet, growth retardation, and low muscle tone with muscle wasting (Burd, et al., 1991; Perry, 1991).

Individuals with Rett syndrome have very significant cognitive limitations. Language, if ever developed, usually regresses to a prelinguistic or **perlocutionary** level. Other areas of development are generally arrested between the developmental ages of 4 and 11 months. However, children do often learn to help in dressing, feeding themselves, and drinking from a cup.

A developmental trend associated with Rett syndrome has been delineated in four widely accepted stages (Hagberg & Witt-Engerstrom, 1986). Stage I is characterized as the onset of the disorder, with symptoms of a developmental halt apparent. A period of relatively rapid deterioration follows in Stage II, lasting months or just a few weeks. A relatively stable period of up to 10 years follows, during which improvements in some symptoms (e.g., seizures, autistic features) are not uncommon. Finally, Stage IV symptoms involve deterioration of motor abilities with muscle wasting and increased spasticity. Those individuals who did learn to walk usually become nonambulatory in Stage IV. Additionally, language and purposeful activity may regress to a very primitive state.

Etiology   At present, there is no known cause of Rett syndrome. However, Perry (1991) reported the findings of several lines of research that have discovered tentative evidence of a cause. The progressive nature of the disability supports theories of a metabolic abnormality. Others have discovered abnormalities in neural transmitters and enzyme functioning in individuals with Rett syndrome. There is also evidence of a genetic etiology, with familial patterns documented.

Treatment   Intervention for children with Rett syndrome currently focuses on treatment of the symptoms rather than the etiology. Medically, children require pharmacological seizure control, physical and occupational therapy, and nutritional monitoring. The developmental prognosis for individuals with Rett syndrome varies considerably. One form of treatment that seems promising for these children is music therapy, which facilitates both movement and social relatedness (Perry, 1991). For families and early educators, this disability can be quite challenging. One parent of a child with Rett syndrome said, "My child will never be considered a poster child. She does not give professionals the satisfaction of making great progress, nor is she terribly social. But I need the same type of investment by professionals as other parents of children with disabilities. The most important thing any educator can do for my child is to love my Mary" (personal communication, C. Maloney, September, 1992). In other words, all the technical and educational jargon or sophisticated intervention strategies in the world could not replace the ability to show parents that someone really cares about their child as a person rather than as a disability.

Tourette Syndrome

Like autism and Rett syndrome, Tourette syndrome is a bewildering and often devastating disability. Until 1972, the syndrome, also referred to as Gilles de la Tourette Syndrome after the French researcher who identified the disorder in 1885, was thought to be quite rare (50 known recorded cases). At that time, the Tourette Syndrome Association was initiated by a distraught father of a child with Tourette syndrome. Since then, Shapiro and Shapiro (1980, 1981) reported that the incidence of Tourette syndrome occurs once in every 2000–10,000 individuals. The most obvious characteristic of individuals with this disorder is the expression of **tics.** While 4% to 23% of all children experience tics (Torup, 1972), Tourette syndrome represents the most severe expression, with 100,000 to 330,000 cases in the United States (Bower, 1990). Tics begin to appear between ages two and seven and are three times as likely to affect boys as girls (Lerer, 1987). Manifest in the form of motor movement or vocalizations, tics have a sudden, unpredictable onset and are purposeless and irregular. Factors such as stress tend to increase the frequency, while sleep thwarts their appearance (Lerer, 1987).

Characteristics As children age, the intensity and form of symptoms also change. Motor tics usually appear first and may begin with a single movement such as an eye blink or head jerk, and usually become more complex (Santos & Massey, 1990). Eventually, children may have whole body involvement including jumping, kicking, squatting, and stomping (Lerer, 1987). Between the ages of 8 and 15, vocal tics may also appear and include barking, whistling, echolalia, grunting, coughing, snorting, and humming. Examples were provided by Santos and Massey (1990, p. 71) "'shut up,' 'stop that,' 'oh, okay,' and 'I've got to.'" Throughout one's lifetime, the tic patterns may vary, and in the early stages of the disorder, remissions may occur in which children are symptom free (Bronheim, 1991; Lerer, 1987).

Until recently, researchers had not acknowledged an "aura" experienced by many individuals with Tourette syndrome that sends them a message to perform a tic or ritual behavior. Their inability to ignore or defy these messages causes individuals another form of anxiety. In instances where persons are able to temporarily avoid performing a tic, the self-control is exerted at great expense. That is, the urge, resisted at one point, must be eventually performed, usually in a more severe form.

In addition to tics, approximately 50% of all children with Tourette syndrome have learning disabilities (Burd, Kauffman, & Kerbeshian, 1992). Burd et al. found a mean IQ of 94 in a sample of 42 children with Tourette syndrome. These findings suggest that the intelligence profiles of individuals with Tourette syndrome spans the normal range. However, there is an absence of research on tic syndromes in individuals with severe disabilities, which could result in inaccurate or inadequate treatment (Crews, Bonaventura, Hay, Steele, & Rowe, 1993).

Not surprisingly, attentional deficits and impulse control are also common in children with Tourette syndrome. Furthermore, Knell and Comings (1993) provided some evidence that Attention Deficit Hyperactivity Disorder and Tourette syndrome are genetically linked. Unfortunately, medical treatment for attentional difficulties may produce the onset or exacerbate the symptoms of Tourette syndrome.

Obsessive compulsive behavior is a third associated disorder in 55% to 74% of cases of Tourette syndrome (Walkup, et al., 1988). The impulse to complete tasks to perfection or to complete certain rituals, such as "evening up," in which actions or materials must be symmetrical, is a unique form of obsessive behavior found in persons with Tourette syndrome (Walkup, et al., 1988). Understandably, individuals may experience excessive fear of expressing their tics or compulsive behaviors in public (Walkup, et al., 1988). In addition to the movement characteristics of Tourette syndrome, these children are particularly vulnerable to psychological distress (Edell & Motta, 1989). Often ridiculed by their peers and misunderstood by teachers, children experience serious anxiety related to social encounters (Bronheim, 1991; Burd, et al., 1992; Lerer, 1987; Levi, 1991).

Etiology Approximately one-third of all children with Tourette syndrome also have **coprolalia,** the involuntary use of vulgar or obscene gestures or language (Levi, 1991). Yet, with concentration, children may be able to suppress tics, though compromising their ability to attend to other tasks (Bronheim, 1991). Because of these characteristics, some claim that the disorder is psychological and that the behaviors are purposeful rather than physical. However, strong evidence suggests that the actual cause is an autosomal dominant genetic disorder (Pauls & Leckman, 1986). Kurlan (1992) hypothesized that the defective gene thought to cause Tourette syndrome results in developmental damage to the area of the brain responsible for primitive motor, vocal, and emotional processes (basal ganglia). He further hypothesized that male sex hormones adversely affect this abnormal brain development, while female sex hormones beneficially influence this development, explaining the differential incidence of Tourette syndrome across genders.

While the precise cause of this disorder is unknown, it is possible that a combination of factors contribute (Cohen, Detlor, Shaywitz, & Leckman, 1992). For example, Bower (1990) reviewed current research and concluded that the basic cause of Tourette syndrome is a genetically caused deficiency of seratonin (chemical) in the brain (neurological), which controls emotions and initiates responses to external stimuli (environmental). According to this theory, individuals with Tourette syndrome inherit two defective genes (one from each parent). It was postulated that approximately 15% of the general population carries at least one of these genes, and that half of the carriers have addictive, compulsive, emotional, or learning problems.

Treatment This disorder can cause heartache for parents as well as children with the disorder. To know that one's child will be ridiculed or mistreated is a lifelong frustration for parents. Children and parents can be comforted by knowing that tics are out of the control of an individual with Tourette syndrome. Informing teachers and parents of other children may also reduce the stigma of tics. Santos and Massey (1990) recommended consideration of the following factors in planning intervention for a child with Tourette syndrome:

1. family's ability to cope and provide support

2. school responsiveness

3. peer group response

4. choice of vocation and acceptance in the work force

5. need for intimacy and long-term relationships

6. family planning

7. access to legal or advocate services

In some cases, medication is given, either for the tics or the associated attentional deficits. For example, Haloperidol may diminish symptoms in some individuals (Bower, 1990) but concurrently introduces the risk of side effects, such as lethargy, poor school performance, and depression, as well as a variety of neurological symptoms (Santos & Massey, 1990). Clonidine, sometimes used as a substitute for Haloperidol, may actually exacerbate tics in some children (Huk, 1989). While relief may be gained, the symptoms rarely subside entirely from medication (Bronheim, 1991). Santos and Massey recommended that medication only be used when the symptoms of Tourette syndrome are so serious that they compromise a child's development. Some behavioral self-management interventions have been effectively used to limit the onset of some of the associated disorders (obsessive-compulsive and attentional), though these treatments may be too sophisticated for preschool age children.

Williams Syndrome (Elfin-Facies Syndrome)

First identified in the early 1960s (Williams, Baratt-Boyes, & Lowe, 1961; Black & Bonham Carter, 1963), Williams syndrome, also known as elfin-facies syndrome, is a relatively rare congenital disorder, affecting 1 in 20,000 to 50,000 live births. The primary features of children with Williams syndrome are abnormal facial structure, cardiac anomalies, mental retardation, dental anomalies, hypercalcemia, and failure to thrive (Swartz, 1981). Additionally, these children are uniformly described as socially affable (Beuren, Schulze, Eberle, Harmjanz, & Apitz, 1964).

Characteristics Abnormal facial features, almost always present, become more distinctive with age. Cumulatively, the constellation of characteristics associated with Williams syndrome make children appear elfin-like: pointed chin, large ears, blue irises, malocclusion of the teeth, wide mouth that appears to be pouting, heavy cheeks, wide set eyes, and broad forehead. A failure to thrive is associated with excessive calcium levels (hypercalcemia) in the infant.

Mild to moderate mental retardation occurs in 95% of children with Williams syndrome (Karmiloff-Smith, 1993). IQ scores are generally in the 50s or 60s with the range being 40–90. However, an unusual combination of cognitive skills is sometimes observed as children typically have proficiency in visual recall and linguistic and abstract areas but difficulty in nonverbal areas of problem solving, mathematics, and motor skills (Finn, 1991; Karmiloff-Smith, 1993; Udwin & Yule, 1991).

Children with Williams syndrome have been consistently characterized as friendly, outgoing, lovable, overly affectionate, charming, and talkative. Yet, behavior problems are also common and sometimes quite severe. Children's behavior has been variously described as impulsive, hyperactive, and self-destructive (Swartz, 1981). In an objective analysis, Tomc, Williamson, and Pauli (1990) found that, compared to average children, those with Williams syndrome had a higher activity level, more negative mood, greater intensity, and greater distractibility. Perhaps as a consequence of these characteristics, these children tend to have poor relationships with their peers (Udwin & Yule, 1991).

Etiology While the etiology of Williams syndrome is unknown, it is suspected that there is a defective gene that normally produces or uses calcitonin, a hormone produced by the thyroid gland to metabolize calcium. Others have suggested that elevated calcium levels in a pregnant mother or neonate causes an imbalance of calcium ions. The identification of a mother and son with Williams syndrome prompted Sadler, Robinson, Verdaasdonk, and Gingell (1993) to hypothesize that the cause is an autosomal dominant inheritance.

Treatment Intervention for children with Williams syndrome, as with many disabilities, is twofold: (1) medical supervision of factors related to failure to thrive (i.e., feeding), cardiac difficulties and hypertension, and management of problems associated with high calcium levels and (2) educational programming focusing on strengthening talents in languages and social skills. Finn (1991) indicated that these children are often very intelligent in certain areas, particularly interpersonal talents. At the same time, compensation for difficulties in problem solving and mathematics is warranted. Children may also need physical or occupational therapy in early intervention. Additionally, the combination of gregarious character and deficient problem solving skills might eventually lead these children into danger. Therefore, parents might be anxious to teach young children with Williams syndrome decision-making in circumstances that are threatening.

As these children grow older and have a tendency to be labeled "difficult," parents may blame themselves for their child's behavior since these children should be "easy" according to the characterization (Tomc, et al., 1990). Counseling parents to relieve the burden of responsibility and training them in behavior management strategies, when necessary, may be helpful.

METABOLISM

This section deals with many of the common metabolic disorders that adversely affect young children. The discussion is limited to conditions that may be seen more frequently within the classroom and is certainly not inclusive of the multitude of disorders that occur. Individual children afflicted with common, as well as rare, conditions that alter normal development require individualized plans for education and inclusion into a community.

Metabolism is the total of all the physical and chemical changes that occur within a human being during each moment of the life cycle. These include all the material and energy transformations (e.g., chemical to mechanical or heat) that occur within living cells. Metabolism is the breaking down of molecular bonds in food sources for the production of energy to be used by cells for their work. The two fundamental processes of metabolism are **anabolism** (building up) and **catabolism** (breaking down). Anabolism converts ingested food into products that can be used by the cells, such as glucose, the single most vital substance necessary for cells to function. Catabolism breaks down substances into simpler structures that can be excreted or converted into energy. This production of energy gives cells the means to work efficiently. Metabolism follows the rules of thermodynamics and produces heat, which is returned to the environment. The heat that is dissipated into the environment is lost through evaporation, radiation, convection, or conduction. Because living organisms are living systems, they are open and constantly exchanging with the environment. This exchange produces a steady state that requires maintenance by a constant input of energy from the environment. The steady state also requires dynamic interactions within human subsystems and with the environment.

Metabolism is under the control of an individual's genetics. Genes produce proteins, which are either part of cellular structure or enzymes. **Enzymes** are complex organic catalysts that induce chemical change in other substances without being changed in the process. For example, the enzyme lactase makes it possible to comfortably digest lactose (milk sugar) in milk. Any gene can be altered during the course of fetal development or may change as the result of adverse physical or environmental factors. Changes (mutations) in genes will, in turn, affect the specific protein for which the gene is responsible. An altered protein or the absence of a specific protein produces errors of metabolism. Most of these errors produce abnormalities of protein, carbohydrate, or fat metabolism.

Hypoglycemia

Hypoglycemia is a condition in which there is a decreased amount of glucose (simple sugar) available for use by cells. Glucose is the single most important substance necessary for brain cells to function. It is also critical for normal functioning of red blood cells, the adrenal glands, and the kidneys (Fajans & Floyd, 1976). Other organs and systems can use other sources for nutrition and energy. When a person takes adequate food, glucose comes from the diet. When one does not eat, glucose is produced by the liver through the act of breaking down stored substances. Lack of sufficient glucose produces a failure in the normal chain of metabolism and results in the death of cells. Many different conditions and disease processes can cause hypoglycemia. These may include genetic defects, stress, nutritional deficiencies, infections, and metabolic errors.

Adults can tolerate lower levels of glucose for longer periods of time than children because of their larger body mass and, more importantly, because they have a smaller brain mass in comparison to the total body size than does a child (Samuels, 1988). Adults can also control blood sugar levels more efficiently by breaking down amino acids into glucose. However, young children have decreased stores of amino acids to utilize for the same process.

Hypoglycemia affects infants and children in different ways and for different reasons. A fetus receives glucose from its mother through the placenta. During the last trimester of pregnancy, stored glucose becomes concentrated in the liver, heart, and skeletal muscles of unborn children. This is to allow for the transition of the fetus after birth. The process requires the metabolism of stored glucose to provide energy for the neonate until sufficient feedings have been initiated to provide external glucose sources. Stress, birth injury, respiratory distress, or other emergencies increase the rate of metabolism and deplete the available stores. This results in decreased glucose levels within the bloodstream. Hypoglycemia produces symptoms of neurological compromise such as jitteriness, decreased activity, and seizures and may be significant enough to cause long-term problems such as learning disabilities or even cerebral palsy (Cole, 1991).

Most hypoglycemic conditions appear later and can be associated with other disease processes. These may include malfunction of the pancreas, drug ingestion, liver disease, kidney disease, infection, hypopituitarism (decrease in function of the pituitary gland), hypothyroidism, and conditions that promote dietary deficiencies such as eating disorders and failure to thrive (Shakir & Amin, 1991). Early diagnosis and treatment is necessary for the prevention of mental retardation in these infants and children. Mental retardation can be found in as many as 80% of those children who do not receive early and effective treatment of hypoglycemia (Ulstrom & Sockalowsky, 1990).

Recognition of those children who are at risk for hypoglycemia and preparation to deal with acute symptoms decrease the possibility of damage from the condition. Children with frequent infections, those with congenital defects who have poor nutrition, those with seizure disorders, and those affected with other disabling conditions require close observation within the educational setting. Symptoms of hypoglycemia may include increased sweating, poor color, decreased attention, sleepiness, seizures, or other symptoms that are specific to an individual child. Chronic hypoglycemia requires a high protein diet to maintain the level of glucose in the blood stream. Awareness by educators and caregivers, along with education about symptoms and treatments, are the keys to decreasing the impact of the condition upon a child.

Galactosemia

Galactosemia is a genetic disorder in which certain people cannot use the nutrient galactose. Galactose is a simple hexose sugar that is normally ingested through the diet, absorbed through the intestinal tract, and converted to glycogen in the liver. Three different inherited disorders can cause an interruption in the normal process for breaking down galactose into glucose. The main source of galactose in the human diet is milk produced by mammals. The principal carbohydrate of these milk products is a form of lactose that is usually broken down in the intestinal tract into glucose and galactose.

Individuals with galactosemia have a cellular deficiency that does not allow this conversion to occur. These individuals develop toxic levels of galactose that may cause failure to thrive; vomiting; cataracts; liver disease; the loss of **albumin,** amino acids, and galactose in the urine; the buildup of acid in the blood stream; and mental retardation (Segal, 1989). If untreated, death occurs.

The treatment for galactosemia is to eliminate galactose, particularly milk products, from the diet. Complete elimination is desired, and during the early phase of treatment, necessary. Failure to comply with treatment results in liver failure followed by death. Casein hydrolysate and soybean formulas are substituted for feeding of infants and children affected with this disease. Care is necessary to educate these children to be aware of sources of galactose in other food sources when they progress to solid foods. Safe food lists are available for parents and caregivers (Koch, Acosta, Donnell, & Lieberman, 1965). No research has shown that diet restrictions can be lifted at any time within the person's life span, though some affected children appear to tolerate milk after puberty. This finding is not consistent in all individuals affected with galactosemia.

Early diagnosis and treatment can prevent the onset of symptoms and development of retardation that occur with this disease. Later recognition and treatment can eliminate symptoms of failure to thrive, gastrointestinal problems, and liver dysfunction but cannot reverse or eliminate cataracts or mental retardation. Even those individuals diagnosed at birth, and treated immediately, may have an increased risk of speech problems and ovarian dysfunction (Donnell & Ng, 1990; Waisbren, Norman, Schnell, & Levy, 1983).

The mental retardation that occurs with both treated and untreated galactosemia can be very subtle or severe. Even children who have normal IQs sometimes have significant learning disabilities, especially related to spatial relationships and mathematics (Fishler, Koch, Connell, & Wenz, 1980). Many of these children also have behavioral problems thought to be associated with either the disease or the psychological effects of severe dietary restrictions.

Phenylketonuria

Phenylketonuria (PKU) is an inherited autosomal recessive inborn error of metabolism. This error results in the inability of individuals to use the essential amino acid phenylalanine. Build-up of phenylalanine results in mental retardation from defective **myelinization** in the brain and degeneration of both gray and white matter (Hayes, Rarback, Berry, & Clancy, 1987).

Many infants born with phenylketonuria are blond with blue eyes and have a fair complexion. Symptoms of untreated cases are vomiting, failure to thrive, short stature, a distinct odor to urine and sweat, seizures, and a rapid progression of mental retardation (Hayes, et al., 1987). This disorder may occur as frequently as 1 in every 15,000 live births in the United States (Nyhan, 1990).

Though previous family history is a marker for diagnosis, this defect cannot be detected by prenatal amniocentesis. Therefore PKU cannot be diagnosed prior to the delivery of an infant. All newborns between 48 and 72 hours of age are initially screened for phenylalanine levels through a simple blood test obtained by sticking the infant's heel. All specimens are sent to a state sponsored laboratory in order to increase the standardization of results. Results are available within two to three weeks of birth.

PKU was the first inherited disease that could be successfully treated with diet. The goal of diet therapy is to restrict the oral intake of phenylalanine, thereby preventing excess buildup in the blood that will cause mental retardation, while still providing an adequate diet for normal growth and development (Hayes, et al., 1987). Any solid foods that are high in protein (cow's milk, meats, dairy products, etc.) are excluded from the diet of children with PKU (Hayes, et al., 1987). Most states within the United States offer assistance to families affected with PKU by providing the dietary supplements essential for normal growth and development. The most commonly used products for infants and children are Lofenalac, a low phenylalanine formula that is used with infants, and Phenyl-Free, a food source that is used with older children.

Current screening programs and available treatment have significantly decreased the incidence of retardation caused by PKU. However, failure to detect the disorder in a newborn (an example may be when there is a home delivery) will result in retardation. Initially, the only symptom may be irritability. This may rapidly evolve to severe vomiting with the sudden onset of seizures. Once neurological symptoms appear, normal recovery without retardation is rare. Affected children also have a decreased life span (Nyhan, 1990).

Families with children affected by PKU require counseling and education as well as positive, ongoing reinforcement of dietary goals to be successful with control of the disease. Success of children and families is dependent on understanding the diet and the reasons for restrictions, making sure that the diet is age-appropriate through the developmental years and decreasing exposure to infections for an affected child (Hayes, et al., 1987). As children get older, it may become increasingly difficult to adequately monitor the diet. Therefore, the entire family must have a commitment to success. Some research has suggested that for PKU (unlike galactosemia) dietary restrictions can be lifted later in life.

Hypothyroidism

Hypothyroidism is a condition in which there is an inadequate production of thyroid hormone. The condition can be present at birth **(cretinism)** or develop at any point during life **(myxedema)** and presents a range of mild to severe symptoms. The **thyroid gland** is located in the neck and produces thyroid hormones, which circulate throughout the body, aiding in the transportation of protein and in the metabolism of fat. They also aid in the synthesis of cholesterol. These hormones are essential to normal development of embryonic and fetal life. By 10 weeks of gestation, the thyroid gland is mature and hormones can be detected in fetal tissue (Torpe-Beeston, 1991).

Congenital hypothyroidism affects as many as 1 out of every 3000 to 5000 children born (Sobel & Saenger, 1989). Pilot programs that screen large numbers of newborn infants in the United States for congenital hypothyroidism were initiated in 1972 (Dussault, Coulombe & Laberge, 1975). This project showed that screening mechanisms were effective in detecting affected infants, thus allowing for early intervention with thyroid replacement therapy. In 1974, mass population infant screening programs were introduced and accepted throughout most of the industrialized world (Fisher, 1983). The treatment consists of medications given orally to affected infants and children.

Some infants born with hypothyroidism will show symptoms before birth. These may include deficiencies in skeletal formation and in linear growth that may be apparent on a perinatal ultrasound. Without a prior history of familial hypothyroidism, perinatal screening may not be done during the course of a pregnancy with the subsequent delivery of obvious but undiagnosed hypothyroidism. These infants will have symptoms that may include lethargy, dry skin, a large tongue (macroglossia), abnormal facial features (broad, flat nose, widely set eyes, and coarse features), and an increased incidence of umbilical hernias. Such infants are at very high risk for growth and developmental retardation (Schimke, 1990).

Most infants suffering from congenital hypothyroidism look normal at birth. Their physical appearance and behavior may be completely within the expected parameters for a newborn (Virtanen, 1988). After birth, symptoms may develop rapidly or appear over the first month of life. Behavioral signs of hypothyroidism may include poor feeding, temperature instability, a hoarse cry, increased size of the abdomen, swelling of the hands and feet, and large fontanels (Virtanen, 1988).

A family history of congenital thyroid dysfunction increases the probability of genetic origins. In fact, many of the functional disorders of the thyroid gland are linked to inheritance. Both autosomal dominant and recessive inheritance patterns have been linked with congenital hypothyroidism (Fisher, 1991). However, it is not yet possible to detect a carrier.

Treatment of congenital hypothyroidism consists of replacing the thyroid hormone. Prior to mass screening, approximately 65% of affected children tested with IQ levels below 85 (Klein, 1985). Current screening and treatment has improved outcomes with most affected children scoring within a normal IQ range and progressing in school at acceptable levels (Fisher & Foley, 1989). This finding is not consistent with newborns delivered with obvious disease. In spite of early and aggressive hormone therapy, these children exhibit delays in motor skills, visual perception skills, and language development (Miculan, Turner, & Paes, 1993).

CONGENITAL HEART DEFECTS

Congenital heart defects are a problem for a significant number of infants and young children. It is estimated that approximately 7.5 out of every 1000 live births in the United States produce an infant with such a defect (Mitchell, Korones, & Berendes, 1971). Furthermore, many genetic disorders and other physical abnormalities are accompanied by heart defects. Most of these infants are ill enough within the neonatal period to require intervention. Consequently, it is estimated that as high as 36% of all neonatal deaths can be attributed to cardiac defects within this period (Mitchell, et al., 1971).

Congenital defects are generally categorized into either cyanotic or noncyanotic abnormalities. Categorization is dependent on the heart's ability to direct blood flow to and from the lungs and then to the general circulation. Situations in which blood bypasses the lungs result in decreased oxygen available to cells and produce a blue-tinged color to the skin, known as **cyanosis.** Diagnosis followed by appropriate treatment is the key to decreasing the general adverse effects of congenital heart defects.

Understanding the differences between fetal circulatory patterns and those required of an infant after birth provides a means for understanding how an affected fetus can survive a significant defect through the period of gestation. Fetal circulation consists of parallel circuits. When fetal blood bypasses the lungs, either the right or left ventricle will pump blood directly to the general circulation (see Figure 6.10). The pressure in either ventricle during this period is similar. This parallel structure allows for fetal survival in spite of a variety of significant cardiac defects. Even if one of the ventricles is completely obstructed, the other ventricle can maintain sufficient blood flow with little effort.

The birth process results in a remarkable change in the blood flow pattern of the infant. With the infants' first breath, blood flows into the lungs and the blood flow from the placenta ceases (see Figure 6.11). At the same time, an increase in the independent breathing of newborns results in oxygenation of the blood from the infant's own lungs, which, in turn, causes closure of the ductus venosus and the narrowing of the ductus arteriosus. Finally, changes in intracardiac pressures result in the functional closure of the foramen ovale. These changes dramatically increase the work of the heart, especially the left ventricle. It is with this demand that many congenital defects will produce symptoms that lead to recognition of an existing cardiac defect.

Most congenital cardiac defects produce symptoms that are diagnosed within the first week of life (Mitchell, et al., 1971). Symptoms may include respiratory distress, a heart rate over 200 beats per minute, a heart murmur, difficulty with feeding, and failure to gain weight. Many of these may persist into childhood (depending on the defect) with the addition of exercise intolerance, poor physical growth, delayed development, recurrent infections, squatting, clubbing of the fingers and toes, and increased blood pressure. Many of these children also have chronic behavior problems, possibly related to repeated hospitalizations.

Certain cardiac defects are known to be associated with certain genetic malformations and maternal conditions. For example, there is an association between Down syndrome and endocardial cushion defects. Males have an increased risk for coarctation of the aorta, aortic stenosis, and transposition of the great vessels; whereas, females have an increased incidence of atrial septal defects. When a mother is diabetic, there is a high risk for significant multiple cardiac defects in the fetus. Congenital rubella is associated with narrowing of the pulmonary arteries and patent ductus arteriosus. Lesions associated with prematurity or low birth weight are also found with an increased incidence of both patent ductus arteriosus and ventricular septal defects (Lambert, Canent, & Hohn, 1966).

Endocardial Cushion Defect

Endocardial cushion defects occur when there is abnormal development of the septum's between the atria and the ventricles, which includes a malformed, deficient, or abnormally attached **mitral valve.** This abnormality results in mixing of oxygenated and nonoxygenated blood between the right and left atria and the right and left ventricles with incompetent valves. This defect may appear as an isolated cardiac defect but more commonly is associated with other malformations and very frequently with Down syndrome.

Figure 6.10/ *Fetal Circulatory Patterns: Most of the blood bypasses the lungs.*

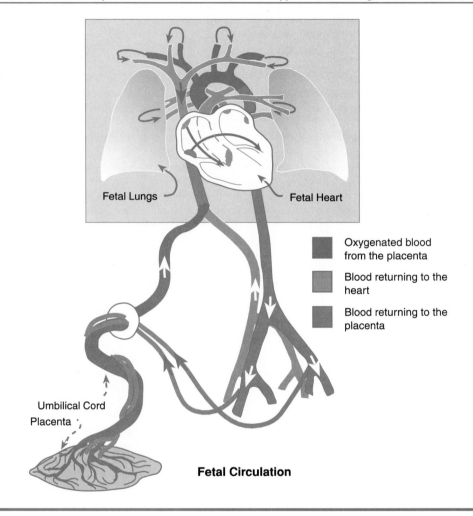

Fetal Lungs

Fetal Heart

Oxygenated blood
from the placenta

Blood returning to the
heart

Blood returning to the
placenta

Umbilical Cord

Placenta

Fetal Circulation

Specific defects of the heart are described in more detail in Appendix A. The congenital heart defects described there include:

Patent Ductus Arteriosus

Ventricular Septal Defect

Atrial Septal Defect

Coarctation of the Aorta

Complete Transposition of the Great Vessels

Tetralogy of Fallot

Hypoplastic Left Heart Syndrome

Figure 6.11/ *Establishment of independent heart and lung function in infants changes the direction of blood flow.*

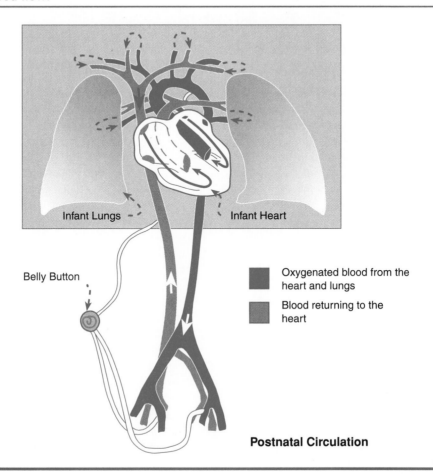

Infant Lungs

Infant Heart

Belly Button

■ Oxygenated blood from the heart and lungs

■ Blood returning to the heart

Postnatal Circulation

GASTROINTESTINAL ANOMALIES

By the time they are born, infants already have much experience with swallowing and gastric emptying. As early as the fourth month of gestation, the gastrointestinal tract is fully formed and functional. The fetus continually swallows fluid and passes it through the stomach into the intestine. After birth, infants experience no new gastrointestinal challenges except the passage of feces and the acts of opening and closing the airway during feeding. This allows an infant to suck, swallow, and breath during feeding. Gastrointestinal maturity is such that infants are capable of fully digesting solids as well as liquids.

Immediately at birth, air enters the stomach from the mouth through the esophagus, filling the stomach and passing into the small intestine. Over the next 12 hours, this air and any food subsequently introduced pass through the small intestine into the large intestine. Anytime during this process feces may be passed. The first stool, called meconium, is very dark and sticky. Failure to pass meconium over the first day of life may mean that an obstruction is present. Physical examination may reveal an obstruction, but more commonly, X-ray studies are used to identify abnormalities when an obstruction is suspected.

The Initial Diagnosis

Interview with David DeWolf

My wife and I have four children. Charles is 11, Maja is 9, Robin, who has Down syndrome, is 7, and Peter is 3. We already had two children when Robin was born and had another child about 3 years later. My wife is basically a full-time mom; with four children you're a full-time mom regardless of what you do.

Robin was born in Oklahoma. Although my wife was 39, we had no particular interest in any kind of prenatal screening, so her disability was a surprise to us when she was born. Priscilla's uncle had Down syndrome, and I had met him early in our marriage, so we were not unfamiliar with the phenomenon. I suppose I'd thought about it, but we were still taken by surprise when she was born. Fortunately, she didn't suffer any of the heart anomalies or stomach problems that are sometimes associated with Down syndrome. I believe about 40% of children with Down syndrome do have some kind of heart anomaly, and I think that about a quarter of kids with Down syndrome do require surgical correction of a valve problem. So far as we can tell, she doesn't have any of those conditions.

Robin was basically a pretty healthy kid. She was born very early in the morning, about 6:30 A.M. and my wife had waited a long time to go the hospital, so I was afraid she was going to have the baby in the car on the way there. We tried to stretch things out so that the doctor would get there in time, and he barely made it when Priscilla gave birth. I was the first one to see Robin, and the moment she was born I had a momentary flash, a fleeting thought that she looked like Uncle Tommy.

I didn't dwell on that thought because so much else was going on and she was basically a happy, healthy little girl. But I remember almost asking one of the nurses, "She doesn't have Down syndrome does she?" I didn't really know quite how to ask that, and then it just seemed like a dumb thing to ask. It was a relatively uncomplicated process until the pediatrician came for his check-up around noon.

We'd had Robin for almost four hours when the pediatrician visited. He picked Robin up and took her to the nursery and did various examinations. He was alert to the possibility of Down syndrome and looked for some of the 50 different characteristics that are found with varying degrees of frequency in children with Down syndrome. He finally identified enough where he felt reasonably confident that his intuition was correct.

I could almost tell by the way he was examining Robin that this was not routine. I could only see him through the glass as he examined her, but there was a sort of look of concern on his face or a kind of seriousness. I just had this sense that there was something going on. And when he came out, I asked him if everything was okay and he said, "Where's Priscilla?"

When we were both present, he said, "I think she has Down syndrome, and we'll have to do more tests." For some reason, by the time he said that, I had forgotten or discounted my earlier intuition, so we were pretty devastated at that point. We began to scramble to try to get some information. No matter how much you know from daily contact with any given disability, whether it's being hearing impaired or any kind of disability that your child might have, once you have a child with that condition, you are desperate for information that will help you plan or locate yourself.

I think the scariest thing for a parent is the uncertainty of not knowing what the future holds. I felt lucky that a disability like Down syndrome has a pretty good baseline of information. Its characteristics are fairly stable; although there are variations such as these heart problems, the general range of

expectations is more reliable than a hearing impairment or a heart defect or some other characteristic that runs a gamut of mild, to moderate, to severe, to fatal. Those are situations where you don't know from one moment to the next what to prepare yourself for, what to brace yourself for. Down syndrome is sufficiently common so that you run into a lot of people who've had the same experience and with whom you can share information. If your child has a more unusual condition and also a condition that's harder to identify, it's a lot more isolating to those parents.

I thought it was really valuable that we got to know Robin as a girl first and a kid with Down syndrome second. I have heard many people say that having advance notice would give them an opportunity to prepare for it. My experience was very contrary to that. I think if we had known in advance that Robin had Down syndrome, and all we knew was a problem, and we didn't have it attached to a cuddly little baby, I think it would have been much more difficult for

us. What made it so easy was that we had a real girl. The glass, so to speak, was more than half full. Everything with the disability came packaged with all these other wonderful things. If you study these conditions by themselves, by looking at a medical textbook, they are far more frightening and disturbing than when you see the condition in the context of a real child.

Lower tract intestinal obstructions, either complete or partial, occur anywhere from the first position of the small bowel (duodenum) through the small bowel and large bowel to the anus. A variety of causes can produce an identical set of symptoms. The success or failure of a surgical repair depends on the mechanics of the obstruction, the location within the tract, and the promptness in diagnosis and initiation of treatment. Lower tract obstructions usually result from either a mechanical failure or a functional failure. Mechanical failures are abnormalities in the formation and/or placement of the tract. Functional failures are abnormalities in the way the gastrointestinal tract works.

Many congenital defects of the gastrointestinal system are possible and often occur with other congenital abnormalities, such as genetic disorders. Anytime an infant is suspected of having a genetic defect, the workup must include examination of the gastrointestinal system.

Cleft Lip and Cleft Palate

Cleft lip and cleft palate (roof of mouth) are commonly occurring defects that may be present as often as 1 out of every 700 live births (Eliason, 1991). Cleft lip and/or palate may occur as an isolated defect (lip or palate), in conjunction with each other, or associated with other congenital abnormalities. A cleft is a division or split that occurs between two tissue planes. Many recognized congenital syndromes present with this defect (e.g., trisomy 13, 15, or 18). The clefts that appear in either the lip or palate are separate defects but there may be a relationship due to the fact that the disruption in normal development occurs during a relative time period in gestational development, between the 5th and 13th week of gestation.

Formation of the lip and palate occurs in stages from about the fifth to twelfth weeks of gestation. It is during this time that the normal fusion process fails, with a cleft occurring. The specific cause for a lip/palate defect is not generally known but may be related to prenatal exposure to teratogens (i.e., maternal alcohol consumption), other anomalies, or possibly to genetic factors (since an increased incidence has been noted in families) (McInerney, 1985).

The cause of isolated defects is different than those appearing with multiple congenital anomaly syndromes, of which more than 300 have been identified (Cohen & Bankier, 1991). Ethnic origins also appear to have some relationship to the occurrence of isolated defects. That is, Native Americans have the highest incidence, while African-Americans have the lowest (Vanderas, 1987).

Cleft lips and palates are classified as unilateral (affecting one side) or bilateral (affecting both sides) and as either complete or incomplete. Approximately 25% of all reported cases involve an isolated cleft lip with another 25% involving an isolated cleft palate (Hardy, 1988). The occurrence of a cleft lip without a cleft palate decreases the potential difficulties that face affected infants.

Clefting of the lip involves a split that affects the lip and gum and may extend upward into the nose. In cases involving bilateral lip clefts, the defect may be extensive enough to join together at a point behind the gum. In these cases a section of the lip and gum appears to hang freely from the septum of the nose. The majority of infants presenting with a bilateral cleft lip also have a cleft palate. The impact of such extensive abnormalities on appearance presents significant problems for families. In many cases the disfigurement is initially so overwhelming that parents experience difficulties in looking past the defect to the infant, and initiation of parent/child bonding is interrupted.

Facial disfigurement (with resulting parental rejection) and feeding difficulties are the two most significant problems that face an infant affected with an isolated cleft lip. Society places a great deal of importance on external appearance, and the face is central to this view. It is vital that health care providers, extended family members, and other individuals involved in providing service give support during the initial bonding experience of new parents of an infant with a cleft lip. This will allow for every opportunity to get past negative feelings and promote normal bonding.

Infants with a cleft lip may have difficulty establishing a normal feeding pattern. Interruption in the integrity of the lip produces the challenge of providing optimum nutrition to foster the necessary growth required before surgical repair can be attempted. Feeding devices are available that can use either breast milk or prepared formulas to promote a feeding pattern that is as close to normal as possible. Many infants with an isolated cleft lip can successfully breast feed. These infants feed using structures within the mouth to express milk from a nipple. Tongue movements assist with this process, but the lip is not essential to establish a successful suck. Referral to appropriate experts within the community can provide support for a successful feeding experience for an infant with an isolated defect.

A cleft palate involves a split in the hard or soft palate or, in some cases, both. Infants who are born with a cleft palate experience a wider variety of problems than do those infants born with an isolated cleft lip. These include facial deformities, speech impairment, hearing loss, infections, feeding, problems and learning disabilities that may or may not be related to either speech or hearing problems.

The potential for failure to thrive because of a decreased ability to eat is a significant problem for infants born with a cleft palate. Feeding problems are generally a result of the physical defect but may also be related to other disabilities. Normal sucking requires the tongue and/or the palate to stabilize the nipple and then to suck milk. This is dependent on the method chosen to feed an infant—breast or bottle. Cleft palates prevent nipple stabilization and create an abnormal suck. Devices such as extended nipples placed on squeeze bottles, flexible tubing placed next to a breast and connected to a bottle of pumped milk, and standard nipples with enlarged holes are available to assist with feeding. Each defect may require adaptation of feeding devices and techniques. Evaluation by an occupational therapist should be made prior to initial discharge from the hospital after birth, and a method of feeding devised. This plan includes parental instruction and referral to appropriate resources within the community for ongoing follow-up.

Another significant problem associated with cleft palate is acute and chronic middle ear infection. Acute infection may be a single episode in a susceptible infant that can be cleared with antibiotic treatment. Chronic infection results from a defective opening between the bacteria laden oral cavity, up the eustachean tubes, to the middle ear space. Surgical repair of the cleft does not significantly decrease the incidence of infection (Yetter, 1992). Therefore, conductive hearing loss from repeated infections is a common occurrence. Though the procedure is controversial, many infants will be placed on antibiotic therapy prophylactically and may even have drain tubes surgically placed through the ear drum, in an effort to reduce infection and subsequent hearing loss.

Speech delay also frequently accompanies a cleft palate. Sucking is necessary to develop muscles used to make speech physically possible. Alterations in the normal sucking process delay the muscle development. Moreover, the presence of a single cavity (nose and mouth) alters the normal sound production. Both the medical condition and the possibility of social isolation decrease the opportunities these infants have for verbal interaction with the adult world, a vital link to the development of speech.

Another problem faced by children with a cleft palate is related to the normal progression of tooth eruption. Dentition is not only delayed, but in many cases, normal tooth formation may be absent. Early evaluation by a dentist with appropriate referral for orthodontics is part of the teaming approach necessary to meet the total needs of the infant and family.

Hearing loss and speech delay lead to speech-related learning disabilities. These may be influenced by the social isolation that frequently results from the facial disfigurement that is part of this defect. In addition, educators sometimes make erroneous assumptions about intelligence in children with facial defects. Richman (1978) found that teachers both underestimated ability and had lower expectations for performance from students with moderate or severe facial disfigurement.

Families of infants who have a cleft palate require a multidisciplinary approach to meet their needs. This teaming should include the primary care physician, plastic surgeon, public health nurse, speech pathologist, audiologist, dentist, social worker, occupational therapist, and educator. This provides for long-term planning to assure that both actual and potential needs of infants and families can be met.

Children whose defects have been successfully repaired may continue to experience alterations in social interactions and with learning. Persistent problems with articulation and with hypernasality of the voice may lead to ongoing anxiety in group interaction and to low self-esteem. Stereotyping must be avoided and identification of personal biases toward the importance of physical attractiveness are important topics in discussion within the team when planning the approach to services for each infant and family affected by this defect.

Details regarding other gastrointestinal anomalies may be found in Appendix A. These include:

Atresia/Stenosis of the Esophagus

Duodenal Atresia

GENITOURINARY SYSTEM

Normal development of the urinary tract (kidneys, tubes, and bladder) is a critical gestational task that frequently can mean the difference between survival and neonatal death. Development of the tubes is well underway by the sixth week of gestation and the bladder begins to form during this time period. By the end of the first trimester, the kidneys, uterus, bladder, and urethra are complete and functional.

Failure of the kidneys to develop is not compatible with neonatal survival. Moreover, many of these infants have other significant genetic malformations that prevent the initiation of dialysis or the consideration of a kidney transplant. Current prenatal technology provides information prior to delivery of a fetus affected with a significant kidney abnormality. A decrease in the amount of amniotic fluid may indicate an abnormality in the urinary tract. Infants and children with genitourinary defects sometimes require surgical accommodation to compensate for their biological problems.

An ostomy is an opening made from an internal tube to an external source to allow for passage of urine or stool from the body. The formation of an ostomy is a surgical procedure. A stoma is the external opening that is on the abdomen at the site of the ostomy. The site is dependent on the reason for creation of the ostomy.

Ostomies are created in the presence of many of the gastrointestinal and genitourinary defects. They may be temporary or permanent depending on the condition requiring their creation. Ostomies placed for urine diversion are generally permanent; whereas ostomies created for stool diversion may frequently be temporary until staged repairs of abnormalities can be successfully accomplished.

A pouch is worn over the external stoma for the collection of urine or stool. This pouch requires careful monitoring to prevent skin irritation from urine or stool. In the absence of other disabilities, a child can be taught to monitor and maintain the external pouch. In situations in which children are neither physically nor mentally able, caregivers or even educators must be adept at both monitoring and maintaining the stoma and pouch. Careful monitoring of an ostomy can prevent foul odors, leakage, and skin irritation. This is essential to promoting self-esteem in the child and allowing a normal lifestyle.

IMPLICATIONS FOR THE TWENTY-FIRST CENTURY

The twenty-first century holds great promise as well as possible pitfalls for humans in terms of their ability to forsee, respond to, and prevent the disabilities discussed in this chapter. Without question, the cause of many inborn variations such as Tourette syndrome and autism will be identified. As in the case of cystic fibrosis, the likelihood of finding a cure is improved with identification of etiology. In fact, it is altogether possible that a treatment will be found to forstall the tragic outcomes of such disabilities as muscular dystrophy, cystic fibrosis, and Rett syndrome. Further delineation of the human genome will identify and describe new disabilities, which were once unclassified, to join recent discoveries, such as Prader-Will syndrome. Prenatal diagnoses will be done earlier and earlier, with greater reliability.

All these changes will alter the "natural" genetic course of the human species. Many disabilities could go the way of Tay-Sachs, selectively eliminated from the gene pool. Others could be treated by replacing defective genes with normal genes to prevent a disease such as sickle cell anemia.

Whether the imminent changes (there is little doubt that such changes will occur) will eventually be healthy for our species or harmful is a question seldom asked. When we get to the point of asking "Do we want 'this variation' or, 'that variation'?" what comes next?

For example, Pueschel (1991) argued against the practice of using prenatal diagnosis to detect Down syndrome, on the grounds that the overriding purpose is to determine whether or not an abortion is needed. Several procedures are available to detect this chromosomal anomaly: amniocentesis, chorionic villus sampling, ultrasonography, and percutaneous umbilical blood sampling. The primary purpose of using prenatal diagnosis is to identify fetuses with defective genetic or structural problems and terminate pregnancies, thereby leading to the prevention of Down syndrome and other disorders.

The arguments for prenatal screening and selective abortions of affected fetuses include:

1. It benefits the individual woman and her family.

2. It also benefits society because such procedures have a eugenic effect in eliminating defective genes from the gene pool.

3. It reduces the financial burden to society.

4. It is preventive medicine.

5. It increases the quality of life for the family.

6. The fetus has a right to be born healthy (Pueschel, 1991, p.186).

Pueschel pointed out various unforseen and ultimately questionable outcomes of prenatal diagnosis. For example, many physicians have been found liable for "negligent genetic counseling" when there was a "wrongful birth" of a child with Down syndrome. Other medical personnel have lost court battles because a specific diagnostic test that might have detected Down syndrome was not conducted. In the latter, parents claimed that they were deprived of the opportunity to make a decision to terminate the affected fetus.

A second issue surrounds the practice in our society of deeming disability as a negative. Many of the arguments mentioned above, for example, are a part of the mythology surrounding persons with Down syndrome. The thoughts of Pearl S. Buck (1973) regarding her daughter illustrate the belief that lives can be richer, not necessarily worsened, by the membership of persons with disabilities:

> In this world, where cruelty prevails in so many aspects of our lives, I would not add the weight of choice to kill rather than to let live. A retarded child, a handicapped person, brings his own gift to life, even to the life of normal human beings. That gift is comprehended in the lessons of patience, understanding, and mercy, lessons which we all need to relive and to practice with one another, whatever we are.

A study conducted by Meryash (1992) may shed the most light on this issue. When women were asked what factors would influence their decision to abort a child with fragile X syndrome, the most salient answer was a fear that the parents' social lives might be disrupted. It is worth noting that women who were more highly educated, had a greater knowledge of fragile X, and had other children with disabilities were more likely to select abortion. Furthermore, the women identified the advice of their physician as an important factor in making a decision to abort. The latter is of concern to Pueschel, who fears that professionals who do not know or work with children with disabilities will be unfairly negative. "Genetic research has the potential for misunderstanding and misapplication; there may be a time when we are tempted to cross the line from curing or preventing a medically burdensome disease to enhancing genetic traits. Society must be able to place wedges in this potential slippery slope" (Kaback, et al., 1993, p. 322).

STUDY GUIDE QUESTIONS

1. How is individual variability related to treatment and prevention?

2. What is genetics?

3. Describe the basic mechanisms of inheritance. Define the following terms in the course of your answer: (1) chromosomes, (2) genes, (3) traits, (4) genetic mapping, (5) chromosomal region, (6) deletion, (7) mutation, (8) protein product, (9) "new genetics," and (10) the human genome.

4. What is the interplay of genetic codes and environmental factors on the cause and treatment of genetic diseases?

5. Describe cellular activity. Define the following terms in the course of your answer: (1) DNA, (2) nucleic acid compound, (3) alleles, (4) homozygote, (5) heterzygotes, (6) genotypes, (7) phenotypes, (8) mitosis, (9) meiosis, (10) gametes, and (11) errors in cell division.

6. How many chromosomes are there within a cell structure? How many of these are autosomes? What is the 23rd pair?

7. Describe single gene disorders.

8. Discuss the relationship among the following: dominant and recessive traits; male and female sex-linked traits.

9. Define chromosome disorder.

10. Define multifactorial disorders and congenital disorders.

11. What are the major types of genetic testing, and which genetic diseases can be most readily diagnosed?

12. What is the purpose of gene therapy? What are the social and ethical implications of gene therapy and advanced genetic testing?

13. What roles do the exocrine glands and the pancreas play in the development of the symptoms of cystic fibrosis?

14. What is meant by "secondary physical complications"?

15. Briefly describe the etiology and treatment of cystic fibrosis.

16. Describe the most common characteristics of Down syndrome and the possible degree of variation from child to child.

17. What are the chief life issues facing persons with Down syndrome?

18. Differentiate between translocation and mosaicism.

19. Describe the chief characteristics of fragile X syndrome.

20. Briefly describe the etiology and treatment needs of children with fragile X syndrome.

21. Describe the primary characteristics, etiology, and treatment of Duchenne muscular dystrophy.

22. What is the most salient characteristic of children with Prader-Willi syndrome?

23. Describe characteristics of development for children with Prader-Willi syndrome during the following phases: (a) neonatal, (b) childhood, and (c) adolescent.

24. What are the chief characteristics of sickle cell disease?

25. The treatment of sickle cell disease has developed slower than other "lower incident disorders." Why might this be?

26. Describe Tay-Sachs disease: (a) population affected, (b) progression of the disease, and (c) life expectancy.

27. What are the primary characteristics and treatment options for children with thalassemia?

28. Describe Turner syndrome: (a) etiology, (b) chief characteristics, and (c) treatment.

29. What are the characteristics of autism?

30. Discuss Cornelia de Lange syndrome including chief characteristics and stereotypic behaviors.

31. Identify the major criteria that must be present for a child to be identified as having Rett syndrome.

32. Describe the four "developmental stages" associated with Rett syndrome.

33. What is the most common manifestation of Tourette syndrome?

34. What percentage of children with Tourette syndrome also experience learning disabilities? What implications does this have for instruction or treatment?

35. What are the main characteristics of children with Williams syndrome?

36. Why is metabolism so basic to human life?

37. How do enzymes assist metabolism?

38. What is hypoglycemia, and why is it so dangerous for very young children?

39. How would you recognize the onset of hypoglycemia?

40. What problems does galactose present for people with galactosemia?

41. What dietary restrictions are necessary in treating galactosemia? What happens if the diet is not followed?

42. How does the build-up of phenylalanine cause mental retardation?

43. What preventive and treatment procedures are used to reduce rates of mental retardation from PKU?

44. What is hypothyroidism, and why is it damaging for young children?

45. What are the signs of hypothyroidism before birth? At birth?

46. How does fetal heart circulation differ from heart function after birth? How does this protect the unborn child?

47. What are the symptoms of congenital cardiac defects?

48. At what point in development is a cleft lip and/or palate formed? What can cause this to happen?

49. Why is counseling especially important for families of very young children with cleft lips and/or palates?

50. What significant problems are associated with cleft lips and/or palates?

51. What is an ostomy, and what kind of care must be given for an ostomy?

REFERENCES

American Psychiatric Association. (1987). *Diagnostic and statistical manual of mental disorders* (3rd ed.). Washington, DC.

Anfenson, M. (January, 1980). The school-age child with cystic fibrosis. *The Journal of School Health,* 26–28.

Armstrong, F. D., Lemanek, K. L., Pegelow, C. H., Gonzalez, J. C., & Martinez, A. (1993). Impact of lifestyle disruptions on parent and child coping, knowledge, and parental discipline in children with Sickle Cell Anemia. *Children's Health Care, 22*(3), 189–203.

Aughton, D. J., & Cassidy, S. B. (1990). Physical features of Prader-Willi syndrome in neonates. *American Journal of Diseases of Children, 144,* 1251–1254.

Beuren, A. J., Schulze, C., Eberle, P., Harmjanz, D., & Apitz, J. (1964). The syndrome of supravalvular aortic stenosis, periperal pulmonary stenosis, mental retardation an disimilar facial appearance. *The American Journal of Cardiology, 13,* 471–483.

Billings, P. R., Beckwith, J., & Alper, J. S. (1992). The genetic analysis of human behavior: A new era? *Social Science and Medicine, 35*(3), 227–238.

Black, S. (1992). The genetics of fragile X syndrome. In B. B. Shopmeyer & F. Lowe (Eds.), *The fragile X child* (pp. 3–17). San Diego: Singular Publishing Group, Inc.

Black, J. A., & Bonham-Carter, R. E. (1963). Association between aortic stenosis and facies of severe infantile hypercalcaemia. *The Lancet, 2,* 745–749.

Bower, B. (July, 1990). The ticcing link. *Science News, 138,* 42–44.

Bronheim, S. (1991). An educator's guide to Tourette syndrome. *Journal of Learning Disabilities, 24,* 17–22.

Brown, R. T., Armstrong, F. D., & Eckman, J. R. (1993). Neurocognitive aspects of pediatric sickle cell disease. *Journal of Learning Disabilities, 26*(1), 33–45.

Bryson, Y., Sakati, N., Nyhan, W. L., & Fish, C. H. (1971). Self-mutilative behavior in the Cornelia de Lange syndrome. *American Journal of Mental Deficiency, 76,* 319–324.

Buck, P. S. (1973). *The child who never grew*. New York: Day.

Burd, L., Kauffman, D. W., & Kerbeshian, J. (1992). Tourette syndrome and learning disabilities. *Journal of Learning Disabilities, 25,* 598–604.

Burd, L., Randall, T., Martsolf, J. T., & Kerbeshian, J. (1991). Rett syndrome symptomatology of institutionalized adults with mental retardation: Comparison of males and females. *American Journal of Mental Retardation, 95,* 596–601.

Butler, M. G. (1990). Prader-Willi syndrome: Current understanding of cause and diagnosis. *American Journal of Medical Genetics, 35,* 319–332.

Cantu, E. S., Stone, J. W., Wing, A. A., Langee, H. R., & Williams, C. A. (1990). Cytogenetic survey for autistic fragile X carriers in a mental retardation center. *American Journal on Mental Retardation, 94,* 442–447.

Chad, K., Jobling, A., & Frail, H. (1990). Metabolic rate: A factor in developing obesity in children with Down syndrome. *American Journal on Mental Retardation, 95*(2), 228–235.

Chua-Lim, C., Moore, R. B., McCleary, G., Shah, A., & Mankad, V. N. (1993). Deficiencies in school readiness skills of children with sickle cell anemia. *Southern Medical Journal, 86*(4), 397–401.

Cohen, D. J., Detlor, J., Shaywitz, B. A., & Leckman, J. F. (1992). Interaction of biological and psychological factors in the natural history of Tourette Syndrome: A paradigm for childhood neuropsychiatric disorders. In A. J. Friedhoff & T. N. Chase (Eds.), *Gilles de la Tourette syndrome* (Vol. 35, pp. 31–40). New York: Raven.

Cohen, M. M., & Bankier, A. (1991). Syndrome delineation involving orofacial clefting. *Cleft Palate Journal, 28,* 119–120.

Cole, M. (1991). New factors associated with the incidence of hypoglycemia: A research study. *Neonatal Network, 10*(4), 47–50.

Crews, W. D., Bonaventura, A., Hay, C. L., Steele W. K., & Rowe, F. B. (1993). Gilles de la Tourette disorder among individuals with severe or profound mental retardation. *Mental Retardation, 31*(1), 25–29.

Curfs, L. M. G., Wiegers, A. M., Sommers, J. R. M., Borghgraef, M., & Fryns, J. P. (1991). Strengths and weaknesses in the cognitive profile of youngsters with Prader-Willi syndrome. *Clinical Genetics, 40,* 430–434.

Cystic Fibrosis Foundation. (1987a). *An introduction to cystic fibrosis.* Bethesda, MD: Cystic Fibrosis Foundation.

Cystic Fibrosis Foundation. (1987b). *The genetics of cystic fibrosis.* Bethesda, MD: Cystic Fibrosis Foundation.

Cystic Fibrosis Foundation. (1987c). *Is an HMO right for you?* Bethesda, MD: Cystic Fibrosis Foundation.

De La Cruz, F. F. (1985). Fragile X syndrome. *American Journal of Mental Deficiency, 90,* 119–123.

Dibble, S.L., & Savedra, M.C. (1988). Cystic fibrosis in adolescence: A new challenge. *Pediatric Nursing, 14,* 299–303.

Donaldson, M. D. C., Chu, C. E., Cooke, A., Wilson, A., Greene, S. A., & Stephenson, J. B. P. (1994). The Prader-Willi syndrome. *Archives of Disease in Children, 70,* 58–63.

Donnell, G., & Ng, W. (1990). Galactosemia. In M. Buyse (Ed.), *Birth defects encyclopedia* (pp. 763–764). Dover, MA: Center for Birth Defects Information Services, Inc.

Downey, J., Elkin, E. J., Ehrhardt, A. A., Meyer-Bahlburg, H. F. L., Bell, J. J., & Morishima, A. (1991). Cognitive ability and everyday functioning in women with Turner syndrome. *Journal of Learning Disabilities, 24*(1), 32–39.

Dussault, J., Coulombe, P., & Laberge, C. (1975). Preliminary report on a mass screening program for neonatal hypothyroidism. *Journal of Pediatrics, 86,* 670–674.

Dykens, E. M., Hodapp, R. M., Ort, S. I., & Leckman, J. F. (1993). Trajectory of adaptive behavior in males with fragile X syndrome. *Journal of Autism and Developmental Disorders, 23,* 135–145.

Dykens, E. M., Hodapp, R. M., Walsh, K., & Nash, L. J. (1992a). Adaptive and maladaptive behavior in Prader-Willi syndrome. *Journal of the American Academy of Child and Adolescent Psychiatry, 31*(6), 1131–1136.

Dykens, E. M., Hodapp, R. M., Walsh, K., & Nash, L. J. (1992b). Profiles, correlates, and trajectories of intelligence in Prader-Willi syndrome. *Journal of the American Academy of Child and Adolescent Psychiatry, 31*(6), 1125–1130.

Eaves, R. C. (1992). Autism. In P. J. McLaughlin & P. Wehman (Eds.), *Developmental disabilities: A handbook for best practices* (pp. 68–81). Stoneham, MA: Butterworth-Heinemann.

Eaves, R. C., & Hopper, J. (1987–88). A factor analysis of psychotic behavior. *Journal of Special Education, 21,* 122–132.

Edell, B. H., & Motta, R. W. (1989). The emotional adjustment of children with Tourette's syndrome. *The Journal of Psychology, 123*(1), 51–57.

Eliason, M. J. (1991). Cleft lip and palate: Developmental effects. *Journal of Pediatric Nursing, 6*(2), 107–113.

Evenhuis, H. M. (1990). The natural history of dementia in Down's syndrome. *Archives of Neurology, 47,* 263–277.

Eyman, R. K., Call, T. L., & White, J. F. (1991). Life expectancy of persons with Down syndrome. *American Journal on Mental Retardation, 95*(6), 603–612.

Fajans, S., & Floyd, J. (1976). Fasting hypoglycemia in adults. *New England Journal of Medicine, 291,* 766–772.

Finn, R. (June, 1991). Different minds. *Discover,* 55–58.

Fisher, D. (1991). Clinical review 19: Management of congenital hypothyroidism. *Journal of Clinical Endocrinology and Metabolism, 72*(3), 523–529.

Fisher, D. (1983). Second International Conference on Neonatal Thyroid Screening: Progress report. *Journal of Pediatrics, 102,* 653–654.

Fisher, D., & Foley, B. (1989). Early treatment of congenital hypothyroidism. *Pediatrics, 83*(5), 785–789.

Fishler, K., & Koch, R. (1991). Mental development in Down syndrome mosaicism. *American Journal of Mental Deficiency, 96,* 345–351.

Gene that causes cystic fibrosis identified. (1989, September). *Cystic Fibrosis Foundation Commitment,* p. 1.

Gil, K. M., Abrams, M. R., Phillips, G., & Williams, D. A. (1992). Sickle cell disease pain: 2. Predicting health care use and activity level at 9-month follow-up. *Journal of Consulting and Clinical Psychology, 60,* 267–273.

Goldman, J. J. (1988). Prader-Willi syndrome in two institutionalized older adults. *Mental Retardation, 26,* 97–102.

Goodban, M. T. (1993). Survey of speech and language skills with prognostic indicators in 116 patients with Cornelia de Lange syndrome. *American Journal of Medical Genetics, 47,* 1059–1063.

Gray, N. T., Bartlett, J. M., Kolasa, K. M., Marcuard, S. P., Holbrook, C. T., & Horner, R. D. (1992). Nutritional status and dietary intake of children with sickle cell anemia. *Journal of Pediatric Hematology/Oncology, 14*(1), 57–61.

Guyer, M. S., & Collins, F. S. (1993). The Human Genome Project and the future of medicine. *AJDC, 147,* 1145–1151.

Haan, E. A. (1990). Ethics and the new genetics. *Journal of Paediatric and Child Health, 26,* 177–179.

Hagberg, B., & Witt-Engerstrom, I. (1986). A suggested staging system for describing impairment profile with increasing age towards adolescence. *American Journal of Medical Genetics, 24,* 377–382.

Hagerman, R. (1992). Medical aspects of the fragile X syndrome. In B. B. Shopmeyer & F. Lowe (Eds.), *The fragile X child* (pp. 19–29). San Diego: Singular Publishing Group.

Hall, J. G., & Gilchrist, D. M. (1990). Turner syndrome and its variants. *Current Issues in Pediatric and Adolescent Endocrinology, 17*(1), 1421–1440.

Hardy, J. D. (1988). *Hardy's textbook of surgery,* 2nd ed. Philadelphia: J. B. Lippincott.

Hawley, P., Jackson, L., & Kurnit, D. (1985). Sixty-four patients with Brachmann-de Lange syndrome: A survey. *American Journal of Medical Genetics, 20,* 453–459.

Hayes, C., Rarback, S., Berry, B., & Clancy, M. (1987). Managing PKU: An update. *Maternal/Child Nursing, 12,* 119–123.

Huk, S. G. (1989). Transient exacerbation of tics in treatment of Tourette's syndrome with Clonidine. *Journal of the American Academy of Child and Adolescent Psychiatry, 28*(4), 583–586.

Hurtig, A., & Viera, A. (1986). *Sickle cell disease: Psychological and psychosocial issues.* Urbana, IL: University of Illinois Press.

James, T. N., & Brown, R. I. (1993). Prader-Willi syndrome: Quality of life issues in home, school and community. *Australian and New Zealand Journal of Developmental Disabilities, 18*(4), 253–260.

Johnson, R. C., & Abelson, R. B. (1969). Intellectual, behavioral, and physical characteristics associated with trisomy, translocation, and mosaic types of Down syndrome. *American Journal of Mental Deficiency, 73*(6), 852–855.

Kaback, M., Lim-Steele, J., Dabholkar, D., Brown, D., Levy, N., & Zeigler, K. (1993). Tay-Sachs Disease—Carrier screening, prenatal diagnosis and the molecular era: An international perspective, 1970–1993. *Journal of American Medical Association, 270,* 2307–2315.

Karmiloff-Smith, A. (April, 1993). Within-domain dissociations in Williams syndrome: A window on the normal mind. Annual Meeting of the Society for Research in Child Development, Plymouth, England. (ERIC Reproduction Document No. ED 363 022).

Keenan, J., Kastner, T., Nathanson, R., Richardson, N., Hinton, J., & Cress, D. (1992). A statewide public and professional education program on fragile X syndrome. *Mental Retardation, 30,* 355–361.

Kennerknecht, I. (1992). A genetic model for the Prader-Willi syndrome and its implication for Angelman syndrome. *Human Genetics, 90,* 91–98.

Klein, R. (1985). Infantile hypothyroidism then and now: The results of neonatal screening. *Current Problems in Pediatrics, 15*(1), 1–58.

Knell, E. R., & Comings, D. E. (1993). Tourette's syndrome and attention-deficit-hyperactivity disorder: Evidence for a genetic relationship. *Journal of Clinical Psychiatry, 54*(9), 331–337.

Koch, R., Acosta, P., Donnell, G., & Lieberman, E. (1965). Nutritional therapy of galactosemia. *Clinical Pediatrics, 4,* 571–578.

Kravetz, S., Weller, A., Tennenbaum, R., Tzuriel, D., & Mintzker, Y. (1992). Plastic surgery on children with

Down syndrome: Parent's perceptions of physical, personal, and social functioning. *Research in Developmental Disabilities, 13,* 145–156.

Krener, P., & Adelman, R. (1988). Parent salvage and sabotage in the care of chronically ill children. *American Journal of Diseased Children, 142,* 945–951.

Kurlan, R. (1992). The pathogenesis of Tourette's syndrome: A possible role for hormonal and excitatory neurotransmitter influences in brain development. *Archives of Neurology, 49,* 874–876.

Lakshaminarayana, P., & Nallasivam, P. (1990). Cornelia de Lange syndrome with ring chromosome 3. *Journal of Medical Genetics, 27,* 404–406.

Lambert, E., Canent, R., & Hohn, A., (1966). Congenital cardiac defects in the newborn: A review of conditions causing death or severe distress in the first month of life. *Pediatrics, 37,* 343–352.

Lerer, R. J. (1987). Motor tics, Tourette syndrome, and learning disabilities. *Journal of Learning Disabilities, 20,* 266–267.

Levi, S. L. (1991). The Tourette Syndrome Association, Inc. *Journal of Learning Disabilities, 24*(1), 16–22.

Liu, J. E., Gzesh, D. J., & Ballas, S. K. (1994). The spectrum of epilepsy in sickle cell anemia. *Journal of Neurological Sciences, 123,* 6–10.

Lynn, D. J., Woda, R. P., & Mendell, J. R. (1994). Respiratory dysfunction in muscular dystrophy and other myopothies. *Clinics in Chest Medicine, 15*(4), 661–674.

Marcell, M. M., & Cohen, S. (1992). Hearing abilities of Down syndrome and other mentally handicapped adolescents. *Research in Developmental Disabilities, 13,* 533–551.

March of Dimes. (1992). *Genetic testing and gene therapy* (No. 09-576-00). White Plains, NY: Author.

March of Dimes. (1987). *Genetic counseling.* Spokane, WA: March of Dimes Birth Defects Foundation.

Mathur, A., Stekol, L., Schatz, D., Maclaren, N. K., Scott, M. L., & Lippe, B. (1991). The parental origin of the single X chromosome in Turner syndrome: Lack of correlation with parental age or clinical phenotype. *American Journal of Human Genetics, 48,* 682–686.

Matson, D. (1969). *Neurosurgery of infancy and childhood.* Springfield, IL: Charles G. Thomas.

Mauk, J. E. (1993). Autism and pervasive developmental disorders. *Pediatric Clinics of North America, 40*(3), 567–578.

May, D. C., & Turnbull, N. (1992). Plastic surgeon's opinions of facial surgery for individuals with Down syndrome. *Mental Retardation, 30*(1), 29–33.

McCauley, E., Kay, T., Ito, J., & Treder, R. (1987). The Turner syndrome: Cognitive deficits, affective discrimination, and behavior problems. *Child Development, 58,* 464–473.

McClennen, S. (1992). Cognitive characteristics, assessment, and intervention in fragile X syndrome. In B. B. Shopmeyer & F. Lowe (Eds.), *The fragile X child* (pp. 33–58). San Diego: Singular Publishing Group, Inc.

McInerny, T. G. (1985). Cleft palate repair—surgical procedure and nursing care. *AORN Journal, 42,* 516–527.

Meryash, D. L. (1985). The fragile X syndrome. (Report No. MF01/PC05). Silver Spring, MD: American Association of University Affiliated Programs for Persons with Developmental Disabilities. (ERIC Document Reproduction Service No. ED 276 194).

Meryash, D. L. (1992). Characteristics of fragile X relatives with different attitudes toward terminating an affected pregnancy. *American Journal of Mental Retardation, 96,* 528–535.

Miculan, J., Turner, S., & Paes, B. (1993). Congenital hypothyroidism: Diagnosis and management. *Neonatal Network, 12*(6), 25–33.

Mitchell, S., Korones, S., & Berendes, H. (1971). Congenital heart disease in 56,109 births. *Circulation, 43,* 323–330.

Nagel, R. L. (1993). Sickle cell anemia is a multigene disease: Sickle painful crises, a case in point. *American Journal of Hematology, 42,* 96–101.

National Institute of Health. (1990). Ethical, legal and social implications of the human genome initiative. *NIH Guide for Grants and Contracts, 19*(4), 12–14.

New treatments predicted. (1989, September). *Cystic Fibrosis Foundation Commitment,* p. 6.

Norwood, W. (1991). Hypoplastic left heart syndrome. *Annuals of Thoracic Surgery, 52,* 688–695.

Nyhan, W. (1990). Phenylketonuria. In M. Buyse (Ed.), *Birth defects encyclopedia* (pp. 1382–1383). Dover, MA: Center for Birth Defects Information Services, Inc.

Otermin-Aquirre, J. (1969). Mongolism and plastic surgery. *Plastic and Reconstructive Surgery, 45,* 411.

Pauls, D. L., & Leckman, J. F. (1986). The inheritance of Gilles de la Tourette syndrome and associated behaviors: Evidence for autosomal dominant transmission. *The New England Journal of Medicine, 315,* 993–997.

Pediatric Pulmonary and Cystic Fibrosis Clinic. (1987). *"Our job is caring...."* Spokane, WA: Deaconess Medical Clinic.

Perry, A. (1991). Rett syndrome: A comprehensive review of the literature. *American Journal of Mental Retardation, 96,* 275–290.

Pollack, C. V. (1993). Emergencies in sickle cell disease. *Emergency Medicine Clinics of North America, 11*(2), 365–378.

Prader, A., Labhart, A., & Willi, H. (1956). Ein syndrom von adipositas, kleinwuchs, kryptorchimus, und oligophrenie nach myotonicartigen zustrand im neugeborenenalter. *Schweizerische Medizinische Wochenschrift, 86,* 1260–1261.

Ptacek, L. J., Johnson, K. J., & Griggs, R. C. (1993). Genetics and the physiology of the myotonic muscle disorders. *The New England Journal of Medicine, 338*(6), 482–489.

Pueschel, S. M. (1991). Ethical considerations relating to prenatal diagnosis of fetuses with Down syndrome. *Mental Retardation, 29*(4), 185–190.

Pueschel, S. M., Jackson, M. D., Giesswein, P., Dean, M. K., & Pezzullo, J. C. (1991). Thyroid function in Down syndrome. *Research in Developmental Disabilities, 12,* 287–296.

Reed, M. L., & Leff, S. E. (1994). Maternal imprinting of human SNRPN, a gene deleted in Prader-Willi syndrome. *Nature Genetics, 6,* 163–167.

Reiss, A. L., & Freund, L. (1990). Fragile X syndrome. *Biological Psychiatry, 27,* 223–240.

Richman, L. (1978). The effect of facial disfigurement on teachers' perception of ability in cleft palate children. *Cleft Palate Journal, 15,* 155–157.

Risley, M. S. (1986). *Chromosome structure and function.* New York: Van Nostrand Reinhold.

Rogers, R. C., & Simensen, R. J. (1987). Fragile X syndrome: A common etiology of mental retardation. *American Journal of Mental Deficiency, 91,* 445–449.

Rovet, J. F. (1990). The cognitive and neuropsychological characteristics of females with Turner syndrome. In D. B. Berch & B. G. Berger (Eds.), *Sex chromosome abnormalities and human behavior* (pp. 38–77). Boulder, CO: Westview.

Rovet, J. F. (1993). The psychoeducational characteristics of children with Turner syndrome. *Journal of Learning Disabilities, 26*(5), 333–341.

Rynders, J. E., & Horrobin, J. M. (1990). Always trainable? Never educable? Updating educational expectations concerning children with Down syndrome. *American Journal on Mental Retardation, 95*(1), 77–83.

Sach, B. P., & Korf, B. (1993). The human genome project: Implications for the practicing obstetrician. *Obstetrics and Gynecology, 81*(3), 458–462.

Sadler, L. S., Robinson, L. K., Verdaasdonk, K. R., & Gingell, R. (1993). The Williams syndrome: Evidence for possible autosomal dominant inheritance. *American Journal of Medical Genetics, 47,* 468–470.

Samuels, M. (1988). Hypoglycemia. In S. Silverstein and D. Frommer (Eds.), *Emergency management of metabolic and endocrine disorders* (pp. 61–75). Rockville, MD: Aspen Publishers, Inc.

Sancho, S., Mongini, T., Tanji, K., Tapscott, S. J., Walker, W. F., Weintraub, H., Miller, A. D., & Miranda, A. F. (1993). Analysis of dystrophin expression after activation of myogenesis in amniocytes, chorionic-villus cells, and fibroblasts. *The New England Journal of Medicine, 329*(13), 915–920.

Santos, C. C., & Massey, E. W. (1990). Tourette's syndrome: Tics, jerks and quirks. *Postgraduate Medicine, 87*(1), 71–74.

Santos, K. E. (1992). Fragile X syndrome: An educator's role in identification prevention, and intervention. *Remedial and Special Education, 13,* 32–39.

Sataloff, R. T., Spiegel, J. R., Hawkshaw, M., Epstein, J. M., & Jackson, L. (1990). Cornelia de Lange syndrome: Otolaryngologic manifestations. *Archives of Otolaryngol Head and Neck Surgery, 116,* 1044–1046.

Schimke, R. (1990). Thyroid, iodide transport defect. In M. Buyse (Ed.), *Birth defects encyclopedia* (pp. 1675–1676). Dover, MA: Center for Birth Defects Information Services, Inc.

Schneiderman, G., Lowden, J. A., & Rae-Grant, Q. (1978, February). Tay-Sachs and related storage diseases: Family planning. *Mental Retardation,* pp. 13–15.

Scientists forecast new approaches for developing treatments. (1989, September). *Cystic Fibrosis Foundation Commitment,* p. 2.

Segal, S. (1989). Disorders of galactose metabolism. In Scriver, C., Beaudet, A., Sly, W., & Valle, D. (Eds.), *The metabolic basis of inherited disease 6th ed.* (pp. 453–480). New York: McGraw-Hill Information Services Company.

Serjeant, G. R. (1985). *Sickle cell disease.* New York: Oxford University Press.

Shakir, K., & Amin, R. (1991). Hypoglycemia. *Critical Care Clinics, 7*(1), 75–87.

Shapiro, A.K., & Shapiro, E. S. (1980). Tic, Tourette, or movement disorder? A guide to early diagnosis. *Diagnosis, 55,* 77–84.

Shapiro, B. S. (1989). The management of pain in sickle cell disease. *Pediatric Clinics of North America, 36,* 1029–1045.

Shapiro, E., & Shapiro, A.K. (1981). Tic disorders. *JAMA, 245,* 1583–1585.

Shapiro, F., & Specht, L. (1993). The diagnosis and orthopaedic treatment of inherited muscular diseases of childhood. *The Journal of Bone and Joint Surgery, 75*(3), 430–454.

Simensen, R. J., & Rogers, R. C. (1989). School psychology and medical diagnosis: The fragile X syndrome. *Psychology in the Schools, 26,* 380–389.

Sobel, E., & Saenger, P. (1989). Hypothyroidism in the new-born. *Pediatrics in Review, 11*(1), 15–20.

Steffens, M. L., Oiler, D. K., Lynch, M., & Urbano, R. C. (1992). Vocal development in infants with Down syndrome and infants who are developing normally. *American Journal on Mental Retardation, 97*(2), 235–246.

Stullenbarger, B., Norris, J., Edgil, A. E., & Prosser, M. J. (1987). Family adaptation to cystic fibrosis. *Pediatric Nursing, 13*, 29–31.

Sudhalter, V., Cohen, I., Silverman, W., & Wolf-Schein, E. G. (1990). Conversational analyses of males with fragile X, Down syndrome and autism: Comparison of the emergence of deviant language. *American Journal of Mental Retardation, 94*, 431–441.

Swartz, S. L. (May, 1981). Williams 'elfin facies' syndrome: A case study. Annual Meeting of Amercan Association on Mental Deficiency, Detroit, MI. (ED Reproduction Document No. ED 208 639).

Temple, C. M., & Carney, R. A. (1993). Intellectual functioning of children with Turner syndrome: A comparison of behavioural phenotypes. *Developmental Medicine and Child Neurology, 35*, 691–698.

Thompson, M. W., McInnes, R. R., & Willard, H. F. (1991). *Genetics in medicine (5th ed.)*. Philadelphia: Saunders.

Thompson, R. J., Gil, K. M., Abrams, M. R., & Phillips, G. (1992). Stress, coping, and psychological adjustment of adults with sickle cell disease. *Journal of Consulting and Clinical Psychology, 60*, 433–440.

Thorpe-Beeston, J. (1991). Maturation of the secretion of thyroid hormone and thyroid stimulating hormone in the fetus. *New England Journal of Medicine, 324*(8), 532–536.

Tomc, S. A., Williamson, N. K., & Pauli, R. M. (1990). Temperament in Williams syndrome. *American Journal of Medical Genetics, 36*, 345–352.

Torup, E. (1972). A follow-up study of children with tics. *Acta Paediatricia Scandinavica, 51*, 261–268.

Udwin, O., & Yule, W. (1991). A cognitive and behavioral phenotype in Williams syndrome. *Journal of Clinical and Experimental Neuropsychology, 13*(2), 232–244.

Ulstrom, R., & Sockalowsky, J. (1990). Hypoglycemia, familial neonatal. In M. Buyse (Ed.), *Birth defects encyclopedia* (pp. 921–922). Dover, MA: Center for Birth Defects Information Services, Inc.

Vanderas, A. P. (1987). Incidence to cleft lip and palate among races: A review. *Cleft Palate Journal, 24*, 216–225.

Virtanen, M. (1988). Manifestations of congenital hypothyroidism during the first week of life. *European Journal of Pediatrics, 147*(3), 270–274.

Wachtel, T. J., & Pueschel, S. M. (1991). Macrocytosis in Down syndrome. *American Journal on Mental Retardation, 95*(4), 417–420.

Waisbren, S., Normal, R., Schnell, R., & Levy, H. (1983). Speech and language deficits in early treated children with galactosemia. *Journal of Pediatrics, 102*, 75–84.

Walkup, J. T., Leckman, J. F., Price, A., Hardin, M., Ort, S. L., & Cohen, D. J. (1988). The relationship between obsessive-compulsive disorder and Tourette syndrome: A twin study. *Psychopharmacology Bulletin, 24*(3), 375–379.

Webster, C. D., Konstantareas, M. M., Oxman, J., & Mack, J. E. (1980). *Autism: New directions in research and education.* New York: Pergamon.

Werthorn, L. A., & McCabe, M. A. (1988). Emerging ethical and legal issues in pediatric psychology. In D. Routh (Ed.), *Handbook of pediatric psychology* (pp. 567–606). New York: Guilford.

Williams, J. C. P., Barratt-Boyes, B. G., & Lowe, J. B. (1961). Supravalvular aortic stenosis. *Circulation, 24*, 1311–1318.

Williams, J. K., Richman, L. C., & Yarbrough, D. B. (1992). Comparison of visual-spatial performance strategy training in children with Turner syndrome and learning disabilities. *Journal of Learning Disabilities, 25*, 658–664.

Wilson, P. G., & Mazzocco, M. M. (1993). Awareness and knowledge of fragile X syndrome among special educators. *Mental retardation, 97*(4), 221–227.

Wolff, P., Gardner, J., Paccia, J., & Lappen, J. (1989). The greeting behavior of fragile X males. *American Journal of Mental Retardation, 93*, 406–411.

Yetter, J. F. (1992). Cleft lip and cleft palate. *American Family Physician, 46*(4), 1211–1219.

Zinn, A. R., Page, D. C., & Fisher, E. M. C. (1993). Turner syndrome: The case of the missing sex chromosome. *Trends in Genetics, 9*(3), 90–93.

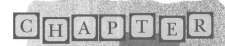

Sensory Impairments and Infections

Sensory impairments, especially in vision and hearing, are common findings in young infants and children experiencing developmental delays. Such impairments are often the result of a significant infection in the neonate or young infant. This chapter focuses on frequently occurring problems with vision and hearing. It also is devoted to the effects of bacterial and viral infections on developing fetuses, neonates, and infants. While some of the diseases resulting from these invasive organisms are negligible, other infections can cause severe and multiple disabilities or even death.

HEARING IMPAIRMENTS

Hearing is the act of receiving and processing sound vibrations. The auditory mechanisms within the ear permit humans to discriminate differential sound waves within their environment. Approximately 1 child in 100 experiences some type of hearing loss and 1 in 1000 children is born deaf (National Institute of Health Consensus Statement [NIHCS], 1993). Of those, 65% are born with a hearing loss, and another 12% develop this disability within their first three years of life.

Hearing Process

The auditory mechanism is functionally separated into three components: external, middle, and inner ear (see Figure 7.1). The **external ear,** consisting of the auricle, auditory canal, and tympanic membrane, is responsible for collecting sound waves. Physical energy is channeled down the auditory canal, where it vibrates the tympanic membrane (ear drum).

The **middle ear** cavity lies beyond the tympanic membrane. Sound vibrations are mechanically transmitted from the tympanic membrane to stimulate, in sequence, three tiny bones: the malleus (hammer), incus (anvil), and stapes (stirrup). The latter is attached to a small opening that leads to the inner ear, referred to as the oval window. The **eustachian tube** intersects the middle ear to form a continuous passage to the throat. The purpose of the eustachian tube is to equalize internal and external air pressure on the tympanic membrane. Excessive buildup of pressure within the middle ear can cause the sensitive tympanic membrane to rupture.

Sound waves traveling to the **inner ear** from the vibration of the tympanic membrane are transmitted through the oval window to the **cochlea** (see Figure 7.2). Tiny nerve endings within the cochlea, referred to as hair cells, are stimulated by the movement of cochlear fluid. The resulting energy (now electrical) is transferred to the temporal area of the brain via the eighth cranial nerve, or **auditory nerve.** Contained within the inner ear are the **vestibule** and the three **semicircular canals;** these structures also contain neural hair cells. Movement of these cells, caused by forces of gravity and motion, provides information through the eighth cranial nerve to the brain regarding the body's equilibrium status.

Figure 7.1/ *Anatomy of the Ear*

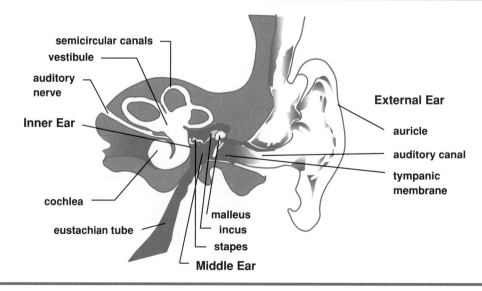

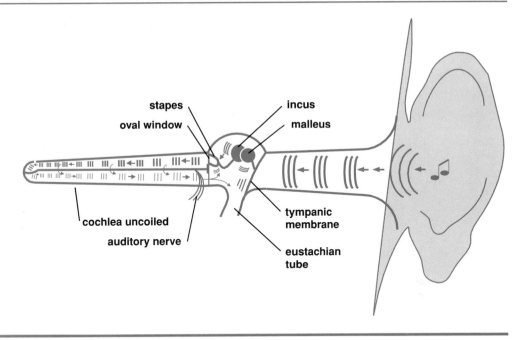

stapes
oval window
incus
malleus
cochlea uncoiled
auditory nerve
tympanic membrane
eustachian tube

Hearing Loss   Sounds are heard along two dimensions: loudness and pitch. Pitch is determined by the frequency of sound waves. Normally, speech sounds range between frequencies of 500 and 2000 cycles per second. Loudness, or sound intensity, is measured in decibels (dB), and hearing is considered normal when sound is audible at 10 dB. Hearing losses, which range from slight (sound audible at 15–25 dB) to profound (sound audible at more than 90 dB), are the result of a variety of insults to the auditory system.

Approximately 50% of hearing losses have an unknown cause (see Table 7.1). The etiology, location, and severity of damage to the ear are variables used in determining immediate and long-range treatment for children with hearing loss. A **conductive hearing loss** is one that disrupts mechanical conduction of sound as it is transferred from the outer ear through the middle ear. Though several factors can contribute to a conductive hearing loss, most causes can be treated through medical intervention. Furthermore, the degree of hearing loss for most conductive etiologies ranges from mild to moderate. The most common cause of hearing loss is **otitis media,** or middle ear disease.

Northern and Downs (1984) found that 76% to 95% of all children contract otitis media, at least once, within the first two years of life. Either viral or bacterial infections cause a buildup of fluid in the middle ear and eustachian tube, which reduces mobility of the membranes and bones necessary to adequately transfer sound intensity to the inner ear. Symptoms of otitis media are a red, bulging tympanic membrane, frequent ear pulling, and irritability. A single infection usually will result in only temporary and mild hearing loss. However, chronic middle ear disease (serous otitis media) can result in a more persistent and significant hearing loss that might substantially interrupt normal acquisition of language. Treatment of otitis media includes myringotomy (tubes placed through the eardrum to drain fluid), antihistimines (to reduce swelling of the eustachian tube), and antibiotics, which will generally work with bacterial infections, even though most middle ear infections are viral.

Table 7.1/ *Factors That Place Children at Risk of Hearing Loss*

Prenatal/Natal Period	After Neonatal Period
Congenital infections 　　Cytomegalo Virus* 　　Rubella* 　　Herpes* 　　Toxoplasmosis* 　　Syphilis*	Head Trauma Neurodegenerative Diseases Childhood Diseases 　　Mumps* 　　Measles*
Craniofacial Anomalies 　　Cleft palate	Bacterial Meningitis*
Low Birth Weight 　　<1,500 grams	
Hyperbilirubinemia 　　Exceeds levels indicating 　　need for exchange transfusion	
Administration of Ototoxic Drugs	
Family History	
Severe Depression at Birth	
Syndromes with Associated Hearing Losses 　　Down syndrome	

* Covered in this chapter

Source: Adapted from Northern, J., & Downs, M. (1984). *Hearing in children* (3rd ed.) Baltimore: Williams & Wilkins.

Conductive hearing losses are common in children with a variety of disabilities. For example, children with Down syndrome are at increased risk of middle ear infection for two reasons:

1. a depressed immune response system

2. an anomoly resulting in a more horizontal than normal eustachian tube, which prevents adequate drainage of the middle ear

Similarly, serous otitis media is quite common in children with cleft palates, whose eustachian tube drainage is hindered by the palate malformation.

Sensorineural hearing losses result from damage to the cochlea or auditory nerve such that the brain does not receive the sound message. Genetic inheritance accounts for approximately 70% to 80% of known abnormalities that result in serious sensorineural hearing loss. Noise pollution can cause sensorineural hearing loss or "noise induced deafness." For example, Bess, Peek, and Chapman (1979) hypothesized that the ambient noise in incubators contributed noise pollution that might result in hearing loss in premature infants.

Intrauterine infections account for a large percentage of serious sensorineural hearing impairments. Toxoplasmosis, maternal rubella contracted during the first trimester, herpes, mumps, syphilis, and cytomegalovirus are all associated with malformations that result in hearing loss. Meningitis, a bacterial infection, is the leading postnatal cause of hearing loss.

Neonates and premature infants are at risk of acquiring hearing losses. For example, asphyxia of infants during delivery may damage the cochlea, resulting in sensorineural hearing loss. High bilirubin levels resulting in severe jaundice may also cause permanent damage to the central nervous system. Other factors include cerebral hemorrhage, apnea, and, in some cases, antibiotic drugs, which can become toxic.

Identification of Hearing Loss

Though the critical period of language development is during the first three years of life, the average age at which children are diagnosed with a hearing loss is close to age three (NIHCS, 1993). The National Institute of Health concluded that one factor contributing to delayed identification is the practice of screening only high risk children—thereby eliminating up to half of those infants with hearing impairments. Early identification of hearing loss would enable families and practitioners to plan and implement a remedial program to enhance cognitive and social development. To broaden the scope of screening practices, while still being realistic in terms of costs, NIH identified new criteria that should be used in determining those infants at highest risk for hearing impairment:

- All infants admitted to Neonatal Intensive Care Units
- All infants with craniofacial anomalies, family history of hearing loss, and a history of intrauterine infections
- Universal screening of all well-babies within the first 3 months
- Any child whose parent(s) indicate concern about hearing
- Any child who fails to attain appropriate language milestones (especially in first 18 months)
- All children who have bacterial meningitis, viral encephalitis, perinatal cytomegalovirus, or chronic otitis media
- All children exposed to excessive noise, ototoxic drugs, or chronic lung disease
- All school-age children

Two tools are considered the most efficient in screening newborns for hearing loss because they measure brain activity rather than physical responses to sound (NIHCS, 1993). The first, auditory brain stem responses (ABS), can be done without sedating an infant and is highly accurate. Evoked otoacoustic emissions (EOAE) is a relatively new procedure that is less costly and complex while still being highly sensitive. A problem with both procedures is the ratio of false positives, with EOAE being the most problematic.

After children are six months old, it is possible to conduct behavioral testing in which they are trained to consistently respond to the emission of a noise. This procedure requires well-trained professionals and is less reliable when used with infants who have developmental delays.

Developmental Implications and Resolutions

Children with hearing losses are identified early when they fail to startle, do not localize sounds, and have delayed acquisition of language milestones. In fact, hearing losses are sometimes misdiagnosed as cognitive delays. The developmental domain most directly affected by hearing loss in infancy is language. However, children with hearing losses generally score within the normal intelligence range when tested on nonverbal measures. Social skills may also be affected since interpersonal communication is considered an essential component of social interactions.

Two factors are related to the interaction between hearing loss and developmental progress. First, it is critical to identify hearing loss early and to provide adaptive intervention at the earliest possible age. Secondly, the age of onset and degree of hearing loss influence the degree to which children's linguistic and cognitive skills will be affected.

There are several augmentative communication systems that should be considered early. Sign language systems, which use hand gestures to communicate, include American Sign

Language (ASL), Signing Exact English (SEE-II), and cued speech. American Sign Language is considered a unique language with its own sentence and word structure (syntax and morphology) and is widely used by adults with deafness. This language is the most efficient manual communication system. By contrast, SEE-II resembles spoken and written English in syntax and morphology and may therefore facilitate the acquisition of written language skills and academic skills.

It is important that children with hearing losses not only learn manual sign, but also be taught to make use of residual hearing, speech (lip) reading, and oral speech to communicate. Since most individuals in our society communicate through speech and do not know manual sign, children will be most able to communicate with hearing persons if they also learn other means to communicate. Yet, even the most observant and well-trained deaf children will not catch a majority of speech messages when relying only on residual hearing and speech reading. **Total communication** combines manual sign with oral methods of communication and is the most frequently adopted approach.

Assistive devices for children with hearing losses include hearing aids, which amplify the sound. These devices should be fitted at an early age to encourage hearing perception necessary for language development. Hearing aids assist but do not replace natural hearing abilities. That is, hearing aids have the disadvantage of amplifying all environmental sounds, including irrelevant auditory stimuli. Additionally, the sounds that are perceived may be distorted. Finally, young children do not automatically link the sounds heard through amplification to the sounds' sources. They must be taught to pay attention to sounds, to orient toward sound sources, and to discriminate between relevant and irrelevant noises. Various amplification devices are available and must be matched specifically to each child's characteristics: age, degree of hearing loss, family environment, and cognitive abilities.

Preschool programs serving children with hearing impairments require some unique considerations. Harrington and Meyers (1992) made the following recommendations:

- Access services by personnel with certification competencies for teachers of preschool children with hearing impairments as delineated by the Council of Education for the Deaf.

- Use transdisciplinary teaming, including an occupational therapist, physical therapist, psychologist, social worker, counselor, audiologist, speech-language pathologist, educator of the deaf, and a parent, to collaborate in assessment and planning.

- Obtain oral interpreters and/or sign interpreters as needed for children with profound deafness in mainstream settings.

- Adapt classrooms so that ceilings and walls use acoustical tiles, floors are carpeted, and visible fire alarm systems are installed.

- Furnish classes with amplification systems (e.g., FM auditory training system), captioning equipment, computer software designed for children with hearing impairments, and telecommunication devices (TDD) to interact with parents who are deaf and members of the deaf community.

As noted by Harrington and Meyers (1992), accommodation of classrooms for children with hearing impairments is expensive and will challenge service providers who are already uncertain of financial resources.

Informing and Working with Parents

Parents of children with hearing losses should receive genetic counseling since a large percentage of these children have inherited their disability. Very early in a child's life, parents of children with deafness must make a decision regarding linguistic instruction that will influence their child's entire life. Those parents who prefer their children be given every chance to become a part of the hearing world are likely to choose an educational program that emphasizes oral communication or total communication. Other parents might feel that a mainstream education would result in social and communicative isolation, particularly since communities of deaf individuals are often very active socially and rely on sign language for communication. While a self-contained manual language does not necessarily preclude integration, this approach is usually paired with a philosophy of isolation and specialized educational programs. Still other parents, due to an absence of community resources or their economic circumstances, feel that they have little choice other than to accept the only services that are offered. Parents must be provided with objective information on the implications of educational choices—and the advocacy skills to negotiate alternative services in areas of restricted options.

The same infections which often cause deafness may also result in visual impairments, either alone or in combination with hearing impairments. The next portion of this chapter considers the diagnosis and treatment of visual impairments.

VISUAL IMPAIRMENTS

Visual acuity is measured by comparing the distance at which a person is able to discriminate an object to the distance at which a person with average visual acuity (20/20) discriminates the same object (see Figure 7.3). For example, what a person with 20/70 vision sees clearly only to 20 feet, a person with average visual acuity would be able to see accurately as far away as 70 feet. A visual impairment is legally defined as a visual acuity of 20/200 or less in the best eye with correction. Additionally, those whose peripheral field of vision is 20 degrees or less are considered legally blind, even though visual acuity might be normal (see Figure 7.4). **Low vision** is assessed when visual acuity is 20/70 or less in the better eye with correction.

While legal blindness is a relatively low incidence disability (1 in 1000), approximately 30% to 70% of children with severe visual loss experience one or more other disabilities (Kirchner, 1988). Further, the overall incidence of visual impairment and blindness rose from 15.6 million in 1978 to 18.8 million in 1989 (Kirchner, 1990). Several factors may influence this overall trend. For example, recent advances in medical technology, which allow very premature and low birth weight infants to survive, has radically increased the incidence of chil-

Figure 7.3/ *Visual Acuity: 20/20 Vision Compared to 20/70 Vision*

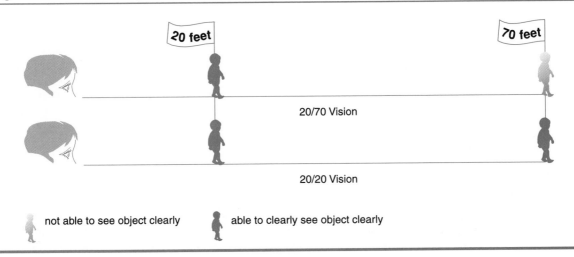

20/70 Vision

20/20 Vision

not able to see object clearly   able to clearly see object clearly

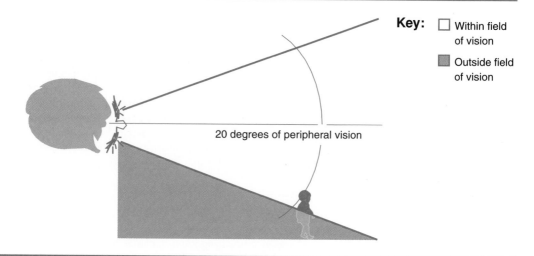

Key:
☐ Within field of vision
■ Outside field of vision

20 degrees of peripheral vision

dren with retinopathy of prematurity (Uslan, 1983). Also, research has demonstrated a relationship between poverty and the incidence of visual impairments, and poverty rates for young children continue to increase. Thus it can be projected that the incidence of visual impairments will also increase. Many causes of visual impairments might be considered preventable. Though an estimated 40 million people worldwide are blind, Goldstein (1980) estimated that two out of three of the cases might be prevented through control of infection and malnutrition.

It is believed that newborns have a visual acuity of 20/200 and that children do not develop normal visual acuity until about age five (Allen & Marotz, 1989). This "developmental visual impairment" combined with infants' cognitive immaturity make assessment of visual impairment unreliable before six months of age (Sheridan, 1969). More important to children and their families than the clinical determination of visual disability is the retention of functional visual abilities. According to Hoon (1991), professionals should emphasize to parents the importance of maximizing a child's **residual vision** for use in everyday activities rather than focusing on visual deficiencies.

Visual Process

Entering light initially strikes the **cornea** of the eye, which serves both a protective and refractive function. The cornea bends the angle of light and channels that light through the fluid-filled anterior chamber. Once the light strikes the **lens,** accommodation takes place, in which the lens changes shape, becoming more or less spherical depending on the nearness of an object or the intensity of light. The elastic properties of the lens permit it to cause a constriction of the iris, which widens the pupil (opening in the eye) to regulate the amount of light entering the vitreous humor **(accommodation).** The **vitreous humor** is a second fluid-filled space lying behind the eye's lens, which maintains the internal pressure of the eye and shape of the eyeball. The rays passing through this chamber intersect at a focal point on or near the **retina.** The retina is a complex neurological network directly linked to the central nervous system; neural fibers from the retina gather to form the optic nerve, which transmits an electrical image to the occipital portion of the brain (see Figure 7.5). Here the visual cortex of the brain perceives and interprets the images.

Refractive Errors Defects in the curvature of cornea and lens or abnormal eyeball shape change the focal point of light rays and are referred to as refractive errors. **Myopia,** or near-

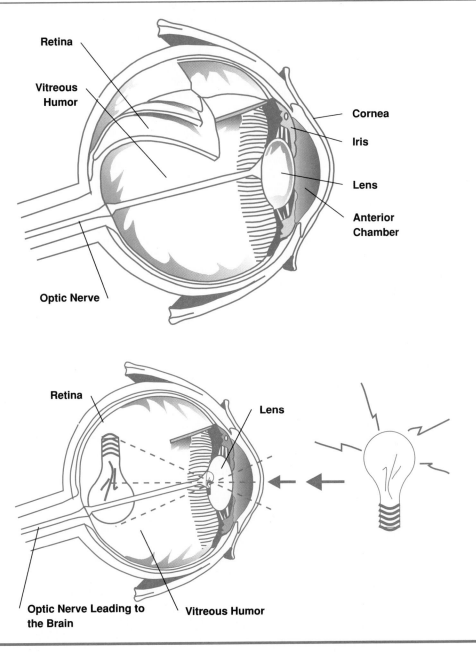

sightedness, results when the shape of the eyeball is abnormally long (or less frequently due to corneal or lens curvature), causing the image of a distant object to converge in front of the retina. Infants who are nearsighted see near objects normally, while images of distant objects are distorted. The opposite is the case of **hyperopia,** or farsightedness, in which far objects are seen with greater acuity than near objects. In this case, the eyeball shape is abnormally short, and the image converges behind the retina. To remediate hyperopia and myopia, eyeglasses or contacts with an appropriately adjusted spherical (section) lens are placed before the eye.

Astigmatism is caused when the cornea is abnormally shaped. An oval-shaped cornea will cause the light to be refracted unevenly. The fuzzy distortion that results from astigmatism can be corrected by using eyeglasses or contacts with parabolic- or toric-shaped lenses. A decrease in accommodation or elasticity of the lens is known as **presbyopia,** the inevitable consequence of aging. Presbyopia causes the focusing function of the eyes to weaken and reduces one's ability to see items close up without correction (i.e., bifocals or trifocals).

Errors in Binocular Vision Six sets of muscles permit the eyes to act in concert to follow a moving object and to focus images correspondingly on both retinas. A disruption in this coordination will upset the correspondence and result in a double image being perceived by the cortex. In a chronic situation, referred to as **amblyopia,** the brain will suppress one of the images and the affected eye will begin to deteriorate in performance. **Strabismus,** also resulting from muscle dysfunction, is when the two eyes do not focus on the same image. One eye may be focused directly at an object and the other eye is turned elsewhere. Strabismus can usually be corrected through lenses, surgery, or muscle exercise programs. Untreated strabismus may progress into amblyopia.

Central Nervous System Dysfunctions In instances where the eye physiology is not impaired, yet a child experiences loss of visual ability, there may be damage to the central nervous system. Damage to the optic nerve or the cerebral tissue within the occipital portion of the brain may cause **cortical visual impairments.** These visual losses may be complete or partial, though researchers have not been able to link the amount or type of loss to specific type of central nervous system damage (Hoon, 1991). Cortical visual loss may be paired with intrauterine and postnatal infection (e.g., syphilis, meningitis), traumatic brain injury (e.g., drowning), perinatal injury (e.g., anoxia), and seizures. Often, this type of visual impairment involves damage to the brain. Mental retardation may accompany cortical visual impairments.

Rhythmic eye twitching or tremors are referred to as **nystagmus.** The etiology of nystagmus may be either neurological or muscular, with the former generally associated with more serious visual impairments.

Causes of Visual Impairment

Perhaps half of all cases of blindness may be genetic in origin (Bateman, 1983). Two common genetic causes of visual impairments are associated with genetic syndromes: albinism and Down syndrome. Down syndrome is a chromosomal aberration that is commonly associated with such visual disorders as severe myopia, cataracts, amblyopia, strabismus, glaucoma, and nystagmus (Shapiro & France, 1985). All children with Down syndrome should have regular ophthalmalogical examinations. Visual impairments accompanying **albinism** are related to a lack of melanin or pigmentosa. The eyes of a child with albinism lack color and are extremely sensitive to light, requiring tinted lenses. Nystagmus is also frequently associated with albinism.

The most common cause of congenital visual impairment is exposure to infections. Rubella may lead to retinopathy, cataracts, glaucoma, and structural malformations. Cytomegalovirus, toxoplasmosis, herpes simplex, and congenital syphilis are associated with visual impairments ranging from lesions to central nervous system malformations. Researchers are also just beginning to understand the relationship between HIV infection and visual impairments in children. A prenatal teratogen that can cause visual impairments is alcohol. Teratogens such as lead may also affect vision postnatally.

A **cataract** is a clouding or opacity of the lens. The location and degree of deviation from transparency caused by the cataract(s) will determine the amount of distortion and obstruction of vision. The treatment of cataracts involves surgery to remove the portion of the lens affected. Corrective lenses are necessary to compensate for the lens lost in surgery.

Glaucoma is caused by a buildup of pressure in the anterior chamber of the eye. In most cases, the onset of glaucoma is unrecognized until much damage has already been done to peripheral vision. Untreated, glaucoma will cause continued serious visual loss or blindness. However, medical treatment (usually medication) can arrest the otherwise progressive degeneration of vision. Since children with other visual losses often have secondary visual problems, they should be observed throughout childhood for signs of glaucoma (i.e., excessive tiredness, severe headaches, dizziness, loss of field vision, and tearing).

Late visual bloomers include those children who, like children with motor, language, and social developmental delays, experience maturational delays in visual ability (Harel, Holtzman, & Feinsod, 1985). These children appear to be blind at birth and during their first months of life, but they typically develop normal visual ability by 18 months to 3 years. Research on delayed visual development is sparse, though it seems that the syndrome is associated with delays in development of specific processes of the central nervous system (e.g., myelination).

Developmental Implications and Resolutions

Children with visual impairments, particularly those with other disabilities, display unusual patterns of eye contact. Yet, one of the first intentional acts of infants is eye gaze. Normal language, cognition, and social skill development, are dependent on eye gaze which sets the occasion for social and language interactions and provides visual memory that enables infants to feel "safe" in exploring their world (Morse, 1991). To mediate the visual attentional differences in children with visual impairments, Morse made the following recommendations to caregivers: develop a trusting interpersonal relationship; establish routine play and social interactions; use clear, colorful (if relevant), and closely spaced cues to attend; reduce irrelevant sensory information.

Children who are visually impaired will usually experience delays in other areas as well, even when they possess normal intelligence. Muscle tone is likely to be hypotonic since normal mobility is impeded (Teplin, 1983). Because language development depends on imitation of mouth movements as well as nonverbal language cues, children who are visually impaired often experience delays in speech development as well as in conversational abilities (Pring, 1984). This inability to see nonverbal cues and subtle forms of language may result in self-orientation or social isolation (Hoon, 1991). Finally, children with blindness frequently present stereotypical behaviors such as rocking or postural abnormalities (Batshaw & Perret, 1988).

One factor affecting the interaction between visual impairments and later functioning is the timing of onset. **Congenital** (born with) blindness and **adventitious** blindness (developed later) differentially affect the type of intervention a child might need. Because adventitious blindness occurs after a child has had opportunities for visual experiences, such children are able to "picture" images of their world conceptually, if not visually, after sight is lost.

The primary goal of early intervention is to have children make the best use of their residual vision. According to Morse (1991), special training is needed to teach infants with blindness to "pay attention." Paying attention requires that infants learn to screen out irrelevant sensory stimuli while vigilantly seeking new information. Additionally, infants must learn to use previously gained information in new situations to make decisions. Very young children can be motivated to use their residual vision if caregivers limit the amount of assistance provided to that which is necessary to ensure safety and success. Beyond that, infants and toddlers should be encouraged to explore, to move independently about their environments, and to risk an occasional bump or bruise to increase mobility.

Prevention of secondary disabilities requires an interdisciplinary approach to give attention to physical development, language acquisition, and social skills. Caregivers can assist in facilitating normal development in other areas by providing enriching experiences with activities, materials, and interactions that make use of residual vision as well as tactile, auditory, kinesthetic, and olfactory senses.

Table 7.2/ *Mobility Devices for Infants and Preschoolers*

Types of Devices	Product Vendor	Advantages
Electronic Travel Aids (ETAs): Electronic devices that detect obstacles and provide users with auditory and/or tactual signals.	Laser Cane: Nurion; Sonicguide: Wormaid International	May be used to teach concepts and stimulate reaching prior to locomotion.
Suspended Movement Devices: Devices suspended from an overhead support that allow freedom of movement within a limited space.	Baby swings: "Jolly Jumpers"	Provide upright movement experiences in space.
Infant Walkers: Wheeled devices with seats that allow infants to propel themselves with their feet.	Commercial walkers	May stimulate child due to change in environment.
Scooterboards: Small wooden, foam, or plastic platforms on wheels.	Cookie Monster Crawl-Along: Educational Teaching Aids; Midline Positioning Scooter: Achievement Products	Allow for independent mobility in prone, supine, and seated positions; provide trunk support for creeping; allow hands to be free to manipulate objects.
Wheelchair Devices: Manual or battery-powered devices that transport nonambulatory children.	Manual devices: Toddler Cart: Achievement Products; Powered devices: Amigo Mini: Amigo	May allow greater independence and exploration.
Cruising Surfaces: Surfaces used to pull to standing position and maintain balance while stepping.	Playpen; Cribs	Provide comfort and stability while moving about the environment; help child to learn about the arrangement of space; provide a training ground for learning to trail.
Push Toys (supported/stooped): Low, weighted toys or objects used for support while walking in a stooped posture.	Large wooden trucks; large beachballs	Allow child to practice balancing in semierect posture; serve as bumpers to protect child from obstacles in path.
Orthopedic Walkers: Therapeutic support devices, without seats, used to assist in walking.	Children's Full Body Suspension Walker: Achievement Products	Serve as bumpers to protect child from obstacles in path.
Walking Hoops and Guiding Sticks: Hoops and sticks used to encourage walking without direct physical contact with another person.	Hula Hoops; PVC pipes	Offer security and support while learning to walk without physical contact with another person.
Riding Roll Toys: Wheeled children's riding toys that are propelled by pushing with the feet.	Tyke Bikes: Environments, Inc.	Are "normal" devices used by nondisabled children; serve as bumpers to protect child from obstacles in path.

Types of Devices	Product Vendor	Advantages
Push Toys (supported/upright): Wheeled children's push toys that offer support while walking upright.	"Tuff Stuff" Shopping Cart: Kaplan	Serve as bumpers to protect child from obstacles in path; are "normal" devices used by nondisabled children.
Walking Ropes: One or two ropes, running horizontally, that serve as tactual guides while walking or running.	Rope; clothesline	Provide practice in trailing; guide child in a straight line while walking or running.
Cane Instruments: Nonrolling devices that may be used in the environment as a bumper and a probe, much as a long cane is used.	Hockey sticks; plastic baseball bats	Are "normal" devices used by nondisabled children; may be arced side to side to clear a complete path in front of child.
Canes: Standard canes modified for young children.	Collapsible or rigid canes: White Cane Instruments for the Blind (WCIB)	May encourage confidence while walking independently; may help child to avoid the development of inappropriate gait patterns; may eliminate the need to remediate skills later on.

Source: Adapted from Clarke, K. L. (1988). Barriers or enablers: Mobility devices for visually impaired and multiply handicapped infants and preschoolers. *Education of the Visually Handicapped, 20,* 115–133.

Informing and Working with Parents

As with any disability, team members who interact with parents should be considerate enough to present any new information related to the visual impairment more than once. It is almost certain that parents who receive a large amount of technical information, especially if this information leads to emotional reactions, will be unable to focus on the details of the conversation. Using the concept of anticipatory guidance, team members can time the delivery of information to intersect with parents' ability to "hear" and a child's need for services. This practice, of course, assumes the need to tailor timing to suit individual children and their families (Hoon, 1991).

Furthermore, information givers should be knowledgeable enough to be able to answer most questions that parents might ask. However, it is worse to give misinformation than to give no information, especially regarding developmental predictions of children's future visual abilities or related developmental prognoses. Whenever possible, vision specialists should assist in informing parents. It may also be appropriate and necessary to explain the nature of the visual loss to children themselves. For example, children with congenital blindness do not recognize a deficiency until they are told and realize how they are different from their peers.

The absence of visual referents that are gained from cumulative visual experiences prevents children with visual impairments from developing conceptual, perceptual, sensory, and body awareness of space and environment. Hence, a primary objective of early intervention should be to train **orientation** skills, which will enable young children with visual impairments to achieve **mobility.** Orientation training is necessary to enable young children with visual impairments to gain a sense of position in space. Children are taught to take advantage of other senses such as touch, smell, and hearing to replace sight. Mobility training should be coupled with orientation, that is, teaching children their location in the room as well as how to move around their environment. According to Clarke (1988), orientation and mobility technology has undergone an exciting evolution during the 1980s (see Table 7.2).

Early Diagnosis

Interview with Marsha Moore

Almost from the very beginning, before he was three weeks old, I had the sinking suspicion that there was something really wrong with Michael. He did not respond to me. He did not quiet to my voice or touch. He would not, maybe could not, make eye contact. He cried day and night, even during bath time or while nursing. He did not nurse well. He was stiff and would not cuddle but rather would arch his back and flail his arms and hands. He was our sixth child, and we were experienced parents, but Michael was not like the rest. We took him several times to our new hometown general practitioner. The doctor believed that Michael was "just colicky" and prescribed a medicine to relieve him (and I suppose the entire family) of the discomfort we all felt.

When Michael was almost four months old, we returned to Denver to visit our previous pediatrician. At first, the appointment was relaxed and friendly. We exchanged small talk about our new home in Wyoming and our other children. Once the examination began, it was apparent that our doctor had that same sinking notion that something was just not right. He examined Michael for several minutes and then called in his physician's assistant and one of his nurses. All three continued to examine Michael, coaxing him to track their pen lights and a squeak toy, pulling him to sit, and checking out his fat, pink perfect little body. I continued to jabber on nervously about all my motherly concerns. In my heart I hoped that I had been foolish to feel so anxious. They said little to each other and absolutely nothing to Jim or me. Perhaps we were expected to read minds! Finally our doctor turned to us and said, "I think Michael is blind."

We had seen Michael reach for toys. We had seen him stare into the lights over the kitchen countertop. We had seen him focus on his mobile over his crib. And although both eyes often crossed and at times seemed disconnected, I still could not believe the diagnosis of "blind." Later, we would find that his vision problems were just the "tip of the iceberg."

Before we left to return home, our pediatrician arranged for us to see a pediatric ophthalmologist and a neurologist and to get a CT scan at a nearby hospital. We had driven almost five hundred miles for medical information and did not want to go home without some answers. It was almost 9 P.M. by the time we left the neurologist's office. Michael had been poked and prodded for almost 12 hours and was tired, over stimulated, and literally "strung out." Jim and I were numb. How could all of this be happening to us?

The results of the CT scan and both examinations were inconclusive. Michael's eyes were healthy. He had strabismus, but there seemed to be no physical reason why he would not be able to see. There was a question, however, as to whether his brain could "see" and whether a label of cortical blindness would be appropriate. The neurologist was guarded in his prognosis. The CT scan showed irregularities in Michael's brain. He acknowledged that Michael's development was a little slow, but we were assured that there was little reason to worry. We were instructed to contact a therapist who worked in the outskirts of Denver. Mike's condition was not "that" delayed and would probably improve as he matured with added infant stimulation. Somehow, neither Jim nor I was convinced.

We drove all night and arrived home early the next morning. We said little to each other during the trip back. I cried, and he sighed! We both recognized that this was only the beginning.

Michael was five months old when he began with his first therapy session in Denver. The therapist was a true godsend. Because we lived so far away, she scheduled the entire afternoon for Michael. We brought the whole family to his first appointment. Therapy was definitely going to be a group effort! All winter long, we worked with Michael on a daily basis, going through the routines that the therapist had taught us and improvising along the way, but we saw little change. Michael had learned to independently roll over, but still was

(continued)

unable to sit up by himself. He could not yet position himself on his hands and knees. He was not even belly crawling. His mode of transportation was either to roll from place to place or to arch and push himself on his back. I spent many hours on the floor with him, trying in every way I knew possible to encourage him to explore his world. I would leave little trails of marshmallows and graham crackers all over the carpet in hope that he would be motivated to creep to get them. We sang to him, read to him, stacked blocks with him. We bought bags of lentils and rice for him to play in. We made pudding finger paints. We purchased vibrating pillows and hot and cold water bottles. At ten months, he was still crying through the night, and although I was still nursing him, he had never made eye contact with me.

He had earlier made somewhat of a small "breakthrough" with Jim. When he was almost eight months old, Jim was playing on the sofa with him; talking, growling, tickling him, when suddenly, Jim whispered "Look, look." I looked over to see that Michael was staring intently at Jim's face. Jim was beaming and did not move for fear that Mike would lose contact. It took only a few seconds before Michael began to cry big alligator tears. Why was this connection so frightening to

Michael? Why did he pull away from us so? What was wrong with *us*? We both felt so helpless!

Our first Wyoming winter seemed very long and very bleak for a multitude of reasons. I stayed in telephone contact with our Denver pediatrician and with the therapist, but we were not able to get back to Denver until April when the snow finally melted and the roads cleared. At that time, Michael saw a battery of specialists at Denver Children's Hospital. He would be a year old in May, and there was still no conclusive diagnosis.

We scheduled a week-long hospital assessment again in July and saw several different "developmental" authorities who worked out of other clinics. These trips were so difficult for Mike. He was in strange places, with strange people, strange routine, strange food. He seemed so disoriented and fussed or cried constantly. Yet, this time we received a diagnosis. Finally, after fourteen months, we had a name to give to what was happening with Mike: infantile autism with severe mental retardation. We were relieved and very sad. How could Michael ever enjoy this type of existence? How could his life be worth anything? We felt so angry. This wasn't fair! What did Michael ever do to deserve something like this? What did any of us do to deserve this? Where do we go from here?

Curriculum specifically designed for infants and toddlers includes precane skills, sensory awareness, trailing, using a sighted guide, and environmental familiarization. Advances in mobility devices for very young children generally consist of modified adult devices, such as shortened long canes, or devices specially designed for children, such as a push toy that provides both support and protection for a toddler who is blind. Selection of appropriate orientation and mobility adaptations should be based on several factors identified by Clarke (1988): a child's motor skills, degree of visual loss, concern for safety of the child and others, adaptability of the child to change required for continuous accommodation, need for formal training, degree of independence in travel required, cost (which can range from several thousand to just a few dollars), the need for maintenance, and the availability of technology. Orientation and mobility (O & M) specialists are available and should be regularly consulted for selection, adaptation, and evaluation of mobility devices for specific children (Clarke, 1988). Individuals with severe vision impairment who are at least 16 years of age, are in good health, and have average or better intelligence and hearing may receive a guide dog.

INFECTIONS

Human beings have been afflicted with both common and complex ailments since the beginning of recorded history. Sore throats, earaches, and fevers commonly interfere with the normal

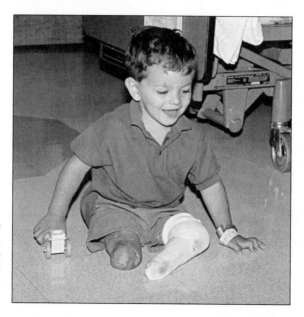

Due to complications associated with meningitis, this child lost part of both legs in early childhood.

activities of daily living. These are generally symptoms of invasion by **biological** agents. The interaction between humans and the microorganisms that cause infection is complex. These biological agents cause damage to human cells by either living on cells or by causing **inflammation** of the cells. Inflammation is caused by the **toxin** given off by the particular **organism** causing a specific infection. This toxin acts like a poison to human cells. Biological agents may travel throughout the body via the bloodstream or by way of the lymph system. The effect of an infection on a particular individual is dependent on the agent involved, the overall physical condition of the individual when exposed to a particular agent, and the age of the person affected.

For some infecting agents, premature babies, term newborns, infants, and young children are affected differently than older children and mature adults. Reactions among very young children may include lowered rather than elevated body temperatures, a decrease instead of increase in the total white blood cell count, and a more rapid progression of an infecting agent producing more significant symptoms. In addition, very young children have immature immune systems and may be less capable of dealing with an infection than an individual with a mature and healthy system. Individuals with compromised immune systems, such as infants with chronic diseases, are also at a much higher risk of developing infection. As a result of these factors, neonates, infants, and young children may have more frequent episodes of significant infections that require more extensive interventions. Biological agents that may cause infections in humans include bacteria, viruses, mycoplasmas, fungi, protozoa, rickettsias, and nematodes. Two of the most common agents are bacteria and viruses.

Bacterial Infections

By adulthood, everyone has experienced an infection. In spite of this, few have actually seen what causes the illness. **Microbes,** or germs, are so small that they can only be seen through a microscope, and **bacteria** are microbes that are found abundantly in nature. Many bacteria are **nonpathogenic,** or incapable of causing disease, and live in harmony with humans. Yet, even bacteria that generally are beneficial can cause significant infections in humans under the right circumstances by becoming **pathogenic.**

Pathogenic bacteria create infections that continue to be a significant cause of infant **morbidity** and **mortality** in the United States, constituting approximately 13% to 45% of neonatal deaths each year (Cole & Cloherty, 1985). Such infections can occur either prior to delivery from an infected mother or shortly after delivery from exposure to infected persons or objects in the environment. An infant's condition can be profoundly affected, depending on the particular organism responsible for a specific infection and the time between exposure to infection and initiation of appropriate treatment. For example, infants infected by **group B streptococcus** may show subtle objective symptoms such as mild respiratory distress, but the infants deteriorate quickly, if not treated, to the point that death may occur. Medical care providers need to use observable signs along with a maternal history and a review of risk factors when deciding whether to start early and aggressive treatment.

A history of poverty may place a child at risk for the development of infections. A direct relationship exists between socioeconomic status and low birth weight, as well as the development of both prenatal and postnatal infections. Naeye and Blanec (1970) concluded that the greater the degree of poverty, the lower an infant's birth weight, and consequently the greater the vulnerability to infection. In their study, poverty was also linked to many of the maternal conditions that lead to low birth weight, such as poor nutrition, lack of prenatal care, drugs, alcohol, smoking, and inadequate attention to chronic disease states, such as hypertension. Appropriate assessment of the physical condition of an infant at delivery provides health care workers with the information necessary to determine risk factors that may indicate the presence of a bacterial agent. Keys to effective treatment of an infected infant are awareness of the possibility of infection, assessment of presenting signs and symptoms, and aggressive treatment of any suspected infection in an at-risk infant.

Infants born through infected amniotic fluid or those who acquire a bacterial infection shortly after birth are at high risk for disability or death from the infection. Initial symptoms of an infection include temperature instability, poor feeding, respiratory distress, low blood sugar, and lethargy. Symptoms may also be as subtle as a lack of appropriate responding to environmental stimulation. Multiple physical system failure can occur very rapidly in an affected newborn. In those infants with multiple system involvement for whom death does not occur, there can be significant long-term developmental effects. Those disabilities occurring most frequently include visual impairment, hearing loss, and mental retardation. Such secondary disabilities may be the result of the infectious process or a result of the treatment used to save an infant's life. Infants experiencing infections at birth, or shortly afterwards, warrant early screening for developmental progress, identification of potential problems, and possible initiation of early intervention programs to provide the opportunity for full development (see Table 7.3).

Chlamydia   **Chlamydia trachomatis** is rapidly becoming the most prevalent of all sexually transmitted diseases in the United States (Centers for Disease Control [CDC], 1989 b). Its high rate directly correlates with the increasing numbers of infants who will be born to infected mothers and thereby contract the infection at birth. Chlamydia trachomatis is among the smallest of currently identified bacteria and resembles a virus because of its size and the manner in which it enters and feeds within the cells. Like a virus, chlamydia contains both RNA and DNA (Sheahan & Seabolt, 1989; Ward, 1983).

Table 7.3/   *General Adverse Effects of Significant Bacterial Infections on Young Children*

Exposure	Effects	Treatment
Prenatal	Visual Impairment	Antibiotics
Environmental	Hearing Impairment	Systems Support
	Mental Retardation	

It is hard to determine how much chlamydia infections contribute to perinatal illness and death. Adverse pregnancy outcomes, most commonly preterm labor, premature rupture of the membranes, and low birth weight appear to have an increased incidence in the presence of the chlamydia infection (Cohen, Veille & Calkins, 1990). There is also an increased incidence of infection among pregnant women of lower socioeconomic means, who are already at increased risk for adverse pregnancy outcomes based on other factors.

Neonatal chlamydial infections have no reported deaths directly related to the infection. However, there may be an increased incidence in mortality related to higher rates of prematurity. Neonates infected with chlamydia experience eye infections and pneumonia. **Conjunctivitis** (inflammation with redness and a discharge of pus from the eye) responds to antibiotic therapy but requires long-term treatment. Occasionally delays in treatment or incomplete treatment with reoccurrence may result in eye changes such as scarring of the conjunctiva or changes in vessels but rarely do these changes alter visual acuity (MacMillan, Weiner, & Lamberson, 1985).

Chlamydia has been recognized as one of the most common causes of pneumonia in infants during the first three months of life (Rettig, 1988). Lung infections, causing pneumonia, occur as a result of chlamydia entering the nose and mouth of the infant during the delivery process and subsequently spreading to the lungs. Respiratory problems can also be the result of a primary infection of the eye that caused conjunctivitis. There has not been definitive determination of any long-term problems associated with chlamydial pneumonia; however, significant abnormalities in respiratory function were noted in studies conducted by Weiss, Newcomb, and Beem (1986) in children being followed after recovery from lung infections.

Viral Infections

Viruses are the smallest infectious agents and are more difficult to identify and control because of their unique properties. Like bacteria, viruses are biological agents but differ from true microorganisms. A virus consists of genetic material, either DNA or RNA, and an enclosing shell of protein. Genetic materials contained in a virus's DNA or RNA make the virus capable of reproducing and attaching itself to susceptible cells. Most viruses have specific cell preferences where they will attach and reproduce. Examples of cell preferences may be nerve, muscle, or blood cells. Once in a host individual, viruses can survive in an inactive state for extended time periods with activation and occasional reactivation periods that produce the disease itself. Other viral infections do not produce recognizable diseases in the infected individual but create a **carrier** state.

Prevention of viral diseases has been accomplished largely through the development of **vaccines.** These consist of either active viral replications that have a decreased capability of causing infection and disease or an inactive virus introduced into the human being to activate the immune system to produce **antibodies.** Through a series of childhood immunizations, many common viral diseases have been nearly eliminated or greatly reduced in early childhood (see Figure 7.6). Once established, antibodies prevent an acute infection if the individual is exposed to an active virus of normal virulence. Potent drugs are continuously being developed to counteract specific viral agents. The success of these drugs in preventing or controlling viral infections has been variable.

Viral infections and many of the common congenital disabilities related to specific agents are frequently discussed under the umbrella of the TORCH infections. Many professionals add syphilis to this group as a separate entity and refer to them as the STORCH infections. In this text, syphilis will be included under other infections (O). The letters TORCH represent toxoplasmosis (T), other infections (O), rubella (R), cytomegalic inclusion virus (C), and herpes (H) (see Table 7.4). Because of the variability in pathology and outcome of these infections, they are usually discussed as independent entities (see Table 7.5).

Toxoplasmosis Pregnant women must be especially careful to avoid infection by **toxoplasmosis** (toxoplasma gondii), a **protozoan,** acquired by humans from contact with the feces of infected cats or birds and from the ingestion of raw or partially cooked meat. This infection is

	Diphtheria, Tetanus, & Pertussis (DTP)	Polio	Measles, Mumps, & Rubella (MMR)	Tetanus Diphtheria	Haemophilus Influenzae Type B (HIb)	Hepatitis B
Birth – 2 weeks						shot
2 months	shot	oral			shot	shot
4 months	shot	oral			shot	
6 months	shot	oral			shot	shot
12–15 months			shot		shot	
15–18 months	shot					
4–6 years	shot	oral	shot			
10–12 years						✳ shot
14–16 years				shot		
Based on National Standards						

✳ shot **if not done earlier, 3-dose series between 11–12 years of age**

shot **immunization delivered by shot**

oral **immunization taken orally**

discussed as part of the TORCH viral infections since the protozoan acts upon the RNA and DNA of the cell in the same manner as viruses. Antibodies are developed following acute infections. This infection can be acquired by a pregnant woman during any stage of pregnancy and subsequently transmitted to an unborn fetus.

Maternal infections during either the first or second trimester appear to be most commonly associated with infections that cross the placenta and affect the fetus **(transplacental).** This occurs when the protozoa cross from the maternal side of the placenta to the fetal side, subsequently infecting the developing fetus. Congenital toxoplasmosis infections (acquired before birth) can cause significant fetal abnormalities. Fetal conditions resulting from an acute infection are dependent on the gestation of the fetus at the time of infection.

Table 7.4/ *TORCH Infections*

T	Toxoplasmosis
O	Other (Varicella-Zoster, Mumps, Rubeola, Syphilis, Hepatitis, HIV/AIDS)
R	Rubella
C	Cytomegalic Inclusion Virus (CMV)
H	Herpes simplex

Table 7.5/ *Characteristics/Outcomes of Congenital Infections*

	Toxo-plasmosis	Chicken-pox	Hepatitis B	Syphilis	HIV/AIDS	Rubella	CMV	Herpes
Blindness	X	X		X		X	X	X
Deafness	X	X		X		X	X	X
Retardation	X	X		X		X	X	X
Seizures	X	X		X		X	X	X
Liver affected			X	X	X		X	
Spleen affected			X	X	X		X	
Hydrocephaly	X	X		X			X	X
Microcephaly	X	X		X		X	X	X
Jaundice			X		X		X	
Brain atrophy	X	X		X		X	X	X
Transmitted at birth		X	X	X	X	X	X	
Transplacental	X	X	X	X	X	X	X	?
"Shed" virus			X	X	X	X	X	X
Hydrops				X				

Prevention of toxoplasmosis can be accomplished by educating women of childbearing age to avoid the ingestion of undercooked meat and contact with excrement from cats and birds. It is also important to recognize that undiagnosed and untreated maternal infections can affect subsequent pregnancies with fetal infections and an increased incidence of in utero fetal death, but this is a rare occurrence.

Fetal effects of congenitally acquired toxoplasmosis often include a classical triad of hydrocephaly, cerebral calcification, and **chorioretinitis** (inflammation of the retina and blood vessels that supply the retina with nutrition) with resulting visual impairment. This triad can be found in approximately 60% of infected infants (Varner & Galask, 1981). Other features commonly associated with congenital toxoplasmosis include microcephaly, deafness, seizures, **encephalitis,** enlargement of the spleen and liver, anemia, jaundice, and mental retardation. The infection itself may not always be apparent at birth and frequently the onset of symptoms is delayed for several months. Treatment of an infected mother may include drug therapy, but most drugs are not effective at treating an infected infant. Though these agents are useful in destroying the harmful protozoa, damage already done to the infected infant cannot be reversed.

The prognosis for infants born with congenital toxoplasmosis infection is poor. As many as 15% of infected infants who are born alive will die within the neonatal period, and 85% of the survivors have severe developmental delays and vision problems (Leclair, 1980). Long-term care includes ongoing assessment for detection of developmental problems and initiation of early intervention programs.

Rubella Rubella, also known as German measles, generally causes minor illness in children but is much more of a problem for a pregnant woman. This viral infection has been preventable by immunization since 1969. A woman may be susceptible if she has not had rubella in the past or has failed to develop sufficient antibodies due to inadequate immunization. An

Encephalitis is a viral or bacterial infection causing inflammation of the brain.

exposed, pregnant woman may pass the infection to her fetus through the placenta. Fetal effects are thought to be the most devastating during the first **trimester;** however, evidence suggests that rubella transmitted during the fourth and fifth month of pregnancy also results in fetal infections and significant fetal effects (Grossman, 1980).

Stillbirth is a common outcome of congenital rubella infection. Other common fetal effects include microcephaly, cataract formation, significant cardiac anomalies, and deafness. Many infants born with congenital infection also demonstrate intrauterine growth retardation (Horstmann, 1982). Infants born with congenital rubella syndrome who suffer from severe intrauterine growth retardation, microcephaly, and other symptoms of central nervous system disease have an 80% mortality rate within the first year of life (Bolognese, Aldinger, & Roberts, 1981). This risk is especially true if these infants also suffer from associated defects such as cardiac malformations. Such abnormalities may be particularly difficult to manage because of the constellation of life-threatening problems associated with rubella syndrome.

Some infants born with congenital rubella have no apparent symptoms at birth. Of these, 70% will show effects of the disease before reaching five years of age. The effects most frequently include hearing loss, cataracts, and symptoms of central nervous system dysfunction, such as seizures and mental retardation (Leclair, 1980). Of concern is the finding that infants with no obvious effects at birth can shed the live virus, infecting others, without caregivers being aware of the condition.

Infants born with congenital rubella syndrome will shed large quantities of active virus from birth and may continue to shed for up to a year. Shedding occurs through the infant's urine, stool, and saliva. The virus is also present in the respiratory tract (Bromberg & Hsia, 1988). Individuals coming into contact with shedding infants need to be aware of the infection in order to take appropriate personal precautions to prevent the spread of the active virus. Health care professionals and caregivers who are not adequately immunized or who have not had a previous rubella infection should refrain from contact with an infant with rubella syndrome. Individuals placed within situations in which exposure may occur (e.g., daycare settings or classrooms) should establish whether they have adequate immunity. This can be done through laboratory testing prior to involvement.

There is no specific treatment once a congenital rubella infection has occurred. A neonate born with rubella needs to be isolated from contact with other infants and nonimmunized children and adults for up to a year. Assessment of the physical and developmental needs of the affected infant is necessary so appropriate early intervention can be planned. Special attention must be paid to any associated defects, especially cardiac, that place infected infants at a higher risk for secondary infections. Infected infants may also have problems related to poor feeding, which can lead to failure to thrive.

Long-term outcomes for infants born with congenital rubella syndrome are poor. Early eye and ear examinations are essential to determine the visual and hearing needs of the affected infant. Referrals to community agencies that provide services for infants with significant disabilities are almost always necessary.

Cytomegalic Inclusion Virus Approximately 80% of adults have antibodies in their blood for **human cytomegalic inclusion viral** infection (CMV) though the causative infection may have produced no noticeable symptoms. Cytomegalic inclusion virus is also the most common congenital viral infection. This medium sized virus is one of the four herpes viruses seen in humans; others are herpes simplex, varicella-zoster (chickenpox), and Epstein-Barr virus. A pregnant woman who becomes infected with CMV, or who experiences a reactivation of a past CMV infection can transmit the virus to her unborn child. Such transmission can cause serious consequences, including brain damage. Prevention of CMV infections is a prime goal of research, though to date no effective prevention or treatment has been established.

More than 90% of primary CMV infections produce no symptoms of disease (Pass, 1985), though a large segment of the general population tests positively by the end of adolescence, indicating a past primary infection. Recent surveys indicate that in the United States approximately 60% of pregnant, middle-class women have CMV antibodies. This rate may be as high as 80% among economically depressed women (Pass, Hutto, & Ricks, 1986; Stagno & Whitley, 1985; Varner & Galask, 1981). This finding, however, does not necessarily indicate immunity to reinfection or reactivation of infection.

Live CMV virus can be transmitted throughout pregnancy, producing congenital neonatal infections at any point prior to delivery. Reported rates of intrauterine transmission to a developing fetus differ significantly, from 20% to 45% (Preece, et al., 1983). Studies have not indicated that primary infection during the first trimester produces more serious complications for the fetus than infection later in the pregnancy (Preece, et al., 1983). This finding does not change the fact that in known infections, fetal effects may be predicted based on the gestational age of the pregnancy when the infection occurred. Cytomegalovirus can cause a significant interruption in the normal developmental progress of a fetus.

Specific congenital anomalies that have been noted in neonates born with congenital CMV infections include microcephaly, deafness, chorioretinitis, optic atrophy, enlarged liver and spleen, platelet destruction, calcifications in solid organs (such as the liver) and the brain, seizures, Dandy-Walker malformations (cystic formations that replace solid structure of the brain), intrauterine growth retardation, congenital heart defects, and abdominal wall defects. Even infants who show no apparent infection at delivery have shown delays in speech and language development on follow-up. These findings raise the possibility that subtle defects are present but not apparent during routine examination (Preece, et al., 1983).

Current treatment for a symptomatic infant is limited. Generally, care is supportive, aimed toward treatment of the symptoms presented by an individual infant. **Antiviral** drugs may be used, especially in infants with life-threatening infection, who display central nervous system symptoms. However, the adverse effects of these drugs must be carefully considered when determining whether the benefits outweigh the risks. Infants born with microcephaly as a result of congenital CMV infection frequently display significant developmental impairment. This finding supports the suggestion that the microcephaly is the result of intrauterine viral encephalitis. Encephalitis frequently results in brain cell death, which causes a halt in brain growth or shrinking of brain tissue.

Infants born with congenital CMV infection shed live virus through urine, stool, and other body fluids, including saliva, throughout their lifetime. Nursing mothers with current infections will also shed live virus through their breast milk, though this resolves once the active infection state is over. The definitive diagnosis of a suspected neonatal infection is made through isolation of the virus from a urine or saliva sample. No specific isolation of infected infants or children is required; however, pregnant women should not care for infected children. Caregivers who are pregnant can also acquire an infection through the handling of infected breast milk. Awareness of an infection or of those infants and children affected with congenital disease is critical in preventing the infection of a pregnant caregiver. The suggestion that a relationship exists between recurrent CMV infections and the development of acquired immune deficiency syndrome (AIDS) in at-risk individuals is also being explored.

Extensive resources may be necessary to meet the developmental needs of infants born with congenital CMV. Assessment of an infant to determine risk for developmental delay and to identify interventions is essential before initial discharge from the hospital. Reassessment of an infected infant must be done at intervals to determine if appropriate programs are in place to meet individual and family needs. Visual screening to identify impairments is a high priority. Neurological assessment to determine if visual disturbances are a result of physical or cortical damage can determine appropriate methods for early intervention.

Developmental impairments related to hearing loss also require monitoring. Current research attempts to identify the best method of early diagnosis of sensorineural hearing loss resulting from congenital CMV infection, especially in infants who present with **asymptomatic** congenital infection. These infants appear to be at significantly increased risk for late onset hearing loss (Hicks, et al., 1993).

Initiation of physical and occupational therapy programs to improve outcomes need to be established and undertaken within the parameters of providing service to the entire family unit. Support services should be provided to parents or caregivers with realistic information based on individual evaluation regarding an infant's long-term outcome.

Herpes   Genital **herpes** infections are among the most common venereal diseases in the United States (Freiji & Sever, 1988; Gast, 1983). In adults, the virus produces itching, burning, soreness, and small blisters in the genital area. The blisters burst to leave small, painful ulcers, which heal within 10 to 21 days. Subsequent attacks tend to occur after sexual intercourse, after sunbathing, or when the affected person is run down. There is no cure for herpes, and sexual activity should be avoided until the symptoms have disappeared.

Herpes simplex virus types 1 and 2 are closely related and share 50% of their basic genetic code (Grossman, 1980). Herpes simplex type 1 is generally associated with oral lesions but can also be present with infection at other body sites. Herpes simplex type 2 is typically associated with genital infection and, as with type 1, can also occur at other body sites. Herpes belong to a larger group of viruses that have common features; included in this category are CMV, varicella-zoster (chickenpox), and Epstein-Barr virus (mononucleosis).

Historically, the primary herpes type 2 infections are self-limiting, lasting up to 21 days. Primary infections usually cause severe discomfort in the genital area (Gast, 1983). Subsequent reactivation of the virus produces less painful infections. Both primary infections and reactivation of the dormant virus result in shedding of live virus. This shedding is of critical importance to a pregnant woman since acquisition of the virus during pregnancy may have adverse effects on a fetus.

The first fatal case of neonatal herpes was described in 1935 by Hass. Neonatal infections are usually acquired during passage through an infected birth canal in a normal vaginal delivery. This makes it vital that pregnant women with a history of genital herpes and their health care providers be certain that no lesions are visible (indicating an active infection) in the vagina, on the cervix, or on the external perineum at the onset of labor (Committee on Fetus and the Newborn, 1980). The presence of lesions or a herpes-positive culture is an indication for delivery by cesarean section.

Women who have a primary herpes type 2 infection during pregnancy may experience more spontaneous abortions and more premature deliveries than those with reactivation of the dormant virus during pregnancy. The risk of neonatal infection also appears to be greater during a primary type 2 infection (Committee on Fetus and the Newborn, 1980). There have been reports of this virus crossing the placenta, but such cases are rare. Evidence suggestive of transplacental infections include the presence of herpetic lesions on the neonate at birth, recovery of the virus from the placenta or cord blood, and the presence of associated congenital anomalies at delivery (Florman, Gershon, Blackett, & Nahmias, 1973; Gagnon, 1968; Sieber, Fulginiti, Brazie, & Umlauf, 1966; Witzleken & Driscoll, 1965).

Neonates exposed to herpes infection generally are without any identifiable symptoms at birth. Symptoms generally begin to appear within the first 6 to 16 days of life, with central nervous system symptoms appearing around day 11 (Committee on Fetus and the Newborn, 1980). These symptoms may include irritability, vomiting, and the onset of seizures (Gast, 1983). It is difficult to diagnose very young children, who may also show symptoms of other disorders and then progress rapidly to herpes encephalitis, though this is not the generally recognized course of the disease (Kohl, 1988). Usually encephalitis does not develop until later in the pattern of herpes infection (Whitley, Yeager, & Kartus, 1983). A rapid progression of the disease decreases the likelihood of success of the treatment.

It is estimated that 50% of neonates who acquire a herpes infection will die. Of those who survive, approximately 30% will have major neurological deficits as a result of the infection (Gast, 1983). Structural damage in the brain results from viral destruction of the gray and white matter. Hence, normal brain growth will be retarded, producing conditions such as hydrocephalus with frequent seizures, reduction in cortical growth with concurrent visual and hearing impairment, and mental retardation.

Specific focal areas of brain infection may frequently be determined in the presence of seizures by EEG (Whitley, Soong, & Linneman, 1982). This finding was the result of research showing that certain types of abnormal electrical activity are associated with herpetic lesions within the brain (Kohl & James, 1985, Whitley, et al., 1982). Measurement of seizure activity utilizing electroencephalography may be useful in tracking herpetic lesions and determining if there is any extension, especially during episodes of reactivation. Antiviral agents have been developed to treat herpes simplex infections in neonates, infants, children, and adults.

Infants who survive systemic herpes infections require developmental assessment and appropriate referrals for services prior to discharge from the hospital. Early intervention planning includes provisions for vision, hearing, physical, and occupational therapy. Caregivers need to be aware that these infants and children can shed active virus from lesions during reactivation phases and should take the appropriate steps to avoid infection. Protection includes covering the lesions and preventing direct contact of the affected area by other children and adults. Since many of these children also have frequent episodes of seizure activity, protective measures (e.g., head gear, removal of dangerous items) are indicated.

Other Viral Infections

Under the "O" or "Other" category of TORCH are a variety of diseases, many of which are common childhood illnesses, such as chickenpox and mumps. Usually, though not always, these illnesses cause only temporary problems for an infant. Even when exposed in utero, there may be no long-term effects to an infant. However, HIV/AIDS, syphilis, and hepatitis are also among the "Other" diseases, and in almost all cases, these illnesses cause severe disabilities and/or death.

Varicella-Zoster (chickenpox and shingles)   Chickenpox is typically a childhood disease but when a pregnant woman becomes infected, her unborn child is at serious risk because of the infection. **Varicella-zoster** (Herpes virus varicella or V-Z virus) is a member of the DNA herpes viruses. Primary infections of varicella virus (chickenpox) produce immunity, though late reactivation of dormant virus residing in nerve cells can result in shingles (zoster) in an older child or adult. However, there is no documentation of adverse effects of reactivated virus with the presentation of shingles in a pregnant woman, fetus, or neonate. Susceptible individuals who experience prolonged contact with infected persons are at a very high risk for developing infection.

Recently a live varicella vaccine has been approved for use in the United States. This has been in use in Europe for many years and has been determined to be effective (Gershon, 1985). Pregnant nonimmune women should avoid contact with people known to be infected with chickenpox. Because the virus is so capable of invading and causing infection, most individuals have acquired immunity through past infection before reaching the childbearing years. Therefore, chickenpox (V-Z virus) rarely occurs during pregnancy. Its incidence is as low as 1 to 7 cases in 10,000 pregnancies (Herrmann, 1982). Yet maternal infections can occur at any point during the pregnancy of a nonimmune mother and will have a significant effect on the neonate. It is estimated that approximately 24% of maternal varicella infections result in transplacental fetal infections (Freiji & Sever, 1988).

Maternal infection that occurs late in the pregnancy can result in severe generalized neonatal infection. Mortality during these infections occurs most frequently from multiple system failure as a result of pneumonia (Herrmann, 1982). Long-term disabilities generally result from central nervous system complications related to the development of encephalitis (Jenkins, 1965). Though rare, older children who develop infection can experience the same complications from the disease. Developmental disabilities in older children are generally related to the effects of encephalitis.

The more serious neonatal effects of V-Z infections result from a maternal infection early in the pregnancy and lead to congenital effects. The increased incidence of either prematurity or stillbirth associated with other viral infections does not appear to be associated with V-Z infections, though other conditions that lead to disabilities are common (Siegel & Fuerst, 1966; Seigel, Fuerst, & Peress, 1966). Congenital varicella-zoster syndrome can result in a condition in which the brain stops growing and shrinks; the remaining space is taken by fluid-filled cysts. Microcephaly, chorioretinitis, cataracts, auditory nerve paralysis, and mental retardation with concurrent seizures can be the consequence. Frequently occurring effects include limb deformities (most commonly involving one extremity), absence of digits, and eye abnormalities. In some cases, congenital infection is followed by skin scarring that frequently occurs on the limb that is deformed (Herrmann, 1982).

Infants born with congenital V-Z effects that involve limb abnormalities require evaluation by orthopedic specialists. Many of these young children will require orthopedic appliances to assure optimum mobility. Assessments of vision and hearing are essential early in the course of planning to determine what developmental needs are present.

Mumps   Another childhood disease that presents risks for pregnant women is mumps, a communicable virus causing swelling of one or both of the parotid glands that are located at the junction of the lower jaw and the neck. Currently, mumps are preventable through immunization with the live attenuated mumps virus vaccine that induces antibody production and protects an individual against acute infection. Acute mumps infections are generally self-limiting, lasting 9 to 14 days, with few complications. Adult males may have inflammation of the testes with subsequent sterilization, and all adults may suffer thyroiditis, pancreatitis, meningitis, and myocarditis. The most common residual effect of a mumps infection is deafness (Korones, 1988).

The risk of fetal effects from maternal mumps is low. There is an increase in spontaneous abortions during the first two trimesters of pregnancy but no obvious increased incidence of premature delivery (Siegel, 1973). There do not appear to be any specific congenital malformations associated with maternal mumps.

Infants exposed to mumps infections require early hearing screening with consistent follow-up. Identification of hearing impairments necessitates inclusion in early intervention programs to prevent secondary delays in other areas of development. Developmental assessments will identify any other areas that may have been affected by the infectious process.

Measles (Rubeola)   Measles virus, also called hard measles, is a communicable virus, like the mumps virus, that also produces a highly contagious infection. The virus is generally spread by droplets carried through the air, thus infecting susceptible individuals through the respiratory tract. Measles vaccine, introduced in 1963, has greatly reduced the incidence of epidemic outbreaks of measles in the United States. With this reduction of infection, the incidence of measles-related deaths has dropped to approximately 0.1% among the general population (Young & Gershon, 1983). Underdeveloped countries have not enjoyed the same progress. Without the availability of vaccine or the advances in technology, these countries experience high infection rates with a significantly increased incidence of related morbidity and mortality. The incidence of measles in these countries is also related to states of chronic protein deficiency (Frank, Orenstein, & Bart, 1985).

The incidence of measles infections among pregnant women has decreased as in the general population. Pregnant women who become infected experience an increased incidence of serious pneumonia, which occasionally results in death (Young & Gershon, 1983). Fetal effects from maternal measles appear to be few. There is an increased incidence of preterm delivery during acute maternal infections, but there is no reported evidence of fetal malformations. Mortality is related to problems associated with prematurity and not directly related to the effects of measles (Gazala, Karplus, & Liberman, 1985; Siegel & Fuerst, 1966; Siegel, 1973).

Measles infections in infants and young children occur consistent with the infection rate of the general population. Those infants and children who do become infected are predisposed to otitis media as a complication of the infection. Pneumonia also occurs and is potentially lethal in combination with the measles. Encephalitis occurs in approximately 1 in every 1000 cases of measles infection and continues to produce a mortality rate of about 10% for those children experiencing this complication (Young & Gershon, 1983). Long-term effects of infection include hearing impairment from ear infections. Viral encephalitis associated with measles can cause visual impairment and interruption in normal brain growth. Still, the goal is prevention, which can be accomplished by immunization of all children along the established guidelines of the American Academy of Pediatrics.

Syphilis Syphilis is a disease that can produce serious illness when contracted by either adults or children. It is generally considered a sexually transmitted disease but can be acquired by contact with infectious lesions that may be present on the mouth, skin, or other mucous membranes or by a fetus through transplacental passage of the infecting organism. Syphilis can also be contracted by an infant through contact with a lesion during the birth process. The disease is caused by a very mobile bacterium, which was identified in 1905 by Schaudinn and Hoffmann, two German scientists. As far back as the late 1400s, the disease represented a widespread health problem throughout the world (Pusey, 1933).

After the discovery of penicillin in the late 1940s, primary and secondary syphilis infections steadily declined in the United States until 1977, when the incidence began a steady increase that continues to the present time (CDC, 1985). A primary infection consists of the development of a lesion, also called a **chancre,** at the site of the contact with an infected person. This chancre is generally painless but highly infectious. There may be the development of multiple chancres with a primary infection. If a primary infection is not detected and appropriately treated with penicillin, it will progress to a secondary, or disseminated, infection. The latter is a **systemic** response to the infection that can have serious effects on many organ systems, especially the kidney and brain. Individuals treated during the secondary stage may continue to have effects from damage to organ systems that occurrred during the active infection. As many as one-third of untreated individuals will progress to **tertiary** disease, late syphilis, which is clinically evident with severe degeneration of organ systems and leads to significant disabilities (Seigel & Washington, 1987).

Pregnancy has no effect on the normal course of syphilis. Pregnant women who acquire an infection require the same diagnosis and treatment course as those individuals who are not pregnant. Furthermore, untreated infection will profoundly affect the outcome of pregnancy since the syphilis bacterium appears to be able to cross the placenta at any time (Harter & Benirschke, 1976). Asymptomatic infections can occur making it more important that standard recommendations for laboratory testing of all pregnant women takes place.

As many as 40% of pregnancies affected with maternal syphilis will result in fetal death (Brunham, Holmes, & Eschenback, 1984). Those infants who survive the pregnancy are frequently affected with intrauterine growth retardation and are frequently premature. Congenital effects from maternal syphilis generally produce significant disabilities. Central nervous system development is altered, resulting in severe mental retardation, visual and hearing impairments, and frequently seizures. Normal bone growth is altered, resulting in orthopedic malformations, and tooth formation is affected.

It has been determined that virtually all infants born to mothers infected with both primary and secondary syphilis will be born with congenital infection, though only 50% will be symptomatic at birth (Fiumara, Fleming, & Downing, 1952; Wendel, 1988). In spite of the relatively low rate, neonatal mortality may be as high as 54% in affected infants, though it has not been determined what percentage of these deaths are related to prematurity and not specifically to infection (Hira, Bhat, & Patel, 1985).

Neonatal effects of congenital infection generally consist of enlargement of the liver and spleen, jaundice, and swelling and destruction to the head of the femur, resulting in major orthopedic deformities. Another common finding is moist skin lesions, particularly located over the palms of the hands and on the soles of the feet. These lesions are highly infectious and caution is vital to prevent spread of the infection in a nursery population.

The degree of developmental disabilities of survivors of congenital syphilis infections is dependent on the gestational age of the fetus when the infection first occurred. Those infants who acquired infection during the first or second trimester of the pregnancy are at high risk for significant neurological delays and for visual and hearing impairments. Inadequate treatment allows a congenital infection to progress toward tertiary infection as it does in the adult. The profound developmental delays caused by this progression leave these infants in need of multidisciplinary services for the infant and family.

The goal of treatment is prevention of both primary infections and further progression of the existing disease state. Comprehensive prenatal care allows for diagnostic testing to determine infection and aggressive treatment to prevent fetal involvement and the subsequent significant affects of congenital syphilis infections.

Hepatitis   Hepatitis is a viral infection that produces systemic damage to the liver. It is a complex disease involving several subtype categories that produce similar symptoms but leave different long-term effects. Many children will be without symptoms; some may proceed to severe, overwhelming, and fatal acute infections; and others suffer progressive, chronic liver failure with **cirrhosis** or even cancer (Diienstaf, Wands, & Koff, 1986).

> Cirrhosis of the liver is the condition in which normal cells are replaced with abnormal fibrous cells that reduce liver functioning.

Hepatitis A virus (HAV) is generally a mild disease and has been referred to as infectious hepatitis. This virus is transmitted through personal contact with food handled by an infected individual. Poor personal hygiene, poor sanitation, and overcrowding greatly increase the potential for spreading HAV infection. Transmission by blood exposure is very rare. Flu-like symptoms and jaundice are the usual symptoms. Infection causes the production of antibodies against HAV, which set up lifetime immunity to further infection. These antibodies begin developing with the onset of an acute infection. HAV infection in children is rarely fatal. Chronic liver disease may result but less than a 0.1% overall mortality rate has been reported (Klein, 1988).

Hepatitis B virus (HBV) is a major health problem throughout the entire world. In the United States, about 300,000 new cases occur each year (CDC, 1989 a). Approximately 16,500 pregnant women infected with hepatitis B give birth every year with almost 3500 of these infants becoming chronic carriers. Twenty-five percent of these babies die from complications of the virus by young adulthood (CDC, 1988 a). Most carriers die from chronic active hepatitis, cirrhosis, or primary liver cancer. The surviving 75% of affected infants can potentially transmit hepatitis virus to family members, personal contacts, and health care providers. This includes daycare providers, teachers, and other children involved in the daycare setting.

Hepatitis B virus is a DNA virus that replicates in the liver. It can infect all body fluids including tears, gastric juices, urine, saliva, and semen. Transmission can occur through puncture wounds, blood transfusions, small cuts, and abrasions and also by absorption through mucous membranes, such as in the mouth or vagina (Boehme, 1985). Screening of pregnant women to determine both acute infection and antibody status is critical. Many of those mothers infected with HBV will not have any symptoms. The Centers for Disease Control suggest that all pregnant women have prenatal screening and absolutely recommend that women who are in risk categories be screened and followed. Women at high risk include:

1. those of Asian, Pacific island, or Alaskan Eskimo descent

2. woman who are Haitian or sub-Saharan African by birth

3. women with acute or chronic liver disease or a history of undiagnosed jaundice

4. IV drug users

5. those with personal contacts with HBV carriers

6. those with multiple episodes of venereal disease or those who are prostitutes

7. women who are sexual partners of hemophiliacs

8. individuals who work in dialysis or renal transplant units

9. individuals who work or live in an institution for persons with mental retardation

10. health care professionals

11. individuals who have tattoos (Summers, Biswas, & Pastorek, 1987)

Laboratory testing identifies women who are in an acute phase of infection through a positive hepatitis B surface antigen. This antigen is present on the surface of the virus and can be detected in the patient's blood serum. The presence of surface antigen indicates acute infection or a carrier state. Those individuals with a positive antigen will be tested for hepatitis B antigen. This is found only in individuals with a positive serum, and its presence is associated with active viral replication indicating the most highly infective state. It is during this time that a pregnant mother is at the highest risk to transmit infection to her fetus. Transmission may occur in as many as 90% of cases (CDC, 1988; Edwards, 1988).

Hepatitis B vaccine provides active immunity against the virus and is given at birth, one month, and six months of age. The Centers for Disease Control recommend that all infants of surface antigen positive mothers be immunized according to this schedule but that ultimately all newborns be immunized. These recommendations can dramatically reduce the incidence of vertical transmission (mother to fetus) but can also reduce the incidence of transmission by other care providers who may contact the infection through provision of services. Teachers, daycare providers, health care workers, social service agency workers, and any other individuals who may have reason to provide service to individuals or families with HBV infections need to strongly consider seeking immunization against the virus. The potential for acquiring HBV virus is significant. The potential loss of productive individuals and resources is as high as the loss encountered with acquired immune deficiency syndrome.

Human Immunodeficiency Virus/Acquired Immune Deficiency Syndrome   The disease known in our society by the familar term AIDS is the outcome or clinical manifestation of infection by a virus called the human immunodeficiency virus (HIV). Persons infected with HIV are said to be HIV positive, and in the early stages of the disease children are nonsymptomatic or the symptoms are mild. As the disease progresses, the symptoms worsen. The most severe manifestation of the disease is referred to as Aquired Immune Deficiency Syndrome or AIDS. Children have a shorter incubation period (12 months) between acquisition of HIV and a transition to AIDS than do adults (8–10 years) (Simonds & Rogers, 1992).

Currently, the HIV infection cannot be identified in the nursery population. However, it has been determined that all infants born to HIV infected mothers have antibodies to HIV. Very rarely do infants have either clinical or laboratory findings that can be diagnostic of infection during the neonatal period. In spite of this, in 1989, over 90% of pediatric cases of AIDS could be traced to perinatally acquired HIV infection. Of these, at least 70% were associated with drug use in a parent (HIV Serosurvey Unit Office of AIDS and HIV Surveillance, 1990). It is estimated that currently over 75% of the pediatric AIDS cases occur in New York, New Jersey, Florida, and Puerto Rico. At least 81% of these have been born to poor people, and in New York City, at least 54% are black, and 36% are Hispanic (AIDS Surveillance Unit, 1990).

The first reported case of AIDS in a child younger than 13 years of age was in 1982 (Oleske, Minnefor, & Cooper, 1983). It is now estimated more than 20,000 HIV infected children reside in the United States. Children usually become infected prenatally through contaminated blood or blood products and, occasionally, through breast milk.

Children infected with HIV represent a population already removed from mainstream health care. Social and economic factors influencing families place these children at high risk

Tuberculosis

Tuberculosis (TB), very common in the United States in the first part of the twentieth century, was nearly eradicated by the 1980s. Now, the incidence of TB is on the rise again. This disease results from a bacterial infection in the lungs. The bacteria spread slowly, transforming into tubules, or tubercles, that cause lung tissue to die. Untreated, active TB can lead to a chronic and even fatal condition. Those with chronic tuberculosis have fevers, loss of weight, night sweats, bloody sputum, difficulty in breathing, and coughing.

Though the incidence of TB is highest among young adults, the period of highest risk for contracting TB is early infancy when babies' immunities are immature. Furthermore, children with some other form of compromised immunity are at greatest risk for acquiring tuberculosis. The disease is highly communicable and transferred from one person to another through airborne respiratory secretions. However, transference of TB from child to child is rare. Well-ventilated rooms and ultraviolet lighting and use of masks will help prevent the spread of TB bacteria.

Today, the threat of contracting TB is increasing for two reasons. First, treatment of the disease requires rigorous compliance with medication protocols. Additionally, the drugs must be

taken until tests indicate that an individual is TB-free (nine months), even though symptoms for the disease may be gone long before tests are negative. Individuals responsible for themselves or their children often fail to complete drug treatment regimens, making themselves more resistant to subsequent treatment. Secondly, a new strain of tuberculosis is drug resistant, even to persons who have never been infected or treated for the disease. Drug resistant strains in the United States may follow the pattern of other countries where supervision and compliance of drug treatment is low. For example, in Southeast Asia, 50% of individuals newly infected with TB have the drug-resistant strain as compared to 7% in the United States. Moreover, south Texas, southern California, and New York City already have a very high prevalence of drug-resistant TB (20%).

Some fear that the rising incidence of TB, combined with its increasing failure to respond to traditional drug therapy, will become epidemic. Yet, this disease pattern may only be the tip of the iceberg when it comes to treating bacterial diseases. Health care workers predict that once-potent medical antibiotics used for other bacterial infections (e.g., influenza) will increasingly be ineffective. Therefore, early childhood educators of the future may be working with more and more children who have persistent or chronic respiratory infections.

Warren, J. (1992). Mycobacterial infections. In S. T. Shulman, J. P. Phair, & H. M. Sommers (Eds.), *The biologic and clinical basis of infectious diseases*, 4th Ed. (pp. 190-207).

for disease progression. Many times maternal risk behaviors continue following childbirth, reducing the probability for either monitoring or intervening in the physical and developmental progression of childhood. Many of these children are abandoned in health care facilities or exposed to poor sanitation and overcrowding that speed up the progression of the infection.

Children infected with HIV may display no symptoms, mild symptoms, serious general symptoms, or the development of full-blown AIDS. These symptoms include failure to thrive, enlarged lymph nodes, enlarged liver and spleen, enlarged heart, chronic bacterial infections, respiratory infections, diarrhea, and fevers. Survival times are shorter for children infected prenatally or during the first year of life, compared to those who contract infection during later childhood and adulthood. Pneumocystis carinii pneumonia is the most common complication of the syndrome that affects survival in very young children. Infants show as much as a 54% infection rate compared to only 16% for older children. The median survival time in perinatal cases after diagnosis with Pneumocystis carinii pneumonia was 1 month. The survival time for infants without pneumonia is greater than 18 months (Caldwell, Fleming, & Oxtoby, 1990).

Failure to thrive is a major problem affecting infants and young children with AIDS. Lactose intolerance and subsequent diarrhea are common findings among the affected pediatric population. Oral lesions due to yeast infections often result from prolonged antibiotic therapy. These lesions are very painful and may cause oral aversion and reduce the child's ability to maintain adequate food intake to support continued health. Consistency in caregivers is important to develop positive relationships that allow for optimum feeding practices.

Current practice for the care of infants of mothers who are either HIV positive or have AIDS is that of support and observation. These infants are usually not treated with antiviral medications unless symptoms develop. Once conversion to HIV positive occurs, medications are initiated to attempt to slow the progression of the disease (Pitt, 1991).

Many medical centers are experiencing an increasing number of infants being abandoned after delivery by positive HIV mothers who are drug abusers and who are unable or unwilling to care for their children. Many of these infants experience conditions related to premature birth or other conditions, including drug addiction, that place them at increased risk for developmental disabilities along with their HIV status. Placement in foster care settings can provide the opportunity to deal with problems that arise as a result of the progression of the HIV status to AIDS.

Advocacy for infants and children affected with both HIV and AIDS is the prime role for those involved with planning care for these children. Prevention of the progression of HIV and AIDS is the goal, but providing a quality of life to those currently affected is the issue. Utilizing a multidisciplinary approach to the many problems encountered by this population is essential for establishing a systematic plan for meeting all the physical, developmental, and emotional needs of these children. Education as part of a comprehensive plan of care for pregnant women will decrease the number of infants born to drug-affected women. Such women are often not only HIV positive but have infections that can and do cause significant physical and developmental problems for the unborn child. Interventions with childbearing women should include prenatal screening, drug and alcohol treatment programs, and attention to social problems. Poverty, crowding, poor sanitation, loss of self-esteem, and the resulting hopelessness that leads people to engage in behaviors that are destructive to themselves and their future must be considered.

Meningitis / Encephalitis

Meningitis and **encephalitis** are both infections that involve the central nervous system with particular concentration in the brain. Though the factors causing these infections may occasionally appear to be the same, the implications for treatment differ depending on the infecting agent. The brain is protected by a fluid-filled sac that surrounds it and the spinal cord. Moreover, the brain matter is intertwined with blood vessels that provide blood flow for the transport of food and oxygen. In the absence of infection involving the central nervous system pressure within the system maintains a steady state, allowing for normal blood flow (see Figure 7.7).

Meningitis Meningitis is a condition in which infection occurs as the result of the entry of bacteria around the surface of the brain, producing inflammation of the **meninges,** the coverings that surround the brain and spinal cord (see Figure 7.8). The meninges are three membranes (i.e. dura mater, pia mater, arachnoid) that are between the skull and brain and also between the vertebral column and the spinal cord. It is in this area that the **cerebrospinal fluid** flows over the surface of the nervous system. Cerebrospinal fluid is a clear, colorless, odorless fluid that resembles water and contains glucose, proteins, salts, and white blood cells. Its function is to protect the nervous system from injury by acting as a shock absorber. It also carries oxygen and nutrition to

Figure 7.7/ *Brain with Uninfected Meninges*

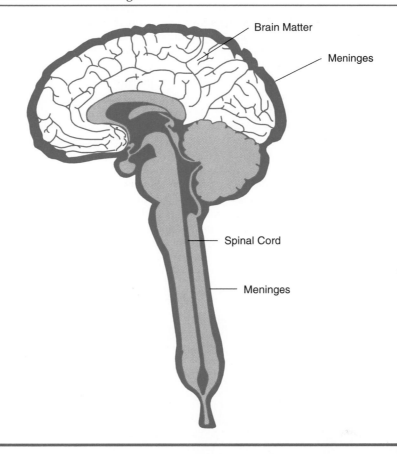

Brain Matter

Meninges

Spinal Cord

Meninges

the nerve cells and takes waste products away to be reabsorbed in the circulatory system. Small blood vessels that are part of the skull's lining act as the mechanism for exchange.

With meningitis, the cerebrospinal fluid becomes cloudy due to the increase of white blood cells in the fluid as the body attempts to fight the infection. Swelling occurs and there also is degeneration of some of the surrounding nerve cells. It is this swelling and nerve destruction that cause the neurological disabilities that sometimes follow an acute case of meningitis. On occasion there may also be an invasion of the infection into the brain matter itself through tears in the meninges. This increases the potential of brain and nerve injury.

Acute meningitis may produce significant symptoms in children, sometimes leading to death within a very short period of time. Death may be the result of either toxin or swelling of the meninges with a concomitant increase in pressure in the skull that blocks the normal blood flow. Loss of oxygen and sugar and the inability of the cells to rid themselves of waste products results, eventually leading to cellular death.

Acute bacterial meningitis is generally a disease of the young or the chronically ill. Immaturity of the immune system in the very young and the compromised immune system of the chronically ill places these individuals at greater risk for developing meningitis. The high incidence of otitis media in children (who have a short eustachian tube) permits easier access of infecting agents to the brain's blood supply. About 12 cases of bacterial meningitis occur for every 100,000 people per year, and approximately 90% of these individuals survive the infection

(Gunderson, 1982). Of those affected, half will have some degree of residual effect. In the case of neonates, half will have severe neurological damage as a result of the infection (Gunderson, 1982). Residual damage ranges from very minor dysfunctions to significant multiple disabilities.

The initial symptoms may include fever, vomiting, severe headache, stiffness of the neck and shoulders, and the onset of seizures and unresponsiveness. The actual diagnosis of meningitis is made through laboratory testing along with a physical examination. A **spinal tap** may reveal cloudy cerebral spinal fluid due to the increased number of white blood cells present in the fluid. Occasionally, the fluid may appear bloody because the tiny blood vessels in the skull's lining break from the increased pressure. Blood and spinal fluid cultures will determine which bacterium is responsible for the current infection. Powerful antibiotics that would be effective against any of the possible organisms are used until a specific organism is identified. Support is initiated to provide optimal care for any other symptoms encountered by an infected infant or child. This may include medication to control temperature, intravenous fluids to provide nutrition, replacement of fluids lost through vomiting, and other supportive measures to assure adequate respiratory function and to maintain a normal heart rate and blood pressure.

Survivors of acute bacterial meningitis may have long-term effects generally associated with the central nervous system. Seizures are common and may be resistant to normal anticonvulsant therapy. The intractable nature of the seizures may be the result of specific focal

> A spinal tap is a procedure in which a needle is inserted into the spine to withdraw cerebral spinal fluid that can then be analyzed.

Figure 7.8/ *Brain Showing Infected and Swollen Meninges*

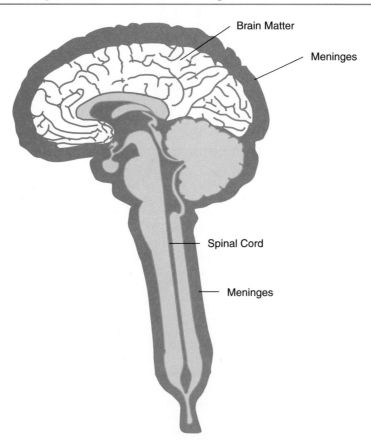

areas of the brain that have been attacked by the disease. Bilateral deafness may occur as a result of pressure placed on the auditory nerve by inflammation of the meninges. Deafness may also be caused by antibiotic therapy needed to eradicate the bacteria. Hydrocephalus frequently occurs because of scar tissue formation in the subarachnoid space that permanently affects the normal fluid pathways for cerebral spinal fluid. Occasionally, brain abscesses may develop that produce symptoms much like those of a brain tumor.

Children with disabilities from meningitis will require extensive services. In addition to the described effects of the infection, many of these children suffer from hyperactivity (along with their seizures), motor involvement (particularly cerebral palsy), and mental retardation. Environmental safety measures are necessary to protect these children from injury during seizures and during periods of erratic behavior. Programs to deal with hearing impairments and visual problems may be part of the general plan when determining services needed for the physical and developmental needs of the infant or child with residual effects from meningitis.

Encephalitis Encephalitis is generally an inflammation of the brain and spinal cord (see Figure 7.9), which may occur as a result of viral or bacterial infection spread by the circulatory system or from movement of infection up neural **axons** to the brain. The infecting agent disperses throughout the brain and to the meninges causing inflammation. A majority of cases of encephalitis are associated with the childhood viral diseases mentioned earlier in this chapter.

Figure 7.9/ *Brain Affected by Encephalitis*

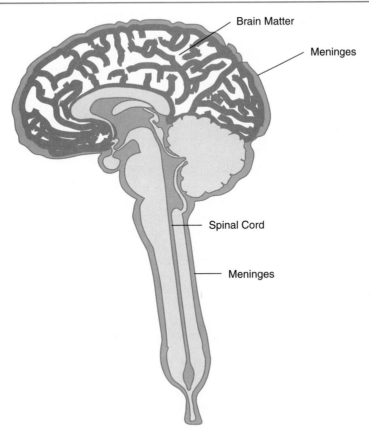

Brain Matter

Meninges

Spinal Cord

Meninges

Most cases of encephalitis in the United States occur during the summer since the major transmitting source is the mosquito (Whaley & Wong, 1989). Some kinds of viruses that eventually lead to encephalitis selectively attack specific types of neurons (as in polio), while others, such as the herpes virus, establish focal areas of infection dispersed throughout the brain. The manner in which dispersion occurs determines the outcome of the nervous system function following an infection.

Encephalitis can be diagnosed when an individual has symptoms of early onset meningitis, but a spinal tap cannot confirm the presence of bacteria. In other words, ruling out meningitis is one part of the diagnosis of encephalitis because symptoms of the two diseases appear to be so similar. Additional diagnostic findings may be a normal white blood cell count and an elevated protein level in the spinal fluid. In this disease, early symptoms include an unsteady gait and seizures,with the later onset of a decreased level of consciousness. Medical measures are initiated to prevent further deterioration of the physical condition. Viral cultures will identify agents responsible for acute encephalitis, or occasionally a brain biopsy itself may be necessary to identify the virus producing the illness. Most cases of viral encephalitis will recover without significant long-term effects. This is not the case with herpes encephalitis, and all virally induced encephalitis can potentially lead to permanent and significant damage. Furthermore, infants born to virally-infected mothers who have experienced in utero viral encephalitis and subsequent interruption in brain growth will be born with severe neurological damage.

Effects of encephalitis on central nervous system function may include severe language disorders or muscle weakness or paralysis on one side of the body. Frequently, focal seizures occur, and EEG findings are sometimes abnormal, indicating the presence of a seizure disorder. Infants and children may experience impairments in vision and hearing, especially with herpes encephalitis. Reactivation of the virus, after the initial recovery from the illness, may further damage the nervous system. Affected children also have an increased incidence of behavior problems and hyperactivity, requiring environmental precautions to assure their safety. Depending upon the severity of the infection, children may experience mental retardation with all the adverse affects of developmental delay.

POSSIBILITIES FOR THE TWENTY-FIRST CENTURY

Implications for Hearing Impairment Technological advances continue to increase the degree of independence and integration of persons with significant hearing losses within society. For example, cochlear implants are electronic devices that can be implanted by surgery to transform sound vibrations into nerve impulses for transmission to the brain. Such transmission stimulates nerve cells for children with bilateral sensorineural hearing loss. The devices do not restore normal hearing, but when used with speech reading, allow a greater understanding of speech. To date, however, cochlear implants have received mixed reviews.

Other innovations, such as computer assisted instruction, have been targeted at increasing language and communication skills for children with deafness but have yet to fulfill their promise. For example, Allen (1986) noted that on the average, students with deafness read at the fourth grade level upon graduation. Though research is still exploratory, preliminary findings suggest that interactive videodisk (IVD) programs may be an efficient means of teaching children with and without hearing impairments such skills as signing and language patterns (Stewart, Gentry, & McLeod, 1991). Interactive videodisk programs have the advantage of permitting children to control a wide range of visual instructional stimuli, to respond to instructional cues, and to immediately receive interactive feedback. Stewart et al. (1991) noted that presently IVD technology may not be practical since, in terms of development and production, it is quite expensive. Moreover, videodisks, once pressed, cannot be edited or revised, unlike computer programs.

People with deafness differ from people with other disabilities in that they have developed their own social communities of peers and deaf culture. Segregation of this culture, largely self-selected, has led to controversy that directly affects parents of very young children with deafness. Even among those who are deaf, persons who acquire deafness adventitiously may be excluded (Darrow, 1993). In fact, Janesick (1990) argued for recognition of the Deaf community (big "D" for congenital deafness) as a distinct cultural and linguistic minority. Contending that inclusion in this community is something to be proud of, proponents of the movement shun attempts to bridge the communication gap.

Educators, researchers, and policy makers in the next decades, in recognition of past paternalism in treatment of persons with hearing impairments (Dubow, 1989), must find a way of giving parents and children options that will enable them to select for themselves either an inclusive or exclusive lifestyle. Advocates of both will continue to challenge the premise of inclusion for this group of children.

Implications for Visual Impairment   Incidence trends, coupled with the finding that between 50% and 75% of children with blindness (Sykanda & Levitt, 1982) also have other disabilities, has significant implications for policy and practice in the next century. Kirchner (1988) indicated that service systems are already overstretched and that if these trends continue, educational systems will be severely taxed.

As children reach preschool and school age, parents will be faced with placement decisions. In the past, most children with blindness were sent to residential schools for the blind. However, with recent inclusion practices, it seems likely that most children with blindness will be served in regular classroom settings, even if these children also have other disabilities. Parents need to be aware of placement options, the implications of these options, and strategies to advocate for the choices made for children with visual impairments. Beginning early with low vision tools (e.g., Braille, large print text, electronic systems, etc.), social skills training, and mobility and orientation training can increase the degree of independence and social competence experienced in these settings by children with visual impairments.

Rapid advancements in electronic/computerized capacities will likely continue to open new doors to academic, domestic, and vocational opportunities for persons with visual impairments. Very young children with visual impairments should be introduced to computer systems. Likewise, team members will be pressed to keep pace with developments in technology that might increase independent functioning while being practical and cost effective for families.

While there has been a realization that advances in medical technology may not always be worth the cost, it is likely that procedures for treating many once untreatable causes of visual impairment will continue to evolve. Like other forms of early intervention, the cost of remediating loss of vision may be far less than the costs of long-term specialized intervention for children and families. While these types of decisions may be taken out of the hands of families and professionals, it is important that institutional decision makers of the twenty-first century are not so shortsighted that the philosophy of empowerment is forgotten.

Implications for Infectious Diseases   All of the infections described in this chapter may have effects ranging from mild to devastating. The most effective way of decreasing the incidence of infections and their effects on children is through education. Many, though not all, infections can be prevented through a more cautious approach to living within our environment and within our society. Both a recognition of cause and an understanding of the nature of the action of bacteria and viruses can make a difference in the approach to prevention and treatment.

1. Into what three components is the auditory mechanism functionally separated? Describe the three practical functions of these components.

2. Along what two dimensions is sound heard?

3. What is the difference between a conductive hearing loss and a sensorineural hearing loss? What are common causes of a conductive hearing loss? Of a sensorineural hearing loss?

4. List the symptoms of otitis media and describe treatment for the infection.

5. What criteria should be used in identifying infants at high risk for hearing impairments according to NIH?

6. What developmental domains are most affected by loss of hearing?

7. Name some sign language systems. Which is the most commonly used approach? Explain the debate in favor of and opposed to manual sign.

8. What are some disadvantages to using hearing aids?

9. List some considerations that should be made when serving preschool children with hearing impairments.

10. Discriminate between blindness and low vision.

11. Describe the visual process.

12. Describe three refractive errors in vision.

13. Name and explain two visual errors caused by a disruption in muscle coordination of the eyes.

14. What are cortical visual impairments?

15. What are common causes of visual impairments?

16. Define and give a brief description of each: glaucoma and cataracts.

17. What recommendations should be given to caregivers in working with children with visual impairments?

18. What is the difference between congenital and adventitious blindness?

19. What might be included in programs specifically designed for infants and toddlers with visual impairments? What factors should be considered in selection of appropriate orientation and mobility adaptations?

20. Define biological agents. How do these agents cause damage to human cells? How do they travel throughout the human body?

21. When do pathogenic bacterial infections occur? What circumstances may affect an infant's outcome?

22. Explain the relationship between socioeconomic status, low birth weight, and infection.

23. Why is appropriate assessment of the physiological status of an infant at delivery important? What are the keys to effective treatment of an infected infant?

24. List the initial symptoms of an infection. What interventions are warranted for infants experiencing infections at, or shortly after, birth to provide opportunity for full development?

25. What are some of the adverse pregnancy outcomes that have an increased incidence in presence of the chlamydia infection? Explain the increased evidence in mortality found with neonatal chlamydial infections.

26. What are viruses and how do they differ from bacteria? How has prevention of viral diseases been accomplished?

27. What are the TORCH diseases? Briefly describe the cause, course, symptoms, and outcomes of each.

28. Explain what is meant by "shedding" of a live virus. How does shedding occur?

29. List characteristics of women who may be at high risk for contracting hepatitis B virus. What individuals should most strongly consider immunization against this virus?

30. How do social and economic factors contribute to placing children with HIV at high risk for disease progression?

31. Explain the differential causes, courses, and outcomes of meningitis and encephalitis. What is the difference between viral meningitis and bacterial meningitis?

REFERENCES

AIDS Surveillance Unit: New York City Department of Health. (1990, March 30). *New York City AIDS Surveillance Report,* 10.

Allen, K. E., & Marotz, L. (1989). *Developmental profiles: Birth-to-six.* Albany, NY: Delmar.

Allen, T. (1986). Patterns of academic achievement among hearing impaired students: 1974 and 1983. In A. Schildroth & M. Karchmer (Eds.), *Deaf children in America* (pp. 161–206).

Bateman, J. B. (1983). Genetics in pediatric ophthamology. *Pediatric Clinics of North America, 30*(6), 1015–1031.

Batshaw, M. L., & Perret, Y. M. (1988). *Children with handicaps: A medical primer.* Baltimore: Paul H. Brookes.

Boehme, T. (1985). Hepatitis B: The nurse-midwife's role in management and prevention. *Journal of Nurse-Midwifery, 30*(2), 79–87.

Bolognese, R., Aldinger, R., & Roberts, N. (1981). Prenatal care in the prevention of infection. *Clinics in Perinatology, 8* (3), 605–615.

Bromberg, M., & Hsia, L. (1988). Rubella in the perinatal period. *The Journal of Perinatal and Neonatal Nursing, 1*(4), 24–32.

Brunham, R., Holmes, K., & Eschenback, D. (1984). Sexually transmitted diseases in pregnancy. In K. Holmes, J. Sparling, & J. Weisner (Eds.), *Sexually transmitted diseases,* New York: McGraw-Hill.

Caldwell, M., Fleming, P., & Oxtoby, M. (1990). National surveillance for pediatric AIDS in the United States (abstract Th. C700). In *Programs and Abstracts of the Sixth International conference on AIDS, Vol. I,* San Francisco, 300.

Centers for Disease Control. (1985). Summary of notifiable diseases, United States. *Morbidity and Mortality Weekly Report, 34*(54), 17.

Centers for Disease Control. (1988). Prevention of perinatal transmission of hepatitis B virus: Prenatal screening of all pregnant women for hepatitis B surface antigen, recommendations of the Immunization Practices Advisory Committee. *Morbidity and Mortality Weekly Report, 37*(2), 341–351.

Centers for Disease Control. (1989 a). *Hepatitis Surveillance Report No. 52, Atlanta 1989.* United States Department of Health and Human Services.

Centers for Disease Control. (1989 b). 1989 STD treatment guidelines. *Morbidity and Mortality Weekly Report, 38* (S-8), 27.

Clarke, K. L. (1988). Barriers or enablers: Mobility devices for visually impaired and multiply handicapped infants and preschoolers. *Education of the Visually Handicapped, 20,* 115–133.

Cohen, I., Veille, J., & Calkins, B. (1990). Improved pregnancy outcome following successful treatment of chlamydial infections. *Journal of the American Medical Association, 263*(23), 3160–3163.

Cole, F., & Cloherty, J. (1985). Infection: Prevention and treatment. In J. Cloherty, & A. Stark (Eds.), *Manual of Neonatal Care.* Boston: Little Brown.

Committee on Fetus and the Newborn. (1980). Perinatal herpes simplex infection. *Pediatrics, 66*(1), 147–149.

Darrow, A. (1993). The role of music in Deaf culture: Implications for music teachers. *JRME, 41*(2), 93–110.

Diienstaf, J., Wands, J., & Koff, R. (1986). Acute viral hepatitis. In Isselbacher, K. (Ed.), *Harrison's Principles of Internal Medicine,* (11th ed.). New York: McGraw-Hill.

Dubow, S. (1989). "Into the turbulent mainstream"—A legal perspective on the weight to be given to the Least Restrictive Environment placement decisions for deaf children. *Journal of Law and Education, 44,* 215–228.

Edwards M. (1988). Hepatitis B serology: Help in interpretation. *Pediatric Clinics of North America, 35*(3), 503–515.

Fiumara, N., Fleming, W., & Downing, J. (1952). The incidence of prenatal syphilis at the Boston City Hospital. *New England Journal of Medicine, 247,* 48–55.

Florman, A., Gershon, A., Blackett, P., & Nahmias, A. (1973). Intrauterine infection with herpes simplex virus: Resultant congenital malformations. *Journal of the American Medical Association, 225* (2), 129–136.

Frank, J., Orenstein, W., & Bart, K. (1985). Major impediments to measles elimination: The modern epidemiology of an ancient disease. *American Journal of Diseases of Childhood, 139,* 881–888.

Freiji, B., & Sever, J. (1988). Herpes virus infections in pregnancy: Risks to embryo, fetus, and neonate. *Clinics in Perinatology, 15*(2), 203–231.

Gagnon, A. (1968). Transplacental inoculation of fatal herpes simplex in the newborn. *Obstetrics and Gynecology, 31,* 682–687.

Gast, M. (1983). Herpes update 1983. *Missouri Perinatal Progress, 5*(4), 1–4.

Gazala, E., Karplus, M., & Liberman, J. (1985). The effect of maternal measles on the fetus. *Pediatric Infectious Diseases, 4,* 203–204.

Gershon, A. (1985). Live attenuated varicella vaccine. *Journal of Infectious Disease, 152,* 859–863.

Goldstein, H. (1980). The reported demography and causes of blindness throughout the world. *Advances in Ophthalmology, 40,* 1–99.

Grossman, J. (1980). Perinatal viral infections. *Clinics in Perinatology, 7* (1), 257–271.

Gunderson, C. (1982). *Clinical Neurology.* Philadelphia: J. B. Lippincott.

Harel, S., Holtzman, M., & Feinsod, M. (1985). The late visual bloomer. In S. Harel & N. Anastasiow (Eds.), *The at-risk infant: Psychosocial medical aspects* (pp. 359–362). Baltimore: Paul H. Brookes.

Harrington, M., & Meyers, H. W. (1992). Preschool programs for the hearing impaired: Young children with hearing disabilities deserve special attention. *Principal, 34–36.*

Harter, C., & Benirschke, K. (1976). Fetal syphilis in the first trimester. *American Journal of Obstetrics and Gynecology, 124,* 368–372.

Hass, M. (1935). Hepto-adrenal necrosis with intranuclear inclusion bodies: Report of a case. *American Journal of Pathology, 11,* 127–128.

Herrmann, K. (1982). Congenital and perinatal varicella. *Clinical Obstetrics and Gynecology, 25*(3), 605–609.

Hicks, R., Fowler, K., Richardson, M., Dahle, A., Adams, L., & Pass, R. (1993). Congenital cytomegalovirus infection and neonatal auditory screening. *The Journal of Pediatrics, 123*(5), 779–782.

Hira, S., Bhat, G., & Patel, J. (1985). Early congenital syphilis: Clinicoradiologic features in 202 patients. *Sexually Transmitted Diseases, 12,* 177–185.

HIV Serosurvey Unit Office of AIDS and HIV Surveillance New York City. (1990). *Department of Health Quarterly Report, 1,* 2–3.

Hoon, A. H. (1991). Visual impairments in children with developmental disabilities. In A. J. Capute & P. J. Accardo (Eds.), *Developmental disabilities in infancy and early childhood* (pp. 395–411). Baltimore: Paul H. Brookes.

Horstmann, D. (1982). Rubella. *Clinical Obstetrics and Gynecology, 25*(3), 585–597.

Janesick, V. J. (1990). Bilingual multicultural education and the deaf: Issues and possibilities. *Journal of Educational Issues of Language Minority Students, 7,* 99–109.

Jenkins, R. (1965). Severe chickenpox encephalopathy. *American Journal of Diseases of Childhood, 110,* 137–145.

Kirchner, C. (1988). National estimates of prevalence and demographics of children with visual impairments. In M. D. Wang, M. D. Reynolds, & H. J. Walberg (Eds.), *Handbook of special education: Research and practice* (Vol. 3, pp. 135–153). Elmsford, NY: Pergamon.

Klein, M. (1988). Hepatitis B virus: Perinatal management. *Perinatal/Neonatal Nursing, 1*(4), 12–23.

Kohl, S. (1988). Herpes simplex virus encephalitis in children. *Pediatric Clinics of North America, 35*(3), 465–483.

Kohl, S., & James, A. (1985). Herpes simplex virus encephalitis during childhood. Importance of brain biopsy diagnosis. *Journal of Pediatrics, 107*(2), 212–215.

Korones, S. (1988). Uncommon virus infections of the mother, fetus and newborn: Influenza, mumps and measles. *Clinics of Perinatology, 15*(2), 259–272.

Leclair, J. (1980). Control of nosocomial neonatal viral infections. *Critical Care Quarterly, 3*(3), 71–77.

MacMillan, J., Weiner, L., & Lamberson, H. (1985). Efficacy of maternal screening and therapy in the prevention of chlamydia infection of the newborn. *Infection, 13,* 263–270.

Morse, M. (1991). Visual gaze behaviors: Considerations in working with visually impaired and multiply handicapped children. *RE:view, 23*(1), 5–15.

Naeye, R., & Blanec W. (1970). Relation of poverty and race to antenatal infection. *New England Journal of Medicine, 283*(11), 555–560.

National Institute of Health Consensus Statement. (March, 1993). *Early identification of hearing impairment in infants and young children.* Volume 11(1), 1–25. Bethesda, MD: NIH.

Northern, J., & Downs, M. (1984). *Hearing in children* (3rd ed.). Baltimore: Williams & Wilkins.

Oleske, J., Minnefor, A., & Cooper, R. (1983). Immune deficiency syndrome in children. *Journal American Medical Association, 249,* 2345–2349.

Pass, R. (1985). Epidemiology and transmission of cytomegalovirus. *Journal of Infectious Diseases, 152,* 243–258.

Pass, R., Hutto, C., & Ricks, R. (1986). Increased rate of cytomegalovirus infection among parents of children attending day-care centers. *New England Journal of Medicine, 314*(22), 1414–1418.

Pitt, J. (1991). Perinatal human immunodeficiency virus infection. *Clinics in Perinatology, 18*(2), 227–239.

Preece, P., Blount, J., Glover, J., Fletcher, G., Peckham, C., & Griffiths, P. (1983). The consequences of primary cytomegalovirus infection in pregnancy. *Archives of Disease in Childhood, 58,* 970–975.

Pring, L. (1984). A comparison of the word recognition processes in blind and sighted children. *Child Development, 55,* 1865–1877.

Pusey, W. (1933). *The History of Syphilis.* Springfield, IL: Charles C. Thomas Publishers.

Rettig, P. (1988). Perinatal infections with Chlamydia Trachomatis. *Clinics in Perinatology, 15*(2), 321–350.

Seigel, D., & Washington, A. (1987). Syphilis: Updated approach to an old disease. *Postgraduate Medicine, 8*(1), 83–90.

Shapiro, M. B., & France, T. D. (1985). The ocular features of Down's syndrome. *American Journal of Ophthalmology, 99,* 659–663.

Sheahan, S., & Seabolt, J. (1989). Chlamydia trachomatis infections: A health problem of infants. *Journal of Pediatric Health Care, 3*(3), 144–149.

Sheridan, M. (1969). Vision screening procedures for very young or handicapped children. In P. Gardiner, R. MacKeith, & V. Smith (Eds.), *Aspects of developmental and pediatric ophthamology (Clinics in Developmental Medicine No. 32, pp. 39–47).* London: Spastics International Medicine Publication.

Sieber, O., Fulginiti, V., Brazie, J., & Umlauf, H. (1966). In utero infection of the fetus by herpes simplex virus. *Journal of Pediatrics, 69,* 30–40.

Siegel, M. (1973). Congenital malformations following chickenpox, measles, mumps and hepatitis: Results of a cohort study. *Journal of the American Medical Association, 226*(13), 1521–1524.

Siegel, M., & Fuerst, H. (1966). Low birth weight and maternal virus diseases. A prospective study of rubella, measles, mumps, chickenpox, and hepatitis. *Journal of the American Medical Association, 197,* 88–92.

Siegel, M., Fuerst, H., & Peress, N. (1966). Comparative fetal mortality in maternal virus diseases. A prospective study on rubella, measles, mumps, chickenpox, and hepatitis. *New England Journal of Medicine, 274,* 768–775.

Simonds, R. J., & Rogers, M. F. (1992). Epidemiology of HIV in children and other populations. In A. C. Crocker, H. J. Cohen, & T. A. Kastner (Eds.), *HIV infection and developmental disabilities: A resource for service providers* (pp. 3–4). Baltimore: Paul H. Brookes.

Stagno, S., & Whitley, R. (1985). Herpes virus infections of pregnancy. Part I. Cytomegalovirus and Epstein-Barr virus infections. *New England Journal of Medicine, 313,* 1270.

Stewart, D. A., Gentry, C. G., & McLeod, R. (1991). Using instructional design principles to produce an IVD to enhance the linguistic environment of deaf children. *Journal of Special Education Technology, 11*(3), 121–135.

Summers, P., Biswas, M., & Pastorek, J. (1987). The pregnant hepatitis B carrier: Evidence favoring comprehensive antepartum screening. *Obstetrics and Gynecology, 69,* 701–704.

Sykanda, A. M., & Levitt, S. (1982). The physiotherapist in the developmental management of the visually impaired child. *Child: Care, Health and Development, 8,* 261–270.

Teplin, S. W. (1983). Development of blind infants and children with retrolental fibroplasia: Implications for physicians. *Pediatrics, 71,* 6–12.

Uslan, M. (1983). Provision of orientation and mobility services in 1990. *Journal of Visual Impairment and Blindness, 77,* 213–215.

Varner, M., & Galask, R. (1981). Perinatal infections. *Perinatology/Neonatology, 5*(1), 37–43.

Ward, M. (1983). Chlamydial classification, development and structure. *British Medical Bulletin, 39,* 109–124.

Warren, J. (1992). Mycobacterial infections. In S.T. Shulman, J.P. Phair, & H.M. Sommers (Eds.), *The biologic and clinical basis of infectious diseases,* 4th ed., pp. 190–207.

Weiss, S., Newcomb, R., & Beem, M. (1986). Pulmonary assessment of children after chlamydial pneumonia in infancy. *Journal of Pediatrics, 108*(5), 659–664.

Wendel, G. (1988). Gestational and congenital syphilis. *Clinics in Perinatology, 15*(2), 287–303.

Whaley, L. F., & Wong, D. L. (1989). *Essentials of pediatric nursing* (3rd ed.). St. Louis: C. V. Mosby.

Whitley, R., Soong, S., & Linneman, C. (1982). Herpes simplex encephalitis-clinical assessment. *Journal of the American Medical Association, 247*(3), 317–320.

Whitley, R., Yeager, A., & Kartus, P. (1983). Neonatal herpes simplex virus infection: Follow-up evaluation of vidarabine therapy. *Pediatrics, 72*(6), 778–785.

Witzleken, C., & Driscoll, S. (1965). Possible transplacental transmission of herpes simplex infection. *Pediatrics, 36,* 192–194.

Young, N., & Gershon, A. (1983). Chickenpox, measles and mumps. In J. Remington & J. Klein (Eds.), *Infectious diseases of the fetus and newborn infant* (2nd ed.). Philadelphia: W. B. Saunders Co., 375.

PART TWO

Once a child has been identified as eligible for early childhood services, life continues, but with considerable complexity. Early childhood professionals should be familiar with the issues and concerns that surround a young child with special needs and that child's family. They must also be prepared to identify support services and options for these families and to understand the evolution of these services and future possibilities. Part Two of this text reviews the history of early childhood services, current legal and applied practices in serving children and their families, and the rights of families.

Historical Interlude

AN HISTORICAL PERSPECTIVE

History is perhaps most accurately described as a series of problems and attempts to resolve these issues. Sometimes solutions result in positive outcomes, but often, solutions also have unintended effects or create new problems. Historical problems usually develop in situations in which people cannot get or keep the things they *need*, particularly for survival. As survival needs are met, problems occur when people cannot get what they *want*, in terms of wealth or personal rights.

Early in the development of a culture, people are most involved in seeking basic needs such as food, shelter, and clothing. As a culture prospers and basic needs are met by a large portion of the population, people work to acquire things they want but don't need, such as wealth. At this point, most societal problems involve economics: people work to accumulate enough wealth to insure access to goods and luxuries, such as art, music, and recreation. Throughout history, wealth has seldom been shared equally by all people, though some societies have been more successful than others at achieving equitable prosperity. Usually, people who have had more wealth have also held more power or rights. Inevitably, economic conflicts and issues of people's rights are interrelated.

When the basic needs of most people have been met and members of that culture are afforded the luxury of concentrating on issues beyond mere survival, a people's sense of rights and values become more prominent. When the rights of children are considered, both economics and cultural values have had a great impact on the regard for young people. The kind of care and services provided to children has always depended on whether or not they were considered assets or deficits in an economic, political, or moral sense. However, even when children's rights, in general, have been protected, children with disabilities have often been treated as a different class and thus treated unequally.

This chapter explores the history of Western culture in terms of its beliefs about the rights of young children and their families. Though it would be preferable to be global in this analysis, it is undeniable that Western civilization has directly influenced the evolution and predominant practice of educational services provided in almost all parts of the world today (Woodill, 1992). This chapter examines how various cultures' perspectives on the rights of children have changed over time, and how cultures have attempted to solve both the economic and civil rights problems these issues present. In addition to looking at the evolution of early childhood services in the United States, this chapter also includes a survey of diverse modern world cultures and the manner in which the very young are served.

THE HISTORY OF CHILDHOOD IN WESTERN CIVILIZATION

This text is sensitive to the ethnocentricity of describing the history of early childhood education from the viewpoint of Western culture. However, study of this discipline reveals that, to know the history of European education (and in particular that of very young children) is to understand educational practices worldwide (Woodill, Bernhard, & Prochner, 1992). Western-style early education has become globally pervasive.

Lloyd deMause (1974) described the history of childhood as a series of stages in which the concept of childhood in Western civilization evolved over the last 2000 years (see Table 8.1). Each stage was marked by great changes in society—changes in the way people were governed, changes in religious beliefs and customs, and changes in the way wealth was distributed (Day, 1983). In general, children in ancient times were treated with indifference, and there was no apparent conception of childhood as a distinct human experience. Perhaps parents could not afford to become attached to children, since their probability of survival was so tenuous. Not until the period from the fourteenth to the seventeenth century did there emerge some notion that childhood was a special time. Even then, economic struggle and survival were so prominent that children were treated with ambivalence and emotional distance.

It was not until the eighteenth century, when religious belief systems developed so strongly, that parents were expected to be responsible for the souls of their children and thus formal education for children grew more important. During the nineteenth century and through the early part of the twentieth century, the concept of childhood evolved to a point that parents were seen as responsible for training their children to be independent and to follow the rules and values of society.

DeMause (1974) regarded current culture as one that recognizes the need for child-directed activity, involving parents in working empathetically toward fulfilling their offspring's

Table 8.1/ *A History of Childhood*

Stage	Date	Problem	Solution
From Bad to Worse **Stage 1:** No apparent conception of childhood	To the fourth century A. D.: the infanticide mode The fourth to thirteenth century: the abandonment mode	Survival depends on pleasing the gods, controlling population, and maintaining a physically strong community.	Eliminate extra mouths to feed; ensure that only the strongest are raised from childhood.
Children Will Be Children **Stage 2:** The emergence of the idea of childhood as a special period	The fourteenth to seventeenth century: the ambivalent mode	Rampant disease and hardship kill many young children.	Remain detached from young children; have many but don't form bonds until they survive early childhood.
Church and State Mix **Stage 3:** Parents begin to feel a responsibility for the soul of the child	The eighteenth century: the intrusive mode	Everlasting salvation of the soul is highest priority; heavenly life beyond this earthly toil is the final reward.	Provide an early education so that children can learn of god's redemption.
Parents Know Best **Stage 4:** Parents become responsible for training the child; a recognition of independence	The nineteenth to the mid-twentieth century: the socialization mode	Industrialization requires an increasing labor base; immigrant parents work long hours and neglect their children.	Provide early childhood care and education to promote productive citizenship among children.
Children Know Best **Stage 5:** Children know better than the parents what they need and involve parents in fulfilling those needs	The mid-twentieth century to the present: the helping mode	Resources are abundant enough that all people should have equal opportunity, including children.	Provide early educational services to children who are poor or disabled to improve their potential for productivity.

expanding and particular needs. Children are no longer seen as helpless, but as thinking, emotional, and responsive individuals who should control their own development. Whether this is an accurate assessment of the current age remains to be demonstrated (Day, 1983).

Stage 1: From Bad to Worse

??BC - 1200 AD
ABANDONMENT MODE

From ancient civilization until the fourth century A.D., many cultures of Western civilization were characterized by their struggles to survive. The solution to crises was often ritualistic sacrifice of children to supplicate the gods or abandonment of children to ensure the survival of the strongest or perhaps to control population (Day, 1983). Historical records show that ritualistic sacrifice of children was practiced in Carthage, Phoenicia, and Ammon.

Children were also murdered in great numbers for nonreligious reasons until well into the fourth century. Cultures in Greece and Rome, among others, abandoned babies on hillsides to die, threw them into the sea or rivers to drown, and even entombed them in large pots. This infanticide may have been to avoid economic crises or to exercise population control. For whatever reason, it is clear that children were not treated protectively or held in special regard.

Children who were born infirm, sickly, or premature were almost always destroyed. Political states like Sparta killed all but the most fit children in order to maintain strength in their society. Though infanticide became a punishable crime by the fourth century, the practice lingered in some places until the eighteenth and nineteenth centuries (deMause, 1974). In these traditional patriarchal societies, the role of women was very different from that in today's Western culture. Women who protested or cried at the slaughter of their children were subjected to fines (Greenleaf, 1978). Perhaps if mothers had possessed more control over their own destinies they could have influenced the treatment of their children as well.

In ancient times, a child was considered to be an adult by age seven (Gordon & Browne, 1993). Formal education of children began at about this same age, though Plato and Aristotle both spoke of the need to educate younger children. Greek education, and virtually all classical European schooling that followed this model, was provided for boys of wealthy families, while girls and children of working-class families were trained for domestic work or trades (Gordon & Browne, 1993). A few insightful ancient Romans provided education at home beginning as soon as a child could talk; some even used systems of rewards for their children's educational gains (Hewes & Hartman, 1974).

The fall of the Roman Empire was followed by centuries of lawlessness and anarchy; people left their villages for the protection of a local baron or king, and schooling ceased to exist (Gordon & Browne, 1993). With no educational system to speak of, even members of the ruling class were seldom taught to write their names or to read. Only monastery schools were available, and these were open only to those entering the priesthood. In medieval times (fifth through thirteenth centuries), childhood was viewed as a period beginning with birth and lasting just beyond infancy. Adults assumed that, in their natural state, children were basically evil and needed to be directed, punished, and corrected in order to learn to follow social rules. Youth were expected to take up the responsibilities of adulthood as quickly as possible, learning the necessary skills of a trade mostly through their parents or through apprenticeship. Survival was the primary goal.

Stage 2: Children Will Be Children

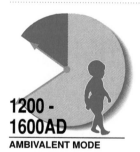

1200 - 1600AD

AMBIVALENT MODE

Well into the seventeenth century, children were commonly beaten, sexually abused, sold into slavery, and abandoned. Even children who were valued by their families were commonly sent away from home to be raised by wet nurses or other families. It was clear that parents were generally ambivalent toward their children.

It could be that the lack of attachment was a psychological survival technique. That is, the rate of infant mortality was so high that more young children were lost to illness or injury than survived childhood. Consequently, it was common practice to have many children in order to ensure that a few children would live. For many years, there were no pictures made of young children nor were formal names given until children had passed the toddler stage.

It is surprising that the recognition of childhood began as early as it did, considering the high infant death rate that persisted from the fourteenth to the seventeenth century (Day, 1983). However, the Renaissance (late 1300s and early 1400s) and the Reformation (fourteenth through sixteenth centuries) brought gradual enlightenment (Gordon & Browne, 1993). Charlemagne of France proclaimed that the nobility should know their letters, a few of the monastery schools maintained libraries, and the craft guilds and apprentice system expanded, all planting seeds of learning that kept education alive if not strong (Gordon & Browne, 1993).

This shift to a more compassionate approach to childhood began in French cities among more affluent families. The gentry of France seemed to find enjoyment in children, who were accepted for the amusement they brought their parents. Philosophers began to theorize about the effect that adult care and nurturance could have on the well-being of children. At the same time, Christian beliefs were spreading, and people began to think about the immortality of a child's soul.

In 1658, Comenius, a Czech educator, wrote *Orbis Pictus* (The World of Pictures), the first picture book for children (Gordon & Browne, 1993). The book was a guide for teachers and emphasized sensory awareness and the study of nature. Comenius believed that education should follow the natural order of things and referred to the "school of the mother's lap." His ideas were later reflected in Montessori's and Piaget's theories of the stages of development.

As an English philosopher of the 1600s, John Locke theorized that children are born neutral, rather than evil, and possess a moral and behavioral "clean slate," or *tabula rasa,* to be written upon by parents, society, education, and the world (Gordon & Browne, 1993). He was one of the first Europeans to promote the idea of individual differences and the need to take the individual learner into account when planning instruction and evaluating progress. Locke recommended that instruction be conducted pleasantly in the areas of business and the Bible. Though Locke's influence was minimal during his life, his ideas were later popularized by Rousseau (Gordon & Browne, 1993).

In 1647, the Massachusetts Bay Colony enacted a law by which all communities of 50 households had to hire a teacher and open a school. If a community had more than 100 families, a Latin grammar school was required. There was no political or moral separation of Christian churches and Christian schools at this time. Indeed, the principle purpose of education was to teach children to read in order to understand the Bible and to study Christian doctrine.

Early life in New England was difficult and, though conditions had improved over the medieval period, as many as 60% to 70% of children under age four died in colonial towns during the "starving season" (Gordon & Browne, 1993). Puritan families showed little overt affection and children were seen as important economic tools, working the land and apprenticed into trades early (Gordon & Browne, 1993). Discipline was harsh and children were expected to obey without question.

By the beginning of the 1700s, most towns provided schooling. However, formal education was still considered unnecessary for children under the age of six or seven years. It was the general belief that young children should stay in the care of their mothers until middle childhood.

Stage 3: Church and State Mix

1600 - 1700AD

INTRUSIVE MODE

By the mid-1700s there was a realization that childhood was developmentally connected to adulthood (Day, 1983). This encouraged consideration of child rearing practices, and society began to place value on disciplined activity and tasks that would foster an appropriate spirit, a fear of God, and a respect for elders. Puritan beliefs supported the idea that children possessed souls that could be saved through devotion to God. Hence, it was expected that parents ensure the education of their children so the latter could begin their studies of Christian doctrine early in life. Consistent with the exacting harshness of Puritan practices, moral and spiritual goodness were often inspired with the birch whip; children were thrashed to drive out evil spirits and to ensure their well-being (Day, 1983; deMause, 1974).

Providing an altogether different view of education, the French scholar Rousseau became an outspoken champion for children. Rousseau departed from the view that children were simply miniature adults (Williams, 1992). In his book *Emile,* in which he raised a hypothetical child to adulthood, Rousseau argued that children should be treated with gentle care early in life and that play and childhood experiences contributed to learning (Day, 1983; Gordon & Browne, 1993; Rousseau, 1969). Rousseau dismissed the idea that children were inherently evil, concluding, on the contrary, that they were naturally good (Gordon & Browne, 1993). The importance of beginning a child's education at birth and treating children with sympathy and compassion was stressed, providing the philosophical basis for early childhood education (Cook, Tessier, & Klein, 1992). He stood against harsh, physical punishment of children and also against education that stressed memorization and recitation. Like others, how-

Living Naturally

Interview with David DeWolf

It's an important thing for our teachers to recognize the need for disabled children to have natural lives and not to be pushed too hard too early. From my perspective, one of the mistakes that you can make is to try so hard to overcome the disability that you push too hard. A parent or a professional can become a little bit like the doctor whose job it is to fight sickness. The doctor views the disease as an enemy and, as sort of a matter of pride, decides he is not going to let this thing take his patient. The doctor uses all his ingenuity and energy to figure out ways to beat the disease.

In dealing with children with disabilities, it is healthy and appropriate to try to ameliorate the effects. Perhaps if the child has a hearing impairment, one thinks, "How can I provide a hearing aid?" or "What new technology or breakthroughs in terms of electronics or whatever can I offer that will compensate and allow the child as normal an experience as possible?"

I think, particularly for kids with a learning disability or a cognitive disability like Down syndrome, there is an impulse to accelerate the educational process, as though you saw a hill coming up ahead of you, and you jammed on the accelerator to get up enough momentum, so when you get to the hill, your momentum will kind of carry you over the top before you've lost your steam. I think some of that is a good idea, but if you're not careful, you can make the child's academic accomplishments overshadow the right to be a child.

Children with disabilities ought to be able to kind of go at their own speed, at their own rate, in what feels good to them in the same way that children without disabilities are allowed to develop whatever talents and abilities they have. That's a difficult balance to strike. I think it's the same balance you have to strike with a normal child. Do I teach my kid to play the violin at the age of four? Suppose I have a tradition in my family of violin players, can I pass that along to my children at the age of four by encouraging them and keeping at them to do this because of the great benefit that I see at the end of the process? They may resent it

now, but they'll thank me for it later when they can see the fruits of all this effort. On the other hand, I can sit back and say, if he wants to, that's great, but I'm not going to push it on him. I think many of the same dynamics are present with a kid who has a disability.

The most important thing is to be sure that what you're doing is really for the child's benefit, rather than for your own psychological benefit. I think that parents who have kids with disabilities are subject to the same kind of competitive streak as everybody else. Some parents want their kid to make the varsity team because it will help them get ahead. We're similarly tempted to think, well, maybe most kids with this condition can only sit there and babble, but by golly, my kid is going to be able to recite the alphabet. That's not all bad, the ambitions that you have for your children to help them achieve, that's part of the reasons that kids do achieve.

But, I think you have to take stock of it periodically to say, is this really for my ego gratification, or is this really because I think my child will genuinely be better for this? Also, it is very important to avoid a denial process. Just like the doctor who appropriately enough is engaged in the fight against disease and death, you can kid yourself into thinking that if you just work hard enough and do enough research in the lab you can beat it.

There is a risk that you get so infatuated with all of the compensatory mechanisms that you think if you just work hard enough and are a devoted enough parent, you can compensate for the disability so that your kid will be just like everybody else. I think that people who work with parents have to be prepared for the parent who won't allow any discussion of the child's limitations, as though it were a kind of sabotage or disloyalty if you ever suggested that something less than normal milestones was acceptable.

In the same way, the doctor occasionally has to say, "I'm sorry, but there's nothing more we can do for your father [child or husband]." There are times, I think, when you have to say, "Your child

is only going to be able to do this and that's just because of the condition that he has." There was a time in which people had unrealistically low expectations of children with Down syndrome. They just wanted to warehouse these kids, or get rid of them. Children with Down syndrome were denied basic opportunities to prove what they could do. So it has become unfashionable to speak discouraging words—to say, "Hey, because your kid has this condition, this is all you should expect."

I think now there is more risk of denial. Both parents and the people who work with children who have disabilities need to accept the fact that their efforts—as worthy as they may be—may be unsuccessful or may prove to be disappointing. They need to understand that you don't have to win this. I think it is particularly important to communicate to the child that whatever they do is acceptable. Just as the parent who wants his kid to play the violin can subconsciously—or not even subconsciously, but overtly—communicate to the kid, "Hey, if you don't do this, if you can't make the varsity team, or accomplish this particular thing which I think is so important, well, you're not really a member of this family, or you're not really worth much, or you must not be trying hard enough." A child with wonderful gifts can be destroyed by the fact that the gifts they have don't measure up to some parent's arbitrary idea of what it is to be a great kid.

Parents who want their kids to be normal have to watch that they don't place such high expectations on their child that the child is taught, in essence, I'm only good to the extent that I outperform my disability expectations. If I'm just a normal handicapped kid, then it's not good enough. I suppose that's a form of equal treatment for parents who push their other kids to be extraordinary. Some parents want their kid with a disability to be extraordinary too. Just as a matter of parenting style, I think that parents have to be gently helped to accept their kids for who they are.

Teachers and other people who work with these kids can help parents see their children

through fresh eyes. Parents of both normal kids and kids with disabilities get stuck with their own perceptions. They don't see their kids the way other people see them, and sometimes it's very important for the teacher to say, "Gee, here's the way this kid looks to me; here's the way I perceive him or her. Maybe you're stuck on something here that doesn't really fit." No parent likes to hear that. Those are tough words to speak to any parent, but I think you can do it if you really care about the child and if you establish some credibility with the parent. You can do it in a subtle and nonjudgmental way, and if you can help the parent get a fresh perspective, that's one of the most important things that I think a teacher can do.

There's nothing wrong with the impulse to "save" a child; it's just that it has to take place within a context of acceptance. Life is limited, and we can't have all we want all the time. A disability is a forced example of learning to accept what you're given, rather than always thinking that life's going to be a series of pleasant experiences.

ever, Rousseau was considered a radical by his contemporaries, and his ideas had little impact on educational practices during his life.

Still, by the late 1700s, several authors extolled humane ways to educate children. For example, Johann Pestalozzi, an Italian-Swiss school teacher, indicated his belief in children's ability to learn through self-discovery (Cook, et al., 1992). He felt that education should be based on the natural development of children, that mothers were the best teachers for very young children, and that the home should be the basic model for teaching and learning. Pestalozzi's ideas were much like Rousseau's, though he was more pragmatic and included principles on how to teach basic skills and the concept of caring for, as well as educating, children (Gordon & Browne, 1993).

Pestalozzi founded the first European school to acknowledge the developmental characteristics of children (Williams, 1992). "Papa" Pestalozzi prescribed parental guidance, strong morality and work ethic, and high intensity work training (Pestalozzi, 1915; Williams, 1992). It was Pestalozzi who coined the phrase, "education should be of the hand, the head, and the heart of the child" (Gordon & Browne, 1993). His humane attitude was a source of present day philosophy in special education where caregivers focus on unique characteristics of children in planning and conducting educational programs.

In 1799, Jean-Marc Itard undertook the first documented efforts to work with a child with special needs (Day, 1983; Itard, 1962). A child, approximately 12 years old, was found living in isolation in the forest near Aveyron, France. Victor, the "Wild Boy of Aveyron," was thought to have been raised by animals, and was described as an "incurable idiot." Itard undertook the task of humanizing the boy, and though he felt he failed, Itard's methods showed that specialized instruction could improve the abilities of children with significant developmental delays.

The first early childhood teachers in America ran "dame schools." These seventeenth- and eighteenth-century "schools" have only recently been researched, as feminist historians have studied the journals and diaries of women who ran the schools (Wyman, 1995). To make ends meet, widowed or young unmarried women held school for very young children in their homes. According to Wyman (1995), dame schools provided a transitional education to students whose mothers had too many children to care for, too many tasks, or too little time. Though no curriculum was available for children of any age, preschoolers at the dame schools were often taught fine motor skills, sewing, knitting, bread making, and rhyming songs. Because the Bible was typically the only reading material available, children learned to read from this text, mostly through rote recitation. It is interesting to note that dame teachers, because they were female, were rarely permitted to go to school themselves after completing their education in a dame school. Therefore, the academic skills taught in dame schools were, by default, rudimentary. By coincidence, however, the resulting practice was quite consistent with current preschool philosophy in which teachers are encouraged to be nurturing and relevant.

Stage 4: Parents Know Best

1800 - 1950AD

SOCIALIZATION MODE

By the nineteenth century, the American and French revolutions had changed the way Western society thought about human rights. It was believed the common person should expect freedom, and concerns were gradually raised about paternalistic treatment of women, children, peasants, and the infirm, who were often treated as property (Day, 1983). Slavery, child labor, and harsh punishment were now considered inhumane. There was movement toward social reform and new voices encouraged parents to raise their children to live self-determined and productive lives.

At the same time, American cities were becoming more industrial and great numbers of immigrants flocked to this country to seek a better life. Rapidly growing cities were heavily populated with foreigners who could barely scratch out an existence and teemed with children whose parents had little time for child rearing activities. Still, parents were assigned the responsibility for guiding their children to good citizenship; children were viewed as the product of parents' competence and attention. Yet, the conviction that the government should intervene in raising the neglected children of immigrants was fueled by an inspired movement to maintain cultural integrity by saving these children (Day, 1983).

Child care centers and public schools developed in response to the needs of working families. By 1828, the Boston Infant School was established as a service to working mothers. The school cared for children from 18 months to 4 years of age. It was open for 13 hours daily in the summer and for 9 hours daily in the winter to accommodate work schedules (Day, 1983).

In 1837, the German educator Froebel created kindergartens (literally translated as "children's garden") and the model quickly spread throughout the world (Day, 1983; Froebel, 1895). Froebel had studied with Pestalozzi, and though he agreed that play should be the medium for children's learning, he altered Pestalozzi's theory to encompass the "self-actualization" of children as a legitimate goal of early childhood (Williams, 1992). Consistent with his desire to build a moral society, Froebel idealistically assumed the potential for perfection in each child. Froebel felt the role of the teacher was to bring a child's inborn capabilities to fruition. He emphasized the use of manipulatives and introduced handiwork projects for children (Williams, 1992).

Froebel started his German kindergarten with children aged 2 to 6 years, focusing on self-directed activities, self-esteem, and self-confidence. Kindergartners were encouraged to play in school, had toys as learning tools, and were educated by trained teachers who joined in the games with playful attitudes (Gordon & Browne, 1993). In his 1826 *Education of Man,* Froebel wrote, "Play is the highest phase of child development—the representation of the inner necessity and impulse." Furthermore, Froebel pushed the radical idea that both men and women should teach young children by being friendly facilitators rather than stern disciplinarians (Gordon & Browne, 1993). Unfortunately, at the time of his death in 1852, Froebel's methods were still being developed, leaving no written guide to explain his ideas (Gordon & Browne, 1993).

Kindergarten in the United States   In 1856, Margaretha Schurz, a German emigrant who had studied under Froebel, opened the first kindergarten in the United States in Watertown, Wisconsin, for German-speaking children (Gordon & Browne, 1993). She frequently traveled to visit other kindergartens or to give inspiring talks about Froebel's system. It was Schurz's inspiration that led Elizabeth Palmer Peabody to open Boston's first English-speaking kindergarten in 1860.

Early kindergartens for children aged three and older were intended to supplement nurturance in the home environment. The goals of these early programs were moral and social growth for children. Women were hired to assist as both teachers and mother-surrogates, even though teaching had traditionally been a male-dominated profession before this time. By now, society had embraced the need for kindergartens, and as with other forms of education, it was affluent families who were the first to take advantage of these services (Cook, et al., 1992). However, because Froebel's underlying philosophy was poorly translated from German to English, most American kindergartens were quite different from what Froebel had intended, and few maintained a spirit of joyous play (Gordon & Browne, 1993).

Social Reform   Following the Civil War, the view that parents were obligated to provide good child rearing was strong enough that parent manuals had been developed to outline a family's responsibilities to its children. There was an increasing emphasis on safe custodial care that could meet children's nutritional, physical, and health needs. Daycare services expanded rapidly with the support of philanthropic women and were clearly seen as an agent for the social reform of poor or neglected children (Day, 1983). The growth of kindergartens from 1880 to 1900 was phenomenal. Free kindergartens were established in Boston in 1877, and St. Louis Superintendent William Harris (influenced by Elizabeth Peabody) established public-school kindergartens district wide before going on to serve as United States Commissioner of Education from 1889–1906. As Commissioner, Harris continued to advocate for public funding of kindergartens.

In the United States, the 1890s were known as the "progressive era," and in some ways served as a turning point for early childhood education. There was a growing national concern for the means by which the poor and immigrants living in cities were forced to exist. Considerable efforts were made to enact child labor laws, establish clean milk distribution centers, and provide for the nurturance of children whose parents needed to work. Kindergartens became an instrument of social reform. These early childhood programs became known as charity kindergartens and included a day-care function (Gordon & Browne, 1993). At the same time, it was generally recognized that some people had greater knowledge and expertise in child development than others.

G. Stanley Hall began the American Child Study Movement, and though he was criticized by his peers, other child advocates and psychologists soon added to the momentum (Day, 1983; Williams, 1992). In 1892, *Children's Rights* was published by Kate Douglas Wiggen; in it she pressed for children's freedom. About the same time, William James, a noted psychologist, argued (like those before him) that children must be active participants in their education process. John Dewey echoed James as an advocate for school reform, insisting that children needed to be actively engaged in order to learn. Dewey emphasized children's direct experience with the natural world and the goal of socializing children as builders of social order and democracy. He believed children should be trained as social beings and participate in role playing and problem-solving that might prepare them to handle societal problems as adults (Gordon & Browne, 1993; Williams, 1992).

By the early 1900s, there was universal acknowledgment that some form of education for three- to five-year-olds was beneficial. Many nursery schools and day-care programs were created, and kindergartens underwent a second evolution. Kindergarten proponents diverged into two groups. Patty Smith Hill, a student and later a colleague of Dewey at Teachers College, Columbia University, was a prominent leader of the Progressive Movement, which emphasized child-oriented rather than regimented kindergarten curricula (Gordon & Browne, 1993). (Patty Smith Hill wrote the song "Happy Birthday" and founded the National Association for Nursery Education, now known as the National Association for the Education of Young Children.) She instituted new ideas to the kindergarten model, such as free play, provided larger blocks, introduced dolls and doll houses, and gave more freedom for creative play. She also introduced the use of workbenches and tools, as well as music and dance.

Of greatest importance, perhaps, was Hill's shift away from Froebel's moralistic "message" and toward more child-directed activity (Day, 1983). By 1925, kindergarten had been transformed. Progressive curricula were more concerned with conformity than morality—a class-related value system was substituted for universal values, and an emphasis was placed on punctuality, cleanliness, responsibility, and sharing.

Patty Smith Hill also promoted nursery schools for children too young for kindergarten and maintained Froebel's belief that young children should learn by doing in a nurturing environment (Gordon & Browne, 1993). Every day, teachers in centers and homes across the country practice the belief that early education should be a garden where adults plant ideas and materials for children to use as they grow at their own pace (Gordon & Browne, 1993). Over 90% of the eligible population in the United States now attends kindergarten. For all practical purposes kindergarten is a universal educational practice in the United States (Warger, 1988).

At the same time that kindergartens were undergoing change, parent-cooperative nursery schools were opened to provide social play for younger children. Usually a morning program was provided for three- to four-year-olds who met three to five days per week. In 1915, a group of wives of faculty at the University of Chicago joined together to establish a nursery school to afford cooperative play experiences for their children and respite for themselves to pursue their own interests. These women were bold enough to claim that time away from their children was important and necessary. In 1926, Smith College opened a nursery school for "conversation of valuable social material," a phrase that described the purpose for the mothers, not for the children. However, the Smith College staff were dedicated to habit training for the children, as were other kindergartens at the time.

The Advent of Child Psychology   In the early 1900s there was a growth of child psychology, as many scholars emerged with advice regarding child rearing and educational practices. In 1907, Maria Montessori, the first female physician in Italy and a noted educator, opened the Casa De Bambini for children of lower income, working class, Roman citizens (Gordon & Browne, 1993). She had been commissioned by the Italian government to serve the educational needs of children living in the tenements. Children from age three attended for six to eight hours each day. The purpose of the preschool was to prepare children for common school and to train them in self-care. Many of the children were labeled mentally retarded, though Montessori sensed that they really lacked proper motivation and environment (Gordon & Browne, 1993).

Montessori believed that education begins at birth and that the early years are the most important for fostering intellectual and social development. She identified what she called "sensitive periods," in which children's natural curiosity makes them especially ready to acquire certain skills and knowledge (Gordon & Browne, 1993). Montessori also believed that any task could be reduced to a series of small steps suitable for a child's learning. Therefore, she developed materials graded in difficulty and emphasizing self-help skills. She emphasized a "prepared environment," meaning that classroom environments set the occasion for children to explore certain materials to engage in activities specifically intended to foster problem-solving and concept formation. She also designed materials, classrooms, and a teaching procedure to prove her points (Gordon & Browne, 1993).

Montessori's curriculum had three major components:

1. Exercises in practical life: hygiene, care of clothing and living space, and skills for self-management

2. Sensorial experiences: didactic materials that would instruct children, such as stacking blocks, series of rods, and wooden cylinders

3. Language development: training on articulation, dialect, and precision in usage (Montessori, 1964)

From 1910 to 1915, Montessori gathered attention in the United States but was criticized by progressive educators as too rigid and constraining. Her work was seemingly forgotten, though interest in Montessori's methods reemerged in the early 1960s. Now, this scholar and teacher can be viewed as one of most influential child psychologists of the century.

In 1914, behavioral psychologists Watson and Thorndike introduced the idea that child development resulted almost entirely from environmental influence (Thorndike, 1913; Watson, 1914). They were convinced that heredity was an inadequate and misleading explanation of human behavior. Thorndike explained that habits were formed by conditioning in which appropriate behavior was rewarded and unwanted behavior stopped because it was either no longer reinforced or was punished (Day, 1983). John Watson emphasized the contribution of specific environmental influences, proposing that parents could make of their children what they wished (Cook, et al., 1992). B. F. Skinner (1904–1990) was the intellectual force behind behavior analysis who proposed a natural science approach to human behavior, moving it away from its early mechanistic focus (Pierce & Epling, 1995). Skinner outlined his theory of operant behavior, discussing basic operant principles and their application to human behavior. He addressed self-control, thinking, the self, and social behaviors. Applied behavior analysis extended the application of behavioral principles to socially important problems. Today, behavioral psychology offers a vast array of effective procedures for the education and training of young children.

A typical child care setting

Gesell, a developmental psychologist, wrote *The Preschool Child* in 1923. In it he too emphasized the importance of the early years. Gesell stated that the preschool period "is biologically the most important period in the development of an individual for the simple but sufficient reason that it comes first in a dynamic sequence; it inevitably influences all subsequent development." He created a normative developmental approach based on keen observation of children at various ages. However, Gesell warned that his "ages and stages" concept could not be interpreted too literally. His norms were not rigid prescriptions, but rather indices of behavior likely to occur (Cook, et al., 1992).

Day Care   Throughout the early 1900s, day cares were considered a component of social welfare and were designed to serve "pathological" families who were incapable of providing proper care for their children. Day care was offered selectively and restrictively to families in hardship and was seen as temporary assistance until families could care for their own children.

During the Great Depression, the need for day care was considerable, and the federal government provided Works Progress Administration (WPA) nursery schools, which hired unemployed teachers in the United States (Gordon & Browne, 1993). In 1937, there were 1900 WPA day cares serving 40,000 children in the United States.

Works Progress Administration day cares were more educational than protective or custodial, and such services were publicly supported during World War II as women were recruited to work in the war industry. The 1941 Lanham Act (Community Facilities Act) gave communities funds to provide support for the war effort; by 1942, the Lanham Act was interpreted to include funding for day care. By 1945, government funded day care was being provided for 1,500,000 children across the United States. Unlike previous programs, child enrollment was based solely on whether the mothers were employed, not on the presence of family pathology. Lanham funds were withdrawn in 1946 when the war ended, and the schools were either turned over to the states or closed (Gordon & Browne, 1993).

Early Childhood Education   Services to young children with special needs seems to be the last piece of an elaborate puzzle. All the other pieces—education, universal education, and education of children with disabilities in public schools—had to come first. The early 1900s also witnessed a seeding of services for children with special needs through the initiation of a variety of programs both in the United States and in Europe. Just before the turn of the century, Alexander Graham Bell, inventor of the telephone and a strong advocate of oral education for the deaf, petitioned the National Education Association to establish a division for the needs of persons with disabilities. The approved division was called the Department of Education of the Deaf, Blind, and the Feebleminded, later shortened to Department of Special Education (Cook, et al., 1992).

In 1904, Alfred Binet was commissioned by France's minister of public instruction to design a test to determine which children could succeed in the public schools and which children needed special attention. The philosophy of the time was to keep children with disabilities in the regular classroom, while creating a method of identification so that teachers would avoid the problem of prejudice that might occur if these children were mistaken for "slackers" or "lazy students" (Cook, et al., 1992).

In 1922, the International Council for Exceptional Children was formed. Its members were an influential advocacy group who worked on behalf of children with special needs (Cook, et al., 1992). The 1930 White House Conference on Child Health and Protection marked the first time special education had received national recognition in the United States. However, prior to World War II, parents were still inclined to isolate children who had severe disabilities, to institutionalize them, or to be unwilling to admit their children needed special services. At the same time, children with mild disabilities received no special services though many were placed in regular classrooms in neighborhood schools (Cook, et al., 1992).

One of the earliest and most dramatic demonstrations of the importance of early intervention was reported in 1939. Skeels and Dye (1939) removed two "hopeless" babies from an orphanage and placed them under the care of adult women with mental retardation who also resided in an institution. After living on the women's ward for six months, the babies' IQs rose by 40 points; a few more months in this setting and their IQs rose to the mid-90s. Skeels and Dye then convinced state authorities to move 13 more children (all but two of whom were classified as mentally retarded and unsuitable for adoption) to the one-on-one care of teenage girls with mental retardation who lived at the institution.

The teenage girls were trained in simple mothering skills, and the children also attended a half-morning kindergarten program at the institution. Twelve other children under age three who remained in the orphanage were used as a comparison group. After two years, the experimental group in the care of the teenage "mothers" averaged a gain of 28 IQ points, while the comparison group that stayed with the orphanage lost an average of 26 IQ points. A follow-up 25 years later by Skeels (1966) showed the experimental group had almost all completed high school, married, and had normal children. By contrast, four of the control children were still institutionalized, and the average education of the group was only third grade. These studies provided substantial support for theories that early environmental experiences influence child development.

After World War II, the public experienced guilt over the numbers of formerly healthy young men who returned from the war in a maimed condition. Consequently, parent organizations developed and directed political pressure toward the improvement of services for people with disabilities, including children. The success of programs for individuals with sensory impairments were a boost to the efforts of advocates for special education. Between 1953 and 1958, there was an increase in enrollment in special education classes by 260% (Cook, et al., 1992). Thus, the age of assisting children with special needs had begun.

Abstract: The Best Day Care There Ever Was

The "best day care that ever was" arose in response to the urgent need to meet production requirements during World War II. In 1943, in Portland, Oregon, 25,000 women were employed to carry out a massive undertaking: the production of tankers and cargo ships desperately needed for the war in Asia. These massive ships were completed, from start to finish, in an unbelievable four days in ship-yards that operated day and night, seven days a week. Five thousand women, working as welders, secretaries, chippers, and burners, were mothers who required day care for their children.

Hence, Edgar Kaiser, general manager of the yards, set about building the finest facilities for a child-care program. Mr. Kaiser began by hiring the best architects to design two children's centers, which would each serve 1,125 children a day and would be open 24 hours a day 364 days a year. The buildings were huge, with round wheel-like plans containing 15 large rooms in the spokes and a protected playground at the central hub. Classrooms were placed at the plant entrances so that every worker passed by, and mothers could drop their children off in the most convenient way.

Kaiser hired only the best professionals—teachers with degrees in child development and three or more years experience. The educators were recruited from every major teacher-training institution in the country. When Kaiser learned the going pay rate for nursery-school work, he exploded, "You can't pay college graduates that!" The pay was raised to match that of other shipyard workers. One hundred teachers, 6 group supervisors, 10 nurses, 5 nutritionists, and 2 family consultants formed an astonishing concentration of experts in child care.

The classrooms were large, and each had storage space and a bathroom with child-sized sinks and toilets. Windows on two sides gave the children views of the shipyards. Two bathtubs were added, high enough that adults did not have to bend over and big enough for children to splash and play in the water. The rooms were filled with carloads of nonbreakable juice glasses, self-feed bibs, cots, sheets, blocks, puzzles, easels, and play equipment.

Kaiser's day-care centers were designed for the needs of working mothers. Each child went through a health test every morning before being admitted. Children who were mildly sick attended an infirmary where nurses and a consulting pediatrician took care of the children in isolated class cubicles, and infirmary teachers provided quiet bed play. The nurses also immunized the children. Three meals and two snacks were provided each day, and the chief nutritionist sent parents a weekly list of meals served and suggestions for additional food to complete an adequate day's diet. Also helpful was the Home Service Food—precooked and packaged meals mothers could purchase and pick up at the center's kitchen.

The centers cared for children from 18 months to 6 years of age and expanded services for school-age children to after school, on Saturdays, and during summer vacations. A commissary provided necessary items like toothbrushes and shoelaces. For a short while, a Mending Service was also in operation, and parents could borrow children's books from the center's library. As James Hymes, Jr., the on-site manager put it, "We thought that anything that saved the working [mother] her time and energy meant she would have more to give to her child."

The Kaiser Centers were in operation for only two years, closing in 1945 when the war in the Pacific was winding down. When the staff separated, they hoped their work would provide a model for excellent day care programs, but the Kaiser Centers were never to be replicated. Though the Kaiser Centers demonstrated that day care could be good for children and mothers, it took a special set of circumstances to bring about full support for working mothers.

Caroline Zinsser, *Working Mother*, October, 1984, pp. 76–78.

1950 - 2000AD
HELPING MODE

By the late 1940s a number of prominent individuals such as Pearl Buck, Roy Rogers and Dale Evans, and the Kennedy family were visibly calling for better education of individuals with special needs. Parents in the 1950s no longer felt the need to hide children with disabilities, and advocacy groups such as the United Cerebral Palsy Association, the National Association for Retarded Citizens, and the American Foundation for the Blind demanded alternatives to institutionalization (Cook, et al., 1992).

Theories of Child Development In the midtwentieth century, new psychological theories regarding childhood became popular in the United States. Freud's psychotherapy concentrated on the affective development of individuals and its connection to early childhood experiences. This view revived a pessimistic attitude toward childhood that had been dormant since the 1700s. According to Freud, childhood was ambiguous, incoherent, and filled with conflict (Freud, 1953). Freud advocated parental permissiveness in order to free children of possible causes of conflict and subsequent neuroses (Cook, et al., 1992). Early childhood education was seen as critical to the social and emotional development of children (Day, 1983).

It was also during the 1950s that Jean Piaget's work became popular in America. Providing an antidote to Freud's pessimism, Piaget proposed that children have an inborn tendency toward adaptation and that through their encounters with the environment they develop categories of knowledge that are remarkably similar among all humans. Piaget, a cognitive psychologist, suggested the purpose of education should be to provide opportunities that allow children to combine experiences into coherent cognitive systems constituting knowledge. He insisted children are active learners and initiators and should direct their own play and learning. The Perry Preschool Project, developed in the late 1950s in Ypsilanti, Michigan, is the most notable Piagetian (cognitive) program (Cook, et al., 1992). However, there is no doubt that Piaget's observations of young children, their translation to theory, and subsequent recommendations for practitioners are the most significant influence of this century on early childhood education policy and practices.

Poverty and Child Development Similar to efforts at the turn of the century to address issues of parental neglect, an interest in poverty and its effect on child development reemerged in the 1950s. During the 1950s, the term "cultural deprivation" was coined. This theory assumed that poor children suffered from a dearth of experiences necessary to meet the demands of a complex and changing world (Day, 1983). A subsequent revolution in early education occurred in America, as curricula were specifically designed for the enrichment of poor children. In 1962, the Baltimore Early Admissions project established preschool programs in public schools explicitly for poor children (Day, 1983). In the same year, the New York City schools arranged an experimental enrichment program for preschool-aged children in three Harlem schools (Day, 1983).

Such remedial efforts were bolstered by scholars like J. M. Hunt, who published *Intelligence and Experience* (1961), arguing against the concept of fixed intelligence and predetermined development. Similarly, William Fowler (1962) suggested that concept formation began during infancy, based on evidence that early verbal stimulation helped the development of memory and knowledge acquisition. This research contradicted Freud's warning that challenging young children's intellect might damage their psychological development (Day, 1983). In 1964, Benjamin Bloom published *Stability and Change in Human Characteristics* in which he claimed that 70% of a person's intellectual aptitude and 50% of the reading skill of young adults was established before the age of nine. Combined, these educators provided ample justification for early intervention (Day, 1983).

Head Start In 1964, the United States government passed the Economic Opportunity Act (EOA), which launched President Lyndon Johnson's ambitious War on Poverty campaign. Eventually, the showcase project for the War on Poverty, the Head Start program, was initiated in 1965 (Bailey & Wolery, 1992). Head Start was the first national enrichment program of preschool education in the United States. It began as a summer program for 560,000 children whose admission was based on their poverty status. As a community action program, Head Start was designed to address the health, nutrition, and education needs of poor families, with the goal of preventing later school failure. Two key features of Head Start are parental participation and health care services.

The Head Start effort was supplemented by the 1965 Elementary and Secondary Education Act, which provided funding to support the creation of preschools for poor children to be directed by public school districts (Day, 1983). It is interesting to note that, until 1965, the federal Children's Bureau still held the position that day care would be disruptive for healthy family relations and that it should be provided only to those families who were not capable of providing adequate care for their children.

Both a strength and a weakness of Head Start were flexible guidelines that allowed individual programs to develop along a wide range of educational approaches (Zigler & Muenchow, 1992). By 1968, there were 14 different variations of Head Start in implementation across the nation. The Westinghouse Learning Corporation and Ohio University conducted an evaluation of the effectiveness of summer and full-year Head Start programs (Cicirelli, Evans, & Schiller, 1969). When the independent evaluators released the Westinghouse Report, it was very damaging to the Head Start effort (Day, 1983).

Researchers found that, despite early gains, summer programs did not produce cognitive or affective gains that persisted into the early elementary grades and that full-year programs had only marginal effects on cognitive development that could still be detected in grades one, two, and three (Smith & Bissell, 1970). Head Start was judged a failure. At the same time, Arthur Jensen (1969), a noted psychological researcher, claimed compensatory education had been tried and had failed. This fueled tremendous debate and controversy.

However, this political and philosophical controversy stimulated early educators to do more to solve the problem of equalizing educational opportunities. It was determined that researchers should identify which early education approaches might have the most success and that intervention should be extended to follow through with poor children into elementary school. By 1969, there were 21 alternative preschool and primary grade curricula being researched under the Head Start Planned Variation program and 20 educational models under Follow Through programs, which served poor children from kindergarten through third grade. In 1970, the Head Start summer programs were discontinued and replaced with full-time, year-round programs serving about 400,000 children.

By the 1970s, the concept of cultural deprivation was discredited (Day, 1983). It became more socially acceptable to recognize that various cultures are different, not deficient (Cole & Bruner, 1972; Labov, 1972). The long-term data on well-run model preschool programs and Follow Through programs revealed positive effects on school performance, special education placement, grade retention, teen pregnancy, delinquency, welfare participation, and employment (Haskins, 1989).

Recent Day Care Efforts In 1971, advocates for national day-care services for all families suffered a serious blow. The National Organization of Women (NOW) had argued for publicly supported, 24-hour on-demand day care as a necessary service for women if they were ever to achieve equitable freedom of opportunity. Though initially supportive, President Richard Nixon, in his first term, vetoed the Comprehensive Child Development Bill, asserting that day care would ruin the American family (Day, 1983). Since that time, the United States has failed even to establish national standards for child care, despite the increasing numbers of children who are cared for outside of the home. Since the 1960s, child development specialists have considered day care as a means by which developmental delays could be remedied or prevented. Day-care needs continue to increase as more mothers are working and as many husbands and wives separate through divorce. Protective care for children is needed. By 1985, the

Department of Education estimated that 2.5 million five-year-olds were enrolled in public preprimary programs and 5 million in private schools (Warger, 1988).

Today, there is scarce and contradictory evidence on the effects of long-term day care attendance by young children. Currently, society's provision of day care is shamefully inadequate in meeting the great demand that exists, and with the rising costs of day care, quality of care is out of reach for parents who must satisfy themselves with any affordable options.

EARLY CHILDHOOD SPECIAL EDUCATION

The first federal law written exclusively for services to preschoolers with special needs was the Handicapped Children's Early Childhood Assistance Act (P. L. 90-538), which was passed in 1968 (Heward & Orlansky, 1992). This act constituted landmark legislation as it represented the first major federal recognition of the importance of early childhood special education (Fallen & Umansky, 1985). The purpose of the bill was to develop model early educational programs for children with disabilities from birth through age eight. These model programs were funded as three-year demonstration grants, called First Chance projects. First Chance directors were required to include parents, to provide inservice training, to evaluate the progress of children served in the program, to coordinate with public schools, and to disseminate information (Cook, et al., 1992).

The First Chance Network began in 1969 with 24 programs funded for one million dollars. Of those 24 projects, 84% continued past their original three-year funding (Fallen & Umansky, 1985). By 1985, there were 173 different First Chance programs throughout the country, and by 1987, over 500 programs had been funded. These projects have developed screening and assessment devices, curriculum materials, parent training programs, and thousands of other print, audiovisual, and support materials for early childhood intervention (Heward & Orlansky, 1992).

The Economic Opportunity and Community Partnership Act of 1974 required that Head Start programs in each state reserve 10% of their enrollment slots for children with disabilities (Fallen & Umansky, 1985). By 1977, 13% of all children enrolled in Head Start programs were classified as disabled, a total of over 36,000 children ("HEW reports," 1978; Heward & Orlansky, 1992). Later, Head Start developed 14 regional Resource Access Projects which provided training and technical assistance to personnel serving children with disabilities in Head Start programs (Fallen & Umansky, 1985).

IDEA of 1975 Head Start's inclusion of children with disabilities was only the first step in extensive federal legislation to provide services to all children with disabilities. The Education of all Handicapped Children Act of 1975 (P. L. 94-142, now renamed Individuals with Disabilities Education Act [IDEA]) mandated a free, appropriate public education for all school-age children with disabilities between the ages of 3 and 21.

The legislation offered an incentive funding program for states whose laws did not conflict to identify and serve children from three to five years of age. However, the preschool incentive of $300 per child was insufficient to stimulate universal services to all preschoolers with disabilities. By the 1980–81 school year, only 16 states provided services for children three to five years of age, and only another 22 states served preschoolers with disabilities age four or five years (Heward & Orlansky, 1992; U. S. Comptroller General, 1981). Even so, in 1986, the states served approximately 75% of children aged three to five years with disabilities, though 31 states did not provide special services for at least part of that age group (Koppelman, 1986). At the same time, services to infants and toddlers from birth to age three were scarce or nonexistent in many states (Koppelman, 1986).

IDEA of 1986 Since its passage in 1975, three bills reauthorized and amended the legislation presented in IDEA. The 1986 bill, P. L. 99-457 had a major impact on services to preschoolers

Table 8.2/ *Recent Landmarks in Early Intervention Services**

Date	Landmark Description
1965	Project Head Start was established to serve 3- and 4-year-olds living in poverty
1968	Handicapped Children's Early Education Program established to fund model preschool programs for children with disabilities
1972	Economic Opportunity Act required Head Start to reserve 10% of its enrollment for children with disabilities
1975	P. L. 94-142, The Education for All Handicapped Children act provided incentive funding for programs serving preschoolers with disabilities ages 3 to 5 years
1986	P. L. 99-457 amends P. L. 94-142 to require services to children age 3 to 5 with disabilities and to provide incentives for programs serving infants and toddlers who are developmentally delayed or at risk of developmental delay
1990	Head Start Expansion and Quality Improvement Act reauthorized and expanded Head Start programs through 1994

Source: Bailey, D. B., & Wolery, M. (1992). *Teaching infants and preschoolers with disabilities.* 2nd Ed., New York: Macmillan Publishing Company.

with disabilities. P. L. 99-457 required states to provide preschool services to very young children with disabilities, ages three to five, and provided new incentive grants to assist states in developing and implementing programs for services to infants and toddlers with disabilities and to their families. To obtain incentive grant funds, states were required to provide services to children from birth to three years of age who were experiencing a developmental delay or had an established risk of later developmental delay. Table 8.2 summarizes recent legislation.

EARLY CHILDHOOD EDUCATION TODAY

Well into the 1990s, early childhood services continued to expand. In 1990, the Head Start Expansion and Quality Improvement Act reauthorized Head Start through 1994 and increased funding so that Head Start could serve more children (Bailey & Wolery, 1992). In the same year, the HCEEP was renamed The Early Education for Handicapped Children Program, which increased the emphasis on identifying and serving infants and toddlers in need, encouraging transition from medical to early intervention services, promoting the use of assisting technology, and serving children prenatally exposed to maternal substance abuse (Bailey & Wolery, 1992).

Three broad historical themes led to the current status of early intervention (Bailey & Wolery, 1992). First, society became concerned about the care and welfare of young children, as evidenced in the passage of legislation to protect and provide services to young children. Second, society demonstrated concern about the rights and needs of individual citizens and minority groups. Changes in advocacy for civil rights, individual rights, women's rights, and disability rights have set the stage for establishing legal rights and improved services for children with disabilities. Finally, a third trend was the increased focus on support for individuals and families as a primary goal of human service programs.

These themes have supported diversity in the population and the way in which service is delivered. Heterogeneity in the kinds of children served has expanded with the inclusion of

Diverse population of children at school

newborns and infants, the improving survival rate of medically fragile infants, the advent of children with AIDS, and the increasing numbers of children who have been affected in utero by exposure to alcohol, cocaine, or other drugs (Bailey & Wolery, 1992). Likewise, the families of these children show greater diversity than in years past.

Despite this increasing diversity, professionals in the field of early childhood share assumptions based on the accumulated knowledge of the profession, knowledge derived from research, theory, cultural values, and clinical experiences. Bailey (1989) summarized the principles of early intervention that have become generally accepted across the profession. Among these shared principles are the following:

1. The quality of a child's physical and social environment has a significant influence on the child's behavior and long-term development.

2. Early intervention is effective in reducing the impact of disabling conditions.

3. Parent involvement is essential for appropriate early intervention.

4. Early intervention is most effective when professionals work together as an interdisciplinary team.

5. Clinicians should teach to a child's strengths rather than focusing on the child's deficits.

6. Intervention must be developmentally based.

7. Individualized assessment is a necessary prerequisite to effective intervention.

8. Skills taught to children with disabilities do not generalize to other contexts unless specific planning and training is designed for such carryover.

If the current best practices in early childhood education could be summed up in one descriptive word, that word would be *natural*. The major goals of early intervention today revolve around a philosophy of normalization. Teachers, parents, and clinicians work toward the child's acquisition of developmentally appropriate skills, they provide services in the natural setting of the home or in integrated classrooms with typical peers, and they emphasize teaching that utilizes normal routines, play activities, and natural contingencies.

Many early childhood professionals embrace the philosophy of developmentally appropriate practice (DAP). Guidelines for DAP encourage teachers to identify children's interests, to arrange the environment to facilitate exploration, and to provide motivating activities (all from the child's perspective). Learning activities and materials used are to be real, concrete, and relevant to young children (Bredekamp, 1987). While DAP guidelines provide a context that makes integration of children with disabilities feasible, some educators warn that DAP may not be a sufficient approach for children with disabilities (Wolery, Strain, & Bailey, 1992). Children with disabilities may require assistance from others, may not learn well on their own, and often have disabilities that interfere with their exploration and interactions.

Despite a long history of increasingly didactic services, today's wisdom of practice dictates a return to more natural settings, empowerment of the family unit, and understanding of the importance of the child's instinctive inclinations. A child is no longer viewed as an isolated entity that can be separated from its environment, treated with standardized educational packages, and returned to the world as a conventional, though small, adult. Children and their families are now viewed as active participants in learning and in teaching.

What will the next phase in the history of early childhood bring? The epilogue to this text considers the predictions of scholars and practitioners from a variety of professional perspectives. Today's students of early childhood special education will take that step into the future and will fashion another generation's past.

CROSS–CULTURAL HISTORY OF CHILDHOOD EDUCATION

Because Western civilizations inhabited and colonized all corners of the globe during the same interval that childhood education in Western culture was evolving, and because Western industrialization has influenced almost every culture, there are distinct commonalities among early

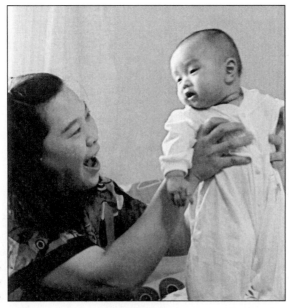

Early education in non-Western cultures reflects the unique heritage of each culture

A Native American Perspective

Interview with James Holden

We know by many of the various demographics available today, what's happening to Native American students. They are overrepresented in remedial programs and badly underrepresented in gifted and talented programs. Unfortunately, the reality is, a lot of that, in my opinion, is because of stereotypic beliefs on the part of the educational community. That's part of it, but another part of it is how we as Native Americans look at ourselves. We tend to think, sometimes, we've lost the ability to know who we are.

Our Indian children today, and our Indian parents, are struggling with who they are. We're dealing with second-, third-, fourth-, and fifth-generation children off the reservation, and parents off the reservation. The circle of life on the reservation is pretty real, but it's also pretty short. The circle of life is you're born, you go to school if you can, you play some sports, often you drink, and you get a job. It seems to repeat itself over and over again across generations.

Unemployment's high, alcoholism is extremely high, emotional, sexual, and physical abuse is extremely high. A lot of Indians believe if they get off the reservation, that will fix them. We get off the reservation, and we run smack into this whole wall of misinformation. If you want to see a third world country, go to a reservation, but don't make a judgment about what it is you see, unless you understand what it is.

Somehow, we as a group, need to get the idea that we must and can walk in two worlds. I want to be able to work and compete in the white man's world. That's fine, there's nothing wrong with that. But I also must have the other foot firmly planted in my roots, my beliefs, and my customs. You know, if you look at the whole warrior society idea, many male Indians are still stuck in that.

What's a warrior? All those stereotypes that whites have about savage warriors have some truth, because that's how we were. Do we treat females differently than our white counterparts? What do you think? Some of us are still stuck back with the warrior mentality.

So, what do we do for children? That's really what it's all about, what we do for children, because if the water of life is our children, and I believe it is, then what are we doing for our children? We must somehow teach them it is right and just to be proud of being Indian. But we also must tell them, what being an Indian is. We can't just say it's living on the reservation. It is who and what we are as a people—our old ways, our oral traditions, our celebrations, and the history of how we have been treated by the dominant culture. A lot of it is just traditional views of Mother Earth getting us back to the basics.

I think, you should start with the smallest of the small. As soon as they're in preschool, what do we teach them? Do we teach them that the girls play with the dolls, and the boys play with the blocks, and all the dolls are white? Or, do we teach them it is all right for the teacher who is

(continued)

REUBEN HOLDEN

male to put on an apron to cook, and it's okay for the girls to put on the construction outfit in play time. That's the way it should be.

Deeper than that, we have to somehow reach them with the idea that diversity is a way of life, and where your place is in that structure of diversity. Our children don't have that sense, when they go back to visit grandfather on a reservation and he's still stuck. Grandfather is still stuck with the idea that it's a white man's school system. Grandmother is stuck with showing her girls the old way because the old way's getting lost. The children today are saying,

"What are you talking about, old way? If it's not video and microwave, I'm not sure I want to know it." But many of us believe there is tremendous value to honoring and understanding the old customs and ideas as a bridge to our past.

Unfortunately, one major problem of Native Americans today is that our agenda is not put on the front burner by many districts because that spot is often already taken by African-Americans or other minority groups. We do not seem to have those powerful speakers and activists who can engage the system in a meaningful way to bring about change.

childhood services in most countries. Unfortunately, Western practices have supplanted traditional educational activities in so many cultures that knowledge and understanding of heritage and customs of various cultures has often been lost. Woodill et al. (1992) compiled brief analyses of early educational practices across the world. In these summaries, the history of childhood education in non-Western cultures is almost always begun with the introduction of services by colonizers. The following synopses, taken from Woodill et al. (1992), provide a sample of cultural histories that reflect a heritage different from that of Western culture.

Albania

Albania has been occupied by foreign governments since the Roman period (Dedja, 1992). The first schools were built by the Greeks, Slavs, and Ottoman Turks. However, a "collective" means has been used to educate young children since the Illyrian tribe. Children were given over to the state for their education at the age of five, where they learned a love of work and were given military training. A national renaissance movement occurred at the beginning of the twentieth century when ideologists such as Sami Frasheri, Naim Frasheri, and Gjerasim Qiriazi envisioned a system of preschool education in the "mother's schools." Still, access to schools was limited, and in 1939, only 10% of Albanian children were considered literate.

In 1913, Parasheevi Qiriazi criticized the predominant Turkish influences and asserted schools were too traditional and heavily affected by Moslem principles. Qiriazi believed preschools should be a transition from family to formal schooling and should emphasize moral development, good behaviors, simple handiwork, mental development, observations of nature, language and proper speech, and physical training. Qiriazi's model provided special schools for children with mental or physical handicaps. These programs would provide a curriculum of practical work skills. However, Qiriazi's curricula were never really implemented, as his work was oppressed by the reign of Ahmet Zog. At the end of Zog's reign, there were only 22 kindergartens in Albania.

Because of widespread destruction during World War II, schools in Albania closed until 1945. In 1946, following the proclamation of the People's Republic of Albania, schools became the property of the people. Nursery school, preschool, and kindergarten services were widely expanded to permit Albanian women to take an equal part in social production. However, traditional education of children, transmitted by families to young children, coexists with state-run preschools.

Until the 1990s, preschool education focused on the socialist pedagogy, whereby teachers constantly worked to link the educational activities with revolutionary practice, life, and production. For example, "preschool children participate in beautifying the kindergarten grounds, watering the plants and flowers, making excursions to work and production centers and the fields (where they learn about the work of cooperative farmers and workers), giving modest aid at building sites and during the country's political campaigns, and cleaning up around memorials, historic monuments, and their own playgrounds" (Dedja, 1992, p. 25). In the 1990s, Albania is again immersed in violent civil conflict. The direction this war will take preschool education is unknown.

Botswana

Traditionally, the families, including extended family members, have been responsible for the education of their own children (Monau, 1992). Grandparents and older siblings were responsible for basic survival needs including health, education, and socialization, while children's parents engaged in agricultural or other economic activities. Families tended to be self-sufficient, "They live, eat, work and play together, consult and help one another in all personal difficulties and share in one another's fortune or even bad luck. . . .Few couples ever live away from the immediate environment of their relatives" (Schapera, 1971, p. 926).

Monau (1992) quoted the former president of Botswana on the importance of self-reliance: "It has always been part of our custom that members of a family should help each other face and overcome the problems of life" (p. 114). This tradition was altered substantially in 1966 when Botswana became independent. Along with economic changes, Botswana experienced long and severe droughts. A subsequent migration of families, first the father and then mother and children, to the urban areas, adversely affected family structure. As women without extended families went to work to supplement their husbands' meager wages, children were increasingly left in the care of older children who were too young to manage their siblings. Though many day-care programs were initiated to address this family crisis, only a small percentage of children have access to such services.

Child-care facilities that do exist are little improvement over home care by siblings. The minimum licensing standard is that teachers are able to read and write. Many are operated in garages or small houses, with perhaps a single toilet for 40 or so children. Though the state is authorized to monitor licensed programs, there is little chance that resources would be available to improve day-care programs that are found in noncompliance. While the concentration of day-care programs is largely preacademic, some are able to provide custodial care only.

One unique preschool program in Botswana is the CHILD-to-Child Program, in which older children in rural areas look after the welfare of younger brothers and sisters. Preschoolers attend the public schools twice a week and are "taught" by older children who select their students (usually siblings). The older students are taught to train the younger children school routines and concepts as well as rudimentary preacademics.

Certified teachers of preschool education in Botswana are trained in Lobatse. Montessori methods and curriculum form the basis of this teacher training. For several reasons, however, experts believe this method is inappropriate. Most importantly, teachers do not adapt the methods and activities to cultural conditions of the people of Botswana. Consequently, many preschool teachers, frustrated with a curriculum that doesn't "fit," resort to formal methods, whereby children are seated in rows, lectured to, and expected to engage in structured academic activities.

People's Republic of China

Laing and Pang (1992) described the history of preschool education in China as a series of stages, beginning in 1949. Prior to this time, early childhood education was based on semifeudal and semicolonial styles of education. After the founding of the People's Republic of China, preschool education was reformed based on Soviet theories of education. During this first stage, preschool education grew in availability, teacher training, and research. In the second stage, "unplanned

growing and consolidation," there was unchecked growth of preschool education, pushed by the extreme left. Education during this period became adult-centered, and ideas such as a children's focus, nutrition, appreciation of art and nature, and use of toys were considered capitalistic and were discouraged. The third period, "seriously damaged," began with the cultural revolution. Preschool children were given military training and taught to engage in "revolutionary criticism." Memorization and recitation from quotations of Mao and giant gymnasiums with organized sports replaced more developmental approaches to early childhood. At the same time, teacher training programs were closed as were many kindergartens themselves. Teachers were prohibited from instructing children and were reassigned to other jobs. The fourth stage began in 1976, and was termed "restoring and vigorously developing stage." Education of young children has become an important part of the overall emphasis on public education. Though not universally available, hundreds of thousands of preschools and kindergartens serve children throughout China.

The two primary foci of preschool education in China are morality (love of motherland, its people, and family) and language. Morality includes teaching children a love of work, more specifically, collective work. This also involves cultural values of altruism, modesty, ability to accept criticism, honesty, respect of adults, use of social manners, hospitality, and a sense of optimism and confidence. There are six components of China's language instruction: (1) articulate and accurate speech in the primary language; (2) enrichment of vocabulary; (3) ability to clearly express wishes and thoughts without inhibition; (4) ability to use descriptive language; (5) enjoyment of songs, stories, story telling, and recitation of 25–30 simple poems; and (6) love of books and radio stories.

Teaching methods in China also vary from traditional Western methods. For example, most activities take place in large groups, with an emphasis on collective play, work, and problem solving. Children also engage in semistructured dramatic role-playing in which they practice real-life activities and language skills. Observation skills are emphasized and specifically taught, so children can use these abilities later across subject areas. Work and daily routines are used to teach good moral habits, so children can learn to be proud of their products and their ability to serve others in the collective. For example, children are assigned to "on duty" groups, and each week the on-duty group designated is responsible for a variety of tasks (e.g., cleaning off the table, feeding the birds, washing the toys, etc.).

Many aspects of Chinese preschool education are unique. However, like most countries worldwide, there is increasing pressure for educators to reform to more Western-style methods.

India

Organized education of children in India began in the nineteenth century when European missionaries introduced the notion of kindergartens (Kaul, 1992). Montessori methods were introduced in India in the 1930s by Marie Montessori herself. At the same time, Mahatma Gandhi was advocating for early childhood education, calling this preschool notion prebasic education.

In the 1940s, Tarabai Modak adapted Montessori education for tribal children. Her *anganwadi* (courtyard centers) literally meant to take education to the doorsteps of tribal children. A major emphasis on early childhood education began in the 1950s and 1960s when the newly independent government established a national agency under social welfare to promote preschool education. Today, however, only 12% of eligible preschoolers are served by any kind of program.

Though the preferred teaching method in India is "playway," in which activities are largely child-directed, there is considerable pressure by parents to provide preschoolers with the prerequisites for formal schooling. National objectives for preschool are physical development, self-help habits, social skills, emotional maturity, aesthetic appreciation, intellectual curiosity, independence and creativity, and expressive communication.

Japan

According to Noguchi, Ogawa, Yoshidawa, and Hashimoto (1992), primitive Japan regarded children as precious, and they were reared within the protection of their tribe. In the dynasty periods (794–1185 A.D.) children of noble families were reared to be cultured women and men. Samuri warriors took charge of the state in the Middle Ages. Consequently, boys were trained to become warriors, and girls were trained to become "womanly" for the sake of the family. The Confucianists gradually changed this philosophy, beginning in the sixteenth century, when they began to advocate for early education.

Self-determination of educational practices altered in the nineteenth century when missionaries earmarked children of poor women for the first "modern" preschools in Japan. Afterwards, the first Froebelian kindergarten was introduced in 1876. The focus, child-centered education, is still considered a central feature of Japanese kindergartens. Industrialization forced an increase in the number of state-sponsored and independent early childhood programs. World War II further increased the need for early childhood care.

In the 1980s, changes in Japanese society, including smaller family size, urbanization, and improved work opportunities for women, led to reform of early childhood services. As a consequence, nursing and education in child care were unified with a new emphasis on "community-based family day care." Currently over 90% of children receive some type of preschool education. For children three and older, the emphasis is on life, play, and health; for children younger than three, the emphasis is on human relations, health, and language development.

The falling birthrate in Japan has led some parents to place greater importance on the educational achievement and competitiveness of their children. However, access to special preschools (e.g., *Juku*, or private schools that prepare children for prestigious private elementary schools) is limited to the children of wealthy parents.

Japan does have early intervention and preschool programs for young children with disabilities. These services are usually provided in special schools of three types: schools for the blind, schools for the deaf, and schools for children with physical and mental disabilities. Children with severe disabilities may be served in the home or in a hospital. Each type of school has its own course of study, relative to the disability of children enrolled.

Liberia

Unlike most other countries in the world, Liberia maintains a traditional educational system and, at the same time, mandates participation in modern schooling (Gormuyor, 1992). Not all, but many, ethnic groups inhabiting Liberia developed a parallel system of educating their youth. Even today, boys are educated in *poros* and girls are educated in *sandes*. In early childhood, boys are secluded from females and noninitiates in groves where they remain for their cultural education and where they will learn the responsibilities placed on them by society. Boys learn survival skills, character, appreciation of art, and to become strong and brave in order to defend their families. Similarly, girls are isolated in a sande, away from males and noninitiates. Girls are taught to perform the roles of females in society, to be loyal and faithful wives. Methods of instruction include discovery, role-playing, games, problem solving, story telling, and learning by doing.

Historically, boys were isolated for four years and girls for three years in their respective institutions. Now, however, families are discouraged from sending their children for more than one year, and traditional education must not interfere with the children's modern Western-style education. United States philanthropic groups, American settlers, and missionaries from the United States introduced Western education to Liberia. The first educational opportunities by colonists, often by barely literate missionaries, were provided to enable children of Liberia to read the Bible. Missions continued to provide the bulk of Western education to children in Liberia into the twentieth century.

Though public schooling increased after World War II, the country still lacks sufficient resources to ensure even elementary education for all children. Thousands of children, especially in the hinterland, go without public schooling. Preschool education in Liberia is very rare, though children four or younger may attend the kindergarten programs that do exist if they show developmental readiness. Educators in this country believe that early education is important and are working toward broadening its availability.

Nigeria

Education in Nigeria has been traced to preliterate times when children's teachers were the mothers or grandmothers who cared for them while others worked on the farm or elsewhere (Aghenta & Omatseye, 1992). Children learned practical skills, such as interpersonal relations and adjusting to the rules and mores of society. Oral tradition constituted instruction, in which children learned through songs, folk tales, and legends. Youth were told about warriors, animals, gods, and the ancestral spirits. An emphasis was also placed on community belonging and achievement through hard work.

Traditional methods of early education were replaced by Western education in the sixteenth century when Portuguese Christian missionaries landed on the West Coast of Africa in 1515. The first school, called the Nursery and Infant Church, was started in 1842 by Methodist missionaries, who were also freed slaves from Sierra Leone. Establishment of public schools by Great Britain, which held colonial rule over Nigeria until 1960, began in the late nineteenth century. By the 1950s, universal free primary school was available in Nigeria.

Preschool programs are available only through private providers. Of these, there are two types of schools. *Akara* are generally run by unemployed semiliterate adults, who care for the children of working parents. School is usually held under a tree or in an unfinished building. These informal schools derive their name from the Yoruba name for fried black-eyed beans, which are given to children to try to appease them and to keep them quiet. More-affluent children attend traditional Western-style nursery schools. Activities include singing, dancing, drawing, listening to African folk tales, playing with toys, and preacademic learning. Nigerian teachers have recently modified Western curricula and activities to reflect traditional African toys and games, as well as supplanting foreign literature with meaningful African stories.

Each state in Nigeria is responsible for running schools for children with disabilities. These are usually segregated programs for children with hearing, visual, and cognitive impairments, as well as programs for the gifted. Children enrolled in state-sponsored schools or institutions usually come from a background of poverty.

Sultanate of Oman

Prior to 1897, when the first Western schooling was introduced by missionaries, children of both genders were served throughout the Sultanate of Oman in *kuttab* (Al-Barwani, 1992). It is believed these schools began shortly after Oman embraced Islam in the seventh century. Basic education was provided to children under the age of 10, in the form of Islamic teachings, arithmetic, and reading and writing of the Arabic language. Teaching in the privately owned *kuttabs* took place under the shade of a tree, in a mosque, in a teacher's home, or in the courtyard. The teachers themselves were appointed, based on their age, their knowledge of Quaran, and their reputations as good citizens of the community. Until the 1970s, most children in rural Oman were still educated in *kuttabs*. Even now, these private schools are held during summer sessions and after school in many communities.

Between 1970 and 1990, Oman moved from having 3 to having 370 Western-style primary schools. Preschool services and day-care programs are scarce since, outside the capital city of Muscat, most women are both uneducated and unemployed. Like *kuttabs,* kindergartens are privately owned. In 1988, Oman adopted and adapted the kindergarten curriculum of Kuwait, which emphasized important concepts and preacademics. Methods of instruction are generally child-centered and based on relevant life experiences.

The first program in Oman for children with disabilities was established in 1989. A center was opened in Bidbid, where children from birth to age 14 are collected and taught skills to help them cope with life. Mothers of children with disabilities also receive training in methods to assist their children.

Summary

These brief descriptions of educational history around the world illustrate the pervasive adoption of Western culture, even in some of the most remote places on Earth. Obviously, Christian religious groups, who dispatched missionaries and priests to colonies in Africa, Asia, and South America, were instrumental in converting indigenous educational methods to Western-style schooling. In most cases, traditional teaching methods were so effectively supplanted that knowledge of the methods themselves is lost or obscure. The industrial age that created a global economy and infiltration of Western culture to all parts of the world helped to institutionalize efforts begun by religiously motivated educators. Now, the information age will surely contribute to an ever-increasing uniformity of educational practices worldwide, in spite of the multicultural emphasis on valuing cultural integrity.

As in the United States, public preschool education in most countries is valued but generally not universally available. Finally, education of preschool children with disabilities, if available, is usually conducted in separate school facilities that emphasize functional skill development rather than using a developmentally appropriate approach.

THE TWENTY-FIRST CENTURY

NOW
POLITICAL MODE

At this writing, there are considerable lobbying efforts focused on returning power and influence over education and public welfare back to state and local agencies. The impetus for this change is a move toward economic restraint necessary to deal with a tremendous national debt and poor income growth among the middle class. It is possible that some states will eliminate early childhood services, particularly those for children with disabilities, which are likely to be viewed as unnecessary luxuries in a time of fiscal crisis. Other facets of early childhood education will also be affected. Training of personnel, which is already hampered by severe cuts in higher education by many states, may become increasingly difficult. Families who currently receive some assistance for their children through various agencies have already seen substantial cuts in services and more are likely.

Of greatest concern is the likelihood that, state by state, standards and practices will vary considerably, based on such factors as revenue generation through the tax base, power of certain voting constituencies, and overall need for early intervention and preschool services by families with children with special needs. Parents may be forced to move from one state to another to receive services, placing a disproportionate burden on those states that elect to provide services. This would be an unfortunate return to an era reminiscent of the 1950s and 1960s.

If there is a silver lining to these predictions, it is the history that has just been presented. The past five centuries have been marked by slow but persistent improvement in attitudes toward and services for very young children. Regressions, when made, have tended to be temporary, with an overall forward progress.

STUDY GUIDE QUESTIONS

1. What is the relationship between human wants and human needs in terms of social priorities?

2. Ancient Western culture was not benevolent toward children. Why? How were children treated?

3. What rationale justified the lack of attachment to children by their parents in medieval culture?

4. What motivated the educational efforts of early American colonists? Why was this purpose so important?

5. Summarize the philosophy of Rousseau and explain how his approach differed from Puritan philosophy.

6. How did social changes in industrial America change child care? What was the larger purpose of child care at this time?

7. Compare Froebel's notion of kindergarten with the practices of today in America.

8. What influence did social reformers have on early education in the late 1800s?

9. Identify the fundamental elements of Montessori's model.

10. Explain why the Skeels and Dye study was so important to early education advocates.

11. In your opinion, why is it impossible to recreate "the best day care that ever was"?

12. In what way was Freud's theory a step backwards in children's psychology?

13. How do the major conclusions of Piaget's theory reflect that of some earlier educators?

14. What were the documented long-term benefits of Head Start and Follow Through?

15. In what ways have First Chance projects influenced early education?

16. What is the relationship between provisions of IDEA legislation of 1975 and IDEA legislation of 1986 in terms of encouraging early childhood services to children who are disabled?

17. What assumptions regarding early intervention are accepted today?

18. Explain how Western notions of child care and early childhood became an influence globally.

19. What cross-cultural practices in child care might be used to enhance early childhood educational practices in the United States?

20. Why might Western educational practices be inappropriate for some cultures?

REFERENCES

Aghenta, J. A., & Omatseye, J. N. (1992). Preschool and primary education in Nigeria. In G. A. Woodill, J. Bernhard, & L. Prochner (Eds.), *International handbook of early childhood education* (pp. 399–406). New York: Garland.

Al-Barwani, T. (1992). Early childhood education in the Sultanate of Oman. In G. A. Woodill, J. Bernhard, & L. Prochner (Eds.), *International handbook of early childhood education* (pp. 407–416). New York: Garland.

Bailey, D. B. (1989). Issues and directions in preparing professionals to work with young handicapped children and their families. In J. J. Gallagher, P. L. Trohanis, & R. M. Clifford (Eds.), *Policy implementation and P. L. 99-457: Planning for young children with special needs* (pp. 97–132). Baltimore: Paul Brookes.

Bailey, D. B., & Wolery, M. (1992). *Teaching infants and preschoolers with disabilities,* 2nd ed., New York: Macmillan Publishing Company.

Bloom, B. (1964). *Stability and change in human characteristics.* New York: Wiley.

Bredekamp, S. (Ed.) (1987). *Developmentally appropriate practice in early childhood programs serving children from birth through age 8.* Washington, DC: National Association for the Education of Young Children.

Cicirelli, V. G., Evans, J. W., & Schiller, J. S. (1969). *The impact of Head Start: An evaluation of the effects of Head Start on children's cognitive and affective development.* Report to the U.S. Office of Economic Opportunity by Westinghouse Learning Corporation and Ohio University. Washington, DC: Government Printing Office.

Cole, M., & Bruner, J. S. (1972). Preliminaries to a theory of cultural differences. In I. J. Gordon (Ed.), *Early childhood education. The seventy-first yearbook of the National Society for the Study of Education, Part II.* Chicago: University of Chicago Press.

Cook, R. E., Tessier, A., & Klein, M. D. (1992). *Adapting early childhood curricula for children with special needs,* 3rd ed., Upper Saddle River, NJ: Merrill/Prentice Hall.

Day, D. E. (1983). *Early childhood education.* Palo Alto, CA: Scott, Foresman and Company.

Dedja, B. (1992). The development of preschool and primary education in People's Socialist republic of Albania. In G. A. Woodill, J. Bernhard, & L. Prochner (Eds.), *International handbook of early childhood education* (pp. 21–30). New York: Garland.

deMause, L. (Ed.) (1974). *The history of childhood.* New York: The Psychohistory Press.

Fallen, N. H., & Umansky, W. (1985). *Young children with special needs,* 2nd ed., Upper Saddle River, NJ: Merrill/Prentice Hall.

Fowler, W. (1962). Cognitive learning in infancy and early childhood. *Psychological Bulletin, 59,* 116–152.

Freud, S. (1953). Three essays on sexuality. In *Standard edition* (Vol. 7). London: Hogarth.

Froebel, F. (1895). *Pedagogics of the kindergarten.* Translated by Josephine Jarvis. New York: Appleton.

Gesell, A. L. (1923). *The preschool child.* New York: Macmillan.

Gordon, A., & Browne, K. W. (1993). *Beginnings and beyond.* Albany, NY: Delmar Publishers.

Gormuyor, J. N. (1992). Early childhood education in Liberia. In G. A. Woodill, J. Bernhard, & L. Prochner (Eds.), *International handbook of early childhood education* (pp. 337–342). New York: Garland.

Greenleaf, B. K. (1978). *Children through the ages: A history of childhood.* New York: McGraw-Hill.

Haskins, R. (1989). Beyond metaphor: The efficacy of early childhood education. *American Psychologist, 44,* 274–282.

HEW reports 13 percent of Head Start children are handicapped. (1978). *Report of Preschool Education,* 10.

Heward, W. L., & Orlansky, M. D. (1992). *Exceptional children,* 4th ed., New York: Macmillan Publishing.

Hewes, D., & Hartman, B. (1974). *Early childhood education: A workbook for administrators.* 2nd Ed., San Francisco: R & E Associates.

Hunt, J. M. (1961). *Intelligence and experience.* New York: Ronald Press.

Itard, J. M. G. (1962). *The wild boy of Aveyron.* New York: Appleton-Century-Crofts.

Jensen, A. R. (1969). How much can we boost I. Q. and scholastic achievement? *Harvard Educational Review, 39,* 1–123.

Kaul, V. (1992). Early childhood education in India. In G. A. Woodill, J. Bernhard, & L. Prochner (Eds.), *International handbook of early childhood education* (pp. 275–292). New York: Garland.

Koppelman, J. (Ed.). (1986). Reagan signs bill expanding services to handicapped preschoolers. *Report to Preschool Programs, 18*(21), 3–4.

Labov, W. (1972). *Language in the inner city.* Philadelphia: University of Pennsylvania Press.

Laing, Z., & Pang, L. (1992). Early childhood education in the People's Republic of China. In G. A. Woodill, J. Bernhard, & L. Prochner (Eds.), *International handbook of early childhood education* (pp. 169–174). New York: Garland.

Monau, R. (1992). Early childhood education in Botswana. In G. A. Woodill, J. Bernhard, & L. Prochner (Eds.), *International handbook of early childhood education* (pp. 111–118). New York: Garland.

Montessori, M. (1964). *The Montessori method.* Cambridge, MA: Robert Bentley.

Noguchi, I., Ogawa, S., Yoshida, T., & Hashimoto, S. (1992). Early education in Japan: From ancient times to the present. In G. A. Woodill, J. Bernhard, & L. Prochner (Eds.), *International handbook of early childhood education* (pp. 317–326). New York: Garland.

Pestalozzi, J. H. (1915). *How Gertrude teaches her children.* (L. E. Holand, & F. C. Turner, Trans.) Syracuse, NY: C. W. Bordeen. (Originally published 1801).

Pierce, W. D., & Epling, W. F. (1995). *Behavior analysis and learning.* Englewood Cliffs, NJ: Prentice Hall.

Rousseau, J. J. (1969). *Emile.* (A. Bloom, Trans.). New York: Basic Books. (Originally published 1762).

Schapera, I. (1971). *Married life in an African tribe.* London: Pelican Books.

Skeels, H. M. (1966). Adult status of children with contrasting early life experiences. *Monographs of the Society for Research in Child Development, 31,* (Serial No. 105).

Skeels, H. M., & Dye, H. B. (1939). A study of the effects of differential stimulation on mentally retarded children. *Convention Proceedings, American Association of Mental Deficiency, 44,* 114–136.

Smith, M. S., & Bissell, J. S. (1970). Report analysis: The impact of Head Start. *Harvard Educational Review, 40,* 51–104.

Thorndike, E. L. (1913). *The psychology of learning.* New York: Teachers College Press, Columbia University.

United States Comptroller General. (1981, September 30). *Disparities still exist in who gets special education.* Report to the chairman, Subcommittee on Select Education, Committee on Education and Labor, House of Representatives of the United States.

Warger, C. (1988). *A resource guide to public school early childhood programs.* Alexandria, VA: Association for Supervision and Curriculum Development.

Watson, J. B. (1914). *Behavior.* New York: Henry Holt.

Williams, L. R. (1992). Determining the curriculum. In C. Seefeldt (Ed.), *The early childhood curriculum; A review of current research* (pp. 1–15) 2nd ed. New York: Teachers College Press.

Wolery, M., Strain, P. S., & Bailey, D. B. (1992). Reaching potentials of children with special needs. In S. Bredekamp & T. Rosegrant (Eds.), *Reaching potentials: Appropriate curriculum and assessment for young children* (Vol. 1) (pp. 92–111). Washington, DC: National Association for the Education of Young Children.

Woodill, G. A. (1992). International early childhood care and education: Historical perspectives. In G. A. Woodill, J. Bernhard, & L. Prochner (Eds.), *International handbook of early childhood education* (pp. 3–10). New York: Garland.

Woodill, G.A., J. Bernhard, & L. Prochner (Eds.). (1992). *International handbook of early childhood education* (pp. 3–10). New York: Garland.

Wyman, A. (January, 1995). The earliest early childhood teachers: Women teachers of America's dame schools. *Young Children,* 29–32.

Zigler, E., & Muenchow, S. (1992). *Head Start: The inside story of America's most successful educational experiment.* New York: Basic Books.

Zinsser, C. (October, 1984). The best day care there ever was. *Working Mother,* 76–78.

Families of Children with Disabilities

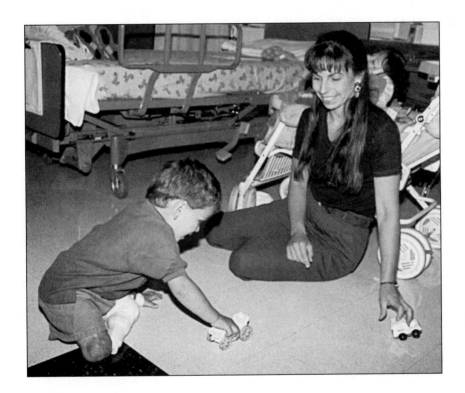

Efforts of the past 20 years to identify and isolate the variables associated with family functioning have fallen short of expected understanding. While some progress has been made, it now appears that neither professionals, parents, nor other caregivers are especially pleased with the current state of practice. Such knowledge of inadequacy is, at best, uncomfortable. This story, told by a mother, exemplifies the frustration of many.

> *There once was a mother of a child with autism. She lived the rather steady life of a mother of an exceptional child in the late 1980s and early 1990s. She accessed resources and participated in an infant and early childhood intervention program. She learned the laws and she learned about the school system. She could speak in*

acronyms as well as anyone. In short, she learned the "politics of service." When her child was 10 years old, she decided to become a special educator and enrolled in a master's degree program. In the course of her studies—in the course of one classroom discussion—she revealed that she was actually rather embarrassed to be associated with special educators. While special educators "knew their content," they had, for the last 10 years, failed to "know her" at all. And in failing to know her, they really had failed to know the needs of her family and her son.

For over three decades, researchers, health care professionals, and educators have occupied themselves with determining the factors that lead to appropriate intervention for infants, toddlers, and preschoolers with special needs. To a lesser extent, these professionals have investigated the processes for developing effective relationships with the parents or caregivers of these children. The perspectives held about parents were many: parent as the chief designer of a child's environment (manager of behaviors), parent as partner in assessment, parent as the agent of intervention (nurse, teacher), parent as advocate, and, sometimes, parent as parent.

Assumptions made about families were equally plentiful. For example, it was long believed that families of children with disabilities adapted to their situations more negatively than families of children without disabilities. Certain researchers hypothesized higher levels of marital disintegration (Farber, 1960), elevated levels of marital dissatisfaction (Friedrich & Friedrich, 1981), and greater psychological dysfunction, especially in mothers (Cummings, Bayley, & Rie, 1966; Holroyd, 1974). Some research assumed that rearing a child with a disability was inherently stressful and that affected families formed a generally homogenous group (Byrne & Cunningham, 1985; Crnic, Friedrich, & Greenberg, 1983; Farber and Rowitz, 1986). Of particular concern were higher levels of disintegration among siblings (Farber, 1960; Gath, 1973; Grossman, 1972). The results of such studies led to the design and implementation of family intervention programs focused on the difficulties experienced by families who received little or no public support.

In the 1980s, due in large part to the escalating volume of parent voices, a number of events altered the relationship between professionals and parents, which had historically been one in which parents were passive recipients of public services. During the 1980s and 1990s, significant changes were made in available service options and the format of those options. Hence, service providers began serious programs of reeducation. At the same time, there were refinements of legal mandates to support families of children with disabilities, including a call for interagency cooperation and coordination. Perhaps most prominently, the posture of parents of children with disabilities shifted from that of being receivers of services to being designers of their own programs. The overall effect of such shifts was a state of current practice that may be ahead of research.

HISTORICAL AND FUTURE POSSIBILITIES

The philosophies guiding work with families of children with disabilities that have emerged in the mid-1990s are substantially different from their predecessors. The most substantial difference is the current understanding of parents or caregivers as managers and the professional as assistant to the parent. This new paradigm has emerged with various names: family-centered services, person-centered services, family empowerment, consumer empowerment, family-driven assessments, and self-determination. Contemporary family-oriented early intervention programs can be traced to the infant and preschool initiatives of the 1960s and 1970s and can be organized in several phases (Weissbourd, 1987; Weissbourd & Kagan, 1989; Zigler & Black, 1989).

During the early 1960s, grass-root initiatives rose from families of children with disabilities. The Family Resource Coalition (FRC) is an example of this self-advocacy. The FRC was an organization of more than 2000 family support programs and was dedicated to the development of community-based programs for supporting and strengthening family functioning (Weissbourd, 1987; Weissbourd & Kagan, 1989; Zigler & Black, 1989).

The 1970s saw greater involvement in special education and early education from state governments. National mandates fostered increased state participation and led to the establishment of policies and programs poised to support and strengthen all families of young children, not just those families deemed most at risk (Weiss, 1989). Still, interventions were generally child-focused with a problem-solution format.

Community-based endeavors supported by federal funding grew in the early 1980s. Family-oriented and community-based efforts were supported by the U.S. Department of Health and Human Services through the Division of Maternal and Child Health. The intent was to make available the supports and resources required by families of health-impaired and medically fragile children (Brewer, McPherson, Magrab, & Hutchins, 1989; Shelton, Jeppson, & Johnson, 1987). Efforts were made to incorporate parents and families as informed and participating members of the intervention team. Interventions included child-focused and parent-focused perspectives.

In the mid-to-late 1980s, yet another shift occurred in the way families and communities responded to persons with disabilities. At least 42 states supported legislative initiatives for persons with developmental disabilities and their families. This movement placed emphasis on the "important role the family members or the community can play in enhancing the lives of persons with disabilities, especially when necessary support services were provided" (U.S. Senate Report 100-113, 1987, pp. 1–2). Services shifted from client-oriented or parent-focused to an approach aimed at establishing partnerships with parents.

During the 1990s, parents and families have worked to recapture their autonomy from public service agencies. Intervention and other supportive opportunities have become family-centered as opposed to parent-child or child oriented. The purpose of intervention today includes the enabling of parents to become long-term, independent, informed advocates for their children (Dunst, 1985; Simeonsson & Bailey, 1990; Meisels & Shonkoff, 1990).

FAMILY AND PROFESSIONAL RELATIONSHIPS

In the decade ahead, it is likely that our most accurate understanding of families of children with disabilities will come from four sources:

1. **family sociology,** which focuses on the enduring dimensions of family life that can be observed in all families (Epstein, Bishop, & Baldwin, 1982; Olson, Russell, & Sprenkle, 1983)

2. **family systems theory,** which approaches families as complex organizations in which internal and external variables affect all members (Walsh, 1980)

3. **family life-cycle theory,** which assumes families have a fairly predictable life cycle governing their growth, development, and functioning (Carter & McGoldrick, 1980)

4. **ethnographic** and other forms of qualitative research generated by parents themselves or by researchers in collaboration with families

Now, as in the future, families are to be regarded as complex systems with their own integrity, fluidity, and organizational coherence (Krauss & Jacobs, 1990).

Current early intervention goals for families of children with disabilities represent a paradigm shift from the professional as leader to the parent as leader. In many cases, the work and the support of families in times of unsteadiness will come from other parents. It is equally possible that parents will be the primary decision makers in much, if not all, of the services provided. Well-educated professionals should be in the position of assisting, not directing—of taking a supporting role, not the leading role.

A Philosophy of Association

Before engaging in professional relationships with families and family systems, it is wise for early childhood professionals to develop and articulate a **philosophy of association.** A philosophy of association is the set of values and guidelines one holds as one interacts with others. In working with families of children with disabilities, a philosophy of association should include attitudes and values about listening and leadership. A well-developed philosophy of association is critical because educators and other professionals are often the first to have sustained and continuous interactions with families. The influence of these professionals is both subtle and obvious; always, it is powerful.

Whether or not it is part of a professional's intent, parents listen carefully to the messages professionals send. Some parents have learned to rely on professionals because they have unwittingly taught parents to do so. A professional voice of authority is commanding and reinforced by so many societal structures that many parents, even in the current and evolving culture of parental empowerment, still question their own judgment when set against the recommendation of a professional. Many parents, especially at the beginning of a working relationship, follow professional advice without much reflection. The implication of this passivity is that professionals control without necessarily intending to do so. The relationship is further complicated by the reality that some parents find comfort in the stability of a professional's guidance. Again, having a well-developed philosophy of association will help professionals and parents remind themselves of the type of relationship they wish to have.

At the beginning of professional associations, it is quite clear that parents need information. Depending on many factors, including caregiver adaptability to a "life script" they did not choose, they may need to rely on professional recommendations more at the beginning of the relationship and less later. They will want to know clearly what a professional or support person thinks is the right way to proceed. At the same time, parents and other caregivers are going to monitor technical competencies, and, in the end, they are going to make a judgment to place or not place their trust in the person(s) hoping to serve them.

For example, one mother who was told by a pediatric specialist that her five-month-old child (later diagnosed with autism) was unresponsive because he was blind, retorted, "He is not blind." That was the beginning of her distrust of professionals. In another case, professionals refused to acknowledge a father's descriptions of his son's myoclonic seizures, assuring the father that his child was tantruming. The father tried to throw his child into the car and rush him to the doctor's office before a seizure ended so that the parents' concerns would be taken seriously. It was only when the father videotaped his son and showed the film to the doctors that diagnostic tests, which confirmed the father's concerns, were ordered.

Should caregivers honor professionals with their trust, that trust is often expansive. The relationship may start with "What are we to do in this situation?" but it will evolve over time to include the service provider's thoughts regarding a broad range of issues not limited to the selection of an appropriate and useful family assessment model or the development of an Individual Family Service Plan (IFSP) or an Individual Education Program (IEP). Without willful intent, the relationship may develop to a point when the focus shifts from professional to personal, for example, how to deal with extended family members or other sensitive personal and family issues.

If a professional associates well with a family, if trust becomes a mutually attained dimension of the parent-professional relationship, services provided will flourish. As time passes, the early role of professional as primary leader should shift to a more inclusive construct of shared leadership. In such a partnership, neither professional nor parent leads or follows alone.

Achieving a level of mutual empowerment begins with the ability to listen well. Depending on a professional's life experiences, educational opportunities, and sophistication of communication skills, an early childhood professional will be able to respond to the explicit and implicit needs of families to varying degrees. Initially, listening well enables a service provider to assume the role each family most needs at any given point: leader, support person, resource, technician, and so on. Unfortunately, listening well is not an innate skill. It must be consciously developed. Like any skill, it is a result of using good techniques, recognizing personal procedures or habits that are ineffective or destructive, and repeatedly using those behaviors and attitudes that are effective. Active, participatory listening requires professionals to be well versed in communication skills and to have an understanding of the psychological dimensions of parenting, family life, and family systems.

Last, early childhood professionals cannot serve well unless there is an established philosophy of leadership. Developing a personal and professional philosophy of leadership helps professionals distinguish between actions that expand one's ego strength and those that truly are a service to others.

The Social Construct of Family

The notion of "family" was more obvious in the 1950s, and the stereotyped idea of a nuclear family held steady until recently. For many years, a commonly accepted definition of a family was a group consisting of two parents with one, two, or more children. Representing a philosophical shift and more inclusive social norms, the definition of family used hereafter is altered and expanded to include a group consisting of at least one child with at least one parent or caregiver.

Whether discussion focuses on families of children with disabilities or families of children without disabilities, the reality is that many family units are not composed of two parents. While statistics vary, it is now probable that professionals supporting families will be working with many families that consist of one parent with one or two children, headed by either a mother or father. Furthermore, in two-parent households, it is likely that families will consist of a blend of children from at least one previous marriage and will consequently include multiple family systems. Other family configurations include:

"One's images of family or parent influences one's ability to interact with a family in an empowering manner."
—*Mary F. Sinclair*

- Extended family members as primary caregivers (grandmother, grandfather, aunt, or uncle)
- Same sex parenting partners
- Families without homes
- Families built through adoption or foster care

Each of these family configurations adds to the complexity of interactions between families and professionals. Table 9.1 highlights some of the factors that may be involved in diverse family structures and the impact of these variations on family relationships with professionals.

Family Needs

All families have a series of needs, though a majority of families do not require the assistance of outside agencies to meet their needs. Family needs were first summarized and identified by Turnbull, Summers, and Brotherson (1984) and have since been expanded and revised by others (Dunst, Trivette, & Deal, 1988). Economic needs head the list and include issues of money for necessities, budgeting financial resources, maintaining a stable income, and saving money for the future. Physical needs and desires are for a clean environment, adequate housing, sufficient heat and water, and safe neighborhoods. Food and clothing requirements necessitate healthy diets and enough appropriate clothes for each season.

Families must have available routine and emergency health care and want to have confidence in their medical and dental professionals. Families need the opportunity to work and

Table 9.1/ *Variables that Make Family-Professional Interaction Challenging*

Situation	Impact
Family structure	Loyalties, power, complex and varying rules under similar conditions, transitions between dwellings, availability of equipment
Child-care requirements	Availability of child care for infants, toddlers, and young children with disabilities, debates with child-care providers about the realities of serving children with disabilities, financial burdens
Single-parent families	Time and resource management, single-parent income, transportation issues, ill-child responsibilities, possible conflict with personal goals, increased need for respite care
Nontraditional partnerships	Prejudice of service providers and local community, debates over "proper parenting authority," legal authority issues
Poverty	Prejudice of service providers toward poor persons, lack of transportation to get to and from services, possible lack of phone services, possible lack of a permanent address
Substance abuse	Immediate impact on the person engaging in the abuse, subsequent impact on immediate and extended family members, inability to keep priorities in desired order, secondary health issues, guilt, shame
Foster care	No long term goals or personal authority, lack of accurate history

to feel job satisfaction and job security. Transportation for family members to and from resources, a means of communicating by telephone, and having contact with relatives are also critical. Many families also seek adult or continuing education opportunities in order to move from inadequate, low-wage jobs to employment that will give their families more security. Opportunities to play and interact with one's own children and to provide appropriate child education and intervention are also critical. Early childhood professionals must not only be aware of these needs but able to identify and recommend community resources that can support families in meeting these needs.

Child care is important in most families, whether it be for help in routine daily care or in emergency situations. The availability and affordability of recreational activities for individual family members and for the total family are also important. An emotional need exists for positive intrafamily relationships, rewarding relationships outside the family, peer companionship, and a sense of belonging to the community. Finally, opportunities to share ethnic or value-related experiences and access to a community of like-minded peers is important.

Family Hardiness

In addition to the basic needs or desires of all families, researchers have identified stressors that may be prominent in families of children with disabilities. **Acute stressors** occur as periodic incidents related to a child's disability; **chronic stressors** include concerns about the future, financial limitations, and society's acceptance of human differences; and last, **transition stressors** are linked to significant milestones, such as entry into school, that occur throughout a child's lifespan. Put in the context of need, Failla and Jones (1991) concluded that, based on these unique stressors, there is a need for family **hardiness.** Hardiness was defined as a constellation of three dimensions that includes:

1. A sense of control or the ability to influence events rather than being controlled by them

2. A commitment to becoming actively involved in events and viewing them as meaningful

3. Recognition of life changes as opportunities for growth and development, not a burden to bear (Kobasa, Maddi, & Puccetti, 1982; Pollack, 1986)

Throughout the course of a child's life, services and providers will come and go. The primary functions and needs of a family may vacillate. Cultural and community norms may expand or contract, and society's acceptance of exceptional persons is uncertain. Funding and research in the area of early childhood education and intervention will undoubtedly pass through highs and lows. What will remain constant in all this will be the children and their families, however formed.

Leadership

Leadership is about spending one's days seeking the truth, acting on that truth, and bringing about the potentiality in another (Peters, 1992; Senge, 1990; Wheatley, 1992). Leadership, in its fullest essence, is about the skillful diminishing of the self in an effort to empower others. Leading is to know and remember that one's own energy (knowledge, skill, wisdom) is to be transferred to others; that the outcome of leadership is not control, but the creation of new freedoms for others.

Leadership is not about being the authority. An authority on a particular subject or issue is a content or technical expert. An expert may or may not be a leader. What an expert has is knowledge—not all the knowledge, and oftentimes not even the right knowledge for a particular situation. The role of an expert is to use that information in response to a need or to help others use information in response to a need. When an expert does not share knowledge but, instead, does for the parents what the parents could do themselves, the professional retains power and consequently keeps the parents in a dependent position. Power is the ability to influence another. Used well, power can empower and make others independent. With such a mental construct or understanding, a powerful individual seeks to teach another what he or she knows.

It is likely that families will rely on professional expertise when they first enter into a working relationship. Many professionals find this transfer of confidence to be highly satisfying and interpret such contributions as giving meaning to their careers. A professional's ego as expert is reinforced, thereby, making it more difficult for him or her to remember that self-diminishment, not self-enhancement, is desired. Because the goal is empowerment, not control, professionals cannot stay in the expert mode for long. Ultimately, power needs to shift so that family members can act confidently on their own behalf. In short, leading well means helping each member gain or regain his or her own energy and reliance on self.

THE EMOTIONAL FUNCTIONING OF FAMILIES

Events of the current decade pose a unique and compelling dilemma for professionals working with families of children who have special needs. From 1960 through 1980, a large body of research was compiled that indicated families of children with disabilities, as compared to families of children without disabilities, were at increased risk for stress (Kazak, 1986) and depression (Cox, Rutter, Newman, & Bartak, 1975), had different family coping strategies or styles (McCubbin, et al., 1982), had less family cohesion (Darling, 1979), had more family strain (Roth, 1982), and experienced greater social isolation (Breslau, 1983). Subsequently, both researchers and theorists assumed that these families had an increased risk of family dysfunction. Research of the 1990s, which focuses less on the pathology of deficiency, has been more expansive and indicates that many of the early research assumptions can be and should be questioned. It now appears that the psychosocial functioning of families of children with disabilities is more like that of families of children without disabilities than it is different from them. Though extensive needs are expressed by all families, those with children who have disabilities face a different set of obstacles.

For many, parenting becomes more difficult from the first moments a disability is diagnosed. After a review of the literature, Moore, Howard, and McLaughlin (1995) concluded that all families have needs; it just so happens that for families of children with disabilities, the obstacles are those of a child with special needs. Other families must deal with issues of poverty, mental illness, child abuse, divorce, drugs, or death of family members, but not of a child with a disability. According to Moore et al., these factors do not make families special, unusual, dysfunctional, or in any way homogeneous.

Parental Responses to Diagnosis of a Disability

Parents unexpectedly faced with the loss of hopes and expectations often proceed through several common stages, ranging from total disbelief and bewilderment to the ability to grasp and control the situation. While every parent or couple responds to a diagnosis of a disability in accord with their own external and internal resources, researchers have found some common themes experienced by many parents. These phases or stages were first identified by Dr. Elizabeth Kubler-Ross in her classic research with cancer patients over two decades ago (Kubler-Ross, 1969) and were initially referred to as the grief cycle.

Over the last decade, professionals working with parents of at-risk infants or infants in crisis have recognized that many, though not all, parents proceed through the same or similar phases (Featherstone, 1980; Turnbull & Turnbull, 1985). Today, many professionals in early childhood refer to Kubler-Ross's reaction cycle as **stage theory response.**

Stage theory response is useful primarily to parents who find that naming their complex emotions helps order them and enables them to talk with others who have similar experiences. Knowledge of stage theory response also helps professionals validate parental emotions.

However, when it is used to label parents or to associate a pathology with a particular stage, stage theory response is badly misused. Perhaps most important, it is necessary to realize that passage through grief, like any other life passage, is not a sign of dysfunction but of normalcy.

The stages, or phases, described are neither sequential nor of equal duration, intensity, or frequency in reoccurrence, either within or across families. Parents often report that the stages overlap and almost always reoccur, often at periods of significant transition. Studies by Allen and Affleck (1985) indicated that for some parents, a stage may last one day or one year. What is important to know and remember about the grief or adjustment process is that knowledge of the process often helps parents to understand that these common emotional behaviors are shared by many others in similar circumstances. The key components of the stage theory, or grief process, as described by Kubler-Ross and subsequent researchers (Francis & Jones, 1984; Seligman & Darling, 1989) are shock and denial, anger and frustration, volatile emotions (hope, isolation, depression), bargaining, and, finally, acceptance or reestablishment. Cook, Tessier, and Klein (1992) outlined several ways in which early childhood professionals can support parents through each of these stages (see Table 9.2).

Anderegg, Vergason, and Smith (1992) studied the grief process with 130 parents. Their work led to the development of a slightly different model still supportive of earlier work. This later research indicated that parents and extended family members pass through three phases:

1. Confronting (denial, blame/guilt, shock)

2. Adjusting (depression, anger, bargaining)

3. Adapting (life-cycle changes, realistic planning, adjusting expectations)

A number of factors account for a family's ability to reach a point of adjustment and acceptance. Among the most significant factors are the characteristics of a child's exceptionality, the degree of exceptionality, and, in particular, the demands of an exceptionality (Turnbull & Turnbull, 1990). Werner and Smith (1982) found that family configuration (e.g., single-parent family, blended family), family size, and the socioeconomic status also affected a family's ability to cope and adjust.

Again, the apparent usefulness of stage theory research is that it gives parents a description of what is happening to them during a period that is otherwise overwhelming and foreign. It provides parents with descriptive language that links their experiences with the experiences of veteran parents. The passage from diagnosis to adaptation is cyclical and complex. Some parents feel they never really move out of a low-grade sadness that seems to permeate their lives. The important thing to remember is that shifts do take place. The early panic that follows the diagnosis of an infant in crisis changes and develops according to healthy patterns of adaptation.

Still, it is necessary to be cautious in applying stage theory response to any particular parent or family. Parents arrive at adjustment in many ways and the sequence and time needed are different for every parent (Allen & Affleck, 1985; Bradley, Knoll, & Agosta, 1992; Schell, 1981). Stage theory response has a distinct psychiatric flavor, which may imply that parents are maladjusted and need counseling when, in fact, they are responding normally (Roos, 1985).

COMMUNICATION BETWEEN PARENTS AND EARLY INTERVENTION PROFESSIONALS

Communication, in its most basic form, is the ability of two or more people to send and receive messages. Of all the skills expected of early childhood professionals, communication skills rank among the most necessary. Based on one of the authors' experience as a parent with a child in a neonatal intensive care unit, Hunt and Marshall (1994) summarized five items to which early childhood professionals must attend if they are to have successful associations

Table 9.2/ *Stage Theory Response and How Professionals Should Support Parents*

Stages and Responses	Support Needed
Shock, Disbelief, and Denial: May be accompanied by feelings of shame, guilt, and unworthiness. Parents may try to deny the existing problems. Parents may go from doctor to doctor seeking opinions. Some may refuse to accept guidance.	Convey to parents that these feelings are appropriate. Listen with acceptance. Help parents focus on ways professionals can work with them to benefit the child. Become active listeners through patience and practice.
Anger and Resentment: Parents may direct anger at the very professionals who are trying to help and be suspicious about a professional's motives. Verbal abuse is common, and parents try to prove the professional to be wrong about their child.	Professionals must be understanding, compassionate, and gently caring. They should get parents busy with child activities that cannot fail. Refuse to blame or react to unreasonable demands.
Bargaining: Parents may work diligently as if to say, "If I do everything you tell me to do, then this problem will go away." If progress is not rapid, they may become severely depressed.	Be empathetic, recognize and accept the natural feelings of parents. Convey an attitude of interest and caring.
Depression and Discouragement: Hopelessness overtakes parents but may make them more likely to request assistance. Parents may be saying "good-bye" to the normal image of the child they held. Parents can begin to focus on productive solutions.	Focus on the positive but avoid overeagerness to get on with the intervention. Give parents activities that will be successful to avoid self-doubt. Avoid all criticism as well as unwarranted praise. Provide access to parent support groups.
Acceptance: Parents have an increasing willingness to do practical, useful activities. The child's needs are recognized, not denied. There may be a conviction that much needs to be done and will make a difference.	Encourage the parents to be patient and set realistic goals. Help parents read their child's cues. Praise the parents for the child's progress. Focus on positive interaction techniques.

Source: Adapted from Cook, R. E., Tessier, A., & Klein, M. D. (1992). *Adapting Early Childhood Curricula for Children with Special Needs.* Upper Saddle River, NJ: Merrill/Prentice Hall.

with parents. Careful reflection on the list reveals that three of the five items deal explicitly or implicitly with communication skills:

1. Do whatever you can to help the parent think of his or her child as a person and an individual.

2. Promote attachment between the parent and the child.

3. Listen.

4. Try not to be judgmental. Talk to parents about your concerns.

5. Get older siblings involved in the child's life as early and as meaningfully as possible.

CASE STUDY

Advice for Teachers

Interview with David DeWolf

The most important thing is to try to treat the child with a disability with as much similarity to other children as possible. Hold them, in so far as possible, to similar expectations—behavioral, cognitive, and emotional. Your instinct is to compensate for their disability, and you think the way to show concern is by doing special things for them to show that you really care. On the other hand, one of the greatest gifts to a child, particularly a child with a disability who may be separated from other children by the physical limitations of their disability, is to really give them a sense of inclusion, that they are really part of a group of children. You have to find the commonality and the points of similarity, which may involve getting past some superficial difference in order to tap into the point at which they're a child no different from any other child. That is an important gift.

As far as treating parents, my advice would be, to be brave in addressing issues. Sometimes, people are afraid to step on toes, and so, they tend to leave things unsaid or unspoken. That leads to confusion or may inadvertently communicate a lack of concern or caring or thought. I know I do this myself. If someone has had a death in the family, I talk about other things, thinking I'm being a good person by keeping their mind off this painful subject, when sometimes what they want to do is talk about that very thing. It requires a bit of courage to address issues in a very straightforward fashion. There is certainly the risk that the parent may be offended, or you may inadvertently touch a sensitive nerve, and you're going to make some mistakes and say the wrong thing. But I think you're better off in the long run—taking some risks, making some mistakes, and getting better at it, than being too cautious about being direct. Even when it's painful, I think that the truth is more healing in the long run than euphemisms.

At the same time, I think that it is important to treat the child's disability in context. This is a child with a disability rather than a disability attached to

a carrier. Sometimes you can get like a doctor; you get so tied up with the disease, and forget that a real live person is connected to it. You may think you're being good by devoting all your professional energy to the disability, but sometimes, you need to pull back and see the disability as a small part of a much larger person. Parents need to be reassured that you love their child. One of the most important things is for them to feel their child is in the hands of someone who really does care about the child.

This may be tough to do. It's hard to like your own children all of the time. But if you can do that and communicate it, that is what parents really appreciate. The bonds between you and the parents are much closer when you make a friend of a child with a disability. Parents can appreciate a teacher or a coach, but they really appreciate

(continued)

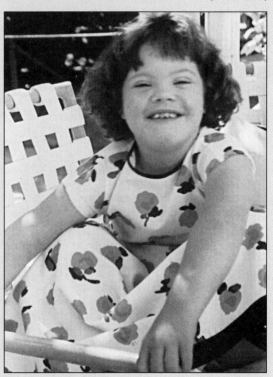

ROBIN DEWOLF

those people who can see in their child that special quality that lots of other people look away from. There are a lot of parents with a child whose disability causes other people to look away. Think of how much that must hurt, and how desperately they want somebody to really like their child and see their child's good qualities.

It's hard to do it all the time, but if you can find the strength to engage at that level, that's the most important thing for a parent. I think that it's far more important than any of the technical skills, though there are many wonderful technical skills that you can learn. As a parent, I would rather have a person who knew nothing about the technical skills, but liked my kid and liked to play with him or work with her. I would pick that person any day over someone who had all of the technical skills in the world, but didn't care.

Communicating well does not mean that each professional should interact with parents according to a rigid set of guidelines. Prerequisite to effective communication is learning the strengths and weaknesses of one's own interaction style and understanding how one's words and actions are interpreted. In short, effective communication grasps, with clarity, the difference between the intent of what is said and the interpretation of the message by the receiver.

For early childhood professionals, communication is complicated by the number of systems in which one must work and the precision of technical languages associated with the many and varied fields. For parents, communication becomes difficult because it involves learning the languages of multiple disciplines, subdisciplines, and agency and interagency systems, nearly all of which are initially foreign. As parents and caregivers are deciphering language, they are also deeply involved in developing a wide range of personal and professional associations.

Communication becomes even more difficult depending on added factors, which may include the complexity of the system of services involved, an individual's ability to engage in assertive communication, and one's ability to deal effectively with stereotypes and judgments. Left unattended, communication can quickly deteriorate into a pattern of parental frustrations and adversarial relationships (Linz, McAnally, & Wieck, 1982). Several basic communication concepts or skills can enhance relationships between parents and professionals. These involve active listening, perception checks, and ways to accurately state needs.

Active Listening

Active listening means that listeners (receivers of information) are attentive to a speaker on multiple levels: hearing, interpreting, sorting, and analyzing (see Table 9.3). It is the opposite of passive listening in which the recipient hears without understanding the intended message and without responding appropriately to the speaker. To illustrate the difference between active and passive listening, and ultimately, the effect they both have on communication and learning, one has only to consider some high school or college level courses.

Classes that are intriguing and stimulating allow the learner/listener to enter into the lecture, discussion, and debate almost effortlessly. In such classes, note-taking takes its proper priority of classroom activities and becomes neither a burden nor an obsession. Classes that employ almost exclusively and methodically the lecture mode, on the other hand, reinforce the dictation response to information (passive listening). Students often take meticulous notes but spend little time in class processing or responding to any of the information. In such cases, the communication is one-way. That is, information passes to the listener, who assumes the passive role.

When active listening is done well, relationships develop between the sender and the listener: partners hear and can respond to what their counterpart is saying; parents and children

Table 9.3/ *Active Listening*

Skills	Description
Hearing	Understands and comprehends the words (spoken or written)
Interpreting	Is attentive to nuances, the larger context of the statement, and the political, cultural, and emotional dimensions of comments
Sorting	Categorizes information with other like information to increase the meaning or clarify intent
Analyzing	Compares information with other knowledge about the topic and draws conclusions

learn that what they have to say is important and respected; and professionals increase the probability that the right supports will be given parents. Unlike passive listening, which involves only one sender, active listening is an inclusive engagement between and among people.

Binding and Freeing Statements

Binding communications are habits of interaction that generally close or diminish the probability of continued conversation. By contrast, freeing communications are those habits of interaction that actually encourage expanded dialogue. The following examples illustrate a few habits that often lead to binding communications:

- Giving an overly enthusiastic response—responses that are generally based on what would be best for you
- Changing the subject without explanation
- Explaining others' behavior by interpreting their history (You act this way because your mother acted this way)
- Providing direct advice and even persuasion (If I were you, this is what I would do)
- Setting up expectations that bind the speaker to the past; this disallows change and innovation (You've never acted this way before; what's wrong?)
- Communicating expectations that bind the speaker to the future (I'm sure you'll figure this out and do such and such)
- Denying feelings (You really don't mean that! Or, You really don't feel that way, do you?)
- Over generalizing (Everyone feels that way); this diminishes the other; makes one feel like one's feelings or experiences really do not matter much
- Approving on personal grounds: praising the other for thinking, feeling, or acting in ways that you agree with, for conforming to your standards
- Disapproving on personal grounds: blaming or censuring the other for thinking, feeling, or acting in ways you do not like
- Commanding and ordering: telling the other what to do (including, Tell me what to do)
- Obligating emotionally: controlling through arousing feelings of shame and inferiority (How can you do this to me when I have done so much for you?)

In summary, **binding statements** are those comments that diminish the listener's desire to continue the conversation. **Freeing statements,** such as "go on," "tell me more," "how do you feel about that?" actually increase the speaker's desire to continue and increase both personal autonomy and power. As a note of caution, professionals must use these statements sincerely and avoid assuming a therapeutic tone.

Avoiding Killer Phrases   Killer phrases range from those comments that discourage further comment to those that break a person's spirit. Appropriately named for the effect they have on communication, killer phrases are generally (though not always), uttered in moments of frustration, anger, or depression. Early childhood professionals should recognize killer phrases and attribute no more to them than indications of weariness. As for the language of professionals, to the greatest extent possible, it should be void of killer phrases. The following are examples of killer phrases:

- It won't work.
- That's a swell idea, but...
- It's not in the budget.
- Good idea, but your family is different.
- It's all right in theory, but can you put it into practice?
- It's too academic (or it's too medical).
- We're rural (or we're too large).
- It's too simplistic.
- It needs more study.
- We've never done it that way.
- I haven't the time.
- I'm not ready for it.
- There are better ways than that!
- You haven't considered...
- Let's not step on anyone's toes.
- Why start anything now?
- The agency won't understand.

It is much easier for a professional to impose hurt on a parent than vice versa since professionals are generally supported in several ways by the power visited on them through training, social norms, and organizational structure. Therefore, the playing field is never level. In consideration of this relationship, professionals should prepare to weather killer phrases aimed at them without bowing to the temptation to respond in kind.

Allow and Respect "No"   Most novice professionals find themselves eager to pass on what they know and to support parents' decisions. Professionals simply do not set out to be offensive or to get in a family's way; yet it happens. It happens, against all intentions, because service providers fail to recognize the more basic needs of families, one of which is to not need a professional support person! In the course of each family or family system, there comes a time when parents and other members of the family want to be left alone. Families may weary of professional conversations and interactions; they may well have priorities not shared by professional support persons.

Not wanting to discourage or seem ungrateful, parents will find various and subtle ways to say "Stay away for now." For a shy parent, avoidance may begin by simply canceling meetings or calling in ill. Others will tell the professional that the timing is bad and reschedule for some distant date. In such situations, it is the responsibility of a professional to analyze the communication as carefully as possible and to draw and confirm a conclusion. When it becomes apparent that a parent is asking for some free space from professionals, support for that request needs to be forthcoming. If professionals are unclear about a parent's actual intent, they need only ask parents directly: "Would you like my assistance? Please feel free to say no." If the parent answers "no," that answer must be accepted with the same dignity afforded the opposite response. In short, allow parents and caregivers to say "no" to your support or services. (After all, it is their legal right to do so.) Then respect them for saying it.

Perception Checks   Sometimes, despite best efforts, it is difficult to draw an accurate conclusion regarding the intent of a speaker. When this happens, it is possible to draw on a communication skill called a **perception check.** A perception check means that listeners check their perception or understanding of what was said (e.g., the parent doesn't want to waste the specialist's Saturday morning) against what the speaker intended to say (e.g., "My oldest child was sick all night, and I'm exhausted. Please leave me alone!"). A perception check is executed not by asking the speaker to repeat what was just said, but by saying, "This is what I understand you to mean . . . ." This pattern allows the initial speaker to confirm or deny the perception.

Perception checks are especially important to use when more than two people are engaged in an interaction. During assessment sessions, in planning meetings, or in family consultations, early childhood professionals may find there is often a good deal of confusion about the intent or content of transactions or interactions. By using any of the following phrases, professionals can help keep the communication lines clear and open.

- I was listening to what you just said. Is (give explanation) what you mean?

- So many people have been offering comments. I'm a bit unsure of your position on (name the issue). Is (give explanation) what you meant?

- You just said, "no." Are you trying to accommodate my schedule, or is there really a better time for us to get together?

These three statements ask for clarification without judging the effectiveness or ability of the speaker.

Paraphrasing   **Paraphrasing** is another technique by which confirmation is obtained by restating the essence of the comment or conversation. In paraphrasing, listeners put into words what they think they have just heard. While a perception check seeks clarification (is this what you meant?), paraphrasing seeks right direction. In the latter, the listener accepts responsibility for interpretation (e.g., "Another way to say what you just said is..." or "So what you just said is..."). Paraphrasing conclusions or using paraphrasing to confirm what is to be done next are the two most commonly used and highly productive forms of paraphrasing.

Descriptions of Behavior versus Description of Feelings   There are a number of ways that parents, siblings, and professionals avoid participating in difficult or sensitive conversations. On one end of a continuum, people avoid engagement in difficult topics by withdrawing. On the other end of the continuum, people avoid a topic by engaging in unrelated conversations or behaviors. While these postures are perhaps admirable during a poker game, they generally complicate family discussions, interdisciplinary work, and most social interactions. When behaviors occur that range from withdrawal to unrelated engagement, there are two issues that must be confronted by listeners. First, what is the person indicating through her or his actions and words, or lack of action or words? Secondly, what is the parent, sibling, or professional really feeling?

Early childhood professionals working with parents and family members need to be especially aware of words, communication styles, and the feelings that ought to correspond to those words or gestures. For example, it is not uncommon to find a parent or professional colleague nodding the "yes" response, only to find out later they don't agree at all with what was being said. Because most human beings often experience a dissonance between what they intellectually believe and how they feel, professionals must be aware of descriptions of behaviors and descriptions of feelings.

Someone wishing to make clear the intent of a participant who suddenly pushes her chair back and withdraws from a discussion can interject, "I've noticed that you pulled out of the conversation [description of behavior]. Would you like to talk about what's going on for you at this time? [asking for description of feelings]." The person may well choose to say nothing because her feelings are still too close to the surface. In this case, the professional may return to the individual after a short while and ask again. The important thing to remember is to rest comfortably with a description of behavior (which is something you can see, feel, and observe) and refrain from making assumptions about feelings based on behavior (only your interpretation). A description of behavior can come from an observer; a description of feelings can come only from the person holding the feelings.

Expectations of Caregivers and Professionals

Most professionals are not too surprised that parents and caregivers draw conclusions about them and their usefulness rather quickly. That is, caregivers tend to conclude in a rather short amount of time whether a professional will be effective or ineffective. The reason this happens has little to do with the person being judged. Rather, it has mostly to do with the experiences caregivers have had with people who appear to be like the professional. For example, a parent who had a series of frustrating professional interactions may well expect the next interaction to be equally frustrating. Knowing that this is bound to happen, professionals must clarify, at the very beginning of their working relationship, what they can and cannot do. The situation will also be helped by a modest amount of self-disclosure. Personal or professional self-disclosure allows parents to learn something unique that may counter stereotyping. Self-disclosure about the following variables almost always assists in keeping stereotypes to a minimum on the part of both professionals and caregivers:

- An individual's spirit of risk-taking
- Willingness to be taught
- Articulation of fears, frustrations, and so on
- Ability to deal with low-level support and approval
- Ability to persevere at a task despite frustration

Strength of the Issue   Naturally, some issues that parents and professionals communicate are more important than others. A professional's or parent's ability to communicate clearly about such issues is influenced by four important variables or elements: (1) belief versus opinion, (2) the power of previous professional interactions, (3) the length of time a behavior or attitude has existed, and (4) a sense of need and the probability of success.

It is important to determine whether the position taken by a parent, sibling, or other family member is the result of a personal or professional belief or self-generated opinion. Opinions are generally much more temporary positions than beliefs. Beliefs tend to be passed down from generation to generation and may or may not be supported by observable data. Opinions are usually readily changed with the presentation of new data while beliefs are resistant to new information that contradicts the long-held view. For example, some cultures continue to view infants with disabilities with disdain. In some of the subcultures of China, for example, infants with disabilities would be a sure sign of dishonor committed by some member of the family. In such situations, it matters little what a concerned professional may

Advice for Teachers

Interview with James Holden

When we have children who enter the school system, I have usually tried to have a conversation with the school nurse, counselor, principal, or teacher to kind of give them some information about a particular child. I know that when school personnel hear a special needs child is coming, the blood pressure goes up, the anticipation goes up, and they start to worry. I wonder how much information to give, so that it doesn't limit the child's opportunities, but gives enough information to say, "We have some concerns about the special needs of this person." I try to give enough information so it gives a picture of what's going on, without giving so much people will be scared to death. One of the things I've said is, "The teachers who have done the best with this child are those who are highly structured, very consistent, and have high expectations."

The biggest problem I have with educators and the children I deal with is that as soon as they know my children are Native American, very often their expectations go down. I think it's important that those of us in education have high expectations for ourselves, for our peers, and for our students. Make sure your expectations are high for all the children and then understand that consistency is important.

Having an awareness or a sensitivity to cultural differences is fine, but carry it to the next step. Talk to parents, not at them, but with them. Find out what it is they want. When I go to an IEP meeting, I make sure my table's arranged so that I'm with those parents. If I can get beside them or between them, that's where I want to sit, because I want to make them feel that I'm part of their side.

I've found you should ask, "What do you think we should do? What else do you want to work with at home?" Usually they'll fill you in, they've got lots of ideas about what they want to do at home, but they've always been too intimidated to say so— especially many of my Indian families. Some families have the attitude, "Well, school's going to take care

of that. I don't have to do it all." So somehow, and I think this is a key for education in general, but early childhood in specific, you must empower parents.

I think we want to let parents know, "This is your program. What is it that you want to do? What is it you want your child to do?" They're going to give you all kinds of ideas. You can then simply say, "Well, gee, let's think a minute, about what we could do at home." The reaction you're going to get is, "You mean, I should be doing this at home too?" "Well sure, we only have him a few hours a day."

I think parents are hungry to be involved. I think that the whole idea of getting parents involved is crucial, particularly when many of them may not have a lot of skill to draw from. We can give them the information they need, and parents of children at this age really do want to do what's best for their children. They are hungry to know what to do. I always had a little weekly paper that would go home to parents. It would focus on the idea that there are lots of things lying around the house that parents can use to work with their children.

THE HOLDEN CHILDREN

say or what data are presented; the belief is unlikely to be substantially altered. To help caregivers in such a culture, a professional must acknowledge the belief as real and guide caregivers to discern if it is a belief they want to continue.

Because opinions are formed in part as a consequence of experience, the best way to examine an opinion is to concentrate on the validity of past history and new information. A grandfather, for example, may be of the opinion that caring for a child with a disability will threaten the integrity of the family. It is likely that the grandfather holds this opinion because sometime in his past, he has observed or heard about the disintegration of a family unit when a child with a disability was born. Until the grandfather is presented with new information, he is likely to retain this opinion.

The nature and relationship between parents and previous teachers, consultants, or support professionals is a critical variable in parents' ability to learn something new instead of continuing the status quo. This is a consequence of past events, which may include relationships with good or favorable professionals or mentors and devastating experiences with poor or offensive professionals. Even subtle characteristics and behavior patterns of professionals who interact with family members have a bearing on outcomes. For example, professionals using unnecessary medical jargon may well remind family members of their nonproductive interaction with a particular physician. Under such conditions, the words themselves become suspect and the speaker is afforded little credibility. There is not much professionals or family members can do about power and influence of previous experiences other than to acknowledge that past experiences account for current dispositions. It is necessary to talk openly and honestly about those experiences that positively or negatively influence one's ability to be successful.

The rootedness of behavior or attitude is determined by the historical context of the behavior. Parents who have established early morning routines around two or three other children are going to have a more difficult time adapting to a different morning ritual to accommodate an infant with special needs than parents who have yet to establish a child-centered morning routine. Every new intervention disrupts some established routine. The longer a routine has been in place, the greater the natural resistance. Even such simple things as loading the car, locating the dog's dish, or the order of meals influence family routines. Changes in these routines are not insignificant. When parents tell professionals they are overwhelmed, it may be that their collection of well-established patterns has been disrupted.

One of the strategies that will be most helpful to parents is the telling of true stories about families in similar positions. Professionals must share these stories with caution, of course, but there is generally nothing more encouraging to caregivers than the knowledge of real outcomes (positive or negative) of others in like situations. If it can be demonstrated through information or stories that the consequence of an activity has been positive for parents in the same circumstances, parents may be more willing to persevere. The contrary is also true. If caregivers hear a professional or associate talking with someone about the futility of an action, they will likely disengage. Most important, then, is the professional's ability to deal truthfully with caregivers and family members. If the probability for success is low (based on both research and experience), say so. This will enable parents and everyone else involved to set proper expectations and prioritize options. It is also necessary to qualify these statements based upon the limitations of research, your own knowledge, and the real possibility of unexplained "miracles."

Special Skills for Communicating with Parents at the Time of Diagnosis

In 1972, Korsch and Negrete investigated typical problems in communication between parents and physicians when difficult news needed to be delivered. Studying the pediatrician-parent interactions in a large urban hospital, Korsch and Negrete found that 76% of the parents felt satisfied with the communication at the time the information was delivered (usually diagnostic information). Yet, follow-up 10 and 30 days later revealed unsettling repercussions:

- 20% of the parents had no idea what was wrong with their child.
- 50% of the parents had no idea of the cause of the illness or disability.
- 26% of the parents had not mentioned their greatest concern about the child because they felt they were not encouraged to do so.
- 38% of the parents complied only in part with the physician's recommendations.
- 11% of the parents did not comply at all with any of the physician's recommendations.

Nearly 25 years have passed since the Korsch and Negrete study. During that time, researchers have taken seriously the importance of determining how best to deliver difficult information to family members. Turnbull and Turnbull in *Families, Professionals, and Exceptionality: A Special Partnership* (1990) take special care to note several specific skills required of those who first introduce a diagnosis of disability to a caregiver. Items of importance to this unique situation include:

- Provide full and honest information about the condition of a child.
- Repeat the information in many different ways and at many different times.
- Try to tell both parents at the same time.
- Avoid a patronizing or condescending attitude.
- Realize parents will need time to filter the information. Always schedule a follow-up meeting.
- Understand that parents may respond with anger. The anger is about the diagnosis —not about you.
- Discuss and practice strategies for informing brothers, sisters, and other family members.

Suggestions for Positive Initial Contact   Be prepared. When you first meet parents, make sure you've done your homework. Learn as much about them as is necessary, taking care not to be too intrusive. Your first encounter should be an interview that is mutual; that is, you interview them, and they interview you. Talk about your value system; inquire and clarify issues about their culture. In short, seek and get the information you need so you can work with them, not against them. In addition, organize your paperwork, ideas, and responses, and make copies available to parents. At the end of this meeting, analyze, along with the caregiver and other participants, the subjective and objective data.

Practice good communication skills. Know and understand the power of your language and the nuances you give it. Listen for judgmental statements; be aware of freeing and binding actions and words. When you communicate poorly, acknowledge such and move on.

Recognize and accept value systems and expectations. Let the family know that you may have little knowledge of the priorities and beliefs that drive their family. However, suggest that you would be open to learning of them if they feel comfortable disclosing such to you. In all cases, privacy is to be maintained and understanding forwarded, both in balance.

Share information in a respectful and confidential manner. Sharing of information will be good when the trust between you is built. Finally, don't rush the meeting or decisions.

CHILDREN AS THE CORE OF FAMILIES AND FAMILIES AS THE CORE OF A WIDER SYSTEM

One of the unique and extraordinary outcomes of legislation supporting services for infants and their families is the requirement for interdisciplinary and interagency cooperation. This aspect of the law requires states and regions to coordinate services to the maximum extent possible. To accomplish this goal, it was required that interagency councils be established to ensure that coordination occurs in a timely and meaningful manner.

The philosophy behind interdisciplinary and interagency coordination is twofold: (1) to ensure that all services are adequately covered without unnecessary duplication, and (2) to facilitate the access of services by parents or other caregivers. Under IDEA, states were invested with financial incentives to provide services for infants and toddlers with disabilities and their families through interdisciplinary agencies. The wisdom of this approach was rooted in the collective observations of a broad range of service providers: The needs of families are so diverse, and in some instances, so extensive, that a single agency approach is too narrow. A family may well need the ongoing support and assistance of a physician, physical therapist, social worker, and financial advisor all at the same time. The spirit of the law was that coordinated services truly facilitate rather than disrupt family life and development.

In addition to coordinating available services, early childhood professionals have committed themselves to using a family-centered approach to those services. This means that the center of all discussion is the family and how a child with a disability is supported and nurtured within that family. Viewing the family from its center (the child) through the family system (a circle around the child) to the community (a circle around the family) is referred to as an **ecologically-based approach to family services.** This is not a new approach. Stories from members of Native American families, for example, reveal that this approach has been in practice for hundreds if not thousands of years. But it is only recently, after failures in attempting to mandate parent participation through IDEA, that many professionals have returned to the ecologically based model (Shelton, Jeppson, & Johnson, 1987).

The family-centered approach ensures that each family receives the unique set of services it requires

An ecological approach to family services and an interagency philosophy places limitations on the independent capacity of interventionists. Professionals must respond not only to the needs as defined from their particular discipline or perspective but from the perspective of the child, the family and its needs and priorities, and the needs and priorities of other professionals. It requires an understanding that professionals are not the primary decision makers because they are not the primary caregivers.

While a professional's role in the past may have been one of contributing expertise, it is now one that should be responsive to the priorities of the family. Above all, families and professionals join in a partnership relationship that is truly collaborative in nature. In its best form, members are mutually engaged in the work to be accomplished and recognize the constraints placed on each other.

An area of considerable constraint and a possible area for conflict between families and professionals that deserves special attention is time and the level of stress that time demands place on a family. Within the last decade, a number of researchers focused attention on the use of time as a critical resource of families with young children with disabilities. McLinden (1990) described time as the critical resource. Indeed, like the earlier studies of Dunlap and Hollingsworth (1977), the amount of time demanded by caregiving responsibilities was the stressor most often mentioned by parents of children with disabilities. Brotherson and Goldstein (1992) described the availability of time within families in the following manner:

> Time is an example of a fundamental resource to family well-being that families can only partially generate and control themselves. To a large extent, a family's time is controlled externally by people, institutions, and events that impose expectations and requirements on the family. Time is a resource when it is available and when it can be negotiated and used; as with other resources, its absence often redefines time as a constraint (p. 509).

While issues of time literally cross thousands of activities, the research of Brotherson and Goldstein (1992) and Brotherson and Martin (1992) found that most critical time issues fell into five categories:

1. Meeting the needs of the whole family

2. Decision making in partnerships

3. Working with the health care system

4. Professional demonstration of respect and sensitivity to families

5. Issues of working within service delivery systems across a variety of programs and agencies

Parents noted four supports that would help them in their use of time. The first of these is a need to fit therapy and education activities into the family's daily routine and environment. Brotherson and Goldstein (1992) wrote that parents' time was used more effectively when therapists integrated activities into the family's daily routines and home environment. Several parents stated that for professionals to know how to truly integrate activities into home life, the professionals had to spend time in their homes. Some parents also used time to frame the issue of transfer of knowledge from clinic to home. In part, this is a time issue, but it is also the issue of effective transferability of skills to the home environment and the material conditions of families' lives. Brotherson and Goldstein (1992) quoted a parent on this issue:

> In the past, the therapist would show me how to do this exercise on a nice round ball and wedges and then she turns around and says, "But you can do this with a dish towel and a beach ball." How am I going to get this together when I go home and try

*to do the exercises she's just told me about? This year we have been getting home
PT and that has been very helpful, because they've got what you've got to work with
and can show me how to work on the living room floor between the TV and stereo.
(pp. 515–516)*

Yet another dimension of the service in the home is the responsibility of professionals
to develop interventions that fit families' schedules and environments. This may mean a radical shift in the working hours of professionals.

It is also critical that professionals listen to what parents know about their child and family.
Perhaps the most common frustration of parents is when professionals discover what families have
already told them. Having to repeat information or wait for the results of clinical assessments only
to confirm what families already know frustrates and humiliates. Parents feel (whether it is true or
not) they were not taken seriously and the information they offered was less than credible. This
frustration frames the broader questions: (1) what information, provided by parents, needs to be
reaffirmed by a professional, and what can be assumed? and (2) how can both parents and professionals learn to share information that results in the best use of time by both parties?

Today, professionals must learn to use technology for therapy and education activities
as a way to work more efficiently. The advent of computer networks, conference call capabilities, faxes, and 800-number phone lines provides communication with families that was
not possible until recently. It is certainly consistent with professional obligation for early childhood educators to teach parents how to access and use those technologies that will free their
time and lead to more consistent and less stressful communication.

Professionals must provide time and consistency to develop trusting relationships with
parents. Professionals who believe they can quickly meet with a family, assess their needs, and
immediately participate in the development of an appropriate IFSP or IEP are badly mistaken.
Time must be invested to develop and to maintain a relationship, even though an IFSP or IEP
cannot be delayed beyond legal time limits. Services may begin while the process of association continues and a partnership is built.

Parents have also reported at least four common impositions on their time: (1) lack of
coordination among professionals, (2) being overwhelmed with therapy and educational
activities, (3) trying to access services not available in the community, and (4) lack of flexible
and family-centered scheduling. In order to respond to these complaints professionals need to
address the lack of flexibility within the structures of their organizations and the inherent difficulty in meeting all the needs of a whole family.

DYSFUNCTION WITHIN A FAMILY:
CHILD ABUSE AND NEGLECT

Unfortunately, a few of the families professionals encounter in early childhood services are
not healthy. Of major concern for the field is the prevention of child abuse and neglect.
Federal agencies such as the National Center on Child Abuse and Neglect and state agencies
concerned with monitoring the degree of child abuse in the United States estimate that
approximately 1 million children are abused annually (National Center on Child Abuse and
Neglect, 1988; 1991).

Of these, many are children with disabilities, though it is unclear whether children who
have disabilities are at greater risk of being abused (Warger, Tewey, & Megivern, 1991). The
purpose of addressing childhood abuse and neglect is to raise the awareness of caregivers,
family members, and early childhood professionals. Abuse of any sort is unacceptable; the
current rate of abuse and neglect among all children is simply intolerable. Despite inconsis-

tencies in definitions and enforcement procedures (McIntyre, 1990) it remains everyone's obligation to help curb this disaster.

Definitions of Abuse

Child abuse is defined in many ways, but perhaps the most common is the definition posited by Garbarino (1987 a,b): child abuse is any willful behavior by parents or guardians that harms a child in their care. Table 9.4 identifies the physical and behavioral indicators that should alert an early childhood special educator to possible abuse. One should note, however, that some of these indicators may also result from a young child's primary disability. Usually, changes in typical behavior to one or more of these indicators may be a warning that abuse is occurring. If evidence points to abuse, professionals must report their suspicions to the appropriate local agency.

It is generally accepted that four areas or types of abuse are included in this broad definition. These have been defined in some detail by The National Center on Child Abuse and Neglect (1989).

1. **Physical Abuse:** characterized by inflicting physical injury by punching, beating, kicking, biting, burning, or otherwise harming a child. Although the injury is not an accident, the parent or caregiver may not have intended to hurt the child.

2. **Child Neglect:** characterized by failure to provide for the child's basic needs. Neglect can be physical, educational, or emotional. Physical neglect includes refusal of, or delay in seeking, health care; abandonment; expulsion from home or not allowing a runaway to return home; and inadequate supervision. Educational neglect includes permission of chronic truancy, failure to enroll a child of mandatory school age, and inattention to a special education need. Emotional neglect includes such actions as chronic or extreme spouse abuse in the child's presence, permission of drug or alcohol use by the child, and refusal of, or failure to provide, needed psychological care.

3. **Sexual Abuse:** includes fondling a child's genitals, intercourse, incest, rape, sodomy, exhibitionism, and sexual exploitation. To be considered child abuse, these acts have to be committed by a parent or guardian responsible for the care of a child.

4. **Emotional Maltreatment:** includes acts or omissions by the parents that have caused, or could cause, serious behavioral, cognitive, emotional, or mental disorders. Psychological maltreatment is a concerted attack on the development of self and social competence. Five forms of psychological maltreatment have been identified:

    a. Rejecting: the refusal to acknowledge the child's worth and needs.

    b. Isolating: cutting the child off from normal social experiences.

    c. Terrorizing: verbally assaulting the child or creating a climate of fear.

    d. Ignoring: being psychologically unavailable.

    e. Corrupting: socializing the child to engage in destructive behavior and reinforcing the deviance.

Historical Context of Abuse in the United States

Child abuse was first recognized as a phenomenon in the United States about 1940 (Kline, 1977). However, it took another 20 years for Kempe and his colleagues to coin and publicize the term *battered child syndrome,* which brought the issue to the nation's attention (Kemp, Silverman, Steele, & Droegemueller, 1962). Still another decade was required before the issue

Table 9.4/ *Symptoms of Child Abuse*

Physical Abuse

Physical indicators:
unexplained bruises, unusual burns, bite marks, fractures or dislocations, abrasions

Behavioral indicators:
reluctant to change clothes in front of others, is withdrawn, self-mutilation, discomfort when others cry, unusual control of crying, dependence or indiscriminate attachment

Child Neglect

Physical indicators:
frequently dirty, unwashed, hungry, inappropriately dressed, tired and listless, has unattended physical problems

Behavioral indicators:
is truant or tardy or arrives early and stays late, begs or steals food, is dependent or detached, states frequent absence of parent

Sexual Abuse

Physical indicators:
pain or itching in genital area, bruises or bleeding in genital area, venereal disease, swollen private parts, difficulty walking or sitting, pain when urinating

Behavioral indicators:
reluctant to change clothes in front of others, is withdrawn, exhibits unusual sexual knowledge, poor peer relationships, is manipulative, is self-conscious, is fearful or anxious

Emotional Maltreatment

Physical indicators:
has a sleep disorder, developmental lags, is hyperactive, has eating disorders

Behavioral indicators:
overly eager to please, seeks out adult contact, anxious, depressed, withdrawn, passive, screams, unable to communicate feelings

---

of childhood abuse and neglect found its way into the legal agenda, in the form of The Child Abuse Prevention and Treatment Act of 1974 (Public Law 93-247). Amended in 1988 under P. L. 100-294 (The Child Abuse Prevention, Adoption, and Family Services Act), the act defines child abuse and neglect as the physical or mental injury, sexual abuse or exploitation, negligent treatment, or maltreatment of children under the age of 18 by a person who is responsible for the child's welfare under circumstances indicating that the child's health or welfare is harmed or threatened thereby.

Synthesis of the Research on Abuse   The critical question, of course, is why would anyone choose to harm a child? There are some indications that abuse stems from a parent's or caregiver's own frustrations, emotional instability, or stresses due to such conditions as poverty or substance abuse. No single cluster of reasons can be found, nor is it possible to classify abusers according to demographic data: abusers come from all socioeconomic, racial, religious, and ethnic groups. Armed with this caveat, a few researchers have tried to identify factors associated with persons who abuse their children.

Abusers tend to have been abused by their parents (Straus, 1983). Abusers are not subjected to significantly more stressful life experiences; however, they tend to perceive that they are more overwhelmed by the stress they experience, and they tend to identify violence as a response to stress (Rosenberg & Reppucci, 1983; Starr, 1983; Straus, 1980; Wolfe, 1985). Some abusers of young children place unrealistic demands on them (Galdston, 1965; Steele & Pollock, 1968). Although males tend to be abusive more often than females, mothers are more likely than fathers to inflict serious injury on a child (Solomon, 1973). Abusers tend to experience a high degree of social isolation, as well as failure to use existing social supports (Garbarino, 1982; Kirkham, Schinke, Schilling, Meltzer, & Norelius, 1986; Salzinger, Kaplan, & Artemyeff, 1983).

Abuse and Special Needs Populations   While there is insufficient reliable, scientific data to draw conclusions about the degree to which children and infants with disabilities are at greater or lesser risk for abuse, a few characteristics have been identified that appear to place certain categories of special needs children at higher than normal risks (Zirpoli, 1986). These are worthy of consideration:

- Premature or low birth weight infants (Fontana, 1971; Klein & Stern, 1971; Lynch & Roberts, 1982)

- Children with difficult temperament, presence of challenging or aggressive behaviors, or behavior disorders (Bousha & Twentyman, 1984; Rusch, Hall, & Griffin, 1986; Zirpoli, Snell, & Loyd, 1987)

- Children with mental disabilities (Elmer, 1967; Nesbit & Karagianis, 1982; Sandgrund, Gaines, & Green, 1974)

A second difficulty in arriving at an accurate assessment of the degree of abuse among young children with disabilities is the complex nature of determining the relationship between a preexisting disability and a disability caused by abuse. Said another way, was the disability preceded by the abusive episode(s), or is it a consequence of abuse and neglect (Ammerman, Van Hasselt, & Hersen, 1988)?

Implications for Early Childhood Professionals

Although social service agencies generally have primary responsibility for child abuse control, legislators have required all professionals with responsibility for children, including early intervention professionals and educators, to report suspected abuse. As of this writing, all 50 states have guidelines mandating that abuse be reported. Unfortunately, the protocols for reporting, even the definition of abuse and neglect, vary substantially from state to state. It is incumbent upon each professional, therefore, to seek an orientation and briefing on the state laws, policies, and procedures that govern the reporting of abuse and neglect. The National Education Association (NEA), the Council for Exceptional Children (CEC), and the National Clearinghouse on Child Abuse and Neglect publish frequently in the areas of identification, prevention, and treatment of child abuse.

FAMILIES IN THE TWENTY-FIRST CENTURY

In a study by Bailey, Palsha, and Simeonsson (1991) early interventionists were found to have only a moderate level of perceived competence in working with families. In fact, their study demonstrated that there was a significantly lower rating of skills in working with families than in working with children. The implications of this study are clear: early childhood educators must attend in a more holistic way to the needs and priorities of families and family systems.

The research of Mahoney, O'Sullivan, and Dennebaum (1990 a,b) gave clear directives for a more holistic approach. Professionals must (1) engage parents in the early intervention system, (2) provide parents with information about their children, (3) help parents implement

Family empowerment is the key to bringing about a more holistic approach to early intervention

instructional activities at home, (4) attend to the well-being of parents and family members, and (5) assist parents to obtain community resources. In the final analysis, however, the single most important perspective must be for early childhood professionals to adopt a philosophy of parent and family empowerment and to obtain the skills necessary to make that empowerment a reality.

The relatively rapid progression of events and philosophies between the early 1960s and middle 1990s led many special educators to imagine a future that was not thought possible a few years ago. Parents and professionals should take a possibility-based approach to life planning that assumes that something not now existing can and will exist in the future. This approach demands community investment in life-long learning, with communities well educated about persons with disabilities who live in their neighborhoods. City or community norms would expect every member of the local school board and every elected official of the city government to answer instantly and correctly the question, "Where can I get the help I need?" Local generic organizations like the YMCA or YWCA and the Girl Scouts and Boy Scouts would require that their staff know how to welcome and support persons with disabilities.

Such a future would emphasize a collaborative, respectful approach to the delivery of services; professionals would hold an intellectual norm of affiliation rather than an attitude of power through authority. Professional assistance would be seen as support and not intrusion. Those who provide information about services would constantly assess their own attitudes and how they are perceived. The model of cooperation would be one in which parents, not professionals, control the process, thereby maintaining and enriching family integrity and dignity.

Parents would not just be acknowledged, but they would be treated as the experts on their children; they would not need to fight for credibility. Parents seeking support could find what they needed through a centralized or coordinated community service agency. The culture would reflect generosity, making those services needed by a child and family available to them at the time they needed it. Child care and respite care for infants, toddlers, and youth with disabilities would be so ingrained that no one would remember to segregate services to those with disabilities.

While these philosophies may appear to be far from full realization, they establish hopes and desires that guide the future. These issues provide the seed for debate, discussion, and research that will frame society's commitment to all persons with disabilities well into the twenty-first century.

STUDY GUIDE QUESTIONS

1. What common assumptions about families of children with disabilities have influenced most past research on these families?

2. How have the perspectives regarding parents and services to children with disabilities changed over the past decade?

3. Give several examples that might be used to illustrate the paradigm shift from professional as leader to parent as leader.

4. Explain what is meant by a philosophy of association and briefly state your own.

5. What are some of the variables that may affect relationships between professionals and families?

6. What are some of the common needs of all families? How might these be intensified for families of children with disabilities?

7. What is meant by family hardiness, and what are the three dimensions of family hardiness?

8. How do authority and leadership differ?

9. Describe the typical stages of the grief process and how they might be misused by professionals.

10. Give your own examples of specific communication skills that should be used and pitfalls that must be avoided when working with families.

11. How should one deliver difficult information to families?

12. What have researchers learned about time as a family resource? What are the implications for early childhood professionals?

13. Briefly define physical abuse, child neglect, sexual abuse, and emotional maltreatment and identify at least two indicators of each.

14. Why are children with disabilities especially at risk for abuse?

15. What are some characteristics of an ideal future for early intervention? What would be necessary for such a vision to become reality?

REFERENCES

Allen, D. A., & Affleck, G. (1985). Are we stereotyping parents? A postscript to Blacker. *Mental Retardation, 23*(4), 200–202.

Ammerman, R. T., Van Hasselt, V. B., & Hersen, M. (1988). Maltreatment of handicapped children: A critical review. *Journal of Family Violence, 3*(1), 53–72.

Anderegg, M. L., Vergason, G. A., & Smith, M. C. (1992). A visual representation of the grief cycle for use by teachers with families of children with disabilities. *Remedial and Special Education, 13,* 17–23.

Bailey, D. B., Palsha, S. A., & Simeonsson, R. J. (1991). Professional skills, concerns, and perceived importance of work with families in early intervention. *Exceptional Children, 58,* 156–165.

Bousha, D. M., & Twentyman, C. U. (1984). Mother-child interactional style in abuse, neglect, and control groups: Naturalistic observations in the home. *Journal of Abnormal Psychology, 93,* 106–114.

Bradley, V. J., Knoll, J., & Agosta, J. M. (Eds.). (1992). *Emerging Issues in Family Support.* Washington, DC: American Association on Mental Retardation.

Breslau, N. (1983). Care of disabled children and women's time issue. *Medical Care, 21,* 620–629.

Brewer, E., McPherson, M., Magrab, P., & Hutchins, V. (1989). Family-centered, community based, coordinated care for children with special health care needs. *Pediatrics, 83,* 1055–1060.

Brotherson, M. J., & Goldstein, B. (1992). Time as a resource and constraint for parents of young children with disabilities: Implications for early intervention services. *Topics in Early Childhood Special Education, 12,* 508–527.

Brotherson, M. J., & Martin, L. H. (1992). Building successful partnerships with families with young children with disabilities: Family, early interventionist, and physician perspectives. Paper presented at the Annual Conference of the Association for the Care of Children's Health, Atlanta.

Byrne, E., & Cunningham, C. (1985). The effects of mentally handicapped children on families—a conceptual review. *Journal of Child Psychology and Psychiatry, 26,* 847–864.

Carter, E., & McGoldrick, M. (1980). *The family life cycle: A framework for family therapy.* New York: Gardner.

Cook, R. E., Tessier, A., & Klein, M. D. (1992). *Adapting early childhood curricula for children with special needs.* Upper Saddle River, NJ: Merrill/Prentice Hall.

Cox, A., Rutter, M., Newman, S., & Bartak, L. (1975). A comparative study of infantile autism and specific developmental receptive language disorders: Parental characteristics. *British Journal of Psychiatry, 126,* 146–159.

Crnic, K., Friedrich, W., & Greenberg, M. (1983). Adaptation of families with mentally retarded children: A model of stress, coping and family ecology. *American Journal of Mental Deficiency, 88,* 125–138.

Cummings, S., Bayley, H., & Rie, H. (1966). Effects of the child's deficiency on the mother: A study of mothers of mentally retarded, chronically ill and neurotic children. *American Journal of Orthopsychiatry, 36,* 595–608.

Darling, R. (1979). *Families against society: A study of reactions to children with birth defects.* London: SAGE.

Dunlap, W. R., & Hollingsworth, J. S. (1977). How does a handicapped child affect the family? Implications for practitioners. *The Family Coordinator, 26,* 286–293.

Dunst, C. J. (1985). Rethinking early intervention. *Analysis and Intervention in Developmental Disabilities, 5,* 165–201.

Dunst, C. J., Trivette, C. M., & Deal, A. G. (1988). *Enabling and empowering families: Principles and guidelines for practice.* Cambridge, MA: Brookline Books.

Elmer, E. (1967). *Children in jeopardy: A study of abused minors and their families.* Pittsburgh: University of Pittsburgh Press.

Epstein N., Bishop, D., & Baldwin, L. (1982). McMaster model of family functioning: A view of the normal family. In F. Walsh (Ed.), *Normal family processes.* New York: Guillford.

Failla, S., & Jones, L. (1991). Families of children with developmental disabilities: An examination of family hardiness. *Research in Nursing and Health, 14,* 41–50.

Farber, B. (1960). Family organization and crisis: Maintenance of integration in families with a severely retarded child. *Monographs of the Society for Research in Child Development, 25,* (1, Serial No. 75).

Farber & Rowitz, L. (1986). Families with a mentally retarded child. In N. R. Ellis & N. W. Bray (Eds.), *International review of research in mental retardation XIV.* Orlando, FL: Academic.

Featherstone, H. (1980). *A difference in the family: Living with a disabled child.* New York: Penguin.

Fontana, V. J. (1971). *The maltreated child.* Springfield, IL: Charles C. Thomas.

Francis, P. L., & Jones, F. A. (1984). Interactions of mothers and their developmentally-delayed infants: Age, parity, and gender effects. *Journal of Clinical Child Psychology, 13*(3), 268–273.

Friedrich, W., & Friedrich, N. (1981). Psychological assets of parents of handicapped and nonhandicapped children. *American Journal of Mental Deficiency, 85,* 551–553.

Galdston, O. (1965). Observations on children who have been physically abused and their parents. *Journal of Psychiatry, 122,* 440–443.

Garbarino, J. (1982). *Children and families in the social environment.* New York: Aldine.

Garbarino, J. (1987a). What can the school do on behalf of the psychologically maltreated child and the community? *School Psychology Review, 16*(2), 181–187.

Garbarino, J. (1987b). The abuse and neglect of special children: An introduction to the issues. In J. Garbarino, P. E. Brookhouser, & K. J. Auathier (Eds.), *Special children, special risks: The maltreatment of children with disabilities.* Hawthorne, NY: Aldinede Gruyter.

Gath, A. (1973). The school-age siblings of mongol children. *British Journal of Psychiatry, 123,* 161–167.

Grossman, F. (1972). *Brothers and sisters of retarded children: An exploratory study.* Syracuse, NY: Syracuse University Press.

Holroyd, J. (1974). The questionnaire on resources and stress: An instrument to measure family response to a handicapped member. *Journal of Community Psychology, 2,* 92–94.

Hunt, N. & Marshall, K. (1994). *Exceptional children and youth.* Boston: Houghton-Mifflin Co.

Kazak, A. E. (1986). Families with physically handicapped children: Social ecology and family systems. *Family Process, 25,* 265–281.

Kempe, C. H., Silverman, F. N., Steele, B. F., & Droegemueller, W. (1962). The battered child syndrome. *The Journal of the American Medical Association, 181,* 17–24.

Kirkham, M. A., Schinke, S. P., Schilling, R. F., Meltzer, N. J., & Norelius, K. L. (1986). Cognitive-behavioral skills, social supports, and child abuse potential among mothers of handicapped children. *Journal of Family Violence, 1*(3), 235–245.

Klein, M., & Stern, L. (1971). Low birth weight and the battered child syndrome. *American Journal of Disabled Children, 122,* 15–18.

Kline, D. F. (1977). *Child abuse and neglect: A primer for school personnel.* Reston, VA: CEC.

Kobasa, S., Maddi, S., & Pucetti, M. (1982). Personality and exercise as buffers in the stress illness relationship. *Journal of Behavior Medicine, 5,* 391–403.

Korsch, B. M., & Negrete, V. F. (1972). Doctor-patient communication. *Scientific American, 227,* 66–74.

Krauss, M. W., & Jacobs, F. (1990). Family assessment: Purposes and techniques. In S. Meisels & J. Shonkoff (Eds.), *Handbook of early childhood intervention.* New York: Cambridge University Press.

Kubler-Ross, E. (1969). *Locus of control: Current trends in theory and research.* Hillsdale, NJ: Earlbaum.

Linz, M. H., McAnally, P., & Wieck C. (Eds.). (1982). *Case management: Historical, current and future perspectives.* Cambridge, MA: Brookline Books.

Lynch, M. A., & Roberts, J. (1982). *Consequences of child abuse.* New York: Academic Press.

Mahoney, G., O'Sullivan, P., & Dennebaum, J. (1990a). Maternal perceptions of early intervention services: A scale for assessing family focused intervention. *Topics in Early Childhood Special Education, 10*(1), 1–15.

Mahoney, G., O'Sullivan, P., & Dennebaum, J. (1990b). A national study of mothers' perceptions of family focused intervention. *Journal of Early Intervention, 14,* 133–146.

McCubbin, H. L., Nevin, R. S., Caulbe, A. E., Larsen, A., Comeau, J. K., & Patterson, J. M. (1982). Family coping with chronic illness: The case of cerebral palsy. In H. I. McCubbin, A. E. Cauble, & J. M. Patterson (Eds.), *Family stress, coping, and social support* (pp. 169–188). Springfield, IL: Thomas.

McIntyre, T. (1990). The teacher's role in cases of suspected child abuse. *Education and Urban Society, 22*(3), 300–306.

McLinden, S. E. (1990). Mothers' and fathers' reports of the effects of a young child with special needs on the family. *Journal of Early Intervention, 14,* 249–259.

Meisels, S., & Shonkoff, J. (Eds.). (1990). *Handbook of early childhood intervention.* New York: Cambridge University Press.

Moore, M. L., Howard, V. F., & McLaughlin, T. F. (In press). *Siblings of children with disabilities: A review and analysis. International Journal of Special Education.*

National Center on Child Abuse and Neglect. (1988). *Study findings: Study of national incidence and prevalence of child abuse and neglect.* Washington, DC: U.S. Department of Human Services, Administration for Children, Youth and Families.

National Center on Child Abuse and Neglect. (1989). *Child abuse and neglect: A shared community concern.* Washington, DC: U.S. Department of Health and Human Services, Publication No. 89-30531.

National Center on Child Abuse and Neglect. (1991). *Study findings: Study of national incidence and prevalence of child abuse and neglect.* Washington, DC: U.S. Department of Human Services, Administration for Children, Youth and Families.

Nesbit, W. C., & Karagianis, L. D. (1982). Child abuse: Exceptionality as a risk factor. *The Alberta Journal of Educational Research, 28,* 69–76.

Olson, D., Russell, C., & Sprenkle, C. (1983). Circumplex model of marital and family systems: 6. Theoretical update. *Family Process, 22,* 69–83.

Peters, T. (1992). *Liberation management: Necessary disorganization for the nanosecond nineties.* New York: Alfred A. Knopf.

Pollack, S. (1986). Human responses to diabetes mellitus. *Western Journal of Nursing Research, 11,* 265–280.

Public Law 100–294. Child Abuse Prevention, Adoption, and Family Service Act of 1988.

Roos, P. (1985). Parents of mentally retarded children—misunderstood and mistreated. In A. P. Turnbull & H. R. Turnbull (Eds.), *Parents speak out: Views from the other side of the two-way mirror* (2nd. ed.), (pp. 245–257). Upper Saddle River, NJ: Merrill/Prentice Hall.

Rosenberg, M. S., & Reppucci, N. D. (1983). Abusive mothers: Perceptions of their own children's behavior. *Journal of Consulting and Clinical Psychology, 51,* 674–682.

Roth, W. (1982). Poverty and the handicapped child. *Children and Youth Services Review, 4,* 67–75.

Rusch, R. G., Hall, J. D., & Griffin, H. C. (1986). Abuse-provoking characteristics of institutionalized mentally retarded individuals. *American Journal of Mental Deficiency, 90,* 618–624.

Salzinger, S., Kaplan, S., & Artemyeff, C. (1983). Mothers' personal social networks and child maltreatment. *Journal of Abnormal Psychology, 92,* 68–76.

Sandgrund, H., Gaines, R., & Green, A. (1974). Child abuse and mental retardation: A problem of cause and effect. *American Journal of Mental Deficiency, 79,* 327–330.

Schell, G. C. (1981). The young handicapped child: A family perspective. *Topics in Early Childhood Special Education, 1,* 21–27.

Seligman, M., & Darling, R. B. (1989). *Ordinary families special children: A systems approach to childhood disability.* New York: The Guilford Press.

Senge, P. (1990). *The fifth discipline: The art and practice of the learning organization.* New York: Doubleday Currency.

Shelton, T. L., Jeppson, E. S., & Johnson, B. (1987). *Family-centered care for children with health care needs.* Washington, DC: Association for the Care of Children's Health.

Simeonsson, R. J., & Bailey, D. B. (1990). Family dimensions in early intervention. In S. J. Meisels & J. P. Shonkoff (Eds.), *Handbook of early intervention,* (pp. 428–444). New York: Cambridge University Press.

Solomon, T. (1973). History and demography of child abuse. *Pediatrics, 51,* 773–776.

Starr, R. H. (1983). A research-based approach to the prediction of child abuse. In R. H. Starr, Jr. (Ed.), *Child abuse prediction: Policy implications,* (pp. 89–133). Chicago: University of Chicago Press.

Steele, B., & Pollock, C. (1968). A psychiatric study of parents who abuse infants and small children. In R. Helfer & C. Kempe (Eds.), *The battered child,* (pp. 89–133). Chicago: University of Chicago Press.

Straus, M. A. (1980). Stress and physical child abuse. *Child abuse and neglect, 4,* 75–88.

Straus, M. A. (1983). Ordinary violence, child abuse and wife beating: What do they all have in common? In D. Finkelhor, R. J. Gelels, G. T. Hotaling, & M. A. Straus (Eds.), *The dark side of families: Current family violence research,* (pp. 194–223). Beverly Hills, CA: Sage.

Turnbull, A. P., Summers, J. A., & Brotherson, M. J. (1984). *Working with families with disabled members: A family systems approach.* Lawrence, KS: University of Kansas, Kansas University Affiliated Facility.

Turnbull, A. P. & Turnbull, H. R. (Eds.). (1985). *Parents speak out: Views from the other side of the two-way mirror* (2nd. ed.), (pp. 245–257). Upper Saddle River, NJ: Merrill/Prentice Hall.

Turnbull, A. P., & Turnbull, H. R. (1990). *Families, professionals, and exceptionality: A special partnership.* Upper Saddle River, NJ: Merrill/Prentice Hall.

United States Senate Report 100–113. (1987). Developmental Disabilities Assistance and Bill of Rights Act Amendments. U.S. 100th Congress, 2nd Session. pp. 1–2.

Walsh, F. (Ed.). (1980). *Normal family processes.* New York: Guilford.

Warger, C., Tewey, S., & Megivern, M. (1991). *Abuse and neglect of exceptional children.* Reston, VA: Council for Exceptional Children.

Weiss, H. (1989). State family support and education programs. *American Journal of Orthopsychiatry, 59,* 32–48.

Weissbourd, B. (1987). A brief history of family support programs. In S. L. Kagan, D. R. Powell, B. Weissbourd, & E. Zigler (Eds.), *America's family support programs,* (pp. 38–56). New Haven, CT: Yale University Press.

Weissbourd, B., & Kagan, S. L. (1989). Family support programs: Catalysts for change. *American Journal of Orthopsychiatry, 59,* 20–31.

Werner, E., & Smith, R. (1982). *Vulnerable but invincible: a study of resilient children.* New York: McGraw-Hill.

Wheatley, M. (1992). *Leadership and the new science—Learning about organization from an orderly universe.* San Francisco: Berrett-Koehler Publishers, Inc.

Wolfe, D. A. (1985). Child-abusive parents: An empirical review and analysis. *Psychological Review, 97,* 462–482.

Zigler, E., & Black, K. B. (1989). America's family support movement: Strengths and limitations. *American Journal of Orthopsychiatry, 59,* 6–19.

Zirpoli, T. J. (1986). Child abuse and children with handicaps. *Remedial and Special Education, 7*(2), 39–48.

Zirpoli, T. J., Snell, M. E., & Loyd, B. H. (1987). Characteristics of persons with mental retardation who have been abused by care givers. *Journal of Special Education, 21*(2), 31–41.

CHAPTER 10

Mandated Services for Young Children

The value of early education and how best to provide these services have been discussed by philosophers, psychologists, educators, and parents for over 2000 years (Ershler, 1992). History reveals three broad trends in American society that have, to some extent, affected early childhood special education in recent years:

1. Concern about the care and welfare of young children
2. Concern with the rights and needs of individual citizens and minority groups
3. Support of human service programs (Bailey & Wolery, 1992)

In recent years, the United States witnessed significant growth in services to preschoolers, national incentives for infant programs, expansion of early intervention to diverse populations and in diverse settings, and new ideas about the goals of early intervention and how services should be provided (Bailey & Wolery, 1992).

This chapter looks in depth at legislation and mandated services for children with disabilities who are from three to five years of age. Such services are federally supported and available throughout the United States. The next chapter will examine recommended discretionary services for infants and toddlers with disabilities and their families. Model programs that exemplify best practices are examined at the end of this chapter. Federal incentives for services to children from birth to age three are ushering in a new phase in intervention for all children with disabilities. Infant and toddler programs are not yet federally mandated but are becoming more commonplace.

INDIVIDUALS WITH DISABILITIES EDUCATION ACT

Foremost in the recent expansion of services was the federal mandate passed in 1975, now known as the Individuals with Disabilities Education Act (IDEA). This "blockbuster legislation" (Goodman, 1976) mandated specific due process protections and services for children with disabilities. Among its provisions were the following:

1. Children with disabilities must receive a free, appropriate education and related services necessary for them to benefit from special education.

2. Children with disabilities must be educated in the **least restrictive environment** appropriate. That is, students with disabilities must be educated with their typical peers to the greatest extent possible.

3. An **individualized education program** (IEP) must be developed by an interdisciplinary team and maintained with yearly reviews for every student with disabilities.

4. Disabilities must be identified on the basis of multiple evaluation procedures that do not discriminate on the basis of race, culture, or language.

5. The rights of children with disabilities and their parents are protected by ensuring parental involvement in planning and placement decisions, confidentiality of records, and opportunities for impartial hearings.

The 1975 legislation required services for children with disabilities from ages 3 to 21. However, those states where public education laws did not include children three to five years of age as part of the school population were not required to begin preschool programs. Still, IDEA was an important breakthrough in 1975 for preschool-aged children with disabilities (Gallagher & Gallagher, 1992). While it fell short of mandating services for all children below traditional school age, it did establish the Preschool Incentive Grant which encouraged states to provide services to children with disabilities ages three to five. Such services were discretionary, at first, but once a state received grant funding, all rights and services of IDEA were assured to each preschool child in that state.

The provisions of IDEA have been reauthorized and amended several times since its initiation. For example, in 1982, President Reagan sought to soften the law and was met by overwhelming opposition from parent advocacy and professional groups (Heward & Orlansky, 1992). As a result, when the law was amended in 1983, Congress reaffirmed the original legislation, while expanding research and services for secondary students making the transition into work settings.

By 1985, parents, professionals, and other advocates were exerting substantial pressure on Congress to expand services to younger children. These groups were armed with the results from efficacy studies, with humanitarian and moral arguments, with examples of model programs, and with evidence of the inequitable availability of already mandated services across states (Safer & Hamilton, 1993). In response, significant changes were made in the law with amendments passed in 1986.

Though only half the states had previously provided a free, appropriate education to children with disabilities who were three to five years old (Safer & Hamilton, 1993), the 1986 amendments of IDEA expanded preschool services to all three-to-five-year-olds with disabilities. Beginning with the 1990–1991 school year, each state was required to serve all preschool children with disabilities with all the rights and protections previously available to school-age children. The regulations for preschool services were similar to those originally included for school-age children, with these differences:

1. Preschoolers do not have to be classified under a specific disability category in order to receive services.

2. The IEP must include information for parents.

3. Preschool services may be provided through a variety of models, including home-based, center-based, or combination programs, and the length of the school day and school year may vary from that of school-aged children.

4. The state education agency must administer preschool special education programs but may contract with other agencies to provide the full range of services needed (Heward & Orlansky, 1992).

In 1990, IDEA was again amended to include autism and traumatic brain injury as two new categories of disability. Schools are now also required to provide transition services to students as they move from school to postschool activities, to be stated directly in the IEPs of students no later than age 16. Rehabilitation counseling and social work services were added to related services.

INDIVIDUALIZED EDUCATION PROGRAM

The IEP is perhaps the principal component of IDEA in terms of classroom services. This document details a specific plan used by preschool education team members on a daily basis. The IEP is specifically outlined in IDEA regulations and contains the following parts:

1. A statement of the child's present levels of performance

2. A statement of **annual goals**

3. A statement of short-term **instructional objectives**

4. A statement of educational services and related services to be provided

5. The date when services will begin and their duration

6. A description of the extent to which the child will be included in regular education settings

7. A statement of evaluation procedures

The IEP must be the product of a team that includes at least the child's teacher, the child's parents, a representative of the local school district other than the teacher, and, when appropriate, the child. Other professionals may also be a part of the team if their expertise is needed to address a specific child's developmental needs; these might include communication disorders specialists, physical therapists, occupational therapists, social workers, counselors, and others. In all cases, a child's parent or guardian must consent to the IEP before it is implemented.

Formats for IEPs vary widely and may go beyond the basic requirements of the law. For example, in the state of Washington during the early 1990s, over 200 different IEP forms were used across different school districts. (A sample IEP is shown in Table 10.1.)

Ideally, an IEP spells out *where* a child is developmentally, *where* the child should be going, *how* she or he will get there, *when* the child will reach specific goals, and *how* to tell if she or he has arrived (Heward & Orlansky, 1992). To ensure that an IEP is continuously relevant, it must be reviewed at least once a year by a child's team. In addition, parents may request a review prior to the annual review date.

Several factors are key to writing a functional IEP. These include:

1. A complete description of the child's current skills and behaviors on which to base future instruction

2. The writing of clear instructional objectives

3. The designation of specially designed instruction and **related services**

4. The identification of the appropriate and least restrictive setting for educational inclusion.

Present Levels of Performance

The first step in IEP development is to translate student evaluation results into practical planning information. IEP teams must use current information, state performance in concise and clear language, and identify specific skills. Teams draw from standardized test scores, medical records, observations, specialist's reports, and parent input. Crucial questions to be addressed are the following:

1. What is the student's current level of mastery in each specified skill area?

2. What is the nature of the specifically designed instruction that should be provided in each skill area? (Strickland & Turnbull, 1990)

Areas to be evaluated include speech and language, motor skills, sensory skills, cognitive skills, social skills, self-help skills, and play skills, as well as others particular to a child's disabling condition. Performance levels should be stated in the positive so that a child's strengths and resources are examined. If there are deficiencies in any area, the kind of intervention recommended for improving that specific skill area should be noted. For example, rather than stating that fine motor skills are not age-appropriate, the present levels of performance should identify concretely what the child can do: "Amos can manipulate large puzzle shapes, use a spoon for eating, and stack blocks. He has not yet acquired the skills to fasten buttons and zippers, use a pencil to draw shapes, or lace his shoes, but these skills could be taught directly by his parents with the assistance of an occupational therapist."

Instructional Objectives

Goals and objectives should be developed collaboratively by the child's IEP team and should consider the assessment information gathered to document a child's present level of performance and the parents' needs and preferences. In general, goals and objectives should address the following areas identified by Noonan and McCormick (1993):

1. Skills that are partially acquired or skills that are demonstrated in some contexts but not others (and can be improved upon or extended)

2. Skills that will permit a child to participate in routine daily activities with nondisabled peers (thus allowing inclusion in a least restrictive setting)

3. Skills that would be instrumental in accomplishing the greatest number of other skills or functional tasks (for example, basic fine motor skills like grasping can lead to self-feeding, dressing, playing with toys, etc.)

4. Skills a child is highly motivated to learn (activities that are self-reinforcing)

5. Skills that will increase opportunities for interactions with nondisabled peers (such as language and play)

6. Skills that will increase participation in future environments (such as handraising and taking turns needed in a kindergarten setting).

An IEP must include specifically developed short-term instructional objectives. These statements describe the expected outcomes of educational intervention within a short-term time frame of one to three months and assist in planning daily activities (Bailey & Wolery, 1992). Any good objective contains three main components: the observable behavior that a child is expected to perform, the conditions or situation under which the behavior is expected, and the criterion or how well the child must perform the behavior (Mager, 1962).

An observable *behavior* is one that can be seen or heard and, therefore, can be measured. "Being kind to others" is a description, not a behavior on which several people could agree. "Handing a toy to another child" is a behavior that could be observed and counted and that most people would accept as a demonstration of kindness. Usually objectives should contain action words that indicate a distinct movement, such as naming, reaching, or stacking. For example, the goal of "joining" in circle activities should be restated as the following behaviors: "*sits* in small group, *answers* questions, *sings* songs, *moves* fingers and hands with the music." By observing these behaviors, it would be clear that a child is joining in circle activities.

The second key component of a good objective is a description of the *conditions* under which the behavior is expected. Conditions are the situation in which learning is to be demonstrated and might include the materials used, the setting in which a behavior is to occur, or the people who would be present when the behavior is performed. Compare these two conditions under which a child is expected to count objects: "Charles will touch and count out loud the number of blocks up to *three blocks that appear one at a time on the computer screen*." "Charles will *stand at the calendar in front of the circle group* and count off *each date of the month* in order, stopping with today's date." Both are good descriptions of conditions, and in both cases, the child is expected to count, but the task of counting under the first set of conditions is probably much easier than performance under the second set of conditions. The second set of conditions implies a much more sophisticated knowledge level and would be influenced by more variables, including the changing number of days in a month, the size of the audience, and the use of numerals rather than semiconcrete images.

Conditions may describe the level of assistance or cueing that will be provided, the kind of audience that will be present, the mode in which the response will take place, and the kind of environmental contingencies present. An example of level of assistance might be: "Using his crutches, Tommy will walk with a friend from the school door to the swings," or at a later time, "Tommy will use a cane to walk alone from the school door to the swings." The kind of audience that will be present makes a difference as well. It is one thing for Darette to sing "Itsy Bitsy Spider" to her mother during bath time, and another for Darette to sing "Itsy Bitsy Spider" on stage for all the parents during the spring festival. The mode of performance can also differ; for example, it is important to indicate if the child will be drawing, using a computer keyboard, or orally telling a simple story. The kind of contingencies needed to ensure a particular performance may vary a great deal as well. For example, Arnold may eat all his soup when

Table 10.1/ *Individualized Educational Program*

Child's name: Jennifer Lovinger   **Birth date:** 6-19-92   **Age:** 38 mos   **School:** Pine Valley, Preschool (3-5)

Parents/Guardians: Lyle & Julia Lovinger   **Address:** W. 1125 Post, Pine Valley   **Telephone:** 328-3520

Reason for referral: Jennifer is an adopted child whose mother was addicted to alcohol and cocaine. Jennifer showed evidence of both in her bloodstream at birth. She was premature and had seizures at delivery. She continued to have tremors for several days as well as increased muscle tone. Jennifer was slow to develop physical skills and lacks age-appropriate self-help skills. She is very active, difficult for Julia and Lyle to control, and has frequent temper tantrums.

Present levels of performance:
Strengths: Jennifer's performance on the test of intelligence fell within the average range expected at this age. She was able to follow directions, imitate line drawings, and complete fine motor tasks. Jennifer is able to place shapes in a box, turn pages of a book and use a peg board competently. Her mother reports that Jennifer can turn door knobs and television and radio dials, and she can manipulate blocks. Jennifer's gross motor skills appear to be at developmentally appropriate levels; she walks, jumps on two feet, and runs with ease. She likes to throw objects and follows them visually. Jennifer sings preschool songs she learned from the television. She has good receptive and expressive language skills. Jennifer has normal hearing and vision.

Areas of concern: Jennifer's self-help skills are delayed and she is not cooperative in tasks such as washing hands, unless it is done very quickly. Jennifer's toilet training is delayed and she does not indicate wet or soiled pants. Jennifer does not hold her own glass when drinking and must be fed with a spoon. She also does not assist in undressing herself. Jennifer has a low frustration tolerance and does not adapt to new situations well. She tantrums frequently, banging her head and biting herself when upset. Her activity level is high, and it is difficult to maintain sustained attention to a task. Jennifer does not tolerate sensory stimulation well. She appeared to be tactilely defensive when touched and overreacted to different textures.

Statement of major annual goals	Specific educational or related support services needed to meet annual goals	Person(s) responsible for providing services—beginning and ending dates
1. Establish self-help skills, including self-feeding, toileting, and hygiene.	A detailed task analysis for each skill area will be used and Jennifer's entry level to each task identified. A system of graduated guidance will be used within self-help routines in the classroom and at home. Completion of each task and independent completion of any step in a task will be consequated with praise and access to a reinforcing activity.	Occupational therapist, special education teacher, and parent. Initiation of service: 9-6-95 Ending date: 8-15-96
2. Reduce temper tantrums in intensity and frequency (to a rate of no more than once a month).	Jennifer will be differentially reinforced for cooperative behavior and for using appropriate ways to say, "no." Each time a temper tantrum occurs, Jennifer will be placed in a chair away from other children and entertaining activities for one minute.	Any classroom staff who are present when these behaviors occur and parents at home. Initiation of service: 9-6-95 Ending date: 8-15-96

348

3. Increase sustained attention to tasks up to a duration of 15 minutes.

Provide structured one-on-one tutoring for short periods each day, initially with the teacher or paraprofessional, later using peer tutors. Use child-selected high-interest materials and allow Jennifer to switch to various objects or toys, gradually requiring longer contact before switching is possible.

Special education teacher and aide.
Initiation of service: 9-6-95
Ending date: 8-15-96

Short Term Objectives

Related annual goal	Observable behavior	Conditions	Criterion	Evaluation & measurement procedures—review dates
1. (a) Establish self-help skills	Jennifer will unbutton and remove her coat, take off her hat, and hang both in her cubby	with no teacher assistance other than verbal direction at the beginning of class each day and after outdoor play	within three minutes of entering the classroom at least twice each day	The parent will record completion of the task and time required at entry each morning and the aide after outdoor play on a record sheet kept in Jennifer's cubby. Reassess procedure in one month.
1. (b) Establish self-help skills	Jennifer will remove her underpants and urinate in the toilet	when taken to the bathroom after snack, after lunch, and after nap, and at any time she requests to use the toilet	within five minutes of arrival at the bathroom each time she is taken	The aide will record time and success using a data sheet kept in the bathroom. Review progress in two months.
1. (c) Establish self-help skills	Jennifer will turn on water, use soap, scrub, and dry her hands	with verbal reminders and physical prompting when needed, after toileting and before eating snack and lunch	requiring no more than one physical prompt and two verbal reminders	The aide will record number of verbal and physical prompts required. Review in two months.
2. (a) Reduce temper tantrums	Jennifer will say "No"	when she does not wish to participate in an activity	without crying, hitting, or running away	Teacher will observe circle time each day and record number of invitations to participate given to Jennifer, times "No" is used and number of times crying, hitting, or running away occurs. Reassess in one month.

Table 10.1/ *Individualized Educational Program (continued)*

2. (b) Reduce temper tantrums	Jennifer will participate	in circle activities when invited to by the teacher	with appropriate singing talking, or hand movements requested	Teacher records number of invitations to participate given to Jennifer, and if she complied appropriately or not. Review in one month, expand to table activities when possible.
3. (a) Increase sustained attention	Jennifer will manipulate, watch, or listen to a toy	which she has selected while working one-on-one with the teacher, aide, or peer for a 15-minute session	for three minutes before switching to another toy	The teacher or aide will use 10-second interval recording to note engagement. Review in one month.
3. (b) Increase sustained attention	Jennifer will sit quietly	during story time	without leaving her seat for three minutes	Aide will use 10-second interval recording to note quiet sitting.

Recommendations and justification for placement:

Jennifer will be integrated into a combination Head Start/School District preschool which serves primarily typical 3-to-5-year-old children from low-income families. This will allow Jennifer to observe appropriate peer models, to have opportunities to learn social and academic skills in preparation for kindergarten, and to engage in age-appropriate activities. A special education teacher is available to work directly with Jennifer and to advise on behavioral and self-help skills. The combination program also offers parent training and support for Jennifer's family.

Date of IEP meeting: August 20, 1995

Persons present—Name/position

Cheryl Howard, Special Education Teacher   Pat Lepper, School District Representative
Julia Fry, Occupational Therapist   Lyle Lovinger, Father
Betty Port, School Psychologist   Julia Lovinger, Mother

Parent Signature

Lyle Lovinger

Julia Lovinger

he is given a bite of ice cream after each bite of soup, or when he is simply praised after each bite. All these factors can have a substantial impact on the quality and strength of a child's overall performance.

The *criterion* of an instructional objective expresses how well a behavior is to be performed to be considered sufficient. Criteria, in some cases may be stated as percentage correct, duration of performance, level of proficiency, topography, or intensity. For example, "Katie will turn and make eye contact when her name is called by the teacher, *90% of the time.*" "Jacob will walk, using only his wheeled walker for assistance, *a distance of 20 feet* across the classroom." "Amy Jo will remove her coat, with assistance unbuttoning, and hang it in her cubby *within five minutes* of entering the classroom."

Criteria should be stated in such a way as to identify consistent levels that are likely to be used and reinforced (Bailey & Wolery, 1992). A child who touches a toy but does not shake it, lift it, listen to it, or in some way have fun with it is not really likely to play with the toy because of its own reinforcing properties. A better criterion for interacting with a toy might be to make it react in some way (rattle, roll, ring, etc.) because it is the toy's reaction that will eventually maintain the behavior of playing with toys.

Criteria should also reach for a high level of proficiency or automaticity that encourages generalization and independent functioning. For example, if the criterion for using "please" is "for 20% of the times a spoonful of food is offered during feeding," then a child is not likely to use the word "please" very often or under new circumstances. On the other hand, if a child is expected to use "please" 90% of the times any adult or child offers toys, food, activities, music, or television, then the child is likely to use "please" very often. "Please" will become automatic when choices are given and may generalize to become a word to request items or activities before they have been offered.

Guidelines for Developing Good Objectives   In summary, any time specific instructional objectives are developed, they should be worthwhile. It is perhaps because so many IEPs are written without thought to individual needs or attention to detail that many teachers see IEPs as a waste of time. The initial investment of thought and time in developing a truly individualized IEP pays off in long-term achievements for the teacher, parent, and child. Bailey and Wolery (1992) suggested the following guidelines for good objectives:

1. They should be developmentally appropriate; that is, they should address skills typical for a child's age and matched to a child's development.

2. Objectives should be **functional.** They should include skills that help a child be more independent, help a child learn a more complex skill, help a child move to a less restrictive environment, or help the family care for the child.

3. Objectives should include skills valued by the parents and significant others.

4. Objectives should be realistic and achievable.

5. Objectives should vary according to a child's stage of learning, including acquisition, mastery, and generalization.

Special Education and Related Services

The next step in IEP development is to decide what strategies, procedures, and materials will help a child achieve the instructional objectives that have been identified and how progress will be monitored (Noonan & McCormick, 1993). That is, an intervention team decides what to teach in order to attain the stated objectives; how to modify or adapt curriculum content, materials, and procedures; and how to arrange the environment to facilitate skill acquisition and generalization.

Special education is, by definition, specially designed instruction that includes adaptations that are significantly different from modifications normally made for typical students and are necessary to offset or reduce the adverse effect of a child's disability (Strickland & Turnbull, 1990). For example, specially designed instruction might include the use of a communication board to help a child initiate interactions and respond to peers in the classroom, the use of peers to model and reinforce offers to play or share toys, or the use of switch-activated toys as reinforcing consequences for verbalizations. Instruction can be modified according to:

1. Levels of assistance provided,

2. The kinds of extrinsic motivation used,

3. The arrangement of the environment and materials,

4. The programming of opportunities for generalization.

It is essential that specially designed instruction be both systematic and naturalistic (Noonan & McCormick, 1993). Students should be exposed to routine schedules, methods of instruction, and management strategies. Systematic instruction emphasizes consistency but does not require unnatural and mechanistic instruction. Educational plans should not be so rigid as to rule out regard for the interests and spontaneity of young children.

For example, specially designed instruction will often include providing assistance through prompting. Prompts may be verbal, gestural, auditory, movement, or picture cues that help a child respond without making errors. Prompts also include models and physical manipulation when necessary. Carefully programmed materials insert and then fade out prompts in such a way that a child can move errorlessly through each lesson.

Specially designed instruction almost always involves "reinforcement-rich" environments in which a child's appropriate responses may be positively **consequated,** making it more likely that the behavior will be repeated. Many natural reinforcers are available, including smiles, hugs, a favorite toy, or a special game. Sometimes the environment must be arranged to make it easier for children to obtain reinforcement for their efforts. For example, teaching during natural routines such as lunch, using age-appropriate and interesting materials, and presenting tasks through fun games and activities all make it more likely that a child's responses can earn reinforcement (Noonan & McCormick, 1993).

Finally, specially designed instruction must address the transfer of skills to other settings, other caregivers, and other appropriate situations. This **generalization** of newly mastered skills is ensured only through systematic and naturalistic procedures. Special education approaches should include the following generalization procedures (Stokes & Baer, 1977):

1. Common materials should be used both in training and in nontraining situations. For example, if a child is learning to use a straw at school, the family should use straws at home too.

2. Naturally occurring contingencies should be emphasized. For example, a child learning to climb steps should be encouraged to climb the steps of a slide and enjoy the quick trip down the slide as a natural reward for her work.

3. Contrived contingencies should be designed to be subtle or not too obvious, so that they can be gradually reduced. For example, a child might get a big handshake for speaking in front of the group but, later, receive a brief squeeze on the hand and, still later, a pat on the hand for the same behavior. Finally, just a wave or salute would be sufficient to maintain the behavior.

4. Generalization should be mediated by providing strategies that assist a child in new situations. Singing the alphabet song in order to remember alphabetical order while in the library is a good example of a strategy most people use.

5. One should use variety in the kinds of prompts, reinforcements, and corrections used from time to time. For example, when giving directions to move from circle to table work, a teacher might sometimes say, "Please sit in your chair at the table," and other times, "Walk to the table quietly."

Related services are those additional support services that allow children to benefit from their educational experience. For example, a child who uses an electric wheelchair may require special lift-van transportation in order to attend school, a child who requires catheterization may need a nurse or paraprofessional to assist in the mechanics of emptying the bladder, and a mobility specialist may train a child who is visually impaired to use a cane to find her way around the school building so she can move independently from the bus to her classroom.

The provision of services to a wide range of eligible children and their families involves the coordinated efforts of many related personnel, including but not limited to, audiologists, nutritionists, nurses, occupational therapists, physicians, psychologists, physical therapists, social workers, speech-language pathologists, and vision specialists (Brown & Rule, 1993). Table 10.2 identifies examples of the related services each professional might provide. All of these personnel concentrate on working with families, addressing child development needs, and coordinating services. In addition, **paraprofessionals** contribute significantly to preschool

Table 10.2/ *Personnel and Related Services*

Professional	Examples of services provided
Audiologist	auditory training, speech-reading, and listening-device orientation and training
Nutritionist	assess food intake, eating behavior, and feeding skills; provide nutrition information and early intervention
Nurse	advise parents and caregivers on basic health needs; develop medical plans to treat developmental problems
Occupational therapist	enhance sensory function and motor skill; select, design, and build assistive seating and orthotic devices
Physician	comprehensive medical care, diagnosis, and treatment; instruct parents and care givers in health care
Psychologist	assess psychological and behavioral needs and resources; plan and provide psychological and developmental interventions
Physical therapist	recommend or build adaptive equipment and mobility devices; recommend and implement environmental modification; teach handling, positioning, and movement techniques to facilitate motor functioning and posture
Social worker	make home visits to evaluate living conditions and parent-child interaction patterns; provide counseling; mobilize community resources
Speech-language pathologist	assess and diagnose communication and oral-motor abilities; provide appropriate therapy for oral-motor and communication skills
Vision specialist	assess visual functioning; provide communication-skills training, orientation and mobility training, and independent living skills training

Source: Adapted from Brown, W., & Rule, S. (1993). Personnel and disciplines in early intervention. In W. Brown, S. K. Thurman, & L. F. Pearl (Eds.), *Family-centered early intervention with infants and toddlers: Innovative cross-disciplinary approaches* (pp. 245–268). Baltimore: Paul H. Brookes.

education in both home and center settings by providing support to teachers and parents or by directly aiding children in daily activities (Brown & Rule, 1993).

Least Restrictive Environment

Another key feature of the IEP is the designation of an appropriate and least restrictive educational setting. IDEA makes it clear that children with disabilities should be placed, to the greatest extent appropriate, with peers who are not disabled. Placing a child with a disability in an environment populated only by other children with disabilities may result in a limited educational experience (Thurman & Widerstrom, 1990). Such a setting does not provide typical role models who facilitate learning language, peer interaction, and other functional skills. Segregation also does not encourage acceptance by peers and adults, nor is it compatible with society's emphasis on pluralism. Finally, no clear evidence exists to suggest that a child with disabilities is better served within a self-contained program, while the benefits of peer modeling and interaction are well documented. Thus, placement in integrated preschool settings is recognized as a goal for children with disabilities.

Still, it would be unwise to place children in settings that do not meet their most pressing needs and the preferences of their parents. A preschool setting is not least restrictive if it fails to provide appropriate services and support. Therefore, the concept of least restrictive should not be considered equivalent to providing one regular program for all children. Legislation and court precedents uphold the need to provide a variety of possible placement opportunities. Least restrictive environments are best facilitated through a continuum of program options which allow a child to enter at any point needed and move on to more or less segregated settings when it is appropriate.

For example, a child who is born with a serious medical problem or physical disability may require a longer than normal hospitalization with the extensive involvement of a team of medical personnel. The hospital or residential setting would be considered the most restrictive on a continuum of placement options but, at this point in the child's life, would be the only appropriate setting for providing the care needed. When this child's health status reaches a satisfactory level, the hospital is likely to discharge the child to home care, sometimes accompanied by medical equipment, such as a respirator or heart monitor. Often, visiting nurses will be assigned to work with the parents and child in the home, and if the child's health continues to be fragile, other early childhood professionals may also provide in-home services.

As the child's strength and stamina increase, placement in a center-based program where the parents and child can work with therapists and special equipment becomes a reasonable option. Perhaps, at first, the child attends only three mornings a week and a physical therapist provides therapy and parent training in a setting where several other families are also present. When the child acquires mobility and speech and language skills, placement in an intensive program five mornings a week might be preferred. As the child grows more independent and shows stable health, placement in a full-time integrated preschool might allow more normal peer interaction. Eventually, this preschooler enrolls in the neighborhood kindergarten program, with consultation from relevant specialists (see Figure 10.1).

As long as an integrated preschool program is properly structured and children are provided training and reinforcement for interaction, this option is clearly the ethical and developmental preference (Thurman & Widerstrom, 1990). A greater availability of child care and other preschool programs for children without special needs makes inclusive settings more accessible to young children with disabilities. However, preschool settings and their curricula should be scrutinized along several dimensions to determine their appropriateness for a particular child and family. Factors that warrant careful consideration are the following: the instructional methods used, experiences and activities provided, how generalization of skills is promoted, the physical environment, curricular adaptations, data collection and evaluation, and the use of technology (Sandall, 1993).

CASE STUDY

Transitioning to Public School

Interview with Tom and Ann Simpson

Tommy just turned three and he learned to walk this summer. He used to really hate physical therapy, and he's always had low muscle tone, even for a Down syndrome child. We've started taking gymnastics classes, and he really likes all that. His fine motor skills are pretty good; he learned to eat right away, but he's real motivated to eat. He's always the best eater in his group. He was the last child in his group to learn to walk, but he was the first child to be able to eat.

Tommy's very social. He likes other children, and he behaves appropriately. He goes to music class, and we're in gym class, and he really acts out a lot less than some of the other normal children. He follows directions to some extent. We have a lot of fun with him because we do all of the preschool things. We go to the library. We go shopping. We go to music class. He does all of that and likes all of it.

I don't think we've really had to readjust our routine for him, except that he's sick an awful lot. He's been in the hospital a couple of times. We did have to adjust to taking him to therapy, which he started when he was just a week or two old. There have been several really kind people along the way who helped us, and his therapist was one of those. He started in a private school intervention program when he was about five months old.

Now, Tommy will be starting with the school district preschool program, and I'm nervous about it. There have already been several miscommunications between me and the school about where he's supposed to go for testing and everything. I thought, "Oh my God, what's going on?" So I just called the teacher and said my son's coming into your program; can I see your classroom? I could tell that most parents don't do that, but I felt I needed to do it. So Tommy and I were introduced to the teachers and the children, and it made me feel more comfortable.

Tommy's new school is in our neighborhood, and they will bus him from our house or from my baby-sitter's house. I felt good about his school; the kids in his special preschool class were verbal and at Tommy's level. I feel he needs to be with the normal kids in his neighborhood school.

I've been to a workshop on transitioning to the public school, and I guess I know as much as anyone else does about what's going to happen. But I decided that I wasn't going to sit passively and wait. I've talked to other parents who live in this area. It's funny, even before Tom was born, we'd see the bus come and the neighbor's wheelchair come out, and I remember thinking, "I wonder who that is." We didn't know our neighbors yet, and they are quiet people. But I talked to the father once about where his daughter went, and he had been happy with the local school program.

The school system is a big bureaucracy, and you've got to interface through all these people, but what you need is a manual to know who to talk to. I don't have much blind faith that it's all going to work out okay. I guess I watch each

(continued)

TOMMY SIMPSON

step a lot more and talk to people more and am a lot more proactive. But yet, I don't want to just beat those guys up because I know what it's like. I work in a big bureaucracy too. I know how things happen, but I also know I have a duty to my child and to myself, to be on top of these things.

Getting Tommy into school reminded me of when Tommy was born. If you put yourself in the hands of the system, you need to know it's designed for its own expediency rather than for your experience and comfort. One thing I have learned is to be proactive about getting my needs and my child's needs met, but always trying to be polite about it. I've talked to a lot of parents who just will take whatever comes, and I guess I'm not willing to do that.

Instructional Methods Early interventionists need to be proficient with a variety of instructional methods in order to meet the needs of children with different disabilities, age levels, cultural beliefs, and family values (Sandall, 1993). Yet, sometimes, educational philosophy dictates which instructional approach is used (Sandall, 1993). A *developmental perspective* is associated with enrichment activities that emphasize a stimulus-rich environment with age-appropriate activities and toys. Play and self-expression are encouraged. The *behavioral perspective* is associated with direct-instruction methods that include a systematic analysis of objectives, sequencing of learning steps, and systematic reinforcement of desired behaviors. Activities and learning tasks are generally teacher-directed. The *interactional and ecological perspectives* place more emphasis on how children and their environments influence each other. These latter perspectives are more often associated with responsive and active-learning techniques, such as milieu teaching, in which the environment is arranged to stimulate a child's interest and behavior on which a teacher can elaborate. These programs would also be described as child-directed and emphasize natural events and routines. Still other programs focus on parents as teachers and emphasize parent-child interactions and support systems for families.

An appropriate program for preschool children with disabilities provides a balance of both highly structured (**teacher-directed**) activities and less structured (**child-directed** or **developmental**) activities. Such scheduling allows direct instruction on specific skills that provide opportunities for skill acquisition, proficiency, and generalization within natural situations. For example, a specific language curriculum could be used during circle time, and a child with a language disability would be systematically prompted to respond appropriately. During free play, the same child might be encouraged to verbalize about an object or activity that is self-selected.

Figure 10.1/ *The Preschool Continuum of Least Restrictive Settings*

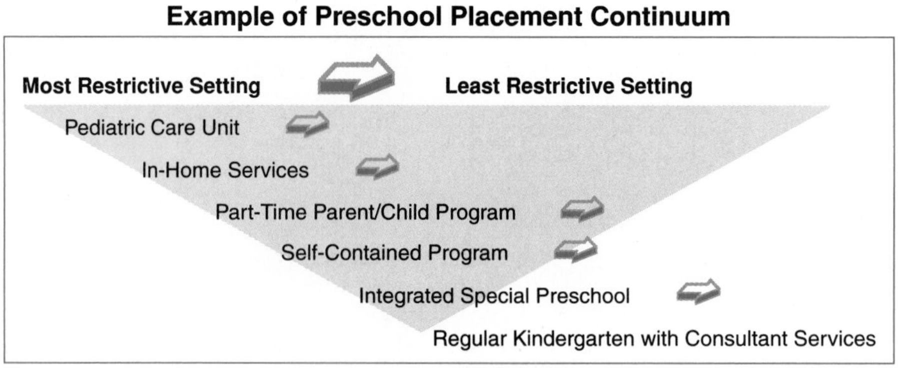

Example of Preschool Placement Continuum

Most Restrictive Setting → Least Restrictive Setting

Pediatric Care Unit

In-Home Services

Part-Time Parent/Child Program

Self-Contained Program

Integrated Special Preschool

Regular Kindergarten with Consultant Services

In addition, generalization is best facilitated if instruction is carried over between both center and home. A center-based program provides opportunities for special instruction and socialization, while well-informed parents can intervene by continuing contingencies for specific behaviors during daily routines in the home setting. For example, a child who is learning to fasten clothing may be highly motivated to button a jacket when the whole class is going outside to the playground. The child's teacher uses this opportunity to instruct by providing partial prompts of physical assistance, as needed during coat buttoning. At home, the parents may use the same system of partial prompts to help the child learn to button clothing in the morning and then, as a reinforcer, allow the child to play outside for a while before boarding the bus for school.

Experiences and Activities   Early development occurs primarily within social contexts (Sandall, 1993). It makes sense then that intervention programs promote social behaviors between infants and their parents/caregivers and between preschoolers and their peers. Activities should also promote engagement or active involvement with the environment (Sandall, 1993). A range of experiences should be provided to accommodate different capability levels and varied interests.

Consider, for example, a four-year-old child, Jonathan, with autism who is included in a preschool program for other four- and five-year-old children. This child is mobile only with the use of a walker, has no expressive or receptive language skills, and engages in **self-stimulation.** Most of the children are able to sit quietly in circle time and listen to the teacher read a story. Jonathan will turn away from the teacher and flap his hands and fingers in this situation. Adjusting for this individual child's interests will help Jonathan participate with the group. For example, using concrete objects or a flannel board increases Jonathan's attentiveness, allowing him to hold something in his hands during the story decreases self-stimulation, and letting Jonathan push the appropriate computer key as the story is told allows him to respond. The other children may even prompt Jonathan to keep his hands quiet as they listen to the story. None of these adaptations make the story less appropriate or less interesting for Jonathan's peers and may, in fact, improve their attention and participation as well.

Generalization   A consistent finding in the research literature is the poor generalization of newly acquired behaviors to functional, less-structured settings by individuals with disabilities (Sandall, 1993). Consequently, programs for young children should emphasize functional, meaningful behaviors that will have many opportunities for practice across settings, people, and materials (Sandall, 1993). Settings should use natural activities, materials, and routines to promote generalization.

A preschool setting considered as a placement for a child with disabilities should be evaluated according to these factors. For example, are all the children responsible for putting away toys, setting the table for lunch, and dressing themselves for recess (all functional behaviors)? Are the children encouraged to play with each other, to verbalize their needs, to engage in group activities (vital for socialization)? Do children take part in regularly scheduled activities such as hand washing, story time, outdoor play, and snack time (routines)?

The Physical Environment   The preschool environment should foster security and trust by being safe, warm, inviting, secure, and predictable (Bailey & Wolery, 1992). Personal identity, opportunities to develop control over their physical surroundings, and a rich and stimulating environment should also be a part of preschool designs (Bailey & Wolery, 1992). The environment should contain child-sized furniture, child-centered displays of their own work, personal storage spaces, and a shelter for escaping from over-stimulation. Numerous activity areas should be available for arts and crafts, reading, sand and water play, housekeeping and dramatic play, wood-working, and outdoor exercise.

Different areas of a room may be more conducive to specific behaviors and routines or specialized instruction. For example, noisy block play should be located away from language activities where a therapist is working on the production of specific speech sounds. A one-way mirror could be located conveniently so that parents may observe instruction or evaluation without distracting a child. Finally, traffic patterns may have to be arranged to accommodate orthopedic equipment such as standing tables or wheelchairs. For some children, it may be necessary to have a ramp to access playground equipment.

Curricular Adaptations   A variety of supports and resources are needed to help adapt activities for individual children (Sandall, 1993). These include access to specialists and technical assistance and availability of specialized materials to accommodate for sensory, motor, health, or other specialized needs. In addition, all services should be delivered at locations close to the family.

For example, specialized feeding equipment, such as a nonslip plate with a lip to catch food, a built-up spoon handle, and a cutaway cup might allow a child to self-feed at lunch with other children. Therapy mats and bolsters should be a part of the classroom furnishings so that physical therapy can be provided without removing a child from the classroom. When not used for therapy, the equipment might make a nice obstacle course for all children. A computer with a touch screen could be used to help a child with severely limited movement to demonstrate cognitive skills and also for art activities or games with the other children.

Data Collection and Evaluation   A necessary component of any preschool program is a set of procedures for collecting and using data to monitor the effects of program efforts (Sandall, 1993). Data should be collected regularly and systematically and used in making educational decisions. Such data might be collected through direct observation of specific child behaviors, through the use of developmental checklists, through permanent product samples, such as videotapes or audiotapes, and through family reporting. Irrespective of the method, it is critical that data be linked to a child's goals or program and used to adjust program activities in accordance with changes in a child's development.

For example, a goal for Courtney, a child with Down syndrome, is to increase verbal interactions with peers. Her preschool teacher decides to observe Courtney on the playground and record how often she asks to play with other children during the daily 15 minutes of outdoor play. The teacher quickly discovers that across a week, Courtney initiated requests to play an average of only once a day, and in every case, the peers did not accept her as a playmate. The teacher then devises a strategy to verbally prompt and praise such requests and to praise peers who play with Courtney. Further data collection shows that requests to play have risen to an average of five per day. Now the teacher can fade out her prompting while continuing to praise interactions with all children.

Technology   Finally, when determining the appropriateness of a placement setting, one should consider technological interventions that may benefit young children. Technology can allow young children opportunities for play, socialization, language, and manipulation of the environment (Sandall, 1993). For example, some simple electronic switches can be activated with as little as an eye blink or a puff of air to operate toys that teach cause and effect. **Augmentative communication** devices, such as an electronic board that speaks when a child touches a picture, allow children who have no capacity for speech or signing to interact with others in a variety of settings. Many preschool language programs are now available on personal computers and can be used with groups of children to stimulate language skills.

In summary, all these factors—experiences and activities, instructional methods, generalization, physical environment, curricular adaptations, data collection and evaluation, and technology—should influence the final placement of any preschool child requiring special education. The critical piece of any IEP is the shared goal of enhancing the child's development and learning (Sandall, 1993). This outcome is reached only through the careful planning of instructional objectives, the deliberate selection of special education and related services that support those objectives, and the appropriate placement of the child in the least restrictive setting that will promote the child's involvement and progress.

Teaching Preschool Children with Disabilities
Tutoring Skills: Effects on Preacademic Behaviors

Children learn by playing, cooperating, and sharing with other children. Even preschool students are capable of playing an active part in their education, and peer tutoring is one method for allowing this to happen. Peer tutoring assists children in acquiring cognitive, language skills, and social skills, and children also seem to enjoy "playing teacher." Even preschoolers with disabilities gain from being tutors and generalize the social skills they develop to other play situations.

In this study, six preschool students with disabilities were taught to use a simple tutoring procedure. Four of the children were selected because they would be attending a regular kindergarten the next year and needed instruction in preacademic skills. Two other children were selected because they had a need for preacademic instruction and social skills training.

Each tutor was trained in the following behaviors:

1. To present a stimulus card (Tutor takes card out of green basket, holding forward, "smiley" face at top, waiting for responses, and placing it in the red basket.)
2. To praise (Tutor tells tutee "good/great job" for a correct answer.)
3. To deliver a stamp (A stamp is placed on a piece of paper by the tutor after he or she delivers a praise statement to the tutee.)
4. To give corrective feedback (Tutor tells tutee the correct answer and waits for response before placing card in the red basket.)

All the tutors were required to meet a criterion of 80% for each particular tutoring behavior for four

D. A. Tabacek, T. F. McLaughlin, & V. F. Howard (1994). *Child & Family Behavior Therapy, 16* (2), 43–63.

consecutive days before moving on to the next tutoring skill.

The stimulus materials consisted of five to eight index cards (5 in. by 8 in.) per student. The cards presented colors, shapes, letters, counting problems, and number identification. The back of each card had a small "smiley" face on the top right hand corner, and the front of each card illustrated the correct response plus two distracters.

Tutoring sessions consisted of the students taking turns as the tutor and the tutee, while the teacher monitored, collected data, and delivered consequences (fruit-flavored cereal) to students who remained on-task. The students were given instructions that related to a particular card, such as "Count the stickers and find the number." The tutee responded by pointing to the hole on the cards next to the chosen response. The tutor could determine accurate responses if the tutee's finger was visible on the opposite side of the card next to the hole that was highlighted with a colored circle.

Some of the students required more training sessions before they could do all the steps in the tutoring procedure correctly, but all eventually mastered the procedure, and all improved in their performance on the preacademic skills taught to a level of at least 90% accuracy. These findings indicated that young children with disabilities could successfully learn reciprocal peer tutoring and gain preacademic skills in the process. In addition, an increase in peer interactions was observed outside the tutoring sessions.

As full inclusion at the preschool level becomes more commonplace, there is a temptation to have the more-capable students serve as the tutor. This research illustrates that such an approach is not necessary since children with even significant disabilities can act as effective tutors and benefit in doing so.

*A variety of
preschool approaches
serve children with
disabilities*

BEST PRACTICES IN PRESCHOOL INTERVENTION

Since the late 1960s, programs for young children with disabilities have proliferated (Karnes & Stayton, 1988). A model program may be defined as one in which the content and operational strategies are clearly conceptualized and defined in a manner that assures internal consistency and coherence (Peterson, 1987). A number of early intervention models have been developed that capture the best of what is known about how to serve young preschool children with disabilities. These models can be characterized by the following (Thurman & Widerstrom, 1990):

1. **Integrated:** Typical children and children with disabilities are served in the same settings; there is supported placement in generic early childhood service sites.

2. **Comprehensive:** A full array of professional services is offered through a transdisciplinary approach and using direct instruction for generalized responding.

3. **Normalized:** Instruction is stressed across a number of settings, age-appropriate materials and strategies are used, contrived reinforcement and aversive control is avoided, and parents are supported.

4. **Adaptable:** Flexible procedures are employed within noncategorical models; emphasis is on the functionality of behavior rather than its developmental form or sequence.

5. **Peer and family referenced:** The curriculum is validated in reference to the child, family, and community; parents are full partners in decision making.

6. **Outcome based:** There is an emphasis on development of skills for future usefulness; transition is carefully planned.

Preschool models are sometimes identified by the location of their service delivery: center based, **home based**, or a combination of the two. Recently, the distinction of family-focus has emerged to identify intervention programs that concentrate on supporting the family rather than providing direct services to children. The following section describes exemplary programs for each of these types.

Center-Based Programs

The most common setting for serving preschoolers with disabilities is in **center-based programs** (Bailey & Wolery, 1992). These children are served in a central location, usually a public school where they attend for 3 to 5 days each week during the school year. Center-based programs can offer a wide range of family services and supports as well as direct services to children. Children who attend group sessions also have increased opportunities for social interaction, which can facilitate their transition into kindergarten settings. The following models serve as demonstrations of center-based programs and were selected based on their effectiveness and integrity of implementation.

Direct Instruction   The **Direct Instruction** model (Bereiter & Engelmann, 1966) was developed to serve low-income preschoolers and later expanded through the federally funded Follow Through program to serve low-income children from kindergarten through third grade. Comprehensive curriculum materials are now available for basic instruction through sixth grade, and a number of remedial programs have been developed that are appropriate for older students in regular and special education.

The preschool program emphasizes academic competence through the development of language, reading, and math skills. The curriculum is highly teacher-directed, fulfilling two major rules for Direct Instruction: "teach more in less time" and "control the details of what happens." More is taught by giving instruction in small groups, maintaining a fast pace for unison responding, carefully sequencing the introduction of new skills, scheduling consistent review, and providing positive consequences to motivate children. The details of instruction are controlled by the use of scripted lessons that incorporate active participation and game formats to encourage responding.

A typical class would be carefully assessed and placed in ability groups of 6 to 12 students (D. Carnine, L. Carnine, Karp, & Weisberg, 1988). These groups change composition often, based on each child's learning rates. Short lessons of 15 to 20 minutes are conducted with each group. The lessons include frequent teacher-pupil verbal interaction through considerable active participation and high levels of engagement, with as many as 10 responses per minute at an 80% to 90% accuracy rate. Specific instruction might total an hour a day, with a teacher and paraprofessional teaching two groups concurrently, while a third group works independently at learning or activity stations. Corresponding activity stations allow children to choose from typical preschool activities such as blocks, books, puzzles, housekeeping, sand and water table, or a computer.

A number of studies have verified the effectiveness of the Direct Instruction approach. Among these was a large longitudinal evaluation conducted by the Seattle public schools (D. Carnine, et al., 1988). Over 2800 economically disadvantaged children participated in Seattle's Direct Instruction preschool program. Of these, only 11% later left high school before graduation, compared to a 17% dropout rate for the control group. Twice as many students were placed in gifted programs, even though 95% of the Direct Instruction students were minority group members who are typically underrepresented in gifted programs. Placement at or above age-appropriate grade levels was 10% higher than that of the control group (Schweinhart & Mazur, 1987).

The High/Scope Perry Preschool Project   The Perry Preschool project began in 1962 as an intervention program for economically disadvantaged children (Weikart, 1988). The program uses the High/Scope Curriculum (Hohmann, Banet, & Weikart, 1979), which is organized around Piagetian principles and the premise that children are active learners who construct their own knowledge from activities they plan and carry out themselves (Weikart, 1988). Primary emphasis is on problem solving, independent thinking, social development, and relationships.

The guiding principle in the High/Scope Curriculum is that children's knowledge comes from direct experience with real objects, talking about real experiences and ideas, and from the application of logical thinking to these events. The teacher's role is to guide and challenge children's awareness and understanding (Weikart, 1988). The daily routine is primarily a plan-do-review sequence in which children make choices and carry out their activities, then recall and represent their experience verbally, pictorially, or through a model (Weikart, 1986). The teacher supports and expands on children's observations at each step. In addition, small-group times are used for more-structured activities, such as cooking and art, and a large-group circle meets to play games, sing, do finger plays, or reenact a special event.

Children with disabilities have been integrated into the Perry preschool model (Ispa & Matz, 1978). Classrooms were set up with two teachers and 15 children, 10 of whom did not have special needs and 5 with disabilities. The High/Scope model allowed each child to work at activities that were developmentally appropriate and self-paced, without infringing on the needs of other children (Ispa & Matz, 1978). Observational data and developmental testing confirmed that the children with disabilities were socially integrated and made gains equivalent to those of typical children in all areas except motor skills.

Over 120 African-American pupils who were either in the Perry Preschool or their non-preschool control group have been studied into adulthood (Berrueta-Clement, Schweinhart, Barnett, Epstein, & Weikart, 1986). The following summarizes these findings to demonstrate the effectiveness of this model (Weikart, 1988):

1. Fewer preschool graduates were classified as mentally retarded (15% vs. 35%)

2. More completed high school (67% vs. 49%)

3. More attended college or job training programs (38% vs. 21%)

4. More preschool graduates held jobs (50% vs. 32%)

5. More supported themselves by their own (or spouse's) earnings (45% vs. 25%)

6. More were satisfied with work (42% vs. 26%)

7. Fewer were arrested for criminal acts (31% vs. 51%)

8. More experienced a lower birth rate (64 children vs. 117 children per 100 women)

9. Fewer were on public assistance (18% vs. 32%)

The High/Scope Curriculum provides a highly effective child-directed approach to preschool education with substantial long-lasting gains.

The Infant, Toddler, and Preschool Research and Intervention Program   The Infant, Toddler, and Preschool Research and Intervention Program (D. Bricker & W. Bricker, 1971, 1972, 1973; W. Bricker & D. Bricker, 1976) began in Nashville, Tennessee, at George Peabody College in 1970 (Thurman & Widerstrom, 1990). The program was originally designed to serve toddlers up to age three years but was later expanded to serve children from birth to five years. About 25% of the children served were typical, about 25% were at-risk for developmental delays, and about half of the group were children with categorical disabilities such as Down syndrome, autism, and so on.

The program emphasizes the use of Piagetian concepts to guide development, while addressing individual programs to promote competencies in each domain. Activities include group and individual language training, gross and fine motor experiences, self-directed tasks, a consistent environment maintained with contingency management techniques, opportunities to develop appropriate cognitive skills, and training in adaptive skills needed for transitions into other settings.

Although the program is child-oriented, there is a heavy emphasis on parent involvement. Parents are asked to participate in their child's classroom at least once a week and project staff provide parent training, counseling, and advocacy.

A major weakness of the program has been its loosely defined evaluation strategy (Thurman & Widerstrom, 1990). Although the Brickers have reported many benefits of the program for children both with and without disabilities, they have not collected data in such a way that it is possible to substantiate these claims.

The Model Preschool Program for Children with Down Syndrome and Other Developmental Delays   The Model Preschool Program was one of the original centers funded by the 1968 Handicapped Children's Early Education Assistance Act (Fewell & Oelwein, 1991). It began at the University of Washington Experimental Education Unit and has been replicated throughout the United States and in many foreign countries. Program goals are as follows:

1. To increase children's rates of development in six skill areas: gross and fine motor, cognition, receptive and expressive communication, and social/self-help

2. To involve parents in carrying over instructional strategies into the home

3. To train university students and others in the field

The program uses a test-teach-test model relying on curriculum-based assessment, systematic and individualized instruction, and guidance through stages of learning, including acquisition, fluency, transfer, and generalization of basic skills. Parents attend their children's classes, master instructional strategies used in the classrooms, and are trained in developmental, academic, and behavioral management techniques used at school. The program has been successfully implemented with children who have diagnoses of mental retardation, severe communication disorders, behavior disorders, neurological impairments, orthopedic impairments, and multiple disabilities. Children have ranged in age from 8 months to 12 years.

An extensive evaluation was conducted for 194 children (of whom 92 had Down syndrome) enrolled in 14 Model Preschool Program sites. During the study, data were taken frequently and shared with the model sites. Parents and staff were trained in adhering to the instructional strategies promoted but were allowed flexibility in class size, staff ratio, and so on. Results showed that, for the total group, the rate of development during intervention was significantly greater than prior to intervention, across all six skills targeted.

Home-Based Programs

There are several advantages to training parents to be teachers for their own children (M. Shearer & D. Shearer, 1979). First, learning takes place in children's natural environments, eliminating the problem of transfer from school to the home. Secondly, there is direct and constant opportunity to intervene on behavior as it occurs naturally. Thirdly, behaviors learned in the natural environment tend be maintained more easily. Finally, training parents gives them the skills to deal with new behaviors as they occur. The Portage project offers an outstanding model for such an approach.

The Portage Project   The Portage Project was initially funded in 1969 by the Bureau of Education for the Handicapped as one of its first demonstration projects (D. Shearer, 1979). The original goals for the project were as follows:

1. To develop an educational service for preschool children with disabilities and their parents living in rural areas of south central Wisconsin

2. To develop a model that was practical, cost effective, and able to be successfully replicated by other programs

3. To make a statement, a single declaration: that parents can teach their own children in their home

The model subsequently developed and provided comprehensive services to a rural area in which no educational service had been previously provided to preschool children with disabilities. The staff's belief was that early intervention should begin as soon as possible and that consultation with parents should begin the moment a child was identified as needing services (D. Shearer, 1979). The program utilized a teacher as change agent who trained parents in their home to work with their own children. Teachers met with each child's family in a one-day-per-week visit of one and a half hours for a period of nine and a half months (M. Shearer & D. Shearer, 1979). Ongoing assessment, curriculum planning, and weekly objectives for parents were provided. Parents maintained a behavioral log describing the activities used and their child's accomplishments in each developmental area.

Both certified special education teachers and paraprofessionals were hired and trained to work as home teachers. Each certified home teacher served about 12 children, and paraprofessional home teachers each served about 10 children. The staff met for inservice one day per week.

Teachers made use of the Early Childhood Curriculum Guide (D. Shearer, et al., 1970) developed by project staff for this purpose. The guide includes a Developmental Sequence Checklist identifying sequential behaviors from birth to five years of age in the areas of cognitive, language, self-help, motor, and socialization skills. The Guide also contains a set of Curriculum Cards that match each of the 450 behaviors on the checklist to behavioral objectives, teaching activities, and materials.

When home teachers visited each week, they brought Curriculum Cards with prescriptive activities and materials to accompany each. The home teacher collected baseline data on each new skill and if performance indicated probable success within a week, then the teacher demonstrated the activity to the parent and later observed the parent carrying out the lesson as described on the Curriculum Card. The home teacher gave feedback and praise to improve parents' teaching skills. Parents carried out the prescribed lessons during the week and recorded the child's performance.

The Portage Project has been successful with children from birth to the mental age of six and has been applied to both typical children and children with disabilities. Measures using the Stanford-Binet and the Cattell Infant Test show that the average project child made 15 months developmental gain in an 8-month period (D. Shearer, & M. Shearer, 1976). Project children also showed significantly greater gains than a group of control children who attended preschool classes serving culturally and economically disadvantaged children (D. Shearer, & M. Shearer, 1976). By 1979, seventy Portage-based replication sites had been subsequently established in the United States and a number in other countries, such as Ecuador, Great Britain, Japan, and Canada (D. Shearer, 1979).

Combination Center- and Home-Based Programs

Programs that utilize both center-based and home-based strategies are able to maximize the benefits of both models. Combination programs can offer a wide range of family services and supports, both at their central location and in the home. The center component allows an efficient use of staff time and ease of supervision. Team members can work closely together but, because of the added home component, can involve parents in both planning and implementation of services. The center services allow children opportunities for socialization, while home services provide for those who are too young or too fragile to take part in group activities.

Multi-Agency Project for Preschoolers (MAPPS) The MAPPS project was developed at Utah State University and works with agencies, including rural preschools for the developmentally delayed, Head Start programs, the Navaho Reservation, Air Force Family Support Centers, and high school programs for adolescent mothers and their families (Karnes & Stayton, 1988). The program is both developmental and behavioral and serves children from birth to five years of age. The focus is to provide parents, caregivers, and teachers with assessment and appropriate intervention curriculum materials for use with individual children.

The MAPPS project serves over 500 children, of whom 20% are Navajo and another 20% Hispanic or African-American. The children have a wide variety of disabling conditions or are at-risk for developmental delay. Each child has an individualized program and the delivery system is based on the individual needs of the children and their families. Parents may choose to have their infants served in the home or in a center; most of the toddlers are served through a combination of home plus center. Children from three to five years of age are mainstreamed into existing preschool and day-care programs, while MAPPS provides child assessment, teacher training, and curriculum materials.

The Curriculum and Monitoring System (Peterson & Sedjo, 1979) developed by the MAPPS project is the primary curriculum used (Karnes & Stayton, 1988). This curriculum provides a developmentally sequenced series of teaching objectives that cover skills normally developed from birth to five years of age. Each skill is task-analyzed and taught in small steps.

Project EDGE   The project for Expanding Developmental Growth through Education (EDGE) is a program for children with Down syndrome. It provides home instruction to infants and center-based preschool instruction to children over 30 months of age (Thurman & Widerstrom, 1990). Project EDGE was first funded through the Handicapped Children's Early Education Program and was based out of the University of Minnesota.

Rynders and Horrobin (1975) described Project EDGE's basic principles in regard to how mothers should work with their young children. These can be summarized as follows: affectionate sensorimotor interaction, an emphasis on speech and language, flexible structure, involvement of nondisabled siblings, and novelty of activities. Mothers are expected to engage in specified training activities for one hour each day using the EDGE curriculum and simple materials. Daily home stimulation continues even after the child begins attending the center-based preschool.

Project EDGE staff provide maternal tutoring and other services, such as respite care and a mobile education unit to lessen maternal stress. An itinerant teacher conducts lessons in the home and provides counseling and instructional support for parents. The mobile unit is used as a classroom on wheels and taken to various locations for child instruction in a classroom-like setting. When compared to a control group, project EDGE children showed positive performance differences in concept formation, expressive language, on-task behavior, and IQ scores (Rynders & Horrobin, 1975).

Family-Focused Programs

These programs are designed primarily to provide assistance and support to family members rather than direct services to children. In most cases, children with disabilities may be attending center programs or receiving intervention through other outlets.

Supporting Extended Family Members (SEFAM)   The SEFAM project is unique in that it does not provide direct services to children. Instead, services are provided to family members who are traditionally underserved: fathers, siblings, and grandfathers (Karnes & Stayton, 1988). The SEFAM project was originally administered solely by the University of Washington, but now each component is housed separately. The Fathers Program is run through the Merrywood School for the Handicapped in Bellevue, Washington, the Grandparents Program is administered by the Advocates for Retarded Citizens of King County, Washington, and the Siblings Program remains with the University of Washington. The SEFAM programs supplement direct service programs for children with disabilities and their families. Staff routinely provide infor-

Jennifer Waritz, The Education Experience

Interview with Tammy Waritz

Jennifer began her early education at a private school for children under the age of three who have disabilities. She attended twice a week, for a couple of hours at a time, and I was deeply involved in her therapy program. It was the most nurturing place we could ever have been. Sometimes it was difficult for us to see other children who weren't as involved as Jennifer, but it was also hard to see children who were more involved. We knew the pain those families were feeling.

The private school was such a supportive and caring environment, a loving and warm place to be. Everyone was very accepting, and they not only worked with Jennifer, they worked with the family. We learned so much from being there. I guess that's why I do the parent advocacy work that I do today. I want to see the system change for families, so they don't have to struggle for the services they need. Jennifer had physical therapy, occupational therapy, and speech therapy twice a week. Her team of professionals taught me so much, helped me learn the system, and helped me gain the knowledge that I needed. They recognized that I was going to be Jennifer's real "case manager," her advocate for the rest of her life, because she doesn't have a voice for herself.

When Jennifer turned three, she was transitioned into a public school self-contained program. That was a scary time for us, because we were leaving the private school where we had been very much involved. (I'm not sure that it's natural for families to separate when the child is only two or three years old.) That Fall, the big yellow school bus pulled up in front of the house, and we were expected to put her on the bus and wave good-bye. The first day I followed the bus to school to make sure that she got off at the right stop; it was still a huge transition for the family.

Jennifer spent two years in a self-contained program, and then the school district initiated a cooperative venture with Head Start to provide an integrated preschool program. The integrated pro-gram was originally set up for children who were much less involved than Jennifer, but I asked for Jennifer to be included, even though I was nervous about the change and wanted to make sure that Jennifer could still go back to the self-contained program if the integrated preschool didn't work for her.

I was afraid of how the other children would treat Jennifer, and I was also worried about how the other parents would react to her. I was afraid there would be so much going on in the regular classroom that she wouldn't be able to learn. For the first three years of her life, all her teaching had been one-on-one, and even in the self-contained program, there had been only six to eight students

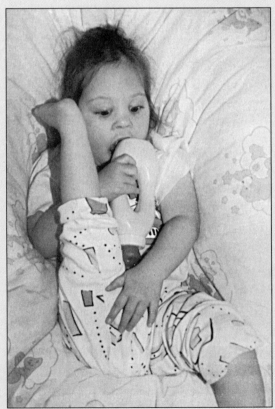

JENNIFER WARITZ

at one time. The Head Start classroom served 12 children, was a regular preschool, and was very energetic, so I was really afraid that Jennifer's needs weren't going to be met.

In fact, Jennifer made more gains in the integrated program in the first year than she had made during her two years in the self-contained program. The social interaction was so important for her. Even though she wasn't on the same level and couldn't do some of the same things, she was always right there with her peers. Jennifer developed a vocabulary of 5 to 10 words and was introduced to a communication board to help her express her needs and wants. We asked that Jennifer stay in the program an additional year, where she continued to develop and make gains that allowed her to be moved right into a regular kindergarten classroom the next year.

Moving into kindergarten was even more difficult because now there was only one teacher and maybe an aide if the teacher was lucky. We requested a full-time aide to assist Jennifer in that environment because we couldn't expect the teacher to meet her needs. Jennifer spent half her day in the regular kindergarten and the other half of her day in a self-contained program for children with developmental impairments. I wanted both programs because of Jennifer's involvement; there are things that she needed to learn in order to be as independent as possible. She deserved the dignity to learn these self-help skills without her peers looking on. The self-contained program provided her with the occupational, physical, and speech therapy she still needed.

Currently, Jennifer is spending about two hours a day and lunch time with her first-grade class. Her aide is still there with her, but we made it clear that we didn't want that person attached to her side, that Jennifer needed to be free to interact naturally in her environment. That's what we've really focused on trying to do. When I went to the first-grade open house, I really didn't know quite how it was going for Jennifer, but there was her own little desk with her name tag and the same little books that everybody else had. When I looked on the other desks in the classroom, I saw they were all doing journals, and Jennifer had one too. Sometimes an adult had helped Jennifer do her journal, but I could see there were children who'd also helped her. In almost every journal on the other students' desks was at least one page with a sentence written about Jennifer in the book. I realized, "She really does belong. She is a member of this classroom."

mation and referral to family members to auxiliary services such as respite care or recreational programs that would benefit the family system. The SEFAM project is based on a family systems orientation. Family members' needs are assessed through formal instruments and addressed through group meetings and newsletters.

PRESCHOOL SERVICES IN THE TWENTY-FIRST CENTURY

The purpose of early childhood special education is the provision of appropriate intervention services that will ultimately assist all children with disabilities. Four fundamental assumptions support this purpose:

1. Children who have disabilities or are at-risk for having disabilities need and have a right to specialized services to enhance their development and the likelihood of success.

2. Families of children with disabilities often experience special needs and stresses.

3. The provision of *earlier* services can mean the achievement of optimal outcomes for children and families.

4. Because of the unique characteristics, needs, and resources of each child and family, no one curriculum or set of services could be expected to meet the needs of all. An individualized approach to service planning and delivery, therefore, is essential. (Bailey & Wolery, 1992, p. 34)

Given these beliefs, several basic service goals for early intervention are apparent (Bailey & Wolery, 1992). First, it is essential that families are supported in achieving their own goals; professionals must serve children in ways that are consistent with family structures, values, needs, and functions. Assisting children in their development requires the promotion of child engagement, independence, and mastery across all the key domains; the final measure of a child's development is successful interaction within a great variety of physical and social environments. Special education must always recognize the primary goal of helping children live lives that are as normal as possible, incorporating all children and their families into mainstream settings and activities. Finally, early intervention must address the prevention of new disabilities or future problems.

Beyond these primary goals for children with disabilities, each early childhood professional must also accept responsibility for pursuing goals important for the culture as a whole (Bailey & Wolery, 1992). The services mandated through IDEA are very new in the history of this society and as such must be protected and supported if they are to be maintained. It is important that special educators continue to increase the public's awareness and acceptance of people with disabilities and their need for early intervention. It is essential that special educators continually and consistently attempt to improve the quality of early intervention services through research and evaluation. Finally, professionals must be active in communicating best practices and disseminating professional knowledge to others in order to promote the availability of quality services. Early childhood professionals must advocate not only for the children and families in their direct care but also for future populations who will face the same challenges.

As this country moves into the next century, the direction preschool intervention services will take depends greatly on the kind of federal leadership that is offered. Currently, there is political movement toward reducing federal governing responsibilities and returning them to the states. Although there have been instances of outstanding leadership at the state level, beleaguered state agencies must already struggle to meet current legislative requirements with few resources (Bricker, 1988). Certainly continued federal resources are required to ensure that all the important issues of early childhood special education are addressed and resolved in ways that lead to the delivery of quality services regardless of state of residence in this nation. Among the issues that need attention in the coming years are these:

1. The improvement of the IEP process toward genuine family involvement

2. The provision of a continuum of preschool services for all children

3. Greater concern for the continuity between early childhood and subsequent education

4. Better preparation of early childhood personnel

It has been reported that most parents are not actively involved in the IEP process, and therefore the process is not valued by many professionals (Bricker, 1988). Family members contribute critically to the development of a functional IEP by relaying assessment information, making decisions about goals and objectives, and participating in the implementation of programs. It is necessary to find new ways to support families in order to encourage participation (Caldwell, 1988). This may necessitate greater creativity and flexibility in the way services are delivered (Bricker, 1988). A greater emphasis on interagency and family collaboration will be essential.

Flexibility must also extend to the kind of placement and service options available as a continuum for intervention and inclusion. It should be a goal to tailor programs to fit families rather than forcing families to fit existing programs (Bricker, 1988). As professionals work toward greater inclusion in natural settings, a merger of early childhood special education and child care should be seen; this might be aptly called "educare," programs that provide care and protection as well as education (Caldwell, 1988). Such settings would also be most natural and convenient for providing the intervention services required of an individual child's education. A real continuum of appropriate services would provide educare for all children—typical, disabled, gifted, at-risk, culturally different, and so on (Caldwell, 1988).

In addition to establishing more opportunities for a continuum of services within preschool, there must also be a continuity between early childhood and subsequent education (Caldwell, 1988). The transition from preschool to school age services should allow us to maximize on the evaluations and curriculum planning already in place, while maintaining already established professional and family relationships, without causing redundant paperwork and time-consuming meetings.

Finally, these changes will not come about successfully without extensive review of the way in which early childhood personnel are prepared (Ludlow & Lombardi, 1992). As practice moves toward inclusive and continuous models for early childhood, more teachers and interventionists trained to work across a variety of categorical labels and across a variety of educational settings are required. All early childhood personnel will need (a) specific course work in special education, (b) methods for infusing special education into more typical educational approaches, and (c) more experience in working collaboratively with other disciplines. Educational specialists will serve in consultant roles to instructional teams and families and will work with more diverse children and settings.

The twenty-first century should achieve the best early childhood education for all young children, regardless of potential or disability (Ludlow & Lombardi, 1992). There should finally be recognition of the crucial nature of the early years of life by the general public (Caldwell, 1988). By the twenty-first century, there will be enough evidence collected to make a persuasive case for a network of quality early childhood programs for all children, provided regardless of social or economic status, appropriate for a range of intellectual or physical needs, and supportive of families and professionals (Caldwell, 1988).

STUDY GUIDE QUESTIONS

1. In what ways were the primary provisions of IDEA of 1975 "blockbuster legislation"? Consider the history of special education in the United States prior to this legislation.

2. In what ways was the original IDEA legislation amended to provide for children three to five years of age?

3. What are the essential components of an IEP?

4. Generate an original example of a clear statement of present levels of performance.

5. Develop a good objective to describe communication targets for a four-year-old child with moderate retardation. Be sure to include the behavior, the conditions, and the criterion.

6. Look carefully at the objective just written, what guidelines for an instructional objective does it already address? How could it be improved it to meet the remaining guidelines?

7. What are the critical characteristics of specially designed instruction?

8. Describe how one might ensure the generalization of conversational skills for a three-year-old child.

9. Describe three specialists who might provide related services to a preschooler (and family) with a hearing impairment. What kinds of support might they provide?

10. Sometimes the same setting is least restrictive for one child but not for another. Give an example of

a child for whom a self-contained preschool program for hearing impaired children might be most appropriate and one of a child for whom it is not.

11. Briefly describe how a teacher-directed program might be different from a child-directed one. What would be the possible advantages and disadvantages of each?

12. How do center-based and home-based programs differ? Design a combined program that would maximize the advantages of each.

REFERENCES

Bailey, D. B., & Wolery, M. (1992). *Teaching infants and preschoolers with disabilities.* 2nd ed., New York: Macmillan Publishing Company.

Bereiter, C., & Engelmann, S. (1966). *Teaching disadvantaged children in the preschool.* Upper Saddle River, NJ: Prentice Hall.

Berrueta–Clement, J. R., Schweinhart, L. J., Barnett, W. S., Epstein, A. S., & Weikart, D. P. (1986). Changed lives: The effects of the Perry Preschool Project on youths through age 19. In F. M. Hechinger (Ed.), *A better start* (pp. 11–40). New York: Walker.

Bricker, D. D. (1988). Commentary: The future of early childhood/special education. *Journal of the Division for Early Childhood, 12*(3), 276–278.

Bricker, D. D., & Bricker, W. A. (1971). Toddler research and intervention project report: Year I. *IMRID Behavior Science Monograph* (No. 20). Nashville, TN: Institute on Mental Retardation and Intellectual Development, George Peabody College.

Bricker, D. D., & Bricker, W. A. (1972). Toddler research and intervention project report: Year II. *IMRID Behavior Science Monograph* (No. 21). Nashville, TN: Institute on Mental Retardation and Intellectual Development, George Peabody College.

Bricker, D. D., & Bricker, W. A. (1973). Infant, toddler and preschool research and intervention project report: Year III. *IMRID Behavior Science Monograph* (No. 23). Nashville, TN: Institute on Mental Retardation and Intellectual Development, George Peabody College.

Bricker, W. A., & Bricker, D. D. (1976). The infant, toddler and preschool research and intervention project. In T. D. Tjossem (Ed.), *Intervention strategies with high risk infants and young children.* Baltimore: University Park Press.

Brown, W., & Rule, S. (1993). Personnel and disciplines in early intervention. In W. Brown, S. K. Thurman, & L. F. Pearl (Eds.), *Family-centered early intervention with infants and toddlers: Innovative cross-disciplinary approaches* (pp. 245–268). Baltimore: Paul H. Brookes.

Caldwell, B. M. (1988, December). Early childhood education in the 21st century. *Exchange,* 13–15.

Carnine, D., Carnine, L., Karp, J., & Weisberg, P. (1988). Kindergarten for economically disadvantaged children: The Direct Instruction component. In C. Warger (Ed.), *A resource guide to public school early childhood programs* (pp. 73–98). Alexandria, VA: Association for Supervision and Curriculum Development.

Ershler, J. L. (1992). Model programs and service delivery approaches in early childhood education. In M. Gettinger, S. N. Elliott, & T. R. Kratochwill (Eds.), *Preschool and early childhood treatment directions* (pp. 7–53). Hillsdale, NJ: Lawrence Erlbaum Associates.

Fewell, R. R., & Oelwein, P. L. (1991). Effective early intervention: Results from the model preschool program for children with Down syndrome and other developmental delays. *Topics in Early Childhood Special Education, 11*(1), 56–68.

Gallagher, K. S., & Gallagher, R. J. (1992). Federal initiatives for exceptional children: The ecology of special education. In D. A. Stegelin (Ed.), *Early childhood education: Policy issues for the 1990s* (pp. 175–193). Norwood, NJ: Ablex Publishing.

Goodman, L. V. (1976). A bill of rights for the handicapped. *American Education, 12*(6), 6–8.

Heward, W. L., & Orlansky, M. D. (1992). *Exceptional children.* 4th ed., New York: Macmillan Publishing.

Hohmann, M., Banet, B., & Weikart, D. P. (1979). *Young children in action: A manual for preschool educators.* Ypsilanti, MI: High/Scope Press.

Ispa, J., & Matz, R. D. (1978). Integrating handicapped preschool children within a cognitively oriented program. In M. J. Guralnick (Ed.), *Early intervention and the integration of handicapped and nonhandicapped children.* Baltimore: University Park Press.

Karnes, M. B., & Stayton, V. D. (1988). Model programs for infants and toddlers with handicaps. In J. B. Jordan, J. J. Gallagher, P. L. Hutinger, & M. B. Karnes (Eds.), *Early childhood special education: Birth to three* (pp. 67–108). Reston, VA: Council for Exceptional Children.

Ludlow, B. L., & Lombardi, T. P. (1992). Special education in the year 2000: Current trends and future developments. *Education and Treatment of Children, 15*(2), 147–162.

Mager, R. F. (1962). *Preparing instructional objectives.* Belmont, CA: Fearon.

Noonan, M. J., & McCormick, L. (1993). *Early intervention in natural environments, methods and procedures.* Pacific Grove, CA: Brooks/Cole.

Peterson, A., & Sedjo, K. (1979). *Curriculum and monitoring system.* New York: Walker Educational Book Corporation.

Peterson, N. L. (1987). *Early intervention for handicapped and at-risk children: An introduction to early childhood special education.* Denver, CO: Love.

Rynders, J. E., & Horrobin, J. M. (1975). Project EDGE: The University of Minnesota's communication stimulation program for Down's syndrome infants. In B. Z. Friedlander, G. M. Sterritt, & G. E. Kirk (Eds.), *Exceptional infant: Assessment and intervention* (Vol. 3). New York: Brunner/Mazel.

Safer, N. D., & Hamilton, J. L. (1993). Legislative context for early intervention services. In W. Brown, S. K. Thurman, & L. F. Pearl (Eds.), *Family-centered early intervention with infants and toddlers: Innovative cross-disciplinary approaches* (pp. 1–19). Baltimore: Paul H. Brookes.

Sandall, S. R. (1993). Curricula for early intervention. In W. Brown, S. K. Thurman, & L. F. Pearl (Eds.), *Family-centered early intervention with infants and toddlers: Innovative cross-disciplinary approaches* (pp. 129–151). Baltimore: Paul H. Brookes.

Schweinhart, L. J., & Mazur, E. (1987). *Prekindergarten programs in urban schools.* Ypsilanti, MI: High/Scope Foundation.

Shearer, D. E. (1979). Introduction. *Portage project readings.* Portage, WI: Portage Project.

Shearer, D. E., & Shearer, M. S. (1976). The Portage Project: A model for early childhood intervention. In T. D. Tjossem (Ed.), *Intervention strategies for high risk infants and young children.* Baltimore: University Park Press.

Shearer, M. S., & Shearer, D. E. (1979). The Portage Project: A model for early childhood education. *Portage project readings.* Portage, WI: Portage Project.

Shearer, D., Billingsley, J., Frohman, S., Hilliard, J., Johnson, F., & Shearer, M. (1970). *Developmental Sequencing Checklist.* Unpublished manuscript, Portage, WI: The Portage Project, Cooperative Educational Service Agency No. 12.

Stokes, T. F., & Baer, D. M. (1977). An implicit technology of generalization. *Journal of Applied Behavior Analysis, 10,* 349–367.

Strickland, B. B., & Turnbull, A. P. (1990). *Developing and implementing individualized education programs.* 3rd ed., Upper Saddle River, NJ: Merrill/Prentice Hall.

Tabacek, D. A., McLaughlin, T. F., & Howard, V. F. (1994). Teaching preschool children with disabilities tutoring skills: Effects on preacademic behaviors. *Child & Family Behavior Therapy, 16*(2), 43–63.

Thurman, S. K., & Widerstrom, A. H. (1990). *Infants and young children with special needs, a developmental and ecological approach.* 2nd ed., Baltimore: Paul H. Brookes.

Weikart, D. P. (1986). Basics for preschoolers: The High/Scope approach. In F. M. Hechinger (Ed.), *A better start* (pp. 83–92). New York: Walker.

Weikart, D. P. (1988). Quality in early childhood education. In C. Warger (Ed.), *A resource guide to public school early childhood programs* (pp. 63–72). Alexandria, VA: Association for Supervision and Curriculum Development.

Discretionary Programs for Very Young Children with Special Needs

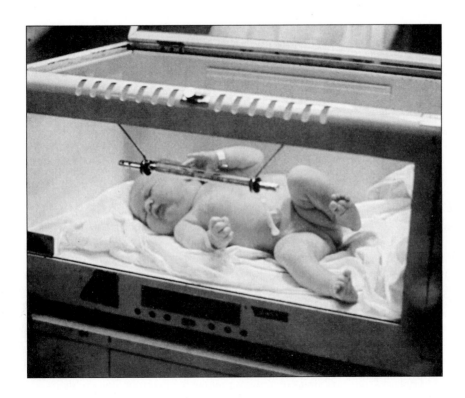

PART A: PRINCIPAL ELEMENTS OF EARLY INTERVENTION

For very young children with special needs, **early intervention** refers to the period between birth and age three. Additionally, the term *early intervention* is used to refer to delivery of services as early as possible in a child's life. The former use of the term is legislated. Even before the passage of P.L. 99-457 in 1986, which gave states an incentive to begin providing comprehensive early intervention, many infants and toddlers with special needs were being served through a variety of programs. These programs may have been funded through such federal entitlements as Title I or, as demonstration projects, through the Handicapped Children's Early

373

Education Programs (HCEEP). Many early intervention programs and models funded through HCEEP had two decades of experience in and evaluation of service to very young children before P.L. 99-457 was passed. It was the knowledge and experience gained through established early intervention programs that encouraged investment in comprehensive services to infants and toddlers for both ethical and practical reasons (Casto & Mastropieri, 1985; Guralnick, 1988).

While infants and toddlers with special needs remain underserved, recent federal legislation prompted a significant increase in the availability and comprehensiveness of services (see Table 11.1). Mention of these changes has been made several times throughout this text. One legislative act, amended on three key occasions, outlines the regulations for serving children with special needs from birth through age six. In 1975, Part B of P.L. 94-142 (1975 Amendments to Education of All Handicapped Children Act—EHA) included initial guidelines for services to preschoolers. The 1986 Amendments to the same law (P.L. 99-457) altered the regulations for preschoolers and added new guidelines for serving infants and toddlers with special needs under Part H. Recently, this law, now referred to as IDEA, was amended in 1991 under P.L. 102-119 to substantively change regulations under both Part B for preschoolers and Part H for infants and toddlers. As can be seen in Table 11.1, each of these revisions to special education law broadened the scope of services available to the youngest children in our society. At this writing, IDEA is again under serious consideration by Congress. Proposed changes to the law could substantially change services to children with special needs. Such issues as individual program planning, categorical labeling, funding methods, and allocation of funding are being considered ("Individuals with," 1995). Some believe that these changes will improve services to very young children (Riley, 1995), while others are more cautious in predicting the future (Lewis, 1995; Penning, 1995).

Public Law 99-457

Amendments to IDEA in 1986 represented the most comprehensive and farsighted commitment to very young children with special needs in our federal history. Specifically, Part H of the law provided substantial discretionary incentives to all states that designed and implemented comprehensive services for infants and toddlers in compliance with federal regulations. Congress passed this law after deliberating the following potential benefits of early intervention to our society:

1. Minimizes the potential for developmental delay and reduces the impact of handicapping conditions

2. Reduces the overall cost of educational services through prevention and attenuation

3. Enhances the capabilities of families to meet the needs of their children

4. Minimizes the likelihood of institutionalization of children with special needs

5. Maximizes the developmental potential of individuals with disabilities to eventually live independently in society (Tucker & Goldstein, 1991)

Initially, states were given five years to come into full compliance with Part H, after which the incentive moneys were to have been withdrawn. However, P.L. 102-119 extended the eligibility window while giving states in full compliance access to full funding (see Appendix B). Other states could be granted up to two one-year "extensions" at a reduced funding level. Several facets of Part H make it unique compared to special education law for school-age children. The most important difference is recognition of the influence an entire family has on the development of children. Consequently, issues such as governance, individualized intervention service plans, services, models of delivery, and service coordination all vary in significant ways from procedures for older children with disabilities.

Table 11.1/ *Legislative History of Special Education and Early Childhood Special Education*

1965	P.L. 89-10	Elementary and Secondary Education Act (ESEA)	Plan intended to equalize educational opportunity for economically under-privileged children
1966	P.L. 89-313	Amendment to ESEA	Authorized grants to universities and state institutions to serve children with disabilities
1966	P.L. 89-750	Amendments to ESEA	Authorized grants to local schools to serve children with disabilities
1969	P.L. 91-230	Amendments to ESEA	Amended P.L. 89-750 and established a core grant program for local educational agencies (This program is known as Part B.)
1974	P.L. 93-380	Amendments to ESEA	Introduced concept of appropriate services to all children with disabilities (Family Education Rights and Privacy Act)
1975	P.L. 94-142	Individuals with Disabilities Education Act (IDEA)— originally named Education for All Handicapped Children Act (EHA)	Mandated public school programs for children with disabilities between the ages of 3 and 21
1983	P.L. 98-199	Amendments to IDEA (EHA)	Established parent training centers and funding for demonstration and research projects in early intervention and early childhood special education
1986	P.L. 99-457	Amendments to IDEA (EHA)	Mandated public education of preschoolers with disabilities and established Part H to assist states to serve infants and toddlers
1990	P.L. 101-476	Amendments to IDEA (EHA)	Amended P.L. 99-457 to mandate transition services and assistive technology to children's IEPs; added disability categories; added related services
1991	P.L. 102-119	Amendments to IDEA	Changed specific language to Part B dealing with preschoolers and Part H with respect to eligibility, related services, IFSPs for preschoolers, LRE, and funding

Interagency Coordination To manage the complex services promised under Part H, a unique governing body was created for early intervention. At the federal level, Part H is coordinated by an Interagency Coordinating Council (ICC), comprised of representatives from 15 different governmental agencies that provide services to infants and toddlers with disabilities and led by the U.S. Department of Education (USDOE). Money allocated under Part H flows from

USDOE to each state's lead agency for the administration of early intervention programs. Many states and territories selected their own Department of Education to administer Part H, while approximately the same number of states designated their Department of Health as the lead agency (Colarusso & Kana, 1991). The remaining states and territories designated other agencies such as Mental Health, Mental Retardation, or Human Resources as their lead agencies (MHLP, 1990). Appointed by the governor, the lead agency provides a single line of authority and is responsible for planning and implementing state and federal Part H regulations. The primary duty of the lead agency is to develop interagency agreements between those parties involved in delivery of services. Agreements must stipulate procedures for such actions as resolution of disputes and payment of service providers.

The governor of each state appoints at least 15 members to the State Interagency Coordinating Council. State ICCs advise and assist their lead agencies in planning for implementation and oversight of Part H requirements. Membership to this committee must include at least 20% parents of children with disabilities, 20% service providers from public or private early intervention programs, one representative from the state legislature, one person involved in early intervention personnel preparation, one state insurance representative, and representatives from other state agencies. In addition to these state level ICCs, many states have created other levels of administration by appointing regional and local ICCs. The latter usually include similar heterogeneous representation and perform the duties of forming local interagency agreements and coordinating and delivering services to families.

Interagency Services When agencies need to coordinate their services to meet the needs of a particular child, it is the lead agency's responsibility to initiate the formal agreement regarding who delivers and pays for early intervention services. Part H funds were not intended to supplant services and funding already provided by public agencies even though the latter might be contracted to provide services to children identified under Part H. For example, if an interagency agreement is formed with the Public Health Department, which already provides audiological assessment and treatment to the community, then Public Health and not the lead agency for early intervention is responsible for the cost of such services. Depending on the services provided and the individual situations of families served, various financial arrangements can be made to ensure that no family is denied services for which they are eligible. Sources of funding include local, state, or federal funding through agencies providing services, a family cost-sharing using a sliding scale, private insurance, and medicaid (Colarusso & Kana, 1991). Colarusso and Kana (1991) listed 16 federal agencies that should be able to contribute to early intervention services through interagency collaboration:

1. Handicapped Infants and Toddlers Program, Education (IDEA Part H)

2. Chapter I Handicapped Program, Education Consolidation and Improvement Act (Chapter I)

3. Services for Deaf-Blind Children and Youth (IDEA Part B)

4. Assistance for Education of All Handicapped Children (IDEA Part B)

5. Head Start Program (Head Start Act)

6. Medicaid, Social Security Act (Medicaid)

7. Maternal and Child Health Block Grants, Social Security Act (Child Welfare)

8. Child Welfare Services Program, Social Security Act (Child Welfare)

9. Developmental Disabilities Basic State Grants Program, Developmental Disabilities Assistance and Bill of Rights (ADD Basic State Grants)

10. Alcohol, Drug Abuse and Mental Health Block Grant Program, Public Health Service Act (Mental Health Block Grant)

11. Community Health Service Program, Public Health Service Act (Community Health)

12. Indian Health Service Program, Indian Health Care Improvement Act (Indian Health)

13. Migrant Health Services Program, Public Health Services Act (Migrant Health)

14. Preventive Health and Health Services Block Grant, Public Health Service Act (Health Block Grant)

15. Health Care for the Homeless Program, Homeless Assistance Act (Health for Homeless)

16. Social Services Block Grant, Social Security Act (Social Services Block Grant)

All these programs have the potential to provide funding for services to infants and toddlers eligible under Part H. The way in which state and local agencies choose to use these and other state and local services varies according to availability and the priorities of ICCs.

In spite of the obvious need to coordinate services across agencies in order to meet the spirit of Part H, this is the element of Part H that has been least effectively implemented (Harbin, Gallagher, Lillie, & Eckland, 1990). Aside from the task of accepting parents as equal partners, the collaboration of multiple agencies in delivery of early intervention must surely be the next greatest challenge. Each of these relationships involves sharing power where power has not been shared in the past.

Childfind   State systems must provide comprehensive **childfind** to ensure that all infants and toddlers who are eligible are found and evaluated. Identification of children through childfind efforts affords early placement of eligible children in programs when they are available, yields data needed for planning budgets and personnel, and assists local and state agencies in long-range planning for special education. Many children who are later served in early intervention were initially identified through statewide informational and screening childfind activities.

Eligible Children   Unlike Part B of IDEA, there are no federal standards or criteria for eligibility of services under Part H. Each state was given the responsibility of determining specific eligibility guidelines for early intervention services. The figures in Table 11.2 illustrate the diversity in criteria that have been established from state to state. In fact, this diversity has caused the U.S. Department of Education to rethink the criteria and to include eligiblity definitions in IDEA (Riley, 1995). In addition to serving children with developmental delays, states were permitted by Congress to serve children who were at-risk of developing a delay later in childhood. Infants and toddlers with developmental delays and those with established risk must be served by states that receive Part H funding. Two other risk categories are discretionary and served at the will of each state: biological/medical risk and environmental risk.

> *Developmental delay:* Infants and toddlers who experience delayed progress or who have fallen significantly below the age related norms in one or more areas have a developmental delay, which may be in communication, physical development, adaptive behavior (feeding, dressing, toileting, etc.), cognition, and social/emotional development. Approximately 4% of infants and toddlers fall into this category.

> *Established risk:* Children who have a diagnosed condition that gives them a high probability of later delays in development have an established risk. Conditions such as Down syndrome, PKU, muscular dystrophy, and sickle cell anemia are examples. Approximately 1% of all infants and toddlers have an established risk condition.

Biological risk: Medical conditions that threaten to compromise a child's health, particularly perinatally, are predictive of later delays. For example, children born anoxic, with low APGAR scores, prematurely, or those who experience meconium aspiration are at-risk for cerebral palsy and other developmental delays but may not have an identified disability or delay (approximately 2% to 3% of infants and toddlers).

Environmental risk: An increasing proportion of children in our society grow up in conditions that place them at risk of developmental delays. Children who live in poverty, whose parents abuse drugs or alcohol, whose primary language is not English, or who are abused are examples of children who are environmentally at-risk. Those who are environmentally at-risk represent at least 25% of our society's infants and toddlers. Because this percentage is so large, most states have elected to leave this discretionary category out of their state plans.

While it seems obvious that children with actual delays should be served, it is probably more practical economically to serve children in the risk categories. Ironically, experts agree that children at-risk are more vulnerable to environmental factors and will have greater problems later on in life than children with diagnosed disabilities (Weiner & Koppelman, 1987). Economic benefits accrue first because so many more children fall into the at-risk groups and, secondly, because relative benefits to our society are gained through *prevention* of delays (i.e., in children who are at-risk for developmental disability) as opposed to *remediation* of disabilities. Still, in times of fiscal restraint, such as we are now experiencing in this country, it is unlikely that the potential long-term cost savings to our society will influence voters to fund expensive preventative educational programs.

In addition to the new categories of services that might be provided under Part H, wisdom prevailed in the labeling of children served. Rather than giving children categorical labels, such as "seriously emotionally disturbed" or "mentally retarded," children and their families are simply identified as "eligible," with services determined and resources allocated according to assessed need. A simple designation of "eligible" avoids the issues of discrimination, testing error, and lowered expectations that are associated with categorical labeling.

Service Coordinator   Imagine a family of a child with significant disabilities receiving early intervention services from three different agencies. There is likely to be confusion and frustration regarding scheduling of appointments, payment for services, and overlap of information and recommendations for home intervention. The attempt by Congress to create an early intervention model that was comprehensive also created the need for a new method of managing the various agencies involved in service delivery for infants and toddlers with special needs. Part H of IDEA called for a "case manager" to assume the responsibility of overseeing the delivery of services to which children and their families were entitled according to the law. "One person, together with the family, actively advocates for services in response to changing needs, and is responsible for implementation of an integrated program of services, in consultation with colleague specialists" (Division of Early Childhood, 1987). The law further states that the professional *most relevant to the needs of a child* and family should serve as that family's case manager. For example, a physical therapist would be most appropriate for a child with muscular dystrophy, while a speech therapist would serve as the case manager for a child with a cleft lip and palate.

Several questions arose simultaneously with the requirement to provide case management. Educators and families asked: Who selects the case manager, the family or the agency? Can families serve as their own case manager? How many children should a case manager serve? What are the qualifications of a case manager? Partly as a result of the ensuing debate to resolve such questions, terminology in the law was changed from case manager to **service coordinator,** which reflects a less clinical and more pragmatic approach to delivery of services. Principles of service coordination generated by parents through a recent survey lend

Table 11.2/ *Examples of Variations in Developmental Delay Criteria from State Definitions*

Alabama	25% delay in one or more areas
Arizona	50% delay in one or more areas
Arkansas	2 SD in one area or 35% delay from birth to 18 months 2 SD in one area, 1.5 SD in two areas, or 25% delay for 18–36 months
Colorado	1.5 SD or equivalent in percentile (7%) or standard scores
Florida	less than 2 months delay: atypical development 2–12 months: 2–month delay in one area 13–24 months: 3–month delay in one area 24–36 months: 4–month delay in one area
Idaho	30% below age or 6–month delay or 2 SD in one area; 1.5 SD in two areas
Illinois	2 SD or 25% delay in one area; 1.5 SD or 20% delay in two or more areas or in one area with additional risk factors
Kansas	25% delay or 1.5 SD in one area; 20% delay or 1 SD in two areas
Kentucky	2 SD in one area; 1.5 SD in two areas or less than 75% developmental quotient
Louisiana	determined by multidisciplinary team
Maine	under 24 months: determined by multidisciplinary team over 24 months: 2 SD or 25% delay in one area or 1.5 SD or 15% delay in two or more areas, or 1 SD or 10% delay with additional risk factors
Maryland	25% delay in one area; atypical development/behavior
Minnesota	cognitive, 1.5 SD; communication, 2 SD; other areas involve clinical opinion and/or 1–2 SD delays
Montana	50% delay in one area or 25% delay in two areas
Nebraska	developmental delay, no criteria
New Jersey	33% delay in one area; 25% delay in two or more areas
North Dakota	50% delay in one area; 25% delay in two or more areas
Ohio	"measurable delay" or not reaching developmental milestones
Oklahoma	50% delay in one area; 25% delay in two or more areas
Oregon	56% to 75% of chronological age in 3 or more areas 40% to 55% of chronological age in 2 areas less than 40% of chronological age in 1 area
Puerto Rico	informed clinical opinion
South Carolina	2 SD or 30% delay in one area; 1.5 SD or 22% delay in two areas
South Dakota	25% or 6 months delay or 1.5 SD
Tennessee	25% delay in two areas; 40% delay in one area
Utah	2 SD or below the 2nd percentile in one area 1.5 SD or below the 7th percentile in two areas 1 SD or below the 16th percentile in three areas
Vermont	observable, measurable delay
Wisconsin	25% delay or 1.3 SD in one area; atypical development; or team decision

Source: Adapted from Shakelford, J. (1992). State/jurisdiction eligibility definition for Part H. *NEC*TAS Notes, 5,* 1–13.

Criteria based upon 1992 state plans.   SD = Standard Deviation understanding to family preferences regarding their relationship with a service coordinator (Early & Poertner, 1993). Parents indicated the following:

1. Parents should have a major role in determining the extent and degree of their participation as service coordinators.

2. Service coordinators should have frequent contact with children, families, and other key participants.

3. A single service coordinator should be responsible for helping families gain access to needed resources.

4. Parents and child should be involved in decision making.

5. Service coordinator roles and functions should support and strengthen family functioning.

Legally, service coordinators have responsibility for ensuring that seven major components of program delivery are completed according to federal and state laws:

1. Coordinating the performance of evaluations and assessments,

2. Facilitating and participating in the development, review, and evaluation of individual family service plans,

3. Assisting families in identifying available service providers,

4. Coordinating and monitoring the delivery of available services,

5. Informing families of the availability of advocacy services,

6. Coordinating with medical and health providers,

7. Facilitating the development of a transition plan to preschool services if appropriate.

It is not necessarily a service coordinator's responsibility to directly provide the services listed above, rather that person makes sure families have access to these services. In fact, the primary goal of service coordinators is to foster family empowerment. Strengthening a family's abilities to coordinate their own services promotes human development and helps build the overall capacity of individuals, families, and communities.

Service coordinators can empower families in several important ways. They can improve families' capacity to master a broad range of skills by providing information to increase knowledge of their child's disability, giving choices and encouraging families to make their own decisions regarding types of services, and showing parents how to access information or perform certain intervention strategies independently. Service coordinators can also improve liaisons and linkages to mobilize social supports within a family's community. Both **primary social supports** (i.e., close family, friends, and neighbors) and **secondary social supports** (e.g., health care providers, educators, and therapists) can provide families with a network capable of enabling them as caregivers of a child with special needs (Dunst, Trivette, & Deal, 1988). Just as service coordinators themselves must be careful to honor the privacy of families, they can work to protect families from other sources of unwarranted intrusion. Being careful to avoid paternalism, service coordinators can serve as advocates for family rights. Finally, service coordinators may be able to minimize stress by making essential resources available in a manner that eliminates or reduces unnecessary work or anxiety.

Since this role is new to special education, there has been much speculation as to the proper training, credentialing, and characteristics of persons serving as service coordinators (Bailey, 1989). According to Berzon and Lowenstein (1984):

> To be effective, the case manager...must possess a high threshold for frustration, a high tolerance for ambiguity, an ability to measure barely perceptible increments,

a sense of humor and an ability to turn to others for support. Personal flexibility, creativity, and persistence are also important. (p. 54)

Such recommendations reflect the importance of engaging in positive, proactive behavior. However, maintaining this attitude has not always been easy for public service professionals. Maroney (1986) described four perspectives taken by many professionals toward parents; some of these views would interfere with the effectiveness of service coordinators:

1. Viewing families as problem-causing and interfering

2. Viewing families as resources to children (with no needs of their own)

3. Viewing families as team participants

4. Viewing families as needing resources (for themselves, independent of child)

"It is not enough for case managers to have the skills to do the tasks of their job, they also need attitudes that support families" (Donner, et al., 1993). These attitudes include: being positive; assigning no blame, no matter what; acknowledging that parents are trying; treating families as the experts on their needs; looking at the world from the parents' perspective; setting priorities based on family desires; and being sensitive to cultural, environmental, racial, religious, and sexual orientation differences.

Procedural Safeguards   States are required to establish a system that protects the fundamental rights of families and children who are eligible for services under Part H. The intent of procedural safeguards is to ensure both that the intended services are not denied to families with eligible children and that an impartial hearing can be requested when families believe their rights are violated. These safeguards are very much like those found under Part B of the same act (IDEA). Federal law and regulations stipulate the following due-process rights (MHLP, 1990):

1. *Access to Records:* Upon the request of parents, all documentation regarding screening, evaluation or assessment data, eligibility determination, development and implementation of IFSP, or other written, audiotaped, or videotaped communication regarding their child and family must be made available for examination.

2. *Notice:* Before initiation or refusal of services (i.e., identification, eligibility, service provision, or placement), parents must receive prior written notification.

3. *Confidentiality:* All personally identifiable information regarding a child or family member must be kept *confidential.* Only after parents have given written consent can information be released, and then it can be released only for the specific purpose for which the permission was given.

4. *Written Parental Consent:* Parents must give written consent before an agency can conduct an assessment or provide services to infants and toddlers. Additionally, agencies must ensure that parents are informed of their right to withdraw consent at any time. This right would be of little value to families who do not understand what "consent" means. Therefore, service providers need to explain information in a family's native language or mode of communication and then ask questions to make sure that family members have understood. As in Part B, states have the right to contest a parent's refusal of an evaluation by filing for a due-process hearing. However, most professionals feel that only in extreme cases (e.g., suspected child abuse or neglect) should a parent's decision to refuse evaluation be challenged.

5. *Surrogate Parents:* Just as with school-age children with disabilities, the state has the responsibility to appoint surrogate parents for any eligible child whose parents cannot

Early Intervention and Integration

Interview with David DeWolf

When Robin was an infant, we were encouraged to take advantage of infant stimulation, and it was all optional—enrichment rather than therapy. To the extent that Robin was in need of services, the need was to accelerate various abilities or to compensate for her otherwise retarded growth rate, but she didn't really need any services that were unique. We did go to a parent support group, and there was a class for kids with Down syndrome through a consortium of parents that had put together a kind of preschool. We went occasionally to that, but Priscilla had planned on being at home anyway, and so we really didn't need any kind of special care.

Robin started going to the special education program at the local elementary school when she was about four or five, basically about kindergarten age. We would go a day or so a week as a kind of preparation for school. We had the idea that Robin would latch on to the school environment, and we had visions that she'd be happy enough for us to be comfortable leaving her there. She never really liked it that much; she liked playing there, and she liked the other children, but until recently, Robin really was not ready (emotionally) to spend a full morning every day in school. She wanted the reassurance of being at home and it stretched her emotionally to go to school day after day.

She started last year going to a preschool three days a week. She was in a combined classroom with special education kids and regular kids of preschool age. This year she started kindergarten, and that's turned out fine. I think she's now, at age seven, developmentally and emotionally at kindergarten age. In some ways she's a little better, in some ways not quite there, but it's certainly well within her range. She is ready to be a kindergartner who learns to go to school and spend all morning at school and do it every day and not just when she feels like it. She also enjoys the sense of maturity and grown-upness about going to school and getting on the bus with her

siblings and riding on it independently. Robin likes accomplishing things and feeling proud.

Now she's in the regular education kindergarten classroom. I can tell by talking to her teacher that it has worked out just fine in terms of her skill level. She's in the pack, in terms of being able to draw things and cut things out and write her name and recognize letters or numbers or whatever, so academically it's appropriate for her. Some things are easier for her, some things are harder for her. She doesn't stand out as being unsuited for that class academically and socially it works out. She's about the right size, so she blends in. That's really neat for her.

My experience has been that she's motivated very strongly by her peers, more so than by her parents. She wants to be accepted by her

ROBIN DEWOLF

peers and to perform and achieve; they are more strict and insistent than her parents. I know, for example, her friend taught her to talk. With us she could grunt, and we could understand what she wanted to say, but when she was with her friend, her friend insisted on more articulate communication. So Robin worked on it and became much more talkative and much more verbal. She learned to do things and be more independent, and that's an effect of the peer relationship that's extremely important. It's just as with my other children, who'll stand on their heads because the kids they hang out with think that's the cool thing to do. We could ask them to do the same thing, and they'd think that we were crazy. The peer phenomenon is a pretty strong instinct, and I hope that will help carry her along.

I suspect at some point that the natural fallout from her condition will cause her to fall behind academically, and perhaps in social ways, and at some point it will simply be hard for her to keep up. I think it may be appropriate to say every third year she stays back. Some of it corresponds physically in that she's simply smaller for her age, so her body size is kind of in synchrony with her academic development. I'm anticipating that there will be some sort of natural slippage as time goes on, and then it's pretty much up to her how far

she wants to push in terms of acquiring adult skills and that sort of thing.

When our youngest (Peter) was born, we had a one in 20 chance of another baby with Down syndrome because of the accumulation of risk factors by that time. That was a tense time, but he's all too normal, and Peter and Robin have just been great friends. I think they always will be great friends. The older children have really benefited from having Robin in our family. I think one of the major benefits they aren't even aware of, is that they have become acclimated to a person with a disability in a way I never was at that age.

Robin's siblings have done a good job of treating her with very few preconceptions. They don't have the baggage that adults have about her abilities and disabilities. They're reaching the age where I think they're more conscious of the embarrassing quality of it, but the experience has really been very good for them. It hasn't come out of their hide; we're lucky in that we were never put in a situation where we had to take something away from one of them just because Robin needed an operation, nor did we have to put her in a special school, so we didn't need to change our lifestyle on some line. There has never been a sense of competition and the natural resentment that I think would come from discrepancies.

be found or are not known or if the child is a ward of the state. This surrogate is responsible for representing absent parents in duties related to evaluation, eligibility, placement, IFSP development, and so on. The state may not appoint a surrogate simply because the parents are considered to be irresponsible.

6. *Continuity of Services:* Analogous to the "stay put" principle, the continuity-of-services right assures that children and their families will continue to receive services throughout any legal proceedings. However, given joint agreement of parents and service provider, services may be withdrawn or changed. If a child has received services, and access to services is the issue under consideration, all services not in dispute should be provided.

7. *Prompt and Unbiased Dispute Resolution:* Both agencies and families may file for an impartial administrative hearing if the rights of either are perceived to have been violated. Each state determines if the regulations for a fair hearing under Part B are to be used or if new regulations will be devised for infants and toddlers. Parents must receive written notification of the resolution within 30 days of filing a request for hearing.

8. *Right to Appeal:* Parents or schools may file a civil action in state or federal courts to appeal a resolution made during the administrative hearing.

9. *Procedures for Resolving Systemic Problems:* Parents and others have the right to file a complaint if it is believed that the state has failed to implement any Part H regulation(s). The state must arrange an independent investigation, with results (and resolution if necessary) completed within 60 days of the complaint.

It is the obligation of each service provider to ensure that due-process rights are made clear to parents. These regulations are complicated and can be intimidating for early childhood professionals and must, therefore, be doubly obscure for many parents new to this field. The fact that we have the privilege of working more closely with parents in early intervention than with parents of older children provides greater opportunity to enhance families self-advocacy by clarifying the law as much as possible.

Assessment

Although Part H of IDEA previously permitted the delivery of services to infants, toddlers, and their families before an IFSP was completed, amendments in P.L. 102-119 now require that an IFSP be developed and have the written consent of parents before services can be delivered. In fact, the entire process of determining eligibility, planning a child's program, implementing the plan, and reviewing progress is similar to that of older children with disabilities (see Figure 11.1).

Differing from assessment of older children, the evaluation process in early intervention has two distinct but interrelated aspects: child assessment, and family assessment. The primary purposes of assessment are to determine if infants are *eligible* for services and to provide sufficient information to *plan* intervention for a child and family. Once a child is determined eligible for services and the initial Family Service Plan is developed, assessment is necessary to measure progress and evaluate the effectiveness of the services provided. Federal regulations also require evaluation and assessment to be conducted in a nondiscriminatory manner.

IDEA Guidelines for Assessment   Each lead agency shall adopt nondiscriminatory evaluation and assessment procedures. The public agencies responsible for the evaluation of children and families under this part shall ensure, at a minimum, that:

1. Tests and other evaluation procedures and materials are administered in the native language of the parents or other modes of communication, unless it is clearly not feasible to do so

2. Any assessment and evaluation procedures and materials that are used are selected and administered so as not to be racially or culturally discriminatory

3. No single procedure is used as the sole criterion for determining a child's eligibility under that part

4. Evaluation and assessments are conducted by qualified personnel

Two basic approaches may be used to conduct assessments. *Formal* assessments are more contrived and generally involve the use of standardized tools. *Informal* assessments are more consistent with current early childhood practices that place emphasis on "natural" methods. While there are advantages and disadvantages to both formal and informal evaluation, there is generally much to be gained from combining the two approaches.

Simeonsson (1986) described three methods of assessment. A **psychometric approach** is used to compare a child to normal standards of development, intelligence, or achievement in order to determine performance discrepancies. In a **behavioral assessment,** practitioners examine factors that govern children's behavior under given conditions. In this approach, the goal of assessment is to determine the controlling impact of setting conditions and consequences on behavior. Finally, manipulation of those conditions are recommended in order to

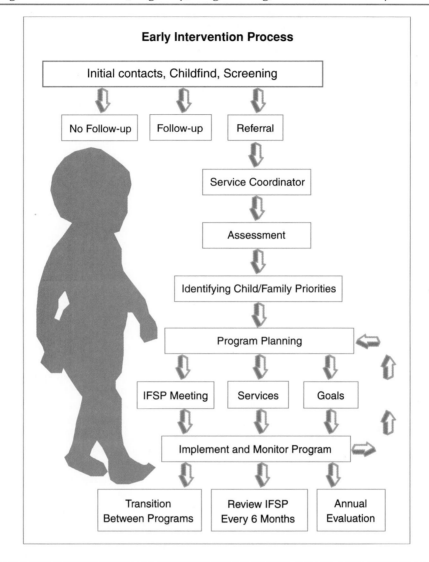

Source: Adapted from Lynch, E., Mendoza, J., & English, K. (1990). *Implementing Individualized Family Service Plans in California: Final Report.* Sacramento: California State Department of Developmental Services.

alter the observed behavior. For example, if a child is 18 months old, and not attempting to make sounds, it may be observed that the child is placed in a playpen for much of the day at a child care center and that when she does attempt to communicate, caregivers often over-look her verbalizations. It would be recommended, therefore, that caregivers provide multiple opportunities for interaction throughout the day and that they begin to consequate verbaliza-tions by imitating or expanding on her communication attempts. A child's age is irrelevant in the **qualitative-developmental** approach to assessment. Early interventionists examine a child's skills, as well as the child's approach to people and tasks. This global approach to assessment provides rich information for program development, which is particularly useful in family-centered intervention.

In addition to these three approaches, a fourth, the **ecological approach,** is currently being used by many early interventionists (Carta, Sainato, & Greenwood, 1988; Sexton, Thompson, Perez, & Rheams, 1990; Thurman & Widerstrom, 1990). Ecological evaluations focus on children, their environment, and the interaction between the two. This approach provides information that is particularly useful in program planning. Since a child's behavior and development are influenced by multiple factors, all these variables need to be considered in evaluation. Therefore, the key to ecological evaluations is to comprehensively analyze a child's *real* environment, taking into account a wide range of variables, including resources and materials, child behaviors, social relationships, and family/adult behaviors, in order to develop a very specific profile.

Child Assessment   It is the purpose of child assessment that most often determines the type and scope of procedures to be used. That is, eligibility is usually determined by a somewhat formal set of procedures, while program design typically involves relatively informal measurement conditions.

Eligibility Determination   Two stages may be involved in eligibility determination. **Screening** is a relatively quick preliminary evaluation used to determine if a child should be referred for more in-depth assessment. Because full evaluations are costly in terms of time and money, screening helps to identify those children who are most likely to need services. On the other hand, there is a drawback to this efficiency. By definition, screening tools are less accurate than follow-up assessment and, therefore, overlook many children who might actually benefit from special services.

Positive screening results lead to a **multifactored diagnostic evaluation** involving professionals from all relevant disciplines. This evaluation must be completed within 45 days of referral. In early intervention, this multidisciplinary team almost always includes parents, an educator, and a communication specialist. The purpose of a team approach to assessment is to have adequate expertise represented in all program areas.

State regulations guide practitioners in determining what data are needed in order to make an eligibility decision (see Table 11.2). Formal assessments use standardized tools, which compare a child's behaviors to those of a standard **norm.** For example, a 10-month-old child's language behaviors are compared to the average language behaviors of children at 10 months of age. With average being the "standard," a significant deviance from the standard indicates that a child may be either delayed or precocious. Standardized tools are also administered in a precise manner and scored according to a set of standard procedures. That is, any variation made in giving the test that is not provided for in the testing manual, such as timing, use of materials, or instructions, renders the results unusable for comparison purposes. Informal assessments may include the use of commercially available or curriculum-referenced tools. Also used are interviews with parents, narrative descriptions of behavior, checklists, and rating scales. These data should be combined with more formal assessment data to make an eligibility determination. If a child is found to be eligible, programs have 45 days from the initial referral to plan and hold an initial IFSP meeting. Services would begin immediately following parental approval of the IFSP.

Program Planning   The most efficient assessment combines eligibility determination with programming evaluation. Due to the developmental nature of both assessment and curriculum design, it is relatively easy in early intervention to use a curriculum-referenced tool to accomplish both purposes. A curriculum-referenced tool is linked to intervention objectives so that the assessment itself is sensitive to relevant behaviors. In early intervention, these tools are generally very practical and measure behaviors in all relevant developmental areas. Some tools are specifically designed to measure very small steps in learning for children with significant disabilities. Others are closely linked to broad developmental milestones and their associated learning objectives.

Day-to-day assessment provides input for dynamic decision making regarding the appropriateness of a child's objectives, intervention strategies, and programming alternatives. Research consistently indicates that continuous measurement (daily or several times a week) is the most effective schedule for assessing child progress on learning objectives. Furthermore, direct observation methods are most useful for daily data collection. Counting the frequency or rate of behaviors (e.g., number of times in a day that child wets), measuring the length of time that a behavior occurs (e.g., duration of independent sitting before falling sideways), and assessing the magnitude of behaviors (e.g., how far will child reach across midline to grasp a toy) are examples of direct data collection.

Curriculum-based tools are also useful for measuring child progress on outcome objectives specified on IFSPs. Review of each IFSP must take place at least every six months since children can progress so rapidly through developmental stages at this early age. The comprehensive reevaluation must be completed at least annually. While it is possible for children to become ineligible for services through rapid development, the at-risk clause of Part H permits agencies to continue services should families be interested.

Family Assessment   To a large extent, family focus is based upon the provisions of P.L. 99-457. Development of IFSPs must include statements about family priorities, which necessitates the assessment of families. However, family assessment is the most sensitive and least well designed component of early intervention programs (Hanson & Lynch, 1989). Yet, families are especially vulnerable during initial diagnostic stages because they are entering a new arena in which they must rely on the integrity and proficiency of strangers. Therefore, parents should only be evaluated voluntarily; assessment for the purpose of defining a family as it relates to care of a child with disabilities is an intrusion to which families of young children without disabilities are not subjected. For these reasons, educators are cautioned to fulfill this legal requirement with wisdom and empathy.

> *Any family assessment that is conducted must be voluntary on the part of the family. If an assessment of the family is carried out, the assessment must be conducted by personnel trained to utilize appropriate methods and procedures, be based on information provided by the family through a personal interview, and incorporate the family's description of its strengths and needs related to enhancing the child's development. (IDEA, 1991)*

All aspects of a family's conduct that might influence their ability to meet the needs of their child with disabilities may be considered in the assessment. P.L. 99–457 directed professionals to include a statement of family strengths and weaknesses on the IFSP (see Figure 11.2). Traditionally, a deficiency model focused attention on family *needs* rather than on their strengths. A more proactive way of looking at families is to concentrate on their relative strengths in formulating plans. Toward that end, the 1991 amendments to Part H redirected educators to include a family-directed assessment of their respective resources, priorities for services, and concerns. Areas of family assessment may include domestic, child-parent interactions, educational, vocational, health, financial, and social domains. Again, while it may not be the responsibility of educational service agencies to provide for all the needs of a family, it is our responsibility to help establish linkages between families and corresponding services.

One approach to family assessment is a traditional format in which professionals survey parents through a standard protocol. In other words, all parents are asked a set of questions regarding specific skills, interests, and needs. Families might be interviewed or asked to fill out a written survey. Either way, professionals take the risk of offending parents who, while seeking help for their children, find the intrusion into their personal and family circumstances unwarranted. The following real account of a parent whose child was enrolled in a public program for low-income families illustrates the point.

I wanted my son in an integrated preschool program but was unprepared for the ordeal. The application process included an assessment of my very personal circumstances. I was asked questions related to the adequacy of our housing and food, whether or not I am on welfare or on legal probation, how I discipline my family, and if we use drugs, alcohol, or birth control.

This parent was from a middle-class family and, therefore, was not accustomed to being treated as if her privacy was less important than the organization's right to ask such questions. It was also apparent that the questions were viewed as perfectly legitimate for families who lived in poverty. We may learn from this example that, while persons who have low incomes

Figure 11.2/ *Comparison of Family Needs and Strengths Across Families of Children with Special Needs*

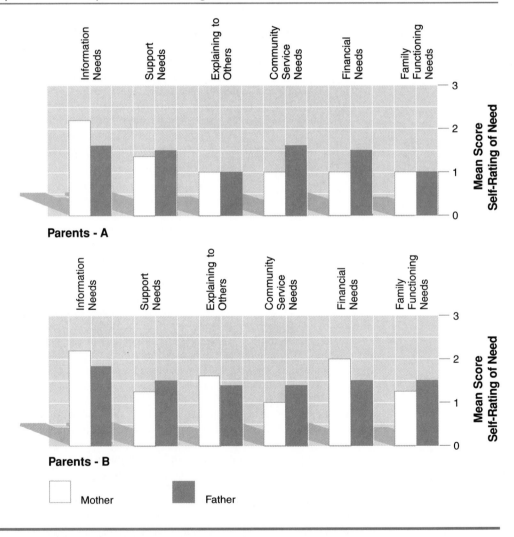

Source: Bailey, D. B., & Simeonsson, R. J. (1988). *Family assessment in early intervention.* Upper Saddle River, NJ: Merrill/Prentice Hall.

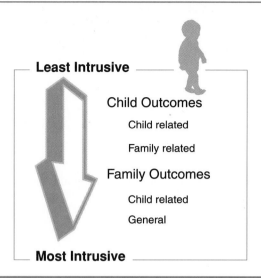

Source: Adapted from Beckman, P. J., & Bristol, M. M. (1991). Issues in developing the IFSP: A framework for establishing family outcomes. *TECSE, 11*(3), 19–31.

are often subjected to intrusive questioning in order to receive other public services, the very implication that a family is deficient could place a barrier between ourselves and that family.

Beckman and Bristol (1991), warned that assessment of families for the purpose of identifying needs of families as opposed to their children's needs could be unwittingly intrusive (see Figure 11.3). Let us take, for example, a child who has cerebral palsy. Traditionally, professionals would concentrate on child-centered needs as they pertain to a variety of developmental areas but, particularly, motor development. Motor assessment, conducted by a physical therapist, can be viewed as minimally intrusive. When the physical therapist attempts to determine if family members have the time, resources, or skills to conduct necessary motor development activities at home then the intrusiveness becomes more substantial, though certainly not unreasonable. Using the same child with cerebral palsy as our example, if the physical therapist concludes that the child requires a wheelchair, the family might be asked about their financial capacity to purchase this child-oriented equipment. Obviously, financial questions can become quite sensitive but, under the circumstances, relevant. The most obvious intrusion and least justifiable questions surround general family needs. For example, the physical therapist, in recognizing that this child is underweight and tends to have chronic upper respiratory infections, might infer that the family lacks the resources to provide adequate nutrition or health care. Asking questions regarding employment status, health care insurance, and mealtime habits represents a very delicate assessment issue that should only be approached with the greatest sensitivity. It is recommended that professionals conduct this assessment informally and only after establishing good rapport with family members (Beckman & Bristol, 1991). Winton and Bailey (1988) suggested an informal four stage process that should be initiated only after professionals and parents have built rapport with each other.

> **Phase I:** *Put family at ease: Describe the purpose, structure, and confidentiality of interview.*

> **Phase II:** *Interview: Family members should do most of the talking after being asked open-ended questions and encouraged to discuss issues that are of importance to them.*

Phase III: *Summary, priority and goal setting: Thoughts and feelings of family members are summarized and needs listed in order of priority. Though professionals may help to articulate family goals, the family itself is given the responsibility for achieving the goals.*

Phase IV: *Ending interview: After summary and articulation of goals, family contributions are acknowledged, while they are encouraged to provide continuous input to the plan.*

Even this amount of structure may be both unnecessary and too overbearing for some families. It is possible that professionals who provide a continuous sounding board and use an IFSP in a dynamic manner will be as effective as those who use a more structured approach.

IFSP Development

With the passage of P.L. 99-457 came the introduction of a new form of documentation that reflected the emphasis on family centered intervention highlighted throughout this text. Individualized Family Service Plans (IFSP) are written plans created for infants and toddlers and their families when eligibility for early intervention is established (see Appendix B). This legal document is the early intervention analog to an Individualized Educational Program (IEP), but is more holistically conceived than the latter. The required components of an IFSP include the following:

1. A *statement of child's developmental status* in the areas of communication, physical, social/emotional, cognitive and adaptive behavior, based upon the completion of a multidisciplinary assessment.

2. If family agrees to its inclusion, a *statement of family priorities, concerns, and resources,* as they relate to enhancement of their child's development.

3. A *statement of the major outcomes* (goals) that the child is expected to achieve, with the criteria for mastery, timelines for implementation and expected completion, and procedures for measuring progress included.

4. A statement of the *specific early intervention services* that must be provided to meet the aforementioned child and family goals. Included are the frequency, duration, location, and method of delivering these services; the payment arrangements, if necessary; and when deemed necessary, a specification of "other" services that may be needed by a family, but are not explicitly required under Part H, and the steps that will be taken to secure those services. While these services may be written into the document, this does not mean that the services must be provided at public expense. Such services might include helping families to identify an agency to provide financial assistance, arranging for the child to access medical-health care services, or helping to prepare insurance papers.

5. Statement of the *dates when services will be initiated and the anticipated duration of services.*

6. The name of the *service coordinator* responsible for assuring that assessment, program planning, and program implementation are provided according to the law.

7. Statement of the steps that will be taken to ensure that a child makes a smooth *transition* from early intervention services to preschool education once a child reaches age three. This includes training parents for the legal and programmatic changes expected.

While IFSPs are intended to serve as a blueprint for services and as a legal agreement with families, there was a conscious effort in the drafting of P.L. 99-457 to avoid some of the pitfalls of legislation regulating the adoption of IEPs in this country. The emphasis is rightly placed on substance of intervention rather than on paperwork compliance. Still, states are far from using IFSPs as effectively as possible. Martin (1989), however, warned us that we should not be easily discouraged:

> I think it would be unrealistic to assume that the new programs for 3- to 5-year olds and for youngsters from birth to 2 years will soon achieve full, high-quality service success either. On the contrary, I think what we have to expect is that we have achieved victory in principle with the passage of the act and that we now begin a long, frustrating process of evolution toward the kinds of quality programs that are necessary. In order to bring about success, we are going to have to be sure that the people who administer the law and the people who are responsible for implementing it understand the intent of the legislation and what their responsibilities are (p. 31).

Selecting IFSP Objectives   As in all areas of education, there is an increasing emphasis on planning children's programs to focus on real life (Notari-Syverson & Shuster, 1995; Stremel, et al., 1992). In the past, objectives for very young children were often based on skills that were evaluated on standardized tests but had little to do with the actual daily activities of infants and their families. For example, parents might be asked to take time each day to teach their child to point to the object named in a set of pictures taken from a commercially available program. Often taught as an isolated skill, parents not only spent time on skills that had little meaning for their child, but there was little chance that such skills would generalize outside the teaching situation. Such activities were contrived in many ways and failed to meet the five guidelines for developing objectives outlined by Notari-Syverson and Shuster (1995):

1. *Functionality:* skills needed to operate as independently as possible in daily routines

2. *Generality:* general rather than specific skills that can be adapted to meet individual needs and used in many situations

3. *Ease of Integration:* skills that will be used naturally in activities and social interactions

4. *Measurability:* skills that can be seen/heard and counted or measured

5. *Hierarchical Relationship:* increasingly complex skills that are logistically sequenced—each new skill building upon a previously learned skill

To provide a sounding board for determining whether or not goals and objectives selected for very young children adhere to the above criteria, Notari-Syverson and Shuster developed a checklist (see Table 11.3). The answer to each question should be "yes" if the goals and objectives meet real life needs.

Natural Routines or the Context for Objections   Naturally occurring routines are well suited for the integration of skill domains. For example, bathing can be the context for language, social interaction, motor (fine and gross) execution, and cognitive growth, as well as for self-help skill development. Instead of planning for integration, skills targeted on IFSPs are often designed to teach skills in isolation (Stremel, et al., 1992). The point of having objectives written so that they can fit into daily caregiver routines is to increase both their relevancy for children and the likelihood that parents will have a reasonable chance of working instruction of objectives into their already demanding lives. On the other hand, Stremel et al. (1992) cautioned that even when objectives are written according to the "family-child routine" standard, parents must be systematically taught to incorporate the objectives into daily activities.

Services Delivered   Several of the components of IFSPs mimic those of IEPs covered in Chapter 10. However, there are three distinct differences. First, the identification of a service coordinator described earlier in this chapter is new. Secondly, the services for which children and their families are eligible include some unique services. Finally, IFSPs must include a plan

Table 11.3/ *Checklist for Writing IFSP Goals and Objectives for Infants and Young Children*

FUNCTIONALITY

1. Will the skill increase the child's ability to interact with people and objects within the daily environment?
The child needs to perform the skill in all or most of the environments in which he or she interacts.

Skill: Places object in container.
Opportunities: Home: Places sweater in drawer, cookie in paper bag.
                  School: Places backpack in cubbyhole, trash in trash bin.
                  Community: Places milk carton in grocery cart, soil in flower pot.

2. Will the skill have to be performed by someone else if the child cannot do it?
The skill is a behavior or event that is critical for completion of daily routines.

Skill: Looks for object in usual location.
Opportunities: Finds coat on coat rack, gets food from cupboard.

GENERALITY

3. Does the skill represent a general concept or class of responses?
The skill emphasizes a generic process, rather than a particular instance.

Skill: Fits objects into defined spaces.
Opportunities: Puts mail in mailbox, places crayon in box, puts cutlery into sorter.

4. Can the skill be adapted or modified for a variety of disabling conditions?
A child's sensory impairment should interfere as little as possible with the performance.

Skill: Correctly activates simple toy.
Opportunities: Motor impairments—Activates light, easy-to-move toys (e.g., balls, rocking horse,
                  toys on wheels, roly-poly toys).
                  Visual impairment—Activates large, bright, noise-making toys (e.g., bells, drums,
                  large rattles).

5. Can the skill be generalized across a variety of settings, materials, and/or people?
The child can perform the skill with interesting materials and in meaningful situations.

Skill: Manipulates two small objects simultaneously.
Opportunities: Home: Builds with small interlocking blocks, threads lace on shoes.
                  School: Sharpens pencil with pencil sharpener.
                  Community: Takes coin out of small wallet.

INSTRUCTIONAL CONTEXT

6. Can the skill be taught in a way that reflects the manner in which the skill will be used in daily environments?
The skill occurs in a naturalistic manner.

Skill: Uses object to obtain another object.
Opportunities: Uses fork to obtain food, broom to rake toy, steps on stool to reach toy shelf.

7. Can the skill be elicited easily by the teacher/parent within classroom/home activities?
The skill can be initiated easily by the child as part of daily routines.

Skill: Stacks objects.
Opportunities: Stacks books, cups/plates, wooden logs.

MEASURABILITY

8. Can the skill be seen or heard?
Different observers must be able to identify the same behavior.

Measurable skill: Gains attention and refers to object, person, and/or event.
Nonmeasurable skill: Experiences a sense of self-importance.

9. **Can the skill be directly counted (e.g., by frequency, duration, distance measures)?**
   The skill represents a well-defined behavior or activity.
   Measurable skill: Grasps pea-sized object.
   Nonmeasurable skill: Has mobility in all fingers.

10. **Does the skill contain or lend itself to determination of performance criteria?**
    The extent and/or degree of accuracy of the skill can be evaluated.
    Measurable skill: Follows one-step directions with contextual cues.
    Nonmeasurable skill: Will increase receptive language skills.

HIERARCHICAL RELATION BETWEEN LONG-RANGE GOAL AND SHORT-TERM OBJECTIVE

11. **Is the short-term objective a developmental subskill or step thought to be critical to the achievement of the long-range goal?**

    Appropriate: Short-term objective—Releases object with each hand.
                        Long-range goal—Places and releases object balanced on top of another object.
    Inappropriate: The short-term objective is a restatement of the same skill as the long-range goal with the addition of an instructional prompt (e.g., Short-term objective—Activates mechanical toy with physical prompt; Long-range goal—Independently activates mechanical toy) or a quantitative limitation to the extent of the skill (e.g., Short-term objective—Stacks five 1-inch blocks; Long-range goal—Stacks ten 1-inch blocks).
                        The short-term objective is not functionally or conceptually related to the long-range goal (e.g., Short-term objective—Releases object voluntarily; Long-range goal—Pokes with index finger).

Source: Notari-Syverson, A. R., & Shuster, S. L. (1995, Winter). Putting real life skills into IEP/IFSPs for infants and young children. *Teaching Exceptional Children,* 29–32. Used with permission.

for a child's transition into other programs once they reach age three. While transition plans are also used for school-age students, it is only when students reach age 16 and are preparing for transition to adulthood that such a plan is required in the IEP.

When children are found eligible for early intervention, assessment of services includes both those that will directly benefit that child and those that will support a child's family. The latter services are intended to indirectly benefit an eligible child by enhancing a family's capability of meeting the child's needs. In other words, if a family or family member has a need that is so great that it prevents nurturance of the child with special needs, that family need is as important to address as the developmental needs of the child. While this practice makes sense, provision of **tertiary services** to families is both costly and complicated.

Services to infants and toddlers and their families can be provided through a myriad of models and agencies (several models will be discussed in Part B of this chapter). Though, traditionally, public and private agencies have been centralized educational facilities, the law permits considerable flexibility in delivery models. It is clear, however, that those who crafted Part H envisioned the coordination of multiple resources; both public and private agencies are to be involved when implicated by the needs of families.

Children who are eligible for early intervention may receive the following types of services if the services themselves render a child's program "appropriate."

1. Audiology

2. Service coordination (automatically provided to all families eligible for services)

3. Family training; counseling and home visits

4. Health services deemed necessary to enable infants and toddlers to benefit from the other early intervention services (This may include clean intermittent catheterization or consultation by health care providers concerning the special medical needs of children eligible for services that will influence the delivery of those services. Specifically, services that are purely medical in nature and surgical services are excluded, as are devices that are used to control or treat a medical condition, as well as medical-health services such as immunizations.)

5. Medical services only for diagnostic and evaluation purposes

6. Nursing services

7. Nutrition services

8. Occupational therapy

9. Physical therapy

10. Social-work services

11. Psychological services

12. Special education

13. Speech-language pathology

14. Transportation (direct and related costs of travel) necessary to enable the child and family to receive early intervention services

15. Vision

16. Assistive-technology devices

This list of services to children is not exhaustive. Other services such as respite care and other family support services should be provided when it is appropriate. In contrast to the services articulated for children, the law is vague about the kind of services that must be made available to families or family members in order to enable the families. In theory, families should receive those services that will permit them to adequately meet the needs of their children with disabilities. The law is so broadly stated that professionals worry about the fiscal and logistical nightmare of serving some families who might be very needy.

Unlike service providers for school-age children under special education law, service providers may charge a fee to families of eligible infants and toddlers (Tucker & Goldstein, 1991). However, services that cannot be charged for under any circumstances are evaluation/assessment and service coordination. Moreover, guidelines that are established to determine payment may not be used to deny services to children or families because of their inability to pay for those services.

Transition Plans

Making the transition from early intervention services to preschool or from preschool to kindergarten can be challenging for parents and for children with disabilities. Transitions include changes in a child's teacher and other personnel, scheduling, transportation, expectations of children and their families, service delivery models, and philosophy of education. To make the movement from early intervention programs to preschool programs smooth, Part H requires that a specific transition plan be developed and included in the IFSP. P.L. 102-119 clarified regulations regarding transition plans, requiring planning to take place at *least 90 days* before a child's third birthday; the family, a representative from the child's early intervention program, and a representative of the school district are to meet to plan transitional activities (Rosenkoetter, Hains, & Fowler, 1994).

Transition Planning Regulations from Part H of IDEA:

1. The IFSP must include the steps to be taken to support the transition of the child, upon reaching age three, to—

   i. Preschool services under Part B to the extent that those services are considered appropriate; or

   ii. Other services that may be available, if appropriate.

2. The steps required in paragraph (h) (1) of this section include—

   i. Discussions with, and training of, parents regarding future placement and other matters related to the child's transition;

   ii. Procedures to prepare the child for changes in service delivery, including steps to help the child adjust to, and function in, a new setting; and

   iii. With parental consent, the transmission of information about the child to the local educational agency to ensure continuity of services, including evaluation and assessment information required in 303.322, and copies of IFSPs that have been developed and implemented in accordance with 3031.340 and 303.346.

While this element of the IFSP is considered critical to efficient service delivery, transition planning is relatively new to special education. Planning for these transitions should begin as early as possible to identify a setting that is most appropriate (Donegan, Fink, Fowler, & Wischnowski, 1995). Early childhood educators work closely with parents to develop a plan that will facilitate adaptation to each child's new environment. The goal of transition planning is to enable children to be as successful as possible in their future environments.

Reasonable transition planning should involve two components. First, early intervention services anticipate the skill requirements needed of children and families in future preschool settings. Early intervention activities leading to skill acquisition and generalization can then be based upon this knowledge. Secondly, transitioning requires coordination between early intervention programs and preschool programs to ensure that schools receiving young children understand a particular child's and family's needs and subsequently develop appropriate individualized programs. More specifically, Noonan and Kilgo (1987) noted that the focus of transition planning would be different based upon organizational perspective. That is, outcomes for administration, parents, professional personnel, and children are necessarily different, though clearly interrelated (see Table 11.4).

Hence, transition planning serves a variety of purposes, all intended to make maximum use of educational services across necessary schooling phases. Toward that end, Noonan and Kilgo (1987) outlined six transition components. While none of these components is new to educators, their function in transition planning is unique.

1. Each member of a *transdisciplinary team* serving children with special needs must operate with attention to priorities included in a child's transition plan in regard to program development, implementation, and evaluation.

2. *Parents should be involved* in developing and evaluating transition plans. In fact, there is strong rationale, since parents are the constant feature in movement from one program to another, that parents actually serve as transition coordinator. To the extent that parents are willing to assume this role, agencies should empower them to do so.

3. *Curriculum planning and assessment* should naturally include individualized priorities. The basis for selection of objectives and transition activities is a prediction that mastery of targeted skills will lead to survival/success in a child's next environment. For example, if a child is transitioning into a program in which the classroom teacher

Table 11.4/ *Differential Goals for Transition Planning Based upon Program Component*

Agency Goals

- Transition planning should minimize the disruption in services or programs delivered to children and their families. Assuming the programming in early intervention is appropriate, every effort should be made to ensure that delivery of those services is neither delayed nor altered substantially.
- Scheduling of transition activities is practical and timely.
- Records that will be useful in planning are transferred to the receiving agency(s) in a timely manner. If records are sent at the beginning of the school year, they will be of little assistance in preparing a child's new environment.
- Strong linkages are formed between programs and agencies to reduce redundancy as well as to enhance communication regarding child and family priorities.

Parent and Personnel Involvement

- Parents and personnel from all agencies are informed of the who, what, where, how, and when of the transition plan.
- Transition plans assist in preparation of the receiving teacher, professionals, and paraprofessionals so that a child can be integrated smoothly into their program.
- Parents are involved in developing transition plans. In order for parents to be partners in the planning, early childhood professionals must make information pertinent regarding choices available to parents.

Program and Curriculum Goals

- Individual Family Service Plans are developed that reflect skills needed in subsequent least restrictive environments.
- Child will be prepared for differences that exist in his or her next environment.
- There is continuity of a child's program from one agency to the next.
- Adjustment to a child's new environment takes place rapidly.
- Transition plans and their outcomes are evaluated.

Source: Adapted from Noonan, M. J., & Kilgo, J. L. (1987). Transition services for early age individuals with severe mental retardation. In R. N. Inacone & R. A. Stodden (Eds.), *Transition issues and directions* (pp. 25–37). Reston, VA: Council for Exceptional Children.

provides children with much autonomy in child-directed free play, experiences in independent play should be included in early intervention.

4. *Interagency cooperation,* leading to smooth transitions, can be facilitated by developing written agreements that identify shared philosophy, responsibilities, and resources. Agencies involved in a child's transition move will be most effective in ensuring continuity of services if all members are represented at IFSP meetings.

5. Transition activities are accompanied by *written documentation in the IFSP.*

6. *Follow-up* of children once they have made the transition to their next environments provides evaluation of the transition plan. Like all other evaluation, this follow-up permits agencies to validate their transition activities and subsequently improve the process for other children in the transition phase.

Before the Transition Destafano, Howe, Horn, & Smith (1991) recommended that planning begin one year prior to the anticipated movement to preschool and should remain in effect until the transition team agrees that a child has made sufficient adjustment to the new environment. The plan itself should answer the following questions (Destefano, et al., 1991, p. 69):

1. What services are available?
2. Which services are appropriate?
3. What steps must be taken before a child can enter the next program?
4. What skills does the next program require?
5. What additional skills does a child need?
6. What can the current program do to help a child succeed in the next program?
7. What is the next program not able to do to make sure a child succeeds?

Activities selected for implementation by transition plans are intended to facilitate the acquisition of survival skills (see Figure 11.4). Survival skills are those that are considered by some to be prerequisites to entry in an early childhood setting. For example, Vincent et al. (1980) noted that skills such as following a three-step direction, completing a task independently, and taking turns were necessary for the survival of kindergarten children with special needs in an integrated setting.

The term "survival" leads to the misconception that if children have not acquired the identified skills prior to transition, they cannot or should not be moved to the next setting until those skills are acquired. This argument is especially potent when decisions of full inclusion are imminent. In fact, transition objectives should be viewed as a means of identifying and working on skills that will enhance independence but not preclude participation in a new environment. Skills not fully acquired prior to transition can be further developed after the transition. Some survival skills are obvious and make sense for all or most children making a transition to preschool or kindergarten. Yet, specificity of objectives should always be individualized.

Transition Until recently, the transition from early intervention to preschool services was often disrupted by political maneuvers. That is, school systems often denied access to children who reached age three in the middle of the school year. At the same time, since these children were no longer eligible for early intervention, they would be required to wait out the period between their third birthday and the beginning of the next school year. In 1991, P.L. 102-119 put an end to this service denial. Under the statutory and regulatory provisions, children with disabilities are eligible for a free appropriate public education upon their third birthday. This conclusion places the burden of transition services upon the state to maintain continuity of services for preschoolers who may either transition to the new preschool regardless of time of year or, upon agreement of participating agencies, remain in the same service program for the remainder of the school year (Colarusso & Kana, 1991).

Posttransition Preparing for posttransition involves communication and planning with personnel in the new environment. Participation of personnel from receiving agencies is the first step. Sharing information regarding a child's assessment as well as child and family priorities precedes decision making regarding placement, curriculum planning, and environmental adaptation. Parents and therapists may want to demonstrate individually developed techniques such as feeding, positioning, or behavior management (Donegan, Fink, Fowler, & Wischnowski, 1995). In some cases, transition activities will include acquisition of necessary adaptive equipment, collaboration with other community agencies, hiring of specialized personnel (e.g., nursing aide), or special transportation considerations. Most importantly, posttransition planning necessitates the continuity of a child's individualized program to build upon progress made in the child's previous environment (see Table 11.5). For example, if a child was working on toilet training in early intervention, whenever practical, preschool personnel will want to use the same routine, methods, and reinforcers after the transition is made.

Figure 11.4/ *Skills Timeline*

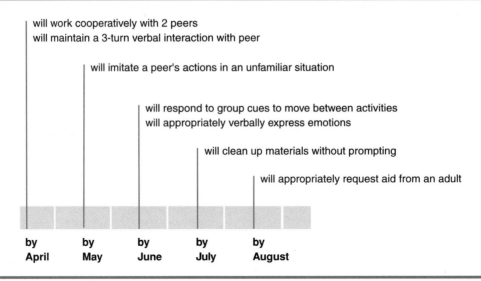

will work cooperatively with 2 peers
will maintain a 3-turn verbal interaction with peer

will imitate a peer's actions in an unfamiliar situation

will respond to group cues to move between activities
will appropriately verbally express emotions

will clean up materials without prompting

will appropriately request aid from an adult

| by April | by May | by June | by July | by August |

Source: Adapted from Rosenkoetter, S. E., Hains, A. H., & Fowler, S. A. (1994). *Bridging early services for children with special needs and their families: A practical guide for transition planning,* p 141. Baltimore: Paul H. Brookes.

PART B: MODELS OF EARLY INTERVENTION

Many excellent models of early intervention have been described in the literature. The purpose of this unit is to include descriptions of some of these projects to illuminate the variability in service delivery models and provide a framework for understanding programs that meet the unique needs of communities and families of children with special needs. Some models are exceptionally well validated, such as SKI*HI, and have been widely adopted. Others, while more obscure, may provide ideas for adapting programs to meet the needs of various groups. Some of the results of projects were disappointing, yet problems often provide us with insight regarding what may or may not work in certain situations. Overall, the projects described in the following pages illustrate the commitment of professionals working in early intervention settings to meet the needs of infants and toddlers with special needs in family-centered, culturally sensitive ways.

SKI*HI

The SKI*HI model was an early HCEEP project funded out of Utah State University in Logan, Utah (Strong, et al., 1994). The purpose of SKI*HI was to provide home-based intervention to infants and preschoolers who had hearing impairments. The primary goals of SKI*HI were (1) to identify children with hearing losses as close as possible to birth and attempt to facilitate linguistic, social, and cognitive growth and (2) to provide families with comprehensive home programming to enable them to adjust to their child's impairment, to support and enjoy their child, and to learn skills to promote development (Strong, et al., 1994). The "heart" of the program is a professional who is trained to make weekly home visits. This Parent Advisor, along with parents and other members of a multidisciplinary team, assesses children, plans programs, and provides appropriate home-based services. In addition to Parent Advisors, other professionals from SKI*HI make home visits when appropriate. In fact, approximately one-fourth of children served have two or more disabilities. Team members may consist of speech therapists, occupational therapists, social workers, and so on. Finally, a large percentage of

Table 11.5/ *Example of IFSP Transition Plan*

IFSP for Sylvia Schmidt
Date of birth: September 12, 19____
Today's date: September 1, 19____

Outcomes	Strategies	Timeline			Evaluation
		Start	End	Check Off	
1. According to their expressed wishes, Mr. & Mrs. Schmidt will learn about the transition process and participate in it in order to make informed transition decisions.	1.a. The family service coordinator (FSC) will meet with the Schmidts to share information about the process, the timeline, and parental rights; to seek permission to exchange information with the school district; and to learn how the Schmidts want to be involved in transition planning.	9-7	9-15		Meeting occurs—case log
	1.b. The FSC will answer questions or locate information to assist the Schmidts in their transition planning.	9-1	9-30		Questions are answered—parent report
	1.c. The Schmidts and the FSC will meet with the representative from the school district to learn the legal context and the local history of services provided to children eligible for special education whose parents chose to enroll them in parochial schools. They will also obtain information about possible placements for Sylvia.	9-15	10-15		Meeting occurs—case log
	1.d. The Schmidts and the FSC will meet with a representative of the diocese to learn about its policy about serving children with disabilities.	9-15	10-15		Meeting occurs—case log
	1.e. The Schmidts and the FSC will meet with the principal at St. Patrick's to discuss Sylvia's possible attendance there next year.	10-15	11-15		Meeting occurs—case log
	1.f. The Daisy Center will share with St. Patrick's any information requested by the Schmidts.	9-15	8-30		Information is shared—parent report
	1.g. Since Sylvia's 90-day transition planning period occurs during the summer, the family and the FSC from the Daisy Center will meet in early spring with a representative from the school district to devise a transition plan for their family and to explore placement options for Sylvia.	2-15	3-15		Meeting occurs—case log; plan is formulated and distributed

Table 11.5/ *Example of IFSP Transition Plan (continued)*

Outcomes	Strategies	Timeline Start	Timeline End	Check Off	Evaluation
	1.h. Mr. & Mrs. Schmidt will attend the state Parent Center's discussion group explaining the IEP process.	9-15	12-15		Schmidts attend class—parent report
	1.i. The FSC will help the Schmidts to locate other families whose children with disabilities are attending parochial schools.	11-15	12-15		Families are located—parent report
2. With parental permission, the Daisy Center will share information, including evaluation results, with the school district in order to ease Sylvia's transition.	2.a. Initial meeting	9-15	10-15		Information is shared—case log
	2.b. 90-day meeting	2-15	3-15		Information is shared—case log
	2.c. Timely exchange of requested information over 12 months	9-15	8-30		Information is shared—case log
3. Sylvia will learn to separate from her mother in order to attend preschool successfully.	3.a. Sylvia and Mrs. Schmidt will attend the toddler playgroup with Mrs. Schmidt absenting herself for longer and longer periods at a time.	9-15	5-25		Note attendance, separation behaviors by mother and Sylvia, and length of separation—parent report
	3.b. Mr. & Mrs. Schmidt will begin to leave Sylvia with a baby-sitter approximately 4 times per month.	11-1	8-30		Checkbook history of babysitting occasions; parents' anecdotal reports
4. Sylvia will cease using her pacifier in order to gain greater acceptance from other children in preschool.	4.a. The Schmidts and the early interventionist will develop and implement a 9-month plan to eliminate Sylvia's use of the pacifier.	10-15	7-15		Pacifier is no longer used—parent report

Outcomes	Strategies	Start	End	Check Off	Evaluation
5. Sylvia will increase eye contact and engagement with objects in order to complete more tasks successfully.	5.a. The Schmidts and the early interventionist will develop a list of activities that Sylvia favors.	9-10	9-20		List developed
	5.b. The interventionist will record data on how often and how long Sylvia gazes at play objects.	9-10	9-30		Data gathered
	5.c. They will plan together how to use these favored activities to increase eye contact and engagement.	9-30	10-20		Plan developed
	5.d. They will implement the plan.	10-20	4-1		Sylvia makes eye contact with objects and plays with them more frequently and for longer periods, according to the interventionist's data
6. Sylvia will comply with 4 one-step directions in order to perform preschool class routines.	6.a. The early interventionist and the Schmidts will teach Sylvia to obey the "look at me" request.	9-15	10-15		Sylvia complies in a natural situation four of five times in a 2-day period
	6.b. The early interventionist and the Schmidts will teach Sylvia to obey the "come" request.	10-15	11-20		Sylvia complies in a natural situation four of five times in a 2-day period
	6.c. The early interventionist and the Schmidts will teach Sylvia to obey the "stop" request.	11-30	2-1		Sylvia complies in a natural situation four to five times in a 2-day period
	6.d. The early interventionist and the Schmidts will teach Sylvia to obey the "wash hands" request.	2-1	4-1		Sylvia complies in a natural situation four of five times in a 2-day period

children, especially those who are older than three, receive some additional form of center-based education.

Home intervention centers around management strategies, language and communication development (including sign language instruction for parents), cognitive development, and more specific strategies such as mobility training for children with multiple disabilities. One of the first tasks of SKI*HI Parent Advisors is to help parents select a communication modality to be used for their children. Parents choose from total communication (aural plus visual), aural/oral communication, as well as other methods, including cued speech. This period of selection usually takes a few months since SKI*HI personnel want to be sure that parents' decisions are made with full understanding of their options and with sufficient individual child and family data to make the decision specific to the child/family needs. Consistent with the literature, which favors aural-plus-visual communication systems, a majority of parents (59%) enrolled in SKI*HI select total communication to learn and use with their children.

In a longitudinal study begun in 1979 and completed in 1991, SKI*HI evaluators determined the following benefits of participation by children with hearing impairments.

1. Children made gains in receptive and expressive language that were greater than would be expected by maturation alone.

2. Children showed increased auditory, communication-language, and vocabulary developmental levels and increased full-time hearing aid use.

3. Parents showed increased ability to manage their child's hearing handicap.

4. Children were identified at an early age and services were promptly delivered.

This widely respected, and now well-validated, model has been adopted nationwide. Over 260 agencies in the United States, Great Britain, and Canada have been trained to replicate SKI*HI components, serving over 5000 children annually (Strong, et al., 1994).

PIPE Project

Like other federally funded projects under HCEEP, the Pueblo Infant Parent Education Project (PIPE) was initiated as a demonstration project and, after funding ran out, was adopted by the state of New Mexico for continuation (PIPE, 1984). Recognizing that the needs of Pueblo families with children with disabilities could not be served in a traditional manner, project staff worked indirectly with families by training Community Health Representatives (CHRs). The CHRs, who were paraprofessionals, conducted child assessments, made home visits, and provided ongoing health care services to infants and toddlers and their families.

Project staff provided monthly inservices to CHRs, as well as providing individual supervision. These CHRs were assumed to have more intimate access and validity within their community by virtue of their own Pueblo membership. Thus, paraprofessionals provided the cultural linkage between a public educational agency and families of infants with disabilities.

The services provided to families were home visits to conduct assessments, training to parents who implemented child intervention programs, and ongoing emotional support to family members. In addition, parent group meetings were held and were facilitated by a social worker from Indian Health Services.

In evaluating the project, it was found that children who participated made modest gains compared to developmental projections. These gains were made in spite of the fact that CHRs were unable to make consistent home visits due to competing obligations to their community health programs. It was also concluded that the parent group meetings were ill-conceived for this group of families. The "apparent lack of success may be attributable to the fact that sharing problems in a 'public' forum is not a traditional part of the culture among this population of parents" (PIPE, 1984, p. 7).

CASE STUDY Isolation

Interview with Marsha Moore

The most difficult thing for me after Michael's diagnosis was the deep sense of guilt I felt. Somehow, I must not be doing all the things that I had done with the other kids. Somehow I had lost my touch. What was wrong with me? Why couldn't I bond with this little boy? Why didn't he know me as his mother? Even though I understood that there was a physical and neurological justification for Michael's delayed development, I felt that somehow the environment I had provided for him just wasn't adequate. I felt responsible for his slow progress, and I think some of the frustrations that I experienced came from the fact that I assumed others looked at me and thought that I must not be doing enough.

After his diagnosis, I made the decision that no one would ever be able to say, "She didn't try!" So I set up a family schedule to work with him. Intervention was a day- and night-process for the entire family. Mike hated it. His brothers and sisters hated it. His dad hated it. I hated it. I think back now and realize that we were really over-stimulating him. The specialists had told us to bring the world to Michael, and that's what we did. Lucky that Michael was a tough little guy. He survived in spite of us all! During this time, we were living in a very small mining town in north-

eastern Wyoming. We felt physically isolated from medical facilities, shopping, entertainment, and civilization in general. We often awakened to find antelope in the backyard! We were socially isolated, as well. Because we had been transferred to the area shortly after Michael's birth, we had only a few acquaintances and no close friends. Our life seemed to be such a struggle, and although we lived there for almost three years, I can only remember bits and pieces about anything during that time. It sounds strange, but when the kids reminisce about neighbors, teachers, and schoolmates, I have a difficult time placing names and faces. For three years, I missed a precious part of life with my husband and my five other children. I guess I didn't have the energy. I suppose my fear and sadness nearly consumed me. All I could think about was helping Michael to "get well."

Perhaps other things really weren't of any importance at that point in time. I think all parents want their circumstances to be the story of a miracle. I wanted Michael's story to have a happy ending. You know, the wonderful stories you see on TV or read about in the newspaper. You think, "My story will be the one that they print, and it will be the miracle."

While the PIPE project was neither large nor an enormously successful program, it does model a unique and credible means of addressing families and children in cultures that the dominant culture cannot assume to understand.

Project Fair Start

As with other ambitious projects, Project Fair Start was designed and initiated to give children who are at risk due to poverty a chance to succeed once they reach school age. In spite of the dismal statistics regarding children who are raised in poverty, Fair Start was based upon "a fragile but pragmatic optimism that we can take steps to extend more of our nation's protections and opportunities to children who were born into poverty" (Larner, Halpern, & Harkavy, 1992, p. 4). Toward that end, Project Fair Start, funded by the Ford Foundation, was launched in the early 1980s. The project had several subprojects serving many different populations, though all possessed similar characteristics. While encouraged to seek solutions to meet the diverse needs of their clientele, programs consistently adhered to the following model:

1. A preventive focus on pregnancy and infancy, offering education, support, and information about appropriate services

2. Targeting low-income groups who are underserved by traditional health and support services because of geographic, cultural, economic, or cognitive barriers

3. Multidisciplinary content, incorporating information about health, nutrition, child development, and social services

4. Implementation through personal contact with paraprofessional outreach workers who are members of the community (Larner, et al., 1992, p. 7)

In summary, the programs targeted very poor families, with very young children, and were served by members of their own community who understood the needs, values, and traditions of their peers. A brief description of four of the programs follows.

Maternal Infant Health Outreach Worker Project (MIHOW)   Centered in rural Appalachia, MIHOW identified pregnant women who were high risk due to age, economics, and education (Clinton, 1992). Of the 413 mothers served, all lived in poverty, their average age was 20, nearly half were married and living with their spouses, two-thirds did not finish high school, and two-thirds were having their first child. Direct service staff for the project were paraprofessional women selected from the communities being served. Referrals were made by members of other agencies who worked in collaboration with MIHOW staff, though participation of families in the program was voluntary. During the pregnancy period, staff focused on prenatal health care and logistical issues of access to health care when there was a lack of money, insurance, identification, and transportation or problems related to literacy and understanding. The goals of intervention for new babies were well-child care, emotional well-being of mothers, and suggestions of activities for parent-child activities that would stimulate child development. To accomplish these goals, MIHOW staff made monthly home visits until a child's first birthday and bimonthly visits until a child's second birthday.

Migrant Farmworker Families   Based in rural agricultural migrant communities of Florida, this program served over 100 families who were mostly of Mexican descent (Winters-Smith & Larner, 1992). Most families served were very poor, had little stable support outside the immediate family, worked grueling hours in the field (often starting at a very young age), were not fluent in English, were illiterate in English and often in Spanish, bore six to eight children, lived in substandard housing, suffered endemic violence and vandalism, and failed to access public services even when they were eligible (e.g., food stamp programs, etc.). Under favorable conditions (i.e., good health, good crops, etc.), migrant farm workers in the 1980s earned less than $4000 per year. In addition, by definition, the frequent movement of families from job to job disrupted services, education, and social and familial support networks. Though a very large percentage of the women involved in the project were in stable relationships with their children's father, there was also frequently a problem of alcoholism and physical abuse in the male-dominated households.

Project staff identified families by canvassing door-to-door, gaining tentative access only because the staff all came from a migrant background themselves. Home visits began during pregnancy and were continued until the child's first birthday. Twelve topics were covered over the period of family participation and included prenatal health care, discomforts of pregnancy, breast-feeding, labor and delivery and family planning, newborn care, motherhood, parenting (including bonding and infant stimulation), immunizations, nutrition, child development, safety, and provision of toys. However, due to the nature of migrant family lives, most families did not complete the entire curriculum, averaging only four or five home visits. Four to six weeks after delivery, most women put their children in child-care centers and resumed their work in the fields, cutting off services since evening visits were not generally welcomed by families who valued this time together. In addition to home visits, project staff held weekly group sessions in each camp. To encourage participation, the staff offered sewing lessons; this forum provided a way to informally help families to access services such as food stamps, housing, clinic cards, and job training.

Adolescent Parent Project To address the increasingly complex issue of teen pregnancy and its inherent risk to the development of very young children, the Adolescent Parent Project was launched in five major cities in the United States (Miller, 1992). Unlike most other teen parent programs, which have been short term in design, the Adolescent Parent Project was intended to serve young mothers from the third trimester of pregnancy through their child's second birthday. Participants in the project were disproportionately poor and minority, tended to live with their mother or other relative, were school dropouts, and had many additional needs.

The intervention model was a weekly meeting format, with each group comprised of 10 to 15 mothers whose pregnancies or babies were at about the same stage of development. The group facilitators, who had been adolescent parents themselves, led discussions on topics including health, child development, education and personal growth, school continuation, and job preparation. These sessions were guided by a 200-page manual that included over 150 modules for the facilitators to cover. Ongoing parenting topics were designed to follow the developmental ages of the groups' children.

Unfortunately, the curriculum and model lacked the necessary flexibility to be responsive to the real needs of young mothers. In spite of the generous incentives offered (i.e., child care, transportation reimbursement, thrift store coupons, entertainment tickets, gift raffles, etc.) attendance was very low. The average mother attended for only about 20 weeks, far less than the planned period of somewhat more than two years. Post hoc analysis indicated that some reasons for low attendance were that the mothers did not believe they needed the information or support provided, they had too many competing needs to attend, the location was inconvenient, and most importantly, the project failed to address their most salient needs, which were centered around peer and boyfriend relationships. It was concluded that, to be successful, teen programs must offer very powerful incentives, such as housing, in order to compete with drugs and money that were contingencies otherwise available.

Haitian Perinatal Intervention Project Haitian immigrants to the United States have had a difficult time achieving the dignity and prosperity hoped for when they fled an impoverished and politically unstable country (Widmayer, Peterson, Calderon, Carnahan, & Wingerd, 1992). The Haitian Perinatal Intervention Project served mothers of high risk infants in two communities in South Florida—one rural agricultural community and one urban community with a tourism economic base. Both communities provided less-than-minimum-wage jobs to most of the participants in the project and generally failed to make accessible the services for which families were eligible. Women participating in the project had emigrated after 1980, were typically living with a man upon whom they were dependent and who hoped to father children in the United States, did not speak English, and had only a few years of formal education, if any. Perhaps because of this background, mothers were motivated to participate in the project, which they believed would improve their children's ability to learn. In spite of this yearning, most mothers also expressed the belief that American schools held poor moral standards and yielded disrespectful and "bad" children.

Project staff were selected based upon their ability to work effectively with Haitian families and to serve as articulate public advocates for their clients. These women were Haitian-American and held a strong commitment to the project and their clients. Visits were made in women's homes every week or two to discuss topics of prenatal nutrition, labor, and delivery. Until the child was 18 months of age, staff continued biweekly home visits, focusing on needs and practices unique to Haitian mothers in the United States. The goal was to provide a culturally compatible link between Haitian and American child rearing. During each visit, mothers received an activity sheet presenting a parent-child task that built as much as possible upon Haitian tradition. Because appointed visits were rarely kept by mothers, staff sometimes drove around their community until they found a mother at home and ready to be visited. If the mother was home but not ready for the visit, the staff might help with household tasks, play with the children, and wait until the mother was prepared, instead of rescheduling the appointment. In addition to child-specific activities, staff also addressed other family needs: immigration paperwork, letters to interpret, information about social services and child-rearing practices.

Besides those projects described, Project Fair Share conducted other programs not included here. The goal of all projects was to address the needs of families and their infants in order to improve the developmental prospects of very young children. An admittedly inadequate evaluation of Fair Share projects revealed that program outcomes were positive but modest (Larner, et al., 1992). Only one project had no positive impact; the Adolescent Parent Project failed to achieve its established objectives. Like other projects whose immediate outcomes are modest, the real test of Fair Share will be the long-term outcomes for children and their families. Though this test is too early to make, most of the project models were assumed and replicated by various agencies after funding by the Ford Foundation was completed.

Family-Centered Programs

Even though a family-centered philosophy of early intervention has been prescribed by leaders in the field and mandated by law for a decade now, practices continue to be largely child centered (Bailey, McWilliam, & Winton, 1992). The following programs were designed to provide a model of family-centered services for infants and toddlers with special needs.

Project Assist   Families served in Project Assist were heterogeneous with respect to income, education, and ethnicity, as were children served with respect to special needs (Beckman, Newcomb, Frank, Brown, & Filer, 1993). Assumptions on which services were based in Project Assist are similar to those outlined earlier in this text, namely:

1. Families are viewed as a system.

2. Families are the primary decision makers for themselves and their child.

3. Families are self-defining.

4. Family concerns change over time.

5. Families vary on multiple dimensions.

Two elements of Project Assist—group support and individual support— provide a continuum of services that support family needs and promote adaptation. However, parents self-selected into the service options and were given the choice of withdrawing at any point. In element one, group support came from other families of children with disabilities who met frequently for six months to share feelings and concerns in a nonjudgmental context. The group was also a source of information and feedback. Group meetings were facilitated by a family therapist and infant specialist in order to create a safe environment. Beckman et al. noted that support groups followed a typical pattern of development. Initially, families tended to respond to topics and questions posed by facilitators. Later, they initiated discussion regarding their child and implications of this child for their family. In the next phase, families solidified relationships with each other and began to work together to problem-solve issues of service delivery. Parents were then invited to move to the second element of the project.

Individual support, the second element of Project Assist, involved home visits to families of children with special needs. However, unlike other forms of home visiting, no direct intervention was provided to children. Rather emotional support was provided through regular discussions about their child and family adaptation. Instrumental support took several forms: staff helped parents prepare for IFSP meetings, accompanied parents on medical visits, provided information on their rights and means of exercising their rights, and linked parents to other community services.

Follow-up interviews of parents who participated in Project Assist indicated that there was a reduced sense of isolation and an increased sense of empowerment, safety, and acceptance, support from other parents, and availability of resources. Parents believed the following elements of the program were important: children were of similar age; parents started the program together, so no one felt like the "new kid" or like an outsider; on-site child care and transportation to group meetings were provided; there was self-determination of support activities; and independence of family support from other services enabled parents to feel more free to discuss frustrations regarding the service system.

Project HAPPEN The goal of Project HAPPEN (Helping Agencies Promote Parent Empowerment through Networking) was to operationalize the family systems approach to service delivery (Deal, Trivette, & Weeldreyer, 1988). In other words, parent empowerment was facilitated through helping families to identify their needs and resources independently. The empowerment mechanism for each family was an already existing support network used by families to meet needs other than those associated with their child with special needs. Deal et al. described the following 12 sequentially implemented components of Project HAPPEN:

1. Visits are made to agencies, service organizations, and other groups in the community. Information is shared, and materials are related to the HAPPEN services. The purpose of these contacts is to develop an understanding of the efforts already made in the community to meet the needs of families.

2. Informal relationships and cooperative agreements are developed with community agencies and groups.

3. Families are referred to the project.

4. An initial home visit to share information is made by project staff at a time convenient to family members.

5. During the first home visit, the family and staff identify needs and the extent to which these needs are being met. The staff helps the family to generate options of action and offer support and information if necessary. Subsequently, a Family Action Plan is developed.

6. On the second home visit, the family identifies people they have had contact with in the past six months: intrafamily, family, informal, and formal. Next, the family determines their satisfaction with and the extent to which support network members help meet identified needs.

7. The child with special needs is evaluated in terms of adaptive behavior. Similarly, family strengths and needs are self-evaluated according to communication skills.

8. Family functioning in terms of empowerment (needs identification, decision making, action, and evaluation) is evaluated.

9. A Family Action Plan is developed, outlining family needs and the person(s) in their support network who will be involved in meeting these needs. The Family Action Plan involves a task analysis of the actions to be taken by families to meet each need.

10. The family carries out the tasks outlined on the Family Action Plan.

11. The Family Action Plan is changed as needs, resources, and level of family empowerment evolves.

12. As the family develops skills and confidence in meeting their needs independently, project staff move to an information and resource role only.

One of the key elements of Project HAPPEN is the evolving role of staff, who move progressively from a community linkage, to mediator, to networker, to resource person. This transition is a reflection of the extent to which families are empowered. To date, however, project coordinators have generated little evaluation of Project HAPPEN outcomes.

Toddler-Parent Play Groups   The Toddler-Parent Play Group Program was described by Popowicz and Haas (1991). The model is included in this section because it demonstrates a serious attempt to empower parents through early intervention. The goal of intervention is to maintain the integrity of parent-child interactions, assuming this relationship is critical to communication improvement. Three essential components of Toddler-Parent Play Groups are:

1. The caregiver is the primary communication partner.

2. The speech/language therapist and family specialist act as participant observers.

3. Intervention techniques involve incidental teaching modeled by therapists.

Toddler-Parent Play Groups were intended to facilitate a nonthreatening child-parent-centered form of intervention in which caregivers were assumed to be the "experts" in their child's development. Also, using a trandisciplinary approach, the aim was to improve the frequency and quality of child communications. To accomplish the goal of empowerment, therapists acted as facilitators to target interventions and then model for parents. Yet, therapists only "told" parents how to interact when parents asked directly. Indirectly, parents were encouraged to analyze their own skills in being responsive, empathetic, setting rules, negotiating, and selecting tools for social play. The following case history illustrates the Toddler-Parent Play Group model.

Sara

C.A.: 2 yr 7 mo
Diagnosis: Developmental Delay
Early Intervention Services: Sara attends the play group with her mother and also attends individual physical therapy.
Speech-Language-Communication Abilities: Sara communicates primarily through intentional communication (using reaching-vocalizing in conjunction with eye gaze to request attention or an object). She has begun to use gross gestures in an imitative context to request "eat" and "more." Phoneme use is limited to vowel sounds and an occasional /m/.
Case History: Sara was born full term and "small for gestational age." She was a failure-to-thrive infant and underwent extensive chromosomal testing, specifically for Cornelia DeLange Syndrome. Her gross/fine motor, oral motor, and cognitive intervention continue to be an important part of her overall programming for communication.
Targeted Communication Goals within the Play Group:
   1. Increase frequency of parent use of child-centered intervention techniques (following child's lead, providing choices to elicit responses).
   2. Increase frequency of child's communicative attempts, specifically gross gestures.

Alyssa

C.A.: 2 yrs 2 months (26 mo)
Diagnosis: Repaired cleft of the soft palate, Pierre Robin syndrome (small mandible, delay in expressive language)
Early Intervention Services: 1/2 hour of individual speech-language per week plus 1 hour in parent-toddler play group per week with her mother and a peer with developmentally appropriate abilities.
Speech Language: Severe articulation delay, 28-month age equivalency in both expressive and receptive language. Speech is characterized by hypernasality and glottal stops. Speech pattern consists of omissions and /k,g,n/ substitutions. Communicative attempts are infrequent and almost always directed towards Alyssa's mother.

Case History: Alyssa was born following an uncomplicated full term pregnancy. She experienced respiratory distress at birth requiring intubation to clear her airways. She had difficulty in nipple feeding for the first few months of life. She received OT/PT services for a period of 6 months (14–20 months) for motor delays.

Target Language Goals within the Play Group:
1. Frequency and maintenance of parent use of child-centered intervention techniques.
2. Frequency of child's communicative attempts, specifically use of vocalization in requesting context.

EARLY INTERVENTION IN THE TWENTY-FIRST CENTURY

While most agencies continue to serve infants and toddlers in a manner that closely resembles the school-aged model for older children, there is the potential for great improvement over a system that, at times, seems to be appreciated by neither families nor professionals. Though the intent of Part H of P.L. 99-457 was noble, as was the intent of the 1975 Amendments to EHA, enthusiasm and compliance from state to state has dwindled over its first decade. In part, such backsliding resulted from economic troubles. Perhaps more important, however, is the lag in commitment of our citizenry to establish early education as a spending priority. Of greater concern is the elimination of funds now being considered in future amendments to IDEA for personnel development; preservice personnel training, specifically early childhood training programs; and research funds for innovation and development. Early intervention has made great use of research and development and personnel training funding in the past. Where will new ideas be tested and validated without the support of public funds?

Aside from the question of whether or not programs will be fully funded in the coming century are issues of program content. Several factors will influence evolution of programs. These include funding for research and research outcomes, educational philosophy, advocacy by parents and professionals, and innovation by practitioners. In concert, professionals across disciplines should continue to make progress in areas that remain unresolved. Specifically, how do we provide comprehensive services to families in rural areas? How do we achieve true partnerships with parents? What methods are most efficacious in devising interagency agreements? How do we best serve culturally different families and their children? Can we make a difference with families who have multiple "crisis" issues in their lives (e.g., teen parents, poverty, parents who are substance abusers, etc.).

In addition to having the benefit of years of research and experience, early intervention under Part H stands the best chance of finding answers to these questions. The inherent flexibility of the law and innovative spirit of practitioners lend themselves well to the diverse families and children who are eligible for services. Additionally, early intervention programs can serve as models to school-age programs that face many of the same challenges.

STUDY GUIDE QUESTIONS

1. Briefly summarize the major achievements in IDEA (first as EHA) in 1975, 1986, and 1991.

2. What rationale were provided as the basis for Part H in passage of P.L. 99-457?

3. How did P.L. 102-119 alter provisions of Part H?

4. Explain the role of ICCs and the relationship between federal, state, and local ICCs.

5. What is the purpose of an interagency agreement?

6. Define and give an example of each of the four categories of eligibility under Part H. What are the criteria for your state?

7. If a child is identified with a hearing impairment, what type of professional would be most appropriate for service coordinator?

8. How would you deliver service coordination to families if you wanted to comply with family preferences identified by Early and Poertner?

9. What are the legal requirements of service coordination?

10. Explain the intent and implied practices of empowerment as the goal of service coordination.

11. Memorize the nine procedural safeguards and be able to explain the meaning of each in terms of preserving the rights of families.

12. Know the regulations regarding assessment procedures under IDEA.

13. Summarize the flow of services to families shown in Figure 11.1.

14. Explain the different purposes of screening and multifactored diagnostic evaluation.

15. What are the timelines from referral of a child to delivery of services?

16. How is ongoing assessment useful in working with infants and toddlers?

17. Why is it advised that family assessment be family-directed?

18. What are the principal steps taken by Winton and Bailey to put parents at ease in conducting assessment?

19. Identify the required components of IFSPs.

20. Develop five goals/objectives, keeping in mind the five principles developed by Notari-Syverson and Shuster.

21. Explain the rationale for using natural routines in planning IFSP objectives.

22. Be familiar with the services available to infants and toddlers eligible for services under Part H.

23. When can families be charged for services included on their IFSP?

24. Explain the purpose and legal requirements of transition planning.

25. How are survival skills best used in transition planning?

26. When is a child eligible for transition to preschool?

27. In what ways are personnel at the "receiving" school responsible for transitions?

28. Describe how each early intervention model described in Part II was family/culture sensitive.

REFERENCES

Bailey, D. B. (1989). Case management in early intervention. *Journal of Early Intervention, 13*(2), 120–134.

Bailey, D. B., McWilliam, P. J., & Winton, P. J. (1992). Building family-centered practices in early intervention: A team-based model for change. *Infants and Young Children, 5*(1), 78–82.

Bailey, D. B., & Simeonsson, R. J. (1988). *Family assessment in early intervention.* Upper Saddle River, NJ: Merrill/Prentice Hall.

Beckman, P. J., & Bristol, M. M. (1991). Issues in developing the IFSP: A framework for establishing family outcomes. *TECSE, 11*(3), 19–31.

Beckman, P. J., Newcomb, S., Frank, N., Brown, L., & Filer, J. (1993). Providing support to families of infants with disabilities. *Journal of Early Intervention, 17*(4), 445–454.

Berzon, P., & Lowenstein, B. (1984). A flexible model of case management. In B. Pepper & H. Ryglewicz (Eds.), *Advances in treating the young adult chronic patient. New Directions for Mental Health Services,* no. 21 (pp. 49–57). San Francisco: Jossey-Bass.

Carta, J. J., Sainato, D. M., & Greenwood, C. R. (1988). Advances in the ecological assessment of childhood instruction for young children with handicaps. In S.L. Odom & M.B. Karnes (Eds.), *Early Intervention for infants and children with handicaps* (pp. 217–239). Baltimore: Paul H. Brookes.

Casto, G., & Mastropieri, M. A. (1985). The efficacy of early intervention programs: A meta-analysis. *Exceptional Children, 52,* 425–435.

Clinton, B. (1992). The maternal infant health outreach worker project: Appalachian communities help their own. In Larner, M., Halpern, R., & Harkavy, O. (Eds.), *Fair Start for children: Lessons learned from seven demonstration projects* (pp. 23–45). New Haven, CT: Yale University Press.

Colarusso, R. P., & Kana, T. G. (1991). Public Law 99–457, Part H, infant and toddler programs: Status and implications. *Focus on Exceptional Children, 23*(8), 1–12.

Deal, A. G., Trivette, C. M., Weeldreyer, J. C. (1988). Family-focused services of the family, infant and preschool program. ERIC Reproduction Services Document No. ED295348

Destafano, D. M., Howe, A. G., Horn, E. M., & Smith, B. A. (1991). *Best practices: Evaluating early childhood special education programs.* Tucson, AZ: Communication Skill Builders.

Division of Early Childhood (DEC). (1987, March). Position statement and recommendations relating to P.L. 99–457 and other federal and state early childhood policies.

Dokecki, P. R., & Heflinger, C. A. (1989). Strengthening families of young children with handicapping conditions: Mapping backward from the "street level." In J. J. Gallagher, P. L. Trohanis, & R. M. Clifford (Eds.), *Policy implementation & P.L. 99–457: Planning for young children with special needs* (pp. 59–84). Baltimore: Paul H. Brookes.

Donegan, M. M., Fink, D. B., Fowler, S. A., & Wischnowski, M. W. (February, 1995). Making the transition to group care. *Exceptional Parent, 29*–31.

Donner, R., Huff, B., Gentry, M., McKinney, D., Duncan, J., Thompson, S., & Silver, P. (Winter/Spring, 1993). Expectations of case management for children with emotional problems: Parent perspectives. *Focal Point,* 5–6.

Dunst, C., Trivette, C., & Deal, A. (1988). *Enabling and empowering families: Principles and guidelines for practice.* Cambridge, MA: Brookline.

Early, T. J., & Poertner, J. (Winter/Spring, 1993). Case management for families and children. *Focal Point,* 1–4.

Guralnick, M. J. (1988). Efficacy research in early childhood special education. In S. L. Odom & M. B. Karnes (Eds.), *Early intervention for infants and children with handicaps: An empirical base* (pp. 75–88). Baltimore: Paul H. Brookes.

Hanson, M. J., & Lynch, E. W. (1989). *Early intervention.* Austin, TX: PRO-ED.

Harbin, G. L., Gallagher, J. J., Lillie, T., & Eckland, J. (1990). *Executive summary: Status of states' progress in implementing Part H, P.L. 99–457, infants and toddlers.* Chapel Hill, NC: Carolina Institute for Child & Family Policy.

Individuals with Disabilities Education Act. (1991). P.L. 102-119.

Individuals with Disabilities Education Act, section by section. (1995). Department of Education. [On line]. Available: Internet http://w.w.w. ed.gov./IDEA/secbysec

Larner, M., Halpern, R., & Harkavy, O. (Eds.) (1992). *Fair Start for children: Lessons learned from seven demonstration projects.* New Haven, CT: Yale University Press.

Lewis, A. C. (1995). Washington commentary: A little secret. *Phi Delta Kappan, 77*(1), 4–5.

Lynch, E., Mendoza, J., & English, K. (1990). *Implementing Individualized Family Service Plans in California: Final report.* Sacramento: California State Department of Developmental Services.

Maroney, R. M. (1986). *Shared responsibility: Families and social policy.* New York: Aldine.

Martin, E. W. (1989). Lessons from implementing P.L. 94–142. In J. J. Gallagher, P. L. Trohanis, & R. M. Clifford (Eds.), *Policy implementation & P.L. 99–457: Planning for young children with special needs* (pp. 19–32). Baltimore: Paul H. Brookes.

MHLP: Early Intervention Advocacy Network Notebook. (January, 1990). *Guide to Part H Law and Regulations.* 2021 L Street N. W., Washington, D.C. 20036.

Miller, S. (1992). The adolescent parents project: Sharing the transition. In Larner, M., Halpern, R., & Harkavy, O. (Eds.), *Fair Start for children: Lessons learned from seven demonstration projects* (pp. 136–158). New Haven, CT: Yale University Press.

Noonan, M. J., & Kilgo, J. L. (1987). Transition services for early age individuals with severe mental retardation. In R. N. Ianacone & R. A. Stodden (Eds.), *Transition issues and directions* (pp. 25–37). Reston, VA: Council for Exceptional Children.

Notari-Syverson, A. R., & Shuster, S. L. (1995, Winter). Putting real life skills into IEP/IFSPs for infants and young children. *Teaching Exceptional Children,* 29–32.

Penning, N. (1995). Federal dateline: A watershed year? Not for school support. *The School Administrator, 52*(9), 25.

Popowicz, L., & Haas, J. (1991, Nov.). *Toddler-Parent playgroups: Empowering parents in language intervention.* Paper presented at the Annual Convention of the American Speech-Language-Hearing Association. Atlanta, GA.

Pueblo Infant Parent Education Project (PIPE Project). (1984). Final Report to U.S. Department of Education. Grant No. G008100234.

Riley, R. W. (June 20, 1995). Testimony before the House Subcommittee on Early Childhood, Youth and Families. [On line]. Available marvel.loc.gov./federal information resources.

Rosenkoetter, S. E., Hains, A. H., & Fowler, S. A. (1994). *Bridging early services for children with special needs and their families: A practical guide for transition planning.* Baltimore: Paul H. Brookes.

Sexton, D., Thompson, B., Perez, J., & Rheams, T. (1990). Maternal versus professional estimates of developmental status for young children with handicaps: An ecological approach. *TECSE, 10*(3), 80–95.

Shakelford, J. (1992). State/jurisdiction eligibility definition for Part H. *NEC*TAS Notes, 5,* 1–13.

Simeonsson, R. J. (1986). *Psychological and developmental assessment of special children.* Boston: Allyn and Bacon.

Stremel, K., Matthews, P., Wilson, R., Molden, V., Yates, C., Busbea, B., & Holston, J. (Dec., 1992). *Facilitating infant/toddler skills in family-child routines.* Paper presented at Council for Exceptional Children/Division of Early Childhood International Conference on Children with Special Needs. ERIC Reproduction Services Document No. 353736.

Strong, C. J., Clark, T. C., Johnson, D., Watkins, S., Barringer, D. G., & Walden, B. E. (1994). SKI*HI home-based programming for children who are deaf or hard of hearing: Recent research findings. *The Transdisciplinary Journal, 4*(1), 25–36.

Thurman, S. K., & Widerstrom, A. H. (1990). *Infants and young children with special needs.* Baltimore: Paul H. Brookes.

Tucker, B. P., & Goldstein, B. A. (1991). *The educational rights of children with disabilities: A guide to federal law.* Horsham, PA: LRP Publications.

Vincent, L. J., Salisbury, C., Walter, G., Brown, P., Gruenwald, L. J., & Powers, M. (1980). Program evaluation and curriculum development in early childhood special education: Criteria of the next environment. In W. Sailor, B. Wilcox, & L. Brown, (Eds.), *Methods of instruction for severely handicapped students.* Baltimore: Paul H. Brookes.

Weiner, R., & Koppleman, J. (1987). *From birth to 5: Serving the youngest handicapped children.* Alexandria, VA: Capital Publications.

Widmayer, S., Peterson, L., Calderon, A., Carnahan, S., & Wingerd, J. L. (1992). The Haitian perinatal intervention project: Bridge to a new culture. In Larner, M., Halpern, R., & Harkavy, O. (Eds.), *Fair Start for children: Lessons learned from seven demonstration projects* (pp. 115–135). New Haven, CT: Yale University Press.

Winters-Smith, C., & Larner, M. (1992). The Fair Start Program: Outreach to migrant farmworker families. In Larner, M., Halpern, R., & Harkavy, O. (Eds.), *Fair Start for children: Lessons learned from seven demonstration projects* (pp. 46–67). New Haven, CT: Yale University Press.

Winton, P., & Bailey, D. (1988). The family-focused interview: A collaborative mechanism for family assessment and goal setting. *Journal of the Division of Early Childhood, 12,* 195–207.

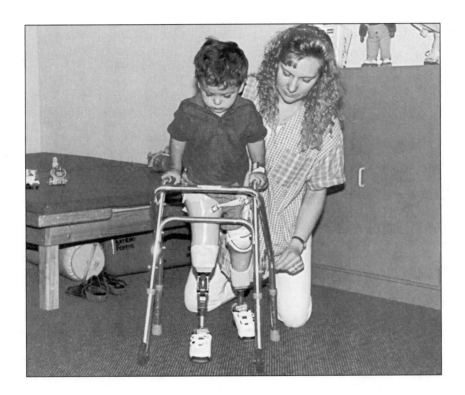

Collaborative Teaming

CHAPTER 12

This chapter explores a phenomenon called **collaborative teaming.** Collaborative teaming—or agreeing to work together to achieve common goals—is the preferred option for service delivery for families with children with disabilities since it has as its first purpose the coordination and interpretation of information from various disciplines including the caregivers. A second purpose of collaborative teaming is to be mutually accountable for the effective design, implementation, and monitoring of strategies to achieve desired goals (Haring, McCormick, & Haring, 1994). Applied effectively, collaborative teaming can achieve results not possible through other, less complex, strategies (Maeroff, 1983; National Commission on Excellence in Education, 1983). If collaborative teaming is implemented poorly, however, teams can create professional and family tension so strong that one might opt for no service at all (Eubanks & Parish, 1987). For this reason, a clear and well developed understanding of collaborative teaming is essential to the delivery of services to very young children with special needs.

RATIONALE FOR COLLABORATION

Before discussing the rationale for collaboration, it is necessary to acknowledge that there are at least two levels of collaboration that are pertinent to this discussion. At the grassroots level, professionals and parents who are directly involved in daily service delivery collaborate to design, implement, and evaluate a child's program. Similarly, on a systems level, multiple agencies collaborate to provide coordinated and comprehensive services to families eligible for early childhood special education. Though the first level is most germane to the following discussion, the second is also critical to well-conceived and well-articulated services to families with very young children with special needs.

Multiple rationale exist for providing coordinated services through a collaborative model. However, the overriding reason for collaboration is efficiency. It is more efficient to treat a child when all professionals are "reading from the same page of the book." The savings in time and money also happens to be a more ecologically valid and, therefore, a more effective model (Dunn, 1987; Dublinske, 1974). Even so, Pugach and Johnson (1995) stated that, "collaboration is acknowledged to have been one of the most glaring, persistently absent characteristics of teachers' work—and the one most in need of being implemented" (p. 11).

Collaboration is often viewed as a response to changes in society itself (Friend & Cook, 1992). In part, innovation in technology has led to an infusion of knowledge and information that exceeds individuals' ability to manage. As a consequence, no single person can be seen as the source of knowledge or the dispenser of decisions. Instead, individuals must be willing to take shared responsibility for both obtaining and sharing their new information. Sharing knowledge and resources, as well as personal skills improves the conceptual and technological understanding of all members (Idol, Nevin, & Paolucci-Whitcomb, 1994). In turn, this cooperation yields more creative and effective programs for children and their families. In other words, collaboration leads to collective induction, or the ability to create solutions together that one person could not generate alone (Thousand & Villa, 1990).

In addition to these practical reasons for participatory decision making, collaboration yields several beneficial side effects. Friend and Cook (1989) referred to these consequences as "emergent characteristics." They found that collaborators developed a higher level of interpersonal trust and, consequently, more respect for other members of their teams. When teams work well together a sense of community also emerges. Team members strengthen one another and the overall outcome of interdependency is a better outcome for the whole. Finally, Friend and Cook (1992) found that rewarding collaborative experiences are generative. That is, people who perceive their work with others to be successful are more likely to seek out and engage in collaborative efforts in the future.

Philosophy and Mode of Delivery

Collaborative teaming is both a philosophy and a specific mode of delivering services. A cooperative, or collaborative, education team is an instructional arrangement of two or more people in schools and communities who share cooperative planning, instructional responsibilities, and evaluation responsibilities for the same students on a regular basis for an extended period of time (Johnson & Johnson, 1991; Thousand & Villa, 1990). Teachers and other professionals work together on an equal footing, regardless of their training, to solve students' problems. Idol et al. (1994) defined collaborative efforts as:

*an interactive process that enables teams of people with diverse expertise to gen-
erate creative solutions to mutually defined problems. The outcome is enhanced,
altered, and produces solutions that are different from those that the individual team
member would produce independently. (p. 1)*

As a philosophy specifically applied to infants and young children with disabilities, McGuigan
(1985) proposed the following rationale for and commitment to collaboration:

Because the needs of individuals requiring support are often multiple;

*because many of the multiple family needs and subsequent sources of interven-
tion overlap and potentially compete with one another;*

*because parents and other family members working in concert with service
providers should be able to expect coordination and valid prioritization and clarity;*

*we, therefore commit ourselves, as professionals who work on behalf of infants and
young children with disabilities, to working with each other toward a common goal.*

*The outcome of this commitment shall be a unified approach to service provision
which has as its purpose the health and growth of the person being served.*

Philosophies or mission statements regarding collaborative teaming may be adopted at
the state level, at the regional level, in local or smaller communities, and even within a particular service agency (e.g., a school, hospital, or specialized clinic). Wherever such a philosophy is adopted, one thing is clear: much effort must be given to learning the skills necessary
for its successful implementation.

Collaborative teaming, as a delivery strategy, exists in contrast to the two most common
service delivery models: **single service** and **action/reaction service.** Single service models
dominated most professional fields until fairly recently. They consist of professionals delivering services in a predominantly isolated and autonomous manner. A familiar example of the
single service approach is characterized by the family practice physician, who works independently but relies on other health care professionals for information and feedback through
professional consultations. Educators often work in a similar isolated fashion. A professional
using this approach to service delivery is solely accountable for implementation of the service
as well as service outcomes.

Action/reaction services or chains of action and reaction might best be characterized by
the following scenario: a physician completes a diagnostic assessment of a young child and
passes on the prescription to the physical therapist, who may, in turn, teach a parent, professional, or paraprofessional how to deliver the treatment or protocol prescribed by the physician. In action/reaction service models, each member in the chain is accountable for learning
and carrying out that member's portion of the service. Accountability is specific to the portion
of the task to be completed and communication may or may not be ongoing once the chain
of service is established.

Contrasting with these relatively insular approaches is the complex notion of collaborative
teaming. While single service models and action/reaction models are best characterized as self-
contained and autonomous, collaboration is a matter of individually talented persons working
together within well-defined parameters that are the mutually established goals of the group.

Both single service and action/reaction models have fostered and been fostered by an
attitude of competition. Yet, competitive behavior stands directly at odds with collaboration.
Perhaps because of this, Morgan (1985) commented that teams do not naturally fall together;
groups can, but teams cannot. While some persons come to groups with the natural skills for
collaboration, most adults in Western cultures must overcome their competitive training and
experience through specific instruction (Kagan, 1991). Kagan warned that early childhood
professionals are ill-prepared for the revolution that is necessary to move away from competitive work and toward collaborative work.

Furthermore, single service or action/reaction services are often favored because they are considered to be easier to manage, less time consuming, and less stressful for the professionals involved. So why then move toward collaborative teaming? The answer is simple. First, while single service and action/reaction models may prove easier for professionals to manage, they are problematic for parents and other caregivers who must try to sort through, interpret, and prioritize information from multiple sources (Zigler & Berman, 1983). Second, as medical and educational models evolved over the last 20 years, it has become obvious that single-approach solutions are not as effective for infants or children as are coordinated services (Trivette, Deal, & Dunst, 1986). These two realizations paved the way for policies and practices aimed at encouraging professionals to collaborate (i.e., co-labor) with parents on behalf of infants and children with special needs (Affleck, Tennen, Allen, & Gershman, 1986; Brickman, et al., 1982; Dunst & Trivette, 1987). Thus, the passage of P.L. 99-457 provided both the opportunity and the necessity for collaboration across disciplines, agencies, and levels of government (Kagan, 1991).

There is yet a third and compelling reason for early childhood professionals to work collaboratively: the ultimate integration of children into cultures and systems of society that are now exclusionary to those with special needs. If early childhood professionals cannot engage in collaborative behavior, how can we ask the same of others? In short, modeling collaborative behaviors is fundamental to the inclusion agenda. Before children can be successfully integrated, professionals must themselves integrate their purposes and talents (Harris, 1987). We should not ask children to do those things that professionals are unwilling to do. Nor is it reasonable to conclude that inclusion can be accomplished without adults working in concert to develop similar goals and plan the necessary components of integration.

In spite of these important reasons to begin using a more collaborative mode, it has been difficult for early childhood special education to accomplish this goal. Educators' history of autonomy prevents "natural" collaboration. Kagan (1991) cited professionalism, turf protection, and an absence of accountability as barriers that isolate educators from other agencies and professionals. To sidestep these barriers, it will take increased *motivation* to seek out the cooperation of others. This motivation might be provided by an inevitable lack of *available resources,* more convincing and practical *research* on collaborative methods, and improved personnel *training* in early childhood training programs. Though the aim of widespread collaboration has yet to be achieved, the establishment of an agreed-upon philosophy and development of some effective collaboration models provides promise of a new era of service to infants and children with special needs.

HIERARCHY OF TEAM CONCEPTS

A team may be made up of both direct service staff and support staff (Haring & McCormick, 1990). **Direct service** staff work with children on a regular basis in a hands-on capacity and may include teachers, teacher's aides, and parents. **Support staff** typically include those professionals who consult, evaluate, train, or serve children and families on a less regular and more peripheral basis. Though the latter usually have some direct contact with children, many programs' budget restrictions do not allow support staff to work directly with all children on a regular basis. These personnel may include physicians, therapists, nurses, administrative personnel, social workers, and bus drivers, for example.

Teams themselves may operate on very different models. Three descriptive terms for various models have evolved over the years: multidisciplinary, interdisciplinary, and transdisciplinary. Though all three models involve some degree of collaboration, in general, they represent a hierarchy ranging from least collaborative (multidisciplinary) to most collaborative (transdisciplinary).

Multidisciplinary Teams

A group of professionals who perform related duties independent of one another comprise a multidisciplinary team. Often, professionals from different disciplines are needed to provide services for a single child. Individuals from these disciplines conduct evaluations and consult independently with no ongoing coordination of information among team members. They are a team by association only, with individual members viewing themselves and their roles as separate from the other members. Communication may consist of individually written reports or by direct interaction. Often, all information is collected by a single service coordinator or sent to one team member who interprets and makes recommendations. In a multidisciplinary team, members exchange information in order to present their goals and plans to other professionals rather than to coordinate across disciplines (Jordan, Gallagher, Hutinger, & Karnes, 1988). Thus, while individual members may be aware of one another's goals, they do not directly assist one another in attempting to meet these goals.

Multidisciplinary models ensure that families receive input from several experts. Collectively, this input permits more informed decision making. Thus, there is less chance that one individual will make a mistake or that the biased opinions of one member will determine the course of a program.

Still, because of the isolated nature of the team, the lack of coordination of information and the minimal interaction among team members, the multidisciplinary approach has obvious weaknesses. The piecing together of information cannot produce a clearly unified approach. There is minimal interaction among its members, which precludes team cohesion and commitment (Jordan, et al., 1988).

Interdisciplinary Teams

Though interdisciplinary teams are comprised of a group of discipline-specific professionals who perform related tasks independently, they interact with one another in a collaborative way to reach mutual goals (Jordan, et al., 1988). These team members share information on a more regular basis than do members of multidisciplinary teams in order to work towards a common goal. The activities and goals of each discipline should, by intent, complement and support those of the other related disciplines. Theoretically, there should be three commitments in an interdisciplinary team mode: a unified service plan, decision making as a group, and the opportunity to interact across the many disciplines. The information flow among team members is, again, usually handled by one person, a service coordinator.

The sharing and coordinating of information is one of the strengths of this model. However, one drawback of interdisciplinary teams is the potential that one or more team members will be unable to yield professional turf. To protect their professional identity, some members may be more rigid in sharing their roles and expertise. This attitude can strain functions of the entire team. Other potential problems arise from the rather ambiguous role that the service coordinator may play. If the service coordinator assumes an autocratic attitude, rather than using sound administrative practices, the decision making and recommendations may be unilateral and not interdisciplinary. The hard feelings this situation creates could reduce the team's productivity and efficiency.

Transdisciplinary Teams

A transdisciplinary team not only performs its related tasks interactively as in interdisciplinary teaming, but expands group interactions by individual members actually sharing their roles. Members become a team through highly coordinated efforts to work together interactively (Jordan, et al., 1988). The term "transdisciplinary" refers to role release, which requires one or possibly two team members to be responsible for all intervention goals. Each member implements program plans in his or her own discipline as well as using skills borrowed from other disciplines to intervene more holistically. Meanwhile, other team members are continually available to offer direct assistance to the primary interventionist(s), through modeling and feedback or consultation.

Members of transdisciplinary teams accept and accentuate one another's knowledge and strengths to benefit both the team and the child (Jordan, et al., 1988). Mutual training in staff development is basic to the concept of role release. This allows each member to perform the disciplinary aspects of the other members' roles. Clearly, the most critical feature of this model is the sharing of information and skills among team members.

The transdisciplinary approach requires participative and collaborative membership of many qualified individuals in order to authorize one person for interaction with the family. To be effectively orchestrated, transdisciplinary teams require the willing input of all staff. While some suggest that this approach has fiscal benefits because there may be a reduction in direct service staff requirements, this in an inaccurate assumption. With too few staff available for consultation, a lone therapist may be called upon to provide services with little or no effective guidance by other team members. "Such programs may feature the crossing of disciplinary boundaries, but only by default. Crossing of boundaries by default is inconsistent with, and inimical to, the transdisciplinary approach" (Healy, Keesee, & Smith, 1989). Professionals and families must reach a collaborative consensus regarding goals, rather than consulting with separate professionals or arriving at decisions independently. This ensures a common purpose among professionals and family members.

Though many disciplines participate in transdisciplinary teaming, the teacher is usually the key figure for encouraging role release (Jordan, et al., 1988). In such a team the teacher's responsibility may be to gather information from various specialists, integrate this information into the intervention procedure, and then implement these recommendations with the help of classroom staff members and parents. In other words, the teacher functions as both an administrative service coordinator and program implementor. In addition, personnel from related service disciplines must be adept at functioning simultaneously as generalists and specialists. Providing therapy in the classroom or other natural environments instead of in a segregated environment is a good example of an effective intervention strategy.

Of particular benefit for a child served by a team approach is that each team member sees the child's problem from his or her own perspective. "Early childhood education has always been an interdisciplinary field with a commitment to the education of the whole child; an understanding of the child as a complete human being is basic to the development of a program concerned with each area of development and learning" (Spodek, Saracho, & Lee, 1986). Sometimes a teacher may be intimidated by the specific knowledge of other specialized team members; however, the generalist perspective that a teacher brings is a necessary part of team dynamics. While specialists have in-depth knowledge, it is confined to a limited area. Teachers, on the other hand, are better able to see the whole child who functions in a variety of settings, both socially and physically.

Although one of the strengths of the transdisciplinary model is the high degree of coordination and interaction, this characteristic may also be its weakness. When many members are included, some individuals may have uncertainty concerning their roles. There may be conflicting expectations regarding individual roles and the feeling that one may lose his or her professional identity in the sharing of roles. Teachers may feel they are required to sacrifice autonomy and flexibility of action. Accustomed to making decisions on their own, teachers must now consult with others to make decisions, justify positions, and make compromises. A transition to the transdisciplinary model is more difficult for professionals who have a history of being isolated from other staff members. Members may need to learn new communication skills in order to resolve any conflicts that arise. In addition, the process of communication requires time to meet with one another, to plan together, and to record decisions (Spodek, et al., 1986). Team leaders must possess expert interpersonal skills to resolve differences, provide support, and facilitate the work of the team, while protecting each member's integrity.

Even with its potential pitfalls, it is generally conceded that the strengths of the transdisciplinary model outweigh its weaknesses. Members may be more willing to accept decisions made by a group and also to implement consensus decisions. There is also the opportunity to learn from other members. For a child, the benefits of such a model would be an increase in services regardless of a restricted budget, less fragmented services, maximized intervention time, holistic treatment, and consistency and continuity of services (Simeonsson, 1986). For professionals and family members, collaboration in this mode means increased skills and breadth of knowledge, and subsequently enhanced effectiveness.

The team configuration used in a particular situation will depend on the administrative policy of the school and service agencies involved and on the comfort and cohesiveness of the professionals serving a particular child. There is no question, however, that teaming across disciplines is a necessary part of services to young children. The greater the ability of the team to interact, to share roles, and to learn, at least the basics, of other members' disciplines, the more unified and complete a child's services are likely to be.

ATTRIBUTES OF COLLABORATIVE TEAMING

Collaborative teaming has been initiated and researched in both regular and special education since the early 1970s (Johnson & Johnson, 1987; Kagan, 1991). While researchers lack agreement as to the essential components of collaborative teaming, at least five elements, or attributes, are common to most models of collaborative, or cooperative, teaming:

1. *There is a common goal or set of goals to which all parties agree.* The first order of business in team conduct is to determine the primary goal of the team. All other decisions, personal and team, should be measured against this fundamental intent. The extent to which some members fail to buy into this goal influences, in direct proportion, the probability of achieving that goal.

2. *There is an agreed-upon strategy for achieving each goal or set of goals (responsibilities).* Members of a team collectively determine the most efficacious method(s). This is not as simple as it sounds. Educators are variously trained to use methods of theory based upon developmental, behavioral, cognitive, psychoanalytic, and eclectic approaches. Additionally, educators are challenged by theoretical models uncommon to their discipline (e.g., a psycholinguistic model used by some communication disorder specialists or a neurodevelopmental model prescribed to by some physical therapists). Even when the goal is quite clear, finding common ground on a method for achieving the goal can be a challenge.

3. *There is a commitment to dignified and meaningful interactions, individual skill development, and task completion.* In short, professional conduct is fundamental to team success.

4. *There is a commitment to interdependence or positive interdependence.* Johnson and Johnson (1991) defined positive interdependence as obligatory dependency of each member to each other member. In other words, teamwork cannot be completed if any one member fails in their responsibility. On the other hand, the entire team celebrates together when success is achieved because it was achieved collectively.

5. *Individuals commit to a shared system of decision making and accountability.* To make the most of each members' time, successful teams submit themselves to an organizational structure that includes such components as leadership selection, role assignments, agendas, and individual and group evaluation.

Face-to-face interaction is an essential part of the collaborative teaming process

While most literature on collaboration is in agreement with the five principles stated above, there also exists considerable variation in prescriptions for the more structural components of collaborative teaming. The following issues are generally considered in different models of collaborative teaming, though divergent recommendations often exist:

1. Process of team formation
2. Structure and guidelines for creating a culture of interdependence
3. Level of explicit training or development of social skills required by team members
4. Nature and quality of reflection and quality of reflection or processing needed to conduct collaborative decision making
5. Nature and role of leadership within a team

In addition to the elements described above several additional factors have been discussed in the literature and are believed necessary if a team is to function successfully and assert that they are indeed co-laboring:

- *Trust.* Smith and Auger (1986) contended that teams must have a way of building and maintaining trust. This trust is generated only over a period of time and, once developed, is the basis for mutual respect and security (Friend & Cook, 1992).

- *Face-to-face interactions.* It is relatively simple today to communicate ideas without actually seeing our colleagues. We can usually E-mail, fax, phone, and voice mail ideas more quickly than scheduling and attending a meeting. However, these types of "interactions" are often not effective as a primary means of communicating. The sacrifice of time and effort made in order to hold meetings will eliminate many misunderstandings and conflicts that can set the team back unnecessarily (Thousand, Villa, & Nevin, 1994).

- *Team members must acquire, refine, and practice small-group interpersonal skills.* As mentioned, there is disagreement about how these skills should be acquired, but most professional educators would agree that committee work can be torturous if decision makers lack basic skills to conduct small-group work.

- *Collaboration should be voluntary.* While individuals can be mandated through policy to work together, collaboration cannot be coerced from individuals (Friend & Cook, 1992).

- *Collaboration requires equity among participants.* Each member of a team must be equally valued, even though certain members may become more pivotal at different points in the process (Friend & Cook, 1992; Morgan, 1985). At other times, these same members are more a part of the supporting cast. In fact, Pugach and Johnson (1989) believed parity to be the defining element of collaboration, and the quality that distinguishes *consultation* from the more preferred model of collaboration. Consultation, which is usually conducted with one member of a team providing the "expertise" to another member of the team, insinuates superiority for the consultant and inferiority for the consultee. Instead of strengthening team members through empowerment and reciprocity, consultant models sustain relationships that are more restrictive and less generative (Johnson & Pugach, 1991). In collaboration, all members of a team are considered "experts" and may serve as consultant and/or consultee at different points in time.

Critical Elements of Collaboration

The remainder of this chapter will explore both the common and variable attributes associated with effective collaborative teams. While it may seem frustrating to have such variability in what different theorists regard as *the* key elements in collaborative models, this lack of uniformity could actually be a desirable feature of team design and process (Kagan, 1991). The flexibility to adapt to different parameters of a program or community may serve to enhance the overall effectiveness of teaming.

A Common Goal or Set of Goals to Which All Parties Agree   Persons new to participating in collaborative teaming on behalf of infants and young children with special needs often think they will be fairly comfortable with this first attribute. After all, it is relatively easy for physician, physical therapist, parents or other caregivers, and educational interventionist, to agree upon an overriding desire to do what is best for the child. The problem is to define what constitutes "best." This lack of agreement is clearly illustrated in the case example of Michael Moore presented in this chapter.

Determining what constitutes the best interest of a child has always been an issue for early childhood professionals. Such issues are presented daily—all of them demand sophisticated attention and discussion. Factors that stand in the way of easy consensus include individual differences in philosophy, religion, politics, economics, values, and experiences. These and other factors help each of us define *best* in a uniquely individual way.

In determining and prioritizing goals, the conversation must be as clear and comprehensive as possible. As early interventionists seek to become vital and reliable members of teams, the following strategies should prove helpful:

1. Be clear about what you know and do not know. You are not expected to know other professional orientations, philosophies, and content as well as you know your own; do not pretend otherwise.

Conflict with the School

Interview with Marsha Moore

It was important to us to live in a school district large enough to provide special education services to Michael; so just before his second birthday, we made the decision to look for employment in a larger town. After a year's search, we moved to Washington state. We focused our search for a home in an area where Michael could be served at a neighborhood school. We contacted the Association for Retarded Citizens to get recommendations for special education preschools. We visited the schools, talked with teachers and administrators, and finally made what we thought to be an informed decision. Two or three days after moving into our new home, and in the middle of unpacking, I called the school district to get information on how I would go about enrolling Michael in preschool. It was mid-August and I felt I didn't have much time to waste.

I was told that no decision would be made until Michael's developmental level could be evaluated by the school psychologist. Several days later, Mike and I drove out to the special education administration building for his assessment. I had dressed Michael in a little "preppy" outfit—short pants, knee socks, saddle shoes. I really had him "spiffed" up. The school psychologist took one look at him and commented that probably the only thing Michael needed was some interaction with some other children. I felt as if I'd just been told that the only problem Michael had was the lack of a stimulating environment, as if I had kept him in a closet all his life. The psychologist never told me outright that I was not providing Michael with the proper early childhood setting, but he clearly insinuated that school would "cure" everything. He also purposefully ignored the medical evaluations from Denver Children's Hospital and stated in a very patronizing manner that Michael was definitely not "autistic," as reported in his medical records. The psychologist "played" with Michael for almost two hours and never managed to get him to respond. Michael was found eligible for special education

preschool because he was two standard deviations below the mean in every domain.

From his office, I was sent over to meet Michael's preschool teacher, who at that point, was already setting up her classroom. We had left home at nine in the morning, and it was now almost noon. Mike was getting cross. He was tired, he was hungry, and he was hot. The teacher sat Mike in the middle of the floor. He immediately stiffened and he threw himself back, banging his head on the carpet, howling loudly. He would not be comforted. She looked at him as if to say, "This is definitely not the kind of child we have in this classroom." She didn't say that, but that was the feeling I got. I was trying so hard to carry on a conversation, trying to be so polite, trying to get a rapport going with this teacher.

As I got up to leave, Michael was still crying. "We'll see you on the first day of school and you will bring him, right?" she instructed. I told her that he probably wouldn't ride the bus for the first few days and that I had planned to bring him to school until he could get adjusted. The teacher continued, "And you will stay with him?" Well, I stayed every day for at least two weeks and then every other day for another month or two because he just hated that new and strange environment. He had never been around other small children and he cried and cried and wanted me to hold him.

Several months into school, right after Halloween, the director of special education phoned me and suggested that another program might be more suitable for Mike. This program was "specifically designed for children like Michael." She arranged to meet me at another school. I went, having no idea what the classroom would be like. When we opened the door, I found a large classroom with 8 or 10 children ranging in age from about 3 to 12 or 13. Only one child could walk, a big boy who was taller than I was. Several children were lying on the floor on mats. One little girl was rocking back and forth on the floor; another was sitting in a rocker and shaking her head. I wondered what program was available for each of these children. Later, I found that the room was called the "Severe and Profound Room," whatever that must mean!

It didn't take me long to realize that all of these other children should be in their own classes and not grouped together; it didn't seem appropriate to me that three-year-olds would be with twelve- or thirteen-year-olds. Whether they were developmentally on the same plateau or not, I just didn't think that was right. I remember feeling my cheeks and my ears getting very flushed. I had never had to fight a school system. I had never even thought about challenging anything that went on in school with my other children. My job as parent had been to support the school. I was a room mother, PTA officer, school carnival chairman. If our children had any problems academically, I had always been able to collaborate with the teacher and often helped my child put in extra time at home. Discipline worked the same way. "So she's talking too much in class, we will see what we can do to take care of that right away." These simple problems were not even considered problems. Now how could I even think of taking a different path than the school suggested?

We visited the room for no more than 20 minutes when I stated that I would not allow Michael to be placed in this environment. The director wanted me to give it a trial run, but I held my ground and flatly refused. I told her I expected her to make the current placement work. I knew nothing of LRE then, but I soon would.

We completed an IEP for the original placement. Mike received a lot of help from an experienced physical therapist who worked for the school district. We were so pleased because by November of that same school year, Mike was up on his hands and knees, ready to crawl. Within a month he was actually pulling himself to stand, and by January he was crawling around. Soon, Mike was able to sit quietly and join circle time, and he was learning to eat finger food at snack time. His teacher, although hesitant towards Michael in the beginning, structured her class in ways that allowed each child to work and learn at their own pace and towards their own goals. Well as you know, all good things must come to an end, and in February, she left school to

have a baby. It's sad to say, but a program is only as good as the teacher.

When Mike started school the next year, the classroom situation was not good. After several conferences with the teacher, I started looking for help from specialists in the community. They recommended many things to facilitate Mike's progress, but the school did not provide what I was convinced he needed. For example, the school refused to work on toilet training although Michael had all the prerequisite skills. Because he did not interact with the other children, he was often left to sit in the corner and watch the other children play, as if he would learn how to play from watching them. The most frustrating thing for me was that the school district disregarded Mike's diagnosis of infantile autism. In fact, they not only disregarded it, but during an IEP meeting, they brought in another school psychologist to tell me that she was an expert on autism and Mike didn't have autism. I realize now that she didn't know what she was talking about, but at the time I didn't know as much and felt very intimated by her professional expertise. I only felt angry and frustrated that they continually reminded me that I did not know my child as well as they knew him. In reality, they did not have a program for children with autism, so therefore, Michael was not autistic.

As the year progressed, I went to school once a week, sometimes twice a week. I was very quiet. If I participated in the circle time, it was only to help Mike do what the other children were doing. I held my tongue and never interrupted any classroom activity, no matter how inappropriate I felt it was. I called the teacher on a monthly basis to check on Mike's progress and ask questions that I felt were pertinent to his program. I often expressed my exasperation that Michael's program was not individualized to meet his needs. I was reminded that the "other" program was the individualized program!

When Michael started preschool the third year in the same classroom, I conferenced with the principal about what I had learned from the community specialist. I felt Mike needed more individual instruction. Mike seemed not to pay any attention to the other children in the classroom, and they were too socially delayed to interact effectively with him. I asked about bringing some

(continued)

kindergarten children into the classroom to act as appropriate role models for all of the children. The principal would not agree to any arrangement I suggested. There was absolutely no room for negotiation. I became more and more assertive, maybe even aggressive. I just got down right ornery.

I invited one of Michael's community autism specialists to visit his classroom in hopes that his recommendations would not fall on deaf ears. He met with the teacher, principal, and special education director and recommended one-on-one assistance, direct instruction, behavioral intervention, and other specifics. All recommendations were totally disregarded. No explanation was given. It was obvious to me that the district had a program, and my child needed to fit that program. It didn't matter that the program was inappropriate for my child. What made me most angry was the reality that there were no data taken during the entire three years that Michael was in the preschool. There was no method to track Michael's progress or lack of progress. To me, that very fact indicated that Michael did not matter much.

Several weeks after the specialist had come in, the principal informed me that I made the teacher uncomfortable and that I was no longer allowed free access to the classroom. I obeyed the rules, but often would watch through the classroom door window until one day, the window blind was pulled. The principal met me in the hallway and asked me please to stay outside the school building unless I was there for a purpose other than to "harass" the teacher.

I was furious! I wrote various certified letters to the teacher, principal, and special education director to document Michael's inappropriate program as well as the unfair and illegal way I had been treated as a parent. I made a request to schedule an IEP meeting and listed the goals and objectives that I believed were appropriate for Michael to work towards. I repeated the recommendations of the specialists I had used as consultants. In the meantime, I shared with the school staff an excellent book on IEP development, underlining everything I was requesting. I took a video to the principal about inclusion in the classroom. My information was politely refused. The school never responded to any of my half dozen certified letters.

Michael's IEP meetings were very tense and very stressful. Communication was terse, and every one of my requests for Michael was met with blank stares, simply no response. I think the school staff thought that if they ignored me, I would go away or perhaps just give up. We must have had at least a dozen meetings, dozens of revised IEP's, and finally, Jim and I went to the superintendent of our school district. We spent less than an hour with him and gave him copies of all the information and documentation we had concerning Michael's program.

Apparently he must have thought that we had some valid concerns. The district hired an aide to work with Michael, and after continued advocacy for an integrated setting, we were finally given a six week trial placement in a regular classroom. We got lucky. Mike had a wonderful first grade teacher who made the placement a successful one, not only for Mike, but for everyone in the classroom. That year marked the beginning of a very different educational path that Michael and our family would follow over the next several years.

2. Listen. And listen some more. Think carefully about what you have heard and your actual ability to analyze it correctly. Do not screen out information at an early stage based on past experiences or personal biases. Consider the relevancy and legitimacy from several perspectives: other parties *including parents,* the literature-base, philosophy of early education, and ethics of professional conduct. The importance of listening was articulated by Friend and Cook (1992). These authors argued that a good listener shows a desire to understand, which increases her or his probability of understanding, and therefore becomes more competent. A person who shows a willingness to listen sufficiently to gain an understanding of others' perspectives is viewed as a committed and valued collaborator. On the other hand, it is sometimes difficult to maintain an attitude of effective listening. Table 12.1 contrasts good listening behaviors with those behaviors that interfere with effective listening.

3. Consider both the short- and long-term consequences of your position and the short- and long-term consequences of the other possibilities placed before the group.

4. Insist upon clarification. If a goal statement is ambiguous or unclear to one person, it may be unclear to others.

5. Check all assumptions underlying a goal before agreeing to support or reject it.

6. In setting goals on behalf of an infant or young child, *be creative.* Develop habits of *conscience and imagination* in order to move beyond personal experiences or the limits of one's education.

Agreement on the Strategy or Strategies for Achieving Each Goal A common failure of teams operating in a collaborative fashion is to cooperatively arrive at goals, assign responsibilities, and then, not agree on strategies for reaching goals. One does not need to explore much of our service intervention history to discover the error of this oversight. When IEPs were initially established in the late 1970s, a student might have as many as three reading goals shared by two or more teachers (e.g., a regular classroom teacher, the resource room special educator, and the Title I specialist). By reviewing case studies of this period, it is possible to discover situations in which a classroom teacher used a linguistic approach, a Title I teacher used an eclectic approach, and the special educator used a phonetic/task analysis approach. The results of such a lack of coordination of strategies were disastrous.

It is easy to assume that the person or persons primarily responsible for a goal will know best how to achieve it, especially if the trust level is high on a team. While this may be true in the majority of cases, it is not always true. Working collaboratively means the team agrees they will take time to specify strategies that accomplish two things. First, collective decision making renders everyone accountable. If a strategy does not work, everyone needs to be part

Table 12.1/ *Comparison of Good Listening Skills with Behaviors that Interfere with Effective Listening*

Listening Skills	Interference of Listening
Rehearse information Mentally repeat information being conveyed	**Rehearsing a response** Anticipating a comment while dialogue is on going
Categorize information Mentally sort information being provided	**Daydreaming** Tuning out all information being provided
Jot down notes Note taking on speaker's content as well as reminders of response to the dialogue	**Stumbling on "Hot" words** Contemplation of a word or topic that interferes with the current discussion, (e.g., institutionalization, etc.)
Select and use a signal to hold responses Rather than taking notes, devise a signal to remind you of your message when the time arises, and in the meantime, you may redirect attention to speaker	**Filtering messages** Selective attention or ignoring of messages to which you do not wish to listen
	Distracted by extraneous details physical, verbal, gestural, or environmental factors that draw attention from the dialogue

Source: Adapted from Friend, M., & Cook, L. (1992). *Interactions: Collaboration skills for school professionals.* New York: Longman.

of analyzing the reasons why the strategy failed and defining one anew. Second, defining strategies helps clarify role responsibilities and expectations among members of the group.

A Commitment to Cooperative Interactions   What does commitment to cooperative interactions really mean? Thousand and Villa (1990) suggested that cooperation means opening ourselves to the will of the group as well as abandoning an individualistic orientation to work. But this simple answer is deceptive. Commitment to cooperative interactions is really a little more dangerous and a little more daring. True implementation means upsetting a bureaucracy's historic affinity for hierarchy and established order. Working in collaboration means entering into the potential uncertainty created when many minds must listen and decide together. It means not having a single boss you can go to for complaints or support. No one person tells others what to do, and no one person will be the sole source of feedback. Collaborative, or cooperative, interactions also mean abandoning personal agendas while asking, "When and how often will the group meet? How much time will be dedicated to each case or each client? How much time will be committed to conversations with collaborators outside of formal group meetings? Who will support me, and whom will I support?"

Commitment to collaborative interactions also means accepting the responsibility to actively engage in conversation. More specifically, team members follow the rules of conversation and converse in such a way as to generate new ideas about issues under consideration. For example, some early childhood professionals are very capable, but very quiet. Silence means nonparticipation and will not do in the world of collaboration. It is essential that those who are quiet learn to speak out, and those who speak too much must learn to balance their input with silence.

Haroutunian-Gordon (1991) identified four rules of conversation that need to be understood and practiced in group problem solving.

1. Offer ideas that are supported by data (research or experience).

2. Ensure that individuals are listening carefully to one another.

3. Uncover and discuss contradictory evidence.

4. Allow members to build on one another's knowledge and comments and to validate new associations of information.

These skills require individual members to find value in collaboration itself. According to Kagan (1991), "Valuing collaboration means valuing empowerment, growth, and diversity. It means moving from programmatic to systematic thinking, from short- to long-term visions" (p. 93).

A Commitment to Positive Interdependence   Positive interdependence involves the recognition among team members that no one person can effectively address the diverse educational, social, medical, and psychological needs of any other person (Thousand & Villa, 1990; Thousand, Villa, & Nevin, 1994). Rather, team members *know* and *feel* that they are all responsible for the overall well-being of the organization and its mission. Four strategies help create a healthy or positive interdependence:

1. Creating a safe place for conversation

2. Developing respect

3. Following a code of association

4. Creating an environment of generosity

Safe Place   Perhaps one of the most difficult tasks is for members of a team to articulate what they feel and know. Conditioned by years of schooling in which the teacher, the textbook, or the law is the dispenser of knowledge and the student is the active respondent, many adults have come to see their role in group work as relatively passive. This is exacerbated in every organization by fear. Fear is instilled in employees whose truthfulness is subsequently stymied by individuals who ignore, ridicule, or discredit the contributions of those whose views are different from their own. Sometimes honesty is punished, and those who are honest are threatened politically or personally. Consequently, persons who fear that they will lose their jobs, their promotions, or their favor with authority wait to be told "the truth" by an authority other than themselves. The result of this unfortunate conditioning is that bright women and men who are experienced listeners, polite, and reflective find the notion of initiating a new line of thinking, especially if it runs contrary to the mainline thinking of the group, to be too dangerous to consider. This passivity limits creativity and imagination—the very talents needed in team problem solving.

If collaborative teams are truly going to serve well, a practice of personal responsibility within a *culture of shared and mutual responsibility* must be developed. For example,

- Members of teams must learn not to let minor issues, which they find contrary to their own thinking or judgment, go unresolved. Differences must be addressed at the time the differences are first identified.

- Members must not be allowed to accept the long ramblings and dominating behaviors of certain members.

- Members must acknowledge the source of their input—whether they are speaking from opinion, fact, experience, intuition, or research.

- Members must confront, with compassion, those individuals or group behaviors that are obstructing the work and direction of the group. Likewise, feedback about tasks or responsibilities well-done is equally necessary.

A special caution is offered to women in this regard: research on female/male interactions during classroom and business meetings reveals that, despite some awareness that they are welcomed to speak freely, women contribute only one-third as much as their male counterparts (Cantor, 1992). Additionally, women report that, in general, they feel their comments are less valued and valuable than those of male colleagues. While it is not within the scope or intent of this chapter to address this issue, both male and female readers are encouraged to further explore their assumptions about formal and informal authority, which may have shades of gender bias—however subtle they may be.

Culture of Respect   Early childhood professionals will be most effective if they not only cooperate with one another but truly collaborate. When done well, members come together to offer perspective, opinion, and recommendations from many different points of view. Again, in our society, members joining collaborative teams bring with them little experience in a group perspective paradigm. Villa, Thousand, Paolucci-Whitcomb, and Nevin (1990) discovered that the learning experiences of most professionals are the consequence of systems built on competition, not collaboration. Indeed, the educational experiences of most professionals and other specialists are highly competitive. Members of collaborative teams find that one of the first lessons is recognition that participating in noncompetitive modes of interaction is difficult after having participated in competitive school cultures for 12 or 16 or 20 years. It takes practice, reflection, analysis, and still more practice to develop a set of habits not previously taught or reinforced.

Johnson, Johnson, and Smith (1991) described a new paradigm for adult education in which teaching actually involved helping others construct knowledge in active ways. Their work, which is applicable to the healthy functioning of collaborative teaming in early childhood special education, found that collaborative interaction models allowed students to work together to increase their own as well as their classmates' learning. The implications of this research are clear: collaborative endeavors promote higher achievement, more positive relationships, and healthier psychological adjustments than individualistic or competitive models.

Code of Association   A commitment to integrity and a readiness or predisposition toward respect are the fundamental starting points for a successful collaborative team. In addition to these dispositions, groups will also be served well by what is sometimes referred to as a code of association—or more simply, who is doing what and when.

While developed codes of association vary greatly based on the goals of the group, they almost always include specification of:

- Number of meetings per year, including anticipated length of meetings
- Team membership (permanent and rotational)
- Personal and group responsibility for evaluation of how the team is functioning
- Process for designating a session facilitator and record keeper
- Identification of logistics manager (who will select place, order coffee, etc.)
- Identification of the agenda manager (who will forward the agenda with specific responsibilities prior to the meeting)
- Development and adherence to rules of confidentiality
- The group's tolerance for or limits to individual arm twisting

Adherence to a code of interdependence implies that members of the group commit themselves to avoidance of highly individualized agendas (Bouton & Garth, 1983). One of the important aspects of interdependence is a concept called **reward interdependence** (Thousand, Villa, & Nevin, 1994). When members of collaborative teams are evaluating feedback from one another, it is especially important for them to remember to structure reward interdependence, that is, the shared rewards and celebrations for a team's work. Reward interdependence means that the work of an individual, or even a subgroup of individuals, does not overshadow the equally important, but possibly less visible, contributions of others. A norm often recommended is that successes are celebrated collectively—no single person receives all the credit. As a result, when goals are reached, all members share in the gratification of having contributed to the achievement. Of course, this strategy can only work if members of the team really do fulfill their respective responsibilities, even if those responsibilities differ in content and effort. When some members must fill their roles and also complete the work of others, dispensing credit to those who did not meet their obligations is likely to be counterproductive and produce a divisive work environment. Therefore, teams must work diligently to ensure that there is both individual and group accountability.

A culture of interdependence includes resource interdependence and role interdependence as well as goal interdependence (Udvari-Solner, 1994). As mentioned earlier, **goal interdependence** occurs when a common goal, or common set of goals, has been established. The goal is considered interdependent if every member of the team has given the goal careful consideration and has actively participated in delineating the strategies that will lead to its fruition. **Resource interdependence** can be engineered by arranging one set of shared materials or distributing information among the group so that single elements of information must be interfaced with others in order to arrive at a more holistic process and outcome. While resource interdependence is often about information, it may also be about equipment sharing, technology links, and so on. Finally, **role interdependence** requires that each group member assumes a specified responsibility that is interconnected to the functioning of other group members. Roles are normally assigned to capitalize on a member's strength, but they can also be arranged so as to compensate for weaknesses. Roles can be task or socially oriented, short- or long-term, and formally stated or informally practiced.

Work Toward an Environment of Generosity   Most professionals today claim busy-ness as a way of life. Because federal and state resources are increasingly limited, good women and men are stretching themselves thin to provide services that are badly underfunded. This condition is not likely to reverse in the next decade, and its consequences on those who serve must be acknowledged. Systems can only function in times of deprivation when there is personal and professional generosity of resources and time. Teams need to develop strategies whereby rules governing resource distribution are flexible, there is reciprocity of resource sharing, and logistics (e.g., proximity, transportation, etc.) of resource sharing are made simple.

If it is to remain healthy and productive over the long haul, one of the responsibilities of a collaborative team is to support its members by being truthful with them when they are functioning at an inadequate level and to help them make adjustments accordingly. The cultural norm of the group should be an understanding that, at one time or another, all members will need assistance and support. Hence, peer feedback and subsequent intervention should be common practice and not seen as an exception, used only in the worst possible situations.

Those who are considered overworkers within a team can also cause problems. For example, overworkers are often denigrated by colleagues who work less because the former tend to receive much attention for both their diligence and their accomplishments. This attention can, in turn, make others feel less worthy and, therefore, resentful. In some schools, teachers who work after contract hours are ostracized by their peers who worked hard to achieve a union victory for reasonable working hours. Often, overworkers themselves are resentful that they must work so hard to complete their jobs to their own satisfaction or the satisfaction of the organization. The latter is increasingly the case when resources become scarce and expectations subsequently increase. To eliminate these problems as much as possible, teams must develop a climate that does not implicitly demand slavish work habits and will find ways to diminish the workloads of those who have taken on more work than they feel is fair. Teams should create an environment in which it is safe to say, "You're asking too much of me." Furthermore, teams need to acknowledge that work volume, within certain parameters, is a personal choice and that members of a team should not be judged by the work/life values of other members of the team. In the true sense of generosity, members give what is best of themselves.

Shared System of Decision Making and Accountability   In the preceding section, some models of shared decision making were introduced. In this section, the notion of commitment to a shared system is the focal point. Members must understand that once a system for decision making is selected, it is the responsibility of each member to adhere in spirit and action to that method. Perhaps nothing is more destructive to the functioning of a collaborative team than a member who adheres to the group's guidelines in session and then proceeds to demean and complain to others once he or she leaves the meeting. Truth of action and perseverance on team goals must prevail both during meetings and outside of meetings.

Shared accountability means that all members of the group are responsible for the integrity and interpretation of data about group effectiveness and the effectiveness of strategies for goals to which the group is committed. Effective group work is influenced by whether or not group members reflect on (process) how well they are functioning. Johnson and Johnson (1991) defined a **process** as an identifiable sequence of events taking place over time. They defined **process goals** as the sequence of events instrumental in achieving outcome goals. **Group processing** may be defined as reflecting on a group session to describe what actions to continue or change. Whether done individually or within the group, the purpose of processing is to clarify and improve the effectiveness of the members in contributing to collaborative efforts to achieve established goals.

Processing seems to bring out the best and worst in some people. Professionals who perceive themselves as high-task personalities are often less than enthusiastic about processing activities. On the other hand, those who often want to avoid the nitty-gritty of hard work, difficult decisions, or increased activities could keep a group paralyzed in processing activities. The challenge, of course, is to engage in enough processing so that members always feel heard, respected, and valued, though not so much processing that members overwhelmingly feel that valuable time is being used nonproductively.

Table 12.2/ *Questions to be Addressed in Evaluating Collaborative Efforts*

Strategy Integrity

- To what extent have we clearly articulated
  a. the delivery method,
  b. the monitoring system,
  c. the goal or immediate outcome, and
  d. the specific roles of those responsible for delivering the intervention, including time?
- To what extent was the strategy delivered as designed?
- If adjustments were made in the delivery strategy, in the evaluation system, and so on, what was the rationale for those changes and what were their effects?
- To what extent was adequate planning done so as to avoid possible problems?

Modeling of Collaboration

- How specifically did those who delivered services provide a model of collaborative intervention?
- How might the collaborative aspect of the planning and delivery be improved in the future?
- Did team members fulfill their agreed-upon roles and responsibilities in the design, implementation, and evaluation components?
- Do team members feel that they were equitably distributed responsibilities (a) during meeting times and (b) during delivery of services?

Health and Functioning of the Team

- Are the team members learning from one another?
- Do team members need more or less support from one another?
- Does the team need additional expertise or does it need to reduce its areas of expertise?
- Is it time for the team to expand or dissolve? If so, for what purpose?

Source: Adapted from Thousand, J. S., Villa, R., & Nevin, A. (1994). *Creativity and collaborative learning.* Baltimore: Paul H. Brookes.

Areas of accountability concerning group effectiveness include the team members' ability to coordinate their actions and work together and the team's acquisition or refinement of skills through the teaming process. These results tell a team how future endeavors might be better designed and conducted. The focal points of evaluation must be the team's performance or evaluation of the integrity of implementation as well as of the outcome itself. Consideration by the team of the evaluative questions presented in Table 12.2 may help foster a sense of group accountability.

Once a team has been formed, the first business of the team will be to create or review the rules or guidelines for operations. Some teams will have or will develop bylaws, which will systematically outline purposes, responsibilities, timelines, and so on. But, if bylaws or guidelines do not yet exist, the first obligation of the team will be to decide how to decide.

There are three widely used decision making methods: (1) **straight vote,** with the majority will upheld, (2) **consensus decision making,** whereby all members of the group must support the goal, and (3) **weighted decision making,** giving greater significance to the will of the parent or another team member most closely aligned with the goal area.

Straight vote, or majority will, represents democracy in action—one person, one vote. The advantage of the straight vote strategy is that it remains the most commonly used method of group decision making and most people are relatively comfortable with it. If they vote anonymously, members can express or register their decision freely. One negative, or no, vote does not upset the will of the majority. The disadvantage is that, while this strategy may be comfortable (especially for persons who dislike conflict), members of the team who voted "no" may well be expected to implement something they do not believe in. This outcome would certainly undermine collaborative efforts and could greatly compromise services to children and their families.

In using a *consensus decision making strategy,* all members of the team must agree on the goal if it is to be adopted. It is essentially an all or nothing approach. The primary advantage of the consensus model is that it forces a good deal of discussion and demands clarity of purpose. Furthermore, members of the team will not be asked to implement something with which they do not agree. The negative aspect of this type of decision making is that many valid goals could be dismissed simply because of disagreement from a single member of the team. In addition, true consensus decision making takes time to learn. A team that adopts this approach of decision making will do well to spend a few hours dedicated to learning the complex nuances of the method.

Weighted decision making actually refers to preferential or priority-opinion voting by selected members of the group. In this system, more value is given to one person's vote than another. The most common approach involves giving parents or caregivers a vote worth three points and everyone else on the team a one-point vote. Another alternative includes establishing the vote weights based on the goal being discussed. If the goal is in the area of communication, for example, the team might weight the vote of the speech professional(s) as two points and that of other members as one point, or of the communication and speech professionals *and* caregivers as two points and of all others as one point. The most significant advantage of this method of decision making is that it puts the authority for the decision with the people who most likely know the most about the goal area. The disadvantage is that a team might erroneously give more weight to a team member than is appropriate or desirable. Some members may feel devalued if the weighting of votes is not absolutely agreed upon with enthusiasm.

BUILDING TEAMS THAT COLLABORATE

The variables presented above are common in the majority of collaborative team-building models. The following is a discussion of variables that have been found by researchers and practitioners to be helpful in designing and implementing team models that are based upon collaboration.

Formation of Collaborative Teams

Collaborative teaming occurs at many levels, from state departments of education and human services to small units within schools and clinical settings. Because of this, a solid set of policies or rules for determining the appropriate constitution of any given team has not been developed. Still, there are some reasonable guidelines that can be used to assist those serving infants and young children with special needs.

Central to all teams should be the parent(s), guardian, and other primary caregivers for an infant or child. Although this seems as though it should be a simple task, it often is not. As many researchers have pointed out, parents may have had negative experiences with professionals. Previous patterns of interaction and confusion over direction lead to parental skepticism about being part of a team. Indeed, very early steps such as the IFSP, and later the IEP, were likely presented in ways that, on the surface, appeared to welcome parental input. However, in most cases, these experiences probably did little to sincerely encourage parents to take active roles on a team. In these cases, goals and objectives that should have been viewed as fluid and flexible—changing and adapting as the family system changed and adapted—often became rigid and didactic. If parents or other primary caregivers are to be truly *meaningful and fully participating* members of a collaborative team, some serious reflec-

CASE STUDY

Advocacy

Interview with Tom and Ann Simpson

Tommy's first physical therapist was a real advocate for him. Right after his birth, we didn't know up from down. We'd never had much to do with the medical field at all—hated hospitals. When Tommy was born, the doctors thought he had a heart problem. We were afraid we were not prepared to be good advocates for a special needs child; it would have been better if it had happened to the family of a nurse or someone who didn't hate all of this medical stuff.

We've had to learn a lot, and people like Tommy's first therapist really helped us. She would talk about what we could do, where we should go, and she was very kind and patient with us. The staff members at his first, private school were also advocates for us; perhaps even more than for Tommy. They trained us and got us up and going. At the private school, we could go to Tommy's class all of the time, and they didn't mind. It actually got to the point where we would help out as much as the aides did. We are looking for that same partnership, at the public school district, but we don't think it's going to be there.

The way we look at it, Tommy's not really a different kid, he's just different the way we're all different. We don't think of him as a special needs kid. We want him to be treated like anybody else, without any special consideration or fear. Tommy's very social, and he's very appropriate. He's just nice, quiet, friendly, kind of shy, and he likes to have fun. He's busy, but he's not out of control. We'd like him to go to school and be happy—have a couple of buddies. A part of us wants to keep him with us forever, and another part of us knows he wants to be on his own.

Our real concern is how well is he going to turn out? You have that concern with every child, handicapped or not, but with Tommy, we think it's

important that he learns to be independent. We have a relative by marriage who is retarded, and he's always been kept in the house and taken care of, so he can't live on his own. We know this man's father is getting pretty old, and his mother has passed away, so who's going to take care of him? He has to be taken care of because that's the way he was raised. We want Tommy to be able to fend for himself to a degree where he can at least live independently. That's our primary concern.

We're trying to save our money, so that it will be there for our daughter's college and for Tommy when he's older. We've been working with people at the Association for Retarded Citizens to network with other parents, just to get to know them. We have this little fantasy about buying Tommy a house and giving it to the state, so they'll let him live there and they'll provide the support. We want him close, but we do envision him being able to live on his own.

It's important that schools help get parents into the proper mind-set for their children's future. The schools should be getting our children with disabilities ready to be with typical kids, and they should be advocates for our children. We want

Tommy Simpson

professionals to look at us as partners instead of adversaries. We both have the same goals. It may look like we are working at cross-purposes, but we really do want the same things for the child. Explain things to us, be kind and open-minded.

Just as every child is different, so every parent is different. That's one thing we've realized working for the parent group. All of the parents are different; they have different expectations and different ideas. We want teachers to be open and listen. They shouldn't be afraid to let us into their turf or territory. They should welcome us. If someone is open and welcoming, we'll be more in tune with what teachers are trying to do.

We think the parents need to learn to listen to the teacher's opinion, too. We parents should not come in with a chip on our shoulder and shouldn't assume the system is going to take care of us. Parents need to be one step ahead and be asking questions but be willing to bend a little bit.

We wouldn't have chosen having Tommy with Down syndrome, but it's made us better people, and it's made our family better. We've all learned a lot from Tommy and grown a lot. Life would have been easier if Tommy had been a regular kid, but life is not always meant to be easy.

tion is required of all other team members. As a point of practice, one of the very first meetings ought to deal specifically with determining how parents have been treated in the past, what their experiences have been in collaborative endeavors, and what might be expected of them in the here and now.

Acknowledging that parents or other primary caregivers are necessary players on any collaborative team, the next step is to identify other people who should be included. Dunst, Trivette, & Deal (1988) pointed out that the potentially most damaging aspect of IFSP development is that a service coordinator is expected to play the role of team leader. The IFSP must contain the name of a service coordinator, who becomes responsible for implementing the plan and coordinating with other agencies and persons. This requirement suggests that the service coordinator, not the family, will play the most active role in securing resources to meet family needs. However, this provision directly threatens a family's ability to become competent decision makers in their child's education and usurps control rather than empowering families. Indeed, this particular requirement of the IFSP violates many of the principles of helping relationships that are known to be both enabling and empowering (Dunst & Trivette, 1987). Perhaps parents themselves ought to identify members of their particular team. As parents begin this process, it may be necessary for them to rely on the expertise of one or more professionals for significant input. With this shift from professional to parental control, the family motivation to be actively involved might be established and sustained. As a caution, however, parents cannot be expected to be satisfied or successful with this new responsibility without some guidance. Suggestions should include information to help parents decide the following: who or what professionals should serve on the team, how many members to select, the implications of team size for group functioning, and logistical considerations regarding team selection (e.g., perhaps selecting members who work in close proximity to one another).

In the formation of a team, it is also important to consider team philosophy regarding how each member is to act once appointed or elected to the team. While potential members should not necessarily be excluded from teams when they do not possess a personal philosophy of collaboration, a prerequisite for selection might be a willingness of new members to learn the skills of collaboration. According to Rappaport (1981), the ability to empower and strengthen families in a way that makes them more competent and capable "requires a breakdown of the typical role relationship(s) between professionals and community people." Collaborative teaming will be a struggle for professionals who have little time to work through the web of conversation necessary for teams to function collaboratively, who are used to being "the expert," and who have little desire or interest in learning the expertise of others.

Partnerships and collaborative efforts are valued over paternalistic approaches because the former implies and conveys the belief that partners are capable individuals who become more capable by sharing knowledge, skills, and resources in a manner that leaves all participants better off after entering into the agreement. This latter belief is perhaps the only fundamental qualification for service on a team.

Identify the Nature and Quantity of Time Given to Climate Setting or Team Building There are few things more annoying than to believe that one's time is being wasted. For some professionals and parents, anything that is not directly related to the final outcome of the task is considered a waste of time. Time spent discovering the interpersonal dynamics of group functioning or dealing with communication styles are issues of secondary importance. However, it is important that professionals not overlook the fact that the quantity and quality of work to be completed is directly affected by the health of the group. For this reason, each member of the group must be secure in the process of group functioning. Thus, determining how much time will be given to team building is one of the most significant steps in achieving collaboration for this decision has as its essence a commitment to proper team functioning.

Personal Responsibility in Collaborative Teaming

As discussed previously, collaborative efforts require both group and individual accountability. In the preceding section, we discussed evaluation of team efficacy and functioning of teams as a whole. The following is a discussion of the efficacy and functioning of individual members on a team. All individuals have different decision-making styles. Since one's ability to consider and react to information and to make decisions is central to successful team functioning, it is useful to identify each team member's natural proclivity for making decisions according to her or his own style.

Hunter Lewis (1990) identified a model that describes six styles of decision making. While other models exist for identifying personal tendencies toward information, conversation, and decision making (e.g., Myers-Briggs Inventory, the Enneogram System, etc.), the Lewis model seems suitable for purposes here. The styles of decision making outlined by Lewis are said to influence what is heard and the credibility given to incoming information. Understanding our own system—and understanding that of other members of the team—is a first step toward effective collaboration. The six personal foundations of decision making identified by Lewis are described below:

Authority. People who rely on an authority figure as their cornerstone of decision making come to a conclusion by taking someone else's word, or through faith in an external authority (e.g., an expert, supervisor, textbook, etc.). Persons with this decision making tendency find comfort and security in detailed codes of operations, handbooks, rules, and bylaws. An affinity toward authority stems from its perceived and often inherent attribute of justice; that is, decisions are always arrived at in like manner for like reasons—the rule, the law, or the code.

Deductive logic. People relying on deductive logic as an avenue for decision making subject their beliefs to the variety of consistency tests that underlie deductive reasoning. For example, a team might be working toward the goal of transitioning a child with a hearing impairment into a regular kindergarten classroom. The team wants to begin training using total communication. A team member using deductive logic might go through the following decision-making steps:

Is the child capable of using both oral and sign language?
If yes, then:
Will the parents agree to and learn the system?
If yes, then:

Is the regular kindergarten teacher prepared to learn the system?
If yes, then:
Is there research indicating that total communication increases peer interactions?
If yes, then:
Begin training immediately in the child's preschool program.

One decision follows directly from another based upon logical reasoning. A strength of this style or system is that it is inherently reasonable. The decision always makes sense if the path of logic has been shown to be a reliable process for reaching conclusions.

Sense experience. People who rely on sense experience to make decision do so by referring only to their own personal experience. For example, have you ever been in a meeting at which someone repeatedly uses the phrase, "That's not my experi-ence"? Or perhaps, something to the effect of, "It was good enough for me; it's good enough for them." Such people gain knowledge and form decisions primarily through their own five senses. Truth is what *they* have lived, not necessarily what other people have lived. People who have this tendency are often passionate about their concerns and directions since the decision represents part of their personal experience.

Emotion. Individuals relying on emotion as their first avenue of decision making believe that their heart should precede their intellectual awareness. They *feel* that something is right or wrong, though they may not be able to provide a rationale for their opinions. Because emotions are so easily affected by constantly changing variables (weather, immediate past activity, etc.) people who adhere to this tendency must be extremely cautious about their initial reactions to a given problem. Particularly problematic with this type of decision making style is an individual's unwillingness to admit that emotions form the basis for their opinions.

Intuition. Intuitive decision making or knowledge is subconscious but is not con-sidered emotional. People who intuit knowledge generally react to subtle cues that are not necessarily understood at the conscious level and may arrive at a conclusion through the merger of many different pieces of information.

Science. Individuals who rely on science as a technique for decision making, rely on sense experiences to collect the observable facts, intuition to develop a testable hypothesis about the facts, logic to develop the test, and testing itself to evaluate the hypothesis. Those aligned with science will need to be convinced that a decision is valid and has a reasonable potential for producing the desired results.

While the six elements discussed above provide a framework for categorizing and labeling our behavior, it is important to avoid pigeonholing individuals by these seemingly discrete systems of decision-making. Rather, all individuals are likely to use all six methods of decision-making, perhaps even simultaneously. It is probably only a matter of degree of align-ment toward particular decision-making styles that clinically separates one from another according to Lewis's model. Yet, it is useful to be aware of potential conflicts between one's own general decision-making method and that of one's colleagues. For example, if a parent on a team tends to use the science approach and the special educator is more likely to use the emotional approach, decision making will be complicated. As in collaboration of any sort, there may be considerable compromise by each participant.

Becoming a Good Collaborator

According to Pugach and Johnson (1995), members of teams can work together, irrespective of their decision-making orientation, if they possess the characteristics of good collaborators. First, good collaborators recognize that many of the problems in public education are a result

Addressing the Challenges of Families with Multiple Risks

The shifts and realities that American families face today reflect growing social concerns that have profound implications for professionals who provide educational, health, and social services. Families have changed dramatically in composition and size, with growing numbers of single-parent households and blended families. Both parents are more likely to be in the workforce, though it has become more difficult for families to stay out of poverty. Parental age is shifting, with more later childbearing at one end of the spectrum and more teen pregnancies at the other. Substance abuse leads to family problems and poses serious threats to caregiving for children. Children across the country are exposed to more violence in their communities and within their own homes. Many of today's families face not just one of these factors but live under the stress of multiple risks.

The stress associated with these many risks can sap parents' physical energy, undermine their sense of competence, and reduce their sense of control over their lives. Parents may find they are so overwhelmed in meeting basic needs that they cannot respond to specific developmental needs of their children. They may find it difficult to follow through or may lack knowledge, resources, or motivation to even access services. When these families must turn to schools or agencies for assistance, they bring the impact of this stress with them. Children from these families may suffer the multiple stresses of poverty, risks from inadequate prenatal care, and the lack of nurturance, structure, and stimulation that would prepare them for life. Finally, these children may see little hope or success for the future.

Social support within the larger community may be a key factor to reducing parents' emotional strain and coercive parenting behavior. However, professionals must understand how to provide this support in effective ways. First, they must recognize that family problems do not come from single causes and, thus, single interventions will probably not be effective. It is helpful in reaching out to multiple-risk families to: (1) provide a wide range of educational, health, and social services, (2) use family associates and paraprofessionals to assist families in gaining access to services, and (3) employ home visitors to enhance contact with children's parents and caregivers. Such comprehensive services require a coordinated interagency response.

Service providers and educators need to engage effective interaction approaches to provide the most appropriate family support. They must give support at the earliest point for children and parents to establish positive and mutually satisfying relationships with one another. They must shift their focus from deficits to an emphasis on child and family strengths, such as cognitive skills, goal-setting behaviors, family stability, and belief systems. Professionals must help build and encourage natural support systems from neighbors, friends, coworkers, and others within the family's community. Service providers must be respectful of cultural differences and able to listen to families as they express their needs, even though they may differ widely from that of the professional.

Service delivery must be comprehensive and coordinated and should provide a continuum of options that are community based and valued by the community members who are being served. Service providers must be advocates for all children, not just those labeled with specific needs. Educators and service providers must be willing to regularly cross traditional professional boundaries in order to offer options and individualize interventions to meet families' and children's needs. They cannot provide an inflexible, uniform, or routine kind of service to all families. Finally, professionals must also go beyond bureaucratic limitations to work with representatives from other agencies and outside the jurisdiction of their own areas.

Only an interactive, multilevel, coordinated approach can address the many challenges of families who experience multiple risks. A broad range of resources and services must be mobilized to counteract these risk factors. One must remember the African proverb "It takes a whole village to raise a child."

Marci J. Hanson and Judith J. Carta. 1995. *Exceptional Children*, *62*(3), pp. 201–212.

of inherent inequities in our society and are, therefore, exceedingly complex. Acknowledging that complexity enables professionals to seek innovative solutions rather than to accept the status quo. This view holds that complexity is a good thing rather than seeing difficult problems as barriers to overcome. Second, good collaborators value the creativity generated by group interdependency. These professionals are willing to accept criticism when solutions are less than successful as well as to share the recognition of team accomplishments. Third, people who enjoy being around others and the social nature of joint problem solving make good collaborators. These professionals respect each other and are willing to tolerate the conflict that is inevitable in human relationships. Collaborators acknowledge and value the intellectual growth that comes with cooperative problem solving. Finally, effective collaborators are willing to invest the time and energy necessary to improve their own professional practice. These professionals know that improving programs for schools is contingent upon their own improvement of professional skills. This understanding prevents professionals from jumping on every new bandwagon or from hastily dispatching creative means of reaching the team's shared goal(s). Apparently, these attributes are neither inborn nor static. Rather, each professional has a personal responsibility to strengthen his or her collaboration skills.

BUILDING TEAMS FOR THE TWENTY-FIRST CENTURY

Even though collaborative teaming is relatively new, there is a tendency to believe that we know much about it. Certainly the research that has been done on this topic has been impressive. Yet, it is disheartening to observe one attempt at collaboration after another, only to find bright and well-meaning women and men not attending to the findings that research and practice has uncovered. Perhaps the task-oriented approaches used for IEP and IFSP planning are getting in the way. Perhaps the overall lack of success in implementing collaborative models stems from professionals' inability to justify the time commitment that collaborative teaming demands of them. These efforts, which are fundamental to collaboration, may be viewed as discretionary since they are *not immediately* related to services needed by families with children who have special needs.

In addition to the elements of collaboration discussed throughout this chapter, Friend and Cook (1990) outlined changes that need to take place in schools and agencies before collaborative efforts can realistically be considered viable; these priorities are professionalism and empowerment (see Figure 12.1). First, professionals, especially educators, need to be trained more rigorously (i.e., higher standards for admission into preservice programs and coursework that is more demanding than current practice). Perhaps, more importantly, personnel training programs need to train teachers to work together collaboratively. The skills in need of training include a willingness to share resources, time, and accountability for outcomes. A part of professionalization should also be training educators and other professionals to use a common language and to trust one another. The second element, empowerment, refers to increasingly giving professionals the responsibility for making decisions that historically were left to administrators. Consistent with site-based management reforms, empowerment is a way of improving professional commitment, respect, and autonomy. Yet, two conditions of empowerment are often overlooked: voluntariness and time. Professionals must come to collaboration on a voluntary basis, and they must be allocated sufficient time to meet and to work toward collective decision making.

Because of the unique mandate given to early childhood professionals to collaborate with and for families, it has been said that we have "the potential to be a guiding light to collaborators as they grapple with the complex issues inherent in today's unique social, political,

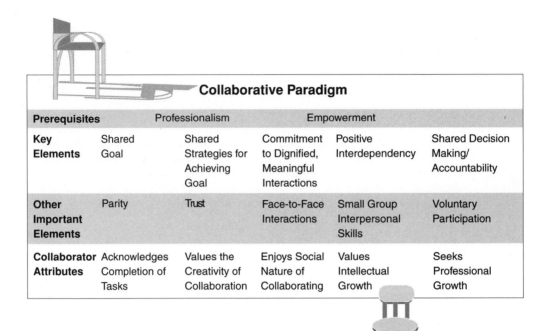

Collaborative Paradigm					
Prerequisites		Professionalism		Empowerment	
Key Elements	Shared Goal	Shared Strategies for Achieving Goal	Commitment to Dignified, Meaningful Interactions	Positive Interdependency	Shared Decision Making/ Accountability
Other Important Elements	Parity	Trust	Face-to-Face Interactions	Small Group Interpersonal Skills	Voluntary Participation
Collaborator Attributes	Acknowledges Completion of Tasks	Values the Creativity of Collaboration	Enjoys Social Nature of Collaborating	Values Intellectual Growth	Seeks Professional Growth

and ideological context" (Kagan, 1991, p. 60). Still, Kagan labeled the current collectivism effort as "naive idealism." She claimed that, as a whole, the movement is unlikely to be a panacea for our country's social ills. On a more modest level, however, she hoped that early childhood special education would be a beacon in the collaboration effort and that collaboration itself will be one necessary tool in efforts to improve care and education for young children with special needs.

It remains clear that parents prefer valid and reliable collaborative teaming efforts. And because serving parents, families, and other caregivers is the primary responsibility of early childhood professionals, perhaps in the years ahead professionals will develop the skills necessary to meet such an expectation.

STUDY GUIDE QUESTIONS

1. In your own words, provide a strong rationale for collaboration rather than working in isolation.

2. Distinguish between the benefits of single service, action/reaction, and collaboration service models.

3. When is a multidisciplinary team a desirable model of collaboration?

4. How is an interdisciplinary team a compromise?

5. What attributes do you think professionals must possess to be good members of transdisciplinary teams?

6. What are five elements that are desirable, if not key elements, in collaborative teaming?

7. Give a unique example for which it is probable that team members will have difficulty in agreeing upon a strategy for achieving a mutually established goal.

8. Why do you think cooperative interactions are difficult to sustain in collaborative efforts?

9. Briefly describe the strategies for building positive interdependency.

10. What kinds of decision-making strategies have you participated in? Have you experienced the benefits/problems of using those strategies that are described in this chapter?

11. What role should parents play in forming teams?

12. What considerations are made in coming to decisions regarding team composition?

13. Why is it necessary, yet controversial, to set aside time to engage in team building?

14. Identify your own decision making style through a process of elimination.

15. What skills do you think you need to work on to become a better collaborator?

16. Friend and Cook identified two elements that are currently missing from early childhood special education and are necessary to support collaboration. Explain.

REFERENCES

Affleck, G., Tennen, H., Allen, D.A., & Gershman, K. (1986). Perceived social support and maternal adaptation during the transition from hospital to home care of high-risk infants. *Infant Mental Health Journal, 7,* 6–18.

Bouton, C., & Garth, R. (1983). *Learning in groups.* San Francisco: Jossey-Bass.

Brinkman, P., Rabinowitz, V., Karuza, J., Coates, D., Cohn, E., & Kidder, L. (1982). Models of helping and coping. *American Psychologist, 37,* 368–384.

Cantor, D.W. (1992). *Women in power: The secrets of leadership.* Boston: Houghton Mifflin.

Dublinske, S. (1974). Planning for child change in language development/remediation programs carried out by teachers and parents. *Language, Speech, and Hearing Services in the Schools, 5,* 225–237.

Dunn, W. (1987, June 18). Occupational therapy must respond. *O.T. Week,* pp. 4–5, 14–15.

Dunst, C.J., & Trivette, C.M. (1987). Enabling and empowering families: Conceptual and intervention issues. *School Psychology Review, 16*(4), 443–456.

Dunst, C. J., Trivette, C., & Deal, A. (1988). *Enabling and empowering families: Principles and guidelines for practice.* Cambridge, MA: Brookline Books.

Eubanks, E., & Parish, R. (1987). An inside view of change in schools. *Phi Delta Kappan, 68*(8), 610–615.

Friend, M., & Cook, L. (1990). Collaboration as a predictor for success in school reform. *Journal of Educational and Psychological Consultation, 1*(1), 69–86.

Friend, M., & Cook, L. (1992). *Interactions: Collaboration skills for school professionals.* New York: Longman.

Hanson, M. J., & Carta, J. J. (1995). Addressing the challenges of families with multiple risks. *Exceptional Children, 62*(3), 201–212.

Haring, N. G., & McCormick, L. (1990). *Exceptional children and youth.* Upper Saddle River, NJ: Merrill/Prentice Hall.

Haring, N.G., McCormick, L., & Haring, T.G. (1994). *Exceptional children and youth.* Upper Saddle River, NJ: Merrill/Prentice Hall.

Haroutunian-Gordon, S. (1991). *Turning the soul: Teaching through conversation in the high school.* Chicago: University of Chicago Press.

Harris, T. (1987, October). A speech and language pathologist's perspective on teaming to accomplish cooperation between and among regular and special educators. Paper presented at Vermont's Least Restrictive Environment Conference, Burlington.

Healy, A., Keesee, P. D., & Smith, B. S. (1989). *Early services for children with special needs: Transactions for family support.* Baltimore: Paul H. Brookes.

Healy, J. M. (1990). *The endangered mind: Why children can't think and what we can do about it.* New York: Touchstone.

Idol, L., Nevin, A., & Paolucci-Whitcomb, P. (1994). *Collaborative consultation* (2nd ed.). Rockville, MD: Aspen Systems Corporation.

Johnson, D.W. (1990). *Reaching out: Interpersonal effectiveness and self-actualization* (4th ed.). Upper Saddle River, NJ: Prentice Hall.

Johnson, D. W., & Johnson, F. P. (1987). *Joining together* (3rd ed.). Upper Saddle River, NJ: Prentice Hall.

Johnson, D.W., & Johnson, F. (1991). *Joining together* (4th ed.). Upper Saddle River, NJ: Prentice Hall.

Johnson, D., Johnson, R., & Smith, K. (1991). Cooperative learning: Increasing college faculty instructional productivity. *ASHE-ERIC Reports on Higher Education.* Washington, DC: ERIC Document No. ED 343465.

Johnson, L. J., & Pugach, M. C. (1991). Peer collaboration: Accommodating students with mild learning and behavior problems. *Exceptional Children, 57*(5), 454–461.

Jordan, J. B., Gallagher, J. J., Hutinger, P. L., & Karnes, M. B. (1988). *Early childhood special education: Birth to three.* Reston, VA: Council for Exceptional Children and its Division for Early Childhood.

Kagan, S. L. (1991). *United we stand: Collaboration for child care and early childhood services.* New York: Teacher's College Press.

Lewis, H. (1991). *A question of values: Six ways we make the personal choices that shape our lives.* San Francisco: Harper.

Maeroff, G. (1983). *Schools and colleges.* Princeton, NJ: Carnegie Foundation for the Advancement of Teaching.

McGuigan, C. (1985). Presentation to the Governor of Minnesota's Blue Ribbon Panel for Early Childhood, Special Education Services. Minneapolis, MN.

Morgan, S. R. (1985). *Children in crisis: A team approach in the schools.* Austin, TX: PRO-ED.

National Commission on Excellence in Education. (1983). *A nation at risk: The imperative for educational reform.* Washington, DC: U.S. Government Printing Office.

Pugach, M. C., & Johnson, L. J. (1989). The challenge of implementing collaboration between general and special education. *Exceptional Children, 56*(3), 232–235.

Pugach, M. C., & Johnson, L. J. (1995). *Collaborative practitioners: Collaborative schools.* Denver, CO: Love.

Rappaport, J. (1981). Terms of empowerment/exemplars of prevention: Toward a theory for community psychology. *American Journal of Community Psychology, 15*(2), 121–128.

Simeonsson, R. J. (1986). *Psychological and developmental assessment of special children.* Boston: Allyn and Bacon.

Smith, S. D., & Auger, K. (1986). Conflict or cooperation? Keys to success in partnerships in education. *Action in Teacher Education, 7*(4), 1–9.

Spodek, B., Saracho, O. N., & Lee, R. C. (1986). *Mainstreaming young children.* Newton, MA: Allyn and Bacon.

Thousand, J. S., & Villa, R. (1990). Sharing expertise and responsibilities through teaching teams. In W. Stainback & S. Stainback (Eds.), *Support networks for inclusion schooling: Interdependent integrated education* (pp. 151–166). Baltimore: Paul H. Brookes.

Thousand, J. S., Villa, R., & Nevin, A. (1994). *Creativity and collaborative learning.* Baltimore: Paul H. Brookes.

Trivette, C. M., Deal, A., & Dunst, C. J. (1986). Family needs, sources of support and professional roles: Critical elements of family systems assessment and intervention. *Diagnostique, 11,* 246–267.

Udvari-Solner, A. (1994). *A decision-making model for curricular adaptations in cooperative groups.* Baltimore: Paul H. Brookes.

Villa, R. A., Thousand, J. S., Paolucci-Whitcomb, P., & Nevin, A. (1990). In search of new paradigms for collaborative consultation. *Journal of Educational and Psychological Consultations, 1,* 279–292.

Zigler, E., & Berman, W. (1983). Discerning the future of early childhood intervention. *American Psychologist, 38,* 894–906.

Issues and Challenges

Early intervention has reached its adolescence,
but there are issues and challenges that must be confronted
before it can emerge into adulthood. (Thurman, 1993, p. 303)

The last 10 years have witnessed a marked escalation in policy efforts at local, state, and national levels on the behalf of young children and their families. For example, the 100th Congress debated over 100 bills related to children and families, an unprecedented number in this country's history (Stegelin, 1993). Many of the key proposals received bipartisan sponsorship, reflecting a universal acceptance of child-related issues as an important part of the political and legislative agenda (Stegelin, 1993). This dramatic increase of interest in child- and family-related legislation seems to have climaxed at a time when the United States is rethinking its responsibility to all citizens. In the very recent past, federal and state governments have cut support and funding for public services. For example, one woman who adopted two boys in 1988, each with severe disabilities, said the agency that initially promised to provide support to her and her sons had dwindled from a large office complex to a corner office with three employees (personal communication, D. Olson, June, 1995). Hence, it is more important than ever that early childhood professionals be knowledgeable of pedagogical, social, and political issues and be active in communicating information about and advocating for children and families. Practitioners, for too long, have been segregated from the policy-making process (Stegelin, 1993).

POLICY ISSUES

> Children and their parents are pioneers in a world where there are no precedents for such simultaneous trends as high mobility, dual-earner parents, minimal extended-family support, single-headed households, and early academic expectations, all converging on the American family, regardless of its particular form or makeup. (Stegelin, 1993, p. 6)

As governments at local, state, and national levels determine policies for the coming century, they must consider a vast array of possibilities and plan for the necessary flexibility to best serve children and families. They will make decisions regarding a number of salient early childhood issues identified by Stegelin, all of which have numerous permutations:

1. Child care for children at all age levels from infancy through school age, both its quality and accessibility

2. Delivery systems for a variety of quality programs such as home-based, center-based, nonprofit, for-profit, school-based, and community-based sites, all requiring extensive collaboration among agencies

3. Funding mechanisms and wage equity—determining ways to pay for services through parent fees, family support and social welfare, employer sponsored benefits, tax credits, public vouchers, purchase of services, federal funds or subsidies, state funds or subsidies, or open enrollment in programs with sliding scales for payment dependent on family incomes

4. Accountability and standards—deciding how outcomes should be measured in terms of child gains and cost effectiveness

5. Programs for impoverished and special needs children that must address family needs as well and determine long-term gains

6. Public school early childhood programs and universal access to early education

7. Developmentally appropriate curriculum and related research in early childhood education

8. Family support systems

Limited Resources

None of these issues are easy to resolve, particularly in a time of limited economic and human resources. Such scarcity may lead to the conclusion that only certain children and their families will be able to receive services (Thurman, 1993). Policy makers and practitioners will be forced to identify the "right" children—those in greatest need of remediation—and to establish criteria for eligibility not only for individual children but also for families. Thus, the development of policy becomes even more complicated and demands the involvement of knowledgeable practicing professionals.

Programs find themselves competing for a piece of a dwindling finite pie (Thurman, 1993). Therefore, decisions must be made wisely, and eligibility criteria must be seen as aspects of a continuum that has as its basis the degree of risk to which an infant or family is exposed. For example, an infant born into poverty but with strong family support systems in place may require less extensive intervention than a child with a disability born into a middle-income family with a single working parent who has become isolated from an active support network. An intervention model that is flexible enough to provide the degree of intervention that is necessary for each of these situations must be developed and supported (Thurman, 1993).

Prevention

Primary among challenges to "earlier intervention" are prevention programs (Thurman, 1993). Whatever can be done, must be done to expand efforts to prevent risk to young children and their families prior to birth. Efforts might include the provision of child-rearing and birthing classes, greater access to prenatal care, increased economic security for families, genetic counseling, and family planning. In order to provide real prevention, these measures must be universal; that is, they must be available to all the population. When appropriate health care is provided to all childbearing women, for example, there will be a reduction in the occurrence of birth defects (Thurman, 1993).

Family-Centered Services

The notion of family-centered services must be expanded in such a way as to accommodate the actual diversity within this country's population and to acknowledge real family empowerment (Thurman, 1993). To do so requires the recognition and acceptance of different social, moral, and cultural values and the development of programs adaptive enough to fit services to needs as identified by family members. Professionals must not dictate to and direct families; rather they must educate, facilitate services that empower families, and cooperate with families.

Professionals need to develop more extensive ways to assess and intervene with families in greater depth (Paget, 1992). For example, it is necessary to involve family members beyond the mother, who has been a traditional focus of services; early childhood professionals may be working more directly with fathers, siblings, and grandparents. It may be important to consider the quality of the marital relationship and to provide support as needed. It may be wise to assess the informal support provided by friends, neighbors, and relatives. It is likely to be necessary to evaluate the formal support provided by professionals and the quality of relationships with particular parents.

Likewise, true family-centered approaches require an increasing awareness of how children with disabilities may disrupt normal family functioning and impede parental effectiveness (Paget, 1992). When invited to do so by families themselves, professionals need to help families identify positive coping strategies and develop models for family adjustment to the stress that may come with the birth of a child with disabilities. Early childhood professionals also must do a better job of working with children and families in the context of particular environmental stressors, such as poverty, unemployment, the death of a parent, family discord, divorce, single-parenting, child maltreatment and abuse, and parental deviance (Pianta & Nimetz, 1992).

Transitions

Family stress becomes particularly critical at times of transition. Professionals need to pay more attention to transitions all along the continuum of childhood and develop deliberate and effective procedures for easing stress at times of transition (Thurman, 1993). Transitions may begin with the child's release from the hospital's NICU to the family's care at home. At home, the next transition may involve therapeutic intervention in either center-based or home-based programs for infants and toddlers. From there, the child is transitioned into the public school systems' preschool programs or other integrated preschool settings. Eventually, the move is made to kindergarten or special classes and continues in numerous grade and program changes and mainstreaming opportunities. Successful transitioning all along this continuum will require greater collaboration and communication among very different agencies, such as hospitals, schools, and public welfare services. More interagency approaches must be developed that can allow this to happen.

Inclusion

Transitioning also implies the goal of integration, particularly into natural settings, that must be responsive to a family's desires and to a child's needs (Thurman, 1993). The definition of mainstreaming must be relaxed to be inclusive of natural and normal experiences for young children. Is it normal for an eight-week-old to be served in a center-based setting? Is it appropriate to insist on the delivery of home-based services when a family would normally be requesting center-based child care for their infant if the child had not been disabled? How can professionals expand opportunities for children with disabilities to participate in common programs for typical children, such as commercial day care or employer-provided nurseries? Too often, no real integration occurs because special programs are devised primarily for children with disabilities and only a few typical children are also enrolled.

Professionals also must do a better job of addressing real inclusion of children with disabilities, inclusion that is not defined by physical proximity but emphasizes significant interaction with peers. Early childhood professionals need to find ways to teach children with disabilities to be adept in producing alternative strategies when an initial social approach does not work. Ultimately, children are truly included only when they develop friendships—mutual child preferences characterized by reciprocity and positive affect (Howes, Droege, & Phillipsen, 1992). That is to say, true integration occurs when the children enjoy and desire one another's company.

Technology

Virtually all early childhood programs will have access to microcomputer technology before the 1990s are over (Clements & Nastasi, 1992). Professionals must be prepared to use computers in the best way possible to benefit young children. Proponents cite evidence to show that computers can be used to enhance social interactions, improve attitudes toward learning, provide intrinsic motivation, facilitate cognitive development, and increase children's sense of competence. Special populations have particularly benefited from computer technology for language development, the acquisition of academic skills, and specialized supports, such as Braille and speech synthesizers. However, there is much to be learned about technology and ways that teachers can best use it, what support and guidance is necessary, how to select appropriate software, how to structure computer activities, and how to encourage independent work (Clements & Nastasi, 1992).

CROSS–DISCIPLINARY PREDICTIONS FOR THE TWENTY-FIRST CENTURY

What does the future hold for young children? Perhaps predictions concerning the twenty-first century are best made by those who stand at the cutting edge, professionals and parents who shape the future as they live each day. In closure, consider the wisdom of a few individuals from diverse fields and perspectives who project how the future will impact the field of early childhood education and service.

An Educator's Projections

Edward Zigler, Professor of Psychology, Yale University, Former Director of U.S. Office of Child Development

Although predicting the future is never certain, it is clear that the twenty-first century will complete many of the changes already begun in the twentieth century. The changes involve the culture's views of young children's development, technological advances, and policy implications in both these areas.

One change concerns child development itself. Compared to only 20 years ago, it is now acknowledged that children develop best within homes, with consistent, caring parents and other adults. This realization has recently been incorporated into an important provision of P. L. 99-457. The IFSP, as opposed to an IEP, formalizes the idea that the "unit of intervention" for young children is as much the family as the child. One can expect to see even more of a focus on family service and support in the future. Leaders at all levels realize that to be effective for the child, families must be an integral part of interventions concerning their children with disabilities.

Medical technology promises to benefit early intervention in developmental disabilities as never before. Premature babies of two pounds or less are now being saved, and revolutionary advances are now occurring in molecular and clinical genetics. Such advances are identifying new genetic causes of mental retardation and refining ways of diagnosing known conditions. Indeed in the decades ahead, virtually all genetic causes of mental retardation will be discovered; over 1000 have already been identified.

Some of these genetic breakthroughs present novel challenges for interventionists. For example, in fragile X syndrome, the most common inherited cause of developmental delay, diagnostic technology includes both prenatal testing and "preimplantation testing." Preimplantation testing, a new choice for families who carry the fragile X marker, involves molecular testing for fragile X in one or two cells of an in vitro fertilized embryo, followed by implantation of embryos without the disorder. In other developments, it is now possible to screen for fragile X syndrome on a large-scale basis, as is currently done for phenylketonuria.

The policy implications of these technological advances are staggering. Does society need to consider the ethical implications of preimplantation testing, or are such decisions best left to families affected by fragile X? If large-scale screening is to be done, exactly who should be screened? Are the costs of such screening programs justifiable if there is no specific "cure" for fragile X? If screening is to be effective, then newly-identified families must not be stigmatized, and supportive services must be available to them, including genetic counseling for at-risk family members. Will policies be in place to meet these challenges in the twenty-first century?

In other ways as well, social policy can provide either a brighter or dimmer future for young children with disabilities. In an age of balanced budgets and social service cuts, how will early intervention laws like P. L. 99-457 work? Exactly what roles will state and federal agencies play in intervention efforts? Right now, the scientific community knows that families are critical to the welfare of young children, but society has not always acted on that knowledge.

What ultimately happens to early intervention in the twenty-first century, then, depends on the interplay between work in child development, genetic and medical technology, and social policy. Perhaps the biggest challenge ahead for workers in each of these three fields is to ensure that social policies are based on both sound developmental research and the best medical technology. Lessons learned in this century from programs such as Head Start and from society's view of children with disabilities as "whole people" suggest a cautious optimism for this ambitious challenge in the century ahead.

An Economist's Projections

John Beck, Professor of Economics, Gonzaga University

Children with disabilities are affected by the same economic trends affecting all children. In recent years, the United States has experienced an increased percentage of children living in families below the poverty line, an increasing percentage of children in single-parent families, and an increased participation of mothers in the labor force.

The percentage of children under 19 in families below the poverty line rose to 20.6% in 1990, after steadily declining from 26% in 1969 (Haveman & Wolfe, 1993, p. 158). This increase in poverty has been attributed to several factors. One factor contributing to increased poverty rates is the decline in the inflation-adjusted value of per family cash transfers to the poor (e.g., Aid to Families with Dependent Children) since 1973. Focusing on cash transfers ignores "in-kind" benefits such as Medicaid, but even including the "near cash" benefit of food stamps along with AFDC, the average annual benefit for a mother with two children and no earnings was only $7,471 in 1991, compared to $10,169 (adjusted for inflation) in 1972 (Haveman & Wolfe, 1993, p. 158). Thus, the incomes of families with children dependent on government programs have declined.

Increased inequality in the earnings of young men (combined with slow growth in average real wages) is a second factor contributing to increased poverty rates. Note that this is a problem of increased inequality in wage and salary income, not a major shift in the distribution of income between labor and capital. A comparison of the proportion of "high earnings jobs" (defined as above 150% of the median wage and salary income) to the proportion of "low earnings jobs" (below 50% of median earnings) for full-time male workers illustrates this increase in inequality. The proportion of "high earnings jobs" increased from 17.2% in 1973 to 20.3% in 1985 while the proportion of "low earnings jobs" increased from 7.7 to 14.4% (Levy & Murnane, 1992).

The increase in single-parent families is of concern because of the loss of the contribution of the second parent's time and attention in raising children and because this is a third factor contributing to increased poverty rates. The percentage of mother-only families with children who are poor was 45.3% in 1990, substantially above the poverty rate for the population as a whole (Haveman & Wolfe, 1993). Without income from a father's earnings, the chances of a family falling below the poverty level increase. The percentage of children living with a single parent has increased from 9.1% in 1960 to 24.7% in 1990 (Haveman & Wolfe, 1993). This is due to both increased birth rates for unmarried teens—approximately 25% of children are currently being born to unwed mothers—and an increase in the percentage of children experiencing dissolution of their parents' marriage—from 19% in the 1960s to 30% in the 1980s (Haveman & Wolfe, 1993).

Another economic trend affecting children is the increased participation of women, particularly mothers of young children, in the labor force. In 1987, 51% of children under age six had mothers in the labor force, compared to 29% in 1970 (Haveman & Wolfe, 1993). Although there is evidence that parental interaction time has a positive effect on children's later educational and economic attainment, the mother's participation in the labor market also has a substantial positive effect on children's attainment, suggesting a "role model" effect (Haveman & Wolfe, 1993). Thus, the net effect of mothers' participation in the labor market is ambiguous.

Will the trends discussed above continue? Such forecasts are highly speculative, but there are some identifiable influences that are unlikely to change. For example, women's participation in the labor force has given them increased work experience. Work experience increases wage rates and raises the cost of withdrawing from the labor force. Furthermore, the observed success of women in the labor force encourages younger women to acquire education and training that will increase their own potential earnings and make continued labor force participation more attractive. Thus, women's higher participation in the labor force is likely to continue.

At this writing, the outcome of "welfare reform" is uncertain, but recent history suggests any possible effects will be modest. Although conservatives may attribute increased birth rates among unwed teenagers to the existence of welfare programs, the facts noted above—that cash welfare benefits adjusted for inflation declined during the period when births to unmarried teenagers increased—suggests that the economic incentives of welfare programs have little effect on behavior in this regard. Changes in the influence of social norms undoubtedly have had more effect on the proportion of children in single-parent families than any economic incentives. Welfare reform might affect poverty among children more directly by changing the amount of cash transfers families receive from government. However, there is reason to believe that disincentive effects may stymie attempts to raise incomes through government transfer programs. For example, Browning (1995) has recently produced simulations showing that the Earned Income Tax Credit actually *reduces* disposable income of most recipients by discouraging work effort. On the other hand, increased government provision of child care, as advocated by Barbara Bergman (1994), would provide increased resources for poor children while encouraging their mothers to increase their own earnings.

A Parent's Projections

Joseph Terhaar, Parent

These reluctant comments are presented from fear and a great sense of trepidation of where we as a society are headed. I hope my views are the product of an oversensitivity to witnessing the current unmet needs of those with disabilities and my emotionally reactive misunderstanding of the political movements and activity of the day.

Over the next 10 years, services for children with disabilities, birth to age six, will be affected more by factors external to the system than by the developments and trends occurring within programs, service provision and practices, and the serving professions themselves.

While business profits have soared in the 1990s and corporations have kept more after-tax profits (no wonder the Dow Jones Industrial average concurrently hit record highs), the average wage earner has made no gain in real income. This is reflected in a long-term trend of a 15% loss of buying power in the average wage since 1973. This trend continued despite four years of economic recovery starting in 1991. The hardest hit middle-class wage earners, the largest tax revenue contributor group, lost more income to taxes than ever before. It is no wonder that the electorate responded so strongly in the 1994 Congressional elections to the Republican promise of a tax cut and less tax burden through a drastic reduction in social service spending. With tax cuts and increased spending for defense, there is less federal money for allocation amid a political environment of insensitivity and intolerance to social needs.

The 104th Republican Congress made clear in budget language and legislation that the cutting of social program support was their raison d'être and not rhetoric. The changes in policy and budget will be the herald of the beginning of the end of federal subsidization of community services for social needs.

Developmental disabilities will be impacted by the reductions in funding and policy changes for many years to come, regardless of the actual longevity of the Republican Congress after 1994. Funding directly serving people with disabilities (e.g., Social Security, Block Grant Funds for disability services, Part H IDEA funds) and dollars that indirectly contribute to opportunities for the development of independence for those with disabilities (AFDC, Medicaid) will be significantly reduced, for adults as well as children. State budgets will follow in kind with reduced funding for disabilities as more revenue will be channeled into prisons and economic development strategies.

The impact will manifest secondarily in the birth to six disabilities service systems.

1. There will be an overall gross reduction in direct service funds and elimination of technical assistance and other secondary support efforts for disabilities services and social welfare programs.

2. Such losses of funding will trigger an austerity of rationing of services and programs for adults. In heeding the survival-of-the-fittest philosophical tenet of Republicanism, leaders in disability advocacy will be forced to ameliorate the lack of available programming by offering opportunities to those who can contribute to their own financial needs through gainful employment. Though many advocates in 1995 subscribe to the need for increasing employment opportunities for people with disabilities, this goal will become the entire menu, with the loss of aspirations for self-fulfillment, self-determination, and a sense of empowerment and choice for those with disabilities.

3. Financial contribution to the economy on the part of those with disabilities will become the key justification for funding of adult services. This will then become the organizing principle that trickles down to children's services. The programs that will survive are those that can demonstrate relevance to future economic contribution by the recipient child. Showing that a piece of equipment or OT/PT services are educationally relevant will be of little value. The question needing to be answered will be, "Will the expenditure in equipment or services contribute to the future employability of the child?" Those planning and structuring programs for children will know that the future is bleak for their students unless the student can command some wage for work. A positive side of the picture will be that inclusion of children with disabilities into integrated service settings will increase. Districts will have to learn fast the lesson of inclusion to reduce the need for social appropriateness programs in middle and high schools. Graduates will not have substantive financial support available without work. Those who can work in integrated social settings will earn much better wages. Those who are less capable socially will still struggle in segregated employment settings at well below minimum wage levels.

4. States with infant and toddler education mandates will escape much of the financial crunch of programs because of an established philosophical base of serving children with disabilities and well-established funding streams. States without mandates that operate on permissive dollars for infant and toddler programs will struggle even more with birth-to-three services.

In difficult financial times, of which there will likely be many to come, the moral imperatives for funding for people with disabilities cannot withstand the intense budget cutting pressures. Only with constitutionally guaranteed funding streams can today's service levels be maintained into the foreseeable future.

A Medical Projection: Fictional Scenario

Carl J. Bodenstein, M.D., Neonatologist of Northwest Neonatology

Jonathan:

Jonathan awoke slowly from his dreamless sleep. Peering through nearly closed eyelids the ever blue surroundings were subtly but perceptibly changed on this awakening. Slightly bluer, ever so slightly. The ever-present tickling was also different. The tiny bubbles passing by were somehow lighter and smaller. At least one familiar and comforting feel, the ever-present mechanical thumping, remained at its rate and volume. Jonathan could not really remember a different volume, but he did remember in some distant past a very different rate, somehow slower and deeper in pitch. Gone too were the weird rumblings, squeaks, and moans that came seemingly out of nowhere and in no predictable pattern. Ah, the current state was so much easier, giving much more time to contemplate the nature of existence and why the subtle changes in his universe had occurred somehow while he was asleep.

Senator Joseph Dodd:

Dodd was tired. His head ached, his stomach growled. Hunger and sleep deprivation were taking their toll. Endless hours of negotiation had led to the Health and Welfare Oversight Committee's decisions. In the morning the announcement would be made: Public funding of dialysis and all organ transplantation would be ended. Finally decades of unconscionable spending for the few at the cost of the many would come to an end. His work almost done, a feeling of pride overcame Dodd. Pride and exhaustion. His hunger would wait. Sleep came quickly. And the never ending nightmares . . .

Jonathan:

Saltier this awakening. And still lighter blue. What now??? The mechanical thumping was different, somehow softer, somehow slower. Ah, this is more pleasant. No cause for alarm. But the elements of the universe added another change. My universe has cooled some, not uncomfortably, but definitely cooler. Time for my exercise. Kick, reach, reach, kick, roll, tumble. Ah, that's enough of that, let's ponder the universe some more. Wet, warm (though cooler this awakening: a new variable), blue, bubbles, salty. And the noises, the mechanical thumping, ever present. But now some other noises, musical with tones and phrases, then a different set of tones, almost as a response. Ah, lots to ponder this awakening.

Senator Joseph Dodd:

Breakfast was one of those damned multigrain patties. Baked. Tasteless, even with the salt substitute. Eva would have to make contact again. It's been three months since the underground had delivered bacon and eggs. What a cost! Ah well, what's a well-paid public servant to do with his wealth anyway? If the constituents ever found out . . . . One more item on the bill— what to do with the Newborn Survival Project. Why, this one's so tough it defies logic. We axed the kidney freaks and those absurd transplant surgeons. Somehow this one is different. I guess people really love kids. But those damn little swimming fetuses! How in the world do they think we'll continue to pay for this? God and religion be damned. This is economics!

Jonathan:

Woow!!! Really different. Shapes through the blue, moving across my field of view. And the wet slightly cooler feel, now on . . . on my eyes. The noises, more rhythmic, more LOUD! Why? What's happening to my universe? To Me?

Senator Joseph Dodd:

Well, progress at last. Pulled every debt out there. Promised away half my stash to boot. Well, I'll be able to secure another delivery later. I just hope my doctor doesn't pick up the ingestion on my monthly blood screen. God though I like that damn bacon!!! The NIH finally caved in. All over. We pull the plug. Monday the damn project will shut down. What did they expect? One million dollars for a fish in a tank. Just because it's "human." Who were they kidding anyway. Future taxpayers my ass!! More dependents, more dilution of the public good. More diversion from the true purpose of modern medicine. Well, it all ends Monday, 8 A.M.

Jonathan:

Gettin' it now. I'm at the center of the universe. Those moving shadows, now clearer, much much clearer, look like me but somehow bigger. The same two keep coming by, their eyes staring in. The one voice, so soft, so pleasant. Ah, sleep and . . . dream.

Monday, 8 A.M. Jonathan:
What?!!! The blue is darkening, the bubbles slowing . . . the pulsing rhythmic beating STOPPED!!! The shadow with the nice sound is here. What's that, it's close, there's liquid from those two dark circles in the big circle. I'm dizzy. I'm faint. I'm not sure. The universe, what's happening? The shape is shaking, the noise from it harsher, shrieking. I'm dizzy. Sleepy, but not normal tired. The universe. What's happening to me?!! MOMMY HELP ME!!!

Tuesday, 7 A.M., Senator Joseph Dodd:
Umh. Ahh! Those little porkers are exquisite. Even if my Doc finds out, I'll bribe him off too!!! Plenty extra resources for the committee now. . . .

A FINAL COMMENT

One of the characteristics that distinguishes professionals from others is that professionals do not punch a time clock; there is no such thing as a 9-to-5 professional day. The commitment and dedication that is brought to early childhood services infuses the values, the priorities, and the purpose of professionals' lives. This implies an inherent pledge, not only to this generation but to the next as well, to continue to advocate for improved programs, to search for more effective treatment, and to establish better collaboration with families. Such devotion has carried the field far beyond its primitive beginnings and will effectively bridge the challenges of transition into the twenty-first century.

REFERENCES

Bergman, B. R. (1994). Curing child poverty in the United States. *American Economic Review, 84,* 76–80.

Browning, E. K. (1995). Effects of the Earned Income Tax Credit on income and welfare. *National Tax Journal, 48,* 23–43.

Clements, D. H., & Nastasi, B. K. (1992). Computers and early childhood education. In M. Gettinger, S. N. Elliott, & T. R. Kratochwill, (Eds.), *Preschool and early childhood treatment directions* (pp. 113–150). Hillsdale, NJ: Lawrence Erlbaum Associates.

Haveman, R., & Wolfe, B. (1993). Children's prospects and children's policy. *Journal of Economic Perspectives, 7,* 153–174.

Howes, C., Droege, K., & Phillipsen, L. (1992). Contribution of peers to socialization in early childhood. In M. Gettinger, S. N. Elliott, & T. R. Kratochwill, (Eds.), *Preschool and early childhood treatment directions* (pp. 113–150). Hillsdale, NJ: Lawrence Erlbaum Associates.

Levy, F., & Murnane, R. J. (1992). U.S. earnings levels and earnings inequities: A review of recent trends and proposed explanations. *Journal of Economic Literature, 30,* 1333–1381.

Paget, K. D. (1992). Parent involvement in early childhood services. In M. Gettinger, S. N. Elliott, & T. R. Kratochwill, (Eds.), *Preschool and early childhood treatment directions* (pp. 89–111). Hillsdale, NJ: Lawrence Erlbaum Associates.

Pianta, R. C., & Nimetz, S. L. (1992). Development of young children in stressful contexts: Theory, assessment, and prevention. In M. Gettinger, S. N. Elliott, & T. R. Kratochwill, (Eds.), *Preschool and early childhood treatment directions* (pp. 151–185). Hillsdale, NJ: Lawrence Erlbaum Associates.

Stegelin, D. A. (1993). Early childhood policy: An introduction. In D. A. Stegelin (Ed.), *Early Childhood education: Policy issues for the 1990s* (pp. 1–18). Norwood, NJ: Ablex Publishing.

Thurman, K. S. (1993). Some perspectives on the continuing challenges in early intervention. In W. Brown, S. K. Thurman, & L. F. Pearl (Eds.), *Family-centered early intervention with infants and toddlers: Innovative cross-disciplinary approaches* (pp. 303–316). Baltimore: Paul H. Brookes.

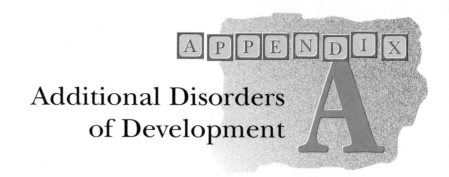

Additional Disorders of Development

NEURAL TUBE DEFECTS

Agenesis of the Corpus Callosum

The corpus callosum is the great commissure (transverse band of nerve fibers) of the brain that runs between the two cerebral hemispheres. This fiber tract allows for information to be transferred from one hemisphere of the brain to the other hemisphere. Agenesis (incomplete development) of this fiber tract decreases the ability of the infant or child to process information.

Agenesis of the corpus callosum may be suspected by findings of prenatal ultrasound but is diagnosed in these infants by computerized tomography (CT scan) after delivery. Frequently this condition is associated with other severe central nervous system abnormalities that may have symptoms of seizures and developmental delays. Some affected children may not have obvious symptoms until normal developmental milestones are not reached. Evaluation for developmental delay will identify the abnormality.

Arnold-Chiari Malformation

Arnold-Chiari malformation also occurs during the period of neural tube closure. It is characterized by displacement of the fourth ventricle and the medulla of the brain into the cervical spinal canal (top of neck), thinning of the medulla of the brain, decreased brain density, and body defects of the skull and spinal column. Hydrocephalus occurs in approximately 95% of cases of Arnold-Chiari malformation. Infants affected with this malformation are severely mentally retarded if they survive the neonatal period (Avery, 1987).

Holoprosencephaly

Holoprosencephaly is the developmental failure of the prosencephalon, the embryonic forebrain, to develop

a cleavage and undergo separation. This leads to a defect in the midline facial development and, in the most severe form, presents with cyclopia (single eye midfacial formation). There is a single cerebral sphere that forms instead of the normal dual hemispheres. This defect is sometimes found with trisomy 13 or trisomy 15. If the infant survives, there is profound mental retardation.

Porencephaly

Porencephaly is the development of abnormal cystic formations or fluid filled cavities in the brain tissue itself. These cysts usually communicate with one of the ventricles. Single or multiple cysts may be present. These replace normal brain tissue. Cystic changes may occur as a result of developmental defects or may develop following an insult to the brain, with subsequent cell death. Once cysts have formed, severe mental retardation occurs. Cyst formation can occur during gestational development or may occur after birth when there has been a significant insult to the brain resulting in cell death.

CONGENITAL HEART DEFECTS

Patent Ductus Arteriosus

The ductus arteriosus is a vessel of fetal circulation that is developed before the sixth week of gestation and allows blood to flow from the pulmonary artery to the aorta, bypassing the lungs. This communicating vessel functionally closes at birth with the changes in pulmonary blood flow. Failure of closure results in blood flow from the aorta backward to the pulmonary artery. Ultimately, this can result in heart failure. The presence

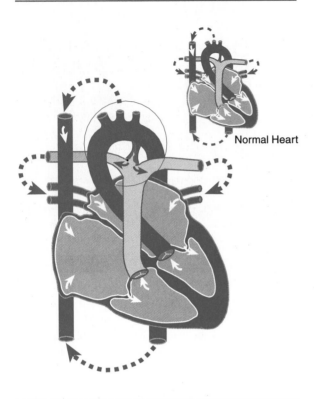

Normal Heart

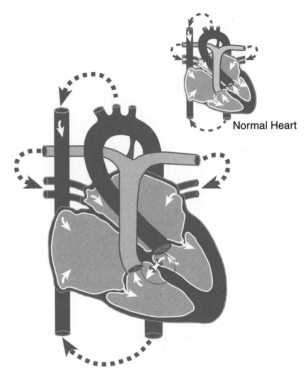

Normal Heart

of a small or partial patent ductus arteriosus may produce no symptoms except for a soft murmur. Treatment is generally not necessary for such small defects. If the defect is larger, and an infant is showing symptoms of heart failure, surgical intervention may be necessary.

Ventricular Septal Defect

A ventricular septal defect (VSD) occurs when there is failure of the septum (tissue wall) between the ventricles to close (lower chambers), allowing blood to flow from the left ventricle (high pressure chamber) across the defect to the right ventricle (low pressure chamber). The interrupted pathway decreases the amount of oxygenated blood available to the general circulation. Frequently occurring in conjunction with complex congenital cardiac defects such as tetralogy of Fallot, VSD has been associated with every other known congenital cardiac disorder.

Lesser VSDs generally require no treatment. Greater defects, especially when also faced with symptoms of heart failure and respiratory distress, require

vigorous medical management. These infants may ultimately require surgical intervention. The majority of severely affected infants have multiple defects or other related malformations. Spontaneous closure may be expected in up to 50% of uncomplicated, isolated defects (Sigman, Perry, & Behrendt, 1977).

Atrial Septal Defect

Like the ventricular defect, an atrial septal defect occurs when there is failure of the septum (wall) between the upper chambers (atria) to close. This defect may occur at either the site of the foramen ovale cordis or at a separate site along the atrial septum. A defect at the site of the foramen ovale cordis usually accompanies other defects. High blood pressure in the right atrium forces the flap open and prevents normal physiological closure. Consequently, blood is pumped into the general circulation that has bypassed the lungs and contains significantly decreased amounts of oxygen.

Isolated atrial septal defects generally require no treatment, especially if the defect is small. Defects that

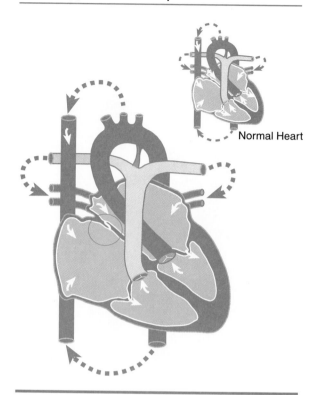

Normal Heart

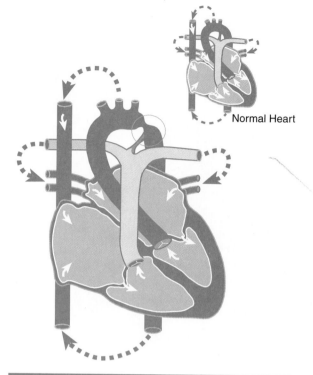

Normal Heart

produce symptoms (e.g., respiratory distress, heart failure) may require surgical closure of the defect. Ironically, many of the atrial septal defects that occur in conjunction with other cardiac defects provide a means to the general circulation of oxygenated blood. Though this blood has decreased levels of oxygen, the defect may be the only means of providing any blood flow to the body. Occasionally, an artificial defect may be created by making a hole between the atria to allow for survival until an infant is able to tolerate surgical intervention for the repair of complex defects.

Coarctation of the Aorta

Coarctation of the aorta is a serious cardiac defect that can affect up to 10% of newborns with serious cardiac conditions (Lock, Bass, & Amplatz, 1983). A narrowed segment of the aorta that generally occurs just above the entrance of the ductus arteriosus into the aorta and obstructs the flow of blood along the normal pathway.

Coarctations are categorized as either simple or complex. Simple coarctations constrict but allow for adequate blood flow into the general circulation.

Complex coarctations present with both narrowing and hypoplasia (underdevelopment) of the aorta and occasionally with an interruption in the formation of the arch. Affected infants have a patent ductus arteriosus that allows blood flow to the lower body. Many of these infants have a small left ventricle from lack of blood flow along the normal pathway. Infants may initially be without symptoms at birth, until the patent ductus arteriosus begins to close over the first week of life. Symptoms then rapidly appear, and death may occur unless a diagnosis is made quickly and treatment is initiated to keep the patent ductus open until surgical repair can be done. Often these infants are at risk of intraventricular hemorrhage caused by increased pressure in the brain.

Complete Transposition of the Great Vessels

Transposition of the great vessels is a cardiac condition in which the pulmonary artery arises from the left ventricle (should arise from the right), and the aorta arises from the right ventricle (should arise from the left). This

Figure App. A.5/ *Complete Transposition of the Great Vessels*

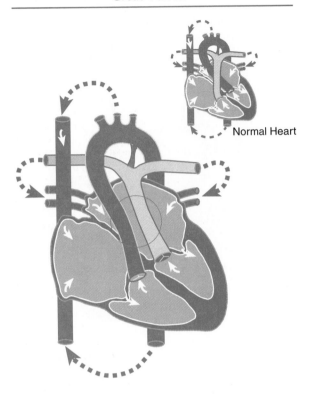

Normal Heart

Figure App. A.6/ *Tetralogy of Fallot*

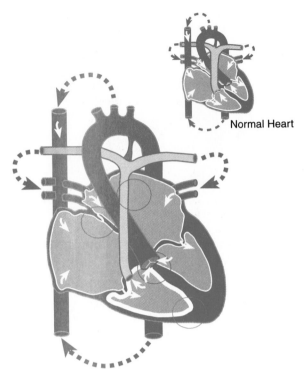

Normal Heart

creates a parallel circulatory pattern in place of the normal series pattern. Blood from the body enters the heart and is immediately recirculated through the body without passing through the lungs. At the same time, blood returning to the heart from the lungs is immediately recirculated through the lungs. The only oxygenated blood flowing to the body is across a patent ductus arteriosus or through an atrial or ventricular septal defect.

Infants born with complete transposition of the great vessels and without a septal defect may become cyanotic very quickly after birth. Immediate surgical intervention to create a hole between the atria is generally sufficient to allow for adequate oxygen delivery to the cells until an infant is of sufficient age and weight for complex surgical repair. Infants born with transposition and a septal defect may be free of symptoms until blood pressure within the lungs is sufficiently elevated to cause enlargement of the heart. Surgical repair within the first year of life significantly reduces the mortality rate from complications from this condition.

Tetralogy of Fallot

Tetralogy of Fallot is one of the most commonly diagnosed cyanotic congenital heart defects in the neonatal period and is also one of the few not generally associated with other congenital malformations. This defect consists of four conditions that must be present. These include a ventricular septal defect, pulmonary stenosis (narrowing of the pulmonary artery), overriding aorta, and hypertrophy (thickening of the wall) of the right ventricle (Pinsky & Arciniegas, 1990).

Initial symptoms in the neonatal period may only be cyanosis and the presence of a murmur. A cardiac catheterization is necessary to determine the exact nature of the multiple defects and to determine if there is more than one defect in the ventricular septum. Supplemental oxygen is frequently necessary during home care of these infants until complete repair can be undertaken. The more severe the initial cyanosis, the poorer the prognosis. New techniques are being developed for surgical repair that are making a difference in the possibility for long-term survival.

Many children affected with tetralogy of Fallot require stage repairs that extend into the school-age years. Attention to individual symptoms of increased oxygen needs (e.g., squatting, change in color, increased respiratory rate, coughing) and predetermined planning for interventions when faced with symptoms allows children to be as involved as possible with a normal educational experience.

Hypoplastic Left Heart Syndrome

Hypoplastic left heart syndrome is a severe defect in development of the left ventricle of the heart. It includes aortic valve atresia (narrowing), mitral valve atresia, aortic hypoplasia (underdevelopment), and severe left ventricle hypoplasia. The result of these multiple defects leaves the left ventricle (main pumping chamber) significantly underdeveloped and incapable of sustaining blood flow to the body. When the ductus arteriosus closes, symptoms rapidly develop and death quickly occurs. Hypoplastic left heart syndrome occurs in approximately 3.5 infants out of every 1000 live births (Norwood, 1991). Genetic abnormalities appear in about 17.5% of affected infants (Ferencz, Boughman, & Meill, 1989). These include Turner's syndrome and Trisomies 13, 18, and 21. Neurological abnormalities may also appear.

Prior to the early 1980s, there was no treatment available for hypoplastic left heart syndrome. Despite the use of hormones to temporarily keep the ductus arteriosus from closing, technology had nothing to offer either for short-term or long-term survival of affected infants. There continues to be a high mortality rate even with advanced surgical techniques, though many treated infants survive to the point of becoming viable candidates for heart transplants. Another advancing option is immediate heart transplant within the neonatal period.

Prior to 1985, no neonates had survived the transplant process. Improved immunosuppressant medications and surgical techniques have drastically improved the survival rates for this defect. The scant availability of organ donors for infant transplants significantly limits the neonatal heart transplant program. A second issue is the long-term commitment needed by families of affected infants, who must maintain lifelong medications and follow-up. Many families choose compassionate care for their infants rather than exposure to the transplant process and all the risks that continue to be part of that process. Compassionate care may include home management with support from medicine, nursing, social services, and hospice-care workers, with the goal of providing infants with a calm, alleviated, and dignified death.

GASTROINTESTINAL ANOMALIES

Atresia/Stenosis of the Esophagus

Atresia (congenital absence of the opening) or stenosis (narrowing of the opening) of the esophagus occurs in approximately 1 in every 4425 live births in the United States (Haight, 1957). This defect is one of the most easily diagnosed and amenable to surgical correction. It frequently occurs in conjunction with a fistula, an abnormal passage from one tube formation to another tube formation, in this case, between the esophagus and the trachea. The ease of surgical repair and the long-term outcome of these infants is dependent on the location of the fistula, the gestational age of the infant, and the presence of other defects or infection.

Isolated esophageal atresia is associated with increased salivation and persistent vomiting. Because there is no connection between the upper segment of the esophagus and the stomach, no air or food can pass through to the stomach. Vomiting increases the risk of developing pneumonia since infants may aspirate saliva or food particles into the lungs. An X ray of the abdomen will show that no air has entered the small bowel. The distance between the two pouches of the esophagus is important to the final outcome. Scar tissue can form around the repair and may be affected by stretching the two ends to connect them together. Prior to the 1970s, the ends were frequently connected by using a section of the small bowel. This required stage repairs with affected infants being temporarily fed via a gastrostomy tube for a variable period of time. New techniques have decreased the need for such drastic methods. Even in cases in which significant distance separates the segments of esophagus, temporary gastrostomy tubes are placed and natural growth then provides the elongation necessary to allow for connection. This can usually occur by about three months of age (Puri, Blake, O'Donnell, & Guiney, 1981).

Esophageal atresia with a tracheal fistula is a more complicated surgical repair. Because there is an opening directly between the lungs and the stomach, there is a high risk for aspiration of stomach acids directly into the lungs. This chemical pneumonia not only causes acute infection but can permanently scar the lung tissue, setting the infant up for chronic lung problems. Infants with atresia and a fistula who have no other obvious anomalies and do not have significant pneumonia are generally repaired immediately. Infants who are small for their gestational age, those with other anomalies, and those with moderate to severe pneumonia are usually delayed until their overall status is more stable. This delay decreases the higher mortality in these compromised infants. Most infants will have a complete repair done during the initial surgery. Occasionally factors such as low weight or infection may require the repair to be done in stages.

Major anomalies that frequently occur in conjunction with esophageal atresia, with or without a fistula, include the absence of an anal opening and other obstructions of the bowel. In addition, Grosfeld and Ballantine (1979) found that as many as 37% of affected infants also had significant congenital cardiac defects.

Duodenal Atresia

Atresia of the bowel is thought to result from decreased blood flow with subsequent loss of oxygen to cells early in embryonic development. This condition is the failure of a tube system to open resulting in complete obstruction in the system. It may affect only a short segment of the bowel or an extended segment or a series of short segments throughout the small bowel.

Duodenal atresia is diagnosed prior to delivery, in many cases, by prenatal ultrasound. The duodenum is the first segment of the small bowel and is connected to the end of the stomach. On the ultrasound video, there is a classic appearance of an enlarged stomach bubble in conjunction with dilatation of the first segment of the small bowel. This phenomenon is frequently referred to as a "double bubble." Vomiting begins shortly after birth, with bile frequently present in the vomitus. Generally, distention of the abdomen is not present. Associated, often severe, congenital malformations are frequently found with duodenal atresia. Studies have shown that other defects are present in as high as 70% of affected infants, with as many as 21% of these having Down syndrome (Guzzetta, Randolph, Anderson, Boyajian, & Eichelberger, 1987). Of those affected, a high percentage also suffers from congenital cardiac defects.

Surgery may be delayed in symptomatic infants until other conditions are stabilized. This may include congenital cardiac conditions or the multitude of problems experienced by the premature infant. In spite of successful surgical repair, the mortality rate for infants suffering from duodenal atresia remains high. Estimates vary from 30% to 65%. Most of these deaths are related to either prematurity or other serious congenital malformations.

Meconium Ileus

Meconium ileus is an obstruction of the bowel caused by abnormally thick and tenacious meconium. It is not a common occurrence but does rank among the top three causes of intestinal obstruction during the neonatal period. Family history can be vital in the early stages of diagnosis with this condition. Previous siblings who have experienced a bowel obstruction or been clinically diagnosed with cystic fibrosis are a marker for diagnosis in the presence of symptoms.

The first noted symptom of intestinal obstruction in meconium ileus is abdominal distention. Normal bowel sounds may be present for an extended period before being lost. There may be obvious dilated loops of bowel noted through observation of the abdomen. These may appear sausage-like and can be freely moved in any direction. Vomiting will occur but may not be noted until more than 24 hours after birth. An absolute symptom will be failure to pass meconium stools within the first day of life.

X-ray examination in conjunction with the physical assessment is the method by which meconium ileus is diagnosed. Medical management is initially used to attempt to relieve the intestinal obstruction. This may consist of enemas along with mineral oil given through a tube passed into the stomach. Care must be taken when giving repeated enemas to the newborn. Dehydration and disturbances in electrolyte balance can occur. If medical attempts fail, then surgery is indicated.

Meconium ileus is present in approximately 10% of infants who have cystic fibrosis and very rarely occurs when cystic fibrosis is not present (Mabogenje, Wang, & Mahour, 1982). Even though these infants generally do not have symptoms of respiratory disease, have negative sweat tests, and recover readily from the intestinal obstruction, pancreatic enzymes are generally started in the neonatal period with the assumption that cystic fibrosis is present.

REFERENCES

Avery, G. (Ed.). (1987). *Neonatology: Pathophysiology and management of the newborn.* (pp. 1111–1112). Philadelphia: J.B. Lippincott Co.

Ferencz, C., Boughman, J., & Neill, C. (1989). Congenital cardiovascular malformations: Questions on inheritance. *Journal of the American College of Cardiology, 14,* 756–763.

Grosfeld, J., & Ballantine, T. (1979). Esophegeal atresia and tracheoesophageal fistula: Effect of delayed thoracotomy on survival. *Surgery, 84,* 394–397.

Guzzetta, P., Randolph, J., Anderson, K., Boyajian, M., & Eichelberger, M. (1987). Surgery of the neonate. In G. Avery (Ed.), *Neonatology: Pathophysiology and management of the newborn* (pp. 944–984). Philadelphia: J.B. Lippincott Co.

Haight, C. (1957). Some observations on esophageal atresias and tracheoesophageal fistulas of congenital origin. *Journal of Thoracic Surgery, 34,* 141–145.

Lock, J., Bass, J., & Amplaz, K. (1983). Balloon dilatation angioplasty of aortic coarctation in infants and children. *Circulation, 68,* 109–112.

Mabogenje, O., Wang, C., & Mahour, H. (1982). Improved survival of neonates with meconium ileus. *Archives of Surgery, 117,* 37–40.

Norwood, W. (1991). Hypoplastic left heart syndrome. *Annuals of Thoracic Surgery, 52,* 688–695.

Pinsky, W., & Arciniegas, E. (1990). Tetralogy of Fallot. *Pediatric Clinics of North America, 37*(1), 179–183.

Puri, P., Blake, N., O'Donnell, B., & Guiney, E. (1981). Delayed primary anastomosis following spontaneous growth of esophegeal segments in esophageal atresia. *Journal of Pediatric Surgery, 16,* 180–184.

Sigman, J., Perry, B., & Behrendt, D. (1977). Ventricular septal defect: Results after repair in infancy. *American Journal of Cardiology, 39,* 66–70.

The following table presents a comparison of the Preschool and Infant/Toddler Programs of the Individuals with Disabilities Education Act and changes made under recent legislation. The information in the table includes both statutory and regulatory provisions for Part B and Part H.

Issue	Preschool (Part B)	Infant/Toddler (Part H)	Recent Changes: P.L. 102-119

Eligibility	3–5 years old
	Same categorical disabilities as for school-age children 6–21 (MR, LD, Seriously Emotionally Disturbed, etc.)
	Who need special services
		Birth to 3 years old
		1. Developmental delay
		2. Established risk
		  • Cognitive
		  • Language
		  • Physical
		  • Psychosocial
		  • Self-help
		Who are in need of early intervention
			Part B
			States may define eligibility: presence of developmental delay in one or more areas (cognitive, social/emotional, motor, adaptive, communication)
			
			Part H
			Changed terminology of developmental delay areas to:
			  • Cognitive
			  • Adaptive
			  • Social/emotional
			  • Physical
			  • Communication

Services	Special education and related services on IEP, same as for school-age children (e.g., audiology, counseling, early identification, diagnostic medical services)	Early Intervention Services documented on IFSP (e.g., audiology, case management, family training, etc.)	**Part H**
			  • Term "case management" changed to "service coordination"
			  • Vision services added
			  • Assistive technology and services
			  • Transportation and related costs added

Issue	Preschool (Part B)	Infant/Toddler (Part H)	Recent Changes: P.L. 102-119
Individualized Plans	Individualized Education Program includes: • Present levels of performance • Annual goals and short-term objectives • Special and related services to be provided, extent of participation in regular education • Projected dates of initiation and duration of services • Evaluation criteria, schedule and procedures • Transition services	Individualized Family Service Plan includes: • Present levels of development • With concurrence of family, a statement of family strengths and needs related to enhancing development of child • Specific early intervention services services needed to achieve child and family outcomes • Projected dates of initiation and duration of services • Name of case manager from the profession most immediately relevant to the child's or family's needs who will be responsible for the IFSP and coordination with other agencies or persons • Steps taken to support transition of child at age three	**Part B** At local or state discretion and with concurrence of the family, an IFSP may be used instead of an IEP, so long as IEP requirements are met **Part H** • A family-directed assessment of the resources, priorities, and concerns of the family replaces a statement of the family's strengths and needs • A statement of the natural environments in which early intervention services would be appropriately provided • Changes "case manager" to "service coordinator" and amends requirement of service coordinator being of the profession related to child's greatest need; allows the service coordinator to be someone who is qualified to carry out the responsibilities of the position as designated under Part H • Requires informed, written consent from parents before services in IFSP are provided. If parents do not provide consent for all services, services for which consent is given must be provided

Issue	Preschool (Part B)	Infant/Toddler (Part H)	Recent Changes: P.L. 102-119
Integration	Least Restrictive Environment is defined: "To the maximum extent appropriate, children with disabilities . . . are educated with children who are not disabled, and that special classes, separate schooling, or other removal of children with disabilities from the regular educational environment occurs only when the nature or severity of the disability is such that education in regular classes with the use of supplementary aids and services cannot be achieved satisfactorily."	No statutory requirement	**Part H** Added a statutory requirement: "To the maximum extent appropriate, [services] are provided in natural environments, including the home and community settings in which children without disabilities participate."
Advisory Council	State Education Advisory Panel • Appointed by governor • Members include: • consumers • parents • teachers • special education administrators • state and local officials	Interagency Coordinating Council • Appointed by governor • Members include: • 15–25 members • 3 parents (B–6)* • 3 providers • one legislator • one personnel trainer • agency representatives *(B = birth)	**Part H** • At least 15 members but no more than 25 • Members include: • 20% parents (1 = B–6; others = B–12) • 20% providers • one legislator • one personnel trainer • one state education agency representative • one state insurance representative • chair may be appointed by the governor or by group, no lead agency representative may serve as chair • May have B–5 focus • Shall advise on transition • Establishes a Federal Interagency Coordinating Council B–5
Participation of Other Agencies	Must meet state standards and be under general supervision of State Education agency	Must meet state standards and be under general supervision of lead agency (if receiving Part H funds)	**Part H** agency must monitor programs used to carry out Part H whether or not receiving Part H funds

Issue	Preschool (Part B)	Infant/Toddler (Part H)	Recent Changes: P.L. 102-119
Implementation Timeline "Mandate"	All eligible children must be receiving services in FY1991 or sanctions are applied.	All eligible children must be receiving service no later than beginning of state's fifth year of participation in the program if the state continues to participate.	**Part H** provides for differential funding that authorizes a maxmum of 2 one-year extensions for states that are unable to meet their fifth-year requirements within 5 years of participation. Funding is at a reduced level for states receiving an extension.
Basis for Allocation of Dollars to State	Preschool children generate funding from both the Part B State Grant Program as well as the Part B—Section 619 (Preschool) Program. Each state receives funds in proportion to the number of children 3–5 years old served on December 1 of the previous year; no state shall receive less than $350,000.	Each state receives funds in proportion to its general population that is B–2 years old, except not less than 5% of the total federal appropriation.	**Part B:** No state shall receive less than $450,000 for administration of preschool grants authorized up to $1500 per child. **Part H:** No state shall receive less than $500,000.
State Use of Funds	At least 75% of funds must flow to local education agencies on a prorated basis; up to 20% of funds may be used at state's discretion; up to 5% of funds may be used for administrative purposes; shall not supplant use for "excess cost."	To plan, develop, and implement statewide system of services; funds cannot be used for services that are provided or paid for through other sources; Part H funds are payor of last resort and are to be distributed equitably across geographic areas; shall not supplant current funding sources.	Allows for flexible use of both **Part B** and **Part H** funds during the year the child turns 3 years of age; allows for the use of both **Part B** and **Part H** funds for the planning of a B–5 seamless system of services.
Cost to Parents	All special education and related services must be at no cost to parents.	State must establish fee scale if state law permits; however, families may not be denied services because of inability to pay; certain services must be provided at no cost: childfind, evaluation and assessment, service coordination, development and review of IFSP, procedural safeguards; if a state provides FAPE from birth, all services are at no charge.	

Source: Adapted from Smith, B. J., Rose, D. F., Ballard, J. B., and Walsh, S. (1992). The Preschool (Part B) and Infant Toddler (Part H) programs of the Individuals with Disabilities Education Act (IDEA) and the 1991 Amendments (P.L. 102-119): Selected comparisons. Washington, DC: USDOE.

APPENDIX C

National Resources

ADOPTIVE PARENTS

Adoptive Families of America
3333 Hwy 100 N
Minneapolis, MN 55422
(800) 372-3300

National Adoption Center
1500 Walnut St, Ste 701
Philadelphia, PA 19102
(800) 862-3678

National Adoption Information Clearinghouse
11426 Rockville Pike, Ste 410
Rockville, MD 20852
(301) 231-6512

ALCOHOL AND DRUG ABUSE

Family Empowerment Network: Support for Families Affected by FAS/FAE
610 Langdon St, Rm 521
Madison, WI 53703
(800) 462-5254
(608) 262-6590
(608) 265-2329 (fax)

Fetal Alcohol Education Program
7 Kent St
Brookline, MA 02164
(617) 739-1424
(617) 566-4019

Fetal Alcohol Network
158 Rosemont Ave
Coatesville, PA 19320-3727
Email-72157.564@compuserve.com

National Association for Perinatal Addiction Research and Education (NAPARE)
200 N Michigan
Chicago, IL 60601
(312) 541-1272
(312) 541-1271 (fax)

National Organization on Fetal Alcohol Syndrome
1815 H St NW, Ste 710
Washington, DC 20006
(202) 785-4585
(202) 466-6456 (fax)

The Fetal Alcohol Syndrome Family Resource Institute
PO Box 2525
Lynnwood, WA 98036
(206) 778-4048

ANGELMAN SYNDROME

Angelman Syndrome Foundation
PO Box 12437
Gainesville, FL 32604
(904) 332-3303

APLASTIC ANEMIA

Aplastic Anemia Foundation of America
PO Box 22689
Baltimore, MD 21203
(800) 747-2820

AUTISM

Autism Research Institute
4182 Adams Ave
San Diego, CA 92116
(619) 281-7165

Autism Society of America
7910 Woodmont Ave, Ste 650
Bethesda, MD 20814
(800) 328-8476
(301) 657-0881
(301) 657-0869 (fax)

Autism Society of Canada
129 Yorkville Ave, #202
Toronto, ON CAN M5R 1C4
(416) 922-0302

Center for Study of Autism
9725 SW Beaverton-Hillsdale Hwy, Ste 230
Beaverton, OR 97005
(503) 643-4121

National Autism Hotline/Autism Services Center
605 Ninth St
Prichard Bldg PO Box 507
Huntington, WV 25710-0507
(304) 525-8014
(304) 525-8026 (fax)

AUTISM AND SENSORY IMPAIRMENTS

Autism and Sensory Impairments Network
c/o Dolores and Alan Bartel
7510 Oceanfront Ave
Virginia Beach, VA 23451
(804) 428-9036

BEREAVEMENT SUPPORT

Compassionate Friends
PO Box 3696
Oak Brook, IL 60522-3696
(708) 990-0010
(708) 990-0246 (fax)

BLINDNESS

American Printing House for the Blind, Inc.
1839 Frankfort Ave
PO Box 6085
Louisville, KY 40206

DVH Newsletter
Division for the Visually Impaired
1920 Association Dr
Reston, VA 22091

Education of the Visually Handicapped
The Alliance
206 N Washington St
Alexandria, VA 22314

Journal of Visual Impairment and Blindness
15 W 16th St
New York, NY 10011

Library Reproduction Service
The Microfilm Co. of CA, Inc.
1977 S Los Angeles St
Los Angeles, CA 90011

New York Lighthouse Low Vision Service
111 E 59th St
New York, NY 10022

National Association for the Visually Handicapped
305 E 24th St
New York, NY 10010

Recording for the Blind, Inc.
20 Rosel Rd
Princeton, NJ 08540

CHROMOSOME 18 AND 13 DISORDERS

Chromosome 18 Registry & Research Society
6302 Fox Head
San Antonio, TX 78247
(210) 657-4968 (voice/fax)

SOFT—Canada: Support Organization for Trisomy 18, 13 and Related Disorders
760 Brant St, Ste 420
Burlington, ON CAN L7R 4B8
(800) 668-0898 (Canada Only)
(905) 632-7755
(905) 632-5997 (fax)

SOFT: Support Organization for Trisomy 18, 13 and Related Disorders
c/o Barb Van Herreweghe
2982 S Union St
Rochester, NY 14624
(716) 594-4621 (voice/fax)

CHROMOSOME DELETIONS

Chromosome Deletion Outreach
Box 280
Driggs, ID 83422
(208) 354-8550

CHROMOSOME INVERSIONS

National Center on Chromosome Inversions
1029 Johnson St
Des Moines, IA 50315
(515) 287-6798 (voice/fax)

CORNELIA DE LANGE SYNDROME

Cornelia de Lange Syndrome Foundation
60 Dyer Ave
Collinsville, CT 06022-1273
(800) 223-8355
(800) 753-2357
(203) 693-0159
(203) 693-6819 (fax)

CRI DU CHAT SYNDROME

5p-Society
11609 Oakmont
Overland Park, KS 66210
(913) 469-8900

CYSTIC FIBROSIS

Canadian Cystic Fibrosis Foundation
2221 Yonge St, Ste 601
Toronto, ON CAN M4S 2B4
(800) 378-2233 (Canada Only)
(416) 485-9149
(416) 485-0960 (fax)

Cystic Fibrosis Foundation
6931 Arlington Rd
Bethesda, MD 20814
(800) 344-4823
(301) 951-4422
(301) 951-6378 (fax)

DEAFNESS

Alexander Graham Bell Association for the Deaf
3417 Volta Place NW
Washington, DC 20007-2778

American Guidance Service
Publishers Bldg
Circle Pines, MN 55014

American Speech-Language-Hearing Association
10801 Rockville Pike
Rockville, MD 20852

Central Institute for the Deaf
818 S Euclid
St. Louis, MO 63132

Council on Education of the Deaf
Gallaudet University
800 Florida Ave NE
Washington, DC 20002

Haren Early Language Resource Center
252 Blon St W, Rm 4-126
Toronto, ON CAN M5S IV6

Infant Hearing Resource
3930 SW Macadam Ave
Portland, OR 97201

Language Centered Curriculum
Texas Education Agency
PO Box 3538
Austin, TX 78764

National Association of the Deaf
814 Thayer Ave
Silver Spring, MD 20910

SKI-HI Institute
Department of Communicative Disorders
Utah State University
Logan, UT 84321

Sign Media, Inc.
4020 Blackburn Ln
Burtonsville, MD 20866

Teaching Resources
100 Boylston St
Boston, MA 02116

DISABLING CONDITIONS

Association for Persons with Severe Handicaps
11210 Greenwood Ave N
Seattle, WA 98133
(206) 361-8870
(206) 361-0113
(206) 361-9208 (fax)

March of Dimes Birth Defect Foundation
1275 Mamaroneck Ave
White Plains, NY 10605
(914) 428-7100
(914) 428-8203 (fax)

National Association of Developmental Disabilities Council
1234 Massachusetts Ave NW, Ste 103
Washington, DC 20005
(202) 347-1234
(202) 347-4023 (fax)

National Early Childhood Technical Assistance System (NEC*TAS)
NEC*TAS Coordinating Office
CB# 8040, Ste 500 NCNB Plaza
University of North Carolina
Chapel Hill, NC 27599-8040
(919) 962-2001
(919) 966-7463 (fax)

National Father's Network (NFN)
The Kindering Center
16120 NE Eighth St
Bellevue, WA 98008
(206) 747-4004
(206) 747-1069 (fax)

National Information Center for Children and Youth with Disabilities (NICHCY)
PO Box 1492
Washington, DC 20013
(800) 695-0285
(202) 884-8441 (fax)

NPND: National Parent Network on Disabilities
1600 Prince St, Ste 115
Alexandria, VA 22314
(703) 684-6763 (voice/TTY)
(703) 836-1232 (fax)

DOWN SYNDROME

Association for Children with Down Syndrome
2616 Martin Ave
Bellmore, NY 11710
(516) 221-4700
(516) 221-4311 (fax)

Canadian Down Syndrome Society
12837 76th Ave, Ste 206
Surrey, BC CAN V3W 2V3
(604) 599-6009
(604) 599-6165 (fax)

International Foundation for Genetic Research
400 Penn Center Blvd, Ste 721
Pittsburgh, PA 15235
(412) 823-6380
(412) 829-7304 (fax)

National Down Syndrome Congress
1605 Chantilly Dr, Ste 250
Atlanta, GA 30324
(800) 232-6372
(404) 633-1555
(404) 633-2917 (fax)

National Down Syndrome Society
666 Broadway, 8th Flr
New York, NY 10012-2317
(800) 221-4602
(212) 460-9330
(212) 979-2873 (fax)

FRAGILE X SYNDROME

FraXa Research Foundation
PO Box 935
West Newbury, MA 01985
(508) 462-1990
Email-fraxa@destek.net

National Fragile X Foundation
1441 York St, Ste 215
Denver, CO 80206
(800) 688-8765
(303) 333-6155
(303) 333-4369 (fax)

GOLDENHAR SYNDROME

Goldenhar Syndrome Research & Information Fund
8829 Gleneagles Ln
Darien, IL 60561
(708) 910-3939
(708) 910-4065 (fax)

GRANDPARENTS RAISING GRANDCHILDREN

American Association of Retired Persons (AARP) Grandparent Information Center
601 E St NW
Washington, DC 20049
(202) 434-2296

Grandparents Reaching Out
c/o Mildred Horn
141 Glensummer Rd
Holbrook, NY 11741
(516) 472-9728

Rocking (Raising Our Children's Kids: An Inter-generational Network of Grandparenting)
c/o Mary Fron
PO Box 96
Niles, MI 49120
(616) 683-9038

HEMOPHILIA

National Hemophilia Foundation
110 Greene St, Rm 303
New York, NY 10012
(212) 219-8180
(212) 966-9247 (fax)

INTERRACIAL FAMILIES

A Place for Us
PO Box 4082
Huntington Beach, CA 92605
(213) 779-1717

Biracial Child Magazine
PO Box 12048
Atlanta, GA 30355
(404) 364-9690

LANGUAGE DISORDERS

TALK: Taking Action Against Language Disorders for Kids
22980 Donna Ln
Bend, OR 97701
(503) 389-0004

LESBIAN AND GAY PARENTS

Gay & Lesbian Parents Coalition International (GLPCI)/Children of Lesbians and Gays Everywhere (COLAGE)
PO Box 50360
Washington, DC 20091
(202) 583-8029

National Center for Lesbian Rights
870 Market St, Ste 570
San Francisco, CA 94102
(415) 392-6257

MENTAL RETARDATION

The Arc
500 E Border St, Ste 300
PO Box 1047
Arlington, TX 76010
(800) 433-5255
(817) 261-6003
(817) 277-0553 (TTY)
(817) 277-3491 (fax)
Email-thearc@metro.com

Voice of the Retarded
5005 Newport Dr, Ste 108
Rolling Meadows, IL 60008
(708) 253-6020

MUSCULAR DYSTROPHY

Muscular Dystrophy Association
3300 E Sunrise Dr
Tucson, AZ 85718-3208
(800) 572-1717
(602) 529-2000
(602) 529-5300 (fax)
Email-74431.2513@compuserve.com

Muscular Dystrophy Association of Canada
150 Eglington Ave E, Ste 400
Toronto, ON CAN M4P 1E8
(800) 567-2873 (Canada Only)
(416) 488-0030
(416) 488-7523

MYOTUBULAR MYOPATHY

X-Linked Myotubular Myopathy Resource Group
2413 Quaker Dr
Texas City, TX 77590
(409) 945-8569

NEUROMETABOLIC DISORDERS

Association for Neurometabolic Disorders
5223 Brookfield Ln
Sylvania, OH 43560-1809
(419) 885-1497

Canadian Society for Metabolic Disease
5301 Ranger Ave
N Vancouver, BC CAN V7R 3M7
(604) 986-2508
(604) 293-7126 (fax)

OBSESSIVE-COMPULSIVE DISORDERS

OC Foundation
PO Box 70
Milford, CT 06460
(203) 878-5669

OPITZ SYNDROME

Opitz Family Network
PO Box 516
Grand Lake, CO 80447
(303) 627-8935

PRADER-WILLI SYNDROME

Prader-Willi Foundation
223 Main St
Port Washington, NY 11050
(800) 253-7993
(516) 944-3173 (fax)

Prader-Willi Syndrome Association
2510 S Brentwood Blvd, Ste 220
St. Louis, MO 63144
(800) 926-4797

Prader-Willi Syndrome International Information Forum
40 Holly Ln
Roslyn Hts, NY 11577
(800) 358-0682
(516) 484-7154 (fax)
Email-visink@delphi.com

RETT SYNDROME

Canadian Rett Syndrome Association
555 Fairway Rd
Kitchener, ON CAN N2C 1X4
(416) 494-1954
(519) 893-1169

International Rett Syndrome Association
9121 Piscataway Rd, Ste 2B
Clinton, MD 20735
(800) 818-7388
(301) 856-3334
(301) 856-3336 (fax)
Email-irsa@paltech.com

SICKLE CELL DISEASE

Sickle Cell Disease Association of America
200 Corporate Pointe, Ste 495
Culver City, CA 90203-7633
(800) 421-8453
(310) 216-6363
(310) 215-3722 (fax)

Triad Sickle Cell Anemia Foundation
1102 E Market St
Greensboro, NC 27420-0964
(800) 733-8297
(910) 274-1507
(910) 275-7984 (fax)

SINGLE PARENTS

National Congress for Men and Children (NCMC)
PO Box 171675
Kansas City, KS 66117
(800) 733-3237

National Fatherhood Initiative
680 Eden Rd, Bldg E
Lancaster, PA 17601
(800) 790-3237

National Organization of Single Mothers
PO box 68
Midland, NC 28107
(704) 888-5437

Parents Without Partners (PWP)
401 N Michign Ave
Chicago, IL 60611
(312) 644-6610

Single Parents Resource Center
141 W 28th St
New York, NY 10001
(212) 947-0221

STEPPARENTS

Stepfamily Association of America
215 Centennial Mall S, Ste 212
Lincoln, NE 68508
(800) 735-0329

The Stepfamily Foundation
333 West End Ave
New York, NY 10023
(212) 877-3244

TEEN PARENTS

National Organization on Adolescent Pregnancy, Parenting, and Prevention
4421-A East West Hwy
Bethesda, MD 20814
(301) 913-0378

TERMINAL ILLNESS

Children's Hospice International
700 Princess St, Lower Level
Alexandria, VA 22314
(800) 242-4453
(703) 684-0330
(703) 684-0226 (fax)

TOURETTE SYNDROME

Tourette Syndrome Association
42-40 Bell Blvd
Bayside, NY 11361-2861
(800) 237-0717
(718) 224-2999
(718) 279-9596 (fax)

Tourette Syndrome Foundation of Canada
238 Davenport Rd, Box 343
Toronto, ON CAN M5R 1J6
(800) 361-3120 (Canada Only)
(416) 351-7757
(416) 351-9267 (fax)

TURNER SYNDROME

Turner's Syndrome Society—Canada
7777 Keele St, Flr 2
Concord, ON CAN L4K 1Y7
(800) 465-6744
(905) 660-7766
(905) 660-7450 (fax)

Turner's Syndrome Society of the US
15500 Wayzata Blvd, #768-214
811 12 Oak Ctr
Wayzata, MN 55391
(612) 475-9944
(612) 475-9949 (fax)
Email-LGTesch@cerfnet.com

VENTILATOR USE

Citizens for Independence in Living & Breathing
78 Golfwood Hts
Etobiocolce, ON CAN M9P 3M2
(416) 244-2248 (voice/fax)

International Ventilator Users Networks
5100 Oakland Ave, #206
St. Louis, MO 63110
(314) 534-0475
(314) 534-5070 (fax)

WILLIAMS SYNDROME

CAWS: Canadian Association for Williams Syndrome
c/o Cathy Wilson
PO Box 2115
Vancouver, BC CAN V6B 3T5
(403) 887-5257

Williams Syndrome Association
PO Box 297
Clawson, MI 48017-0297
(810) 541-3630
(810) 541-3631 (fax)

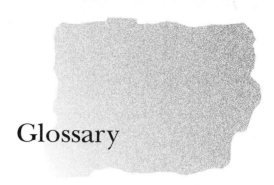

Glossary

abduction: limbs move outward, away from the body

abruptio placenta: separation of placenta from the walls of the uterus prior to delivery

absence seizure: momentary interruption of ongoing activity with a brief, blank stare

accommodation (mental): changing an existing mental schema (pattern) to fit new information

accommodation (visual): the process by which the eye adjusts to focus on near objects

action/reaction service model: professionals work together only in the sense that they prescribe or teach another member of the chain that is linked by a common client

active listening: attentiveness to a speaker on multiple levels: hearing, interpreting, sorting, and analyzing

acute stressors: events that place strain on a family and occur as periodic incidents related to a child's disability

adaptable intervention model: flexible procedures employed within noncategorical models, emphasizing the functionality of behavior rather than its developmental form or sequence

adaptive reflexes: *See* postural reflexes.

adaptive skills: problem solving, responding appropriately to environmental demands

adduction: limbs move in toward the body

adolescent stage: time starting at about 10 to 16 years of age, depending on physical maturity, and extending to adulthood

adventitious blindness: blindness aquired after birth

advocacy: favoring and supporting the needs or cause of another

albinism: a congenital condition characterized by a lack of the pigment that gives color to skin, hair, and eyes

albumin: the most abundant protein in the body

alleles: one of two alternative versions of a gene with complementary alleles residing on each of the two chromosomes in a pair

amblyopia: dimness of vision not due to organic defect or refractive errors

amniocentesis: a procedure in which fluid is removed from the sac surrounding the fetus to determine if the fetus carries a genetic anomaly

amniotic sac: the membrane that surrounds the fetus and contains fluid that protects the fetus from physical shocks and maintains a constant temperature

anabolism: the conversion of ingested food into products that can be used by the cells

anemia: a condition in which the amount of oxygen-carrying hemoglobin is below normal in the blood

anencephaly: a congenital malformation in which the brain does not develop and the skull, which would normally cover the brain, is absent

annual goals: targets for improvement that should be reached within one year's time

anomaly: a deviation in physical development

antibodies: a protein produced by the body in response to the presence of an antigen (chemical substance that causes the body to produce specific antibodies) and is capable of combining specifically with the antigen

antiviral: a group of drugs used to treat infection by a virus

aphasia: defect in or loss of the power of expression by speech, writing, or signs, or of comprehension of spoken or written language, due to disease or injury of the brain centers

apnea of prematurity: breathing pauses due to immature central nervous system

arachnoid: the delicate membrane interposed between the dura mater and the pia mater and, with them, constituting the meninges

arteriogram: a procedure in which a dye is injected into the bloodstream and is detected by X ray to produce an image of blood flow

asphyxia: loss of consciousness from interruption of breathing as in suffocation or drowning

associative play: individual children play with other children engaging in similar or even identical activities

astigmatism: a visual defect caused by unequal curvatures of the refractile surfaces (cornea, lens) of the eye, resulting in light rays from a point not coming to focus at a point on the retina

asymmetrical tonic neck reflex (ATNR): a primitive reflex in which the limbs are extended on the side of the body toward which the head is turned but flexed on the opposite side; also called "fencer's reflex"

asymptomatic: showing no symptoms

at-risk: used to refer to that class of infants who have been exposed to any one of a number of medical or environmental factors that may contribute to later developmental delay

ataxia: cerebral damage that causes difficulty with coordination and balance

athetosis: variable muscle tone caused by noncortical cerebral damage, producing slow, writhing, and excessive movement

atrophy: a condition in which muscles that are not used shrink in size; a condition in which the brain stops growing and shrinks, with the resulting space in the skull filling with fluid-filled cysts

attachment: emotional bonding to another person

attention deficit hyperactivity disorder (ADHD): a combination of characteristics including inattention, impulsivity, and hyperactivity

attitude of science: the use of parsimony and empirical research to determine what is true

auditory nerve: vehicle of transmission of electrical energy from the ear to the temporal area of the brain

augmentative communication: using appliances or systems to enhance a child's natural communication skills

autosome: any of the chromosomes other than the sex (X and Y) chromosomes in humans of which there are 22 pairs

axon: the nerve-cell process that carries impulses away from the nerve-cell body; any long nerve-cell process

babble: a combination of consonant and vowel sounds uttered by infants at about four months of age as they gain oral-motor control

Babinski reflex: a reflex in which stimulation applied to the sole of an infant's foot results in the infant spreading his or her toes

bacteria: a large group of typically one-celled, microscopic organisms widely distributed in air, water, soil, and the bodies of living plants and animals

behavioral assessment: examination of factors that govern children's behavior under given conditions

best practice: instructional and collaborative procedures based on current research and knowledge

binding statements: habits of interaction that generally close or diminish the probability of continued conversation

biologic agents: microorganisms that cause damage to human cells by either living on cells or by causing inflammation of the cells and that travel throughout the body via the bloodstream or lymphatic system

biological risks: medical conditions that threaten to compromise a child's health, particularly perinatally, and are predictive of later delays

blended families: families including stepchildren and stepparents

bonding: attachment between infant and caregiver

bound morphemes: morphemes that cannot stand alone in meaning (-ed, -ing, etc.)

breath-holding spells: involuntary holding of breath

bronchopulmonary dysplasia: chronic lung disease resulting from respiratory distress syndrome

cardiovascular system: organ system including heart, veins, and arteries

carrier: individual who possesses a gene for a trait but does not express the characteristics

catabolism: in a living organism, the breakdown of substances into simpler structures that can be excreted or converted into energy

cataract: clouding or opacity of the lens of the eye

center-based programs: programs in which children are served in a central location

central nervous system (CNS): the brain and spinal cord

cephalo-caudal: the sequence of growth and development of motor skills that is progressively downward from head, to neck, to trunk, to hips, to legs, to feet, to toes

cerebral palsy: a nonprogressive neuromuscular condition affecting muscle tone, movement, reflexes, and posture

cerebrospinal fluid: a clear, colorless, odorless fluid that resembles water, is produced from blood through secretion and diffusion between the vascular system and the choroid plexuses in the brain, and protects the nervous system from injury by acting as a shock absorber

chancre: a lesion at the site of contact with an infected person

child abuse: the willful behavior by parents or guardians that harms a child in their care

child-directed instruction: flexible instruction that follows a child's lead in terms of interests and motivation

childfind: federally mandated process of identifying children from birth to age six who have devel-opmental delays or are at-risk for develop-mental delays

child neglect: failure to provide a child's basic needs of either a physical, educational, or emotional nature

chlamydia trachomatis: a microorganism that causes various genital, eye, and lymph node infections

chorionic villus sampling: testing a small tissue sample from the chorion, or outer sac that surrounds the fetus, to determine if the fetus carries a genetic anomaly

chorioretinitis: inflammation of the retina and choroid

chromosome disorders: disorders caused by whole chromosomes or chromosome segments rather than a single gene or combination of genes

chromosomes: the basic genetic units that stay constant within a species and across generations (For example, normal human cells contain a complement of 46 chromosomes or 23 pairs.)

chronic: long-term or frequently occurring; applied to a disease that is not acute

chronic stressors: constant pressure or strain on a family caused by concerns related to a child's disability

cirrhosis: interstitial inflammation of an organ, particularly the liver

cleft lip: a split in facial tissue that affects the lip and gum and may extend upward into the nose and may occur with a cleft palate

cleft palate: a split in facial tissue that affects the hard or soft palate (roof of mouth) and may occur with a cleft lip

clonic seizure: alternate contraction and relaxation of muscles

cochlea: the portion of the inner ear associated with the reception of sound waves, which lies in a cavity in the temporal bone and is shaped like a snail shell

code of association: in group work, establishes who is doing what and when

cognition: thinking, mental processes

cognitive-developmental approach: a theory about how children learn that recognizes a natural, fixed sequence in which thinking processes emerge

cognitive indifference: failure to interact or show recognition; e. g., gaze avoidance, blank expression

collaboration: an interactive process that enables teams of people with diverse expertise to generate creative solutions to mutually defined problems

collaborative consultation: when teachers and other professionals work together on an equal footing to solve students' problems

collaborative teaming: members agree to work together collectively to achieve common goals

communication: the ability of two or more people to send and receive messages; the most necessary skill of both parents and childhood educators

complex sentence: a sentence that contains at least one independent clause and at least one subordinate or dependent clause

compound sentence: a sentence that contains more than one independent clause and combines two or more ideas in a single sentence by using conjunctions, relative pronouns, or other linguistic linkages

comprehensive intervention model: a full array of professional services offered through a transdisciplinary approach

Computerized Axial Tomography (CAT or CT): a procedure that uses X rays to view several plains of the body at one time to produce a three-dimensional image of body tissue

conceptual system: a set of principles that articulate a body of knowledge

concrete operations: the stage of cognitive development (at age 7–11 years) when children can use real objects to logically solve problems

conductive hearing loss: disruption of mechanical conduction of sound as it is transferred from the outer ear through the middle ear

congenital: present at birth

congenital heart defect: an abnormality of the heart present at birth

conjunctivitis: an inflammation of the conjunctiva, the membrane that lines the insides of the eyelids and covers the cornea, which can be caused by a number of irritants such as dust, smoke, wind, pollutants in the air, and excessive glare

consensus building: guiding groups in decision making based on group agreement

consensus decision making: a process in which all members of a group must agree to a decision before action is taken, and if any one member disagrees with a decision, it is aborted

consequate: to follow, contingent upon a specific behavior

consolidation: when disorganized behavior is replaced by more advanced developmental skills

contractures: a condition in which muscles and tendons shorten, causing rigidity and joint immobility

conversational postulates: subtle conversational rules that allow humans to converse in a reciprocal manner (i.e., initiating, turn taking, questioning, repairing a breakdown in conversation, maintaining interactions, and closing a conversation)

cooing: vowel sound production that requires little motor control or use of the articulators (tongue, lips, palate, and teeth), which usually occurs in infants during the perlocutionary stage

cooperative interactions: opening oneself to the will of the group and abandoning individualistic orientation to the work

cooperative play: children engage in organized play activities

coordination of secondary schemata: a level of learning characterized by ability to understand and manipulate the environment

coprolalia: involuntary use of vulgar or obscene gestures or language

cornea: the transparent epithelium (tissue covering internal and external surfaces) and connective tissue membrane that covers the anterior portion of the eye, which refracts light rays and channels that light through the fluid-filled anterior chamber

corrected gestational age: age adjusted to reflect premature delivery

cortical blindness: blindness that results when brain function interferes with processing of visual images

cortical visual impairments: a condition in which eye physiology is not impaired, yet there is a loss of visual ability caused by damage to the optic nerve or the cerebral tissue within the occipital portion of the brain

crawl: coordination of arms and legs to move across a surface on the abdomen

cretinism: condition characterized by mental retardation, stunted growth, and coarse facial features caused by a disorder of the thyroid

cruising: a child's movement by stepping sideways while holding on to furniture or some structure for support

cultural competence: a program's ability to honor and respect those beliefs, interpersonal styles, attitudes, and behaviors both of families who are clients and the multicultural staff who are providing services

culturally sensitive: awareness of different values and practices of divergent ethnic and cultural groups

cyanosis: a blue-tinged color to the skin, which can occur when blood bypasses the lungs, resulting in decreased oxygen being available to cells

cytomegalic inclusion viral infection (CMV): one of the family of herpes viruses that is common and produces no symptoms in adults but can cause malformations and brain damage to an unborn child

demographics: statistical characteristics of human populations

dentition: the development of teeth

description of feelings: an account of feelings that can come only from the person holding the feelings

development: occurs when the complexity of a child's behavior increases

developmental delay: delayed progress experienced by infants and toddlers in one or more developmental areas: communication, physical development, adaptive behavior (feeding, dressing, toileting, etc.), cognition, and social/emotional development

developmental instruction: instruction that matches a child's abilities and interests according to age, skills, and cognitive level

developmental milestones: major indexes of development identified across developmental areas and across years and used to measure developmental progress

diabetes: any disorder characterized by excessive urine excretion, usually caused when the pancreas produces insufficient insulin

diplegia: cerebral palsy affecting all four extremities of the body, with greater involvement of the legs than of the trunk and arms

direct instruction: an educational model in which instruction occurs in small groups, using a fast pace for unison responding and a careful sequencing of new skills, consistent review, and positive consequences

direct service delivery: a procedure in which services are delivered directly to a client rather than consulting with or training another person to deliver the prescribed services

dominant gene: a gene that possesses sufficient genetic information for a characteristic to be expressed when only one allele carries the gene

duodenal atresia: a narrowing of the intestine

dyskinesia: a condition caused by noncortical cerebral damage (*See* athetosis.)

early childhood stage: time from three years to six years of age

early intervention: period from birth to age three when services can be delivered under Part H of IDEA to infants and toddlers with developmental delays or at-risk conditions

ecological approach to assessment: evaluations focus on children, their environment, and the interaction between the two

ecologically-based approach to family services: an approach in which services arise out of the perspective of viewing the family from its center (the child) out through the family system and then the community

electroencephalography: a procedure that measures electrical potentials on the scalp to produce an analysis of brain activity

embedding: a process in which children add clauses internally to sentences (develops at 4 to 13 years of age)

embryonic stage: begins in the third week of pregnancy when cell differentiation permits the emergence of the central nervous system and circulatory system and is completed by the eighth week of gestation

emotional maltreatment: acts or omissions by the parents or caregivers that have caused or could cause serious behavioral, cognitive, emotional, or mental disorders

empirical: relying on observation and experimentation

empowerment: encouraging individual reliance on self and providing understandable and practical information that can be used by families

encephalitis: inflammation of the brain

endoscopy: a procedure in which a viewing tube is inserted into the body

environmental risks: environmental conditions, such as poverty or abuse, that place infants and toddlers at-risk for developmental delays

enzymes: complex organic catalysts that induce chemical change in other substances without being changed in the process

epilepsy: a condition of recurrent seizures

equilibrium reflex: the reflex that involuntarily causes the body to realign its trunk to a vertical posture after the body moves or is moved out of midline

errors in binocular vision: a disruption in the coordination of six sets of muscles that permit the eyes to act in concert to follow a moving object and focus images correspondingly on both retinas

established risks: diagnosed conditions that give infants and toddlers high probability of later delays in development

ethical standards: accepted professional guidelines for conduct

ethnographic: research involving observation of a social setting over an extended period

eustachian tube: a continuous passage from the middle ear to the throat that acts as a safety tube, equalizing internal and external air pressure on the tympanic membrane

excited: activated to perform a function

exocrine glands: glands that secrete substances onto an inner surface of an organ or outside the body, such as salivary or sweat glands

exosystem: societal structures, such as local and state agencies or advocacy groups, that affect a child's life

expressive affect: behaviors related to interacting or associating with others, for example, smiling

expressive language: coded output message emitted by a child or adult

extension: the straightening of a joint that changes the angle between bones that meet in the joint; the opposite of flexion

external ear: the part of the ear responsible for collecting sound waves, consisting of the auricle, auditory canal, and tympanic membrane

extrapyramidal: outside the pyramidal nerve group; used to refer to noncortical cerebral damage

extremely low birth weight: less than 750 g (1 lb 10 oz)

failure to thrive: delay in physical and neurological growth in infancy and early childhood due to organic or environmental causes

family hardiness: a constellation of three dimensions: (1) control: the ability to influence events, (2) commitment: active involvement in events, and (3) challenge: viewing changes as opportunities for growth and development

family life-cycle theory: posits that families have a fairly predictable life cycle governing their growth, development, and functioning

family sociology: universally enduring observable dimensions of family life

family systems theory: approaches families as complex organizations in which internal and external variables affect all members

Fetal Alcohol Effects (FAE): moderate birth defects caused by prenatal exposure to alcohol

Fetal Alcohol Syndrome (FAS): serious birth defects caused by prenatal exposure to alcohol

fetal blood sampling: a blood sample withdrawn from the umbilical cord to determine if the fetus carries a genetic anomaly

fetal stage: the stage of pregnancy from the ninth week through the ninth month

fine pincer grasp: grasp using the tips of the thumb and index finger in opposition

flexion: the bending of a joint; the opposite of extension

formal operations: the stage of cognitive development (at age 11 years and older) when humans develop abstract thinking; can classify and sort

freeing statements: habits of interaction that actually encourage expanded dialogue

free morphemes: morphemes that can stand alone in meaning (bottle, cup, etc.)

full inclusion: to accept an individual with a disability as a full-time member of a regular social group and as a contributing participant

functional skills: of immediate or future usefulness in the environment, such as self-feeding or mobility

functionality: degree to which skills are needed to operate as independently as possible in daily activities

galactosemia: a genetic disorder in which a person cannot break down galactose into usable glucose

gametes: the cells involved in reproduction (A sperm is a male gamete, and an ovum is a female gamete. These germ cells have one half the number of chromosomes, one from each chromosome pair. When a sperm and ovum join during conception, the resultant cell has a full set of chromosomes, one of each chromosome pair from each parent.)

gastrointestinal system: the part of the digestive system that consists of the mouth, esophagus, stomach, and intestine

generality: general rather than specific skills that can be adapted to meet individual needs and used in many situations

generalization: transfer of skills to other settings, other caregivers, and other appropriate situations

genes: regions of a chromosome made up of molecules that collectively define a particular trait

genetic mapping: a process of learning the genetic code of humans by charting the relationships between specific genes and individual chromosomes

genitourinary system: the reproductive organs and the urinary tract

genotype: the combination of alleles inherited for a particular trait within an individual (The genotype can only be determined through cellular testing since the trait determined by the genotype may or may not be expressed.)

gestation: the period of intrauterine fetal development

gestational diabetes: acquisition of diabetes during pregnancy

glaucoma: a condition characterized by a buildup of pressure in the anterior chamber of the eye

goal interdependence: establishment of a common goal or set of goals, including delineation of strategies that should lead to fruition, after careful consideration and active participation by each team member

grasp reflex: flexion of the hand in response to stimulation of the palm

gravida: the medical term for a pregnant woman; often used with a number to indicate the number of pregnancies a woman has had (a 3-gravida)

group B streptococcus: a group of bacteria from the streptococcus family

group processing: reflection by a group to determine what actions should be continued and what group behaviors should be changed in order to make collaborative efforts more effective

habituate: to selectively ignore irrelevant stimuli (capacity to screen interfering stimuli)

handling: therapeutic preparation for movement and positioning

head righting: an attempt to hold the head in an upright position that occurs when an infant's trunk is pushed out of an upright position

hemiplegia: cerebral palsy affecting one side of the body

hemoglobin: component of red blood cells that enables them to transport oxygen and carbon dioxide

herpes: infection with the herpes simplex virus, causing small, painful blisters on the skin

heterozygote pair: when an individual has two different alleles for a particular trait (For example, a child who receives a normal gene from one parent and a gene for cystic fibrosis from the other parent will not express the disease from this heterozygote pair since the gene for cystic fibrosis is not dominant.)

home-based programs: programs in which children are served in their homes with instruction given primarily to the parents or caregivers

homozygote pair: when an individual has identical alleles for a certain trait (For example, when the gene for cystic fibrosis is inherited from both mother and father , the alleles form a homozygote pair and the child will express the disease.)

hydrocephalus: a condition in which there is an excessive accumulation of cerebrospinal fluid in the ventricles of the brain, causing the head to increase in size beyond two standard deviations above the mean on the standard growth chart

hydrops: extreme swelling in all tissue spaces resulting in destruction of the normal development and functioning of organs

hypercalcemia: excessively high levels of calcium

hyperextension: the movement of extension beyond that needed to straighten a limb

hyperopia: farsightedness; a condition in which parallel light rays come to focus beyond the retina because the refractile system is too weak or the eyeball is flattened

hypertonia: high muscle tone that limits joint movement

hypoglycemia: a condition in which there is a decreased amount of glucose available for use by cells

hypothermia: low body core temperature

hypothyroidism: a condition in which there is an inadequate production of thyroid hormone

hypotonia: low muscle tone that allows excessive joint movement

hypoxia: decreased oxygen flow

illocutionary stage: a stage of language development in which infants communicate intentionally, but are still using mostly nonverbal signals to direct adult attention (develops at 8 to 15 months)

imitation: copy another's behavior

inclusion: to take in as a part of the whole (*See* full inclusion.)

incontinence: inability to retain urine or feces

Individualized Education Program (IEP): an intervention plan developed by a team for a child (age 3–21 years) with a disability; includes a report of current performance, annual goals, instructional objectives, special education and related services, and an evaluation proposal

Individualized Family Service Plan (IFSP): an intervention plan developed by a team for an infant or toddler (birth to age 3) with a disability and for the child's family; includes identification of strengths and needs, a statement of expected outcomes, intervention and support services, and evaluation proposals for the child and the family

Individuals with Disabilities Education Act (IDEA): current federal legislation regarding the education of children with disabilities, the 1990, P. L. 101: 476 amendment of the original Education for all Handicapped Children Act; provides for a free, appropriate education for all children with disabilities ages 3 to 21 and encourages services to infants and toddlers with disabilities or at-risk for developmental delay

infancy period: time from 30 days to 12 months of age

inflammation: redness, swelling, heat, and pain in tissue caused by injury or infection

inhibited: prevented from activating when not needed

inner ear: a fluid filled chamber located in the temporal bone medial to the middle ear, containing the cochlea, the vestibule, and the semicircular canals

instructional objectives: expected outcomes of educational intervention within a short-term time frame; should state the observable behavior, the conditions or situation under which the behavior is expected, and the criterion, or how well the child must perform the behavior

integrated intervention model: typical children and children with disabilities are served in the same settings

integumentary system: organ system including skin, nails, hair, glands, muscles, ligaments, tendons, and fat tissue

Interagency Coordinating Council (ICC): agencies at the federal, state, and local levels that provide administration and service delivery for infants and toddlers with special needs

interdisciplinary approach: the combination of expertise from several disciplines for evaluating, planning, and implementing intervention

interdisciplinary model: a group whose members perform related tasks independently but interact collaboratively to meet goals

intraventricular hemorrhage: bleeding in the brain

invasive: a procedure that penetrates the body (such as surgery)

involvement: degree to which a child is affected motorically; ranges from mild to severe

ischemia: death of cells/tissue due to decreased blood flow and oxygen supply

isolettes: artificial environments used to warm and shelter a premature or ill infant

karyotype: the number and configuration of chromosomes

kin: immediate and extended family

kinship care: child care, housing, and so on, provided by members of the immediate or extended family other than the parents

labor: process by which mother expels the fetus in three stages: (1) dilation of the cervix; (2) passage of fetus through the birth canal; (3) separation and expulsion of the placenta

language: a symbolic communication system comprised of a set of rules for structure and content

language, content of: a child's knowledge of word meanings and the interrelationship between words

language, form of: the structure of language: phonology, syntax, and morphemes

language use: the way in which children communicate in social contexts

late visual bloomers: those children who, like children with motor, language, and social developmental delays, experience maturational delays in visual ability, appearing to be blind at birth and during their first months of life, but usually developing normal visual ability by 18 months to 3 years of age

least restrictive environment: students with disabilities must be educated with their typical peers to the greatest extent possible; the most appropriate setting in which a child with a disability can be with typical peers to the greatest extent possible

lens: transparent convex structure of the eye just behind the pupil, whose curvature can be altered to focus on near or far objects

lipid: an organic compound composed of carbon, hydrogen, and oxygen that is usually insoluble in water, but soluble in alcohol, ether, and chloroform; examples: fats, phospholipids, steroids, and prostaglandins

localization: identification of the orientation of a sound source

locutionary stage: a stage of language development in which infants communicate both conventionally (words and sentences) and intentionally

low birth weight: less than 2800 g (6 lb 3 oz)

low vision: visual acuity at or less than 20/70 in the better eye with correction

macrosystem: the cultural and legislative/judicial contexts that affect a child, for example, IDEA legislation

magnetic resonance imaging (MRI): a procedure that uses magnetic force to draw ions to the edges of an internal organ to produce an image of normal and abnormal tissues

mainstreaming: children who have a disability participate in programs designed for typical children in areas where their disability does not affect their performance

maternal infections: illness in a pregnant woman

maternal obesity: degree of excessive weight in a pregnant woman

maturation: the universally observed sequence of biological changes as one ages; permits the development of psychological functions to evolve

Mean Length Utterance (MLU): an index of the sophistication of a child's language, acquired by measuring the frequency of morphemes in children's utterances

meconinum: the thick, sticky, greenish-black feces passed by infants during the first day or two after birth

meconium aspiration: when the dark sticky mucous in the intestine of a fetus is expelled before birth and inhaled as the infant takes its first breaths

meiosis: cell division that produces sex cells, in which chromosomes divide and produce half the complement of 46 chromosomes in each of the resulting gametes

meninges: the covering that consists of three layers (arachnoid, dura mater, and pia mater) and surrounds the brain and spinal cord

meningitis: a condition in which infection occurs as the result of the entry of bacteria, producing inflammation of the meninges, which is the covering that surrounds the brain and spinal cord

meningocele: a neural tube defect that involves a soft tissue mass that is covered by skin, and does not contain nerves or nerve roots

mesosystem: relationships among microsystems in which a child sometimes spends time, for example, the relationship between teacher and parent

metabolism: a collective term for all the chemical processes that take place in the body

microbes: germs that are so small that they can only be seen through a microscope

microcephaly: very small head and brain; head circumference that falls at least two standard deviations below the mean on a standard growth chart for age

micropremature infant: an infant born at less than 600 g (1 lb 5 oz) or less than 25 weeks gestation

microsystem: the immediate environment in which a child spends the majority of time, for example, the childcare center

middle childhood stage: time from about 6 to 10 years of age

middle ear: a small air-filled chamber medial to the tympanic membrane containing three tiny bones: the malleus (hammer), incus (anvil), and stapes (stirrup)

milestones: behavioral markers or accomplishments of development

mitosis: cell division that produces two identical daughter cells, each containing the full set of 46 chromosomes; occurs in all body cell reproduction in which chromosomes replicate and the cell divides once to create two identical cells, as in the regeneration of skin cells

mitral valve: valve between the left atrium and the left ventricle; permits the left ventricle to contract and pump blood out the aorta without regurgitation of blood back into left atrium

mobility: degree to which individual is able to move around her or his environment independently, with or without adaptive equipment

monoplegia: cerebral palsy affecting one extremity of the body

morbidity: diseased; pertaining to disease

moro reflex: a symmetrical abduction and extension of the arms followed by an adduction when a child's head is suddenly dropped backwards (as if the child were embracing something)

morpheme: the smallest part of a word that possesses meaning

morphological development: evolution of word structure and word parts

morphological inflections: bound morphemes or small word units that change the meaning of words (e.g.,'s, -ed, pre-, etc.)

mortality: the death rate; the ratio of total number of deaths to the total number in the population

mosaicism: a portion of cells have 46 chromosomes and another percentage of the cells have a deletion or an extra chromosome

multidisciplinary team: a group whose members work independently but meet to exchange information and to present goals and progress reports

multifactored diagnostic evaluation: administration of more than one test to determine the presence of a disability; tests should be administered in all areas relevant to a child's perceived needs

myelin: lipid material with protein arranged in layers around many axons to increase efficiency of electrical transmission during neural activity; gives white matter in the brain its color

myelinization: production of myelin around an axon

myelomeningocele: a condition in which both the spinal cord and its covering, the meninges, push through a spinal defect to the surface

myoclonic seizure: brief, shock-like muscle contractions

myopathies: diseases of muscle, usually degenerative

myopia: nearsightedness; a condition in which parallel light rays come to focus in front of the retina because the refractile system is too strong or the eyeball is elongated

myxedema: thickening and coarsening of the skin caused by hypothyroidism

natal: pertaining to birth—before, during, and immediately after

natural routines: activities that normally take place in the daily routine of infants and toddlers and their families

negative sentences: statements using "no," "not," "can't," and so on

neonate: an infant during the first four weeks after birth

neural tube defects: disorders in the development, closure, and formation of the neural groove, the vertebral column (which houses the spinal cord), or other soft tissue structures surrounding the nerves

neurological system: organ system including, brain, spinal cord, and nerves

neuromuscular: relating to the coordination of the central nervous system and the muscular-skeletal systems

neurons: cells responsible for receiving and sending messages

noncontingent helping: providing assistance without effort or request from the recipient

nondisjunction during meiosis: an incomplete detachment of the pairs of cells occurring during cell division to create either an ovum or sperm

nonimmune: not related to the antigen-antibody response

noninvasive: a procedure that does not involve penetrating the body (such as ultrasonography)

nonpathogenic: incapable of causing disease

normal development: a sequence of changes across time that is very similar for all children

normalized intervention model: instruction that is stressed across a number of settings, using age-appropriate materials and strategies, avoiding contrived reinforcement and aversive control, and supporting parents

norms: statistically determined age levels for developmental milestones

nutrition: adequate intake of nourishment

nystagmus: rapid involuntary oscillations or tremors of the eyeball; may be horizontal, vertical, or rotary

object permanence: the understanding that objects continue to exist even when they are out of sight

occipital: the back section of the head

organism: a total living form; one individual

orientation: conceptual, perceptual, sensory, and body awareness of space and environment

ostomy: an opening made from an internal tube to an external source, allowing for passage of urine or stool from the body (usually to a collection pouch)

otitis media (middle ear disease): an inflammatory disease of the middle ear; may be acute otitis media or serous otitis media

outcome-based intervention model: an emphasis on development of skills for future usefulness

overextension: children's language usage that commonly occurs due to a limited repertoire of words or when categories are defined too broadly, for example, referring to all men as "Daddy"

ovum: an unfertilized female sex cell; egg

P. L. 94-142: the original 1975 Education for All Handicapped Children Act, which mandated specific due process protections and services for children with disabilities

P. L. 99-457: the 1986 Education of the Handicapped Act Amendments, which expanded special education services to all 3- to 5-year-olds with disabilities and provided incentives and guidelines for services to infants and toddlers with disabilities

palmar grasp: grasping an object in the palm of the hand

parachute reflex: extension of arms and legs toward the surface that results when an infant is held in a horizontal position and prone, and then lowered toward the floor

parallel play: children play independently even though they are near other children and engaged in similar activities

paraphrasing: the practice of the listener restating the heart of the conversation in order to confirm and clarify what was meant

paraplegia: cerebral palsy affecting the lower extremities of the body

paraprofessionals: staff who assist licensed or certified intervention specialists

parity: number of live births delivered by a woman

parsimony: the adoption of the simplest assumption in the formulation of a theory or the interpretation of data

Part H: the section of P. L. 99-457 that specifies the provision of special education services to

infants and toddlers who are disabled or at-risk for developmental delay

passive affect: behaviors typical of self-involvement, for example, hoarding objects

patent ductus ateriosis: when the opening between the aorta and the pulmonary artery, which permits blood to bypass the lungs prenatally and normally closes shortly after birth, stays open after birth and diminishes flow from the aorta

pathogenic: capable of causing disease

peer and family referenced intervention model: when the curriculum is validated in reference to the child, family, and community with parents as full partners in decision making

perception checks: when a listener checks his or her perception or understanding of what was said in the course of a conversation in order to open up and clarify the communication

perceptual abilities: a child's ability to make use of information received through the six senses or modalities: auditory, visual, kinesthetic, gustatory, olfactory, and tactile

perinatal: relating to the period just before or just after birth

perlocutionary stage: a stage of linguistic development in which infants' language is unintentional and unconventional (develops at birth to 6–8 months).

phenotype: refers to the observable expression, or appearance, of a genetically inherited characteristic in an individual

phenylketonuria (PKU): an inherited disorder in which the enzyme that converts phenylalanine (an amino acid) into tyrosine (another amino acid) is defective, with the resulting build-up of phyenylalanine causing mental retardation

philosophy of association: a set of guidelines that includes values about listening and leadership, support of one another, and constant self-assessment of attitudes

phoneme: the smallest unit of sound that signals a meaningful difference; generally divided into consonants and vowels

phonological development: development of vocal sound production

phonology: the study of speech sounds

physical abuse: the infliction of physical injur by punching, beating, kicking, biting, burning, or otherwise harming a child, whether or not the parents or caregivers intended to do so

placebo: a chemically inert substance given in place of a drug—sometimes has a positive effect if the person believes it will

placenta: a fleshy mass made up of villi or projectiles that insert themselves into the lining of the uterus

placenta previa: a condition in which the placenta implants itself near the cervix rather than the top of the uterus

plantar reflex: observed when pressure applied to the ball of an infant's foot is followed by flexion of the toes around the stimulus

plasticity: the quality of being plastic, or capable of being molded; in regard to neural function

polypeptide: three or more amino acids joined together

positioning: treatment of postural and reflex abnormalities by careful, symmetrical placement and support of the body

positive interdependence: the dependency of each group member on each other member—successes and failures are collective deeds

postnatal: occurring after birth, with reference to the newborn

postural reflexes (adaptive reflexes): involuntary responses that supplement movement while preventing injury

predictive utility: providing accurate forecasts about what will happen

preexisting diabetes: diabetes that developed prior to pregnancy

prehensile grasp: opposition of the thumb to the other fingers of the hand

premature labor: prior to 37 weeks of gestation

premature rupture of membranes: membranes of the water sac surrounding the fetus break prior to 37th week of pregnancy

prenatal: preceding birth

preoperational stage: stage during which children reason through linguistic input and personal knowledge

presbyopia: loss of the eyes' ability to accommodate; the loss of elasticity of the lens of the eye that causes the near point to recede

present levels of performance: use of current evaluation information to summarize skills and abilities

presuppositions: judgments made about the listener in a conversation that allow us to modify the content and style of the communication (These judgments include assessment of social status, educational or developmental level, closeness of relationships, etc.)

primary circular reactions: learning to coordinate movements through repetition

primary social supports: informal support network comprised of close family, friends, and neighbors

primitive reflexes: involuntary motor responses to specific stimuli that interfere with movement if persistent

proactive stance: working to influence others positively toward a particular position

procedural safeguards: rights guaranteed to families of children eligible for services under IDEA

process goals: the sequence of decision-making events leading to outcome goals

prolapse of umbilical cord: baby presses on the umbilical cord during delivery and decreases or stops blood flow (and oxygen supply)

prone: position of lying facedown on one's abdomen

protective extension: reaching an arm out to prevent falling when pushed out of midline, either from sitting or standing position

protozoan: a member of the phylum comprising the simplest forms of the animal kingdom; a unicellular organism

proximal-distal: sequence of development that progresses from the center of the body outward toward the extremities

psychological maltreatment: a concerted attack on the development of self and social competence, such as rejecting, isolating, terrorizing, ignoring, and corrupting

psychometric approach: assessment comparing a child to normal standards of development, intelligence, or achievement in order to determine performance discrepancies

pulmonary: concerning or affected by the lungs

quadriplegia: cerebral palsy affecting all four extremities of the body

qualitative-developmental assessment: assessment in which a child's skills, as well as the child's approach to people and tasks, are evaluated according to a developmental sequence

range of normalcy: lower and upper limits of age at which developmental milestones are attained

range of reaction: the extent to which environment is likely to influence the sequence of development within individual children

receptive language: understanding of a message sent by another individual

recessive gene: a gene that does not possess sufficient genetic information for the characteristic to be expressed unless the gene is carried on both alleles

refinement: sequence of development that progresses from large muscle control to small muscle control

reflex integration: the disappearance of involuntary reflexes to allow for normal motor development

refractive errors: defects in the curvature of cornea and lens, or abnormal eyeball shape, that change the focal point of light rays

reinforcement: a change in stimulus, contingent upon a response, that results in an increase in the probability of that response

related services: additional support services that allow children to benefit from their educational experience

relative clauses: a part of a sentence that describes a subject, for example, "I want a doll *that wets.*"

renal system: organ system including kidneys and bladder

replicate: to demonstrate again with the same results

residual vision: visual ability remaining to an individual with a visual loss

resource interdependence: the arrangement or sharing of a single set of materials, equipment, information, and so on

respiratory distress syndrome: collapse of alveoli in the lungs due to lack of surfactant production in premature infants

respiratory system: organ system including lungs and airways

retina: the innermost layer of the eye; the neural layer containing the receptors for light

retinopathy of prematurity (ROP): overgrowth of connective tissue in the eyes due to excess oxygen given to premature infants; oxygenation that causes damage to the blood vessels supplying the retina and, in severe cases, detachment of the retina

reward interdependence: the collective expression of shared rewards and criticisms for a team's work

Rh sensitization: blood type incompatibility of mother and fetus that causes a buildup of antigens in mother's blood

role interdependence: when each member assumes an interconnected, yet specific responsibility that capitalizes on his or her strengths

rooting reflex: occurs when an infant's cheek is lightly stroked and, in response, infant's head turns toward the stimulus

rubella: commonly called German measles; caused by a virus that usually produces only mild upper respiratory symptoms and a rash in the infected individual; can cause severe damage to a fetus and can result in spontaneous abortion

savant: an individual shows extreme aptitude in one area (e.g., music or mathematics)

scoliosis: spinal curvature of the lower back

screening: a relatively quick preliminary evaluation used to determine if a child should be referred for more in-depth assessment

secondary circular reactions: learning to control or focus movements through repetition to produce interesting simulation

secondary social supports: formal sources of support, such as health care providers, educators, and therapists, that are usually more temporary than primary social supports

seizure: abnormal electrical discharges in the brain that cause the body to tremor, lose consciousness, or move in uncontrollable ways

self-help skills: independent care including eating, dressing, toileting, and other personal responsibilities

self-stimulation: sensory input from personal tactile, visual, auditory, or other physical activity that ignores other people or objects in the environment (such as hand-flapping, lip smacking, biting, etc.)

semantic relationship: combinations of two or more words that possess more meaning than any one of the words uttered in isolation

semicircular canals: three canals in the temporal bone that lie approximately at right angles to one another, containing receptors for equilibrium, specifically for rotation

sensorimotor stage: takes place from birth to age two; represents children's primitive exploration of their environment, wherein children attempt to integrate sensory information with their own movement

sensorineural hearing loss: results from damage to the cochlea or auditory nerve

serum: plasma minus its clotting proteins

service coordinator: person assigned to family of a child with special needs who is responsible for seeing that family and child receive all the services for which they are eligible under Part H of IDEA

sex-linked disorders: transmitted through the parents on a sex chromsome (X or Y) so that it is common for individuals of only one gender to express the disorder

sexual abuse: includes fondling a child's genitals, intercourse, incest, rape, sodomy, exhibitionism, and sexual exploitation committed by a parent or caregiver of a child

shunting: procedure that requires the surgical placement of a soft pliable plastic tube between the ventricle and either the heart or the peritoneal cavity in the abdomen to drain off excess cerebral spinal fluid

sickle cell crisis: in persons with sickle cell disease, frequent and severe painful episodes

single service model: professionals work predominantly in isolation

social-affective play: interaction between adult and child that elicits pleasure responses from the child

socioeconomic: relating to income and social factors

solitary play: a child is involved with his or her own play and does not interact with others

spastic cerebral palsy: cerebral damage in which the muscles tighten and resist efforts to move

special education: specially designed instruction that includes adaptations that are significantly different from modifications normally made for typical students and are necessary to offset or reduce the adverse effects of the child's disability

spectator play: a young child observes the play of others but does not attempt to join them

speech acts: the speaker's intentions or purposes for communicating

speech: communication produced through spoken words using oral-motor functions

spina bifida: refers to an incomplete spinal column and the relationship of the spinal cord and contents to the defect

spina bifida occulta: a defect in the vertebrae covering the spinal cord, with no exposure of the neural membranes or any evidence of nerve tissue in the defect

spinal tap: a procedure in which a hollow needle is used to draw cerebrospinal fluid from the spinal canal

spirochete: a highly coiled bacterium; a general term applied to any organism of the order Spirochaetales, which includes the causative organisms of syphilis

stage theory response: the naming and sequential ordering of complex emotions that are normal under a given set of circumstances

startle reflex: occurs when a sudden noise or movement causes a child to throw its arms away from the body and then back toward the midline

status epilepticus: a prolonged seizure of 15 minutes or more that is a life-threatening condition

stepping reflex: step-like response that occurs when a child is held in a vertical position so that its feet touch a surface

strabismus: a condition in which the optical axes of the two eyes are not parallel; cross-eyed

straight vote decision making: when each member of a group has one vote

substance abuse: use of illicit drugs or excessive use of legal substances

sucking reflex: *See* swallow reflex.

supine: positioned horizontally on the back with the face upward

support staff: professionals who consult, evaluate, train, or serve children in an indirect manner or on a less than regular basis

survival skills: skills that are considered useful in making the transition from one program to the next as smooth as possible for a child

swallow reflex: works in combination with the sucking reflex; when fully developed a child has good tongue control and lip closure; also present is the ability to move food from the front to the back of the mouth and to control the path of food to the esophagus, and then to the stomach

symmetrical tonic neck reflex (STNR): reflex such that when head falls forward, arms flex and legs extend; when head falls back, arms extend and legs flex

syntax: rules that govern structural patterns of language utterances and sentences

systemic: pertaining to or affecting the body as a whole

teacher-directed instruction: highly structured instruction planned in advance and guided by the teacher

temperament: characteristic emotional response

teratogen: any agent or factor that causes physical defects in a developing embryo

term pregnancy: gestational period of at least 38 weeks

tertiary: third in order, as in tertiary service delivery in which a professional serves a parent who, in turn, serves a child

tertiary services: indirect services that benefit children or their families (For example, when service providers enable parents to implement activities to assist in the development of their children, the child is receiving tertiary services from the professional.)

thyroid gland: an important organ of the endocrine system that helps control metabolism

tics: purposeless and irregular behavior such as motor movement or vocalizations with unpredictable onset

toddler stage: time from 1 year to 3 years of age

tonic-clonic seizure: rigid muscular contraction and rapid alternation of contraction and relaxation of muscles

total communication: a combination of manual signing with oral methods of communication

toxemia of pregnancy: elevated maternal blood pressure during pregnancy

toxin: a poison

toxoplasmosis: a protozoan that is acquired by humans from contact with the feces of infected cats or birds and from the ingestion of raw or partially cooked meat; may result in premature delivery or spontaneous abortion

tracking: ability to follow moving objects with the eyes in several directions (vertically and horizontally)

transdisciplinary model: a group whose members share roles and combine assessment and treatment tasks so that they may be carried out by one professional

transfer: ability to take short steps for small distances between furniture or other supporting objects without holding on

transition: change in growth and development that may result in unpredictable behavior or regression

transition plan: formal written plan that indicates activities and responsibility for those activities that will make the move from one program to the next as smoothly as possible

transition stressors: pressure on a family related to a child's disability and occurring at significant milestones in life

translocation: the existence of extra chromosomal material, which has become attached to another chromosome, varying in size from a piece of one arm to an entire chromosome

transplancental: substance crosses from maternal to fetal bloodstream, or vice versa, via the placenta

trimester: a period of three months, usually pertaining to gestational periods, for example, second trimester

triplegia: cerebral palsy affecting three extremities of the body

trisomy 21: the presence of an extra number 21 chromosome, which causes Down syndrome

ultrasonography: a procedure that uses high-frequency sound waves to produce an image of an internal organ

umbilical cord: the cord that joins the bloodstream of the fetus at the abdomen to the bloodstream of the mother via the uterine lining

underextension: children's language usage that occurs when categories are defined too narrowly (For example, a young child may use the word "chair" when referring to a high chair or table chair, but not include the rocking chair or kitchen stool in the category.)

vaccines: consist of either active viral replications with decreased virulence or an inactive virus introduced into the human being to activate the immune system to produce antibodies, preventing an acute infection

varicella-zoster: a virus related to herpes responsible for chickenpox and shingles

ventricles: fluid filled sacs that occupy space within and around the brain mass

very low birth weight: less than 1500 g (3 lb 5 oz)

vestibule: a small cavity or space at the entrance to a canal, such as that in the inner ear

viable: the age at which the fetus has the potential to live outside of the womb, about 26 to 28 months

viruses: the smallest known types of infectious agent that invade cells, take over, and make copies of themselves

visual acuity: acuteness of vision; the power of the visual apparatus to distinguish visual detail, such as recognizing a letter of the alphabet

vitreous humor: the colorless, transparent gel filling the cavity of the eye behind the lens

weighted decision making: when some members of a group receive priority in voting, so that their votes count more heavily in decision making than other members' votes

Index

Page numbers in italics indicate illustrations pertinent to the entry.

characteristics of, 213
diagnosis of, 252–253
families and, 311–312
resources on, 466
Autosomal dominant genes, 189
Autosomal recessive genes, *188,* 194
Autosomes, 185

Babbling, 86
Babinski reflex, 77
Baby Doe legislation, 175
Bacteria, 254
Bacterial infections, 254–256
effects on young children, 255
Baltimore Early Admissions project,
295
Barriers, to inclusion, 9–12
Battered child syndrome, 333–334
Becker muscular dystrophy, 203
Behavior
of children with prenatal drug
exposure, 123–124
descriptions of, 325–326
of homeless children, 17
language use and, 91–92
measurable, 347
tutoring and, 359
Behavioral assessment approach,
384–385
Behavioral genetics, 185
Behavioral psychology, 291
Behavior analysis, 4–5
principles of, 6
Bell, Alexander Graham, 293
Bereavement support, resources on,
466
Best practice concept, 2
Binding statements, and freeing
statements, 323–326
Binet, Alfred, 293
Binocular vision, errors in, 248
Biological agents, 154
inflammation and, 254
Biological risk, 378
Biology, intelligence and, 63–64
Birthrate, in foreign-born families, 14
Birth weight. *See also* Prematurity
cigarette smoking and, 125
low, 134
very low, 134–135
Blended families, 18
Blindness. *See* Visual impairment
Bloom, Benjamin, 295
Body control, lower, 82
Body proportions, 47, *47*
Body systems, prematurity and,
116–118

Bonding, 67
Bone growth, 50
Botswana, early childhood education
in, 303
Bound morpheme, 88
Brachmann de Lange syndrome,
213–214
Brain. *See also* Congenital physical
malformations
encephalitis and, 271–272
fetal, 102
growth of, 49–50
herpes virus and, 261–262
meningitis and, 268–271
microcephaly and, 176
plasticity of, 56–57
voluntary and reflexive motor
control in, *49*
Brain injury, hypoxic-ischemic,
132–133, 134
Breath-holding spells, 166
Bronchopulmonary dysplasia (BPD),
135, 139
Bronfenbrenner, U., 30
Brooks, Eve, 32

Cancer, 192
Canes, 251
Cardiovascular system, 48
prematurity and, 117
Caregivers, expectations of, 326–328
Carriers, 188
Carrier state, 256
Catabolism, 219
Cataract, 248
CAT scan. *See* Computerized Axial
Tomography (CAT, CT scan)
Caucasians, 13
poverty and, 16
public school enrollments by, 14
Causality, and cerebral palsy chil-
dren, *161*
Cell division, Down syndrome and,
198
Center-based programs
combined with home-based
programs, 364–365
preschool, 361–363
Central nervous system, visual dys-
functions and, 248
Cephalo-caudal development,
47–48, 79
Cerebral palsy, 154–164
categorization by body parts, 157
causes in low birth weight
infants, 162
characteristics of, 157–158

diagnostic criteria for, 158
etiology of, 160–163
object permanence and causality
tests, *161*
treatment of, 163–164
Cerebrospinal fluid, 268–270
Chancre, 264
Chickenpox, 262–263
Child abuse and neglect, 333–335
historical context of, 333–335
population of abused, 335
poverty and, 16–17
research on, 334–335
symptoms of, 334
Child Abuse Prevention, Adoption,
and Family Services Act (1988),
334
Child Abuse Prevention and
Treatment Act (1974), 334
Child assessment, 386–387
Childbearing, poverty and, 18
Child care
development and, 66
need for, 32
Child-centered model. *See* Family
systems model
Child development
poverty and, 295
theories of, 295
Child-directed activities, 356
Childfind, 377
Child neglect, 333
symptoms of, 334
Child psychology, origins of,
291–292
Children. *See also* Growth and devel-
opment; Infants
eligible for government services,
377–378
in families, 329–332
growth and development of,
46–53
history of childhood in Western
civilization, 282–297
impact of homelessness on,
17–18
Children's Defense Fund, 33
Children's Rights (Wiggen), 290
China. *See* People's Republic of
China
Chlamydia trachomatis, 255–256
Chomsky, Noam, 85
Chorionic villus sampling, 193
Chorioretinitis, 258
Christianity, child-rearing and,
284, 285
Chromosome deletions, resources on,
467

Chromosome 18 and 13 disorders, resources on, 466–467
Chromosome inversions, resources on, 467
Chromosomes, 184, 185–186
　　abnormalities in, *191*, 191–192
　　arranged sequentially in pairs, *185*
Chronic diseases, of mother, 121
Cigarette smoking, prenatal effect of, 124–125
Civil Rights Act (1965), 8
Clauses, relative, 88
Cleft lip and palate, 192, 227–229
　　language development and, 92
Coarctation of aorta, 455, *455*
Cocaine/crack
　　children exposed to, 54–55
　　prenatal impact of, 123–124
Cochlea, 240
Code of Ethical Conduct, of National Association for the Education of Young Children, 31
Cognition, 61, 94–99. *See also* Cognitive development
　　autism and, 212
　　theories of, 96–99
Cognitive development
　　milestones of, 100–101
　　Piaget's approach to, 96–99
Collaboration. *See also* Teams
　　attributes of, 419–431
　　building teams for, 431–437
　　critical elements of, 421–431
　　in early intervention, 30–31
　　hierarchy of team concepts in, 416–419
　　for meeting child's needs, 26–31
　　paradigms for, 438
　　personal responsibility in, 434–435
　　professional, 2
　　rationale for, 414–416
　　successful, 435–437
Colors, language development and, 91
Combination center- and home-based programs, 364–365
Comenius, 285
Communication, 61–62. *See also* Language development
　　active listening and, 322–323
　　binding and freeing statements in, 323–326
　　by infants, 84
　　between parents and professionals, 319–329
　　with parents at time of diagnosis, 328–329

in teams, 419–420
Communication systems, for hearing impaired, 243–244
Community Facilities Act. *See* Lanham Act
Complete transposition of great vessels, 455–456, *456*
Complex sentences, 88
Compound sentences, 88
Comprehensive Child Development Bill, 296
Comprehensive preschool programs, 360
Computerized Axial Tomography (CAT, CT scan), 151
Computers
　　development and, 70, 71–72
　　technology and, 444
Concepts, language and, 85
Conceptual system, 4
Concrete operations stage, 97, 99
Conditions, for behavior, 347
Conductive hearing loss, 241
Conflict, with school, 422–424
Congenital conditions. *See also* Infections
　　genetic, 192
　　heart defects, 222–224, *225*, 453–457
　　infections and, 258
　　physical malformations, 170–178
　　in visual impairment, 249
Conjunctivitis, 256
Consensus building, 26
Consequated responses, 352
Consolidation, 58
Constitution of the United States, equal protection under, 8
Content
　　of language, 86
　　language development and, 89–91
Contractures, 203
Control. *See* Family, empowerment of
Conversational postulates, 91
Cooing, 86
Cooperative play, 108
Coordination
　　of secondary schemata, 98
　　of services, 378–381
Coprolalia, 217
Cornea, 246
Cornelia de Lange syndrome, 213–214
　　resources on, 467
Corpus callosum, agenesis of, 453
Corrected gestational age, 118
Cortical visual impairments, 248

Costs. *See* Financial resources
Council for Exceptional Children (CEC), child abuse and, 335
Crack. *See* Cocaine/crack
Crawling, 81
Cretinism, 222
Cri du chat syndrome, resources on, 467
Criteria, for instructional objective, 351
Cross-cultural history, of childhood education, 300–307
Cross-disciplinary predictions, 445–450
Cruising, 82
Cruising surfaces, 250
Crying, as communication, 84
Cued speech, 244
Cultural competence, 16
Cultural deprivation, concept of, 295–296
Cultural sensitivity, 2, 13–16, 327
Cultural values, 61
Culture. *See* Cross-cultural history
Curriculum, for individual children, 358
Curriculum and Monitoring System, 365
Cyanosis, 223
Cystic fibrosis, 186, 187, 193–195
　　resources on, 467
Cytomegalic inclusion virus, 259–261

Dame schools, 288
Data collection and evaluation, 358
Day care, 292
　　Kaiser Centers and, 294
　　recent efforts in, 296–297
Deafness. *See* Hearing impairments
Decision making
　　in collaborative teams, 429–431
　　methods for, 430–431
　　styles of, 434–435
Deductive logic, in decision making, 434–435
Delivery, problems in, 131–132
Delivery strategy, collaborative teaming for, 415
DeMause, Lloyd, 282–283
Demographics
　　cultural sensitivity and, 13
　　on family, 66
　　shifts in, 15 (fig.)
Dentition, 50
　　eruption and loss of primary and permanent teeth, *51*
Department of Special Education, 293

Eligibility. *See also* Assessment
  assessment of, 384–390
  for government services, 377–378
Embedding, 88
Embryonic stage, 44
Emile (Rousseau), 285
Emotion(s)
  in decision making, 435
  of families with special-needs children, 318–319
Emotional maltreatment, 333
  symptoms of, 334
Empirical approach, 3–4
Empirical testing, 4–5
Empowerment, of family, 2, 21–22, 24–26
Encephalitis, 258, 271–272
  varicella-zoster and, 262
Endocardial cushion defect, 223
Endoscopy, 154
Environment
  cocaine and, 54
  for collaborative teams, 428–429
  IDEA and, 344
  for IEP, 354–359
  intelligence and, 63–64
  prenatal factors and, 192
Environmental risk, 378
Enzymes, 219
Epilepsy, 165–166
Equal Protection Clause, of Fourteenth Amendment, 8
Equilibrium reflex, 79
Erikson, Erik, psychosocial development stages of, 102, 103
Established risk, 377
Ethics
  importance of, 31–33
  plastic surgery for Down syndrome, 196
  of professional, 2
Ethnicity, development and, 70
Ethnographic research, 313
Etiology, of ADHD, 170
Eustachian tube, 240
Evaluation, of collaborative efforts, 430. *See also* Data collection and evaluation
Evoked otoacoustic emissions (EOAE), 243
Exceptional children. *See* Special needs children
Excited neurons, seizures and, 164–165
Exocrine glands, 193
Exosystems, 30
Expanding Developmental Growth

through Education (EDGE). *See* Project EDGE
Experiences, development and, 69
Expressive language, 85
  development of, 89–91
Extension, 77
  and muscle tone, 79
External ear, 240
Extinction, 6
Extrapyramidal damage, 157
Extremely low birth weight infants, 135–136
Eye, functioning of, 246–248, *247*. *See also* Visual impairment
Eye contact, 83

Face-to-face interaction, in teams, 420
Facial expression, 83
Facts, scientific attitude toward, 3
Failure to thrive, 135, 142–145
Fair Start. *See* Project Fair Start
Familial hypercholesteremia, 188
Families, Professionals, and Exceptionality: A Special Partnership (Turnbull and Turnbull), 329
Family(ies)
  assessment of, 387–390
  of children with disabilities, 311–340
  comparison of needs and strengths of, *388*
  composition of, 18–21
  defined, 22–24
  development and, 66
  divorce and, 20
  dysfunction in, 332–335
  ecological mapping of, *23*
  emotional functioning of, 318–319
  empowerment of, 2, 21–22, 24–26
  future relations with, 335–337
  hardiness of, 317
  isolation of, 403
  kinship care and, 20
  with multiple risks, 436
  needs of, 316–317
  as part of system, 329–332
  possibilities for, 312–313
  professional relationships with, 313–318
  as service context, 21–26
  social construct of, 315–316
  time use by, 27–28
Family adaptation hypothesis, 25

Family-centered programs and services, 365–367, 406–409, 443–444
Family life-cycle theory, 313
Family Resource Coalition (FRC), 312–313
Family service planning, 21
Family services, ecologically-based approach to, 330–332
Family sociology, 313
Family systems model, 22–24
Family systems theory, 313
Farsightedness. *See* Hyperopia
Fathers
  and "motherese," 94
  in parent-professional interactions, 24
Federal agencies, 376–377
Federal government. *See* Government
Feeding, of cerebral palsy children, 159. *See also* Eating skills; Malnutrition
Feelings, descriptions of, 325-326. *See also* Emotion(s)
Fencer's reflex, 77
Fetal Alcohol Effects (FAE), 122–123
Fetal alcohol syndrome (FAS), 122–123
  parent's perspective on, 126–127
Fetal blood sampling, 193
Fetal brain, engineering of, 102
Fetus, 45. *See also* At-risk infants; Pregnancy; Prenatal conditions
  development of, *44*
  phases of, *45*
Financial resources, problems with, 19–20
Fine motor development, 62, 82–84
  refinement of, 85
Fine pincer grasp, 84, *84*
First Chance Networks, 297
Flexed extremities, 77
Flexing, and muscle tone, 79
Fordham Institute for Innovation in Social Policy, 66
Form, of language, 86
Formal operations stage, 97, 99
Formative analysis, in future, 112
Foster care systems, 20, 68–69
Fourteenth Amendment, Equal Protection Clause of, 8
Fowler, William, 295
Fragile X syndrome, 190, 201–203
  resources on, 469
France, children in, 284
Freeing statements, and binding statements, 323–326
Free morpheme, 88
Freud, Sigmund, 295

tion, 282–297
cross-cultural, 300, 307
HIV/AIDS, 262, 266–268
Holoprosencephaly, 453
Home-based programs, 363–364
combined with center-based
programs, 364–365
Home environment, cocaine and, 54
Homeless families, 17
Homosexual parents. See Gay parents
Homozygote, 186
Howard, V. F., 54
Human cytomegalic inclusion viral
infection (CMV), 259–261
Human development. See
Development
Human Genome Project, 184
Human immunodeficiency virus. See
HIV/AIDS
Hunt, J. M., 295
Huntington's disease, 188
Hydrocephalus, 176–178
Hyperactivity. See Attention deficit
hyperactivity disorder (ADHD)
Hyperopia, 247–248
Hypertension, pregnancy-induced,
129
Hypertonia, 79, 157
Hypoglycemia, 219–220
Hypoplastic left heart syndrome, 457
Hypothermia, 135, 140
Hypothyroidism, 222
Hypotonia, 79, 157, 196–197
Hypoxia, 132–133, 134

IDEA. See Individuals with
Disabilities Education Act (IDEA)
Identification, eligibility, program-
ming, and review, for early inter-
vention services, 385
IEP. See Individualized Education
Program (IEP)
IFSP. See Individualized Family
Service Plans (IFSP); Individual
Family Service Plan (IFSP)
Illness. See Infections
Illocutionary stage, 86
Imaging, as diagnostic tools, 151, 152
Imitation, 98
of words, 92
Immigrants, 14
Impulsivity. See Attention deficit
hyperactivity disorder (ADHD)
Inattention. See Attention deficit
hyperactivity disorder (ADHD)
Inclusion, 5–13, 298–299, 444
attitude toward, 2

defined, 5–8
justification for, 8–9
opposition to, 9–12
Independence, 61
India, early childhood education in,
304
Individualized Education Program
(IEP), 314, 344, 345–359
least restrictive environment for,
354–359
sample of, 348–350
team for, 26
Individualized Family Service Plans
(IFSP), 314, 390–394
checklist for writing goals and
objectives, 392–393
sample transition plan, 399–401
Individuals with Disabilities
Education Act (IDEA) (1975), 6–7,
297–298, 344–345, 374
assessment for services eligibility
and, 384
and changes under recent legislation, 461–464
transition planning regulations
from, 395–396
Infancy period, 51, 53
Infant, Toddler, and Preschool
Research and Intervention Program,
362–363
Infants. See also Development;
Growth and development;
Neonates
as active learners, 55–56
brain plasticity and, 56–57
competencies of, 53–55
developmental sequencing of, 56
micropremature, 118
mobility devices for, 250–251
multidimensional development
of, 56
social activity of, 55
specialized skills of, 56
Infections. See also Development
bacterial, 254–256
congenital, 258
future implications for, 273
of mother, 121
sensory impairments and,
239–277
viral, 256–262
Inflammation, 254
Information sources. See Resources
Inheritance, 46. See also Genetic
disorders; Genetics; Metabolic
conditions
dominant genes and, 188–189
recessive gene and, 187–188

sex linked, 189–190, 190
Inhibited neurons, seizures and, 165
Initial contact, 329
Inner ear, 240
Institutionalization, alternatives to,
295
Instructional methods, in IEP, 356–357
Instructional objectives, for IEP, 345,
346–351
Integrated preschool programs, 360
Integrated reflexes, 76
Integration, 444
early intervention and, 382–383
inclusion and, 7
as reason for collaboration, 416
Integumentary system, 50
prematurity and, 118
Intelligence, IQ and, 69
Intelligence and Experience (Hunt),
295
Interaction, face-to-face, 420
Interagency Coordinating Council
(ICC), 375
Interagency coordination, 375–376
Interagency services, 376–377
Interdependence, in collaborative
teams, 426–429
Interdisciplinary approach, to meeting
child's needs, 26–31
Interdisciplinary-interagency coopera-
tion, 330
Interdisciplinary teams, 28–29, 417
International Classification of
Epileptic Seizures, 165
International Council for Exceptional
Children, 293
Interpersonal skills, in teams, 420
Interracial families, resources on, 469
Intervention, 298
collaboration in, 30–31
families in, 22
goals for, 368–369
methods of, 3
time and, 27–28
Intraventricular hemorrhage (IVH),
135, 140
Intuition, in decision making, 435
Invasive diagnostic tools, 150
Involvement, in cerebral palsy, 158
IQ. See also Intelligence
of children with FAS, 122
environment and, 69
Ischemia, 132–133, 134
Isolation, of family, 403
Isolettes, 118
Itard, Jean-Marc, 288
IVH. See Intraventricular hemorrhage
(IVH)

James, William, 290
Japan, early childhood education in, 305
Johnson, Lyndon, 295
Juku, 305

Kaiser, Edgar, 294
Karyotype, 186
Killer phrases, 324
Kindergarten
    of Froebel, 289
    in United States, 289
Kinship care, 20
Knowledge-base, for services to children, 9
Kozol, Jonathan, 14
Kuttabs, 307

Labeling, segregation and, 10
Labor
    maternal/infant complications in, 131–132, 134
    premature, 128, 131
Language.
    development, 84–94
    expressive, 89–91
    factors affecting, 92–94
    form, content, and use of, 86
    form and, 86–88
    language use and, 91–92
    milestones of, 93–94
    morphological development, 88
    signing and, *90*
    skill development in, 61–62
    symbolic systems as, 84
    unconventional, 84
Language disorders, resources on, 469
Lanham Act (Community Facilities Act) (1941), 292
Late visual bloomers, 249
Latin America, immigrants from, 14
Law, professional behavior and, 22
Leadership, professional-family relationships and, 317–318
Learners, infants as, 55–56
Learning. *See also* Development
    cognition and, 94–99
    critical periods of, 57–58
Least Restrictive Environment (LRE), 6–8
    in IEP, 354–359
    legal foundation of, 8–9
Legal system, inclusion under, 8–9
Legislation. *See also* legislation by name

early intervention and, 373–384
and interdisciplinary-interagency cooperation, 329–330
Lens, 246
Lesbian and gay parents, resources for, 469
Lesch-Nyhan syndrome, 212
Liberia, early childhood education in, 305–306
Life-cycle theory, 313
Linguists. *See* Language development
Lipids, 209
Listening
    in collaborative teams, 424–425
    in family-professional communication, 322–323
Local Education Agencies (LEA), 7
Locke, John, 285
Locutionary stage, 86
Logic. *See* Deductive logic
Low birth weight infants, 134
    cerebral palsy and, 162
    neutral thermoregulation and, 139–140
Lower body control, 82
Lung function, *225*

MacDonald, K., 55
Macrosystems, 30
Magnetic resonance imaging (MRI), 151
Mainstreaming, 5–6
Majority minorities, 14
Malformations, congenital physical, 170–178
Malnutrition, signs of, 159
Mandated services, 343–371
Manual language, 84
Mapping, genetic, 184
MAPPS project, 364–365
Marijuana, prenatal effects of, 125–127
Marriage, families of children with disabilities and, 312
Massachusetts Bay Colony, children in, 285
Maternal conditions, pregnancy and, 119–121
Maternal Infant Health Outreach Worker Project (MIHOW), 404
Maternal obesity, 121
Maturation, 46
Mean Length Utterance (MLU), 88
Measles (rubeola), 263–264
Meconium, 133
    aspiration syndrome, 133, 134
    ileus, 458

Medicaid, 20
Medication. *See* Drugs
Medicine, point of view of, 448–450
Meiosis, *185,* 186
    compared with mitosis, *187*
Memory. *See also* Cognitive development
    habituation paradigm and, 94–96
    long-term, 99
Meninges, 268
Meningitis, 254, 268–271
Meningocele, 173
Mental retardation. *See also* conditions by name
    and cerebral palsy, 160
    in Cornelia de Lange syndrome, 213
    Down syndrome and, 195
    resources on, 470
Mesosystems, 30
Metabolic conditions, 219–222
    galactosemia, 220–221
    hypoclycemia, 219–220
    hypothyroidism, 222
    PKU (phenylketonuria), 221–222
Metabolic problems, 192
Methamphetamine, prenatal impact of, 123–124
Microbes, 254
Microcephaly, 176, 213
Microcomputers. *See* Technology
Micropremature infants, 118
    ethics and, 137–138
Microsystems, 30
Middle childhood stage, 51
Middle ear, 240
Migrant Farmworker Families program, 404–405
Milestones, developmental, 75–76
Minorities. *See also* Cultural sensitivity
    poverty and, 16
    special education services to, 14
Minority status, risk and, 21
Mitosis, *185,* 186
    compared with meiosis, *187*
Mitral valve, 223
Mobility, 251
Mobility devices, for infants and preschoolers, 250–251
Modak, Tarabi, 304
Model Preschool Program, 363
Models, of early intervention, 398–409
Montessori, Maria, 285, 291
Moral development, 61
Morbidity, 254
Moro reflex, 77, *77*

Tetralogy of Fallot, *456,* 456–457
Thalassemia, 210
Therapy, gene, 193
Thorndike, E. L., 291
Thurman, K. S., 441
Thyroid gland, 222
Time, as resource and constraint, 27–28
Timelines, skills, *398*
Title I, 373
Tobacco. *See* Cigarette smoking
Toddler-Parent Play Group Program, 408–409
Toddler stage, 51, 53
    vocabulary of, 90
Toileting skills, 111
Tonic-clonic seizures, 166
    treatment for, 169
TORCH viral infections, 257
Total communication, 144
Tourette syndrome, 216–218
    resources on, 472
Toxemia of pregnancy, 128, 129
Toxin, 254
Toxoplasmosis, 256–258
Tracking, 83
Training, of special preschool teachers, 12
Transdisciplinary teams, 29, 417–419
Transferring, 82
Transition plans, from early intervention services, 394–397
Transitions, 444
Translocation trisomy, 197
Transplacental infections, 257
Transposition of great vessels, 455–456, *456*
Treatment
    of ADHD, 170
    of autism, 212–213
    of cerebral palsy, 163–164
    of cystic fibrosis, 193–194
    of Down syndrome, 200–201
    of fragile X syndrome, 203
    for generalized tonic-clonic seizures, 169
    of muscular dystrophy, 204–205
    of otitis media, 241
    of Prader-Willi syndrome, 206
    of Rett syndrome, 215–216
    of seizures, 166–168
    of sickle cell disease, 208–209
    of thalassemia, 210
    of Tourette syndrome, 217–218

of Turner syndrome, 211
of Williams syndrome, 218–219
Trimester, infections during first, 259
Trisomy disorders, 200
    trisomy 21, 197
Trust, in teams, 420
Tuberculosis (TB), 267
Turnbull, A. P., 329
Turnbull, H. R., 329
Turner syndrome, 191, 210–211
    resources on, 472
Tutoring skills, 359
Twin studies, 63, 64

Ultrasonography, 152–153
Umbilical cord, 44
    problems in delivery and, 132, 134
Unconventional language, 84
Underextension, of word use, 90
United Cerebral Palsy Association, 295
United States
    kindergartens in, 289
    social reform in, 289–291
U.S. Department of Education (USDOE), 375–376
U.S. Department of Health and Human Services, support from, 313
University of Chicago, nursery school at, 290
Utah State University. *See* SKI*HI model

Vaccines, 256
Values, cultural, 61
Varicella-zoster (V-Z), 262–263
Ventilator use, resources on, 472
Ventricular peritoneal shunt, 140
Ventricular septal defect (VSD), 454, *454*
Very low birth weight, 134–136
Vestibule, 240
Viability, 116, 120
Viral infections, 256
    cytomegalic inclusion virus, 259–261
    encephalitis, 271–272
    hepatitis, 265–266
    HIV/AIDS, 266–268
    measles (rubeola), 263–264
    meningitis, 268–271

mumps, 263
rubella, 258–259
syphilis, 264–265
toxoplasmosis, 256–258
tuberculosis, 267
varicella-zoster (V-Z), 262–263
Vision, measuring, 245–246
Visual acuity, 245
Visual impairment, 245–253
    causes of, 248–249
    development implications and resolutions, 249
    diagnosis of, 252–253
    future implications for, 272–273
    resources on, 466
Vitreous humor, 246
Vocabulary, development of, 90. *See also* Language
Vocational Rehabilitation Act, 8

Walkers, infant and orthopedic, 250
Walking hoops, 250
Walking ropes, 251
War on Poverty, 295
Watson, John, 291
Weight
    and growth, 50–51
    infant, *52*
Westinghouse Learning Corporation, 295
Wheelchair devices, 250
White House Conference on Child Health and Protection (1930), 293
Wiggen, Kate Douglas, 290
Williams, B. F., 54
Williams syndrome (Elfin-Facies syndrome), 218–219
    resources on, 472
Words. *See* Language development
Working poor families, 18–20
Work patterns, child care and, 66
Works Progress Administration (WPA), nursery schools of, 292

X chromosome, 189–190
X rays, 150

Y chromosome, 189–190

Zigler, Edward, 445–446